Domestic Service and the Formation of European Identity

Antoinette Fauve-Chamoux (Ed.)

Domestic Service and the Formation of European Identity

Understanding the Globalization of Domestic Work, 16th–21st Centuries

PETER LANG
Bern · Berlin · Bruxelles · Frankfurt am Main · New York · Oxford · Wien

Bibliographic information published by Die Deutsche Bibliothek
Die Deutsche Bibliothek lists this publication in the Deutsche National-bibliografie; detailed bibliographic data is available on the Internet at ‹http://dnb.ddb.de›.

British Library and Library of Congress Cataloguing-in-Publication Data:
A catalogue record for this book is available from *The British Library*, Great Britain, and from *The Library of Congress*, USA.

Published with support of the European Union (Contract n°: HPSE–CT2001-50012), and the help of Centre de Recherches Historiques/ Centre National de la Recherche Scientifique, Ecole des Hautes Etudes en Sciences Sociales (Paris), France.

Text design: Carlo Dottor Communication
Cover illustration: Camille Pissarro: *The Little Country Maid*, 1882
© Tate, London 2004
Cover design: Thomas Jaberg, Peter Lang AG

ISBN 3-03910-589-2
US-ISBN 0-8204-7042-2

Hochfeldstrasse 32, Postfach 746, CH-3000 Bern 9, Switzerland
info@peterlang.com, www.peterlang.com, www.peterlang.net

Printed in Germany

Forword

The Editor dedicates this book, with deep gratitude, on the one hand to the modest nannies and "bonnes-à-tout-faire" of all ages and forgotten family names, who looked after her in childhood, alleviating for her mother and grand-mothers the weight of daily household and family duties, so allowing them enough freedom to develop some professional and social life, and, on the other hand, to all current home helpers, immigrant "maids" of Paris and other European cities, "women-of-all-work", looking after the young and the aged family members when she and her female colleagues teach, write or meet, this means so many trustable and representative figures of the current globalization of home help and care, without whom life would be far more difficult and the European "Servant Project" less successful.

Antoinette Fauve-Chamoux

Acknowledgements

The Editor wishes to express her appreciation of the encouragement and daily help she received from the Centre de Recherches Historiques of the Ecole des Hautes Etudes en Sciences Sociales/Centre National de la Recherche Scientifique (France), this academic institution being responsible for the publication of this book, as principal contractor in the European Servant Project. She is grateful to Professor Suzy Pasleau, University of Liège, Laboratoire de Recherches sur les Sociétés Industrielles (Belgium), who assumed the coordination of the European Servant Project and to Isabelle Schopp for her permanent assistance in this task. All planned Seminars were co-organized beautifully by European colleagues, Suzy Pasleau (Bruxelles, Belgium, December 2001), Regina Schulte (European University Institute of Florence, Italy, February 2002), Sølvi Sogner (University of Oslo, Departement of History, Norway, June 2002), Carmen Sarasúa (Autonomous University of Barcelona, Department of Economics and Economic History, Spain, December 2002), Richard Wall (University of Essex, Department of History, United Kingdom, May 2003), and John Komlos, Ludwig-Maximilians University of Munich, Economic History Institute, Germany, September 2003), with respectively the local help of Eliane Gubin (Université Libre de Bruxelles, Groupe interdisciplinaire d'Etudes sur les Femmes and Fonds Suzanne Tassier), Pothiti Hantzaroula, Hans Henrik Bull, Beatrice Moring, Helma Lutz, Belinda Waterman, Liliane Komlos and Christiane Artz in Paris. She would like to express her gratitude to Katherine Tschopp of Peter Lang AG, Carlo Dottor, Janet Marcus, Mary Louise Nagata and Raffaella Sarti for their assistance in preparing the manuscript.

Table of Contents

PART II
DOMESTIC SERVICE AND THE EVOLUTION OF LAW

PART III
THE MAID, THE MASTER AND THE FAMILY

PART IV
SERVANT ADAPTABILITY TO THE LABOUR MARKET, PAST AND PRESENT

PART V
SOME PORTRAITS

List of Contributors

BLACKETT, Adelle, University McGill (Canada) and Labour Law and Labour Relations Specialist at the International Labour Organisation, Geneva (Switzerland)

COOPER, Sheila McIsaac, University of Indiana (Indianapolis), Department of History (United States)

DUBERT, Isidro, University of Santiago de Compostela, Department of History (Spain)

EWAN, Elisabeth, University of Guelph, Department of History (Canada)

FAUVE-CHAMOUX, Antoinette, Centre de Recherches Historiques, Ecole des Hautes Etudes en Sciences Sociales/CNRS, Paris (France)

FIALOVÁ, Ludmila, Charles University, Prague, Department of Demography and Geodemography (Czech Republic)

HANTZAROULA, Pothiti, European University Institute (Florence), (Italy) and University of Thessaly, Volos (Greece)

IGLESIAS ESTEPA, Raquel, University of Santiago de Compostela, Department of History (Spain)

ISAKSEN, Louise Widding, University of Bergen, Department of Sociology (Norway)

JAEHRLING, Karen, Institute for Work and Technology, Gelsenkirchen (Germany)

LUNDH, Christer, University of Lund, Department of Economic History (Sweden)

LUTZ, Helma, University of Muenster, Department of Education and Social Sciences (Germany)

LYNCH-BRENNAN, Margaret, University of the State of New York, State Education Department (United States)

MARTÍN CASARES, Aurelia, University of Granada, Department of Social Anthropology (Spain)

MAGAT, Margaret, Center for Folklore and Ethnography, University of Pennsylvania (United States)

MOOSVI, Shireen, Aligarh Muslim University, Department of History (India)

MORING, Beatrice, University of Essex, Department of History (United Kingdom)

NAGATA, Mary Louise, Centre de Recherches Historiques, EHESS/CNRS, Paris (France)

ÖZYEGIN, Gül, Williamsburg, College of William and Mary, Sociology and Women's Studies Program (United States)

PARREÑAS, Rhacel Salazar, University of California, Davis, Asian American Studies (United States)

PASLEAU, Suzy, University of Liège, Laboratoire de Recherches sur les Sociétés Industrielles (Belgium)

REY CASTELAO, Ofelia, University of Santiago de Compostela, Department of History (Spain)

SARASÚA, Carmen, Autonomous University of Barcelona, Department of Economics and Economic History (Spain)

SCHWALGIN, Susanne, University of Muenster, Department of Education and Social Sciences (Germany)

SCHOPP, Isabelle, University of Liège, Laboratoire de Recherches sur les Sociétés Industrielles (Belgium)

SOGNER, Sølvi, University of Oslo, Department of History (Norway)

VIKSTRÖM, Marie-Christine (Lotta), Umeå University, Department of Historical Demography (Sweden)

WALL, Richard, University of Essex, Department of History (United Kingdom)

WALTER, Bronwen, Anglia Polytechnic University (Cambridge), Irish Diaspora Studies (United Kingdom)

List of Illustrations

Introduction

Antoinette FAUVE-CHAMOUX

The condition of European servants has never been a poor field of interest or research until now. We may be surprised at the number of paintings[1] and texts which, century after century, describe the lives and conditions of those who constituted perhaps the most important part of the active population. We could also appreciate a full list of studies, mainly monographs, which the thema gave rise to in more recent past decades.[2] But time came for a systematization of this interest and for an extension of its perspectives: first for comparative research, to which the European area was first evidently to give the necessary background for two types of inquiries. One of them concerns the broad economic significance of an apparently purely "domestic" activity (after all, domestic service was a specific form, maybe the first one, of non-permanent employment contracts), the second one in its deep social significance as a factor of social cohesion and European identification.

These are the major concern which inspired the initiators of the *Servant Project*.[3] This book is an attempt to determinate with some accuracy the role of servants, past and present, in the multi-secular process of socio-economic transition and urbanization which affected European societies. As domesticity, even in remote times, meant some local, regional or transnational migration, this study might also help in understanding the contemporary long distance labour migrations linked to new domestic and

1 See Giles Waterfield, Anne French and Matthew Craske (eds), *Below Stairs, 400 years of servants' portaits*, National Portrait Gallery, London, 2003.

2 For the best overview of the related bibliography, see the Servant Project online Library Database: http://www.uniurb.it/Servantproject/
Content Referee: Raffaella Sarti, Maria Casalini with the help of Helma Lutz and Susanne Schwalgin.

3 *Servant Project* is the acronym for "The socio-economic role of males and females in domestic service as a factor of European identity" (Contract n°: HPSE–CT2001-50012), Project financed within the Key Action Improving the Socio-economic knowledge Base, 2001–2004).
All information on the project may be found on: http://www.servantproject.com/

family service as well as care systems related to demographic and social changes.

Domestic Service Past and Present and the Formation of European Identity: The Servant Project

The purpose of the Servant Project network[4] was not only to study the socio-economic role of domestic service since the Renaissance and how it contributed to forming a European identity, but to understand the contemporary long distance labour migrations linked to new domestic and family service, and care systems related to demographic and social changes.

We could no longer be satisfied with an approach to the socio-economic development of Europe that mostly ignored the servant population and its variances across time and country, this means 10 to 20 percent of the working population (Fauve-Chamoux and Fialova 1997). This is particularly true when we consider the fact that they were the youngest and the most mobile elements – men and women – in these populations and therefore the most open to innovation, even if servants of very young ages tended to disappear in many European regions (with some exceptions, as shown by Fauve-Chamoux 2004 for the Central Pyrénées, or Waris 2004 for Estonia).[5] We may suspect how much weight they had in the socio-cultural mixture and in changes in mentality. We might also assume that these young people, living often in wealthier and more learned households than their family of origin, would have felt dissatisfied, and as a consequence more concerned about social promotion, but,

4 The Coordinator of the Servant Project was Professeur Suzy Pasleau, LERIDOC (Laboratoire de Recherches sur les Sociétés Industrielles), Université de Liège, Belgium. The Servant Thematic Network gathered together twenty Institutes or Departments, dependent on nineteen Universities or European High Schools, in the fields of Social Sciences, Economics (labour market, female labour), History, Demography, Statistics, etc. Besides a coordinator, principal contractors and members, several experts were invited. The detailed structure and composition of the Network may be fund in Annex, below.

5 In Estonia, it was common to take young girls into the household as foster-children, partly so that they could look after the smaller children in the family

before our European project, the state of the research did not allow any conclusion whatsoever, because we had not a comprehensive knowledge of this servant class. Of course, we did rely on a number of case studies – some of them useful and enlightening – but their approach of such a wide field of research was too varied to allow for comparative study. Hence our effort to associate, within the *Servant Project*, different groups of research working on a common thematic and to stimulate collaboration between historians and social scientists of the present times. It implied building a scholarly network[6] and pan-European compatible databanks. A preliminary Conference held in Brussels, December 2001, "Bonnes pour le service. Déclin, professionnalisation et émigration de la domesticité, Europe–Canada, 19e–20e siècles" was soon published as a special issue of *Sextant* (Gubin and Piette 2001). This process had already begun informally before a European network came into existence in the framework of a European Project: the first international meeting devoted to domestic service was held in 1996, *Le phénomène de la Domesticité en Europe, XVIe–XXe siècles,* Departement of Sociology, Charles University, Pragua (Czech Republic). It was followed by a series of conferences and sessions including: "Women's employment, marriage age and population change", International Conference held at University of New Delhi, sponsored by the International Commission for Historical Demography (CIDH), March 1997; "Domestic Service: comparing European models", Social Science History Association (SSHA), Chicago, November 1998; "Living in the City", University La Sapienza, International Conference sponsored by the CIDH, September 1999 (Sonnino 2004); "Domestic Service in comparative perspective", Third European Social Science History Conference (ESSHC), Amsterdam, March 2000. We were happy, thanks to all partners of the

6 Five seminars were organized during the *Servant Project*, on the following topics:
- First Seminar in Florence, "Servants and changes in mentality (16th–20th centuries)", 14–16th February 2002;
- 2nd Seminar in Oslo, "Domestic service and the emergence of a new conception of labour in Europe", 13–15th June 2002;
- 3rd Seminar in Barcelona, "Domestic service and the evolution of the law", 12–15th December 2002;
- 4th Seminar in Essex, "Domestic service, a factor of social revival in Europe", 8–10th May 2003;
- 5th Seminar in Munich, "The modelization of domestic service", 8–11th September 2003.

Project,[7] members and invited experts, to cover the whole Europe (West/East; North/South) and to be able to compare Europe and extra-European countries as Canada (Lacelle 1987, Barber 1991, de Groot and Ouellet 2001, Baillargeon 2001), USA (Lynch-Brennan's chapter below, Harzig 1997), India, Japan, Australia (Robinson 1988, Hetherington 2002), particularly in the present days, considered as an age of globalization). One of our main aims was to furnish information to policy makers. While discussing the appropriate themas, to that end, four research objectives emerged during our early meetings, with the proposal to cover them in an interdisciplinary socio-economic approach. These following four research themas are therefore considered in the successive parts of this book.

1. Domestic service, life course and social renewal,
2. Domestic service and the evolution of law,
3. Servants and changes in mentality: the relationship between the maid, the master and the family,
4. Servant adaptability to the labour market, past and present.

Domestic Service, Life Course and Social Renewal

Domestic service was often a "life-cycle occupation", as Peter Laslett called it in *The World we have Lost* (Laslett 1965). Many chapters in the present volume trace how it acted as one of the factors of social renewal all over Europe, be it a temporary or a lifetime occupation (R. Wall, B. Moring, C. Lundh, L. Vikström, I. Dubert, O. Rey Castelao and R. Iglesias, L. Fialová in the present volume). The first theme discussed in this volume – domestic service and social renewal – is doubtlessly the best documented one, for it being the reason that it always appears, under one or another form, in statistical studies. Inquiries about migration, about the growing number of households headed by women living alone, about professional feminization, etc., brought much useful information, but they do not always suggest identical conclusions.

7 See in Annex the list of members and partners of the Servant project network.

The "servant" population has been said to make up 17 percent of the urban adult population (aged more than 15) in seventeenth century Europe (Cipolla 1976). However, at that time, being a servant was only a transitory moment of one's life course and, for many women, a stage before marriage as well as an opportunity to amass wages and marry at a higher social level. It interested essentially young people, but there was a change in the eighteenth century, especially for women. Their growing migration to town, during the early modern period, affected the matrimonial market conditions (Fauve-Chamoux and Sogner 1994). Celibacy was too often the lot of these young populations drawn to town by economic crisis from their villages where they could no longer earn their subsistence. In such conditions, the transitory stage of domestic service – with its moral dangers stressed by so many contemporary thinkers as Thomas Robert Malthus in his first *Essay on the Principle of Population* (1798)[8] – lasted far longer than expected, often beyond the limits of the normal age at marriage, and could become a permanent occupation.

Service was a key factor in the growing urbanization of past European societies and is still nowadays a key motivation for immigration to Europe. Beyond apprenticeship, another pattern of education emerged independent of the old guild system: domestic service was in Europe a *sui generis* mechanism for geographical and social mixing. It may be considered as providing to young people, during a moment of there life course, a strong motivation to pursue social promotion. Whether domestic service was mostly a "life-cycle" occupation remains subject to discussion: examples of men and women in service during all their entire life can be seen, but, in the old days, the great majority of male and female servants used to quit this dependant position to get married. Besides the problem of definition of what is a domestic servant or "family help" and his/her tasks, present authors have considered both servants and slaves and have included persons working for institutions (nursing homes, hospitals, convents).

8 First *Essay on the Principle of Population as it affects the future improvement of society with remarks on the speculations of Mr. Godwin, M. Condorcet and other writers*, 1798 (published anonymously), J. Johnson, London, Chap. IV and Chap. VII.

Domestic Service and the Evolution of Law

Many of the essays gathered in this book present the definition and evolution of the servant's duty according to various laws and customs (particularly S. Sogner, A. Martín Casares, M. L. Nagata, K. Jaehrling, A. Blackett). Specific labour laws emerged from the contractual practices between servants and employers. We know for early modern times that the courts were increasingly concerned with the matter. Their sanctions are documented, especially in England, but we cannot generalize. In France, so it appears, civil and ecclesiastical courts usually sided with the female servants when they were seduced and became pregnant by their employer or a fellow manservant. In that case, we may point out a crucial difference between European societies and slave states, where the master's law always triumphed.

More generally, there is no doubt that specific labor laws were in formation rather early in many countries. It appears that this process had a true European dimension. An important question is if and to what extent these labor laws may be considered as antecessors to more recent labor laws enacted after associations and trade unions were recognized as legitimate. A general answer to this question would be all the more important since this would be a clear and rare case of transition from private family law to social labor law. Some chapters in this book answer partly this question. Authors stress the emergence and consolidation of servants' rights (social welfare, rest times, the constitution of brotherhoods, dowries, sponsorships, etc.) and the differences between countries and mentalities. We notice the growing possibility of juridical claims (for instance in cases of unpaid wages, sexual harassment, etc.[9] or in cases of professional misconduct – sanctions and punishment by time and country). In our age of globalization, it is time for reducing gender inequalities among migrant workers, as shown by R. Parreñas. Mary Louise Nagata brings an interesting comparative long view on labor migrations and legal and political environment of domestic service in Japan from 1600 to 1937.

9 A recent book, written by a Philipina women, a mother of four children left in her home country, maid in Abu Dhabi and later in Paris, gives some striking testimony of "new slavery" (Medina-Sirven 2004).

Servants and Changes in Mentality: the Relationship between the Maid, the Master and the Family

On this point, sources are numerous in Europe, some were already well explored, as in England (S. Cooper in the present volume), but without enough comparative or statistical perspective – if any – on an European scale. Of course, the easiest sources to study were the literary ones (Schulte and Hantzaroula 2001), but how are we to treat them rigorously? We find servants in every comedy, the author being Molière, Marivaux or Beaumarchais (Deloffre 1996)[10] or in every *mémoire*; they usually are rogue and impertinent, their masters hard-hearted and miserly. There are so many similarities that we ought only to mistrust these descriptions when not corroborated from other sources liable to a statistical approach (length of employment, motivations in the sentences of courts, career after first employment). We know that, in this area of research, a lot remains to be done. Another difficult theme could lead us to revealing results: the domestic service and the churches. The research by Renate Durr (1995), who conducted a thorough analysis of exceptional documents about the attitude of the Lutheran church versus servants in pre-modern times, could be amplified.

What we know much better is how important was the role of domestic service as a stage in the life course and as a self-regulating parameter in demographically growing societies with generally late and selective marriages. Pre-industrial family formation models developed both by John Hajnal (1965, 1982, 1983) and Peter Laslett suggest clearly a correlation between the number of servants and high rates of celibacy, as well as growing numbers of illegitimate births.

A further overall European survey of servants and their families (descent and descendants) based on census would throw some more light on their individual and familial behavior and show how specific they were. However, the situations were very complex, according to time, place and socio-economic context. Creating further consistent maps on an European scale would not be an easy task, even if past and present migration patterns are actively studied (Rosental 1999, Barjot and Faron 2002), and if

10 For example: Molière, *L'Avare*; Marivaux, *Le Petit Maître corrigé*, or *Le Jeu de l'Amour et du Hasard*.

well-archived oral sources are now available in many European countries (especially Greece, Balkanic countries, Belgium, France and central Europa).[11] In the present volume, some authors describe the long path which leads from merging into the employer's household to individualistic behaviour emphasizing the long time it took for individualistic self affirmation. We have good reasons to think that servants did play a role in the emergence of the modern family pattern (free choice of spouse, conjugal family, concubinage, illegitimacy). We discover also new fascinating models of globalization of domestic service in present time, be it in Italy (M. Magat), Germany (H. Lutz and S. Schwalgin), Greece (P. Hantzaroula) or Turkey (G. Özyegin).

Servant Adaptability to the Labour Market, Past and Present

Being highly adaptable to the labour market, domestic service favoured the emergence of a new conception of labour in Europe with the appearance of precarious or short time labour contracts. Until now, we had a fair knowledge of labor only in the framework of guilds, where labor was carefully structured according to a hierarchical system, with apparently inescapable rules of apprenticeship going back to the Middle Ages. On the contrary, the contact between the servant and the employing household allows for many kinds of adaptation. Elisabeth Ewan gives various fascinating examples of by-employments in sixteenth-century Scottish towns. Furthermore, what employers expected from servants changed with time.

Employment of servants was, above all, a matter of supply and demand in a shifting market, for a duration which everyone, employer and servant alike, knew to be relatively short. These servants were not exactly organized along class lines, but rather regrouped according to age, common rural origin, etc. People only joined such groups temporarily rather than for the whole life course, although the period of domestic service continuously lengthened as time moved on, as matrimonial projects were increasingly doomed to failure. Carmen Sarasúa shows to what extent traditions

11 Cf. Karl Kaser's projects at Institut für Geschichte, University of Graz (Austria).

and constructed roles shape supply and demand concerning domestic service remuneration.

In Europe, this labour market depended mostly on recruiting networks, but our knowledge of them up to now was very limited, for the past as for the present. Shireeen Moosvi brings an interesting long-term comparative perspective on Indian servants, male and female. Real employment agencies appeared during the eighteenth century, which we may consider the ancestors of our agencies for short term jobs. Bronwen Walter dedicates her chapter to Irish domestic servants in England, while Margaret Lynch-Brennan retraces the difficult conditions of living of Irish servants in Northern America. Nowadays, recruiting agencies and large employment networks dominate the recruitment system, including the internet. The globalization of care systems creates new patterns of institutions and large interactions, as shown by Lise W. Isaksen, Suzy Pasleau and Isabelle Schopp. We observe for example in Europe some unification of remuneration levels according to skills and tasks. The sexual division of labour encourages the long trend of feminization and professionalization of domestic service that generalized during the nineteenth century (Sarti 1997). Consequences of this globalization of service and care givers on both families of origin and family of employers are part of today's policy makers concern.

The Essays in this Volume

The papers selected for the present volume are only a sample of the intense studies and discussions which the Servant Project network helped to promote. Many other papers were discussed in one or another of the five seminars we held. Facing such affluent themas of research and suggestions, the editor's task would have been an impossible one without the support of the Editorial Committee[12] helping to choose among so many

12 The Editorial Committee was composed of: Antoinette Fauve-Chamoux, John Komlos, Suzy Pasleau, Carmen Sarasúa, Regina Schulte, Sølvi Sogner, Richard Wall, as principal contractants. Raffaella Sarti was invited to participate.

papers with high scientific qualifications.[13] Since some papers presented in French had been already published in Belgium as a special issue of *Sextant* (Gubin and Piette 2001), it was decided that this present volume would be in English. Other related meetings offered some more opportunities of dissemination of the network activities which are going on and enlarging.[14] Forthcoming *Proceedings*, edited by Suzy Pasleau and Isabelle Schopp will offer a larger view of the Servant Project contribution to this so important field of research and contemporary preoccupation: the labour condition of private household helpers and care givers living in Europe – be their situation legal or not –, their individual and gender characteristics, origin, motivation and cultural identity, facing their own family and also their communities of origin and destination.

References

BAILLARGEON, Denyse, 2001, "'Sur les berceaux, je veille'. Les aides-maternelles de la Fédération nationale Saint-Jean-Baptiste et la professionnalisation des domestiques (1928–1940)", in Eliane GUBIN and Valérie PIETTE (eds), *Sextant*, numero 15–16, Université Libre de Bruxelles, pp. 203–235.

13 This volume should have been edited jointly by Antoinette Fauve-Chamoux and Raffaella Sarti, Researcher in Early Modern History at the University of Urbino, Italy and associate member of the Centre de Recherches Historiques, EHESS/CNRS, Paris. Because of scientific disagreements between us, we decided to go back to the original project submitted to the European Commission, according to which Antoinette Fauve-Chamoux was the only editor of the final selective publication. Nevertheless, the present volume has profited from Raffaella Sarti's work, even though the parts she had written have in the end not been included here.

14 "Making a career in domestic service: a comparative perspective", 4th European Social Science History Conference (ESSHC), Den Hague, February 2002; "Domestic service old and new" and "Domestic Service in comparative perspective: the long view (16th–20th centuries)", Session 29, XIIIth International Congress of Economic History, Buenos Aires, Argentine, July 2002; "Servants and children. The role of domestic personnel in upbringing and education of master's children (16th–21st centuries)", 5th European Social Science History Conference (ESSHC), Humboldt University, Berlin, Germany, March 2004; "Domestic service and domestic servants", 20th International Congress of Historical Sciences (CISH) and International Commission for Historical Demography (ICHD), University of New South Wales, Sydney, Australia, July 2005.

BARBER, Marilyn, 1991, *Immigrant domestic servants in Canada*, Ottawa, Canadian Historical Association.

BARJOT, Dominique and FARON, Olivier (eds), 2002, *Migrations, cycle de vie familial et marché du travail*, Société de Démographie Historique/Association Française d'histoire économique, Paris.

CIPOLLA, Carlo M., 1976, *Before the Industrial Revolution: European Society and Economy, 1000–1700,* New York, Norton.

De GROOT, Raphaëlle and OUELLET, Elisabeth (eds), 2001, *Plus que parfaits, les aides familiales à Montréal, 1850–2000,* Montréal, Les Editions du remue-ménage.

DELOFFRE, Frederic, 1996, "Introduction", *Marivaux, théâtre complet*, Paris, Garnier, 1996.

DURR, Renate, 1995, *Mägde in der Stadt. Das Beispiel Schwäbisch Hall in der Frühen Neuzeit*, Frankfurt a. M./New York, Campus Verlag.

FAUVE-CHAMOUX, Antoinette, 1997, "Pour une histoire européenne du service domestique à l'époque préindustrielle", in Antoinette FAUVE-CHAMOUX and Ludmila FIALOVA (eds), *Le phénomène de la domesticité en Europe, XVIe–XXe siècles. Acta Demographica*, XIII, Praha, Ceská Demografická Sociologický Ústav av CR, pp. 57–73.

–, 1998a, "Servants in Preindustrial Europe: Gender Differences", *Historical Social Research/Historische Sozialforschung*, 23, 172, pp. 112–129.

–, 1998b, "Le surplus des femmes en France préindustrielle et le rôle de la domesticité", *Population*, 2–3, pp. 359–378.

–, 2001, "Domesticité: Etat de la question. Apport de l'historiographie internationale", *Sextant*, 15–16, pp. 9–32.

–, 2004, "Patterns of leaving 'house' in a 19th century stem-family society", in Frans VAN POPPEL, Michel ORIS and James LEE (eds), *Leaving Home in Western and Eastern Societies, 16th–20th centuries*, Bern, Peter Lang, pp. 199–220.

FAUVE-CHAMOUX, Antoinette and FIALOVA, Ludmila (eds), 1997, *Le phénomène de la domesticité en Europe, XVIe-XXe siècles*, Praha, Ceská Demografická Sociologicka, Acta Demographica, XIII.

FAUVE-CHAMOUX, Antoinette and SOGNER, Sølvi (eds), 1994, *Socio-economic consequences of sex-ratios in historical perspective, 1500–1980*, Milan, Universita Bocconi.

GUBIN, Eliane and PIETTE, Valérie (eds), 2001, *Sextant*, 15–16, Université Libre de Bruxelles.

HAJNAL, John, 1965, "European Marriage Patterns in Perspective", *Population in History*, David V. GLASS and D. E. C. EVERSLEY (eds), London, Arnold, pp. 101–140.

–, 1982, "Household formation patterns in historical perspective", *Population and Development Review*, 8, 3, pp. 449–494.

–, 1983, "Two kinds of pre-industrial household formation system", *Family Forms in Historic Europe,* Cambridge, Cambridge University Press, pp. 79–90.

HARZIG, Christiane (ed.), 1997, *Peasant maids-City women, From European countryside to urban America,* Ithaca, Cornell University Press.

HETHERINGTON, Penelope, 2002, *Settlers, servants and slaves, Aboriginal and European Children in 19th century Western Australia*, Crawley, University of Western Australia Press.

LACELLE, Claudette, 1987, *Les domestiques en milieu urbain canadien au XIXe siècle*, Ottawa, Environnement Canada.
LASLETT, Peter, 1965, *The World we have Lost*, London, Methuen.
MEDINA-SIRVEN, Vilma, 2004, *Pour le meilleur et pour le pire*, Paris, Michel Lafon.
ROBINSON, Portia, 1988, *The women of Botany Bay, a reinterpretation of the role of women in the origins of Australian society*, Sydney, Macquarie Library.
ROSENTAL, Paul-André, 1999, *Les sentiers invisibles. Espaces, familles et migrations au XIXe siècle*, Paris, EHESS.
SARTI, Raffaella, 1997, "Notes on the feminization of domestic service. Bologna as a case study (18th–19th centuries)", in Antoinette FAUVE-CHAMOUX and Ludmila FIALOVA (eds), *Le phénomène de la domesticité en Europe, XVIe–XXe siècles, Acta Demographica*, XIII, pp. 125–163.
SCHULTE, Regina and HANTZAROULA Pothiti (eds), 2001, *Narratives of the Servant*, European University Institute, San Domenico (Firenze), EUI Working Paper HEC N° 2001/1.
SONNINO, Eugenio (ed.), 2004, *Living in the City*, Roma, Università degli Studi La Sapienza.
WARIS, Elina, 2004, "The family and marriage in southern Estonia", in Tapio HÄMYNEN, Jukka PARTANEN and Yury SHIKALOV (eds), *Family life on Northwestern margins of imperial Russia*, Joensuun, Joensuu University Press, pp. 333–358.

Annex

Servant Project Network Composition and Structure

1. Coordinator

University of Liège, Belgium, Laboratoire de Recherches sur les Sociétés Industrielles: Suzy PASLEAU and Isabelle SCHOPP.

2. Principal contractors

Ecole des Hautes Etudes en Sciences Sociales (Paris), France, Centre de Recherches Historiques/Centre National de la Recherches Scientifique (CNRS): Antoinette FAUVE-CHAMOUX, Raffaella SARTI, Mary Louise POWELL-NAGATA and Marie-Pierre ARRIZABALAGA.

Autonomous University of Barcelona, Spain, Department of Economics and Economic History: Carmen SARASÚA and Raquel IGLESIAS ESTEPA.
European University Institute (Florence), Italy, Department of History and Civilization: Regina SCHULTE, Pothiti HANTZAROULA and Karen DIEHL.
Ludwig-Maximilians University of Munich, Germany, Economic History Institute: John KOMLOS.
University of Essex, United Kingdom, Department of History: Beatrice MORING, Richard WALL and Matthew WOOLLARD.
University of Oslo, Norway, Department of History: Sølvi SOGNER.

3. *Members*

1. Members dependent on coordinator

Charles University (Prague), Czech Republic, Department of Demography and Geodemography: Ludmila FIALOVA.
Ecole Moyenne de l'Etat "Primo Levi" (Milan), Italy: Claudia ALEMANI.
Umeå University, Sweden, Department of historical Demography: Lotta VIKSTRÖM and Stefan WARG.
University of Białystok, Poland, Institute of History: Cezary KUKLO and Małgorzata KAMECKA.
University of Lund, Sweden, Department of Economic History: Christer LUNDH.
University of Santiago of Compostela, Spain, Department of History: Isidro DUBERT GARCIA and Ofelia REY CASTELAO.

2. Members dependent on principal contractors

University of Florence, Italy, Department of Historical and Geographical Studies: Maria CASALINI and Jean-Baptiste SALINARI (associated to Ecole des Hautes Etudes en Sciences Sociales / CNRS, Paris, Centre de Recherches Historiques.
University of Nijmegen, The Netherlands, Department of History: Angélique JANSSENS.
Oriental Universitary Institute (Naples), Italy, Department of Social Sciences: Angiolina ARRU.

University of Geneva, Switzerland, Département d'Histoire économique: Anne-Lise HEAD-KÖNIG.

University of Münster, Germany, Department of Education and Social Sciences: Helma LUTZ and Susanne SCHWALGIN.

Hungarian Central Statistical Office, Hungary, Hungary Demographic Research Institute: Tamas FARAGO.

4. *Experts*

Jacqueline ANDALL, Assistant in Italian Studies, University of Bath, United Kingdom.

Bridget ANDERSON, Anthropologist, University of Oxford, United Kingdom.

Mary BELLHOUSE, Professor of Political Science, Providence College (Rhode Island), United States.

Adelle BLACKETT, Assistant Professor of Law, University McGill, Canada and Labour Law and Labour Relations Specialist at the International Labour Organisation (Geneva).

Sjoukje BOTMAN, Doctoral candidate, University of Amsterdam, The Netherlands.

Giulia CALVI, Professor of Early-Modern History Renaissance, University of Sienna, Italy.

Giovanna CAMPANI, Professor of Intercultural Education, University of Florence, Italy.

Sheila McISAAC COOPER, Professor of History (retired), University of Indiana (Indianapolis), United States.

Beatrice CRAIG, Associate Professor in History, University of Ottawa, Canada.

Tracy DENNISON, Doctoral candidate in History, University of Cambridge, United Kingdom.

Renate DÜRR, Assistant in Modern History, University of Frankfurt, Germany.

Otto EIBEN, Professor of Human Biology (retired), Eotvos Lorand University (Budapest), Hungary.

Elisabeth EWAN, Professor of History, University of Guelph, Canada.

Esther FISCHER-HOMBERGER, Psychotherapeutic practice (Berne), Swizterland.

Edward HIGGS, Senior lecturer (History), University of Essex, United Kingdom.

Artemigia IOLI, Representative for the sector of domestic employees FILCAMS-CGIL, Italy.

Karen JAEHRLING, Researcher, Institute for Work and Technology, Gelsenkirchen, Germany.

Valerie LAFLAMME, Doctoral candidate in History, University of Montréal, Canada.

Margaret LYNCH-BRENNAN, Department of Education, University of the State of New York, United States.

Margaret MAGAT, Doctoral candidate in Folklore and Folklife, University of Pennsylvania, United States.

Tomas MANTECON, Professor in Modern History, University of Cantabria, Spain.

Aurelia MARTÍN CASARES, Assistant Professor of Social Anthropology, University of Granada, Spain.

Sabine N. MERZ, Research Assistant in Sociology, University of Massachusetts (Amherst), United States.

Shireen MOOSVI, Professor of History, Aligarh Muslim University, India.

Maria del Carmen MUNOZ RUIZ, Research Grant in Contemporary Histor, University Complutense of Madrid, Spain.

Gül ÖZYEGIN, Associate Professor of Sociology and Women's Studies Program, College of William and Mary, Williamsburg, United States.

Richard PAPING, Associate Professor Economic and Social History, University of Groningen, The Netherlands.

Rhacel PARREÑAS, Assistant Professor in Women's Studies and Asian American Studies, University of Wisconsin (Madison), United States.

Ralph ROTTE, Institute of Political Sciences, University of Aachen, Germany.

Ellen SCHRUMPF, Associate Professor of History, Telemark University College, Norway.

Leonard David SCHWARZ, Senior Lecturer in Modern History, University of Birmingham, United Kingdom.

Francesca SCRINZI, Doctoral candidate in Sociology, SOLIIS URMIS-University of Nice-Sophia Antipolis, France.

Kyoko SHINOZAKI, Doctoral candidate in Gender Studies, University of Ochanomizu (Tokyo), Japan and University of Muenster, Germany.

Carolyn STEEDMAN, Professor of History, University of Warwick, United Kingdom.

Gunnar THORVALDSEN, Researcher, Norwegian Historical Data Centre, University of Tromsø, Norway.

Eleonore VON OERTZEN, Lecturer, Technische Universität, Berlin, Germany.

Bronwen WALTER, Professor of Irish Diaspora Studies, Anglia Polytechnic University (Cambridge), United Kingdom.

Peter WARD, Professor of History, University of British Columbia (Vancouver), Canada.

Lise WIDDING ISAKSEN, Associate Professor of Sociology, University of Bergen, Norway.

Part I

Domestic Service, Life Course and Social renewal in Europe

The Social and Economic Significance of Servant Migration

Richard WALL

Writing in 1812 Mary Leadbeater counselled against Irish girls moving to London in search of higher wages in domestic service (Leadbeater 1812, 32–5).[1] The argument is presented in the form of dialogue between two peasant women, one who was tempted by the prospect of the high wages which servants could earn in London and the other who was content to remain in Ireland. First she attempted to undermine the economic rationale on the basis that only a disciplined and trained workforce would secure such wages. These standards, Leadbeater continued, Irish girls could not hope to meet even when they had previously held good service positions in Dublin. That argument failing to convince, she then urged that it would be unfair to seek out the support of relatives who had families of their own to support, and ended by raising the spectre for the girl without either friends in London or place (as a servant), of the inevitable fall into immorality. This last argument proved decisive and both girls stayed in Ireland.

It is not necessary to confuse Leadbeater's stereotypes with reality to appreciate that she raised important issues concerning the motivation for migration by servants and some of risks this might entail. These issues we will now consider further by broadening the perspective to encompass the significance of migration of servants for their parents and community as well as for their own life history.

1 This paper has benefited from points raised when it was first presented at the conference "Domestic service as a factor of social renewal in Europe", Wivenhoe House, University of Essex, 8–11 May 2003. Special thanks are due to the discussant, Edward Higgs. I would also like to thank my colleague in the University of Essex, Matthew Woollard, for assistance and advice in extracting data sets from the 1851 Census of Great Britain.

The Servant

Advantages conferred by service in another community include the opportunity to make new friends, increase the number of potential marriage partners, experience a different working environment and the possibility of social advancement. These supplemented what might be expected from any service post: training in housekeeping skills, a better diet, although this did not always materialise, and introduction to an employer whose patronage, a reward for loyal service, might be activated to protect living standards in later life. It is relatively easy from autobiographies, diaries, correspondence and oral history to document individual instances of such benefits from service but much more difficult to generalise. In the 1820s, for example, Mary Russell Mitford recorded a social visit she had paid to an invaluable former servant who had married and moved to another community, necessitating a carriage drive of some two hours (Mitford 1936, 31–9, 147–54; first published 1824–1832). In 1913 another grateful employer remembered a former servant with a Christmas gift (Dick to wife 26 December 1913, letter in possession of daughter). More practical help followed as the former servant's family grew and aged: transport to a convalescent home arranged for the war-injured husband; better employment for the eldest son (information from daughter). But it is impossible to determine the frequency of such contacts. Various factors, however, imply that relatively few former servants could depend on assistance from former employers: the short contracts served (McBride 1976, 76), the time needed to maintain contact, sensitivities about differences in status, and the impression that such contact was a return for exceptional service, founded on mutual respect while in service. In this context it may be significant that Elisabeth Shackleton recorded only three requests for character references from or on behalf of former servants between 1770 and 1781. They are heavily outnumbered by her correspondence searching for new servants (34 letters, see Vickery 1998, Appendix 5, 387–9).

Evidence is equally hard to come by concerning the relevance over the longer term of the housewifery skills that might be acquired from domestic service. The apprenticing of girls to housewifery both privately and by the parish between the sixteenth and nineteenth centuries indicates that contemporaries justified the system on this basis. Autobiographies (from a much later period) confirm that skills were acquired: from other more experienced servants in wealthier households, and directly from the employer in others. In an example of the latter, the employer of Winifred Foley, newly arrived in London in 1928 from Gloucestershire at the age of 14, demonstrated how each chore should be performed until too exhausted to tackle the stairs she sent her to the local store in search of eggs (Foley 1974, 162). Whether any skills learnt could be applied later in her own home when the servant married depended largely on the size of the social and economic gulf that separated mistress and servant. This may mean that service skills were more relevant to the servant during the era of "life-cycle service" before 1800, when (following Sheila Cooper) servants were often the social equals of their employers in that they would hire servants themselves later in their lives whereas after 1800 it increasingly became a class as well as an age specific employment. In the case of Winifred Foley, although employed in a relatively modest household, the ability to light a gas mantle was of no use in a home which lacked gas. Service in a grander household employing many servants generated routines and flaunted luxuries that were simply irrelevant out of service. Jean Rennie, for example, at the age of 18 in her first service post as third housekeeper in Argyllshire in 1924, was horrified at the large portions and waste at servants' tea. Nor she added had she ever encountered a domestic servant, male or female, who was satisfied with the food served them (life history as reported in Burnett 1974, 237).

From an earlier period Mary Leadbeater, as might be anticipated, was more sanguine about the acquisition of skills in service that could be applied in later life, commending the care the mistress took in making butter as this would help her friend should she ever acquire a cow of her own (Leadbeater 1812, 25–6). Leadbeater, however, was less pleased when contemplating, in her fictional scenario, the carrying through into married life a passion for drinking tea acquired while in service (Leadbeater 1812, 49). Flora Thompson recalling life in a hamlet on the borders of Northamptonshire and Oxfordshire towards the end of the nineteenth century, also noted (but without a hint of condemnation) that married women who had been in good service positions prior to marriage would meet to chat and drink tea, sharing the cost. According to Thompson, the conversation was lighter and more refined than at other gatherings of women from the neighbourhood (Thompson 1945, 108). However, although such forms of socialising may well have developed out of experience gained in domestic service, other explanations are possible such as changes in the behaviour of younger cohorts. Most of the women participating in these tea drinkings were said by Flora Thompson to be under 40.

The issue of whether servants benefited from a better diet than could be provided by their parents is also not as easily determined as it might at first appear. Most of the girls like Jean Rennie who accepted even humble posts in gentry households probably did eat well even when other decisions made by employers provided evidence of meanness and lack of consideration (see the summary of Jean Rennie's account of her second period of service in Burnett 1974, 243 which reports her mistress's Christmas gift of material for a dress for work and the master's reclaiming from a fellow servant of the 'fortune' sixpence he had found in the Christmas pudding). The provision by such households of better food in quantity may have compensated to some extent for the spatial as well as the social distance that could separate employer and many of the more humble employees in wealthy households (Meldrum 2000, 86). Modest households provided more opportunity for companionship between mistress and servant but this could be at the expense of a very inadequate diet. In the 1920s Winifred Foley's sister had accepted lower wages to continue in the service of an impoverished maiden lady. This enabled her to spend her time mending old clothes, embroidering tablecloths and painting woodwork while her mistress attended to the washing up and dusting, tasks which her sister hated. The diet, however was poor. For breakfast, the mistress bought the cheapest streaky bacon and fried bread, sharing it with her servant in a way that one morning the mistress had the bacon and the servant the bread, while on the next the servant had the bacon and the mistress the bread (Foley 1984, 27). In her second and third service posts, Winifred Foley herself ate only poorly, in the former because of her employer's poverty and in the latter due to meanness and the employing family trying to live in a style that exceeded their income (Foley 1974, 177, 187–90). This third employer provided his servant with less and poorer quality food than they allowed themselves. It needs to be remembered, however, that these accounts of life in domestic service come from an era late in the evolution of domestic service as an institution. For earlier times there is little direct evidence of how well servants were fed. It would seem likely though that there was less inequality in the diets of master and servant particularly when service was life cycle in character in that the servants of today were the masters and mistresses of tomorrow and when employer and employee ate from the same table. On the other hand, genteel poverty was not a creation of the twentieth century. Elisabeth Gaskell described the elegant poverty of the ladies of a quiet Cheshire village in her novel *Cranford* first published in 1851 and many of the widows and spinsters who were enumerated in the lists of inhabitants of the seventeenth and eighteenth century as keeping a servant were probably in no better position to feed them adequately, surviving as they did on fixed incomes and divided inheritances (Wall 2002) than were the employers of Winifred Foley in the 1920s.

Table 1. Residence of children of labourers and craftsmen resident in Cardington in 1782 who were in service

Location	*Males (%)*	*Females (%)*
Cardington	45	17
Elsewhere within 8 km	32	55
8–16 km.	10	3
16 km. + (excl. London)[1]	7	10
London	5	14
All	100	100
N[2]	40	29

1 Excludes 2 males at sea and 5 soldiers.
2 Includes 1 craftsman and 4 unmarried girls not specified as servants.
Source: Calculated from Schofield 1970, pp. 268–9, Table III.

Table 2. Unmarried children aged 10+ of labourers and craftsmen resident in Cardington, Bedfordshire, in 1782 who were in service

Residence	*Males (%)*	*Females (%)*	*Sex Ratio*[1]
At Home	62	78	75.6
Service	38	22	156.0
N	104	111	93.7

1 Males per 100 females.
Source: Calculated from Schofield, 1970, 265, Table II. Count of servants in Schofield adjusted to exclude 2 males at sea, 5 soldiers and 1 craftsman, and 4 unmarried girls resident outside the parental home but not said to be in service; 3 male apprentices are included.

The longer term impact of spells of service also need consideration, in particular the opportunity they provided to move from parish to parish and from country to town, and in the process build up experience of work which could help secure further employment (possibly on a part-time basis) when married. It is well known that the population of England in the past was extremely mobile. Reconstitutions of parish registers suggest that on average about two thirds of those born in a village would reside elsewhere as adults (Souden 1984). It is also known that "snapshot" enumerations of communities in pre-industrial England reveal that servants were housed by some poor households as well as many wealthy ones, that at the time of the enumeration around a third of men and women aged between 15 and 24 could be in service (Laslett 1977, 34; Laslett 1965, 14; Laslett 1972, 154) and that servants frequently changed positions and their parishes of residence. These features of the social structure would seem to be related but in the absence of detailed life histories of the sort that can be compiled from population registers, it is impossible to determine what proportion of servants met their future spouse while they were in service in another parish and then set up home either there or in their partner's home parish. Mary Russell Mitford noted that at 14 all the village girls disappeared into service in neighbouring towns but that some (the proportion left unspecified) returned to marry (Mitford 1936, 136–7).

A detailed study of the migration patterns of servants whose parents, labourers and journeymen craftsmen, were resident in the Bedfordshire parish of Cardington in 1782 was carried out some years ago by Schofield (Schofield 1970). His results are reproduced in a slightly amended form in Table 1 and reveal that, when the census was taken, somewhat over half of their sons and more than 80 percent of their daughters over the age of 10 and then in service had gone to live in other parishes. The proportions ever entering service in another parish would of course be higher as, by the time the list was drawn up, some of the children would have left service while others were still (or currently) resident in the parental home. Five percent of their sons and 14 percent of their daughters were in service in London, some 80 kilometres to the south. However, just over half of the girls were in service in the county town at a distance of only 4 kilometres (cf. Baker 1973, 58). If these proportions are then compared with the locations of those children of the labourers and craftsmen who had married (Schofield 1970, 258–9), it emerges that lower proportions of the married sons resided locally (25 percent) and that higher proportions lived in London (31 percent). The residence patterns of the married daughters differed less markedly from those in service although fewer

(39 percent) were living outside Cardington but within 8 kilometres (which would include Bedford) and more over 8 kilometres but within 16 kilometres of Cardington (18 percent). It would thus seem clear that if Cardington can be considered representative, residence when in service was not a good predictor of residence when married. However some qualifications are in order. First, there were some distinctive aspects of the local economy (the significance of these is considered later); secondly, that the married children were not the children who had been in service but their elder (usually) siblings and thirdly, that service may have influenced the choice of marriage partner and provided the training that made it possible later for the sons to find employment in London even if it did not directly dictate the location of later residence.

The enumeration of Cardington in line with other lists does not indicate the precise duties of these servants. Many undoubtedly might best be described as farm servants or trade assistants. However, there was a nebulous border between such "productive" work and domestic tasks. The migration patterns of domestic servants where such servants can be identified also do not appear to be markedly different. Elisabeth Shackleton for example in her attempts to recruit servants between 1770 and 1781 for successive homes on the borders of Yorkshire and Lancashire drew on a network where the average distance between her home and the contact (usually a former or potential employer of a servant) was 22 kilometres. A quarter were within 9 kilometres although this may be unrepresentative as servants recruited locally may not have generated correspondence (details compiled from Vickery 1998, 387–9 with the aid of a modern gazetteer).

The second issue that requires consideration is the impact of service employment on future work histories. Autobiographies and oral histories can be invaluable in this connection. Those that I have consulted indicate very little strategic thinking governed the choice of a service post even on the part of those entering service in the 1920s. As Winifred Foley put it "for girls, going into service was the only future. There was no employment for us in the village" (Foley 1974, 141). She settled on a post in London, advertised in the *Daily Herald* with about as much thought of the realities as the foolish (but fictional) Irish girl counselled by Mary Leadbeater early in the previous century. Older girls from the village had become servants in Cheltenham or Bristol. Winifred, however, would aim higher and try London (*ibid.*, 146).

Even in the absence of strategic thinking, service could prove useful for later working history. Burnett's potted biographies of the servants stories he included in *Useful Toil* are informative (Burnett 1974). Of those we have mentioned above, Jean Rennie became manageress of the American Red Cross Services Club in Greenock and later cook to a firm of solicitors. Winifred Foley worked sometime as a waitress in a teashop and after marriage and while her family was growing up took the "classic" path into charring and part-time domestic work. Of the other women not previously mentioned, Lavinia Swainbank referred to her final service post prior to marriage as enabling her "to complete my training to be a good housewife" (*ibid.*, 221) while Lilian Westall after wartime munitions work acted for twelve years as an escort to deaf children. In all four cases work as a servant could be said to have helped steer these women in later years into particular types of employment as different service type employments emerged and domestic service in its purer form declined in popularity. Many more life histories, however, are required to determine the typicality of their experiences.

The question of whether domestic service facilitated social mobility is a different one. Evidence again is limited but in a study conducted two decades ago, Penelope Wilcox argued, based on an analysis of the civil registers of Cambridge between 1847 and 1901 that women who reported that they were in service when they married were more likely to marry into a lower social class than that of their fathers, than were women from the same social class who were not in service (Wilcox 1982, 31–2). Wilcox also considered whether service raised the age at which they married, concluding that there was some evidence that it did during the period before 1870, regardless of parental status, but that after 1870, for reasons that were not clear, women in domestic service from lower class backgrounds tended to marry earlier than other women from the same class (*ibid.*, 29, 33).

The Parental Family

It has already been demonstrated through Table 1 that one of the consequences of service for parents was that the majority of their children would reside outside their parish of current residence although not necessarily at any great distance. This means that despite the long hours which servants had to work, they might still meet on the servant's afternoon off. Winifred Foley, however, did not find this sufficient. Her departures from her first two posts were occasioned by a crisis in the parental family involving the illness of a younger sister, and homesickness. Her decisions, taken almost as hurriedly, to place herself immediately back in service but elsewhere were motivated by the realisation that the parental economy could not afford to support her at home (as even Leadbeater's Irish peasant girl with her dreams of London also appreciated, Leadbeater 1812, 36). It is on the economic significance of the departure of children from the parental home for service that the following account is focused.

If we again use the experience of Cardington by way of example, we can see that many more males than females entered service: 38 percent of the unmarried sons compared with just 22 percent of the unmarried daughters over the age of ten (see Table 2). The effect was to distort further the already low sex ratio in the offspring group so that were four daughters at home for every three sons. Keeping the girls at home (and out of service) were earning opportunities spinning linen and jersey and making lace (Baker 1973). Where such proto-industrial employments were not available, much higher proportions of daughters can be expected to have moved into service leaving the sex ratio of the offspring group within the parental household skewed in favour of sons. This was the typical situation in England in the nineteenth century (for evidence of changes in the patterns of leaving home, see Wall 1987).

The impact on the parental budget of some children being away in service will have varied according to the cost saved by not having to maintain those children at home, whether the parents had to bear the cost of providing the servant's uniform (which Foley 1974, 147 reports as the standard practice) and whether the girl in service could (and would) pass on some of her earnings to her parents. The main consideration, however, was the number of children who remained within the parental home and whether they were able to contribute significant sums to the parental economy. In the absence of direct evidence on how incomes were distributed within families, simulated populations can be created to examine the likely effects on family budgets of the absence of children in service. A simple exercise of this sort is attempted below based on the income of a labouring household in Essex at the end of the eighteenth century of

11.53 shillings per week (£30 per annum) allowing for subsidiary earnings (Sokoll 1993, 122).

The first aspect to consider is how family income may have been apportioned between family members. In earlier work on these lines (Wall 1994) the assumption has been made that male household heads consumed half as much again of the resources of the household than was at the disposal of their wives, and that sons and other males over the age of 15 a quarter more. Children aged between 10 and 14, it was assumed, consumed 75 percent of the share of an adult woman and children over 1 but under 10 half as much. A scenario on these lines embodies a considerable degree of inequality in access to the resources of the household although considerably less equality than would apply if women (and children) had to survive on what they could earn. These are of course just estimates but they appear to be in line with the limited budget evidence on the consumption of food by individual members of working class households in the middle of the nineteenth century (Wall 1994, 332, note 17) and differences in the wages allowed to those male and female servants who boarded out in the late seventeenth and early eighteenth centuries (women were paid 75 percent of the male allowance in the former period and 80 percent in the latter, see Meldrum 2000, 198).

The second issue to consider is the variation in income per head following from differences in the size and composition of households. Time and space preclude a full simulation exercise and in its absence, the most promising course is to apply the consumption indices specified above to different types of household. We may begin with the case of a household comprising, in addition to the daughter in service, one child aged 10–14 and three under 10 plus both parents. Such a family would have an income per head, distributed as suggested above, of 2 shillings per week if they had to support all members of the family including the daughter in service. However, this income would rise by just over 20 percent to 2.43 shillings per head if the daughter could be placed in service at minimal cost to the parental budget (and the Poor Law might assume responsibility for some of these costs in the event of poverty, see Wall 2003, 115–7). The incentive to enter service in these circumstances is obvious. It was a situation that families were likely to face once the eldest child (if a girl) reached the age of 14.

The second case we might consider is one where the family was of similar size and composition but with the difference that there is also an older brother still resident in the household. Family income in this case is measured with greater uncertainty as the estimate of family income will need to be altered depending on what proportion of his earnings he shared with other members of his family. If his potential earnings are ignored, then the estimates indicate an income per head of 1.92 shillings per week with the daughter out of service, and 3.42 shillings if they were added to the family's budget. In each case sending the daughter to service would raise income by some 15 percent. The final example would be more typical of a family during a later phase of development where the daughter was the youngest of the surviving children and the only child at home. This family received the largest proportionate gain from the daughter entering service, increasing income per head by 29 percent from 3.29 shillings to 4.61 shillings per week. Of course the proportionate increase in income may not always have been the critical factor governing entry into service as an income above a certain level may have lessened the need for a daughter to leave. There was also useful work (unpaid) that a girl might undertake in the parental home, care of younger children, nursing of an ill or elderly parent that might be of more value to a family than the income foregone.

A final point to bear in mind though is that the economic advantage to the parents of placing their daughters in service increased if the daughter transferred some of her modest earnings to her parents. Winifred Foley reported this in the 1920s (Foley 1974, 116, 166) but in the days before postal orders this must have been less easy for those in service at some distance from their parents. Servants earnings, however, were meagre and the contribution to the parental budget (if made) must have been modest. Meldrum (2000, 188) reports annual wages of £6–£7 paid to men in service in London in the 1740s and of £4–£5 to women. In Chelsea, some 5 kilometres to the south-west and at the time a kind of satellite village, women in service earned perhaps a little less. Over the course of the nineteenth century, money wages increased so that by the 1913 a housemaid could be paid £24 a year (according to a servants account book in my possession; for the nineteenth century, see McBride 1976, 62). However, girls entering service at the age of 14 would be paid much less. In the 1920s Winifred Foley, for example, was earning £13 a year in her second service post in the Cotswolds (Burnett 1974, 227). For the late eighteenth century we might therefore estimate the earnings of a girl of similar age as about £2 per annum. This estimate assumes constancy in the ratio between adult and adolescent earnings and there is reason to consider that it may over-estimate the earnings of an adolescent. In the 1790s, for example, the Overseers of the Poor for the Essex parish of Ardleigh were paying an adult woman just 6 pence a week for housework (equating to an annual rate of £1 6 shillings, see Wall 2002, 118). A contribution of this magnitude to the family budget of six (case 1 above) would be a modest 4 percent. More significant might be the arrival from the daughter of cast-off clothes from her employer's family, an event which Flora Thompson remembers as occasioning some excitement in the village (Thompson 1945, 102).

Table 3. Birthplace regions of servants resident in certain districts of West London in 1851 and in Middlesex

Enumeration District		*Middlesex (%)*	*Other South Eastern Counties*[1] *(%)*	*Elsewhere (%)*	*N*
601	Kensington	27	39	34	262
602	Fulham	30	28	41	92
603	Chelsea	21	38	41	66
604	Mayfair	16	34	49	271
605	Belgrave	42	38	20	50
606	St Margaret	22	46	32	153
607	Berwick St.	28	32	40	121
Total		24	37	39	1015
Middlesex (1660–1750)		24[2]	28	48	651

1 Defined to approximate definition of Meldrum and includes Surrey, Kent, Herts, Essex, Sussex, Hants, Bucks, Beds, Oxon, Berks, Northants, Cambs, Lincs, Rutland, Hunts, Suffolk and Norfolk.

2 London and Westminster with parts of Middlesex, Surrey and Kent within the metropolis in this period.

Sources: 1851: Economic and Social Research Council (ESRC) Data Archive; 1660–1750 as reported in Church Court depositions. Calculated from Meldrum 2000, p. 19.

The Employer

Given that employment of the servant within and around the household involved in many cases, particularly in more modest households, frequent contact between master, mistress and servant, it is worth considering what an employer might have "learnt" from the servant as well as the servant from the employer. As a rule, however, historians have paid scant attention to this aspect of servanthood. Accounts of a number of sexual associations of the more salacious sort are retold by Meldrum. The autobiographies also refer to the efforts servant girls frequently had to make to repulse unwanted attentions from male members of the household. In their search for household labour some potential employers were willing to offer the prospect of companionship as a sort of compensation for the drudgery of servanthood and even an eventual inheritance (Foley 1974, 182). At a more prosaic level, there can be little doubt that employers did access servant networks in order to recruit new staff, with, for example, a younger sister joining or replacing an older one. It is quite clear, however, that a number of forces hindered the development of close personal relationships between master (and mistress) and employee. These barriers included, notably, the hierarchies within the household, based first mainly on age (before 1800) and later mostly on class, the different priorities of master and servant with the latter, particularly when young, missing the parental home, and in the larger households, the development of a servant "culture" with its own hierarchies from butler and cook to third housemaid. On the other hand, relationships between mistress and servant were probably at their most fluid when age, relative poverty or illness rendered the employer dependent on her sole (female) servant.

The Local Community

In the final section of this paper, we turn to the impact of the migration of servants on the wider community, focusing in particular on the experience of specific areas of London and adjacent communities. Table 3 has been compiled from a random sample of the census enumeration schedules from the 1851 census of Great Britain (data supplied by the Economic and

Social Research Council [ESRC] Data Archive). The census records the birthplaces of almost all those persons enumerated but unfortunately not how long those born elsewhere had lived in the area. In the case of servants this means, for example, that we cannot tell whether they had migrated directly to London from their place of birth in order to enter service (like Winifred Foley) or alternatively had lived elsewhere in or out of service, or had moved at some earlier point, perhaps with their parents. Nevertheless the Table does indicate the considerable distance that separated the birthplaces of many servants from the districts of West London where they were in service in 1851. Only a quarter were locally born, even in the broad sense that they had been born in the same county (Middlesex). Somewhat over a third had moved within the region (again broadly defined) with a similar proportion having been born in areas of the country most distant from London. Further analysis (not included in Table 3) revealed that 2 percent of the servants had been born in Wales, another 2 percent in Scotland and 8 percent in Ireland; 3 percent were foreign born. The definition of locally born can be modified in a number of ways. If, for example, it is changed to include also those servants born in Surrey (which included parishes immediately south of these districts), and with less justification, Kent, as even its metropolitan parts were more distant, this would raise the proportion defined as locally born to 34 percent and lower the proportion born non locally but within the region to 27 percent.

There is also evidence in Table 3 of considerable variation between districts in the proportions born locally or further away: for example the proportions of servants claiming to have been born in Middlesex range from 16 percent in Mayfair to 42 percent in Belgrave. The reason for the variation is not evident. Random variation, given the small size of some of the servant populations, may explain some of the variation but another factor is likely to have been the operation of different recruitment policies by different employers, particularly on the part of those who held country estates as well as keeping a house in London.

The country has been divided in this way to facilitate comparison with the migration patterns of London servants between 1660 and 1750 derived from the details witnesses provided to the church courts (Table 3, last row, following Meldrum 2000). Little change is evident in the migration patterns of servants between this earlier period and 1851 as regards the proportions born either locally or elsewhere. Admittedly the comparison is not exact as Meldrum used information on the servant's parish of birth to identify the proportion of servants born in London rather than in Middlesex. The former he defined as those parts of the counties of Middlesex, Surrey and Kent lying within the metropolitan area, and included the rest of these counties in his construction of the region of South and East England outside of London. He did not specify the exact areas involved but by 1851 the metropolis would in any case have expanded considerably and there would be little point in trying to replicate it here in connection with 1851. However, examination of data on parish of birth from the census of 1851 in combination with information on the extension of housing developments provided by a contemporary map would reveal the proportion of servants born in the metropolitan area as of 1851 although not in the metropolitan area as it was constituted in the year of their birth. The amount of work involved in identifying this area would, however, be considerable. In the meantime the comparison provided by Table 3 based on the proportion of servants born in Middlesex must suffice. This comparison should thus be considered as offering only a rough approximation to Meldrum's definition of the metropolitan area in that, included in the count, would be some servants born in the non metropolitan parts of Middlesex while servants from metropolitan parts of Kent and Surrey have been excluded.

The diversity of servants' birthplaces is also in evidence in Table 4. In 1851 England, Wales and Scotland were divided into 89 counties. Fifty of these appeared among the birthplaces of the 250 England born servants resident in Mayfair in the same year. Even the 46 servants resident in the Belgrave district produced 17 different counties as birthplaces. In most districts there was just one or two servants originating from a particular county (Table 4, last column). The mean number of servants per county was larger because of the much larger proportions born in certain counties, such as Middlesex (see Table 3). However, very few counties other than Middlesex, Surrey and Kent contributed more than 5 percent of the total number of servants in any of the seven districts (just Essex, Hampshire and Yorkshire on one occasion each).

A further perspective on the impact on the local community of migration by servants is provided by documentation that was produced during the collection of Poll Taxes at the end of the seventeenth century. Payments due in connection with some of these taxes were collected quarterly or even, on rare occasions, monthly (Arkell 1992, 159), necessitating searches by collectors for taxpayers listed at the beginning of the year. Table 5 has been compiled from the Poll Tax returns for the parishes of St Clement Danes (an urban parish just outside the London city walls) and Chelsea (then a satellite village of London) for the year 1698–9 and shows the number of taxpayers who had "disappeared" due to migration by the time the collectors came to demand payment. Persons listed as not paying due to poverty or having died since the list was drawn up have been excluded.

In considering the evidence on migration patterns provided by the Poll Taxes two points need to be kept in mind. The first is that they are returns of taxpayers and not lists of entire populations. Large sections of the population were liable (including servants) but persons in receipt of poor relief together with those deemed too poor to contribute to the church and poor rates were exempted (Arkell 1992, 151, 156; Alexander 1992, 186). The total number of migrants is therefore under-estimated as is the rate of migration if poorer sections within the population were more mobile. The second point worth considering is the impact of evasion. There are two problems. First, some persons may have escaped listing altogether. The second is that other persons, having been initially listed as liable for the tax, may have moved to avoid payment. The latter type of evasion is the more serious in the present context as if it had occurred on any significant scale, it would result in inflated estimates of the number of migrants. There can be little room for doubt that there was some evasion. Contemporaries suspected as much and some individual instances were documented (details from Cooper 1992, 207–8). However, although the extent of evasion was (and remains) difficult to determine, Cooper's verdict after careful examination of payment of the Poll Taxes in King's Lynn is that evasion primarily concerned avoidance or under-payment of the surtaxes rather than of the standard charge (*ibid.*, 208).

The evidence that the Poll Taxes provide on the extent of migration in the late seventeenth century is thus not easy to adjust for omissions. It has to be taken on trust or rejected. Here we take it in trust as it provides considerable detail on the migration patterns of large sections of the population. Four sub-populations have been identified: servants, lodgers, under-tenants and householders with their families. It needs to be emphasised that the terms "under-tenant" and "householder", unlike that of servant and lodger, are not to be found in the records but have been introduced here to distinguish those individuals reported as formerly resident in the house of another person but who were not described as lodgers (and termed here under-tenants) from both lodgers and other persons who as they were identified only by their names have been considered as members of principal households. Admittedly such distinctions place considerable faith in the consistency of the list maker and the distinction between lodger and under-tenant, and even between under-tenant and householder, may be misleading in suggesting the presence within the local population of distinct sub-groups. However, I would argue that for the present, the categories are best kept apart in case further analysis reveals important differences in the behaviour of the two groups either in terms of migration or family composition.

Proceeding in this way, the final two columns of Table 5 thus indicate that servants contributed 15 percent of all migrations in St Clement Danes, lodgers and under-tenants about a quarter each, and householders about a third. Servants contributed a much larger proportion to the pool of migrants in the satellite village of Chelsea where approximately four in every ten migrations involved a servant. However, as in St Clement Danes, about a third of migrations in Chelsea were made by householders and members of their families. On the other hand, lodgers and under-tenants, particularly the latter, formed much smaller proportions of the migrants than in St Clement Danes. It would seem likely that this reflects differences in the social structure of the two parishes (fewer lodgers and under-tenants in the population of Chelsea).

Unfortunately as the initial list of taxpayers for either Chelsea or St Clement Danes appears not to have survived, it is impossible to establish the proportion of servants who moved during 1697–8 of the total in residence at the start of the year or to determine whether servants were more likely to migrate than, say, householders or other groups in the population. However, it would seem plausible that those with a less secure footing in the community such as lodgers, under-tenants and particularly servants were more prone than householders to move in and out of a parish and comparison of the annual lists of the inhabitants of other parishes compiled under the Marriage Duty Act of 1694 certainly indicates this to be the case (work in progress on lists of inhabitants in the library of the Cambridge Group). The Poll Tax also implies that more migration was undertaken by women than by men (Table 5, last row). This was particularly marked in the case of Chelsea but caution is advisable in interpreting this finding because the sex of many of the Chelsea migrants was not recorded.

Table 4. Birthplace counties of servants resident in certain districts of West London in 1851. Mean and median number of servants per county

		Servants per county[1]		
District	*Servants (N)*	*Birthplace: Counties (N)*[1]	*Mean*	*Median*
Kensington	236	37	6.4	3
Fulham	77	23	3.3	1
Chelsea	56	22	2.5	1
Mayfair	250	50	5.0	2
Belgrave	46	17	2.7	1
St Margaret	126	30	4.2	2.5
Berwick St.	99	22	4.5	2.5

1 At the time England, Wales and Scotland contained 89 counties. Servants whose place of birth was recorded as Wales, Scotland, Ireland or foreign have been excluded.

Table 5. Residents of two Middlesex of St Clement Danes and Chelsea migrating during 1698–99

	Males		*Females*		*Persons*[1]	
Position in Household	St Clement Danes (%)	Chelsea (%)	St Clement Danes (%)	Chelsea (%)	St Clement Danes (%)	Chelsea (%)
Servants	4	21	24	33	15	42
Lodgers[2]	36	8	20	17	26	19
Under-Tenants[2,3]	26	8	23	10	24	8
Family of Household Head	34	62	33	40	35	32
All Migrants (N)	160	24	185	42	355	120

1 Includes migrants whose sex was not specified.
2 With in some cases accompanying family members.
3 Persons described as having resided at the house of another but who were not specified as lodgers.

Sources: Corporation of London Record Office 40/114 Estreats into the Exchequer. The return is dated on the basis of references in the returns to the quarterly poll and the detail on the various Poll Taxes in Arkell 1992, 179–80.

Of the recorded male migrants, roughly a fifth in Chelsea were servants but only 4 percent of those in St. Clement Danes. Of the female migrants, servants contributed a quarter of migrations in St. Clement Danes and a third of those in Chelsea. Higher proportions of migrations by servants in both parishes would of course be suggested if we were to measure the migration outflow in terms of the number of migrating groups instead of individuals (as in Table 5). However, as this would involve counting the migration of an entire household as the equivalent of the migration of a solitary servant, it was considered that the more effective way to measure the extent of migration on the community was to record the number of individuals who had migrated.

Moreover, not all migrations by servants involved a servant leaving a household. Some moved when the whole household relocated. Others left at the same time as other servants but without the householder's family, the records often not making clear whether they left for the same or different destinations. In Chelsea most migrations by servants occurred when the household itself moved. As Table 6 makes clear just 30 percent of migrations by servants occurred as a result of individual servants leaving a household. In St Clement Danes, on the other hand, household migrations involving servants constituted a much smaller percentage of migrations by servants. Almost two thirds of the servants who moved had left their previous posts.

Table 6. Forms of servant migration from parishes of St Clement Danes and Chelsea during 1698–99

Type	*St Clement Danes (%)*	*Chelsea (%)*
Individual	65	30
Household moves	27	58
Other Servants also move	8	12
N	52	50

Source: As Table 5.

Table 7 sets out the evidence available on the intended destinations of the people who had moved away. This evidence has to be treated with caution as in many cases the collectors despite their best endeavours could not discover from the remaining members of the household or from neighbours where the individuals had stated they were going. Incomplete though the evidence is, it is worth consideration given that so little is known about migration within and around London and between London and the provinces. For example about a quarter of all migrations by servants in St Clement Danes involved servants moving out of London and into provinces.

Table 7. Distance moved by migrant servants in parishes of St Clement Danes and Chelsea during 1698–99

St Clement Danes	*Distance moved*	*Servants (%)*	*Lodgers[1] (%)*	*Under-tenants[2] (%)*	*Family of Household Head (%)*
	Local[3]	28	38	32	46
	City[4]	11	10	5	12
	Suburbs[5]	25	16	16	21
	Provinces[6]	25	28	38	12
	Wales	3	2	3	0
	Ireland	0	5	3	4
	Overseas	5	2	3	0
	At Sea	3	0	0	5
	All	100	100	100	100
	N	36	61	37	76
	% unknown	31	42	54	48
Chelsea	Local[3]	0	60	0	7
	City[4]	14	0	33	18
	Suburbs[5]	43	40	33	39
	Provinces[6]	14	0	33	7
	Wales	0	0	0	4
	Ireland	14	0	0	7
	Overseas	14	0	0	4
	At Sea	0	0	0	4
	All	100	100	100	100
	N	14	5	3	28
	% unknown	72	78	57	30

1 Including in some cases accompanying family members.
2 Persons described as having resided at the house of another but who were not specified as lodgers.
3 A specified address within half a mile of previous residence or same parish.
4 London within the city walls or in the case of Chelsea references to London.
5 Areas immediately adjacent to London.
6 Remainder of England.
Source: As Table 5.

It seems likely (but cannot be proven) that this was return migration with servants returning to areas or even the same houses (when they moved as part of the household) where they had previously been in service. Fourteen percent of servants also moved to the provinces from Chelsea. Another 14 percent relocated to Ireland. However, much migration by servants involved no great distances. In St Clement Danes, for instance, just over a quarter of servants were still within half a mile of their former residence after the move. A further one in ten had entered other areas of the city (which shared a border with St Clement Danes) or were to be found in the immediately adjacent suburbs. The position in Chelsea differed a little with more suburban but no local moves (possibly because the collectors responsible for smaller and less tightly packed population than the collectors in St Clement Danes, did not need to make a record of migration within the parish).

The migration patterns of servants, lodgers and householders are also set out in Table 7 for comparative purposes and indicate a broad similarity in migration destinations. In this period it may be that neither class nor geographical origin separated employer and servant. In the nineteenth century it was to be different.

Conclusion

The aim of this paper has been to assess the social and economic significance of the migration of servants for the servant, her or his parental family and employer and the local community. A variety of sources have been used, some qualitative and some quantitative, and methodologies outlined which when developed further should yield more insights particularly into the benefits accruing to the parental budget of daughters moving into service where their maintenance costs were met by the employer. Limitations as well as the potential of different sources have been stressed. For example, the evidence on servant migration in the two seventeenth century populations selected for study as presented in Table 5 reveals how many servants had migrated since enumeration at the start of the year and what proportion this constituted of total migration, and for some, how far they moved but not how many servants had moved in to replace them either from elsewhere or by recruitment from the local population. The number of posts for servants is likely to have varied from community to community with the result that some communities as well families (cf. Table 1) shed labour while others gained.

Another instance of sources that provide an incomplete perspective on migration, arises in connection with the analysis of migration patterns in the nineteenth century. For certain areas of West London it has been possible to show that three quarters of the persons then in service has been born outside the home county of Middlesex but not how many of those who had been born in these areas were in service elsewhere in 1851. Such an approach would, however, be feasible with two later censuses (1881 and 1901) by accessing the birthplace information in the machine-readable versions of these censuses (available respectively from the ESRC Data Archive and the Public Record Office). Neither in the case of seventeenth or nineteenth centuries, however, do the records reveal the social significance to the servant of migration, whether local, regional or international. This only becomes clearer when servants speak or write of their own experiences of service. A review of this type of evidence stressed the variety of those experiences and the difficulty of establishing any general patterns. Even in the 1920s when most service posts no longer combined domestic duties with agricultural, industrial or retail tasks, service was very varied. In service in a middle class household in straightened circumstances in the 1920s, Winifred Foley recalled that she was a housemaid in the morning, a parlour maid in the afternoon, then nanny to the children for outings and finally a washerwoman in the evenings (Foley 1974, 184–185). In her immediately previous post, she had effectively been a nursing assistant, having to undress her elderly mistress for bed and help her onto the night commode; in her next she was a farm servant near Abergavenny (*ibid.*, 175; Burnett 1974, 227). In reality these were six different jobs but Winifred Foley moved with little evident difficulty between them.

The advantages she and other servants gained from their service, however are difficult to quantify. The potential offered by service both immediate and in the medium and long term is clear enough: the opportunity to meet new friends, widen the circle of potential marriage partners, experience of different working environments and financial assistance in married life from grateful former employers. In individual instances such benefits can be documented but the evidence does not exist to suggest that most servants received them. Even some apparent consequences of having worked as a domestic service such as the type of employment undertaken by former servants later in life were in fact not part of some strategic plan by servants when entering service but reflected instead the internal structure of the service labour market.

References

ALEXANDER, James, 1992, "The City Revealed: An Analysis of the 1692 Poll Tax and the 1693 4s. Aid in London", in Kevin SCHURER and Tom ARKELL (eds), *Surveying the People. The Interpretation and Use of Document Sources for the Study of Population in the Later Seventeenth Century*, Matlock, Local Population Studies, pp. 181–200.

ARKELL, Tom, 1992, "An Examination of the Poll Taxes of the Later Seventeenth Century, the Marriage Duty Act and Gregory King", in Kevin SCHURER and Tom ARKELL (eds), *Surveying the People. The Interpretation and Use of Document Sources for the Study of Population in the Later Seventeenth Century*, Matlock, Local Population Studies, pp. 142–180.

BAKER, David, 1973, *The Inhabitants of Cardington in 1782*, Bedfordshire Historical Record Society 52.

BURNETT, John (ed.), 1974, *Useful Toil. Autobiographies of Working People from the 1820s to the 1920s*, London, Allen Lane.

COOPER, Sheila, 1992, "Household Form and Composition in King's Lynn: A Reconstruction Based on the Poll Taxes of 1689–1702", in Kevin SCHURER and Tom ARKELL (eds), *Surveying the People. The Interpretation and Use of Document Sources for the Study of Population in the Later Seventeenth Century*, Matlock, Local Population Studies, pp. 201–221.

–, 2002 "Service or Servitude? The Decline and Demise of Life-Cycle Service in England". Unpublished Paper.

FOLEY, Winifred, 1974, *A Child in the Forest*, London, British Broadcasting Corporation.

–, 1984, *In and Out of the Forest*, London, Century Publishing Co.

GASKELL, Elizabeth Cleghorn, n.d. (first edn 1851–53), *Cranford*, London, Odham.

LASLETT, Peter, 1965, *The World We Have Lost*, New York, Charles Scribner's Sons.

–, 1977, *Family Life and Illicit Love in Earlier Generations*, Cambridge, Cambridge University Press.

–, 1972, "Mean Household Size in England since the Sixteenth Century", in Peter LASLETT and Richard WALL (eds), *Household and Family in Past Time*, Cambridge, Cambridge University Press, pp. 125–158.

LEADBEATER, Mary, 1812, *Dialogues among the Irish Peasantry*, Dublin, J. and J. Carrick for John Cumming and Willliam Watson.

MCBRIDE, Theresa M., 1976, *The Domestic Revolution. The Modernisation of Household Service in England and France, 1820–1920,* London, Croom Helm.

MELDRUM, Tim, 2000, *Domestic Service and Gender 1660–1750. Life and Work in the London Household*, Harlow, Pearson Education.
MITFORD, Mary Russell, 1936 (first edn 1824–1832), *Our Village*, London, J. M. Dent and Sons.
SCHOFIELD, Roger S., 1970, "Age-Specific Mobility in an Eighteenth Century Rural English Parish", *Annales de Démographie Historique*, pp. 261–274.
SOKOLL, Thomas, 1993, *Household and Family among the Poor. The Case of Two Essex Communities in the Late Eighteenth and Early Nineteenth Centuries*, Bochum, Universitätsverlag Dr. N. Brockmeyer.
SOUDEN, David, 1984, "Movers and Stayers in Family Reconstitution Populations", *Local Population Studies*, pp. 11–28.
THOMPSON, Flora, 1945, *Lark Rise to Candleford*, Oxford, Oxford University Press.
VICKERY, Amanda, 1998, *The Gentleman's Daughter. Women's Lives in Georgian England*, New Haven and London, Yale University Press.
WALL, Richard, 1987, "Leaving home and the Process of Household formation in Pre-Industrial England", *Continuity and Change,* 2,1, pp. 77–101.
–, 1994, "Some Implications of the Earnings, Income and Expenditure Patterns of Married Women in Populations in the Past" in John HENDERSON and Richard WALL (eds), *Poor Women and Children in the European Past*, London, Routledge, pp. 312–335.
–, 2002, "Wealth and Household Economies of Propertied Widows in England 1700–1900". Unpublished Paper.
–, 2003, "Families in Crisis and the English Poor Law as Exemplified by the Relief Programme in the Essex Parish of Ardleigh 1795–97", in Emiko OCHIAI (ed.), *The Logic of Female Succession: Rethinking Patriarchy and Patrilineality in Global and Historical Perspective*, Kyoto, International Research Center for Japanese Studies, pp. 101–127.
WILCOX, Penelope, 1982, "Marriage, Mobility and Domestic Service in Victorian Cambridge", *Local Population Studies,* 29, pp. 19–34.

Migration, Servanthood and Assimilation in a New Environment

Beatrice MORING

Servanthood was for a large part of the population, in seventeenth and eighteenth century Sweden and Finland, a life-cycle phenomenon. Even though there were individuals who spent their lives in the service of other people, the majority of servants were between 15 and 30 years of age. The medieval legislation regulating society in these countries until 1734, and still incorporated in the new law code, made it possible for fathers to exercise considerable control over their unmarried daughters. However, the girls could enter service without parental permission and had sole control over their earnings. The likely place for entering employment for most young people was another farm in the home village or parish but when some experience had been accumulated some did venture further away. A number of migration studies of the pre-industrial period in Finland and Sweden show that although there was considerable migration of young people, particularly before marriage, short distance migration was by far the most common. Life course studies also show that most men tended to remain in or return to their parish of birth or a place not far from their relatives.

The issue of distance is, however, relative not absolute. When a transport link exists, a place distant in miles can become close because of frequent contact. The people in this study lived within the sphere of influence of a growing city, as much a part of their life as it was of the people living in adjacent parishes to this capital. However they reached it over the sea. They came from coastal parishes on the Aland islands and parishes along the south western coast of Finland.

The angle of observation will not be that of their experiences as servants in the town but of their assimilation into a new environment. The period of service was a means to an end, accumulation of capital, marriage and establishing oneself as a householder. Being a servant for life was a sign of failure in seventeenth and eighteenth century Stockholm just as it was in the countryside. The women in this study succeeded in finding a partner and becoming mistresses of their own households, the ultimate goal for a servant girl. However the circumstances of their life varied: some achieved relative opulence, others died in poverty.

The Backdrop and the Growing Capital

The town of Stockholm experienced considerable expansion during the seventeenth century. The country was engaged in successful warfare in central Europe, in Poland and with Denmark. The capital of the growing kingdom developed from a relatively small market town with 10,000 inhabitants in 1620 to a metropolis of 60,000 in the 1690s (in a Nordic context). Through this phase of development the numbers of deaths in the town continuously exceeded those of births and therefore the increase in population was a result of in-migration. However, the change experienced by the town was not only a change in numbers but also in structure. The capital of a rising power needed a suitable face. When the body of king Gustavus Adolphus was brought home from Germany the funeral had to be postponed because the centre of the town needed improvement. In the sixteenth century it was still customary for the court to move from one part of the county to the other, consuming taxes in the form of agricultural produce in the region of origin. The central administration followed the King on these travels. While this used to be a perfectly normal procedure, the conversion of tax goods, destined for the crown, into grain and money, made possible the concentration of administration in the capital. The seventeenth century saw the construction of several prominent government buildings and a number of noblemen engaged in the central administration saw fit to build town residences for themselves. The main body of the Navy with its docks and shipyards was stationed on one of the islands in Stockholm until 1679. New town plans were designed for the northern and the southern parts of the town, and the activity in house-building, shipbuilding and street-construction attracted people with building skills and interested in earning money. The sector of sea-transport increased as did activity in the harbour and with the increase in population the demands for food, clothing and services multiplied.[1]

Contacts over the Baltic

The migrants to Stockholm came from all parts of the kingdom, however the main part of the migrants from the eastern side of the Baltic had their roots in western Finland. Traditionally selling what he produced in the capital had been the right of any subject but the restrictive trade ideology of the seventeenth century promoted the founding of many market towns in Finland, thus inducing or forcing the population to trade there. While the main trade centres for the eastern part of the country had been Vyborg, Reval and later St Petersburg, the population of the Southwest and the Northwest turned towards Stockholm. Even though restrictions were created for trade from north-western Finland, the coastal area and archipelago of the southwest retained their trading rights with Stockholm. The population of the south-western islands transported fish in their own vessels and returned with grain and salt, the price of which was usually lower in Stockholm than in the towns of Finland. For the islanders the capital was the nearest town and, in addition to fish, logs and firewood were transported, since, even for those of the south-western mainland, the trip was only a matter of a couple of days. Between 1670 and 1705 the customs registers of Stockholm show a yearly import of between 2,000 and 3,500 barrels of Baltic herring (200–500 tonnes) per year from the parish of Korpo-Houtskar, in the Southwest archipelago, for all years that have been examined. The other point of contact between this area and Stock-

1 Gustaf Utterström, *Stockholms folkmängd 1663–1763*, Stockholm, Särtr. ur Historiska studier tillägnade Nils Ahnlund, 1949, pp. 271–273; Gustaf Utterström, *Jordbrukets arbetare; levnadsvillkor och arbetsliv på landsbygden från frihetstiden till mitten av 1800-talet*, Stockholm, Tidens förlag, 1957; Åke Meyerson, "Befolkningen pá Södermalm ár 1676", *Sallskapet Sankt Eriks Arsbok,* 1943, p. 90; Axel Zettersten, *Svenska flottans historia 1635–1680*, Norrtelje, Norrtelje tidnings boktr., 1903, pp. 152–154; Werner Pursche, *Timmermansämbetet i Stockholm före 1700*, Stockholm, Stockholms byggmästarefören, 1979, p. 91; Albert Sandklef, *Allmogesjöfart påSveriges västkust 1575–1850*, Lund, Gleerup, 1973.

holm was the guild of fishermen and fish-merchants. In medieval times this guild had managed to gain monopoly on fishing and fish trading within the town gates. During the following centuries the situation became more complicated and the guild-members started buying in fish along the Swedish and Finnish coast, transporting it alive in special vessels for marketing. The trading took place in specified ports along the coast continuously used by the guild. It is thus not surprising that the south-western islands, with an economy heavily relying on fishing, were well represented on the trading routes.[2]

The contacts were there and the town might have had a certain attraction for young people, particularly for those who did not envisage their chances of succession to a farm being very great. The eighteenth century communion books in the parish of Korpo record persons leaving for Stockholm, alone or in the frame of the fishing guilds. The restrictive economic doctrine of the seventeenth century included efforts in controlling both economy and migration. The continuous warfare put considerable strains on society. The urgent need of soldiers created a favourable climate for restrictive measures; these measures had implications for the everyday life of ordinary people. As long as the servants of the nobility were exempt from military service, the farmers had to attract servants through increasing wages. At that point the nobility petitioned in the parliament for the imposition of a maximum wage in Sweden-Finland as it was the case in Denmark. The nobility wanted wage control and a restriction of the numbers of male servants the farmers were allowed to employ. Some of these restrictions were reflected in the Regulations on Service of 1686. By the 1690s voices were raised not only for the need of permanent employment of everybody but also for restricting mobility of potential servants. The local interests might have dictated anti migration attitudes, but the Navy was recruiting skilled carpenters and boat builders from coastal Finland. The farmers' representatives of the Aland islands complained in 1693 that "the country is emptied of people", "farmhands and maids cannot be found and the local quotas for the Navy cannot be filled". The result was a compulsory "passport" for migration to Stockholm. However, with the frequent trips to the town, regulations were not gener-

2 Beatrice Moring, *Skärgårdsbor. Hushåll, familj och demografi i finländsk kustbygd på 1600-, 1700- och 1800-talen,* Helsingfors, Fonska veten skaps-societeten, 1994, p. 45; *Id.*, "Den gyllene staden", *Alandsk Odling,* 1986, pp. 66–67; Ernst Söderlund, "Stockholms fiskkoparambete", *Studier i ekonomi och historia*, Uppsala, 1944, p. 260.

ally observed, even though fines had been imposed. To catch somebody and prove that his intention had been to transport someone to Stockholm and leave the person there was almost impossible. People left for economic as well as for personal reasons. The seventeenth century visitation protocols show that when people wanted to get out of engagements or entanglements, Sweden, and particularly Stockholm, was the place to disappear to. In the 1630s, 40s and 50s it seems that women as often as men left their partners and disappeared in the town.[3]

Migration Size

It is almost impossible to reliably estimate the size of Finnish migration to Stockholm in absence of a registration of birthplace at death. The estimated number of people born in Finland who died in Stockholm during the seventeenth and the eighteenth century hover around 4,000 in the southern part of the town, an area of dense Finnish settlement. Six percent of the town population is one figure that has been proposed for the seventeenth century. In one of these parishes, Katarina, between 28 and 11 percent of those who put their banns up in the 1650s and 1660s, had been born on the Finnish side of the Baltic. The proportion between 1670 and 1710 moved between 14 and 6 percent. The absolute numbers remains the same but as the parish grew the proportion decreased. Those of the second generation would of course be recorded as born in the parish. Altogether about a thousand Finnish migrants were recorded between 1654 and 1711, 30 percent originated from the south-western region. In 1645, 46 out of 82 members of the Carpenters Guild were of Finnish origin, in 1644, 21 out of 27 members of the Fishermens' Guild were from the eastern side of the Baltic. In 1654–1736, 228 people with roots in south-western coastal Finland married in Katarina parish, 66 in the Finnish parish (1664–1760) and 24 in the parishes of Hedvig Eleonora, Maria and Skeppsholm in Stockholm. 81 persons with similar background left inventoried property in 1650–1750. Altogether 399 people have been traced, about half of them being women. The reason for settling in southern Stockholm was the cheaper housing prices outside the old town boundary. In addition to this

3 *Acta Visitatoria 1637–1666*, p. 182; B. Moring, *Skärgårdsbor*, p. 92.

the services in Katarina were in Swedish, the language spoken in the archipelago. Most of the persons found in the Finnish parish originated from the south-western mainland with a different linguistic background.[4]

The Country Girl in an Urban Setting

Unmarried female migrants worked as maids. This is however not to be understood as engaged in housework only. Finnish girls seem to have been popular as maids first in Stockholm and later in St Petersburg because of their diligence and cleanliness (the same qualities stated in the twentieth century for Finnish *au pair* girls and hospital nurses in Britain and Germany). Being a "piga" (servant girl) in seventeenth and eighteenth century Stockholm could mean a number of things. When the 35 bakers and 7 bakers' widows in 1740–41 had altogether 140 servant girls in their households and 54 brewers and 14 brewers' widows had 157 servant girls, it is highly unlikely that all these were engaged in housework. A girl would do the same work as a young male but never ask for an apprentice contract or compete as a master.[5] The attraction of a position in Stockholm was among other things better wages – 20 daler copper –, board and clothing (1678 appendix 4) while the earnings in western Finland were 5–10 daler, board and clothing.[6] The environment was not necessarily as hostile as one might imagine. Some girls migrated in pairs with their sisters, others formed links in networks of first and second generation migrants taking care of recent arrivals. The probate inventories show groups of sib-

4 Parish registers of Katarina, Maria, Skeppsholm, Hedvig Eleonora, Finska parishes Stockholm, Guild Registers, Stockholm City Archive; G. Utterström, *Stockholms folkmängd*; Volmar Bergh, "Tukholman sumalaisia menneinä vuosisatoina", *Historiallinen Arkisto,* 1961, 57, pp. 218, 224, 275; B. Osterlund, "Finlandsk befolkning pa Sodermalm under 1600-talets senare halft", *Studier och handlingar rorande Stockholms Historia,* Stockholm, Stadsarkivet, 1966, pp. 222–223, 333.

5 Ernst Söderlund, *Stockholms hantverkarklass 1720–1772,* Stockholm, Stockholms Kommunalförvalig, 1943, pp. 177, 304–305.

6 Jorma Wilmi, *Isäntäväet ja palvelusväen pito 1600-luvulla,* Jyväskylä, Jyväskylän yliopisto, 1991, p. 194, Appendix 4.

lings, some in Stockholm, some on the other side of the Baltic. The banns registers sometimes record information about employment and/or residence with relatives.

Table 1. Occupational structure of women born in south-western Finland marrying in Stockholm, 1654–1760, and of their partners

Husbands		*Migrant women*	
Sailors Royal Navy	23	Maids	85
Sailors Merchant Navy	16	Widows	24
Fishermen	10	Unmarried	4
Craftsmen and apprentices in carpentry	11	Fallen	3
Bricklaying	4	No occupation	20
Textiles and shoes	10		
Metal-production	3		
Other crafts	8		
Transport	6		
Harbour work	7		
Tradesmen	4		
Guards, soldiers	9		
Customs officer	1		
Other skilled	6		
Employed in private household	6		
Day labourer	2		
Refugee	2		
Unknown	8		
Total	*136*	*Total*	*136*

Sources: Banns registers of Katarina parish 1654–1736 and the Finnish parish 1664–1760.

> Anna Svensdotter Berg born in Aland, worked at her brother's "a merchant in the Town, with Claes Olofsson Lindeberg born in Uppland working at Petter Mynders' the tobacconist". (13 September 1690, Katarina parish, banns register)
>
> Margareta Staphansdotter born in Aland, maid formerly employed by the shopkeeper Erik Halvardson with Anders Larson Drake, bricklayers' apprentice, born in the parish. (12 November 1692, Katarina parish, banns register)

It is not easy to determine what the relationship was like between servant girls and their employers. In some cases there could be a considerable amount of solidarity. Stockholm seems to have been the location par excellence for runaway brides, absconding servants or partners; it is also fairly obvious that both at the place of origin and in the new environment people were covering the tracks of the migrants. In 1644 the Church court records of Aland include an account of a man trying to retrieve his bride to be who had left him and found a position in Stockholm. When the local clergy and authorities tried to trace her both she and her employer left town for an unknown address and remained hidden until the situation calmed down.[7]

On the other hand relations could be quite difficult. Sweden-Finland was not a country really plagued by witch-hunts. However, one of the few instances of such a hunt in Stockholm involved three Finnish servant girls. Two of these were clearly only general troublemakers trying to get their own back from neighbours and other locals. The third however was ready to face execution as long as she took her mistress with her, to whom she said after their arrest: "You should have given me better food." Another example of bad relations can be found in a court case of compensation claims by a girl, who came to her uncle in Stockholm at the age of 20, believing in his promises to treat her as a daughter, and worked for him without wages for ten years.[8]

Where it has been possible to determine the ages at first marriage of the Finnish servant girls, a similarity to what can be gleaned in other localities seems to be the case. The girls seem to have married between the ages of 23 and 35 for the first time. The number of remarriages of young widows should also be noted. There are some instances of the woman giving birth to a pre-marital child. The clergyman registered the girl as a "fallen woman" when making the note of the banns. However in the three known cases the couple was about to legalise the relationship. The child was the result of the commonly practiced pre-marital co-habitation or sex that generally can be observed in the case of children being born soon after the wedding.[9]

After marriage a number of women would continue earning but in a different way. If their husband kept a shop or a workshop it would be run as a family enterprise. The Pauli wool manufacture in the southern sub-

7 *Acta Visitatoria 1637–1666*, pp. 8, 32, 38, 122, 182; *Consistorum Ecclesiasticum Aboa protocols 1658–1666*, p. 432.

8 Kari Tarkiainen, *Finnarnas historia i Sverige,* Helsinfkors, Finska historiska samf., 1990, p. 108; Per Anders Fogelström, "Haxorna i Katarina", *Historia kring Stockholm*, Stockholm, Wahlstöm & Widstrand, 1966.

9 Katarina parish registers.

urbs gave out knitting-work, to be performed in the home, to soldiers' wives, sailors' wives, carpenters' wives, building labourers' wives and to paupers. The wives of the town fishermen's and fish merchants' guild were doing the actual hawking, while their husbands bought and transported the fish. The boatmen's wives augmented the family income by wet-nursing.[10]

In the eighteenth century it became legal for a woman who had learnt a craft to apply for a licence from the magistrates and to engage in it. In general the licences were only granted to widows. Out of the 850 workshops in Stockholm 1676, 50 were run by widows. Sewing, the knitting of stockings, lace-making and spinning were not subject to guild regulations and could therefore be practiced by anybody. The taxation register of 1676 lists females occupied as spinners, stocking knitters, lace-makers, seamstresses, washerwomen, wigmakers, broom-makers, midwives and wet-nurses. In addition to this the list records women occupied in sand-carrying, salt-carrying, lime-mixing, bricklaying and laying out corpses.[11] When the Italian Lorenzo Magalotti visited Sweden in 1674 and wrote a travel book he recorded with great interest women working as rowers, water-carriers, street-sweepers and workers in bath-houses.[12]

Partners

The occupational structure of the partners of female migrants shows a considerable concentration of sea-connected occupations, 37 out of 136 husbands. In addition, 14 were in the building trade and 12 worked in connection with the harbour or transport; 5 were guards and soldiers; 14 had mastered or were apprenticed for a craft of some kind and some were unskilled manual workers. With a few exceptions the higher strata in society were not represented. About 50 percent of the partners were born in Stockholm while 25 percent were Finnish migrants, the rest were born in

10 Eli Heckscher, *Sveriges ekonomiska Historia*, Stockholm, Bonnier, 1949, pp. 633–634; Söderlund, "Stockholms fiskkoparambete", p. 260; Kekke Stadin, "Den gömda och glömda arbetskraften. Stadskvinnor i produktionen under 1600 och 1700-talen", *Historisk tidskrift*, 1980, 3, pp. 309–311.

11 Å. Meyerson, "Befolkningen", pp. 105–107.

12 Lorenzo Magalotti, *Sverige under år 1674*, Stockholm, Rediviva, 1986 (reprint).

Sweden outside the capital and probably of a social standing similar to the migrants'. It is not unlikely that the residential proximity or proximity of workplace had a decided influence on partner choice. The southern parts of town were famed for their opulence. Widows engaged in their husbands' trade might have had contacts with his colleagues but also possessed skills desirable from the point of view of a person with a similar occupation. A widow with a workshop would of course be looking for somebody to continue the work if she decided to remarry. The probate inventories show that at the end of life some tradesmen had prospered, men in the navy and army had in some cases reached officers rank, the civil servants had made some progress and those engaged in transport on land or sea had put aside a little bit of money. However, very few of the migrant women married into an easy and luxurious existence.[13]

Table 2. Occupational structure of husbands of women migrated from south-western Finland dying in Stockholm, 1650–1750, leaving property of some kind

Sailors Navy	1
Sailors	3
Skippers	3
Fishing trade	5
Building trade	5
Textile manufacturer	4
Butcher	1
Soldiers, guards	6
Merchant	3
Customs or state employee	5
Assorted manufacture	5
Gravedigger	1
Gardener	1
Others	4
Total	*48*

Sources: Stockholm City Archive (SSA), Probate inventories of the town of Stockholm.

13 Parish registers, banns lists; probate inventories 1731: 994; 1739/2: 535, Stockholm City Archive (SSA).

Money, a Home or Destitution

The probate inventories have preserved detailed information about the wealth of people in seventeenth century Stockholm. From the 55 inventories concerning women with roots in south-western Finland and the Aland islands, it appears that some had managed to accumulate considerable amounts of worldly possessions while others were almost destitute.

Table 3a. Contents and value of properties left by widowed women with roots in south-western Finland dying in Stockholm, 1650–1750, (in daler copper)

Occupation of husband	*Value of house*	*Estate in total*	*Debts*	*Total Daler copper*
Inspector of hospital	9,000	26,047	17,304	9,277
Master blacksmith	2,200	3,189		3,189
Officer				1,665
Government official	1,200	2,180	603	1,577
Tailor		2,082	636	1,446
Tailor	2,000	2,157	2,344	–
Tailor	450	942	60	882
Corporal in the Guard		1,345		1,345
Gravedigger		1,229		1,229
Bailiff		927		927
Skipper		1,902	3,302	–
Skipper				416
Fishtrader	800	1,167		1,167
Fishtrader	450	641	438	203
Fishtrader		306		306
Soldier	300	523		523
Farmer	200	457	39	418
Brickmaker	250			250
Buttonmaker		988	1,456	–
Broommaker		125	98	27
Boatman		116	106	9.3
Carpenter at the Palace		63.2	123	–
Gardener		45.4	124	–
Unmarried servant girl				275

Sources: See Table 2.

The widow of the inspector of the hospital in Danvik, Margareta Steen, left a house-property worth 9,000 daler copper, a carved monument for her grave worth 1,020 daler, gold, silver, clothes, furniture, carriages etc. worth 11,500 daler and in addition 4,000 daler in ready money. Even, with debts as high as 17,304 daler, there were still more than 9,000 daler for the nephews and nieces to inherit (see Table 3a). The itemised list shows that the widow was engaged in some kind of trade, as textile merchandise to the value of 6,400 daler was found in the house. It is however possible that the wealth of the family was not only the result of the generous salary paid to the inspector but some useful sidelines the position had made possible.[14]

The brewer and merchant Erich Erichsson Strom left a house of 7,000 daler and brewery items, money, metal objects, clothing, household goods, animals etc. worth another 3,000. The debts of the business were no less than 7,400 daler, therefore the estate was seemingly not as prosperous as at first sight. However, the widow Christina Ludvigsdotter kept a firm grip on what was left and clearly managed to negotiate with the creditors. When she died three years later, not only she did still reside in the same house, now worth 8,000 daler, but she was also running the brewery business (the house was literally over-flowing in beer and alcohol). She left no less than 15,000 dalers worth of property to be divided between her own and her husbands' relatives.[15]

Only some of the families listed house-property worth 1,000 daler or more. A property of 500 daler or less was much more common. There is reason to remember however that probate inventories after women's death do not necessarily reflect correctly the total wealth of the household or the standard of living when both parties were alive. While one might expect the widows, in absence of a male breadwinner, to have fewer assets than the married women, this was not necessarily the case. Some widows had been in a situation where they were consuming their little capital and borrowing to cover their expenses. Some other widows clearly engaged in trade evidenced by the presence of newly manufactured goods ready for sale. There are also several examples of outstanding claims indicating money-lending activities.[16] The town legislation awarded half of the marriage property to the wife, but there might have been an inclination by

14 SSA, Probate inventories 1734/2: 193.

15 SSA, Probate inventories 1736/2: 75; 1739/2: 535.

16 SSA, Probate inventories 1705: 993; 1745/1: 1168; 1735/1: 1189.

husbands to try to avoid payments out of the household. Whenever it came to legal issue, the father would be the guardian and claims by the wife's siblings were not taken into consideration. If the couple was childless, however, the situation was different. Pinning the wife's property down to her personal effects would then be in the husbands' interest.

Table 3b. Contents and value of property left by women with roots in south-western Finland dying in Stockholm, 1650–1750, before their husbands

Occupation of husband	*Value of house*	*Estate in total*	*Debts*	*Total*
Textile merchant	2,400	8,800		8,800
Textile merchant	2,500	4,835	5,120	–
Textile merchant	2,100 (2 houses)	5,531	7,101	–
Unknown	1,000	778		1,778
Sailor	800	977		977
Sailor	150	211		211
Sailor		182	58	122
Ships carpenter	400	220		660
Fisherman (Town Guild)	800	1,751		1,751
Fisherman (Town Guild)	300	400		400
Carters assistant	150	360		360
Bricklayers assistant		321		178
Tobacco spinner		634		634
Harbour worker		115	128	–
Butcher		–		–
Alderman of the guard		–		–
Corporal		–		–
Guardsman		–		–
Guardsman		–		–
Spraymakers apprentice		–		–

Sources: See Table 2.

One golden ring was listed as one of the few items made of precious metals among the possessions of poor wives or widows. Sometimes a silver spoon can also be found. Pewter pots or copper kettles were not uncommon and cooking utensils made of iron were staples. A scattering of Bibles and hymn books were also present. While the opulent had horses for driving or for their trade and cows if there was a business need, the poor sometimes kept pigs. The items found in almost every inventory however were clothes and underwear. In some cases only the house is mentioned and specifications of contents are not to be found.[17]

Merchants and brewers were part of the opulent strata in society. Without capital it was impossible to attain this position.[18] The fish-merchants seem to have coped reasonably well, many left a house and nets, boats or parts of boats, salting equipment etc. in addition to ordinary household goods. For example the widow of guild fisherman Erich Larson Fisk left a house with reasonable household goods, fishing boats, fishing equipment, clothing etc. Her niece arranged a funeral in style, using up two thirds of the assets (cf. Appendix 1).

Sailors and boatmen had to rely on the crown as paymaster and were therefore not very wealthy. Brita Nilsdotter a boatman's widow left 116 daler copper as clothes, bedding and some cash, while the debts amounted to 106 daler. The sailors' wife Gertrud Erichsdotter, had a golden ring, pots and pans, some clothing and bedding worth 182 daler and debts of 58 daler. Beata Persdotter had married a sailor in the merchant navy and was therefore better off, they owned two little houses in Katarina parish worth 800 daler together, her wedding ring was only valued to 6 daler, but she had candle sticks, plates, tankards and bottles, a copper tea-kettle and a metal watering can for her garden. In addition to the pine bed and bedding, clothes, chests etc. she had a mirror on her wall and left no less than 977 daler. The carpenters' widow Elisabet Matsdotter left some clothing, bedding, her wedding ring and her husbands tools, altogether worth 63 daler but she had accumulated debts up to 123 daler, among other things for medicine bought on credit. The most destitute people who had an inventory made left nothing, among these was the wife of a spray-maker's apprentice, the only precious thing in the house was the three-year-old girl.[19]

The probate inventories provide information about the location of migrants' households. The majority of these were situated in the south, Sodermalm, some in the north, on Norrmalm, or on Ladugardslandet, none in the "Town". The (old) town had restrictions as to what kind of buildings could be constructed and was considered a desirable location. The inhabitants of this part of the town were generally more opulent than those

17 Probate inventories 1743/1: 831, 1735/1, 1745/1: 1168.

18 E. Söderlund, *Stockholms hantverkarklass*, pp. 177, 181.

19 SSA, Probate inventories 1734/1: 122; 1745/2; 1748/2; 1733/3: 242; 1729/1: 1051.

in the southern or the northern part. However, the more recently incorporated areas were not totally dominated by poor folk, even in these parts reasonably wealthy people did occasionally settle. Norrmalm was primarily crown land and a large part of the inhabitants were engaged in the Navy or worked on the naval shipyards. Some were soldiers or worked for the crown in some other capacity.

Table 3c. Contents and value of property left by husbands of women with roots in south-western Finland dying in Stockholm, 1650–1750, before their wives

Occupation of husband	*Value of house*	*Estate in total*	*Debts*	*Total*
Brewer, shopkeeper	7,000	10,634	7,468	3,165
Sailweaver		1,525	77	1,448
Portofficial	900	983		983
Skipper	800	879	555	324
Skipper	600	670	837	–
Fisherman (Town Guild)	400	949	70	879
Sailor	200	748	277	471
Mintworker	400	515	315	200
Carpenter	200	200		200
Carpenter	125	250		250

Sources: See Table 2.

The southern part of the town was the centre for the carpenters. In the 1640s while the war was still on, the crown forced a number of the carpenters into service on the Royal shipyard.[20] Meyerson describes the southern part of town as extremely diverse. On the same plot a number of buildings could have been erected. Sometimes two houses with or without basement and loft, workshops, baking houses and outbuildings were jogging one another. The carpenters in the southern and northern part of town often built so called "aland cottages" with one heated room. Some carpenters' families acquired extra income by renting out rooms, which indicates that either the cottage was somewhat bigger or that the carpenter possessed several small buildings. There are examples in the probate invento-

20 W. Pursche, *Timmermansämbetet*, pp. 90–94.

ries of persons owning "two small cottages". Magalotti describes the buildings in the following manner:

> In the country side and the small towns most houses are built of wood and the most opulent ones of them look like the one in the drawing I have provided. The farmers and the poor live in houses of inferior quality. They only have fireplaces made of bricks, the roofs are covered with bark from the trees and grass is grown on top. In the summertime this is an appealing sight.[21]

The probate inventories listed the contents of the households in great detail. Commonly you find pine furniture: beds, cupboards, tables, chairs and sometimes chests. Most households had bedclothes: sheets, pillows, blankets and sometimes a *rya* (tapestry used in bedding and for travel). Iron cooking utensils and pewter tankards were also common. Most people left woollen trousers, skirts and jackets, linen shirts and underclothes. The wealthy households differed from the poor ones through the value of the house-property, the presence of cash and some gold or silver items, workshops with large quantities of raw materials, valuable items used for production of goods, horses and cattle, carts and carriages. The items within the houses, although more numerous, were not particularly different. Charles Ogier comments in his diary, after a visit to the house of Jacob de la Gardie, one of the highest-ranking noblemen in Sweden, on the sparse interior decoration of the building. Instead of tapestries and textiles, silks and brocades, upholstery and tablecloths, he found solid wooden furniture, good food in faience bowls and no frills.[22] It seems that wealth was shown in the form of imposing houses and expensive clothing but not in decoration of the home. The poor and really destitute left nothing but their bedding and the clothes they were wearing.

While the number of boatmen, carpenters, sailors, labourers and apprentices are considerable in the banns' registers, their proportion among those leaving inventoried property is much less prominent. It has to be remembered that one list reflects the early part of life while the other one records the situation at the end of it. Some individuals probably did advance economically over their lifetime and would therefore move out of one group into another.

21 Å. Meyerson, "Befolkningen"; Pursche, *Timmermansämbetet,* pp. 314–321; L. Magalotti, *Sverige*, pp. 10–12.

22 Charles Ogier, *Från Sveriges storhetstid: franske legationssekreteraren Charles Ogiers dagbok under ambassaden i Sverige 1634–1635,* Stockholm, Norstedt, 1914.

Table 4a. Estimates of income per year for certain occupational groups in 17th century Stockholm

Boatmen	64 daler silver + house, food and uniform
Carpenters RN	85–135 daler silver
Carpenters Civ.	90–145 daler silver*
Bricklayers	77–150 daler silver
Housepainters	55 daler silver
Barrelmakers	64 daler silver
Sailmakers	80–90 daler silver
Sailweavers	200 daler silver
Town guards	72 dalers + percentage of fines
Male servant	50 daler copper

Sources: Zettersten 1903, pp. 73, 218–222; Pursche 1979, pp. 299–301; Swensk 1946, p. 75, 1678, 11.7.
* calculation based on information about income per day.

Table 4b. Income per year for certain occupational groups in Stockholm, early 18th century

Apprentices	48 daler silver[1], 80 daler silver[2] + board and bread
Sailors	120 daler silver (8 working months per year)
Matros	80 daler silver (8 w.m.y)
Steersman	224 daler silver (8 w.m.y)
Skipper	320 daler siler (8 w.m.y)[3]
Male servant	16,5 daler silver plus board and bread, set of clothing
Female servant	8 daler silver plus board and bread, set of clothing[4]
Garden worker	16 daler silver[5]
Maid	5 dale silver[5]
Builder	160–220 daler silver (8 w.m.y)[6]
Carpenters apprentice	120–240 daler silver
Carpentryworker	100–200 daler silver[7]

1 1720s and 1730s.
2 1740s.
3 1756 calculation based on monthly earnings.
4 1739.
5 1734 listed in probate inventory.
6 calculation base on daily earnings.
7 1750, calculation based on daily earnings.
Sources: E. Söderlund 1943 pp. 270–272; A. Sandklef 1973, pp. 134–135; G. Utterström 1957, p. 446. Appendix; Probate inventories Stockholm 1734/1: 763.

On the other hand it is quite likely that some did remain in the same social group all through their lifetime. Because not everybody left enough to have their few possessions listed, the analysis of the income of some of the occupational groups will try to approach their destinies.

Income

The seventeenth and the eighteenth centuries are not a time of statistics on wages. Whatever information can be acquired originates in different sources and therefore a study of variation in the short term is out of the question. Those employed by the Navy, the town and the crown would hardly experience much change in their income. On the other hand, the carpenters working on the free market would see changes in their income even within the span of one year. Finding information about income for all the occupational groups that recruited Finnish migrants is not possible. Only those in the building trade, on the sea, apprentices and labourers are included in this part of the study. Those who had risen to positions of wealth leave a mark in the probate inventories.

The boatmen of the Royal Navy were paid 64 daler silver per year, the recruitment union called *rote* paid an additional 10 dalers and provided a cottage. Because of the constant shortness of Navy funds, the wages were often converted into payments in kind. The ship's carpenters of the navy had wages of between 85 and 135 daler silver per year. However, the bad navy economy could result in occasional payments in kind, and more than often in no payment at all. As a result the carpenters had to look for work in town to support themselves. The situation of the navy bricklayers, drillers, ship's painters and other craftsmen was the same.[23] The carpenters in town were paid by day. Between the 15 of September and 15 of March, the working day was shorter due to lack of day-light.[24] The calculations in the table on income are based on the assumption that the carpenters found work both during winter and summer (Table 4a).

An examination of wages during the early part of the eighteenth century again raises the question of monthly, weekly and daily payments.

23 A. Zettersten, *Svenska flottans*, pp. 213–214, 222, 244.
24 W. Pursche, *Timmermansämbetet*, pp. 156, 299–301.

There were no guarantees for employment all year round, especially within the building sector. This problem has been noted and the calculation has in many cases been done for active employment eight months of the year. The sailors of the merchant navy sailed out "in spring", and returned in the middle of December. During the time when the waters were covered with ice, sailing was impossible.

Prices and Consumption

The best information about prices and consumption in seventeenth century Stockholm can be acquired from Zettersten's *Svenska flottans (The History of the Swedish Navy)*. The Navy was at this time dependent on acquisition on goods from various parts of the kingdom. Taxation was still based on goods instead of money and a part of the taxes went directly to the Army and the Navy. When the deliveries were insufficient, it became necessary to buy goods at market price, sometimes even in Stockholm. The information provided in the next table refers to purchases in the 1650s, 1660s and 1670s and, for the eighteenth century, to Jörberg's *History of prices*. Jörberg's price estimates are based on market prices not only in Stockholm but in the region of central Sweden.[25]

The calculations about consumption are based on the Naval rates of 1643, 1660 and 1680. The main reason for the choice is the absence of other information for this century, in addition to the fact that the Navy could not grossly underfeed the men while keeping them fit enough to work, but the finances were in such a state that we may safely assume that no excessive liberties were taken. A comparison with the food rations within the merchant navy in 1759 shows similar levels. The table shows the estimated yearly consumption of a working adult male and the price of the same. In addition the need of clothing as seen by the naval authorities has been added. This amount was an absolute minimum, not sufficient in cold winters, with the ensuing fatal consequences (Table 5).

The amounts and distribution of food items are roughly on line with Hannerberg's calculations for seventeenth century agrarian communities in Sweden. While older estimates and calculations assumed 2–3 barrels of

25 Lennart Jörberg, *A history of prices in Sweden 1732–1914*, Lund, Gleerup, 1972.

grain per person and year, later revaluations have fixed the amount of grain to 1–2 barrels per active adult. Mats Isacson's calculations include larger amounts of home grown root-crops and milk products in the diet of a seventeenth century farming household than those presented in the table. However, it is necessary to note that the opportunities for growing large quantities of turnips or cabbage in the town of Stockholm were more limited.[26]

Table 5. Estimate of yearly consumption of food and clothing, amount and price, 17th and 18th century Stockholm

		17th century	*18th century*
Herring	1 lisp 16 pounds	3 daler silver	3 daler silver
Baltic herring	2 lisp 8 pounds	1½ daler silver	2 daler silver
Meat	7 lisp	7½ daler silver	12 daler silver
Cereal, flour	1.5 barrel	6 daler silver	10½ daler silver
Salt	1 lisp 4 pounds	¾ daler silver	¾ daler silver
Butter	3 lisp	6 daler silver	13½ daler silver
Peas	½ barrell	3 daler silver	3 daler silver
Beer	8 barrells	27 daler silver	27 daler silver
Total		*54¾ daler silver*	*71¾ daler silver*
Clothes, adult male/ year			
Trousers and jacket, coarse wool		1 daler	10 ore silver
Prime quality wool		12 daler	30 ore silver
Long trousers, coarse wool		1 daler	28 ore silver
Prime quality		17 daler	5 ore silver
2 shirts		2 daler	10 ore silver
Woollen socks, 1 pair			16 ore silver
Shoes		1 daler	11 ore silver
Total		*6 dalers 1 ore (or 21 dalers 10 ore)*	

Sources: A. Zettersten 1903, pp. 239, 243, 280–297; Jörberg 1972, pp. 133, 149, 197, 312, 323, 359, 366, 382 (the large quantities of beer caused by calculations based on male consumption, however beer was a staple in the 16th and 17th centuries and particularly in urban areas safer than water or milk).

The considerable quantity of beer in the calculation is partly based on consumption in the navy and partly on Swensk who claims that the daily

26 David Hannerberg, *Svenskt agrarsamhälle under 1200 är, Stockholm,* 1971, Stockholm, Läromedelsforagen, pp. 111–117; M. Isacson, "Heckscher", *Sveriges Ekonomiska*, 1949; N. Friberg, *Dalarnas befolkning, Stockholm,* 1956, p. 413.

consumption of an adult man in seventeenth century Stockholm was about 2.5 litres a day. It is also known that 20 percent of the daily intake of calories by farmhands and maids on the royal farms in sixteenth century Sweden were to ascribe to beer consumption.[27] In this context it should be pointed out that the alcohol content of the beer was not particularly high at this time. People in densely populated areas were reluctant to drink water, and with good reason. The proximity of dung-heaps to wells was a constant problem. People in the poorer parts of the town did keep animals if they could and in addition to animals there was the presence of human refuse. The mortality in Stockholm was very high because the environment was far from healthy, without in-migration the population of the town would have had problems in keeping up the numbers. The passion for coffee in the eighteenth and nineteenth centuries introduced a drink made with boiled water, but in the seventeenth century, the choice lay between low-alcoholic dark beer, beer, water and milk-products (not to be recommended in warm weather). The prevalent mean of food-preservation was salting, which increased the need of drink. The brewers in Stockholm were prosperous, although it is very likely that beer was produced in the home of the poor when possible. In this case the beer in the calculation should be replaced by barley, malt and hops bringing the amount of expenditure down.

The calculation in the table does not include house-rent, firewood nor food and clothes for the wife and children. While there was resistance against married apprentices in the seventeenth century the building sector was more liberal and married apprentices were common already in the 1670s. A comparison between the seventeenth and the early eighteenth century shows slightly higher wages and prices but this is to a large extent the result of inflation and monetary reform. Söderlund has calculated a minimum expenditure of 1.5–2 copper daler per day for a workers' family in the 1740s. A builders' labourer earned about 2 copper daler during a summer-working-day and therefore many experienced a miserable life in wintertime.[28]

Even though this calculation is very rudimentary, it shows reasonably clearly that a number of occupational groups did not make enough money to support themselves and a family. The fishermen added to their income

27 J. Swensk, "Stadsvaktens foregangare", *Sallskapet Sankt Eriks Arsbok,* 1946, p. 63; D. Hannerberg, *Svenskt agrarsamhalle,* p. 111.

28 E. Söderlund, *Stockholms hantverkarklass,* pp. 270–277.

by renting out rooms. 5–6 percent of the households in the northern and southern part of the town kept a cow and almost as many a pig in the 1670s. Some of the cows can be located in the probate inventories of the migrants, however, milk was an unusual drink with meals and the purpose was likely butter-making.[29] The observations on economic activity among married women should be recalled here. A skilled and diligent stocking-knitter was able to earn as much as 100 copper daler per year. There is even a case of a woman earning 260 copper daler from making 115 pairs of stockings. However, earnings of 50 or 30 daler were not unusual. Some of the female knitters at Pauli wool-manufacture did not work during the part of the summer when carpenters were paid more for "summer working hours" and sailors were earning. Spinning at home was another way of making extra money for the family. The income of these women was approximately 20–30 copper daler per year. After the age of six, children could participate in this type of work.[30]

A study of the 1674 taxation register shows larger households in the "Town" than on the outskirts. Although the proportion of households without children was slightly higher in the more opulent part of the town those with many children was also higher. The workers could not afford large families. Söderlund has described how the economic standard of the 1740s can be seen in the number of children per household, using cross-sectional data. While the brewers had on average 2.3 children in the household, the shoemakers had only 0.85 and the apprentices even fewer.[31] Although there were no legal restrictions about entering service it seems that the idea of staying in the parental home until confirmation already had penetrated the ideology by the early eighteenth century. In 1730 the vast majority of children did not leave home until after the age of 15, more than 20 percent of the girls not until the age of 20. A small minority entered service between the ages of 11 and 15. Interestingly enough the lowest strata in Stockholm seemed to hold on to their young children more than the intermediate group which secured apprentice contracts for their sons when they reached the legal age of 14.[32] So far there are no data on the socio-economic distribution of infant mortality for this period.

29 Å. Meyerson, "Befolkningen", pp. 92–96.
30 E. Heckscher, *Sveriges ekonomiska,* 1949, pp. 630–637.
31 Å. Meyerson, "Befolkningen", p. 90; E. Söderlund, *Stockholms hantverkarklass,* pp. 125–127.
32 S. Hedenborg, *Det gatfulla folket*, Stockholm, 1997, pp. 70–74, 81.

Conclusion

In view of what has been shown in this paper it can be concluded that the prospects of girls migrating from south-western Finland to Stockholm were neither extremely good nor extremely bad. The geographic settlement patterns indicate that they moved to the parts of the town where there were other migrants, even friends or relatives. The frequent contacts between their regions of origin and the town also probably meant that their capacity to orientate in the new environment were better than for people arriving in the town for the first time in their lives. While being a maid was the female occupation, it is not possible to determine what kind of work it actually involved in the new environment. One can however say with a fair amount of confidence, that only for a relatively small number was it exclusively housework of the kind associated with being a maid in a nineteenth century urban environment. The brewers and bakers and carters employed women for a number of tasks including tending to animals and milking cows. The more specialised craftsmen probably needed general assistance with less demanding tasks while the small households employed maids for housework.

Their origin in coastal societies with maritime occupations, shipbuilding and carpentry seems to have had effect on partner choice even though most marriages were contracted with men born in Stockholm or other parts of Sweden. It is hardly surprising that girls with knowledge of fish and fishing became wives of fish-traders where the family engaged in various aspects of the economic activity. In other cases possibly the partner was sought within the social environment where most of the migrants settled, the areas dominated by people engaged in the crafts or manual labour. The social networks can occasionally be glimpsed but their workings can not be clarified.

Many women married a man able to provide them with a house of their own although in most cases one of reasonable but not astoundingly high standard. The contents of the households were adequate but when a surplus was accumulated it was put into the business, not into consumption, apart from buying expensive clothes. Those who married men in insecure sectors of employment probably assisted in keeping the family. This was witnessed by the occupational activity of the wives of soldiers, boatmen, carpenters etc. The property could also be put to use through the renting out of rooms. In some cases the family economy was augmented by keeping livestock, an activity only possible in the parts of the town where we find these women. Some did not manage to accumulate anything. The selectiveness of the probate inventories unfortunately excludes a large part of the migrants who settled in the town and lost all connections to their place of origin.

We do not know how many women had very high hopes about the golden opportunities in town. Marriage was certainly an option for many but whether their standard of living was better or worse than it would have been in their home region is difficult to tell.

Appendix 1

1745. Probate inventory of Gertrud Erichsdotter wife of Lars Andersson Gedda, sailor

She was survived by husband and 2 daughters Margareta 16 years old and Anna Lisa 10 years old. Gertrud was born on the Aland islands, worked as a maid and married Lars in Katarina parish in Stockholm 1726.

Property in daler copper:

- One golden ring 12 d, silver spoon 7: 1 d, 3 pewter plates 3 d, frying pan and saucepan of iron 2 d.
- Clothes: 3 skirts, one ordinary 4 d, two of better quality at 15 d, cardigans, bonnets, altogether 66 d.
- Textiles: table cloths, sheets, curtains 22: 16 d, Bedding: mattresses, pillows, bedcovers 48: 16 d.
- Furniture: Pine cupboards, several chests, table and chairs 14: 16 d. Altogether 182 daler.

Debts 58 d, percentage for the poor 1: 4½ d, Remains 122 daler

Source: Probate inventories Stockholm 1745/2: 416; 24.12 1726 Katarina parish, banns registers (SSA).

Appendix 2

The funeral costs of Anna Staffansdotter Lind widow of Erich Larson Fisk, fish-trader

It is not clear whether the opulent funeral was the wish of the deceased or her sister's daughter Anna, whose husband was a fish-trader and a member of the same guild as Erich Larson. It is however possible that the expectations of the society went along these lines. Of the total assets of 640 daler a massive part was wiped out by the costs of the funeral.

- Fee for vicar and Holy communion, 12 daler
- Coffin and laying out, 90 daler
- To the Church, 51 daler
- 12 men to carry the coffin, 28.4 daler
- Callers, 15 daler
- Clergyman, 15 daler
- Wine, 42 daler
- 2 barrels of double beer, 1 barrel of single beer, 60 daler
- Fresh meat, dry meat, vodka and crackers, 30 daler.

Total costs, 438.20 daler
(Examples of funeral costs of other individuals during the same time period: 164 daler for a soldier's widow, 60 daler for a tailor's widow)

Source: Probate inventories (SSA), 1729/2/1: 173.

Appendix 3

Inventory of Brita Tornstrom wife of tobaccospinner Isac Lund, childless

The husband left 16 years ago for England where it is said he contracted a new marriage.

Ready money 180 daler. Objects of gold and silver 56 d, other metals 20 d. Clothes 75,20 daler, underwear 103 d, bedding 74 d, furniture 146 d, books 26 d. Money lent out 300 daler. Altogether 982 daler. Funeral 176 daler, debts 166 daler. Remains 634 daler for the nephews and nieces in Aland.
List of books owned by Brita: The Holy Bible 15 daler, The New Testament 2 daler, hymn book and 6 religious booklets among the *Jesu bok* (The Book of Jesus) by John Graham and Thomas de Kempis' *Andeliga Betractelser*.

Source: Probate inventories (SSA) Stockholm, 1735/1: 1189.

Appendix 4

Value of certain items in the probate inventories

- Pig 8 daler copper (1678), pig 10 daler (1682), male pig 19 daler (1739)
- Cow 24 daler (1736), 36 daler (1739)
- Horse 30 daler (1705), 60 daler (1736), 50 daler (1739)
- Barrell of Rye 15 daler
- Male servants wages 50 daler copper (1678) Female servants wages 20 daler copper (1678).

Source: Probate inventories Stockholm (SSA) 1678.11.7, 1682; 763, 1705.

Appendix 5

1715 Beata Persdotter, maid, born in Aland, married Petter Larsson Gran, sailor, born in Harnosand
1721 Beata Persdotter Berg, born in Aland, widow of Petter Gran, sailor, married Joseph Sigfridsson Flink, sailor, born in Ostrobothnia
1748 Inventory of Beata Persdotter, wife of sailor Joseph Flink, 1 son Johan Flink sailor

- House in Sodermalm, Katarina parish 800 daler
- Golden ring 6 daler, Pewter items 20 daler
- Copper, brass 15 daler, Iron and tin 5.16 daler
- Clothes 45.24, Textiles 15.24
- Bedding 47.16
- Pine bed with etc, pine table, 3 chests, 2 cupboards, 1 mirror.

Total 977.16 daler

Sources: Probate inventories Stockholm 1748/2:336, Katarina parish banns registers (SSA).

Appendix 6 – Sources and Structures

The data-sources used are primarily banns' registers of the parishes that record place of birth, Katarina parish (the Finnish parish). Secondarily probate inventories after individuals dying in Stockholm and listing close kin, i.e. parents or siblings, living in South Western Finland. In addition to this, numerous studies on living conditions of various socio-economic and occupational groups in seventeenth century Stockholm and the history of wages and prices in the seventeenth and eighteenth centuries have been used.

Even though it was necessary to provide the clergyman with a document about your identity and marital status when you wanted to get married, this type of documentation has hardly ever been preserved for times earlier than the nineteenth century. Although the clergyman had access to information about the previous parish of residence and usually about the parish of birth, this information was not necessarily included in the register of banns or marriages. Katarina parish is an exception to this rule as the place of birth was systematically registered in this newly created parish, for everybody who married between 1654 and 1736. In 1737 the system is changed and the information omitted. The Finnish parish registers place of birth between 1664 and 1760. An examination of Maria, Klara, Jakob och Johannes, Hedvig Eleonora, Skeppshoms, Svea livgardes bataljons, showed only very sporadic registration of place of birth. As Katarina parish is situated in Sodermalm, the area where Finns reputedly settled, the data-situation can be viewed in reasonably positive light.

In addition to the origin of individuals the banns registers provide information about occupation thereby making it possible to see how the migrants oriented in their new environment, just when they were about to establish a family. The other dataset, the probate inventories provide a glimpse of what the migrants had been able to achieve in material sense. The prime drawback with this dataset is that persons who did not leave live issue in Stockholm figure more prominently when the records are used from this perspective. The law guaranteed children of the body the right to inherit, together with the spouse, thereby parents or sisters and brothers would usually not be listed if there were children. This means that probably a large proportion of people who had established themselves never come under observation. However, when studying the seventeenth century one must be grateful for whatever data-sources can be found. The inventories give us a chance of studying not only how much money the migrants had accumulated but also what kind of houses they had and the location of these houses, the contents of their homes in the form of precious metals, furniture, clothes, bedding, animals etc. We can also see the differences in chances to accumulate property according to social groups.

Male Occupations

A study of the male occupations of the migrants shows a considerable diversity, however the men of marrying age do show a preference for maritime occupations and carpentry. Indeed it does not seem totally unfounded to presume that the recruitment of people with particular skills initiated with the sixteenth century did go on in later centuries. On the other hand it is of course possible to object to this on the grounds of the selectiveness of the sample; perhaps a very large number of the migrants spent years as unskilled labourers or in the service of other people before they married; 51 men out of 145 were registered as having sea connected occupations and 25 others were in the building trade; 4 were guards and soldiers and 4 occupied in activities around the port; 13 were day labourers and 7 employed in private households in various capacities; 14 were engaged in various stages of food-, textile or metal-production. The structure among the migrants found in the probate inventories is quite similar but the proportion of more opulent merchants, innkeepers and persons having advanced higher up in the ships' hierarchies is more prominent.[33]

33 Main sources are: Katarina parish, banns' registers the Finnish parish; Probate inventories Stockholm; V. Bergh 1965, p. 209; Axel Zettersten, *Svenska flottans historia*, Norrtelje, Norrtelje tidnings boktr., 1903, p. 244.

Life-Cycle Servants in Nineteenth Century Sweden: Norms and Practice

Christer LUNDH

The system of life-cycle servanthood, which was well established in Sweden in the nineteenth century, was based on rural custom and regulated by special Servant Acts from the seventeenth century.[1] From legislation we know the rules that structured the lives of young farmhands and maids, and our knowledge of the servant institution is based to a large extent on normative sources.[2] We know considerably less about how important such rules were in practice. Did servants and masters arrange their relations in ways that the legislation stipulated, or was the local practice much different? The relative lack of knowledge in this respect is the point of departure for this paper, in which the legal status of servants is contrasted with servants' actions as they appear in demographic and ethnological sources.

Two main sources are used in this study. The first one is family reconstructions of four parishes in western Scania, the southernmost part of Sweden. This data is gathered in the Scanian Demographic Database.[3] By using this data, it is possible to quantify certain demographic variables, and better understand the functioning of the servant system. Thus, the distribution of servants by sex, age and civil status could be studied, together with the turnover of servants.[4]

The second main source is ethnological reports on conditions in the countryside in Scania during the second half of the nineteenth century, gathered in the Folk Life Archives in Lund. By studying these reports, it is

1 The research was conducted within the projects "Age at Marriage in Sweden, 1750–1900. Trends and Regional Variations" and "Wage Formation and Labour Market Integration in Sweden 1860–1914" funded by the Swedish Council for Research in the Humanities and Social Sciences.

2 For a detailed analysis of the legislation, see Winroth 1878.

3 The Scanian Demographic Database is a collaborative project between the Regional Archives in Lund and the Research Group in Population Economics at the Department of Economic History, Lund University.

4 For a general ethnological description of the servant system, see Svensson 1943 and Granlund 1944.

possible to establish the occurrence of a certain practice (but not its frequency) of importance to the servant system. Reports based on a questionlist dealing with various aspects of the relationship between masters and servants[5] are used, together with some other reports that relate to the subject of "servants" in other respects.

The Servant Act of 1833

Ever since the middle of the seventeenth century, employment conditions in agriculture had been regulated in certain Servant Acts *(tjänstehjonsstadgarna).* Legislation changed several times, and the last Servant Act was passed in 1833, which was valid throughout the nineteenth century and was not abolished until 1926.[6] In this section, the norms of this Act are briefly presented.

The Servant Act regulated the relation between master and servant in several ways, and was therefore normative for the employment agreements that were made between individual employers and servants. The decision to take up service or to hire a servant was made freely, but as soon as the employment agreement was made, a relation of subordination and superiority was also established. Even though an individual employment agreement was made freely by the two parties involved, a servant could not refrain from all employment offers. The Servant Act made it compulsory for anybody who did not own or lease land, or possess other sources of income, to find employment as a servant. This was a relic of the mercantilist era, once introduced to provide labour at reasonable wages to estates and peasants. The work obligation was not abolished until 1885.

The Servant Act did not explicitly say anything about who was intended to be a servant. The law used the word "servant", never sex-specific words like "farmhands" or "maids". Nothing in the act said anything about the required age of servants. In three paragraphs the hiring of

5 See Folk Life Archives in Lund (LUF) 105.

6 The act was named "Kongl. Maj:ts Förnyade Nådiga Lego-Stadga för Husbönder och Tjänstehjon: Gifwen Stockholms Slott den 23 November 1833".

children (including foster children) or adults that were not legally competent was regulated. In such cases it was the parents (or foster parents) or any other guardian that made the employment agreement on behalf of the under-aged.

In a similar way, any required social origin of servants was not stipulated in the act. However, the work obligation probably meant in practice that people of lower social status, with or without land, were more likely to be servants than people from rich homes. Only once in the act was the social origin of servants touched upon, when one paragraph said that the children of poor parents could be hired as servants. Anybody with a business enterprise who needed to hire servants as labour and had enough financial resources to provide for them, could be a master. As long as the servants were used as labour, he could hire as many as he wanted.

The Servant Act regulated the rights and liabilities of masters and servants, once an agreement on employment was made. It was the duty of a master to instruct the servants on how to do their work tasks and treat them politely and according to their deserts. He also had to provide the servant with proper food and lodging. If a servant was ill, the master was obliged to see to that he or she was nursed, but he could, if he wanted, deduct the costs for a doctor or medicine from the servant's wage. If a servant stayed for a long time (from the age of 30 until old age), the master was obliged to provide for and take care of the servant until he or she died.

According to the Servant Act a servant had to be devout, diligent, sober and decent. He or she also had to be faithful and obedient to the master and could not shirk work tasks that were assigned by the master. Besides the description of the general qualities of a servant, the act included a list of things that a servant was explicitly not allowed to do. He or she could not be disobedient to the master or mistress, show unfounded discontent over the food, steal or treat a fire or the master's property in a careless way. Neither could the servant visit inns or other places where alcoholic beverages were served, or without permission leave the master's house or stay out all night.

The way that employment agreements were made and terminated was also regulated in the Servant Act. The period of employment for servants was one year in rural areas, and only in exceptional circumstances could the employment contract be broken during this period. In the late summer, from 26 July to 24 August, both employers and servants had the right to terminate an employment contract. This could have been discussed earlier in the year, but it had to be repeated during the period of notice. As proof of notice, the servant was given a testimonial *(orlovssedel)* confirming that he/she was free to take up new employment, and which contained the employer's opinion of his/her work performance and moral qualities. If neither partner terminated the contract during the period of notice, it meant that the farmhand or maid continued to work for the same employer for a further year.

If a servant agreed to work for a new master during the coming employment period, an employment contract was made. For the new employer the testimonial provided evidence that he, without the risk of a claim for compensation from a previous employer, could employ the servant concerned. The Servant Act stipulated that the employment contract had to affirm that the servant's *orlovssedel* was kept by the master, and that it contained the agreement terms of wage compensation and other privileges including cash payments of part of the wage paid out in advance. This paragraph indicates that the lawmaker had written employment contracts in mind, even though the act did not explicitly make *written* agreements compulsory. Furthermore, another paragraph of the act regulated disputes in cases when, for instance, a written employment contract was lacking, which indicates that oral contracts were also accepted.

During the period of notice and for two more months, the servants had to continue to work for their old masters. The period of employment did not come to an end until 24 October, which was the official Moving Day. For seven days from the moving day, servants moved from the old to the new employers, thereby experiencing a free week. On the seventh day after the moving day the new employment period started. From his or her old master, the servant received a supplementary testimonial *(afskedsbetyg)*, covering the period after the employment contract was made and including the master's opinion on his or her work performance and moral qualities in this period.

Several paragraphs in the Servant Act regulated how the parties involved in the hiring process were supposed to behave, how matters in dispute were to be settled and how misbehaviour was to be compensated by claims adjustments.

The master could not refuse if he was asked for the servant's *orlovssedel*, and his opinion on the servant's performance and qualities had to be fair. In this way, the servant's right to look for new employer was guaranteed. In order to protect employers against unfair competition, the Servant Act forbade the attracting of other employers' workers during an ongoing employment year. Employment contracts that had not been drawn up according to the rules of the act could be declared invalid and be revoked. Disputes in such matters could be settled by mediation within the village or in a civil court.

Once the employment agreement was made, it was binding for the parties involved. It could not be abolished without the approval of both parties. Servants were forbidden to leave during the employment period. If anybody did, the master had the right to have him or her captured and brought back by the parish constable. In such cases, the servant was to pay for the harm and be deprived of half of his or her wage.

Norms and Practice

Male and Female Servants

The Servant Act was quite precise on who could be a master, but was neutral on the sex, age or social origin of a servant. From demographic sources we know that both male and female servants were frequent. In the migration registers of the parishes of Halmstad, Hög, Kävlinge and Sireköpinge in 1831–35, 269 farmhands and 266 maids were registered as moving into one of the parishes (Lundh 1996).

The demand for domestic servants of both sexes could be derived from the way that production was organised at a farmstead in those days. From ethnological sources we know that the work tasks were quite different for male and female servants (Löfgren 1975a, 1975b, 1982). Farmhands took care of the horses, worked in the fields in the summer, and threshed grain in the winter, while the maids took care of the milking, looked after the animals and did the household chores.

Thus, the demand for both male and female servants stemmed from the work organization at a farm. At a farmstead with mixed farming the demand for labour was determined by the acreage and the number of horses or oxen and other animals (colts, cattle, pigs, sheep, geese etc.). On small farms of about 10 to 15 acres and a pair of horses/oxen, the need was generally just one maid and one farmhand. On middle-sized farms of about 50 to 60 acres of flat land, and somewhat smaller in woodland areas, where there were two pairs of horses there were often two maids and two farmhands (Dribe and Lundh 2002).

Age Structure

The Servant Act did not stipulate that a servant was to be of a particular age, but the way the act was written indicates that a servant was normally in his/her teens or older, but seldom very old. For under-aged children their were special rules, and a person under the age 21, who was living in the parental home, was not allowed to go into service in another household without the parents' permission. Once a person had left the parental home, he or she was free to change employer without permission from the parents. As was mentioned, the act also stipulated that the master had to provide for and take care of a servant that stayed for a long time (from the age of 30 until old age). All such special rules indicate that it was unusual for a servant to be under-age or to be very old.

This picture is confirmed by the age specific migration into the parishes of Hög and Kävlinge in 1831–1840. As can be seen in figure 1, as many as 84–90 percent of the servants were in the ages 15–30. Some of the young servants were orphans and taken care of as foster children or as servant lads or young maids, or were children of unmarried maids. The proportion of servants under 15 was 8 percent for both girls and boys. Servants who were over 30 were quite rare. Here we find no more than 3 percent of the maids and 8 percent of the farmhands (Lundh 1996).

The same age distribution of servants could be found in other sources as well, for instance in the catechetical examination registers, and it corresponds well to the average age at leaving the parental home in this area (Lundh 1996). Dribe calculates the medium age at leaving home to be 16–17 in the four parishes of Halmstad, Hög, Kävlinge and Sireköpinge in 1829–1866. Less than 10 percent left home before the age of 15, but at 21 no more than one third were still living in the parental home. Consequently, almost two thirds moved out while they were in the ages 15–21. Ninety percent of those who left home moved within the same parish or within a radius of 15 kilometres. Only 2 or 3 percent left the parental home for marriage – among peasants 3–6 percent. Thus, the vast majority left the parental home in order to work as a servant in another household (Dribe 2000).

Figure 1. Age distribution of servant immigrants into Hög and Kävlinge parishes, 1831–1840

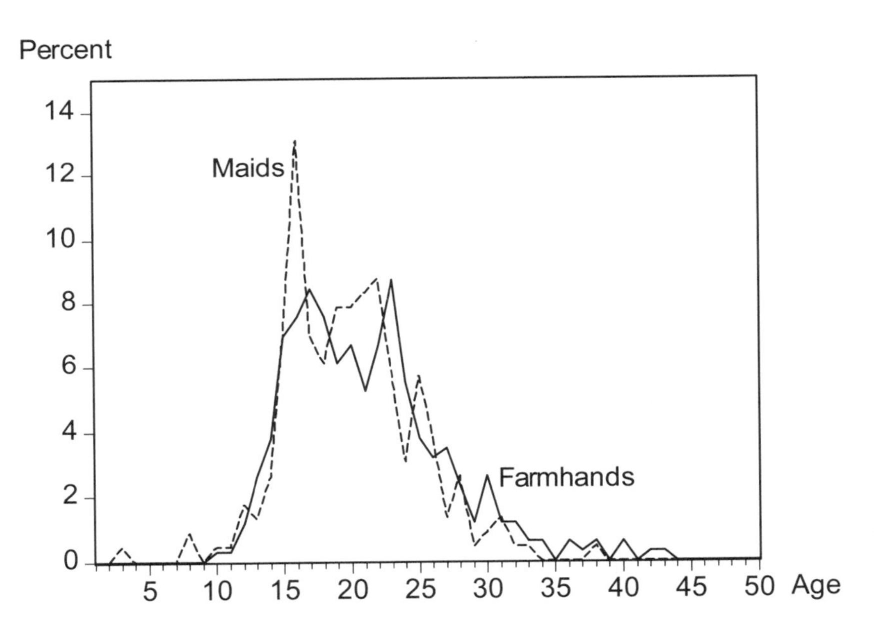

Source: The migration registers of Hög and Kävlinge, The Regional Archives in Lund.

The age distribution among servants corresponded to the demand for labour given by the work organisation at a farmstead. On the farm work tasks were divided according to gender, and within each gender according to age, employment duration and skill. Normally the master and mistress were the oldest and filled the positions requiring the greatest skills in their respective areas (Dribe and Lundh 2002).

Servants were often labelled "first" and "second" farmhand or maid, according to their position in the work hierarchy. Among the male servants, the first farmhand was the oldest and most qualified. He was about 22 or older and was able to do the qualified work tasks on the farm, for instance to be the work leader for the other farmhands, to sow by hand and to repair equipment. The second farmhand, usually aged between 16 and 22, was less experienced and skilful than the first farmhand but could plough with horses and carry out other tasks meant for grown men (Dribe and Lundh 2005).

In a similar way, the first maid, most often over 20, was the oldest and the most qualified on the female side. Her duties were to feed all the animals except the horses, to milk the cows and to be responsible for the work in the barn. She was also supposed to help in the fields at harvest time and to lead, with the housewife, the work involved in washing, baking, brewing, spinning and weaving. The second maid was usually younger, between 16 and 20 years, and less qualified. She took care of the household work indoors, under the supervision of the housewife, and looked after the children (Dribe and Lundh 2005).

On larger farms or estates there could be several servants with roughly the same tasks, status and wage as second farmhands or maids. Thus, "first" and "second" servants formed the bulk of the hired labour in peasant households. At the age of 20–22, a servant probably reached the top of his or her carrier. The next step was to marry and form a family, and this required an own household and an own farm or croft – to stay as a servant for additional decades was considered to be a "failure". Therefore, there were few that continued as servants for life – to most young people, the work as a servant was just a phase in life.

On larger farms, especially during the summer, there were certain work tasks for minor children as well. Younger boys, around 10–15 years old, ran errands and fed the animals on larger farms or took care of geese and sheep during the summer. Some were hired only in the summer, while others were employed on a yearly basis. On larger farms there could also be younger maids aged between 10 and 15 who took over the task of looking after the children from the second maid. The maids were employed on a yearly basis, while young nursery maids sometimes were employed only in the summer, especially if they were very young (Dribe and Lundh 2005).

Civil Status

Nothing is stipulated in the Servant Acts on the civil status of a servant. However, the fact that a servant was supposed to live in the master's house, with board and lodging included in the employment agreement, indicates that the legislation assumed that a servant was unmarried. This is confirmed in demographic sources. Only in rare cases were domestic servants married.

Among servant migrants into the parishes of Hög and Kävlinge in 1831–1840 as many as 98 percent were unmarried (Lundh 1999a). When a young couple married, they normally moved into an own household, and quit their work as domestic servants. To be able to marry, they had to find another job and a house to live in. In those days, the job market and the housing market were often combined, so that the house went with the job. For young people of peasant origin, this meant that they could take over the family farm, or use the compensation from a sibling who was taking it over, to buy another property. Young people of poorer origin could not expect to get a farm, but could negotiate a tenancy contract with some landowner for a croft or cottage in exchange for rent in work or money.

The servant system was an institutional precondition for the relatively late marriages that characterised the Swedish marriage pattern. While waiting to get married, young people worked as servants for a period of their lives. Laslett's term "life-cycle servants" is well suited to the Swedish system (Laslett 1977). From previous studies, we know that the average marriage age was quite high in this area. In the period 1811–1860, the mean age at first marriage was 27 for women and 29 for men (Lundh 1997).[7] In the course of the nineteenth century the marriage age decreased for landless and semilandless groups (Lundh 1998). This development probably reflected an increase in the possibility of the landless to get access to jobs and dwellings as commercialisation of agriculture and industrialisation progressed.

7 The parishes included in the study are Ekeby, Frillestad, Halmstad, Hög, Kävlinge, Sireköpinge and Stenestad, all situated in western Scania.

Social Origin

While the Servant Act did not say anything about the social background of servants, it did about the masters. To be a master, one had to be self-supporting and not an object of the work obligation of the law. In rural areas this meant that a master could be a civil servant (priest, officer etc.), a farmer or landlord, or a mine owner, whose business was good enough to bear the costs and who needed domestic servants for labour. Thus, indirectly we can conclude that a servant could be anybody who lacked these resources. Since a servant was supposed to live in the master's household, young and unmarried people, who had left the parental home and intended to marry and form a family later on, were well suited for the role of servant.

It has been established that servants were recruited from all social groups including the peasant group itself. Regardless of sex and social background, the vast majority of young people worked as servants before they married. One study calculates that the probability of becoming a servant prior to marriage was 85–90 percent in the parishes of Halmstad, Hög, Kävlinge and Sireköpinge in 1740–1859 (Lundh 1999b). Thus, there is no doubt that servanthood in rural areas was an important institution that affected the life courses of young people, even those from peasant homes. However, there was an over-representation of young people from landless or semilandless families in the recruitment of servants (Eriksson and Rogers 1978; Lundh 1999a–b).

In the eighteenth and early nineteenth century the occupation of servant was not a lifetime job but a temporary one. Servanthood was a phase in young peoples' lives, between childhood in the parental home and the life as a grown up and married with an own household. Children from peasant homes worked as servants for some time, but still had a good opportunity of progressing to the position of a married farmer or farmer's wife later on.

In the second half of the nineteenth century the character of the servant institution was partly changed. The combination of a rapidly growing population, commercialisation of agriculture and industrialisation brought about a process of downward social mobility. Work as a servant was no longer a temporary job, but became a first step to permanent wage labour. Peasants became reluctant to send their sons or daughters to work as servants, and kept them at the farmstead. Over-representation of servants from non-peasant homes increased, and, for young people of peasant origin, working as a servant increased the risk of becoming a permanent wage labourer (Lundh 1999a).

Moving Day and Employment Turnover

The Servant Act stipulated that 24 October was to be the Moving Day and the new employment period was to start seven days later. In between was a free week. Consequently, there were strong institutional reasons for migrations to be concentrated in October or November. Of all the dated servant migrations from the parishes of Halmstad, Hög, Kävlinge and Sireköpinge in the period 1825–1844, 78 per cent occurred in October and a further 12 per cent in November. The remaining 10 percent of the moves were equally distributed over the year except for a minor concentration to April. This may be due to the fact that contracts for a farm, croft or cottage at the estates often contained a moving day in the spring (Lundh 1999b).

The Servant Act stipulated a yearly employment period and regulated the terms for renewal or termination of employment contracts. The yearly employment period was a guarantee of available domestic labour for the master, and of continuous board and lodging for the servant. But the act was not a guarantee that servants would stay for longer periods than a year, even though one can suspect that this was the norm of the lawmaker. One study reports widespread disapproval of the extensive servant turnover in the eighteenth and early nineteenth centuries in the Swedish Diet of the Four Estates *(ståndsriksdagen)* and among peasants all over the country (Harnesk 1990). There is also ethnological evidence from the latter half of the nineteenth century that peasants were not in favour of a large turnover of servants. On the contrary, from Scania there are several reports, from the latter part of the nineteenth century, of masters favouring farmhands and maids they were satisfied with and wanted to keep or reward for loyal service (Dribe and Lundh 2005).

Even though the norm might have been a long-term relation between a master and a servant, in reality servants changed employers quite frequently. In the parishes of Halmstad, Hög, Kävlinge and Sireköpinge in 1829–1867 a servant moved on average eight times between the ages of

15 and 30, including the first move out of the parental home and, in some cases, a final move to get married. Thus, the turnover of servants was impressive. About 60 percent stayed only for one year with the same employer, and another 23 percent moved after two years (Dribe and Lundh 2005).

The extensive servant mobility has been found to have its incentives deeply rooted in the local rural economy. About half of the moves of a servant could be due to advancement within the social hierarchy that characterised rural life. For a boy, a servant career started with the employment as a herder lad, later to become a second farmhand and a first farmhand, and ended when the servant left life-cycle service to get married and establish a new household on a farm, croft or in a cottage. Three of four years on average would then be spent on one and the same farm. Besides this structural basis for the frequent changes of employment by servants, there were a lot of other reasons. A servant might have been dissatisfied with the standard of board and lodging, got into a conflict with the master or anyone else in the household, or moved to find a marriage partner. A master might have wanted to substitute adult children for a servant, and in times of bad harvests the demand for male labour, or the master's capacity to pay, might have been reduced. A master might also have wanted to prevent his grown up children from being too closely involved with one of the servants (Dribe and Lundh 2005).

Breach of Contract, Mediation and Award

The Servant Act presupposed the existence of a written testimonial. This document was the previous master's judgement on the servant's work capacity and loyalty, which was to be handed over to the new master who kept it during the employment period. As far as employment contracts were concerned, the act was formulated as if written documents were the normal form, but written contracts were not compulsory.

Very few written testimonials and employment contracts are preserved for posterity. Such documents were normally kept in private hands and were seldom registered by official authorities who were obliged to file them. Probably, most employment contracts were oral. In times when oral contracts were common, certain ceremonies were used to confirm an agreement, for instance a handshake in front of witnesses. From ethnological sources we know that the giving and accepting of a payment in advance was a quite frequent way to ratify the employment contract.

The rights and duties of masters and servants were regulated in the Servant Act, as was how to handle disputes and breaches of contract in many detailed situations. That conflicts occurred and that the agreements were sometimes violated are witnessed in ethnological sources. Servants who were careless or disobedient to the master were punished by deductions from their wages or were dismissed. Only in rare cases were younger servants physically punished according to the ethnological reports. Servants who left during the employment period without serving for the period of notice lost their wages due and did not get a testimonial from the master, which probably made it difficult to get a new job. Even though the master had the right to get the runaway brought back by the district police, the ethnological reports mention that he seldom utilised it (Dribe and Lundh 2005).

Sometimes the disputes were taken to the District court for award or judgement. According to ethnological sources the most common disputes concerned assault and absconding. As far as I know, there is no study yet of such disputes based on court archives, which could shed new light on the relation between masters and servants in the nineteenth century.

Concluding Remarks

Far too much of our knowledge of the servant system is based on the normative source of the Servant Act. This Act tells us how the lawmaker wanted the system to work. But the law does not tell us the realities of everyday life in rural Sweden in the nineteenth century – from such a source it is not possible to say anything about the practice of the servant system. Yet, the servant institution is often described in the way the system was intended to work by the lawmaker, not as it really worked in practice.

This paper has gathered some facts on the practice of the servant system. As is obvious, our knowledge is mainly based on demographic sources, informing us of the existence and frequency of phenomena. Ethnological evidence provides supplementary information on the occurrence of customs and behaviour. One important source that has not yet been used is court records of disputes. By using such a source, it would be possible to expand our knowledge on what was acceptable and what was not in the relation between masters and servants.

References

DRIBE, Martin, 2000, *Leaving Home in a Peasant Society. Economic Fluctuations, Household Dynamics and Youth Migration in Southern Sweden, 1829–1866*, Södertälje, Almqvist & Wiksell International.

DRIBE, Martin and LUNDH, Christer, 2005, "People on the Move. Determinants of Servant Migration in Nineteenth Century Sweden", *Continuity and Change*, 20, 1, pp. 55–94.

ERIKSSON, Ingrid and ROGERS, John, 1978, *Rural labor and population change: social and demographic developments in East-central Sweden during the nineteenth century*, Uppsala/Stockholm, Almqvist and Wiksell International.

GRANLUND, John, 1944, "Arbetsorganisation", in Andreas LINDBLOM (ed.), *Arbetaren i Helg och Söcken. Kulturhistoriska studier. II Vardag och fest*, Stockholm, Tidens förlag, pp. 61–114.

HARNESK, Börje, 1990, *Legofolk. Drängar, pigor och bönder i 1700 och 1800-talens Sverige*, Umeå, Umeå University.

Kongl. Maj:ts Förnyade Nådiga Lego-Stadga för Husbönder och Tjänstehjon: Gifwen Stockholms Slott den 23 November 1833, Swensk Författnings-Samling, nr 43, 1833.

LASLETT, Peter, 1977, *Family Life and Illicit Love in Earlier Generations*, Cambridge, Cambridge University Press.

LUNDH, Christer, 1996, "Youth Migration in a Life-Cycle Perspective", *Lund Papers in Economic History*, no. 52.

–, 1997, "The World of Hajnal Revisited. Marriage Patterns in Sweden 1650–1990", *Lund Papers in Economic History*, no. 60.

–, 1998, *Nuptiality in Pre-industrial Sweden*. Paper presented at the EurAsian Project conference "Nuptiality and Family Formation in Comparative Eurasian Perspective", Beijing University, 25–29 December 1998, Peking.

–, 1999a, "The Social Mobility of Servants in Rural Sweden, 1740–1894", *Continuity and Change*, 14, pp. 57–89.

–, 1999b, "Servant Migration in Sweden in the Early Nineteenth Century", *Journal of Family History*, 24, pp. 53–74.

LÖFGREN, Orvar, 1975a, "Arbeitsteilung und Geschlechterrollen in Schweden", *Ethnologia Scandinavica*, 5, pp. 49–72.
–, 1975b, *Arbetsfördelning och könsroller i bondesamhället: kontinuitet och förändring: ett diskussionskompendium*, Lund, Etnologiska inst. med Folklivsarkivet.
–, 1982, "Kvinnfolksgöra: om arbetsdelning i bondesamhället", *Kvinnovetenskaplig tidskrift*, 3, p. 3.
SVENSSON, Sigfrid, 1943, "Böndernas tjänstefol", in Andreas LINDBLOM (ed.), *Arbetaren i Helg och Söcken. Kulturhistoriska studier. I Hus och hem*, Stockholm, Tidens förlag, pp. 117–130.
WINROTH, Alfred Ossian, 1878, *Tjenstehjonsförhållandet enligt svensk rätt*, Uppsala, Uppsala universitets årsskrift.

Female Domestic Servants in Sundsvall

A Swedish Sawmill Town, during Industrialization

Marie-Christine (Lotta) VIKSTRÖM

Introduction

A long time ago, in the year of 1879 to be precise, there were five female servants living in the town of Sundsvall. You might never have heard of Sundsvall but it definitely existed, just as did the five women. You can still visit this thriving town. In the 1870s, however, everything had just started. The surrounding sawmills provided economic strength, virgin forest gave fuel for it, and the sea waited to carry off the fruit of the forest to the rest of the world. Sundsvall was getting stronger, bigger and more popular in people's eyes, since it had jobs to offer, a future within it. It is no wonder that this town attracted migrants who were arriving in thousands, most to seek employment in the sawmill industry.

However, to carry planks and saw timber all day long was regarded as men's, not women's, work. And according to the parish registers our five women seem mostly to have worked as domestic servants *(piga)*.[1] In 1879 all of them were relatively young and still unmarried. Märta Westerstrand was the oldest, 35 years of age. Selma Wallmark was only aged 17 whereas Anna Helena Bolin just had reached the age of 25. Then there

1 *Piga* was the Swedish term for unmarried women involved in the domestic sector even though the parish registers cannot give complete information on what kind of domestic work they were performing. The term *piga* was however frequently used and might not always include a domestic employment. Cf. under the heading of "Women's work in quantitative sources" below.

were Amanda Rådberg and Lina Ågren, aged 28 and 34 respectively. Except for the latter woman, a native, all of them were migrants.[2]

Even though Sundsvall primarily attracted men or families, also single women had good reasons to move to or live in this town. There were hundreds of solitary men, hundreds of hungry workers and thousands of dirty shirts that all needed a woman's service. Furthermore, there was a growing middle class able to pay for domestic service. A woman knew the art of cooking a meal and scrubbing a floor, and she knew how to sew, wash and iron. The single men had to have someone to care for their laundry and also needed to eat. We should not forget, however, the potential risks that could befall women in a town crowded with men. With the increasing labor and partner market, there was likely an involuntary sexual market in which some women had to take part to earn their daily bread. As a matter of fact, the police inspector Hellman reported that about 60–100 prostitutes were living in the town at the beginning of 1879 (SP 1879-02-01). In order to find a place to have a drink or two, the people in Sundsvall did not have to look far. In 1879 no less than 226 public houses and inns (ST 1879-08-05) were found in a town populated by only 9,000 individuals (Tedebrand 1997, 101). It is hardly surprisingly, that slightly more than 1,000 persons were found guilty of abusing alcohol the previous year (SP 1879-02-20).

Then what about our five servants? Of course, not all of them remained unmarried. Neither did they remain in Sundsvall for the rest of their lives even though one woman died at young age in 1884. Another gave birth to two illegitimate children. This is vital information generated from the parish registers. However, like every other source, parish records can only offer one perspective of the past. Seen from another point of view, things might look differently. As a matter of fact, the five women had other occupations than those given by the parish registers. The local newspapers tell us that Amanda Rådberg in fact was involved in the fashion trade (ST 1879-08-07). However, as they also report her bankruptcy in August 1879, her business obviously did not do very well. Perhaps the sawmill strike earlier that year had caused some damage to her trade, and people had other things than hats and clothes to worry about when times were

2 The five women's identity-numbers according to the Demographic Data Base (DDB), Umeå University, Sweden, are as follows: Märta Westerstrand (844001556), Selma Wallmark (862002185), Anna Helena Bolin (852002658), Amanda Rådberg (851001711), Lina Ågren (845001325).

rough. Nevertheless, on her arrival in 1875, the parish records report Amanda as being a *piga,* an occupation she held until 1881 according to similar source. At the age of 30, she married the 35 year-old bookkeeper Olof Forsell. Amanda's business background might explain the relatively high social status of her husband. Even though of course it could happen, servants seldom married civil officials. Interestingly enough, the parish records indicate that Amanda had been found guilty of some sexual indecency in 1875, the year she had left Stockholm for Sundsvall. This does not seem to have hindered her prospects though. Perhaps the fact that Amanda's sexual misconduct never bore visible fruit in terms of illegitimate children, facilitated her life, work and marriage in Sundsvall.

Märta Westerstrand also earned her living, but not by performing the type of work usually linked to servants. Perhaps Märta's two illegitimate children, born in 1873 and 1876, stopped her from doing domestic duties away from home. In an ad printed the summer of 1879, Märta revealed that if the readers just bring her some cloth she had the skill to sew almost anything on the machine (SP 1879-06-19). This was likely the only way for her to make a living and at the same time keep an eye on her children. According to the parish registers, however, Märta was reported as being an unwed mother and *piga* throughout her Sundsvall residency from 1872 to 1892. There is not a word about her skill in sewing.

Yet another *piga*, the Sundsvall born Lina Ågren, was engaged in other work. Instead of serving people in their households, she invited hungry people to her home where she offered them something to eat (ST 1879-12-06). Even though the parish registers obviously fail to give complete occupational information in her case too, they reveal that Lina kept her position as *piga* until she married a customs officer in 1884 at the age of 39. She was sixteen years younger than her husband who married for the second time.

The two remaining servants, Anna Helena Bolin and Selma Wallmark, also found other ways to pay for their daily life in 1879. As they both appear in the newspapers' police-reports, they did not behave as decent women should. Anna Helena was accused of sexual indecency and drunkenness. According to the newspaper this was the third time she fell foul of the law and sent to jail. The parish records reveal nothing of this, except from that the minister sometime has noted "defenseless" ahead of *piga*, which might indicate that she was not doing all right. Indirectly, the parish records also suggest why, since Anna Helena was of poor origin and fatherless. Within three years her mother would die too. Administratively, she was living in a neighboring parish, Tynderö, but it seems as if she spent her time in Sundsvall. Furthermore, the parish records reveal that this "fallen" woman never married. Most likely, Anna Helena was never employed as domestic servant, at least not for extended periods. From the 1880s onwards, she lacks occupational data in the parish registers. Somehow, however, Anna Helena survived and maybe she did by having sold her body even though she never bore illegitimate children.

Similar to Anna Helena Bolin, the servant Selma Wallmark originated from the surrounding district. She too committed a crime in 1879, but of a different nature. At the time, she was only 17 years old. As both her parents were dead according to the parish records, Selma and her siblings probably had to make use of all their skills and knowledge to earn their living. One day in the summer of 1879, young Selma went to a shoe shop in Sundsvall pretending she was the servant of a teacher in the town (ST 1879-06-19). Apparently, Selma played her role well, as she gained a pair of shoes for the teacher's wife on his credit. After some time, however, she was caught and sent to spend three months and three days in jail. Five years later she died of pneumonia, still reported as being a *piga*.

Unlike most fairy tales this servant story did not have a happy ending. It shows, though, what life and occupation looked like for five Sundsvall women in transitional times as industrialization and migration hit their town. Having viewed these five women's experience of life and labor, the following questions related to women's work according to different sources could be addressed. How did lone women support themselves? Did a servant actually work as a servant, and was a demoiselle always a non-working delicate lady? Furthermore, what source is in position to offer the most sufficient information regarding women's occupations?

Apart from time and place, the profession tends to influence the individual's identity. Occupation usually has an impact on people's geographic and demographic behavior (cf. Alter 1988, 150ff.; Janssens 1998, 256ff.).[3] The kind of work we do might affect the way we migrate or

3 Some scholars find a strong correlation between women's occupation and demographic behavior. According to George Alter 1988 (150–152), one theory suggests that women's increased participation on the labor market made them less inclined to marry. In opposite to this, another theory assumes that this increase made it possible for women to marry at a younger age. Angélique Janssens argues that the women's type of employment influenced marriage pattern (1998, 255ff.). Hence, women working in

marry. However, the demographic and socio-geographical background also forms one explanatory factor to people's occupation. Of great importance too, is the context and the socio-economic preconditions associated with it, as this affects our life opportunities as well. Having this information at hand, there is a chance to approach past people's experience and get a better idea of why they behaved as they did, or as in this study, why women show up in one particular occupation.

The above issues create difficulties in relation to women in the past. In comparison to information on men, most sources neglect women's historical presence or group them together with dominant expectations. However, it is not totally impossible to trace them and their various activities on the labor market. This survey seeks a deeper understanding not only of women workers in general but of domestic servants in particular. The purpose is to analyze a range of different data since they tend to treat the activity of women differently. Of course historians are aware of that this is often the case, not only in relation to women. It is another thing, however, to tell what the differences look like. This study shows at least 289 individual examples of to what extent differing sources disagree regarding women's occupations.

Women's Work in Quantitative Sources

Historians dealing with urban areas during the transition towards modern society cannot avoid encountering a large number of women, and particularly domestic servants. Thus there are millions of them in old censuses and parish records stored all over Europe. Since the 1970s, many servants have also become known to us through efforts made by scholars searching for a better understanding of their life, labor and demographic path (Alter 1988; Carlsson 1977; Hietala and Nilsson 1999; Katzman 1978; Matovic 1984; Davidoff and Westover 1986; Davidoff and Hall 1987; John 1986;

---

industries did not parallel the pattern of domestic servants who were employed in a familial context. For a more thorough discussion about this issue, see Vikström 2003a, 246–251.

Jorde 1995; Hudson and Lee 1990; Pinchbeck 1930; Tilly and Scott 1978).[4]

We now know a great deal about women workers engaged in probably the most common occupation for women living in the nineteenth century. Nevertheless, most quantitative data deliver incomplete information on their occupations in the eighteenth and nineteenth centuries. They were recorded for a purpose that does not fit today's desire to trace women on the labor market. Domestic servants, though, appear frequently. In fact there are so many of them that the broad definition of their work causes troubles. First, the domestic occupation covered different duties, and thus diverse statuses. Second, the status of a servant also depended on the household in which she served. Third, in Sweden a *piga*, i.e. maidservant, could be the daughter of almost any man belonging to the working or even the middle class. These circumstances make it hard to tell exactly what characterized a servant or the work she did. As was just shown, women reported as being *pigor* (maidservants) according to the parish registers did not always work as domestic servants. Nevertheless, there is usually no other choice than to let the sources decide whether women were servants or not. This principle will also guide this study.

There also was a considerable under-registration of the actual work of spinsters, defined in the Swedish records as *demoiselles*, for instance. All of them were not sitting at home doing embroidery. They too sometimes needed to work to make ends meet (e.g. Anderson 1984, 377–393; Davidoff and Westover 1986, 9–12; Hufton 1984, 355–376; Pinchbeck 1930, 287–303; Vicinus 1985, 10–45). Probably, few of them had wealthy fathers or kin at hand ready to pay for their daily life. However, to take up a servant employment was not always considered a suitable occupation for a woman belonging to the lower middle class or above. For them, starting businesses and trading formed one survival strategy (Alter 1989, 105–111; Davidoff and Hall 1987, 272–315).

4 There has, of course, been considerable historical writing on women's work, particularly as regards their conditions during industrialization. Only a few major works of certain interest are above considered.

Sundsvall, the Sawmill Town

For a long time it looked as if the industrial revolution would never cross the Swedish borders. While almost every part of Western Europe was affected by industrialization and urbanization there were nothing but small towns in Sweden, with one single exception: Stockholm, the capital. Urbanization thus proceeded at a slow pace. In 1900, four out of five Swedes were still living in rural Sweden (Nilsson 1989; Samuelsson 1985; Thomas 1941, 19–23, 112–166).

From the 1870s onwards things happened quickly regarding the speed of industrialization. Important explanatory factors related to this change were the free trade and Sweden's abundance of natural resources, such as watercourse and forest. In the county of Sundsvall, the latter key factors were easily found. This place was perfect for establishing sawmills, particularly since Sundsvall's harbor and the Gulf of Botnia were readily available to carry off the timber to Europe where the demand for timber was increasing. Together with the improving technical knowledge, the invention of the steam-driven mill made the Sundsvall district one of the fastest growing regions in Europe in the 1870s. In times of population pressure and increasing emigration due to the famine years in 1867–68, the region soon became known as an alternative destination sometimes called 'Little America'. The migrants went in tandem with this industrial development and dramatically built on the population growth in the town. In 1860, only about 4,500 people were living in Sundsvall. Twenty years later the population consisted of slightly more than 9,300 inhabitants (Figure 1). Seen from an international horizon Sundsvall could hardly be considered a large town. From a demographic point of view, though, it has been shown that this small town functioned as any large city elsewhere in Europe (Brändström and Tedebrand 1995; Edvinsson 1992).

Initially, mostly young men and families took the road to Sundsvall or the surrounding parishes because of the type of work the sawmill industry demanded but soon the labor market widened. Since Sundsvall provided for the necessary banks and the harbor, it soon became the center for the trade and commerce (Björklund 1997, 7–39; Ericsson 1997, 137–154, Svanberg 1999). In only a couple of decades this development changed the town's socio-economic structure. Pre-industrial occupations, connected to primarily fishing and handicraft, were rapidly replaced by new occupations linked to the white- and blue-collar sector. Because of all the underreported season laborers who were temporarily living in the town, there are reasons to believe that the large number of unskilled workers was even more pronounced. Estimations based on the late 1870s suggest that about 3,000 male laborers stayed in Sundsvall without having told the minister about their residence (Åslund 1878, 271).

Figure 1. Population development in Sundsvall 1860–92. Number of men and women, number of women reported as being *pigor* (maidservants), number of men connected to the upper and middle class, and proportion of *pigor* among all women in Sundsvall (N/10,000)

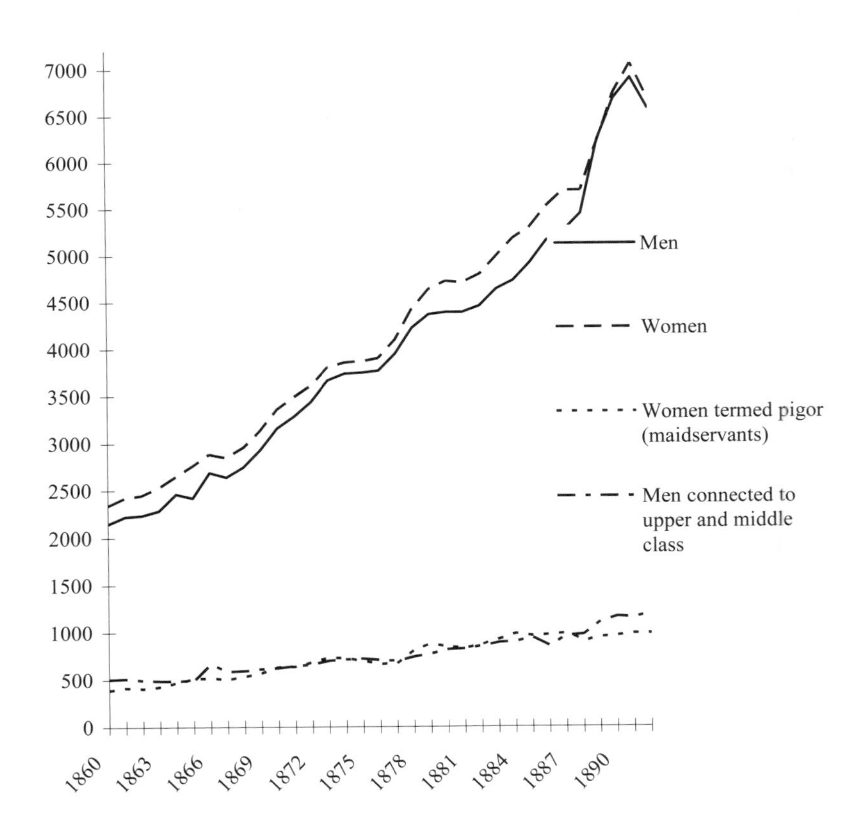

Source: Parish registers, DDB, Umeå University.

Although the sawmills mainly supported men's labor, the economic development probably also generated favorable job opportunities for women in Sundsvall. In addition to taking up domestic employment in the increasing numbers of middle- and upper-class households, the town was populated by men who needed a woman's services. Basically, the female labor market consisted of one single but broad field, the service sector. Except for a minor brewery and some tobacco production, there were no other industries, such as a garment industry, ready to employ them. Figure 1 shows, however, that the town's ratio of *pigor* (maidservants) did not parallel the general growth regarding the total number of women. Besides of a possible under-registration, Figure 1 indicates that women probably found other occupations over time. As the business and professional sector developed and offered employment at the end of the century, women were not only limited to domestic service.

Due to the development of the sawmills a predominantly male demographic profile characterized Sundsvall. Usually, the urban demand for domestic service caused a surplus of females in towns. In Sweden, 121 women for every 100 men were living in urban areas in 1870. This typical surplus was not seen in Sundsvall and especially not during the latter period of the nineteenth century (Figure 1). In 1870, there were only 111 women in 100 men in the town. Twenty years later, the similar ratio consisted of only 101 women (*Historisk Statistik* 1969, Table 4, 46ff.; Tedebrand 1997, 126ff.).

In short, it seems as if a young woman had at least two good reasons to live in, or move to, this town: job and love. Perhaps, these prospects were particularly prosperous in a "male" town as was Sundsvall?

Definitions and Data Set – a Combination of Quantitative and Qualitative Sources

This study is based on varied sources. The major material consists of parish registers computerized by the Demographic Data Base (DDB) at Umeå University, Sweden. These sources include the nineteenth century until 1893. Thus this year ends the industrial interval below considered. To judge the occupational quality of the parish records, three other kinds of sources are addressed. These are termed *the alternative sources* and are manually linked to the parish registers where the women's names worked as the linking factor. Thanks to the computerized registers, this identification process was made possible, but even when identified, the necessary criterion to have one woman's occupation reported that paralleled in time in both the alternative sources and the parish registers, made many women impossible to consider. When comparing two different sources on an individual level, it is of vital importance to secure their identity.

Before dealing with the alternative sources more in detail a few comments on the Swedish parish records are made as there is reason to call them into question when it comes to analyzing women's occupation. Despite being known as possibly the best parish records in the world, the Swedish registers share some of the international shortcomings initially mentioned. Because of the heavy in-migration both the parish records and the poll taxes in Sundsvall fail to provide information about the households in which *pigor* might have served. Hence, the different statuses of maidservants cannot be related to the status of their masters.

The actual occupation of wives and spinsters is seldom reported or sometimes masked behind the occupation of their husbands or fathers. In this study, some spinsters will nevertheless be regarded, as they were also likely to hold a servant employment. Spinsters who lack occupation, but have a title reported in the parish registers, are labelled *title-women.* They consisted of *fröknar, demoiseller, mamseller* or *jungfrur*, which suggest they were daughters of men belonging to the middle or upper classes even though that was not always the case. In addition, in the end of nineteenth-century Sweden some titles underwent an inflation, as working class girls started to label themselves *jungfru* or *mamsell*, for instance (Carlsson 1977, 16). They probably did so in order to increase their status and prospects on the labor market.

When studying Sundsvall's newspapers in the year of 1879, the many problems connected to women's work in the parish registers came into view. Contrary to the latter source women frequently played an active part on the local labor market according to the newspapers. They were cleaning, ironing, washing, and busy selling various goods and services related to domestic, catering, and fashion trade. Assuming that the newspaper-women really were living in Sundvall and their names did not belong to the most common name categories, this information was enough to identify them in the computerized parish registers. It was thus possible to link some newspaper-women to the quantitative source in order to add their demographic data and compare the occupational data from two totally different sources. Below, Table 1 shows the frequency of identified newspaper-women in this respect. All of them were unmarried, born between 1830 and 1860 and thus in the age of 18–49 when they for various reasons showed up in the local newspapers the year of 1879.

To get more comparable cases, patient records were addressed. Hence 216 unmarried female patients with an occupation reported in the patient records have been linked to the parish registers.[5] All of them were born 1841–1864 and visited the Sundsvall hospital during the 1862–1889 period at an age of 15–44. Additionally, they have exclusively reported Sundsvall as their place of living. According to previous efforts, the patient records give a fair socio-economic picture of the town's population (Brändström 1988, 14; Brändström 1995). Patient records also tend to better cover women's occupation as they separate ordinary maids *(piga)* from more "qualified" domestic servants *(tjänstepiga, tjänsteflicka, tjänstekvinna)*. Some prostitute women also appear in these sources.

Yet another source was utilized. For selected years in the 1860–93 period, this material consists of the National Board of Trade's business statistics where individuals in possession of a business permit for trade or crafts were annually registered.[6] These lists had two purposes. First, they formed the basis for the countrywide published statistics. Second, they were the basis for personal taxation of the businessmen (Svanberg 1999, 57–65). Because of the taxation, there is a risk of not finding everyone engaged in the business life. Nevertheless, businesswomen seem to emerge more frequently in this kind of statistics than is the case in the parish records (Alter 1988, 105–111). Hence forty six unmarried women born 1830–1860 have been drawn from this material and manually linked to the computerized parish records in order to add the comparable occupational and demographic data.

According to Table 1 conflicts between the sources are not hard to find. Apparently, the patient records form the source most likely to paral-

5 The Demographic Data Base has created a preliminary link between the parish registers and patient records. In this analysis, this link has been manually checked and completed to get the necessary information for the women under study.

6 For the 1860–1893 period single years per decade were analyzed in the following order: 1860, 1863, 1865, 1868; 1870, 1873, 1875 and so forth until the year of 1893. Many thanks to Mikael Svanberg, who has supplied me with this material. In his thesis, he focuses on the business and life of tradesmen living in Sundsvall during the second part of the nineteenth century (Svanberg 1999).

lel the occupational structure reported by the parish registers. However, this holds true only in about 50 percent of the cases.

Table 1. The degree of disagreement between the alternative sources and the parish records as regards women's occupation reported single years during the 1860–1893 period in the town of Sundsvall[7]

Alternative sources	*In comparison to occupation reported in the parish records*			*Total*	
Type of source	Agreement	Minor disagreement	Major disagreement	N	%
Patient records	50.5	17.1	32.4	216	100
Business statistics	23.9	4.3	71.7	46	100
Local newspapers	22.2	7.4	70.4	27	100
Total	*43.6*	*14.2*	*42.2*	*289*	*100*

Sources: Parish registers, Sundsvall, DDB; Patient records, Sundsvall, DDB; Business statistics, Sundsvall, Riksarkivet, Stockholm; Sundsvall's local newspapers 1879, Umeå University.
Explanations: In the table major disagreements refer to women who according to the source comparison changed social group in the classification applied in this study (cf. Table 2). The category of minor disagreements considers occupational changes within one particular social group.

7 In this study the socio-economic classification is modified but based on the following classification.

Men	Women
Upper class	
1. Large-scale business entrepreneurs	1. Small-scale entrepreneurs and civil officials,
2. Higher civil officials	2. Title-women *(demoiseller, mamseller, jungfrur-fröknar),*
	3. Skilled and unskilled laborers (seamstresses, cooks, female manual laborers)
Middle class	
3. Small-scale entrepreneurs in trade and industry, master artisans and craftsmen; farmers	
4. Lower civil officials	4. *Pigor* (maidservants)
	5. Occupation unknown
Working class	
5. Skilled laborers, craftsmen and artisans below the rank of master	
6. Unskilled laborers; farm hands	

Concerning the other alternative sources the similar figure consists of 20–25 percent. These results put the parish records in some doubt.

Table 2. Comparison of the women's occupational status between the parish records and the alternative sources

Alternative Sources Social groups	Parish records Social groups							*Total*	
	1	2	3	4	5	6	Occupa-tion unknown	%	N
1. Business entrepreneurs & civil officials	100	52.2	40.0	33.3	5.8	–	24.0	20.4	59
2. Title-women	–	15.0	10.0	–	3.6	–	18.0	7.6	22
3. Skilled & unskilled labor-ers	–	7.5	40.0	–	7.2	–	6.0	7.6	22
4. Domestic servants	–	7.5	–	33.3	21.4	–	14.0	16.3	47
5. *Pigor* (maid-servants)	–	15.0	10.0	33.3	60.7	–	20.0	41.5	120
6. Prostitutes	–	2.5	–	–	5.4	–	18.0	6.6	19
Total %	100	100	100	100	100	0	100	100	289
(N) (parish records)	(18)	(40)	(10)	(3)	(168)		(50)		

Sources: See Table 1.
Explanations: The category of title-women includes women reported as having no occupation, yet a title, such as demoiselles, for instance. In contrast to the social group of pigor, i.e. maidservants, the category of domestic servants consists of pigor who according to the alternative sources were more qualified and probably employed as servants.

Occupational Structure According to the Different Sources

Table 2 displays what the above source conflict looked like more in detail. The women's social status based on the occupation reported in the alternative sources is compared to that offered by the parish records the same year. According to the parish registers, fifty women lacked occupational information, but the alternative sources indicate what they were up to. These women were in fact engaged in domestic service, petty commerce or trade. Furthermore, the alternative sources reveal there were fifty nine women located to the first social group, whereas the parish records suggest they were only eighteen. The latter sources report them as being *demoiselles* or having no occupation at all. Apparently, some were working as *pigor* (maidservants), whereas others turned up in the third social group formed by seamstresses.

Pigor (maidservants) predominate in Table 2, just as they probably did in the female labor market in Sundsvall. The newspapers of 1879 show many ads where people asked for servants. Women too frequently advertised their domestic service and skill, so there definitely tended to be a great labor market for servants. Unfortunately, the women's name is seldom printed in this kind of advertisement, only a signature or a reference number appears. This makes them impossible to identify in the computerized parish registers. In their ads they often stress their skill but tend to be rather modest about their salary requirements. It seems as if they were well aware of their low societal position and probably did not dare to ask or expect too much of a possible employer. In some ads though, servants express a desire regarding the households in which they would like to serve, usually in 'better' households. Perhaps the women behind these want ads had long experienced the servant sector and thus had the skill and confidence to bring such claims. Even though these unsigned ads deny us the details regarding the female originators, they show at least some of the different status connected to servants, likely depending on their skill and years in the domestic business. Yet another type of servants obviously preferred to serve lone men or widowers. Hypothetically, these women were primarily looking for a man, not a master. To marry was one way to escape domestic employment, even though many wives kept performing domestic duties in order to build on the family economy.

In Table 2 the group of identified *pigor* is divided into two separate categories labelled *pigor* (maidservants) and *domestic servants*. The latter had more qualified titles reported in the alternative sources *(tjänstepiga, tjänsteflicka, tjänstekvinna, hushållerska)*, which suggest that they were probably employed as servants or housekeepers. Their professional title indicates that they served wealthier households. The category of *pigor* (maidservants) covers those reported as being only *pigor*. In their case we cannot be that sure of that they really were employed servants, even though that was probably the case. The fact that the majority of the servants in the parish records also show up in the domestic sector according to the alternative sources, further confirms this. However, Table 2 also suggests that servants sometimes were doing something else in reality. About 14 percent out of the 168 *pigor* (maidservants) were engaged in petty commerce or worked as seamstresses. Obviously, about 5 percent were regarded as being prostitutes, at least at the time of measurement.

Contemporary guardians of law and order deeply worried about the frequent domestic work many live-in-servants performed in households exclusively formed by male laborers engaged in the sawmill industries (ST 1879-09-04).[8] This mixing of unrelated men and women under the same roof was regarded as morally unhealthy.

The predominance of *pigor* or servants on the nineteenth-century female labor market is well known. Even though women were regarded as a suitable cheap labor force in the dynamic garment industries, they were not particularly welcome to work outdoors in dirty industries (Alter 1988; Berg 1993, 26–36; Hareven 1982, 189–218; Tilly and Scott 1978, 81–88). The "male" sawmill industry in Sundsvall is yet another example of that. In the sawmills, women's work was hardly held high. Due to the strike in 1879, an official investigation of the working conditions in the Sundsvall district was initiated in 1880. This investigation strongly recommended that the few women engaged in the sawmill industry immediately should be liberated from their dirty duties.[9] It looks as if the bad times were just perfect to remind everyone of the ideology of separate spheres in order to save the jobs for the "breadwinner-men" and let women stick to their decent and domestic field of the labor market (Vikström 2003a, 254–256). They and their usually low salaries should not compete with men's occupational need. Consequently, during the course of the nineteenth century this occupation underwent a "feminization", which soon made the men leave the servant employment (Davidoff 1999, 29; Dubert 1999, 218–221;

8 In 1879, the ethnographer, liberal politician and publisher Ernst Beckman (1850–1924) visited the Sundsvall area to observe people earning their living from the sawmill industry. A lot of things bothered him such as the abuse of alcohol and the poor state of people's health and housing. Some of his articles were published in the local newspapers 1879. For a further information, see Vikström 2003, 256–259. A summary of Beckman's articles is published, see Björk and Schnell 1979.

9 See *Betänkande angående åtgärder till förbättrande af de vid sågverken i trakten af Sundsvall anstälde arbetarnas ställning*, Sundsvall 1880, 33ff., 51ff.

McBride 1978, 241). For men there was other, better paid, work to do. Women had definitely less choices.

That the servant profession was connected to long days of hard work is indicated by the newspapers. In October 1879, they tell us about a sympathizing farmer in the county of Sundsvall, *Västernorrlands län*. He had invented a scrubbing-machine to facilitate the work for his urban serving "sisters" (ST 1879-10-23). Few women stayed however a lifetime in this profession. Basically, it was a pre-marital experience where young women achieved some domestic skill, built on their dowry, and maybe learned a few favorable things from the middle class they sometimes served. Then, it was time to marry. Hence, doing domestic service was a life-cycle phenomenon, which Hajnal and later Laslett have emphasized with a certain respect to Western Europe (Hajnal 1965; Laslett 1977).

According to some scholars, servants' domestic skills, their dowry, and the fact that they because of their work frequently interacted with middle or upper class people, made them popular on the local urban labor and partner market (Broom and Smith 1963, 321–34; McBride 1976, 82–98). Consequently, the term "bridging occupation" is sometimes applied to conceptualize the upward potential servants were able to achieve by marrying.[10] It is possible that some of the businesswomen in Table 2 had gained some experience in doing trade from having served households related to the business sector, since some of them had previously been employed as domestic servants according to the parish registers.

In short, Table 2 reveals a confusion regarding the actual employment of women. According to the alternative sources their occupation ought to be defined differently in the parish registers, at least during one single year in late nineteenth century Sundsvall. However, women's work was often casual and irregular. Probably, many women only engaged in one specific occupation as long as they needed or were able to hold this position. *Tjänstehjonsstadgan*, the Hired or Household Servants Act, made especially servants mobile on the urban labor market around Michaelmas in the fall (Lundh 1996, 14; Vikström 2003a, 23). Occasionally, or perhaps permanently, they earned some money from trading, sewing or even prostitution. The alternative sources identify the multi-occupational and part-time work of urban women more accurately than parish records. The

10 Already in 1963, the sociologists Broom and Smith described the domestic service as a "bridging occupation", since they considered that servants were especially able to achieve upward social mobility.

alternative sources also suggest that women often participated in the informal labor market that was often neglected in official statistics.

The Women's Socio-Economic Background and Access to Family Networks

The socio-economic background might offer keys to the occupations that individuals chose. Whenever possible, the social status of the women is linked to their father's occupation and this information is found in the parish registers. This method is sometimes applied among scholars dealing with women's status and social mobility (e.g. Alter 1988, 98–102; Janssens 1998, 261ff.; Moch 1983, 171–78; Sewell 1985, 272–312; Wilcox 1981, 198–200). Unfortunately, the father is only identified for about every third woman. The occupation reported when he was at the mid or top of his career, i.e. at the age of 40–50, has been given priority.

Table 3 shows that the higher the occupational status of the women, the higher the status of the fathers. About every fourth woman in the first social strata had a father belonging to the first or second social groups. This suggests these women had probably learned something about trade. It is also possible that their fathers, because of their knowledge, money and network of customers and commercial contacts, were able to facilitate their daughters' business aspirations. These relatively wealthy fathers might also explain why a few teachers show up among the civil officials included in the first social group. Their fathers could afford such education. These women were likely prepared to do work and service not exclusively linked to domestic service.

Table 3 also identifies an access to family networks. Having a father around meant there usually was a mother and possibly siblings. Social ties tend to positively affect individuals involved in them (e.g. Aronson, Fagerlund and Samuelsson 1999; Hareven 1982, 85–119; Brändström and Ericsson 1995, 264–271). These potential relationships could have assisted the women but they could not guarantee their urban path. Almost every second prostitute had a father nearby and he was usually a labor. As is below discussed, a majority of the two types of maidservants were in-migrants and thus there is less information available about their fathers. Although a few were daughters of men classified as small-scale entrepreneurs, civil officials of farmers, they mainly originated from the working class. They usually had little alternative but to enter the broad sector of domestic service because they probably lacked networks and material resources to improve their occupational situation.

Table 3. Occupational status among the women and their fathers' status at the age of 40–50. In case of the fathers, the information is based on parish records. Alternative sources are used in case of the women

Alternative sources Social group of the women	*Parish records* Social group of their fathers					Total	
	1. Large-scale entrepreneurs & higher civil officials	2. Small-scale entrepreneurs & lower civil officials; farmers	3. Skilled laborers	4. Un-skilled laborers; crofters	No father reported	%	N
1. Business entrepreneurs & civil officials	3.4	20.3	6.8	1.7	67.8	100	59
2. Title-women	–	9.1	18.2	27.3	45.5	100	22
3. Skilled & unskilled laborers	4.5	18.2	4.5	4.5	68.2	100	22
4. Domestic servants	–	2.1	8.5	17.0	72.3	100	47
5. *Pigor* (maidservants)	–	5.8	5.8	18.3	70.0	100	120
6. Prostitutes	5.3	–	–	42.1	52.6	100	19
Total %	1.4	9.0	6.9	12.5	66.8	100	289
(N)	(4)	(26)	(20)	(36)	(193)		

Source: See Table 1
Explanations: See Table 1.

The results of Table 3 relates to Pierre Bourdieu's concept of the socio-cultural capital and its impact on human behaviour (Bourdieu 1994, 247–310; Svanberg 1999, 148–156; Vikström 2003a, 265–266). Broadly conceived, people's failure or success in an occupation depends on their socio-economic and cultural background. Although economic growth offered expanded opportunities for women's inclusion on the labor market, especially servants could not break into entirely new fields because of gendered constraints and their socio-economic background that was determined by their fathers' status. Table 3 offers only a few examples of working-class daughters who did not follow the path predicted by Bourdieu. Albertina Edstedt was one such case. In 1868 she was born in the neighbouring parish of Skön where her father was a crofter. According to both the business statistics of 1893 and the parish registers of 1891, the year of her in-migration, she had used her culinary skills to become the owner of a café in Sundsvall.

Probably, women's various domestic skill made them well able to leave traditional household service to take up employment in the growing sector of business, or even start minor catering and fashion trade. In late nineteenth-century society, the commercial activities had also become somewhat easier to perform for women such as Albertina Edstedt.

The Women's Geographical Background and Age

A few words about the women's geographical background and age will close this study, as knowing this sheds further light onto their occupations in Sundsvall. According to Table 4, a majority of the titled women were from urban centers and especially Sundsvall, their home town. A pronounced urban origin is also found among women in the first social group. This background must have stimulated their goals to enter business as urban labor markets in general were more open and diverse. These women had likely developed their business skills in other towns.

Those labelled domestic servants came to a larger degree than *pigor* from urban areas. This suggests that they might have had a domestic career in other towns and this would explain why they had a more specified position. The age at which they performed their work also suggests their level of experience. The domestic servants were slightly older than were the *pigor* as their mean age was 27.9 but for *pigor* the corresponding figure was 24.4.

The women in business and civil service were considerably older, i.e. 34.8. They were probably considered too old to be servants and had also passed the stage in life when marriages usually occurred. No wonder these women were doing business. Perhaps these demographic circumstances, more than a desire for economic independence, explain why they engaged in their trades. It is difficult to say whether they chose to remain single to better control their property or if the failure to find a supporting husband drove them into various business. However, the large marriage market for women in Sundsvall ought to have also favored these women.

Table 4. The women's geographical origin according to different social groups. The occupational status is based on the alternative sources, the place of birth on the parish registers

Alternative sources Social group of the women	*Parish records* Urban or local origin according to place of birth				Total
	Sundsvall	Other towns	The Sundsvall district	Other non-urban areas	N
1. Business entrepreneurs & civil officials	13.6	37.2	5.1	44.1	59
2. Title-women	27.3	27.2	13.6	31.9	22
3. Skilled & unskilled laborers	13.6	9.1	22.7	54.6	22
4. Domestic servants	8.5	19.1	17.0	55.4	47
5. *Pigor* (maidservants)	7.5	9.2	20.8	62.5	120
6. Prostitutes	5.3	10.5	31.6	52.7	19
Total % (N)	10.7	18.0	17.3	54.0	289

Source: See previous table.

In comparison to the other social categories in Table 4, the large group of *pigor* lacked urban background. Scholars have found that female migrants gradually replaced the urban native women working as maids. They argue that women already established in towns were able to use their better knowledge of the local labor market and larger access to various networks to find better employment (Dubert 1999, 221ff.; Fauve-Chamoux 1998, 119ff.; Higgs 1983, 208; McBride 1976, 34–48; Sewell 1985, 208–210). Consequently, the occupation of servants became "ruralized", i.e. dominated by women of rural origin. Table 4 indicates that this pattern was also evident in Sundsvall.

Increasingly, scholars now turn their focus to higher structural levels by discussing the mediating role of domestic servants and their work in times of turbulent transitions such as those that characterized the nineteenth century. Servants and their domestic skills became part of a larger process, i.e. the economic transformation from agricultural to urban-industrial production. The nineteenth century witnessed an increase in numbers of domestic servants who showed a preference for going to towns. It is now believed that their "inproductive" domestic work facilitated the transition towards today's modern society (Berg 1993, 23ff.) By attracting so many rural women, this was a "bridging occupation" (Broom and Smith 1963, 321–334) that made it easier for them to cope with this transitional stage (e.g. McBride 1974, 63ff.; Gyáni 1998, 31–34). Industry would never have been able to employ the growing proletariat that populated the rural parts of Europe. As people moved from the countryside to towns or industrial centers, and from one occupation to another, the increasing demand for domestic servants' universal skills particularly guided women through this socio-economic phase.

If not through social networks the process of urban adjustment of young females in Sundsvall probably occurred while they were employed as servants. These women indirectly both contributed to and lived off the economic development in the town and surrounding area although the labor market it generated had mainly a male profile. There was reciprocal and complementary need for domestic service. On the one hand, and for means of subsistence, women searched for work where it was easily found. On the other hand, Sundsvall and its many male inhabitants could not have managed without the kind of services *pigor* performed. These women contributed to the process of industrialization and urbanization, and helped keep the industrial and commercial wheels turning.

Concluding Remarks

For some or single years in the late nineteenth century, Sundsvall formed the heart and home for the 289 women in this study. Most of them surely worked, but exactly what they did to earn their living is an issue. To know how individuals in the past managed to pay for their daily bread is crucial for historians searching for a deeper understanding of women's historical paths since – exclusive from time, place and gender – occupation forms a crucial part of one's life and behaviour. This study shows however that one of the most utilized historical sources, the parish registers, reports incomplete information on women's occupation including the domestic work of servants. Alternative sources such as patient records, business statistics and not least local newspapers, are better than quantitative data at covering the often multi-occupational and part-time work of urban women.

Obviously, domestic servants could not always be regarded as servants. Some were in fact engaged in petty commerce, even though this particularly held true for titled women and spinsters reported as having no occupation at all according to the parish registers. Sometimes, these latter women even performed domestic duties. Sundsvall's newspapers suggest that women frequently offered their various skills related to typical female fields and not entirely to the serving sector but also the fashion and catering trade. Explanatory factors for their favourable labor market are found in the male profile of the sawmill town that in addition lacked typical female industries. It was crowded with men that all needed a woman's service.

The fact that two sources are in conflict concerning women's occupations may only add to the confusion about how these women found their means of subsistence, but there is reason to ask why the parish registers report incomplete data about women's work although they acknowledge that they were mainly located to the domestic field. Even though reforms finally improved women's legal, economic and social positions, the late nineteenth century still could be considered a man's world divided by the ideology of separate spheres. Although the household-based production lost ground in favour of industrial goods and growing markets even in nineteenth-century Sweden, women were not exactly welcome in the widened labor market and public sphere. This place was primarily reserved for men supporting their wives and children. A woman was usually little or nothing on her own, but as daughter, wife or employed by a master she became noticeable by being related to a man.

It was also a man, the minister, who put pen to paper and by doing so he defined a woman and her work in the parish registers. He had to follow the instructions given by the state and consider the patriarchal message of the Bible. The same likely held for many collectors of the business statistics and the doctors or hospital administrators who registered the patient records. They were men, just as the ministers, even though they did not have to regard religious issues or had to cover as much information as the clergy. But maybe the minister did not ask the woman herself about her work, but asked her father, master or husband, or the head of the household to which she belonged. If so, she was viewed through the eye of a male beholder.

Hypothetically, the stereotyped classification of women's work, all the non-working wives and the over-registration of *pigor* (maidservants) found in most quantitative data, probably represents what women should be doing, rather than what they really were doing to earn their living or to facilitate the survival of their family. The ideal image of the male breadwinner influenced the official under-registration of women's occupations. Those who either asked for, or made these records, were often committed to dominant thoughts of their historical time and setting. Thus sources reflect the ideologies and gender regimes of their time.

This might explain why a conflict appears when comparing sources of different natures as has been shown here. As domestic servants, though, young women were never in conflict with the ideal of being a true woman. Therefore, they tend to be more frequently employed as servants in quantitative data, than in past society.

References

Unpublished Sources

The Demographic Data Base (DDB).
Computerized parish registers 1800–1893.
Computerized patient records from the hospital in Sundsvall 1844–1889.
Riksarkivet, Kommerskollegii kammarkontors arkiv.
National Board of Trade's Business Statistics, the town of Sundsvall 1860, 1863, 1865, 1868, 1870, 1873, 1875, 1878, 1880, 1883, 1885, 1888, 1890, 1893.

Published Sources

Local newspapers 1879.
Sundsvalls-Posten (SP) 1879-01-01–1879-03-22.

Sundsvalls Tidning (ST) 1879-03-22–1879-12-30.
Betänkande angående åtgärder till förbättrande af de vid sågverken i trakten af Sundsvall anstälde arbetarnas ställnin, Sundsvall, 1880.
Åslund, Daniel. 1878. *Beskrivning öfver Westernorrlands län.* Härnösand.

Secondary Sources

ALTER, George, 1988, *Family and the Female Life Course. The Women of Verviers, Belgium, 1849–1880*, Madison, The University of Wisconsin Press.

ANDERSON, Michael, 1984, "The Social Position of Spinsters in Mid-Victorian Britain", *Journal of Family History*, 9, 4, pp. 377–393.

ARONSSON, Peter, FAGERLUND, Solveig and SAMUELSON, Jan (eds), 1999, *Nätverk i historisk forskning – metafor, metod eller teori,* Växjö, Växjö Universitet.

BERG, Maxine, 1993, "What Difference did Women's Work Make to the Industrial Revolution?", *History Workshop Journal,* Spring, pp. 22–44.

BINFORD, Henry, 1975, "Never Trust the Census Maker, even when he's dead", *Urban History Yearbook*, pp. 22–28.

BJÖRKLUND, Jörgen, 1997, "Tillväxt och differentiering. Näringslivet 1870–1940", in Lars-Göran TEDEBRAND (ed.), *Sundsvalls Historia*, Del 2, Sundsvall, Stadshistoriska Kommittén, pp. 7–65.

BOURDIEU, Pierre, 1994, *Kultursociologiska texter: I urval av Donald Broady och Mikael Palm,* Stockholm, Stehag.

BRÄNDSTRÖM, Anders, 1988, "Myt eller verklighet? Patienter på Sundsvalls lasarett 1844–1900", in Anders BRÄNDSTRÖM, Tom ERICSSON, Agneta GUILLEMOT and L. LUNDMARK (eds), *Historia nu. 18 Umeåforskare om det förflutna,* Umeå, Umeå universitet, Historiska institutionen, Forskningsrapport no. 4, pp. 9–28.

–, 1995, "A Life After Dismissal? Patient's Life Histories at a Swedish County Hospital, 1845-1890", in Robert JÜTTE and John WOODWARD (eds), *Coping with Sickness. Historical Aspects of Health Care in a European Perspective,* Sheffield, European Association for the History of Medicine and Health Publications, pp. 93–119.

BRÄNDSTRÖM, Anders and TEDEBRAND, Lars-Göran, 1995, *Swedish Urban Demography during Industrialization,* Umeå, Umeå universitet, The Demographic Data Base, Report no. 10.

BROOM, L. and SMITH, J. H., 1963, "Bridging Occupations", *British Journal of Sociology,* XIV, pp. 321–34.

CARLSSON, Sten, 1977, *Fröknar, mamseller, jungfrur och fröknar. Ogifta kvinnor i det svenska ståndssamhället,* Uppsala, Uppsala universitet Studia Historica Upsaliensia, no. 90.

DAVIDOFF, Leonore, 1995, *Worlds Between. Historical Perspectives on Gender & Class,* Oxford, Polity Press.

–, 1999, *The Family Story. Blood, Contract and Intimacy, 1830–1960*, London, Addison Wesley Longman.

DAVIDOFF, Leonore and HALL, Catherine, 1987, *Family fortunes. Men and Women of the English Middle Class 1780–1850,* London, Butler & Tanner [1994].

DAVIDOFF, Leonore and WESTOVER, Belinda, 1986, *Our Work, Our Lives, Our Words. Women's History and Women's Work,* Basingstoke, Macmillan Education.

DUBERT, Isidro, 1999, "Domestic Service and Social Modernization in Urban Galicia, 1752–1920", *Continuity and Change*, 14, 2, pp. 207–226.

EDVINSSON, Sören, 1992, *Den osunda staden. Sociala skillnader i dödlighet i 1800-talets Sundsvall*, Umeå, Umeå universitet, Demografiska Databasen.

ERICSSON, Tom, 1997, "Välstånd och välmåga. Borgerskapet 1850–1900", in Lars-Göran TEDEBRAND (ed.), *Sundsvalls Historia.* Del 2, Sundsvall, Stadshistoriska Kommittén, pp. 137–154.

FAUVE-CHAMOUX, Antoinette, 1998, "Servants in Preindustrial Europe: Gender Differences", *Historical Social Research,* 1/2, pp. 112–129.

GYÁNI, Gábor, 1998, "Patterns of Women's Work in Hungary, 1900–1930", *European Review of History,* 1, pp. 25–38.

HAJNAL, John, 1965, "European Marriage Patterns in Perspective", in D. V. GLASS and D. E. C. EVERSLEY (eds), *Population in History*, London, Edvard Arnold, pp. 101–143.

HAREVEN, Tamara K., 1982, *Family Time and Industrial Time,* Cambridge, Cambridge University Press.

HIETALA, Marjatta and NILSSON, Lars (eds), 1999, *Women in Towns. The Social Position of Urban Women in a Historical Context,* Stockholm, Stads- och kommunhistoriska institutet.

HIGGS, Edward, 1983, "Domestic Service and Households in Victorian England", *Social History,* 2, pp. 201–210.

–, "Domestic Service and Household Production", in Angela V. JOHN (ed.), *Unequal Opportunities. Women's Employment in England 1800–1918*, Oxford, Basil Blackwell, pp. 125–150.

HILL, Bridget, 1993, "Women, Work and the Census: a Problem for Historians of Women", *History Workshop Journal,* Spring, pp. 69–94.

HUDSON, Pat and LEE, Robert W., 1990, *Women's Work and the Family Economy in Historical Perspective,* Manchester, Manchester University Press.

HUFTON, Olwen, 1984, "Women Without Men: Widows and Spinsters in Britain and France in the Eighteenth Century", *Journal of Family History*, 9, 4, pp. 355–376.

JANSSENS, Angélique, 1998, "Class, Work and Religion in the Female Life Course – The Case of a Dutch Textile Town: Enschede, 1880–1940", *Historical Social Research*, 1/2, pp. 254–274.

JOHN, Angela V., 1986, *Unequal Opportunities. Women's Employment in England 1800–1918,* Oxford, Basil Blackwell.

JORDE, Tine Susanne, 1995, *Stockholms Tjenstepiker under industrialiseringen*, Stockholm, Stads- och kommunhistoriska institutet.

KATZMAN, David M., 1978, *Seven Days A Week. Women and Domestic Service in Industrializing America,* New York, Oxford University Press.

KRONBORG, Bo and NILSSON, Thomas, 1975, *Stadsflyttare. Industrialisering, migration och social mobilitet med utgångspunkt från Halmstad, 1870–1910,* Uppsala, Uppsala universitet.

LASLETT, Peter, 1977, "Characteristics of the Western Family Considered over Time", in *Id., Family Life and Illicit Love in Earlier Generations,* Cambridge, Cambridge University Press, pp. 12–49.

LUNDBERG, Anna, *Care and Coercion. Medical Knowledge, Social Policy and Patients in Sweden 1785–1903,* Umeå, The Demographic Data Base.

LUNDH, Christer, 1996, "Youth Migration in a Life-Cycle Perspective", *Lund Papers in Economic History*, 52, pp. 1–27.

MATOVIC, Margareta R., 1984, *Stockholmsäktenskap. Familjebildning och partnerval i Stockholm 1850–1890,* Stockholm, Liber Förlag.

MCBRIDE, Theresa M., 1974, "Social Mobility For the Lower Classes: Domestic Servants in France", *Journal of Social History*, 1, pp. 63–78.

–, 1976, *The Domestic Revolution: The Modernization of Household Service in England and France, 1820–1920,* London, Croom Helm.

MOCH, Leslie Page, 1983, *Paths to the City. Regional Migration in Nineteenth-Century France*, London, Sage Publications.

NILSSON, Lars, 1989, *Den urbana transitionen: tätorterna i svensk samhällsomvandling 1800–1980,* Stockholm, Stadshistoriska institutet.

PINCHBECK, Ivy, 1930, *Women Workers and the Industrial Revolution 1750–1850,* London, Augustus M. Kelley [1969].

SAMUELSSON, Kurt, 1985, *Industrisamhällets framväxt 1850–1914,* Stockholm, Industriförbundet.

SEWELL, William H., 1985, *Structure and Mobility. The Men and Women of Marseille, 1820–1870,* Cambridge, Cambridge University Press.

SVANBERG, Mikael, 1999, *Företagsamhet föder framgång. Yrkeskarriärer och sociala nätverk bland företagarna i Sundsvall,* Umeå, Umeå universitet, Institutionen för historiska studier, Forskningsrapport no. 13.

TEDEBRAND, Lars-Göran, 1997, "Befolkningsutveckling och social struktur i Sundsvall efter 1860", in Lars-Göran TEDEBRAND (ed.), *Sundsvalls Historia,* Del 2, Sundsvall, Stadshistoriska Kommittén, pp. 101–136.

THOMAS, Dorothy Swaine, 1941, *Social and Economic Aspects of Swedish Population Movements 1750–1933,* New York, Macmillan.

TILLY, Louise and SCOTT, Joan W., 1978, *Women, Work and Family,* New York, Holt.

VICINUS, Martha, 1985, *Independent Women. Work and Community for Single Women 1850–1920,* London, Virago.

VIKSTRÖM, Marie-Christine (Lotta), 2003a, *Gendered Routes and Courses: The Socio-Spatial Mobility of Migrants in Nineteenth-Century Sundsvall, Sweden*, Umeå, Umeå University.

–, 2003b, "Different Sources, Different Answers: Aspects on Women's Work in Sundsvall, Sweden, 1860–1893", *Interchange,* 3/4, pp. 241–259.

WILCOX, Penelope, 1981, "Marriage, Mobility and Domestic Service", *Annales de Démographie Historique*, pp. 195–205.

Agricultural Work, Social Structure and Labour Markets of the Rural Domestic Service in Galicia in the Mid-Eighteenth Century

Isidro DUBERT

The Uneven Geographical Concentration of Domestic Service

Previous studies on the rural domestic service in the *Ancien Régime* have tended to treat its different facets and implications as unrelated topics.[1] As a result, some authors have taken pains to study its role within the framework of the family economies of that sector of the peasantry that were able to make use of its services. Others, taking a more demographic point of view, have considered its role as another of the components of the household or have established its importance therein according to the social position that the head of the family occupied in the rural society under study. Nevertheless, when the afore-mentioned authors have attempted to explain the uneven concentration of the rural domestic service in the regional areas under study, they have ended up, as a rule, relating this to the different types of agricultural economy that existed within each one of these areas. That is to say, they have related this difference in concentration to the existence in each area of different frameworks of agricultural work, from which, moreover, they have derived the internal and external characteristics that constituted the labour markets of the servants.

On this matter, and to provide an example, A. Kussmaul and P. R. H. Hinde each showed in their day how in England, well after 1750, certain types of rural domestic service, such as the *servants in husbandry*, managed to maintain a notable presence in the North and West of the country.

1 Research for this paper has been financed by Xunta de Galicia, Secretaria Xeral de Investigación e Desenvolvemento, *Servicio doméstico e mercados de traballo na Galicia de fin do Antigo Réxime, séculos XVIII–XIX*, PGIDIT02PXIA21001PR.

That is, in a world characterized by the predominance of an archaic agricultural economy, based on small farms that, in order to function properly, required a more or less stable and permanent workforce that was made up basically of servants, to whom access was gained thanks to the creation of renewable annual contracts. On the other hand, in the South and East of England their number was hardly significant, due largely to the mechanization of an agriculture that was carried out on large cereal farms whose productive necessities generated seasonal work that was covered by an abundance of day labourers.[2]

This rationale, that of the existence of different frameworks of agricultural work in the same regional area, has also been used by other researchers to resolve the same problem in socio-productive contexts that bear little similarity to that of the English. Fernando Mikelarena, for example, made use of it in his research on the ancient Kingdom of Navarre (Northeast of Spain) at the end of the eighteenth century, while trying to uncover the reason for the uneven geographical distribution of rural domestic service in that area. Broadly speaking, he aimed to offer a coherent interpretation of both the net decrease in number and the feminization that the rural Navarran domestic service underwent as we move from North to South, traveling from the mountain valleys of the western Pyrenees to the river plains close to the course of the river Ebro. In other words, in the transition from areas in which an agriculture characterized by its lack of technical development was carried out at the hands of small-scale peasants (who, in order to survive, were obliged to accumulate a vast amount of human work on small-sized farms and to take care of a large number of livestock, all of which was possible for one sector of the peasantry thanks to the systematic employment of servants), to those southern localities where unirrigated cereal agriculture was carried out on large farms. This was a fallow agriculture, a system that was effective thanks to a workforce made up of day labourers. Not in vain did 42 percent of the families of this area in 1787 subsist partly thanks to their seasonal work on the lands of a few important landowners.[3]

2 Ann Kussmaul, *Servants in husbandry in Early Modern England*, Cambridge, Cambridge University Press, 1981, p. 24f.; P. R. Andrew Hinde, "L'influenza del servizio rurale doméstico sulla demografía inglese, 1850–1914", *Quaderni Storici*, 68, 2, 1988, pp. 544ff.

3 Fernando Mikelarena, *Demografía y Familia en la Navarra tradicional*, Pamplona, Gobierno de Navarra, 1995, pp. 41 and 296ff.

Likewise, and still within the Iberian Peninsula, only this time further to the west, in Galicia, a region of some 30,000 km^2, it has recently been noted how this same rationale contributes to clarifying the uneven distribution and spatial concentration of its rural domestic service in the course of the second half of the eighteenth century.[4] In fact, the extensive participation of domestics in the family economies of inland Galician households was, in principle, closely related to the practice of an agriculture based on the cultivation of rye interspersed with fallow periods on small-sized farms,[5] of some 2.7 H^a on average; the exploitation of scrubland (where 25 percent of the total harvest came from) and the care of a large number of livestock. As in the North of Navarre, this type of agriculture, along with the effects derived from the fact that the stem family was the predominant socio-familiar norm, entailing, for example, the existence of an inegalitarian hereditary system, favoured the emergence and employment of servants as an agricultural workforce. This is revealed, for example, by the fact that 22.5 percent of the households of the area made use of their services (Map 1). In comparison, farm sizes in the rest of Galicia oscillated at around 1–1.5 H^a. From the point of view of production, this reduced size was compensated for by the implementation of a subsistence poly-culture, made possible thanks to a system of ternary rotations that guaranteed at least three harvests in two years, and which also benefited from the integration of cattle in the farms.[6]

4 Isidro Dubert, "The Domestic Service of Rural Galicia, 1752-1787: Labour Markets, Gender and Social Structure", paper handed to the meeting *Domestic Service, as a Factor of Social Renewal in Europe*, Essex, 7–11 May 2003.

5 With respect to the use of the term farm, it must be borne in mind that the farming landscape in Galicia during the *Ancien Régime* bore no similarity to that of England, with its country houses with their granary, stable and other outbuildings, surrounded by arable land and grazing for the livestock, and separated from each other by fenced fields. In contrast, the most common situation in Galicia was for the peasants to live in hamlets along side the members of the other social groups and to work their lands, which were made up of a large number of small plots dispersed throughout the parish.

6 Hortensio Sobrado, *Las Tierras de Lugo en la Edad Moderna. Economía campesina, Familia y Herencia, 1500–1860*, A Coruña, Fundación Pedro Barrié de la Maza, 2001, pp. 204ff.; Pergeto Saavedra, *Economía, Política y Sociedad en Galicia: La Provincia de Mondoñedo, 1480–1830,* Madrid, Xunta de Galicia, Consellería de Presidencia, 1985, pp. 145ff.; José Manuel Perez Garciá, *Un modelo de sociedad rural de Antiguo Régimen en la Galicia costera: La Península del Salnés*, Santiago de Compostela, Universidad de Santiago de Compostela, 1979, pp. 154ff.

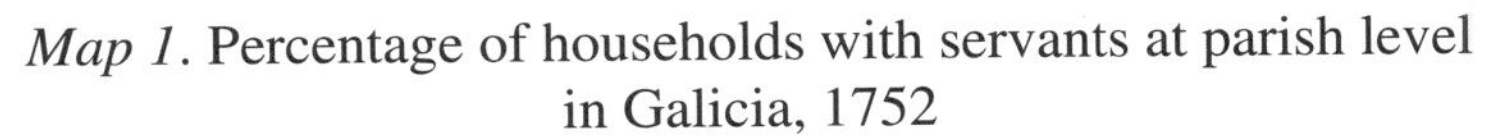

Map 1. Percentage of households with servants at parish level in Galicia, 1752

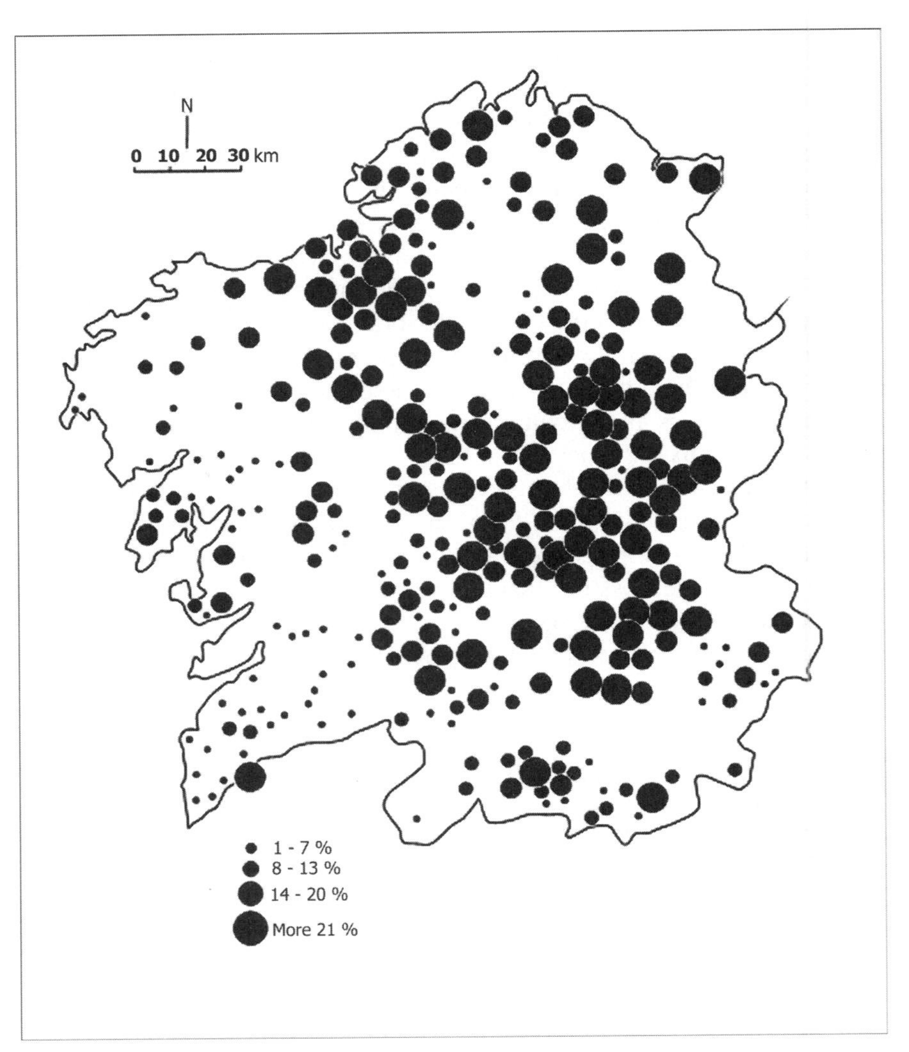

In this particular context, domestics were scarce and the great majority of them were women, as reflected by their presence in barely 10 percent of households and the fact that 65 percent of them were maids.

As can be appreciated, and apart from the different socio-productive and labour structures associated with the different agricultural frameworks that existed in Europe at the end of the *Ancien Régime*, it would seem evident that the spatial variations relative to the increase or decrease in concentration of the English, Navarran or Galician rural domestic service, can be explained in the final instance thanks to the agricultural work frameworks existing within their respective regional areas. However, we should not lose sight of the fact that this conclusion has been reached, in some cases, after having studied what happened to the peasant economies that used servant help, and in other cases, by associating the afore-mentioned spatial variations with the use that those economies might have made of the afore-mentioned servants. Either way, both cases presuppose that domestic staff were abundant in certain geographical areas because their particular economic, social or family circumstances favoured their occurrence, but above all, and what is of prime importance, because these circumstances permitted the peasants to have domestics at their disposal[7]. With this in mind, the question is finding out whether they actually did, or rather, to what extent.

This last consideration may have unsettled the reader who followed me up until here, although it should be fully understandable if one remembers that, in the world of the *Ancien Régime,* domestic service, rural or otherwise, was characterized by its uneven distribution from a social point of view. In other words, and simplifying almost to the point of caricature, domestic service was a luxury, a form of ostentation, a display of wealth and power on the part of the dominant classes. If this was the case, it is obvious that the overworked argument of spatial variations that we have been referring to cannot fully explain what happened to the afore mentioned domestic service without also taking into account the social framework it was related to.[8] Hence, it would appear that the picture we gave

7 A. Kussmaul, *Servants in husbandry*, p. 24; Thomas Martin Devine, "Scottish Farm Service in the Agricultural Revolution", in Thomas Martin Devine (ed.), *Farm Servants and Labour in Lowland Scotland, 1770–1914,* Edinburgh, John Donald Publishers LTD, 1984, pp. 9ff.; P. R. A. Hinde, "L'influenza del servizio rural", p. 544; Michael Mitterauer, "Peasant and non-peasant family forms in relation to the physical environment and the local economy", *Journal of Family History*, 17, 2, 1992, pp. 139–159; F. Mikelarena, *Demografía y Familia en la Navarra tradicional*, pp. 296ff.; I. Dubert, "Labour markets".

8 Peter Laslett, "Servi e servizio nella struttura sociale europea", *Quaderni Storici*, 68, 2, 1988, pp. 345–354.

until now of the existence, working and characteristics of the labour markets of the rural domestic service is based on what happened to a determined segment of the peasantry, consequently giving us an incomplete and biased impression of the problem in question.

On the other hand, by adopting a perspective based on the social framework, it becomes clear, at least for the case of Galicia, that the different formulas of agricultural work that existed in its heartland form only a part of the explanation that could be offered to account for the uneven intensity of servants' concentration in this region. Meanwhile, the results obtained by this means enable us to reveal a labour market of which today nothing is known. In order to proceed along these lines, use has been made of the information obtained from a systematic random sample on 8 percent, carried out on the more than 3,600 rural communities that existed in Galicia in 1752.[9] This has involved working with data concerning more than 22,000 households that belonged to at least 311 rural parishes.

Composition of the Social Framework, Unequal Spatial Distribution of the Rural Domestic Service and Configuration of their Labour Markets

The data contained in Table 1 show us how, in rural Galicia, 73.6 percent of the households were headed by peasants; it is therefore logical that in them were to be found at least two out of every three domestic staff member registered in 1752. What is more striking is that, in the households run by clergymen or noblemen *(hidalgos)* – 2.1 percent and 2.3 percent of the total respectively –, 13.2 percent and 9.9 percent of all Galician servants were employed. These figures indicate in themselves the narrow and intense relationship that the members of the elite established with the components of the domestic service in the rural world. A relationship that, without a doubt, is even more clearly demonstrated if the panorama is

9 Isidro Dubert, *Historia de la Familia en Galicia durante la Época Moderna, 1550–1830. Estructura, modelos hereditarios y conflictividad*, A Coruña, Editorial do Castro, 1992, pp. 15ff.

contemplated in relative terms, that is to say, by taking account of the presence of servants in the households of each socio-professional category under consideration. By doing so, we can focus on studying the domestics in the setting of their most immediate work sphere, which, at the same time will allow us to swiftly obtain a first impression of how their labour markets were externally structured.

Following this approach, we find that 75.2 percent of the households that were run by a clergyman (2.1 percent of the total) had servants and that, in 68.1 percent of cases there were more than two, being female in 58.7 percent of cases. Despite this, these were still small households, made up of scarcely four people (3.8 people/household), of whom at least two had been contracted to attend to the chores of the parish house or to the rural patrimony of the parish run by the clergyman in question. In order of importance, the clergy was followed by the nobility *(hidalguía)*, whose members headed 2.3 percent of the registered families, with 50.9 percent of them employing domestics and 65.1 percent of these having two or more. Nevertheless, these do not appear to have been directly responsible for the dimensions reached by the households of these lower levels of Spanish nobility (6.6 people/household). This is revealed by the fact that they made up only 22.6 percent of the household inhabitants or that, without including them, these households continued to be, on average, 20 percent larger than those of the remaining social categories under consideration. It was, moreover, a domestic service that was composed equally of both sexes and whose chores were more specialized than those of the clergy, as demonstrated by the presence of administrators, butlers, pageboys, coachmen, waiters, kitchen maids, etc.

Moving away from the elite, we find individuals linked to administration and commerce, 2.1 percent of the total, and those making up "other professions", 1.2 percent of households. When taken together, only 12–17 percent of them had domestic staff, who were women in two out of three cases. Even so, in the mid eighteenth century, both sectors convey a picture that is very different from that shown by the peasantry as a whole, from whose 73.6 percent of households the servants were absent in 89.4 percent of cases.

Table 1. Distribution of servants within the social framework of rural Galicia, 1752

	A.	B.	C.	D.	E.	F.
Nobility *(Hidalguía)*	2.3	50.9	9.9	22.6	65.1	50.1
Clergymen	2.1	75.2	13.2	48.0	68.1	58.7
Peasantry	73.6	10.6	65.8	2.7	20.7	59.6
Craftsmen &Wage earner	5.0	8.2	3.4	3.1	16.1	61.6
Administration & Commerce	2.1	16.7	2.9	7.6	41.2	59.6
Other professions	1.2	11.9	1.2	5.6	34.4	58.0
Women without profession	13.8	3.1	3.6	0.7	19.4	60.3
Total	100	11.8	100	4.3	31.9	57.3

A. Social Framework; B. Percentage of households with servants; C. Distribution of servants within households of each socio-professional category considered; D. Percentage of servants with respect to the total number of household inhabitants; E. Percentage of households with two or more servants; F. Percentage of maids among servants.
Source: Author's own calculations from the provincial historical archives (El Catastro de Ensenada, 1752).
Note: Number of cases: 22,926 households; 4,476 domestic servants (male and female).

Their limited capacity for contracting this work force, despite taking in two thirds of them in absolute numbers, contrasts with the fact that 23 percent of Galician servants were concentrated in those 3 percent of households headed by members of the clergy and nobility *(hidalguía)*. This indicates that the domestic service in rural Galicia was distributed across society following rules based on the different possibilities that derived from the unequal distribution and use of property, and the richness of the land. Their presence, therefore, tended to be more pronounced in those social sectors which, although a minority, had greater scope and socio-economic potential in the sphere of class-society. In contrast, the presence of servants tended to be weaker in those groups which, despite being the social majority, lacked this scope and potential. The latter constituted a group that, within the set of feudal-type socio-productive relations, was both subordinate to and dependent on the elites. With this in mind, it is not surprising that the 10.6 percent of peasant families with servants corresponded, broadly speaking, with the 11 percent of peasants who controlled 37.4 percent of the cultivated land in the coastal areas of western Galicia, or with the 13–15 percent who owned and had exclusive use of up to 46.5 percent of the land in inland Galicia. In both cases, these were people with farms that were larger than the average 4 H[a], whose productive capacity not only covered the basic necessities of the household, but also allowed attribution of part of the harvest and of the livestock to the numerous fairs and weekly markets that were celebrated in their respective localities.[10] They were, thus, the elite of the peasantry, despite the fact that the 10.6 percent of families mentioned were attended in 79.3 percent of cases by a single servant, who in 60 percent of these cases was a woman.

This feminine predominance among the domestic staff of the peasantry not only highlights the reproductive nature that their work assumed in the sphere of their respective family economies, but also contributes to qualifying the idea that hiring this peculiar workforce met the direct labour necessities of the farms, similar to what would happen in other European contexts.[11] In order to understand this, we should remember the character of Galician agriculture, whose immediate objective was not market production. There we deal with a subsistence agriculture immersed in a set of feudal-type socio-productive relations, in which the collection and use of income, and not the direct working of the land, were what established social differences. So, running appropriately this type of agriculture did not imply using a permanent work force, at least in principle: the main part of the agricultural workload was taken on by the household members. Only when this load was excessive did they turn to the combination of neighbours, friends and relatives, via a mutual help system whose mission was not so much to encourage the birth of a class of day labourers, but rather to strengthen and guarantee social cohesion in the peasant communities.[12] Under these conditions, the presence of servants in the households

10 P. Saavedra, *Economía, Política y Sociedad en Galicia*, pp. 454ff.

11 A. Kussmaul, *Servants in husbandry*, pp. 49ff.; Alistair Orr, "Farm Servants and Farm Labour in the Forth Valley and South-East Lowland", in T. M. Devine (ed.), *Farm Servants and Labour*, pp. 30ff.; W. Robert Lee, "Women's Work and the Family: some Demographic Implication of Gender-Specific Rural Work Patterns in the XIXth Century Germany", in Pat Hudson et W. Robert Lee (eds), *Women's Work and the Family Economy in historical perspective*, Manchester, Manchester University Press, 1990, pp. 54ff.; Deborah Simonton, *A History of European Women's Work, 1700 to the Present*, London-New York, Routledge, 1998, pp. 32ff.

12 Raúl Iturra, *Antropología económica de la Galicia rural*, Santiago de Compostela, Xunta de Galicia, Consellería de Presidencia e Administración Pública, 1988, pp. 75ff.; José María Cardesin, *Tierra, trabajo y reproducción social en una aldea gallega, siglos XVIII–XIX: muerte de unos, vida de otros*, Madrid, Ministerio de Alimentación, Pesca y Alimentación, Secretaría General Técnica, 1992, pp. 135ff.

enabled, in two out of three cases, the family workforce rather to concentrate on increasing the farm's productive profitability, with the maids taking on the reproductive tasks relative to the domestic economy. The final rung of this social scale was made up of craftsmen or those who depended on a salary in order to survive, 5 percent of the total number of households, of which only 8.2 percent had domestic staff (Table 1).

Summing up, from this panorama of servants' presence within the households in 1752, we can appreciate their particular tendency to group around the sectors of the social elite in the different socio-professional categories considered. In addition, it brings to light the existence, in the world of rural Galicia, of a labour market that was segmented from a social point of view, and that apparently tended to become more complex and structured as it moved from the base to the apex of the social pyramid. Nevertheless, this panorama evidently omits the uneven importance of this market in the region.

In this sense, it takes for granted that the labour opportunities offered by the different social groups under consideration were the same in the whole of Galicia. However, this was not the case, as for example can be inferred from the data contained in Map 1. For this reason, an individualized analysis of the geographical behaviour expressed by some of the main socio-professional categories that tended more frequently to use domestic staff in 1752 would help us to understand the particular spatial disposition adopted by a significant part of this labour market. There is no doubt that this procedure will help us to break this impression of uniformity, as well as to determine what other factors influenced the regional distribution of domestic staff, and to give us a broader view than the explanatory potential implicit in the existence of different frameworks of agricultural work. In order to progress in this direction, and for obvious reasons, we focused on nobility *(hidalguía)* and secular clergy. Firstly, because in relative terms they were the main employers of domestic service and, secondly, because they both lived off the peasant income and did not directly work the land.

If 9.9 percent of all the Galician domestic staff worked in 2.3 percent of the households belonging to the nobility, their tendency to concentrate in inland Galicia will become clear when it is noted that 47 percent of noble families registered in 1752 lived in rural communities situated within this specific area. The mapping of the percentages of the nobility's households with respect to the total number of those in each parish, echoes their tendency to have the greatest values in those places where the presence of the domestic service was more intense (Map 2). In the same way, while 13.2 percent of all the domestic staff registered in rural Galicia were employed in 2.3 percent of the households headed by a clergyman, the corresponding mapping of the percentage of these households related to the total of those in each parish, shows again that the percentages were higher in the localities of inland Galicia (Map 3). All the data would indicate that we should focus our attention on what happened in that area. Hence, the social framework study of the population living in the area reveals that, unlike what happened in Galicia as a whole (Table 1), one out of every ten households was in the hands of that elite made up of the nobility (7.1 percent of the total) and the clergy (3.0 percent of the total), which, taken together, provided occupation for 45 percent of the total number of servants in this area.

Broadly speaking, such data indicate that the particular make-up of the prevailing social framework in each geographical zone allows in itself a good understanding of the unequal concentration of domestic service in the space that up until now has not been taken into account by researchers. An understanding which justifies setting aside the overworked explanation of the existence of different frameworks of agricultural work, explanation to which we referred throughout this paper. Accordingly, it is unquestionable that the specific nature of the social framework of inland Galicia, aside from the historical causes which made it possible,[13] contributed to the creation and definition of an important segment of the labour market wherein our servants evolved, clarifying to a certain extent their tendency to concentrate in this specific area. As always, we must not lose sight of the fact that the domestic necessities of the nobility's country homes, or the attention required by the parish homes, only made up the upper levels of this labour market. The lower levels were formed by fulfilling the necessities of the family economies of a certain sector of the peasantry; a fulfilment linked in its case to an agricultural framework that had nothing in common with those existing in other parts of Galicia.

Thus, in principle, the tendency of the peasant households that employed servants to be concentrated in inland Galicia is of less surprise to the researcher than the behaviour shown by the clergy or the nobility, which, let us not forget, bore a strict relation with the series of historical

13 Ramón Villares, *La propiedad de la tierra en Galicia, 1560–1936*, Madrid, Siglo XXI, 1982, pp. 98ff.

circumstances that facilitated the relevance that both classes acquired within their social framework.

Conclusion

The analysis of the presence of servants in the households of the different socio-professional groups under consideration, along with the subsequent mapping of those groups, has served to reveal that the traditional explanation given for the uneven spatial distribution of the domestic service in the regional areas under study is incomplete. An explanation, as is common knowledge, based on the existence of different agricultural work structures within each of these regional areas, and which implicitly includes the definition of the internal and external characteristics of the domestic service labour markets.

In contrast, the results of the current investigation reveal that in the afore-mentioned definition, the particular composition adopted by the social framework in the different territorial spheres of one and the same regional area played a leading role. This is due to the contribution of certain social strata in generating important labour opportunities for potential servants in some areas and not in others, which, in the final instance, is related to the greater or lesser degree of concentration therein. Thus, if it is indeed true that in inland Galicia the abundance of those servants had its origin in a determined series of causes (a property structure; a form of organization of agricultural tasks; a socio-familiar reality deeply impregnated with the spirit of the stem family; the practice of an inegalitarian hereditary system, etc.), it is also true that they did not make full sense without taking into account the peculiarities that were happening concurrently in the social framework of the area. Without them, that is to say, without the importance of the role of the clergy and the nobility, neither the afore-mentioned internal and external characteristics of that labour market, nor the mere existence of domestic service can be explained coherently.

Map 2. Percentage of households headed by nobility (hidalgos) at parish level in Galicia, 1752

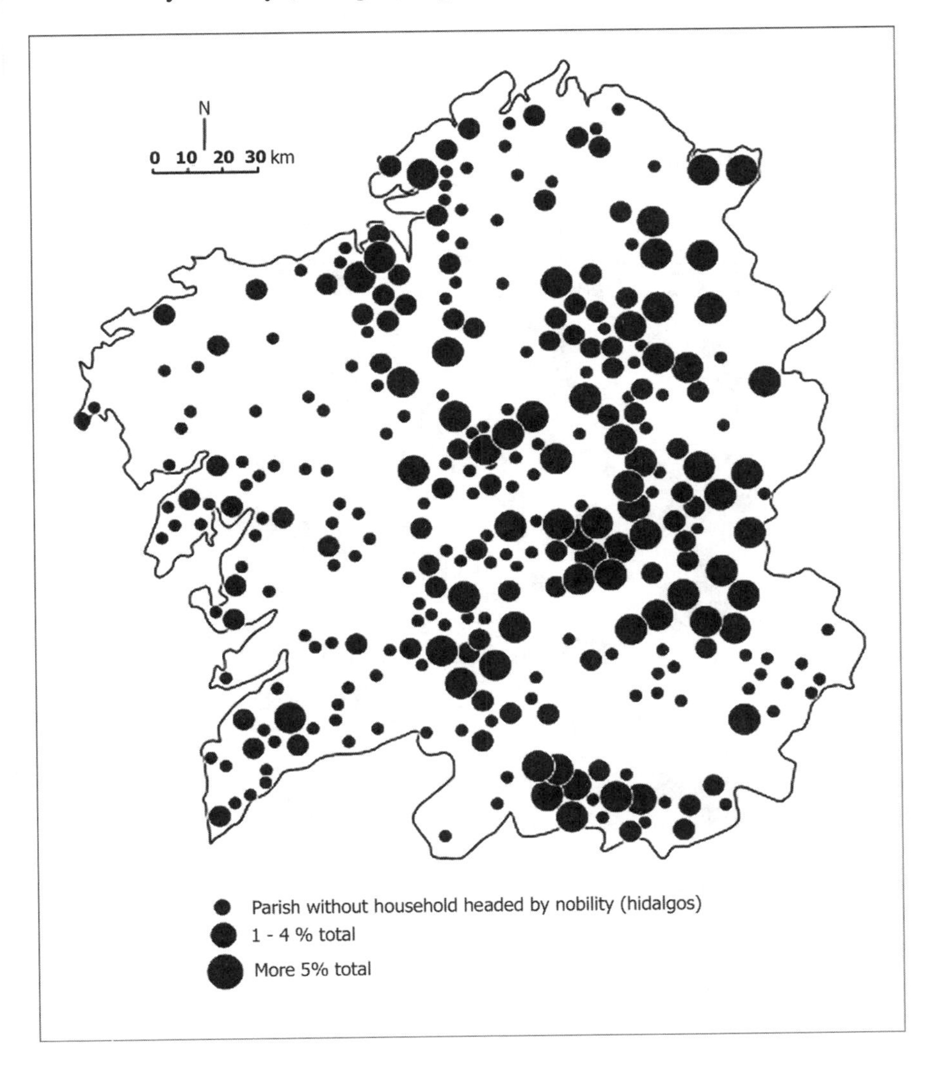

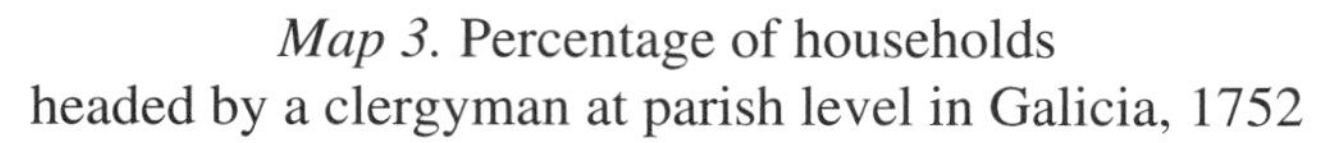

Map 3. Percentage of households
headed by a clergyman at parish level in Galicia, 1752

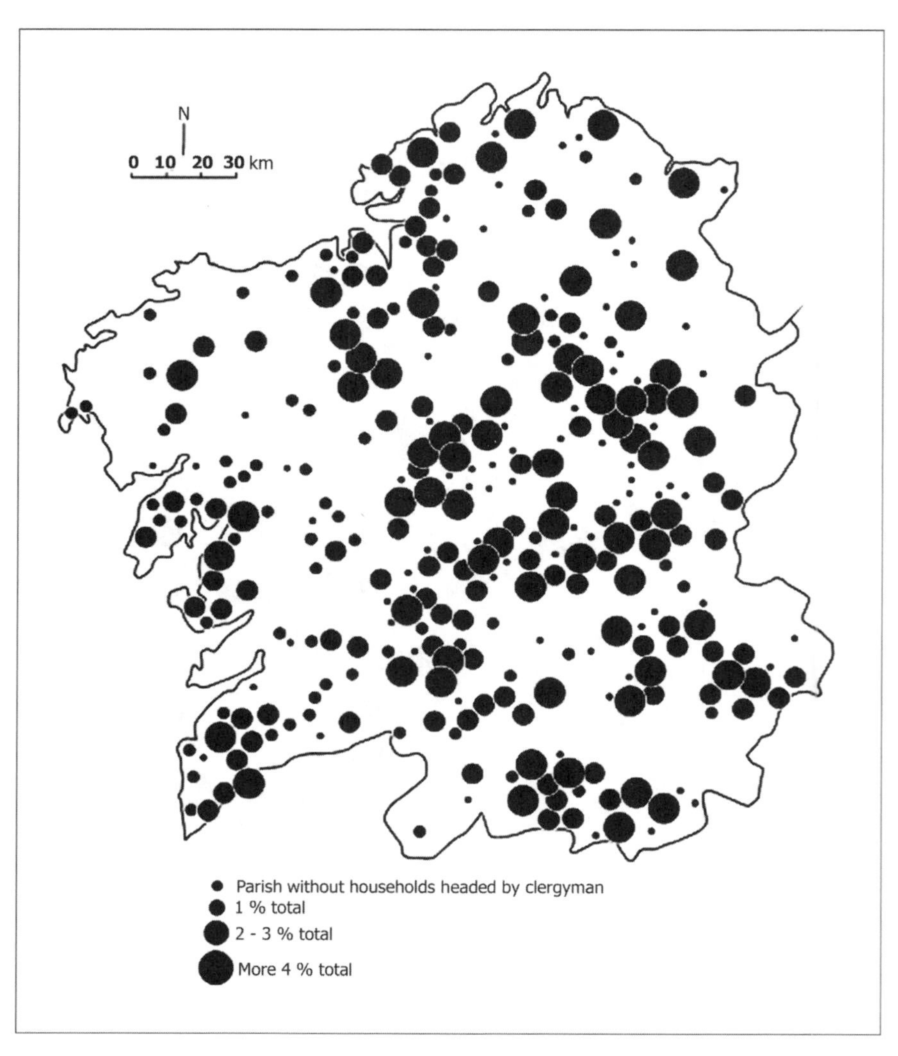

Domestic Service in Spain, 1750–1836

The Domestic Servants of the Clergy

Ofelia REY CASTELAO and Raquel IGLESIAS ESTEPA

The conditions of Spanish servants in the eighteenth and early nineteenth centuries might depend not only on their sex, age, fitness for work and training, and on the wealth or social status of their employers, but also on their employers' legal status as private individuals or institutions. In conformity with the scheme sketched at the Barcelona meeting,[1] here we shall consider all those persons who performed domestic service in ecclesiastical institutions, specifically monasteries and convents. The persistence of these institutions in time facilitates examination of the conditions of their servants and of the dependence of these conditions on the conditions and circumstances of the institutions themselves – in particular, as we shall see, the measures taken against the religious orders in the early nineteenth century had dramatic consequences for their servants.

The institutions in which the servants of the Roman catholic clergy served were not, of course, "normal" homes. Nevertheless, according to the notion of how servants should be treated that was shared by the religious orders and the Church in general, the households of the clergy, whether regular or secular, were as families, each with a father at its head.

At least in theory, the Council of Trent (1563) had provided the clergy with guidelines that were in general extracted from the Bible and from the behaviour required of the Christian family; in particular, the "families" of the clergy were distinguished by the requirement that they should reinforce the reputation of the head of the family through exemplary behav-

1 Ofelia Rey Castelao, "Le service domestique sous les règles des ordres religieux (la Couronne de Castille à la fin de l'Ancien Régime)", paper presented at the seminar *Domestic service and the evolution of the law. III Seminar of the EU Network on the Socio-Economic Role of Domestic Service as a Factor of European Identity,* Barcelona, 12–15 December 2002.

iour, by conforming to social norms that were more rigid than those to which other families were subject. The contribution of household servants to the maintenance of their master's reputation was in fact two-fold, since they did so not only through their behaviour, but also by their very existence, numbers, and appearance.

Numerous testimonies by both secular and regular clergy support this account of the Church's attitude to servants. In 1579, for example, the Archbishop of Santiago, in a letter addressed to a friar appointed Bishop of Calahorra,[2] recommended that he devotes as much attention to managing his household as to governing his see, and that his residence should "smell more like a monastery than a palace"; to which end he should treat his servants justly from the start, establishing agreements with respect to their wages and paydays, and bonuses to recompense their virtue. For the Archbishop the greatest virtue was industriousness, and care should be taken to choose young men with multiple talents allowing them to fulfil various functions. The aim was for the household to resemble a convent in its sobriety, the servants dressing and eating with the same austerity as their master in return for security. This arrangement would ensure fidelity, especially in times of trial.

The same theory was expounded in 1715 by the Franciscan friar Fr. Arbiol in *La familia regulada con doctrina de la Sagrada Escritura*, a book taking its inspiration chiefly from the Gospel that underlines the importance of not taking on an excessive number of servants (a sign of vanity) and of choosing them wisely (because of the difficulty of getting rid of them – above all because of what they might disclose about the life of the household); once taken into service, a fair wage should be agreed, together with living conditions and duties, in return for which their master should care for their worldly and spiritual well-being. And in 1743 the Benedictine Fr. Sarmiento,[3] writing to justify the discrepancy between the poverty prescribed by the rule of the Order and the relative luxury in which the monks actually lived, again stressed the idea of a family with abundant reasons for maintaining an extensive domestic service and, ac-

2 *Memorias brebes de las cosas más notables de el Señor Don Francisco Blanco de Salcedo, Obispo de Orense y Málaga y Arzobispo de Santiago*, 11.v, circa 1600.

3 *Manifiesto del recibo de las rentas de los monasterios de la religion de san benito; y en que se emplean*. Sacado y presentado al Consejo por el Rvmo. P. Mtro. Fr. Martín Sarmiento, benedictino. Cronista general de su Religión: y de Indias por el Rey N.S.: en carta a un amigo que le consulta. Madrid. Año de 1743.

cording to him, more than sufficient rules for its government. This theory may be confronted with two objections: firstly, as noted above, it was in principle forbidden for the religious orders to have servants, because to have them contradicted the vow of poverty and because the rules of the orders explicitly forbade it; and secondly, the servants who, in spite of being forbidden, were present, with the acquiescence of superiors, in all convents, were not treated on an equal footing with other inmates. In these hierarchichal, paternalistic, minutely organized institutions, choir monks, choir nuns and novices were waited on by a numerous domestic service comprising on the one hand servants proper and on the other lay brothers or lay sisters.

In the eighteenth century, in male monasteries of the monastic (i.e. non-mendicant) orders, 31 percent of the inmates were servants and another 7 percent were lay brothers, making a total of 38 percent of the inmates devoted to domestic service. Even among the mendicant orders the total domestic service accounted for 29 percent of inmates, although in this case 23 percent were lay friars and only 6 percent servants. Overall, servants made up about 19 percent of the total population of male monasteries, and in female convents, in which the domestic service comprised both men and women, it made up about 30 percent of the population. In 1797, there were 1,655 male and 4,366 female servants in female monasteries. True, for both male and female monasteries there were considerable differences among different geographical areas, but these are attributable to differences in income, in numbers of monks and nuns, and in the distribution of the population among the various orders.

Servants

The large number of servants was of constant concern to the higher echelons of the religious orders, partly because the servants altered the life of their communities and partly because they contradicted the ideal of poverty. The exact number of servants in each convent is not easy to ascertain, because the records sometimes do and sometimes do not include the personal servants of monks and nuns that employed them; but in any case it was often deemed excessive by the authorities of the orders. The recurrent social criticism of this sign of wealth became increasingly frequent in the eighteenth century, especially after the 1760s, and the orders responded by insisting on a reduction in the domestic service, and in some cases, such as the barefooted Carmelite nuns, in the prohibition of all servants (although lay sisters were allowed); but these instructions were in practice never followed, even when the religious orders were in danger of being suppressed by the government.

As an example, we may take the case of the Benedictine nuns. The internal regulations of their convents contradicted the rule of the order not only by consenting to the employment of female servants attending the community as a whole, but also by allowing that abbesses or ex-abbesses, and nuns who were sick or aged more than 65 years, to employ personal maids as long as they were not paid from the income of the convent. In addition, gentlewomen residing in the convent were allowed maids for whose board and lodging they paid. Further justification for the presence of servants was a regulation forbidding cooking in the nuns' cells. The minimum age for maids in the Benedictine convents was twelve years; as in other orders, their character was examined prior to admission to ensure their honesty and good habits, and they were required to dress modestly and behave discreetly. Their situation was relatively comfortable, that of personal maids because their conditions were linked to the status and habits of their mistresses and that of the communal servants because they had board and lodging and received a wage. Differences among the orders as to the wages paid were considerable, but have not yet been investigated in depth.

As in other orders, the Benedictine authorities were concerned about the internal problems of fraternization arising from the proliferation of servants in their nunneries, and about the adverse effect on external attitudes towards the order, since the existence of such large domestic staffs reinforced the notion that the monks and nuns were parasites living off the labours of others; but recurrent attempts to remedy the situation had little or no effect. Towards the end of the seventeenth century, the convent of San Paio de Antealtares in Santiago de Compostela was cautioned because of the excessive number of personal servants, and ordered to allow only those who were needed to care for nuns with serious illness who could keep them in their cells and maintain these servants from their own income; but in 1753 the forty eight nuns of this community were attended by six or seven communal servants and no fewer than twenty seven personal maids.[4] Even one of the city's more modest communities, the Dominicans of the Convent of Belvís, were reproved in this latter year for the same reason, the Visitor instructing them not to replace personal maids who left service, but instead to increase the number of lay sisters, who were expected to be more decorous and attentive to their duties.[5]

The situation was much the same in the male Benedictine communities. Although it was recommended that domestic tasks be performed by lay brothers, male servants of appropriately sober habits were allowed, subject to the permission of the authorities of the order, if the number of lay brothers was insufficient.[6] In theory, personal servants were not allowed, and communal servants were only to attend elderly, sick or high-ranking monks; but in practice the large numbers of lay brothers and communal servants in Benedictine monasteries were supplemented by the monks' personal servants, who were paid from the monks' own pockets and lived in their cells. All attempts to correct this situation failed.

For example, in 1654 the Monastery of San Martín Pinario in Santiago de Compostela was reminded by the Visitor of the Superior General's prohibition of servants, and the abbot was encouraged to admit more lay brothers to carry out domestic tasks; but in the visit of 1666 it was again necessary to insist that the only monks allowed to have servants were those who needed them for their duties; and the Visitor of 1688 gave in to the inevitable, ordering merely that no monk have more than one personal

4 Serrana Rial García, *Mujer y actividad económica en la Galicia Moderna. La inserción de las mujeres en la producción económica rural y urbana*, Santiago, Universidade de Santiago de Compostela, 2003, pp. 485ff.; Eduardo Montegut Contreras, "Servicio doméstico y educación en los conventos femeninos del Antiguo Régimen, siglo XVIII", *Torre de los Lujanes*, 15, 1990, p. 119.

5 Baudilio Barreiro Mallón, "El monacato femenino en la Edad Moderna: demografía y estructura social", *1º Congreso Internacional del Monacato femenino en España, Portugal y América, 1492–1992*, León, Universidade de León, 1999, vol. 2, p. 57.

6 "Que ni del todo se quiten los criados a los que los hubieran menester... ni permitan que haya más que los que de ningún modo se puede escusar. Y a estos no se les consientan habitos indecentes a nuestro estado, ni profanos, ni que tengan cosa alguna de seda, sino que anden con habito de sacerdotes [...] Y para que el abuso del número de criados se ataje con más rigor y severidad, mandamos que ningún monge [...] (excepto los Generales pasados) pueda tener criado sin licencia in scriptis del Reverendísimo General" (Constituciones de la Congregación de N.G.P. San Benito de España, published in Valladolid).

servant.[7] In 1701, in another campaign against deviation from the rule, a *carta acordada* – a letter of rebuke from the higher authorities of the order – established that no-one could have a servant without express licence, but concessions again followed: in 1706 higher-ranking members of the community were allowed personal servants, although the number of communal servants was limited to two. In 1729 a *carta acordada* reproached the monks for not taking their meals together in the refectory, an omission due to their having their servants cook for them in their cells;[8] and in an assembly of 1741 the need for special licence for personal servants was again reiterated – as was prohibition of the entry of pages into the monks' cells – in a period in which numerous documents denounced the relaxation of monasterial austerity, describing the easy life of regular monks as that of laymen living together with only worldly cares. The Visitor of 1752 was even obliged to impose punishment for the presence of servants with their own servants. At the beginning of the nineteenth century things were no better: in 1806 the Benedictine authorities once more decreed that the only monks allowed servants were abbots, monks with important duties (preachers, confessors, administrators), and the sick; all others were to be attended by lay brothers. But once more, the decree was ignored and things went on as before.[9]

As far as we know, the servants themselves had no complaints, being better off than servants in other situations; in eighteenth-century Santiago, for example, the wages of convent servants – which, if the convent rules were followed, were paid punctually when due – were substantially higher than those of persons serving in hospitals and public charities.[10]

The recorded expenses of San Martín Pinario in 1742 included the money wages of a grain storeman (200 *reales* a year), two cooks and two cook's assistants (total 570 *reales*), four men to attend the threshing floor and carts (total 400 *reales*), four stable lads (528 *reales*), washerwomen (429 *reales*) and four footmen (560 *reales*), as well as those of three barbers and a farrier; a total of 874.5 bushels of wheat (31,798 litres) that was paid in kind to active, elderly and invalid servants; and the food and foot-

7 Archivo Histórico Diocesano de Santiago, San Martín, leg. 21.

8 Archivo Histórico Diocesano de Santiago, San Martín, leg. 64/18, s.f.

9 Ernesto Zaragoza Pascual, *Los Generales de la Congregación de San Benito*, Silos, Abadía, 1987, p. 99.

10 Baudilio Barreiro Mallón and Ofelia Rey Castelao, *Pobres, enfermos y peregrinos. La red asistencial gallega a fines del Antiguo Régimen*, Santiago, Consorcio de Santiago, 1999.

ware of twenty other servants employed in domestic offices. In 1769 there were thirty servants living within or without the monastery, with a total annual salary of 1,245 *reales* plus board, lodging and clothing.

A chronicle written in the mid-eighteenth century by a Franciscan friar of the Colegio de Misiones de Propaganda Fide in Herbón[11] mentions the services of the inhabitants of the village in which the Colegio was located: a seamstress, a tailor, a weaver, two washerwomen, three men "to look after the rams, the vegetable garden and the sacristy", and an unspecified number of youths sent out to collect alms. These servants were paid both a money wage – which amounted to less than 2 percent of the total expenses of the Colegio – and in kind, the latter payment taking the form of the same kinds of inferior cereal – rye and maize – as were distributed as alms to the poor.

Wage differences among servants depended on several factors. Although one must undoubtedly have been the difference between communal and personal servants, we know little of the wages of the latter because of the private nature of their relationship; all we know for certain is that personal servants had board, lodging and clothing assured because they lived in their master's or mistress' cell in exchange for preparing their food and clothes, keeping them company, running errands and bringing them news of the outside world. Communal servants were subject to the regulations of their convent and, as we have already seen above, their wages depended on its resources. Male servants were generally paid more than female servants, but not always: in the Monastery of San Paio in Santiago,[12] the men servants of the vicars received the same annual salary as the communal maidservants during most of the eighteenth century, and following 1787 their salary was less than that of the maidservants (though

11 Fray Antonio de Herosa, *Memoria de las cosas notables de este convento de Herbón*, ms. Archivo de la Provincia Franciscana de Santiago, s.r.

12 María Concepción Burgo López, *Un dominio monástico femenino en la Edad Moderna. El monasterio benedictino de San Paio de Antealtares*, Santiago, 1986, Tesis de Doctorado inédita, 1037ff.; *Id.*, "Política económica y gestión administrativa en las entidades monásticas femeninas", *1° Congreso Internacional sobre del Monacato femenino*, León, 1993, vol. 2, p. 569; *Id.*, "La economía del monasterio de S. Payo de Antealtares en el s. XVII", *Obradoiro de Historia Moderna*, 1990, p. 47; *Id.*, "La importancia de los ingresos dotales en la economía monástica femenina durante la Edad Moderna", in *Jubilatio*, Santiago, Universidade de Santiago, 1987, I, p. 351; M. García Colombas, *Las señoras de San Payo. Historia de las monjas benedictinas de San Pelayo de Antealtares*, Santiago, Caja de Ahoros de Galicia, 1980.

so was their workload). Greater differences derived from the type of work done, but differences in money wages such as those exemplified above are not necessarily a faithful reflection of differences in total wage, which included wages paid in kind (generally as grain). For example, in San Paio, in the period 1717–1726, the total wage of chambermaids was 22 percent higher than that of cloister washerwomen, 31 percent higher than that of chapel washerwomen, and between 37 percent and 62 percent higher than those of lower-level servants; however, since chambermaids and washerwomen alike were paid 16 bushels of rye a year (the amount estimated as sufficient for the needs of an average family), the corresponding money-wage differential was larger; Table 1 (and Table 2) shows similar differences between real total wage and money-wage differentials for other classes of servant.

During most of the eighteenth century wages in kind remained constant while the price of grain increased steadily, so that the money value of servants' salaries rose considerably.[13] At the same time, however, the income of the monasteries – rents and tithes – was increasingly paid in money rather than grain. As a result, the real income of the monasteries fell, creating economic difficulties that worsened steadily over the last 30 years of the eighteenth century and by 1800 had become critical. Because of these difficulties, towards the end of the century all the Galician monasteries that have been studied decided to suppress payment of wages in kind other than board, lodging and clothing. In San Paio this occurred in the year 1787, the money equivalent of the former grain wage being calculated on the basis of the average price of grain over the preceding few years (the opportunity was also taken to adjust the salaries of some servants upwards or downwards). Once the new money-only wages were fixed, the continuing inflation rapidly reduced the real value of servants'

13 In many cases, money wages also remained constant, so that the ratio of the real worth of wages paid in kind to that of money wages increased markedly. For example, in the Convent of Santa Clara in Santiago de Compostela, kitchen maids were paid 44 reales and 16 bushels of rye from the beginning of the eighteenth century until its end, when wages in kind were suppressed (María del Carmen Alvariño Alejandro, *El dominio de Santa Clara ante la Desamortización*, Tesis de licenciatura, Santiago, 1972). Ofelia Rey Castelao, "Las economías monásticas femeninas ante la crisis del Antiguo Régimen", *1º Congreso Internacional del Monacato femenino,* León, 1999, vol. 2, p. 105; *Id.*, "El clero regular gallego en la Edad Moderna: evaluación de su poder económico", in Fiorenzo Landi (ed.), *Accumulation and dissolution of large estates of the regular clergy in Early Modern Europe*, Rimini, Guaraldi, 1999, p. 235.

salaries: over the decade 1777–1786 the annual salaries of the best-paid servants were equivalent to 22.6 bushels of rye (823.1 litres), but in the decade 1797–1807 to only 10.7 bushels (388.5 litres). We know of no protests on the part of the servants during this period, possibly because their guaranteed wages and extras (board, lodging and clothing) still meant that they were better off than servants in private homes or other institutions. But for many, things changed dramatically in 1809 when the closure of convents ordered by Joseph Bonaparte left thousands with no lodging and no wages, a crisis that was to be repeated in 1820 and 1836. The situation of those made redundant was in many cases worsened by their employment in convents not having fitted them for other kinds of work, even as servants in private homes. Also, a goodly proportion were elderly and/or sick and had no family to turn to.

Summing up, the paternalistic system that prevailed in Spanish convents until 1836 guaranteed satisfaction of the basic necessities of the domestic staff who served in them: board, lodging and clothing were provided (extras that were not to be scorned in times of scarcity or soaring prices such as the crisis of 1768–69), and when age or infirmity made them unable to work they were maintained in the convents or paid a pension. In return, they in most cases not only rendered their services, but also relinquished the possibility of forming a family of their own. But when in 1809, 1820 and 1836 liberal governments suppressed increasing numbers of convents, the measures adopted to allow other former convent inmates to earn a living completely ignored the servants, who were in many cases left without any means of supporting themselves.

Lay Brothers

In most Spanish monasteries of the eighteenth century, some 10–15 percent of inmates were lay brothers or lay sisters.[14] In Benedictine monaster-

14 Exceptions with larger numbers of lay inmates are exemplified by the Colegio de Misiones in Herbón, which in 1749 had, besides its servants, 10 lay brothers for just 17 friars (in 1808 there were 10 lay brothers for 16 friars, and in 1835 there were 11 for

ies they could legitimately be admitted only with the express permission of the authorities of the order and after providing proof that they were honest, of clean habits, and came from Christian families. Their dress distinguished them from the choir monks, but like these they attended divine offices.

During their noviciate they performed the most menial tasks (cleaning, sweeping, bedmaking, slop-pail emptying etc.) under the watchful eye of a monk who, as their master, would "teach and punish them". At the weekly chapter meetings, which lay brothers as well as choir monks attended, they might be the object of complaints, but did not themselves have any right to complain of others. They ate in the refectory (but only after the choir monks), were inferior in rank not only to choir monks who had taken their vows but also to novices, and they were not to be addressed as "Father".

The Cistercians had similar but more explicit regulations concerning lay brothers, who were again identified as such by distinctive dress. Aspiring lay brothers had to be healthy and strong, without any physical impediment preventing their performing their work, and leaving no debts in the outside world upon entry into the monastery. During their noviciate they were under the authority of a novice-master who was to "instruct them in obedience and humility, explaining the obligations and labours they would face" and teaching them to pray. Their conduct was examined every four months, and information on their families and habits was sought. They began the day with prayers before going to work, and on Sundays and feast days they received extra lessons on religious subjects. Because of the physical nature of their work they were excused from fasting (except on Fridays). As among the Benedictines, they took their meals only after the choir monks, and might be complained about but not admitted to make complaints. They were denied the possibility of subsequently rising to be choir monks, however excellent their behaviour. This "professionalization" of the lay brothers was advantageous to the Cistercian community, and at the same time allowed them a certain relaxation of religious observance.

Although all the monks and lay brothers of a given order shared vows of poverty, their communities were extremely hierarchical and composed of rigid strata based on priesthood, age and occupation. Although the

---

19 friars). This large proportion of lay brothers was justified by the monks devoting most of their time to preparing themselves for their missionary work.

status of lay brothers was not the same as that of the monastery servants, the difference between choir monks and lay brothers reflected the uncrossable division that existed in society in general between the ruling classes and the common people. Lay brothers were thus a class apart, whose function was to serve the choir monks, usually by performing domestic chores (notably cooking), by working monastery land, by begging in the surrounding towns and villages, or by acting as companions or servants to the higher-ranking monks. Their only education concerned Christian doctrine, religious rites and the rules of their order, and they had no right to speak or vote in chapter (something that the liberal government of 1820–23 was unsuccessfully urged to remedy by the Franciscan lay brothers). Their reasons for entering and remaining in their monastery were their vocation and/or their lack of any other livelihood: although, as noted above, monasterial economies were in crisis by the end of the eighteenth century – especially in Andalusia and wherever monasterial income was based on tithes and other forms of rent derived from agriculture – lay brothers still enjoyed guaranteed board and lodging and a standard of living equivalent to that of the middle classes of the day. By 1820 this number had fallen by 28 percent to 33,544, and in 1835 there were 1,940 monasteries housing 30,906 religious. The female convents were not suppressed in 1820–23, but the number of nuns likewise fell from 24,007 in 1797 to 15,130 in 1836, although there were still new admissions (usually of young women with no prospects of marriage). These drops in numbers were initiated during the War of Independence, when Joseph Bonaparte ordered the closure of numerous convents. This was later followed by the closure of all male convents with less than twelve monks or friars by the liberal government of 1820–1823, and in 1836 by the disamortizations of Mendizabal.

The closures of 1820–23 affected 8,111 monks and friars. Many of the choir monks who abandoned their convents did so voluntarily, because they were given pensions or parish livings or other posts, and were freed of the rigours of convent life. Lay brothers who had acquired higher training in their convents (as musicians, apothecaries, etc.) also had relatively few problems. However, the majority of lay brothers had no professional training allowing them to earn a living; in most cases they could not be supported by their families, which were usually poor (for this very reason many future lay brothers were put into the care of convents as children); and upon taking their vows had relinquished any inheritance. Their conditions were precarious in spite of provisions having been made for them, too, to receive small pensions.

In 1823 the absolutist monarchy of Fernando VII not only allowed the return of vocational monks and friars to their convents, but also removed all ex-monks and ex-friars from their parish livings and suppressed their pensions, so forcing the return of those who had left voluntarily. In 1825 the Franciscan Provincial, Fr. Casiano Agero, testified that "many, deprived of their employment, have been left in deepest poverty".[15] Given that their exclaustration had meant their breaking the rules of the orders, the conditions of their return were the object of discrepancy between the Pope, the monarchy and the religious orders themselves: the Pope, through the Spanish nuncio, favoured their being readmitted subject merely to their taking part in appropriate spiritual exercises; the monarchy and its government proposed that readmitted religious lose all privileges and be obliged to repeat their noviciate; while the religious orders were inclined to impose readmission conditions on a case-by-case basis. On 26 April 1824, the view of the monarchy prevailed.[16]

Following 1836, lay brothers were left in much the same situation as following 1820, except that now the numbers of exclaustrated religious were much larger: the population of lay brothers living in Spanish monasteries (12,581 in 1797 – 12,117 in male, and 464 in female monasteries) was reduced in 1835.

The papal representatives and the authorities of the religious orders negotiated solutions to the problems faced by those who could voice their preoccupations in chapter, but did next to nothing for lay brothers (although the ecclesiastical commission charged with negotiating the conditions of convent closures did ask the government to allow lay brothers to

15 Manuel Revuelta, *Política religiosa de los liberales en el s. XIX. Trienio Constitucional,* Madrid, C.S.I.C., Escuela de Historia Moderna, 1973, pp. 339–340; *Id., La Exclaustración (1833–1840)*, Madrid, Editorial Católica, 1976.

16 The readmitted friars who had left their convents voluntarily – the "liberal" friars – were mainly young or lay brothers. It was this group that, following 1833, would side with Isabel II in her succession dispute with her uncle, Don Carlos. In fact, numerous lay brothers enrolled in the queen's army, whereas most monks and friars directly or indirectly supported Don Carlos, who promised the conservation of all their privileges. However, there were exceptions: in 1834 the lay brothers of Franciscan convents in Viana and Rentería deserted to join Don Carlos' army. Those who supported the liberal government but desired the continuance of the monasteries were disappointed when their extinction was decreed in 1836.

continue to live in their convents, under episcopal supervision, while undergoing training – to be established by the government – that would fit them for life in the outside world).

Table 1. Population of lay brothers in 1835

	N.	%
"Sacerdotes in sacris"	16,785	54.3
"Ordenados in sacris"	2,013	6.5
"Coristas"	5,641	18.2
"Legos"	5,763	18.6
"Novicios"	704	2.4
Total	30,906	100.0

Source: M. Revuelta, *Política religiosa de los liberales*, Madrid, C.S.I.C., Escuela de Historia Moderna, 1973, p. 339.

Since the decree of March 8th 1836 provided for pensions to be paid to unemployed exclaustrated monks and friars, efforts were made to find them employment, and lay brothers were next in order of preference as regards placements in the churches, charities and hospitals; also, some young, moderately well-educated lay brothers were awarded scholarships to allow them to finish their training in seminars or colleges; but these alleviatory measures were not pursued systematically.[17]

Table 2. Pensions paid in 1820 and 1836

	1820		1836	
Age	Monks	Lay brothers	Monks	Lay brothers
+60 years	6,600	2,200	2,190	1,460
50 to 60 years	4,400	2,200	1,825	1,095
-50 years	3,300	1,100	1,460	1,095*

* 2 years only.

Furthermore, to the criteria used to determine the size of pensions following 1820 (mainly the difference between lay brothers and choir monks,

17 Juan Sáez Marín, *Datos sobre la Iglesia Española Contemporánea, 1768–1868*, Madrid, Editora Nacional, San Agostin, 1975, pp. 203ff., Exposición dirigida a S.M. el 25 de julio de 1836 por la Real Junta Eclesiástica, Madrid, 1836.

but also age) was added a further criterion distinguishing between lay brothers who were infirm or older than 40 years and those who were healthy and younger than 40 years, who would be paid a pension only for 2 years: in 1808 the 2,056 Spanish male monasteries housed 46,568 religious (monks, novices and lay brothers).

Thus, whereas in 1837 a pension was paid by the State to 7,904 lay brothers exclaustrated in 1835 (33 percent of the total number of religious who were exclaustrated at that date, Jesuits apart),[18] by 1840 this number had fallen to 1,971 (16 percent of the surviving religious), allowing a drop in the total sum paid in pensions from 37,911,455 *reales* (26 percent paid to lay brothers, the rest to choir monks) to 27,609,423 (11 percent paid to lay brothers). It is difficult to determine how many religious – often of advanced age – were left without work, without training (even for service in private homes), and with no families to turn to; but in 1844 the moderate liberal government recognized their situation to the extent of raising the number of pensions paid to lay brothers to 2,106.

18 Note that the convents of the Basque country were not closed down.

Domestic Staff in the Czech Lands at the Turn of the 19th and 20th Centuries in the Light of Statistical Figures

Ludmila FIALOVÁ

Although the population living in the Czech Lands had been regularly counted since the mid-eighteenth century, the effort at gaining the total number of domestic staff till the second half of the nineteenth century has faced big problems. With the exception of the years 1762–1768 the category "domestic staff" is lacking in the classification of population according to profession. It only reappears in the 1857 census and from this year onwards it remained a permanent part of the classifications until 1930, when over 150,000 people were put into the category "domestic staff". However, since 1950 the censuses have no longer recorded the category "domestic staff" and it was no longer present in the classifications of professions used for the examination of unemployment in intercensal periods. As a result, the number and possibly structure of the domestic staff in the Czech Lands can only be traced on the basis of statistical data for roughly 80 years.

The domestic staff at the turn of the nineteenth and twentieth centuries has not stood in the focus of interest. The researchers who have paid a detailed attention to the development of social and professional structure of the population of the Czech Lands usually put the domestic staff among workers' professions and possibly among the economic sector of the employer and they did not consider it as a group of population. When analysing the composition of the population in 1930, Antonín Boháč, e.g., only gives domestic staff as a social category within the industrial population, and does not mention it at all among the farming population (Boháč 1936, 62). A similar approach was adopted by Zdeněk Pavlík, who tried to examine the long-standing trends of the changes in social and professional structure of the Czech Lands on the basis of the data from population counts and censuses (Pavlík 1959). No detailed mention is made about domestic staff even by Pavla Horská, who studied very thoroughly the social structure of the population of Czech Lands and the methodological problems of its examination (Horská 1972; 1982a; 1983). Evidently, this was to some extent associated with the fact that this was a relatively small group, whose size tended to decrease. The work in domestic services was among the least attractive ones and it was considered as inferior. The notion of "housemaid" was almost identical with the notion of "poor maid".

On the other hand, the employment of domestic staff was among major characteristics of social status. Analyses of social structure of the population often described how many households could afford to have servants and how many of them. Differences in the employment of domestic staff in Prague households were therefore used for the delineation of social position of individual households when studying the social and ethnic development of the population in Prague at the end of the nineteenth century by such authors as Jan Havránek, who took a keen interest in the demographic and social development of the city (Havránek 1970), and Gary B. Cohen, who was primarily interested in ethnic development (Cohen 2000). By the same token, the size and structure of the domestic staff is an integral part of analyses of the development of the Jewish population in Moravia, as conducted by Ludmila Nesládková and Lumír Dokoupil (Nesládková and Dokoupil 1997) or Jana Helemíková (Helemíková 2001). The question of employment was also tackled by Jana Brabencová in her study of the mobility of population of Nymburk at the turn of the nineteenth and twentieth centuries (Brabencová 1991). These studies were based on archives material, mostly analysing census sheets. This made it possible to get the information whose statistical value significantly exceeded that of the published statistical data.

"Domestic Staff" as a Category in Statistical Approach

The oldest count describing the population in the Czech Lands in 1754 was basically confined to the acquisition of data about the number of population and its composition according to age and sex, partly also according to the marital status. In 1762–1769 the counts were widened to describe the social aspect, too. However, the preserved data are much fragmentary and often just reflect the contemporary structure of society.

The clergymen, noblemen and clerks are followed by the domestic staff and then by burghers, trades people, serfs and the poor in asylums. The list of the individual categories makes it clear that at present it is difficult to specify who exactly was counted in the "domestic staff"; the table even does not clearly show whether the population in question included both sexes or just men – only when the data are compared with the figures from next years one can judge that the information about profession only related to men. In 1780–1850 the male population of the Czech Lands is usually classified in a more detailed way, comprising clergymen, noblemen, clerks, and notables, burghers (including craftsmen and artists) and farmers. Although during these seventy years the classification was somewhat modified, it never explicitly included the group "servants" or "domestic staff". Moreover, only men were sorted by profession (Pavlík 1959).

Table 1. Domestic staff in the Czech Lands from 1857 to 1930: proportion in the total population and in the total economically active population

Year	Number of domestic staff members	*The proportion of domestic staff in:*		
		Total population	The economically active people	Wage earners
1857	155 400	2.18	6.31	8.15
1869	317 767	4.17	7.77	9.49
1880	314 625	3.79	8.13	11.18
1890	135 920	1.56	3.07	3.88
1900	160 620	1.70	3.51	5.94
1910	152 547	1.50	3.14	5.35
1921	149 668	1.50	3.45	5.23
1930	152 318	1.43	2.99	4.60

Notes: The economically active population is here defined according to Z. Pavlík (1959), i.e. people with regular employment as wage earners, clerks, workers or labourers and domestic staff.

From 1857 onwards the category "domestic staff" was permanently recorded within the classification of population by social and professional status. But it was so not only under various names, but also according to various definitions. In 1857 one can probably find the persons who can be included in this category in the group "other servants" because the previous group contains "auxiliary workers in agriculture, industry and trade".

The independent category "domestic staff" appears in 1869. However, it is also in agriculture and the subgroup "permanent servants" is only defined in agriculture. One can believe that the subgroup "permanent servants" was to a large extent identical with the notion of "farm labourers", which was at that time a frequent name for wage earners in agriculture. However, both among the male and female farm labourers it was very difficult to distinguish the persons who would be in the current approach classified as workers or auxiliary workers from the men and women who really worked as domestic servants. In the 1880 census the subgroup "permanent servants" was no longer defined in agriculture, but the disunity in classification and above all in the enumeration of the people making their living in agriculture survived.

From 1869 onwards the Austrian statistical service applied a new approach to the classification of population according to its social position. Based on the relationship to the profession, it placed individual persons into big social groups whose definition and names gradually changed, but their substance remained the same. Judging by the position in profession it distinguishes the "independents", which means owners of companies or their tenants (including people with a liberal profession and those living from rents and subsidies); the category also included asylums inmates, people without any profession and beggars, which means all those who had a self-sufficient source of livelihood (but since they did not have to work, not all of them would be considered as economically active according to today's criteria). Clerks and workers were put into independent categories. The next category included the people dependent on a breadwinner and the third category contained domestic staff. As one can see, the contemporary statistics considered domestic staff as quite a distinct category, which escaped the usual distinction into working and dependent people. This classification was hardly changed in the subsequent years and after Czechoslovakia was established the population censuses used the same methods.

As noted by authors such as Pavla Horská, there was obviously disunity when various professions and persons were sorted into groups of professions and the position in a profession in the Austrian statistical practice (Horská 1984, 57). Some groups of auxiliary workers were evidently classified as domestic staff and on the other hand some groups of domestic staff were often counted among the workers; as a result, when studying the development of basic social groups, the data of the Austrian statistics can serve just for a general look and comparison in time can bring about misleading results.

The fact that domestic staff was considered as an independent category within the profession is a favourable circumstance. Thanks to this, almost all characteristics under which the population was sorted within a census were as a rule available. From 1880 onwards, the classification by sex and since 1890 by sex and marital status, from 1900 onwards also according to religious denomination and possibly also ethnic origin, was used (in 1900–1910 according to the colloquial speech of the person in question when the census was taken and from 1921 onwards according to the mother tongue or the ethnic group). Since 1910 one can also see the classification of households by the number of servants. Understandably, one can best examine the structure of domestic staff by the profession of employer, which had been provided in big detail since 1890.

As a result, there is available a relatively large set of information which can thoroughly describe the domestic staff. I have just selected the most basic data, those which directly concern the domestic staff – the number and structure by age and sex –, and those which clearly specify the employer or the households employing domestic staff.

The Number of Domestic Servants

In 1762 a total of 104,180 people were classified in the group "servants" in the Czech Lands. Although within the Christian population this was the second most numerous group just after the serfs (who numbered about 1,900,000), it only accounted for 4.8 percent of the total population. In this year the count found 57,057 Christian servants (4.3 percent), whose number rose to 86,450 (4.8 percent) by 1768. At the same time the number of Jewish servants rose from 1,559 to 1,943 (the percentage fell from 21.1 percent to 10.7 percent of the people with Jewish denomination). Unlike the Christian population, the category accounted for a much larger portion of Jewish population. However, there remains the question of who was effectively included in the domestic staff in Jewish households and who was in the Christian households. In 1780–1850 the category "servants" or "domestic staff" was not named among the professions into which the population was sorted.

In 1857 the category "other servants" contained roughly 155,000 people, but in 1869 and 1880 the category "domestic staff" included over 300,000 persons.[1] The 1890 census found so far the smallest number of the persons working as domestic staff, just under 136,000. However, the significant oscillation of the number cannot probably be a reason to speak about any changes in the social environment. Instead, the big alterations reflect the changes in the method of data processing after the population census was taken, as noted by Horská (Horská 1984). In 1900–1930 the proportion of the persons placed in the category "domestic staff" did not much change and it was estimated at about 150,000.

Zdeněk Pavlík tried in 1959 to convert the data from the Austrian and Czechoslovak statistics in order to extract information about the distribution of population according to its economic activity and social groups or sector of the national economy. According to his findings within the economically active population (which however did not include *rentiers* and house owners, but unlike the contemporary statistics he included just the domestic staff), the proportion of the persons enumerated as domestic staff did not significantly change in the individual censuses taken in the second half of the nineteenth century and it eventually remained stable at about 3 percent of the economically active population (Pavlík 1959) (Table 1).

As one can see, in the second third of the nineteenth century the category domestic staff included every eighth to twelfth employed person, which basically meant one tenth of all wage earners, who were as well clerks, workers and day labourers. The fact that between 1880 and 1890 the domestic staff statistically fell by 178,000, which was a 57 percent decline over ten years, indicates the above-mentioned change in the method of data processing for the profession of population rather than a real decline since at that time the number of day labourers increased by 135,000. From 1890 to 1930, the domestic staff accounted for less than 2

1 After 1918 (the Constitution of Czechoslovakia), the (Czechoslovak) State Statistical Office had calculated a new important data referring to population of the new state including the distribution of population according to its economic activity in older period. The official information was that in 1880 there were 234,251 persons (18,066 men and 216,195 women) working as domestic staff on the territory which was, since 1918, part of Czechoslovakia. Unfortunately now we do not know the method of this recalculation.

percent of the total population and the already small proportion was further slightly diminishing in the course of these years to less than 1.5 percent at the end of the period under observation. Moreover, domestic staff included a diminishing proportion of economically active people as well as wage earners. In 1930 just 4.6 percent of wage earners made their living in domestic service.

Domestic Staff According to Sectors

The fact that from 1880 onwards the domestic staff members were, similarly to the dependent population, carefully classified according to their employer, seemingly makes it easily possible to ascertain the structure of domestic staff according to the sector of employer. However, this is hampered by the contemporary classification of individual groups of profession, which was continually changing, although after 1890 the changes were just minor. As a rule, the domestic staff members were placed among the persons who belonged with their livelihood to the sector of employer and in analyses they were counted among the workers who were there, too.

However, from 1890 onwards the groups of profession, which numbered from 29 in 1890 to 34 in 1930, were put together into four major classes (sectors) of the national economy: A (agriculture, forestry and water management), B (industry and construction), C (trade and transport), D all the rest (usually army, civil and public service, but also education and health care, etc.). This allows a swift orientation on how many persons depended with their livelihood on the development of a relevant sector, with the exception of the non-productive sector, which also embraced the persons who did not depend on anyone for their incomes, but did not work either. The sector D also contained such "professions" as *rentiers*, asylum inmates, etc., but their members were placed by the contemporary statistical service among the "independents" (Horská 1982b). Since the class D differed internally in the individual years, the comparison in time of its individual groups is problematic. But just this class employed a large portion of domestic staff.

From 1890 onwards, within the classification of population by groups of profession there was also the group "independently executed domestic service", which also included "domestic service, laundering, cleaning, etc". This group, too, was defined within the fourth sector (D).

The statisticians seem to have faced the biggest problems from the beginning when having to define the persons making domestic works in agriculture and subsequently having to place them into the classification of employment. In 1869 people executing domestic services were classified irrespective of the sector of their employers. Apart from 317,000 "servants in domestic services" the census also recorded another 865,000 "permanent servants" in agriculture – apparently the people who were in subsequent years classified among agricultural workers or day labourers. This is why I did not place them into domestic staff. The 1880 census found in agriculture more than 131,000 domestic staff members, but in 1890 just 10,000, and in 1900 almost 20,000. The oscillations in the next years can be explained by a permanent decline in the importance of agricultural production for the Czech Lands in which a swift industrialisation was under way and possibly by the impact of the First World War on employment, which was reflected in the falling number of domestic staff in the country in the first decade of the twentieth century and its rise after the end of the war. By 1930 the number of domestic staff members working in agriculture fell again (Table 2).

Table 2. Domestic staff according to sectors of national economy in the Czech Lands in 1869–1930

Year	Agriculture (A)	Industry (B)	Trade (C)	Rest (D)	Total
1869	–	–	–	–	317,767
1880	131,758	65,200	30,222	87,445	314,625
1890	10,494	49,612	32,934	42,880	135,920
1900	19,989	58,133	34,170	48,328	160,620
1910	16,194	40,350	44,198	51,805	152,547
1921	25,359	39,286	41,572	43,451	149,668
1930	10,786	41,126	49,451	50,955	152,318

In industry, too, serious oscillations in the number of domestic staff members reflect more changes in classification rather than the real development. It may be that the people employed in the households of trades people or owners of small industrial companies could have been recorded in 1880 as domestic servants, while in 1890 they were counted as workers or day labourers, whereas in 1900 again as servants. But still the number of domestic servants bound to the industrial sector was evidently falling on the eve of the First World War. A minimum number of domestic staff members was found in the 1921 census, while in 1930 there was a higher number of servants in the households of industrialists and trade people, even exceeding that in 1910. But this was still just 41,000, which meant only about one quarter of all domestic servants.

On the other hand, it was easier to classify domestic staff within the sector of trade and transport, where the position and relationship with the employer was obviously more clear-cut. The 1880 census recorded in this sphere as men servants or housemaids 30,000 men and women and their number was continually rising until 1910, when it exceeded 44,000. After a slight decline in the First World War, the number of domestic staff members in the sector of trade surged to almost 50,000 by 1930. One can say that from this angle the households of traders were the most successful social class because they employed an increasing number of servants – every third housemaid was employed in some of the households we place into this class (hauliers played only a negligible role) by 1930.

If agriculture and industry are, in keeping with usual practice, considered as productive spheres, these fields employed as long ago as 1880 a smaller proportion of domestic staff than the non-productive sphere (trade and other spheres, which may include the households of the people working in the civil service, liberal professions, education and health care, but also rentiers, etc.) and the proportion was still decreasing. While in 1880 the biggest number of domestic servants was found in the households of people bound with their livelihood to agriculture, by 1890 in the households of trades people and industrialists, from 1900 onwards the domestic servants mostly found employment in the households of clerks, people with a liberal profession, rentiers, etc. Out of the 100 domestic servants some 60 worked in this year in the households which can be placed in the non-productive sphere, whereas by the 1930 census the figure was 66, which meant two thirds of them.

Apart from the households of traders, in the non-productive sphere domestic staff was employed in a large number in the households of clerks in the civil and public service. The big group of clerks also included employees of the educational and health care sectors. The fact that one fifth of all domestic servants was employed just in the households of these people is not very surprising because both senior government officials and teachers at secondary schools and universities were, just like doctors, an acknowledged group of society and their living standards both allowed and required the employment of domestic staff. A specific class of population, included in this group, was made up of clergymen who also usually employed domestic staff.[2] A large proportion of households of just this social group, which as a rule could not afford to employ more than one servant, also explains the fact that there was on average one manservant or housemaid in these households.

Domestic servants were traditionally employed also in the households of the people whose property was big enough and who did not have to work directly. The statistics called these people rentiers and house owners.

It is likely that the elites (aristocracy, big landholders, bankers, industrialists, and rich traders), which also employed the biggest number of domestic staff, were classified according to the dominant source of income either as owners of big agricultural or industrial holdings or they also could have been recorded in this group of rentiers and house owners. Quite different data from 1880 as against the following years are due more to the method of data conversion than to any real changes in the level of employment of domestic staff (Table 3).

Table 3. The proportion of domestic staff in the Czech Lands employed in the non-productive sector (trade, civil and public service, others) in 1880–1930

<table>
<tr><th rowspan="4">Year</th><th colspan="6">Out of 100 domestic staff members, their employment was in the following sectors:</th></tr>
<tr><th rowspan="3">Trade (C)</th><th colspan="5">(D)</th></tr>
<tr><th rowspan="2">Total</th><th colspan="4">Of whom their employers:</th></tr>
<tr><th>Clerks in the civil and public service</th><th>Other liberal professions</th><th>Rentiers and house owners</th><th>Army</th></tr>
<tr><td>1880</td><td>9.6</td><td>27.8</td><td>5.4</td><td>1.1</td><td>7.1</td><td>0.3</td></tr>
<tr><td>1890</td><td>24.2</td><td>31.5</td><td>10.0</td><td>1.1</td><td>10.7</td><td>0.9</td></tr>
<tr><td>1900</td><td>21.3</td><td>30.1</td><td>17.0</td><td>0.8</td><td>6.5</td><td>1.0</td></tr>
<tr><td>1910</td><td>29.0</td><td>34.0</td><td>18.8</td><td>0.7</td><td>9.4</td><td>1.2</td></tr>
<tr><td>1921</td><td>27.8</td><td>29.0</td><td colspan="2">16.5</td><td>11.0</td><td>0.8</td></tr>
<tr><td>1930</td><td>32.5</td><td>33.5</td><td colspan="2">18.1</td><td>14.1</td><td>0.8</td></tr>
</table>

2 In 1880 the clergymen engaged 6,703 maidservants, i.e. 2.1 percent of total sum of domestic staff.

Domestic services mostly gave jobs to women. There was an extremely small percentage of men which was constantly shrinking – to just under 1 percent by 1930.

Structure by Sex and Age

The 1880 census found among domestic servants over 70,000 men, whereas the figure fell to less than 5,000 by 1890. The number of women included in this social group between the 1880 and 1890 censuses also slumped (from 241,000 to 131,000), but their proportion inordinately grew – from 77 percent to 96 percent. The considerable discrepancy in the structure by sex of the domestic staff in 1880 compared with the following years indicates that in this year the category of domestic staff largely included agricultural workers and day labourers, probably in keeping with the surviving tradition when wage earners employed at large estates as well as small agricultural holdings were not clearly distinguished according to the type of work they executed. Therefore statistical classification was not quite clear-cut (Table 4).

Table 4. Domestic staff in the Czech Lands in 1857–1930 according to sex

Year	Total	Men	Women	Men per 100 women
1857	155,400	–	–	–
1869	317,767	–	–	–
1880	314,625	73,014	241,611	30.22
1890	135,920	4,921	130,999	3.76
1900	160,620	3,495	157,125	2.22
1910	152,547	2,648	149,899	1.77
1921	149,668	1,992	147,676	1.35
1930	152,318	896	151,422	0.59

Understandably, the employment of women in domestic services was strongly connected with their qualification. Although there was almost no illiteracy in the Czech Lands, young women had only rarely a higher than elementary education and this type of education was often ended sooner than among boys. In the country in particular early ending of compulsory school attendance (after six years of schooling, which means at the age of

12) occurred much more often among girls than boys as recently as the beginning of the twentieth century. Parents effectively pleaded the girl's duty to help in the farming when requesting ending of education for their daughters (this was the only plausible reason for an early completion of education and it could only apply to agriculture). The possibility of ending the compulsory school attendance just after six years was only cancelled in 1922 (Bulíř, 1990, 11–12). In general, the rising level of education in female population was reflected in its ability to work in a broad spectrum of professions. While in 1880 almost every fifth employed woman was classified in the category of domestic staff, it was only every seventh woman by 1930. The structure of employment of women by the main sectors also reflected changes in the employment of population during the era as a whole because the proportion of persons employed in agriculture was constantly falling to the benefit of employment not only in industry, but later also in trade and service, which corresponded with the contemporary development of the economy (Table 5).

Table 5. The structure of employed women in the Czech Lands according to the sphere of their activity in 1880–1930

Year	Agriculture	Industry	Trade	Public services	Domestic staff	Total
1880	43.5	35.2	1.0	1.2	19.0	100
1890	67.8	20.5	2.5	1.5	7.6	100
1900	43.1	32.2	4.9	3.2	16.5	100
1910	39.1	37.9	4.9	4.2	14.0	100
1921	30.9	35.5	6.1	12.5	14.9	100
1930	17.1	43.6	9.0	15.7	14.5	100

Note: Without the category "independent", but including liberal professions.

The exceptional character of employment of women in domestic services is also illustrated by a comparison with other spheres as regards the proportion of women employed in the whole relevant sphere. In agriculture this was just under one half, although their proportion was constantly falling (the 1930 census found that the proportion of the women employed in agriculture was still more than 45 percent). The figure was in various branches of industry roughly one quarter and in trade approximately one fifth. But from 1880 to 1930 the proportion of women and men working in the public sector considerably changed. This was doubly true of the civil service, education, health care and other fields, in which the initial less than one-fifth proportion of women employed in these spheres rose to over 40 percent during the fifty years. On the other hand, domestic services were still dominated by women during the whole period under observation and, since the proportion of women in domestic services was gradually rising, the profession became by 1930 a pure women's affair.

A similar trend in the importance of domestic services in employment is indicated by the differences in the intensity of employment of men and women and the proportion of domestic services in their employment. In this case, too, the statistics only gives some gross global data which are not fully comparable in time. But they make it quite plain how important the employment in domestic service was for women. Some 15 percent of all employed women worked as housemaids as recently as the inter-war period (Table 6).

Table 6. Intensity of employment of the population over 15 by sex and the proportion of women employed in individual sectors from the total of employed people in the Czech Lands in 1880–1930

Year	Proportion of employed from the population over 15		Proportion of women employed in individual sectors of all employed people			
	Men	*Women*	*Agriculture*	*Industry*	*Trade*	*Dom. staff*
1880	58.5	43.8	54.3	33.6	16.9	76.8
1890	68.1	55.9	64.4	27.6	24.6	96.4
1900	61.4	29.2	49.5	22.4	20.1	97.8
1910	63.0	30.8	51.4	25.2	16.9	98.3
1921	59.3	25.9	46.9	23.7	18.1	98.7
1930	59.5	24.7	45.4	24.3	19.4	99.4

Note: see Table 2.

The structure of domestic staff by sex in the main sectors of the economy indicates (irrespective of major discrepancies concerning the presence of men servants and housemaids) where there was the biggest demand for male manpower in domestic services. Here, too, the data were evidently twisted in the time series, as is obvious from the comparison between years 1880 and 1890. But one can still infer that a slightly higher presence of men among domestic staff was maintained in agriculture (it accounted for one fifth to one third of men servants) throughout the period under observation. The smallest number of men servants was employed in the households of traders: the figures were 16 percent in 1900 and 22 percent in 1921, while it was reportedly less than 4 percent in 1880.

Given the probable overestimation of domestic staff in agriculture the proportion of domestic staff in the sphere of trade was probably higher in this year, too. One fourth to one third of men servants were employed in the households of "others", which meant the persons employed in the civil and public service, rentiers, persons with liberal professions, etc. A comparison of the proportion of men and women employed as domestic staff is highly interesting for the sector agriculture, which accounted for a steadily falling number of housemaids (it was less than 7 percent by 1930), but it still employed over one third of all men servants. These were perhaps the men servants employed by big landowners who were often of noble origin and some of these servants were coachmen and later also personal drivers (Table 7).

Marital Status of Domestic Staff

There was a majority of single persons among the men and women employed in the domestic staff, especially in the case of women. Among them there was a considerably higher number of at least once married men than at least once married women. Given their low total number, these were not any significant social groups among men. In 1890, e.g., out of 4,921 men working as men servants 75 percent were still single, and in 1900 they were 84 percent out of 3,495. The situation was different by women. The housemaids' marital status was much more clear-cut. As many as 90–95 percent of the women employed in domestic services were usually single. Married and widowed women were rather exceptional in this social group. There were about 1–2 percent of married women in domestic services. The most clear-cut was the marital status of the women serving in agriculture, which usually meant in the country – there the proportion of single women among housemaids was up to 95 percent. Widowed (later also divorced) women taken together did not account for more than 4–5 percent and the proportion of married women was quite negligible – as little as 1–2 percent. In other spheres, where one can assume that employment was mainly an affair of urban areas, the proportion of married, widowed and divorced housemaids was on average higher by 5 percentage points. In the towns there was an evidently higher proportion of widows among housemaids.

Table 7. The structure of domestic staff according to the sectors of national economy and sex (percentage) in 1880–1930

Sector	*A-Agriculture*	*B-Industry*	*C-Trade*	*D-Rest*	*Total*
		1880			
Total	41.88	20.72	9.61	27.79	100.00
Men	62.39	11.32	3.69	22.61	100.00
Women	35.68	23.57	11.39	29.36	100.00
		1890			
Total	7.72	36.50	24.23	31.55	100.00
Men	19.93	28.23	21.03	30.81	100.00
Women	7.26	36.81	24.35	31.58	100.00
		1900			
Total	12.44	36.19	21.27	30.09	100.00
Men	22.72	27.93	15.97	33.39	100.00
Women	12.22	36.38	21.39	30.01	100.00
		1910			
Total	10.62	26.45	28.97	33.96	100.00
Men	30.82	20.43	16.92	31.84	100.00
Women	10.26	26.56	29.19	34.00	100.00
		1921			
Total	16.94	26.25	27.78	29.03	100.00
Men	31.07	21.49	21.64	25.80	100.00
Women	16.75	26.31	27.86	29.08	100.00
		1930			
Total	7.08	27.00	32.47	33.45	100.00
Men	37.05	21.76	17.19	24.00	100.00
Women	6.90	27.03	32.56	33.51	100.00

It is true that after becoming widows some older women returned to the service, which meant for them a source of livelihood. This also happened in the households in the non-agricultural environment. One can infer that these were mostly women who had had some experience with this sort of livelihood before their marriage and that working conditions for the employment of these women were probably somewhat more favourable (Table 8).

Table 8. Women employed as housemaids in agriculture and other spheres by marital status in 1880–1930

Year	*The percentage of housemaids in:*							
	Agriculture				Other sectors of economy			
	Single	Married	Widows	Divorced	Single	Married	Widows	Divorced
1890	93.0	–	–	–	90.5	–	–	–
1900	93.1	–	–	–	85.9	–	–	–
1910	95.4	1.0	3.6	–	89.3	1.6	9.1	–
1921	93.5	1.6	4.0	0.8	90.3	2.2	6.9	0.6
1930	94.6	1.4	2.8	1.2	87.6	2.9	8.2	1.4

Composition of Domestic Staff by Age

Concerning housemaids, mention must be maid of age structure. Services were mostly a domain of women at younger age. One half of housemaids was usually younger than 20 years and another third was aged 20–30 years. Only 2–3 percent were over 60. It is impossible to ignore some differences, which still survived in the structure of domestic staff according to individual sectors or differences between the domestic servants working in agriculture and in other sectors.

Although almost 80 percent of all housemaids were under 30, there was a slightly higher proportion of younger housemaids under 20 years in agriculture, while in other spheres the proportion of the youngest housemaids was still somewhat lower to the benefit of older girls. This may be connected with two circumstances: first, the length of school attendance in the country was usually shorter than in the towns until 1922, second, average age at marriage of single brides was usually lower in the country. Since the girls left service after concluding marriage, their proportion at the age of 20–30 years was on average lower in the country than in towns where the age at marriage was slightly higher and exceeded 25 years (Fialová 1985).

As a result, to be employed as a housemaid was a significant source of livelihood for young single women. This is also evidenced by the intensity of employment of single women in the position of domestic staff by age. Out of the single women aged 20–40 years about one eighth worked as housemaids, whereas at higher age the proportion was slightly falling. There was no major breakthrough over the forty-year period when data allowed examination of their age structure. Only in the years after the First World War, the intensity of employment in the youngest age group (under 20 years) started to decline considerably.

The combination of the age of housemaids and their marital status proves that work in domestic services was sought by single women as a suitable source of livelihood before a marriage. For most of them this was not any affair for their lifetime, a number of them had no qualification at all at the beginning. They mainly sought livelihood or acquisition of experience with large household management. After a couple of years they often left the service because they usually found a partner for their marriage. Obviously, just a part of them kept the job of a housemaid for a longer time, especially those who failed in their effort to get married. And the service was subsequently sought again by widowed women who stayed without any means after they had become widows. In general, the group was clearly defined along these lines, and the domestic service *de facto* meant a shorter or longer period in the life of some women who obtained that way the money required to establish their own household.

Conclusion

The proportion of the people employed in domestic services did not much change between the last quarter of the nineteenth century and the end of the first third of the twentieth century. This was evidently caused by a demand for housemaids because the system of management of middle-class households employing the domestic staff did not much change and the social status of these households still required the employment of a housemaid. Although the number of housemaids was falling in the long run in the households of the people living of agriculture and industry as well as various crafts, the fall was compensated by their joining the households of trade people, people with liberal professions and *rentiers*. Nevertheless, the proportion of households employing housemaids was not very high. Usually there was just one housemaid in a household with domestic staff and their number was more or less constant.

Evidently, the work in domestic services was a relatively short-term affair, not considered as being a life-long job – so there was no great change since the eighteenth century. This is indicated by the fact that there were some 90–95 percent of single women among those employed in domestic services. The occurrence of married and widowed women was rather exceptional and they made their living more often in the holdings of farmers than in the households of the people from other economic sectors. One half of the women employed in domestic services was usually younger than 20 years, and another third was aged 20–30 years. Those over 60 years accounted for only 2–3 percent of single housemaids.

Sources

Bevölkerung und Viehstand der im Reichsrathe vertretenen Königsreiche und Länder nach der Zählung vom 31. December 1869. II. Heft – Bevölkerung nach dem Berufe und Beschäftigung. Wien, K. K. Hof- u. Staatsdr., 1871.

Die Ergebnisse der Volkszählung und der mit derselben verbundenen Zählung der häuslichen Nutzthiere vom 31. December 1880 in den im Reichsrathe vertretenen Königreichen und Ländern, Oesterreichische Statistik I, Heft 3, Wien, K. K. Hof- u. Staatsdr., 1882.

Die Ergebnisse der Volkszählung vom 31. December 1890 in den im Reichsrathe vertretenen Königreichen und Ländern, Oesterreichische Statistik XXXIII, Wien, K. K. Hof- u. Staatsdr., 1894.

Die Ergebnisse der Volkszählung vom 31. December 1900 in den im Reichsrathe vertretenen Königreichen und Ländern, Oesterreichische Statistik LXIV, Wien, K. K. Hof- u. Staatsdr., 1902.

Die Ergebnisse der Volkszählung vom 31. December 1910 in den im Reichsrathe vertretenen Königreichen und Ländern, Oesterreichische Statistik NF III, Wien, K. K. Hof- u. Staatsdr., 1916.

Obyvatelstvo českých zemí v letech 1754–1918, díl I. 1754–1865, Česká statistika řada Dem, Praha, Česky statistický úřad, 1978, tab. 11, pp. 49–50.

Sčítání v republice Československé ze dne 15. února 1921, Československá statistika 21, Praha, Státn í úřad Statistický, 1925.

Sčítání v republice Československé ze dne 1. prosince 1930, Československá statistika 113, Praha, Státn í úřad Statistický, 1935.

References

BOHÁČ, Antonín, 1936, "Obyvatelstvo v Československé republice", *Československá vlastivěda*, řada II. Národopis, Praha Sfinx Bohumil Janda, p. 62.

BRABENCOVÁ, Jana, 1991, "Vliv migrace na věkovou a social strukturu obyvatelstva města Nymburka na přelomu 19. a 20. století", *Historická demografie,* 15, pp. 99–121.

BULÍŘ, Michal, 1990, *Základní školství v ČR (Retrospektiva let 1780–1989)*, 2. vydání (doplněné), Praha, Český statistický úřad, 1990.

COHEN, Gary B., 2000, *Němci v Praze 1861–1914*, Nakladatelství Carolinum Praha.

FIALOVÁ, Ludmila, 1985, "Příspěvek k˙možnostem studia sňatečnosti v˙českých zemích za demografické revoluce", *Historická demografie,* 9, pp. 89–122.

HAVRÁNEK, Jan, 1966, "Social Classes, Nationality Ratios and Demographic Trends in Prague 1880–1900", *Historica,* 13, Praha, pp. 171–208.

–, 1970, "Demografický vývoj Prahy v druhé polovině 19. století", *Pražský sborník historický*, 1969/1970, pp. 70–105.

–, 1973, "Úloha měst v populačním vývoji 19. století. Příklad Prahy", *Demografie,* 15, pp. 229–234.

–, 1979, "Češi v severočeských a západočeských městech v letech 1880–1930", *Ústecký sborník historický*, Ústí nad Labem, pp. 227–253.

HELEMÍKOVÁ, Jana, 2001, "Židé v Jevíčku od poloviny 19 století do roku 1938", *Historická demografie,* 25, pp. 139–155.

HORSKÁ, Pavla, 1972, "Pokus o využití rakouských statistik pro studium společenského rozvrstvení českých zemí v 2. polovině 19. století", *Československý časopis historický,* 20, pp. 648–676.

–, 1982a, "K otázce sociálního vývoje českých zemí na přelomu 19. a 20. století", *Sborník historický*, 29, Praha, pp. 119–177.

–, 1982b, "Kategorie 'samostatný' v rakouské statistice povolání (Příklad Českých zemí)", *Československý časopis historický,* 30, pp. 547–579.

–, 1983, "K ekonomické aktivitě žen na přelomu 19. a 20. století (Příklad Českých zemí)", *Československý časopis historický,* 31, pp. 711–743.

–, 1984, "Několik poznámek k vývoji socio-profesního kódu rakouské statistiky povolání", *Sborník k dějinám 19. a 20. století*, 9, Praha, pp. 41–59.

NESLÁDKOVÁ, Ludmila and DOKOUPIL, Lumír, 1997, "Židovská minorita na Moravě a její služebnictvo v době utváření moderní společnosti (1869–1938)", *Historická demografie,* 21, pp. 149–174.

PAVLÍK, Zdeněk, 1959, "Dynamika hospodářsko-společenské struktury obyvatelstva českých zemí", *Demografie,* 1, č. 3, pp. 145–155.

Fig. 1
A Lady Writing a Letter with Her Maid. Jan Vermeer, 1670, National Gallery of Ireland.

Fig. 2
The Hon. John and the Hon. Thomas Hamilton with a Negro Servant.
William Aikman, 1728, The Mellerstain Trust.

Fig. 3
The Governess. Jean-Baptiste Siméon Chardin, 1738, National Gallery of Canada, Ottawa.

Fig. 4
Back from the Market (La Pourvoyeuse).
Jean-Baptiste Siméon Chardin, 1739, Musée du Louvre (RMN), Paris.

Fig. 5
Chocolate Maid. Jean-Etienne Liotard, c. 1744–45,
Staatliche Kuntsammlungen Dresden.

Fig. 6
Thomas Hodges, College servant. L.L., 1768,
The Warden and scholars of New College, Oxford.
A male domestic servant living in a rich institution:
the disable College servant is wearing a tankard and
a bundle of clay pipes.

Fig. 7
A Lady's Maid Soaping Linen. Henry Robert Morland, c. 1765–82, Tate Gallery, London.

Fig. 8
The Cook. François Bonvin, 1846, Musée de Mulhouse.

Fig. 9
The Indiscreet Servant. François Bonvin, painted 1871,
Collection Tanenbaum, Toronto.

Fig. 10
Woman at the Fountain. François Bonvin, 1858,
The Walters Art Gallery, Baltimore.

Fig. 11
Maids of All Work. John Finnie, 1864–65, The Geffrye Museum, London.

Fig. 12
Her First Place. George Dunlop Leslie, c. 1885,
Courtesy Christopher Wood Gallery, London.

Part II

Domestic Service and the Evolution of Law

The Legal Status of Servants in Norway from the Seventeenth to the Twentieth Century

Sølvi SOGNER

> There are some positions in society which are of a kind that those who have them, can not be liberated unless the group as such becomes extinct.

These are the words of a prominent Norwegian labour historian with clear reference to domestic service.[1] In today's society, to be politically correct, everybody physically fit is expected to take care themselves of their personal and domestic needs. An important distinction is made between personal service and care. Care for the children, the sick, the handicapped and the aged people is alone acceptable.

Industrialization, technological development, a market based rather than a household based production system, a differential job spectrum – open to both women and men – have all influenced the service institution. So has the politico-ideological development, forcefully advocating liberty, equality and democratic ideas, and castigating all remnants of personal exploitation, with domestic service high on the list of unacceptable activities. Service was seen as a *dependent* position, and as such unacceptable in an egalitarian society. To serve – once a highly evaluated undertaking – has over time lost its appeal, concomitant with an upgrading of personal freedom. The medieval Popes would call themselves *servus servorum Dei,* and maybe the Pope still does. Kings would use such terms in their royal mottos, like *Ik dien.* Linguistic remnants are still found in polite terms, archaically or ironically – "your humble servant".

By the 1950s, servants were in reality an extinct species in Norway. A survey by sociologists and lawyers on a representative sample of housewives and housemaids in Oslo regarding the impact of labour-legislation

1 Edvard Bull, "Fra bøndenes og husmennenes samfunn til den organiserte kapitalisme", in Edvard Bull, *Retten til en fortid*, Oslo, 1981, p. 15.

on the servant occupation in its terminal phase, concluded with the following thesis:[2]

> The occupational relationship and the role expectations between a family and its domestic servants were patterned throughout a long tradition in a society with a preponderance of *Gemeinschaft*-characteristics. In Sir Henry Maine's terms, it was for a very long time a status-relationship and not based upon contract. The *Gesellschaft*-characteristics that today dominate in most other occupations of industrial society have not left the same marks on this time-honoured relationship. But neither do present conditions permit a continuation of a relationship on a genuine *Gemeinschaft*-basis. While the role of the housemaid is wavering between these two occupational models, its incumbents are escaping from the field as statistics show beyond any doubt. Attempts to restore the balance in the relationship through legislation has not been very successful in reversing this trend.[3]

And they added: "Few occupations have a longer tradition, and in few do more traditional patterns survive. An ahistorical approach to this occupational role would therefore of necessity be misleading".

This paper will look at the historical development of legislation with reference to the service institution in Norway. All inhabitants were directly subjugated to the same national law code from the 1270s. The judicial system required private charge in a majority of cases for a matter to be heard in court. It was thus dependent upon the initiative of ordinary men and women to bring suit. From the Middle Ages farmers were responsible for passing judgment at the local court, and the participation of laymen in the legal procedure was retained for a long time. A systematic investigation, based on legal practice, of the long term development of the servant institution will hopefully be carried out in the future.

Empirical studies of service in Norway, often based on oral sources, exist for the twentieth century.[4] A series of MA-theses from the 1970s

2 V. Aubert, T. Eckhoff and K. Sveri, *En lov i søkelyset*, Oslo, 1952; Vilhelm Aubert, "The Housemaid – An Occupational Role in Crisis", *Acta Sociologica*, Vol. I, 1955, pp. 149–158.

3 Aubert 1955, p. 149.

4 Dagfinn Slettan, *Dreng og taus i Verdal,* Oslo, 1978; Irene Storvik, "Hushjelpene i det norske bysamfunn i mellomkrigstida – med særlig vekt på Tromsø. Hushjelphold, levekår og organisering", unprinted MA-thesis in history, UiTø, 1982; Merete Wishman, "Han ville ha meg sånn hjemmekvinne. Middelklassehusmødre i Trondheim 1900–1940", unprinted MA-thesis in history, UiT, 1983; Anna Avdem, ... *gjort kva gjerast skulle. Om arbeid og levekår for kvinner på Lesja ca. 1910–1930*, Oslo, 1984; Sølvi Sogner, Hege Brit Randsborg and Eli Fure, *Fra stua full til tobarnskull*, Oslo, 1984; Ståle Dyrvik, "Hushaldsutviklinga i Norge 1800–1920", *Odense University*

onwards give empirical evidence of the development during the nineteenth century.[5] Further back in time less has been written, but some research exists.[6]

Service Obligatory According to Norwegian Law at Least from the 1200s Onwards

In the Middle Ages, the most important economic sector, agriculture, had low productivity, and human energy was in great demand. The need for labour was pronounced, and the institution of service was most important to make the wheels of production go round sufficiently fast for society to survive.[7] Servants were found in most households, even in the most modest. Slavery had been abolished in Norway between ca. 1150–1250 under

Studies in History and Social Sciences, Vol. 96. *Familien i forandring i 18- og 1900-tallet*, Odense, 1986, 33–38; Sølvi Sogner, *Far sjøl i stua*, Oslo, 1990.

5 Ellen Schrumpf, "Tjenestepike–spørsmålet i Kristiania. Tjenestepikenes kår og organisering ca. 1880–1900", unprinted MA-thesis in history, UiO, 1978; Dagfinn Slettan, Dreng og taus i Verdal, Oslo, 1978; Brita E. Wiig, "Tjenestepikehold i Kristiania i 1875", unprinted MA-thesis in history, UiO, 1980; Jan Oldervoll, "Det store oppbrotet", in Sivert Langholm & Francis Sejersted (eds), *Vandringer. Festskrift til Ingrid Semmingsen*, Oslo, 1980, 91–107; Turid Birkenes, "Byfødte og småbyfødte tjenestejenter i Kristiania i 1860-og 1870-årene", unprinted MA-thesis in history, UiO, 1983; Irene Gunnhild Iversen, "Tenestejentene i Bergen 1865–1990. Strilejenter, bergenstauser og andre tyende", unprinted MA-thesis in history, UiB, 1997.

6 Hans Magne Kvalvåg, "Tjenere som samfunnsgruppe. En undersøkelse av tjenerforhold og tjenernes lønnsnivå hos oppsitterne i det søndenfjeldske Norge", unprinted MA-thesis in history, UiB, 1974; Leif Ødegaard, "Tjenestefolk som samfunnsgruppe. En undersøkelse omkring tjenerhold og tjenerlønn i ulike sosiale lag fra Romsdal til og med Finnmark fogderi, basert på et skattemanntall fra 1711", unprinted MA-thesis in history, UiB, 1975; Ståle Dyrvik m.fl., *Norsk økonomisk historie*, Bergen, 1979, 192–193; Sølvi Sogner, "Hva kan tingbøkene fortelle om barns rettsstilling på 1600-tallet?", in Dag Michalsen and Knut Sprauten (eds), *Rett og historie. Festskrift til Gudmund Sandvik.* Oslo, 1997, pp. 82–89.

7 Carlo M. Cipolla, *Before the Industrial Revolution. European Society and Economy 1000–1700*, 1976. Third edition. London, 1993, pp. 54ff.

the influence of the Christianized State, the end of the Viking raids and slave import, and gradually former slaves became lease or free holders.[8]

Already in the middle of the thirteenth century complaints were made that "everybody now wants to go trading and no one wants to work for the farmers".[9] Later, the same complaint was repeated, again and again. Legal precautions were taken to secure enough labour and at reasonable wage. According to King Magnus Lagabøter's nationwide law 1274–1276 people with restricted property were not allowed, from Easter to Michaelmas, to go travelling in order to trade. In 1291 a general order was given that every able-bodied man or woman of restricted means was obliged to take service. Later amendments to the law, in 1364 and 1383, raised the property threshold, and laid down that the period of hiring oneself out in obligatory service was to be a full year, thus restricting the free mobility of poor people in towns as well as in the countryside. According to a royal amendment in 1384 the King's officials were responsible for supplying the "good men" in the country with workers: "... in autumn and spring the bailiffs shall drive from the towns all men and women able to work in the fields, and who have not taken steady service with the farmers".[10]

The social pattern was characterized by small farmers – either free holders or lease holders – acting within an egalitarian culture, with no serfs and no feudal system. A restricted elite based its main income on rent from individual farmers, not on manor farming. Estate or manor farming was atypical. Farm land for corn growing was limited, for climatic and topographic reasons – large areas of the country being too elevated or too far North. Norway has been a net importer of cereals from medieval time, and cattle raising has been more important than cereal growing. Individual farms or farm parcels were cultivated individually, and as a rule dependent on additional resource exploitation.

8 Tore Iversen, *Trelldommen: norsk slaveri i middelalderen*, Bergen, 1994.

9 The Frostating Law, quoted in Halvdan Koht, *Norsk bondereising*, (1926), Oslo, 1975, who discusses these questions more fully, pp. 21ff., and gives references.

10 Norges gamle Love III, R. Keyser (ed.), Christiania, 1846–95, p. 220.

The Situation of Male Servants: Alternative Opportunities

The existence and character of the rich resources outside of ordinary agriculture had an important impact on the development of the service institution. Rich fisheries were exploited for export from medieval time, and could be freely exploited for anyone able to handle a fishing line; rich forests – exploited for export from the early modern period – were likewise freely exploitable for anyone able to handle an axe. From about 1500 the economy became steadily more export-orientated and capitalistic – now also including export of minerals, copper and silver, and shipping.[11] The army and the navy represented other new work possibilities for men. Within this economy, a wide range of independent economic opportunities opened up for males, outside of service, more attractive and better paid. A telling example is how the farmers in the neighbourhood of the copper mines in Trøndelag at first made good money themselves by letting their servants work for the mining company, while paying the servants their traditional annual pay.[12] Within the existing gender-differentiated work pattern male jobs were thus the first to be professionalized, and we see that male servants disappear early. Before 1700 we lack quantitative information, but already by 1700 there was only one male servant for every two female servants.

In the 1500s we find a series of ordinances aimed at securing the supply of servants.[13] In 1539 all idle men – except tailors, shoemakers and ordinary carpenters – are ordered to take service for the duration of a year or half a year. 1557: Servants are not allowed to trade in the countryside on their own behalf. 1562: Servants in yearly service shall give notice three months in advance. Nobody can hire a servant who has left his former master without testimony, lest he pays a fine of 100 marks to the former master. 1582: Lots of idle people do not take service, but carry on a trade and the like, and for this reason servants are difficult to come by.

11 Sølvi Sogner and Hilde Sandvik, "Minors in law, partners in work, equals in worth? Women in the Norwegian economy in the 16th to the 18th centuries", in Simonetta Cavaiciocchi (ed.), *La donna nell'economia secc. XIII–XVIII*, Prato, 1990, pp. 633–653.

12 Knut Sprauten, personal communication.

13 *Lover og forordninger 1537–1605. Norsk lovstoff i sammendrag*. Edited by Harald Winge, Oslo, 1988.

Hence, the district governor and the bailiffs must see to that these people enter service or are punished.

Also, all through the same sixteenth century all tax levies have special provisions for servants. The wording of the ordinance indicates in a series of cases that servants will pay taxes on income other than their ordinary servant wages:[14] 1539: "servants who grow cereals"; 1544: "every servant man who has a trade"; 1546: "every cottar, idle man or servant man who uses the sea, a craft or a trade"; 1574: "every man on the coast who goes fishing"; 1574: "artisans, servant men, idle men, saw mill men"; in 1582 the whole gamut of taxable males is listed: "farmers, servants with full pay, cottars, settlers, servants with half pay, men on the coast who fish, rowers who are of age, every servant man who rows but is not of age, skippers, mates".

For men, alternative occupations to being a servant were a clear option, no matter the letter of the law and the obligatory service provision. Being one's own man was more attractive, than being somebody else's. This was true, probably economically but undoubtedly statuswise. If we make a quick sally forward in time, we see that when in 1814, one – for its time – extremely liberal constitution extended the vote to large contingents of the male population, it withheld the vote from "dependents", that is persons in the service of others – universal suffrage for men only came in 1899. The egalitarian ethos of society worked contrary to the ethos of service.

Law Revisions in the Seventeenth Century

In the seventeenth century, the new developments were well under way, and the need was felt for a law revision. *King Christian IVs Law* of 1604, however, was to all intents and purposes only a translation from old Norse of the national law of the 1270s. But later legislation, such as *Christian IV's Reces 1643*, while upholding and underpinning ancient norms, makes an important point of vagrancy: by upholding obligatory service for unsettled young people, society is also protecting itself against vagrancy. Chapter

14 See in H. Winge, nos. 27/13, 38, 46, 323, 335, 476.

21, book 2 treats, very characteristically, and in that order: servants, vagrants and beggars.[15]

Of servants: Servants, men and boys, wherever they serve, are legally obliged to give notice 8 weeks before moving day. If the master unduly detains them, they must declare themselves free of service at the thing or in the presence of some of the people of the parish. Does the master as a consequence hurt them bodily, he is liable to punishment. The vicar is duty bound (and punished if he detains them more than half a day) to give them proof thereof, if the ending of the service is lawfully notified, also that they are free to marry, unless they are married or betrothed to somebody. For this, the vicar receives 2 shillings from servants who work for full pay, 1 shilling from women and those who work for half pay. Does a servant or servant boy leave his service illegally, he has forfeited half his annual wage, half to his master and half to the master's master, and the person who hires him, wittingly, to pay twice as much to the rightful master and master's master.

Vagrants to be detained: If there are vagrants, who are healthy and who cannot prove that they are willing to serve for a just wage where needed, they shall immediately be arrested, unarmed if they have any rifles or guns, and be sentenced to the number of months or years in iron that they deserve, and suffer the punishment.

In even greater detail, but in the same vein, provisions regarding service were spelled out in *King Christian V's Norwegian Law 1687,* 3 – 21: "On Servants in the Countryside and in the Towns, Lodgers and Vagrants".[16] In the same Codex, 6 – 5: "On Children's Misdemeanours towards Parents, as well as those of Husbands and Wives", we find:

- *Article 5:* The Master may correct his children and servants with a stick or a branch, but not with a weapon. But if he inflicts them with a wound, with the sharp edge of a blade, or maims them, or hurts their health, he shall be punished as if a stranger had done the harm.
- *Article 6:* The Mistress has the same rights over her children and her servants.

These two articles are not included in the general section of the law dealing with servants, but in the section dealing with family authority. The

15 Christian den fjerdes recess 1643, Oslo, 1981, 2-21-1,2,3. My translation.

16 Reprinted Stavanger 1982. The section "Om Tienistefolk paa Landet og i Kiøbstæderne, Inderster og Løsgængere" is found pp. 155–158.

servants' position within the family – the character of which is a much discussed phenomenon – is here highlighted. Except for this last provision, the right of the Master and the Mistress to punish the servant bodily, these laws say nothing explicitly on how the servant is to be treated, but leaves it to local custom.

The law lays down the obligation to serve for unmarried men and women who do not have an acceptable alternative – such as running a farm, using an important trade or craft. It stipulates in great detail the conditions of how the contract with the employer is to be entered into, upheld and dissolved. The servant has clear rights within this contracting system. Labour contracts must be of a year's or half a year's duration, and can only be dissolved twice a year, at specified dates.

Interesting are the provisions directed at making a clear distinction between service and day labour. To work for a daily wage is obviously seen as a privileged position. Except for seasonal occupations like fishermen, sailors and threshers during the quiet seasons, only married people or people domiciled at farms may work for a daily wage – married people or domiciled people, not unmarried, unsettled people. Also, the right to take in lodgers is regulated. So, the escape route out of the obligatory service through marriage, getting a place to live and working as day labourers seems closed for the majority. Nobody must be idle. The main purpose seems twofold: to secure labour for the farmers, and to avoid social dropouts, vagrancy, beggary.

The 1687 Codex remained in force, and was even strengthened during the following century. According to a decree of August 9, 1754, farmers were no longer allowed to have more unmarried children above the age of 18 at home than were needed for the running of the farm. Cottars were similarly only allowed to keep at home one son and one daughter above the age of 16. All others were obliged to enter service for at least a year. Bailiffs and sheriffs should see to that the law was complied with. Also, it was forbidden to raise wages above traditional level, or give servants extra emoluments.

The Enforcement of the Law

As already mentioned, we lack systematic research as regards how these severe legal restrictions were practiced. It is indicated that local public servants at times enforced them.[17] But there are also indications that reality was less bleak than might be expected.

In Sweden the situation and the legal system were comparable to the Norwegian system. And a Swedish thesis argues that "the legislation probably did not work. No one paid any attention to the many prohibitive rules included in the law. In practice there seems to have been a rather free labour market in operation".[18] There is even a quotation relating to a statement in 1734 to the effect that the strictness of the Swedish service law was of no avail, as it only served to drive servants away to other places, i.a. to Norway [sic], in order to find a more liberal situation![19]

The cottar system in Norway such as it developed from the late seventeenth century onwards served as a safety valve. From 1670 the taxation system of Norway was based on the existing matriculated farms, and only farmers paid taxes. Each farm paid a set tax. If the farmer set up a cottage within the boundaries of his farm, he could let it to a cottar in return for lease money and labour prestations. The farmer could thus improve upon the value of his farm and secure a steady supply of labour, while taxes all the time remained the same. Cottars, on the other hand, paid no taxes, had a place to live and work to do, and were free to marry and raise a family. In fact, cottars are, to all intents and purposes, actual farm servants, only they are married farm servants and listed under a different category. At the same time, by being married, they constitute a recruiting potential for a real social group, which the unmarried servants could never aspire to become.

17 Anna Tranberg, *Ringsakboka,* Brumundal, 1993, pp. 237–245.

18 Börje Harnesk, *Legofolk. Drängar, pigor och bönder i 1700- och 1800-talens Sverige,* Umeå, 1990, p. 230.

19 B. Harnesk, p. 51.

Service Becomes the Domain of Country Born Women

The nineteenth century saw the appearance for full of a new lower class social group – consisting of cottars, day labourers, and unspecified workers – and also of a new middle class. Servants, however, could not and did not develop into a social group. Service remained on the whole a life-cycle phenomenon.

Service continued, for a time, as a training ground for children and young people. Training for a profession or to become an artisan had long been reserved for restricted groups, whereas service had been an option for everybody. Compulsory school attendance to the exclusion of other activities had to await a richer public economy in late nineteenth and beginning of the twentieth century. The traditional, almost universal character of service for all was fast disappearing through the impact of the new opportunities opening up for young people.

More liberal attitudes also came to the fore in the nineteenth century. The old servant laws seemed more and more archaic and out of step with the changing of the times. Revisions were made. The decree of 1754 was abolished in 1854. In 1891 the specific right of the Master to punish the servant bodily was abolished. Interestingly, however, the right of parents to punish their children corporally was not abolished until 1972, an indication that in the nineteenth century at least, if not before, a distinction was made between own children and servants!

In the 1890s the question of domestic service was put on the public agenda.[20] By now service had become an all-feminine profession. As we saw above, by 1700 there were two female servants for every male servant. In 1800 and 1850 the sexual proportion was still the same. But by 1900 there were four female servants for every male servant. This trend only continued. Service was the most important profession for women until the Second World War. In the nineteenth century there were more maids in towns than in the country, relative to the population, but this changed in the twentieth century, when industry provided alternative occupations also for women. Urban girls preferred industry to maid service, whereas country girls migrated to town to find work. As domestic in-living servants they found a place to live along with the job. Keeping a

20 See E. Schrumpf's thesis.

servant was steadily becoming more of a middle class and not a universal phenomenon. A class or cultural divide between mistress and maid tended to develop to the dissatisfaction of both. The initiative to revise the old servant law was typically initiated in urban surroundings.

Revisions of the Servant Law

Three times in the course of the few years from 1891–1900, female servants in Oslo organized in unions, demanding legal protection of their working rights. These first unions did not survive. Not until 1910 did a servant girls' union survive, and then only under the wings of the Labour Party. The servants claimed higher wages, improved working conditions, public hiring offices, and a new law regulating their specific profession. The law from 1687 did not function in their interest. It provided few if any rights for the servant, and left it up to the master and mistress of the house to decide on wages and leisure time. Conditions varied a great deal, according to local custom. A vigorous public debate ensued, between those who supported the servant girls on the one side and their employers on the other side. The cause was considered a threat against the "family", and hence a threat against society.

The rights and duties of master and servant respectively were asymmetric in the law, and specifications dealt mostly with the conclusion and the dissolution of the contract itself. In the course of the nineteenth century some few additions had been made to the old law of 1687. E.g. if the servant fell ill, the Master should pay for doctor's assistance during four weeks, but if the disease was immorally contracted, such as a venereal disease, the servant might be immediately dismissed. The same was true if she became pregnant. She could also be dismissed immediately if she proved untrue, was intoxicated, disobedient or recalcitrant. Obedience on the part of the servant was absolute. Only twice a year was it allowed to give notice. Working hours, leisure time, kind of work, lodging, food were not mentioned in the law at all.

Both parties felt uncomfortable with the situation. The first initiative to initiate a law more in concordance with the time came from the employers. In 1895 the housewives made a petition to the Department of Justice. Nothing happened. Again in 1898 a new petition was made, now to the Parliament. In order to create a better understanding between employers and employees, a system with testimonials was proposed, authorized by the police, and with the introduction of certain sanctions.

The servants' union disagreed. Their solution to the problems was to do away with private hiring offices and establish public ones instead. They claimed two weeks' notice for both parts, sickness assistance for up to six weeks, and declared police authorized testimonials unacceptable. Also, they demanded set working hours, a free afternoon per week, and free every other Sunday.

A parliamentary committee discussed the petition. A legal proposal was passed by a unanimous Parliament 1898, to the expressed satisfaction of the servant girls' union. The proposal was transmitted to the Justice Department. A committee was set up to revise the law. 560 local governments and 80 organizations were contacted, all venting the view of the employers. The servant girls' union was not contacted; but it may have been dissolved at this time. In 1902 a law proposal was made, far more conservative than the proposal which the Parliament had voted for four years earlier. It was not discussed, however, because of "lack of time", but there was no debate the following year either. Then it was withdrawn – a new government was in doubt about the contents, and whether a law reform was actually needed.

The revision of the law was not resumed until the 1930s. The new law was passed only in 1948, replacing the old law of 1687.[21] First it was temporary, after 1963 permanent. At this late date, law regulations of working hours and free time lagged behind realities. The parliamentary debate demonstrates that the politicians were well aware that they were only legalizing existing conditions, and not creating new reforms. The number of domestic servants was dwindling fast at this late date, approaching zero, and the servants' terms of work negotiable to their advantage.

At this late date men servants were history long since. The law text uses the gender neutral word "house help" about the servant, but when a personal pronoun is needed, it is always "she" and "her", e.g. in §5: "*She* has the right to one bath per week, in so far as the employer has a bath that can be used."

21 The full text in V. Aubert *et al.*, 1952, pp. 185–190.

Norms and Practice

The paper has mostly been concerned with norms, and hardly at all with practice, given the state of the art. We note with interest that the lawmakers in 1948 felt that they were only legalizing an already existing practice, a custom that had developed independently of the letter of the law. The historic lawmakers had not concerned themselves with the actual living and working conditions of the servants. This side of the matter had been left to local custom. The State has traditionally been reticent when it comes to intervening directly in family and household matters. And servants had, traditionally, been members of the family household. In the twentieth century this was no longer the case, at least not in the same way as it had presumably been before, and at least not in urban surroundings. When it took so long to make the much-needed revisions of the archaic servant law, it may be because of the difficulties envisaged. Housewife and housemaid were the only remaining agents at work in a very private arena, an arena undergoing fundamental changes, where angels, let alone lawmakers, might well fear to tread.

Domestic Service in Spain

Legislation, Gender and Social Practice

Aurelia MARTÍN CASARES

Throughout the history of Europe, domestic service has been filled basically by three categories of people: a) women of low economic status – we either call them maids, slaves, servants, or simply wives, daughters and mothers, b) slaves in times of slavery, and c) women immigrants when natives refuse the miserable wages and conditions offered. In Roman and Medieval Spain, domestic work was mainly performed by slaves and semi-enslaved serfs. In Early Modern Spain there were several kinds of domestic workers: a) humble relatives coming from rural areas who worked for food, lodging and dress, and had no work contract, b) maids and servants who had service contracts whose clauses were rarely fulfilled, c) young apprentices in workshops who also performed domestic work, d) slaves without any rights, and e) women – wives, daughters, etc. – who could not pay a servant of their own.[1]

In this chapter I shall analyse the emphasis and omissions of Spanish legislation – from the medieval code of the "Siete Partidas" to the "Nueva Recopilación de Leyes del Reino" compiled by Philip II – and compare it with reality, pointing out the distance between law and social practice. I shall also study the different status of the groups of domestic workers mentioned above, which underlies the sexual division of labour as well as the social perception of gender disparities, both in law and social practice. Legislation in Medieval and Early Modern Spain focused on several major fields such as: a) the affirmation of royal power, b) the regulation of taxes for the royal treasury, c) the regulation of the judiciary system and the administration of the State, and d) the transmission of patrimony and heri-

1 I would like to thank Laure Ortiz, professor of law in the University of Toulouse-Le Mirail (France) for her guidance in my research on the history of Spanish legislation regarding slavery and domestic service.

tage through the strengthening of patrilinearity and long term monogamy, punishing adultery and incest. Laws were clearly conceived to preserve the privileges of wealthy people and noblemen. Poor and insignificant social groups, such as free and slave domestic workers, only appear in a limited though significant number of legal dispositions.

Although domestic work involves a large number of people and includes multiple activities, it has not left many documentary traces. For the study of laws regarding domestic workers I have based my research primarily on legislative and court sources (legislative compilations, royal decrees, edicts and local ordinances) preserved in several Spanish Archives as well as in the Library of the Faculty of Law of the University of Granada and I have used notarial sources (service contracts, testaments, contracts of sale and purchase of slaves, licenses for working, etc.) for the study of the composition of the group and their standard of living.[2] I have also explored literary sources and have realized that Spanish Literature of the Golden Age is an amazing compound of facts and details concerning domestic service that needs to be systematically revised.

Slave and free domestic service was widespread and brought together an important number of people.[3] It was mainly an urban phenomenon, although the boundary between urban and rural life was very imprecise at the time. If there is a unifying characteristic in the domestic sector it is precisely its association with the home, since the duty of domestic workers was to cover the needs generated by the household. But contrary to the image of domestic workers being confined to the interior of the house, they performed a large number of productive activities outside the house in public spaces. Consequently, it is common to find the following expression in most service contracts: "The minor will serve in your house and outside it in whatever way you may order."[4] If the house had land or gardens, domestic work could include crop-growing and gardening. Thus, the jobs executed by domestic workers varied greatly depending on the social status of the master and the configuration of his property.

2 I have analyzed more than 3,000 documents from different archives in Spain on the topic of slavery and domestic service since I started the investigation for my doctoral thesis up till the present day.

3 Aurelia Martín Casares, *La esclavitud en la Granada del siglo XVI: género, raza y etnicidad*, Granada, Editorial Universidad de Granada, 2000, pp. 256–258.

4 "La menor os servirá en vuestra casa y fuera della en lo que mandáredes."

Free and slave domestic workers lived and slept in their masters' houses, so supervision of their productivity was constant and they were available twenty-four hours a day. They depended on their landlord for all basic needs and in many cases they worked only for food (mainly left-overs), housing (small cold rooms) and clothing, since they needed working clothes. The life and working conditions of most domestic workers were, in most cases, cruel. However, the group of domestic workers was very heterogeneous and circumstances and status varies widely. There were many factors that influenced the quality of their life, such as their professional position on the staff, their relationship with other servants, their own capacity to bear an unjust situation, the masters' character, the size of the house, etc.

The Panorama of Legislation in the Middle Ages: The 13th Century Code of the *Siete Partidas*

The territory we call Spain nowadays was a Muslim kingdom in medieval times. The penetration of Islam started in the eighth century and by the eleventh century only small territories in the north were still Christian. Islamic legislation – *sharia* – was obviously the rule at the time. The Christian army advanced from north to south during the next two centuries and by the thirteenth century the only Muslim territory in Spain was the Kingdom of Granada (consisting of the southern Andalusian provinces of Malága, Granada and Almería). Spain was at the time a mosaic of kingdoms (León, Castile, Navarre, Aragon y Catalonia) with diverse forms of legislation: local "fueros", "ordenamientos" and unwritten consuetudinal laws. The panorama was confusing, intricate and conflicting. The most important legislative compilation in the Christian territories in the Middle Ages was the "Siete Partidas", a code of law that Alfonso X "el sabio" (the learned) commissioned in order to reform the existing situation. This code of law, based mainly on Roman legislation and Spanish custom, was compiled between 1251 and 1265. Its intention was to regulate the chaotic legal situation in order to provide norms and legal dispositions that would guide future monarchs.

Slavery

Slavery was regulated and justified in the fourth section of the "Siete Partidas", the thirteenth century code mentioned above. The first law of the fourth section states that slavery is the "establishment that old times' people made so that persons who were naturally free became slaves under the property of others".[5] It affirms that the Spanish word "siervo" comes from the Latin term "servare" which means "to keep" ("guardare") in Romance (old Castilian) and the explanation given to the etymology is that in older times captives were killed, but emperors later decided to keep them and make use of them as slaves.[6] There were three ways of becoming a slave: through war, birth or sale.[7] War against the Spanish Muslims resulted in many prisoners being enslaved. Birth status was attributable to the condition of the mother. The law established that a child was a slave if the mother was a slave, no matter whether the father was free, and likewise the offspring of a free woman was equally free even if the father was a slave.[8]

It's worth pointing out that if women transmitted slavery, patrilinearity was imperative for the transmission of patrimony and nobility. The question is, why paternity was not important in slavery. The link between mother and progeny has always been obvious since babies are born from their bodies, but paternity is not evident. Since patrilineal consanguinity could not be confirmed unless women were locked up, the transmission of heritage through the father was an artificial rule. Slavery points up the difficulties of knowing who is the father, and therefore makes it clear that patrilinearity was a social invention. Slavery refers back to natural values,

5 Ley 1, Título XXI, Partida 4º.

6 "Servidumbre es postura é establecimiento que fizieron antiguamente las gentes por la qual los omes que eran naturalmente libres, se fazen siervos é se meten à señorío de otro, contra razón de natura. E siervo tomó este nome de una palabra que llaman en latín servare, que quiere dezir tanto en romance como guardar. E esta guarda fue establecida por los emperadores. Ca antiguamente todos cuantos cativavan, mataban. Mas los Emperadores tuvieron por bien y mandaron que los non matassen, mas que los guardasen y se sirviesen de ellos." Ley 1º, Título XXI, Partida 4ª.

7 "E son tres maneras de siervos. La primera es de los que se captivan en tiempos de guerra, la segunda es de los que nascen de siervas. La tercera es quando alguno es libre y se deja vender." Ley 1º, Título XXI, Partida 4ª.

8 If the mother had been freed during pregnancy, the child would also be free. Ley 2, Título XXI, Partida 4ª.

and since there was no patrimony to inherit there was no sense in vindicating patrilinearity. Ownership of land, monarchy and other privileges were transmitted man to man in Early Modern times, but since there was no honour, distinction or wealth to distribute in the case of slaves, there was no need to claim artificial patrilinear succession.

For a person to sell himself/herself legally into slavery, the medieval code of the Siete Partidas stipulates five requirements: 1) his/her consent, 2) the reception of a fraction of the price, 3) the knowledge that he/she is a free person, 4) the purchaser has to think that he/she is a slave, 5) the person sold has to be over 20 years old.[9]

The owner has the right to do whatever he/she wants with his/her slave except for killing or injuring him/her, or letting him/her starve to death unless the judge orders it so. But if the proprietor finds his slave with his wife or daughter he has the right to kill him.[10] This last clause is meant to protect patrilinearity since this was always in doubt. At the same time, slaves ill-treated by their owner could complain to the judge and if found to be true they could be sold to another purchaser who would pay the former owner.

Slaves had no right to property and they could only be witnesses in exceptional cases.[11] Christians could be sold to other Christians but it was not permitted for a free Muslim or Jew to have a Christian slave.[12] The law contemplates the liberation of the slave and defines freedom as the power everyone naturally has to make what he/she wants if not forbidden by legislation.

Criados

I would like to point out that the precise meaning of the terminology employed to designate domestic workers in medieval legislation is difficult to

9 "La una que él mismo consienta de su grado que lo vendan. La segunda que tome parte del precio. La tercera que sea sabidor que es libre. La quarta que aquel que lo compra crea que es siervo. La quinta que aquel que se faze vender, que aya veynte años arriba." Ley 1, Título XXI, Partida 4ª.

10 Ley 6, Título XXI, Partida 4ª.

11 Ley 5, Título XII, Partida 5ª.

12 Ley 8º, Título XX, Partida 4ª.

interpret, since the Spanish words "siervo" (serf), "cautivo" (captive) and "esclavo" (slave) are used as synonyms in the Siete Partidas, while the word "criado" (servant) has specific connotations although sometimes it can be interchangeable with the others. It is in fact crucial to know that the Spanish noun "criados/as", used up to the present time to designate domestic servants, means literally "those who have been brought up in the home". Etymologically, the root "criar" signifies to breed animals or to raise people. The law concerning "criados" in the Siete Partidas is under the section dedicated to "siervos" (serfs, servants) but it says that people who have been raised in the household and have no blood affiliation to the landlord cannot be exploited as servants, because a person who raises a child at home has no right over his/her properties, as well as no right to enslave or to put him/her to serve.[13] The law probably forbids the master who has raised a child to treat him/her as a slave or a servant because of social abuse. The younger the child raised by the master, the greater the control and manipulation of his/her behaviour and feelings. Just think of the celebrated fairytale "Cinderella".

The Unification of Spain and the Centralization of Early Modern Legislation

Spanish legislation tended towards centralization along with the unification of the country. In the fifteenth century, the marriage of Ferdinand and Isabel, the Catholic monarchs, entailed the union of the kingdom of Castile and the kingdom of Aragon, although at the time Castile and Aragon had different coinage and a tax had to be paid to cross the frontier. But the kingdom of Granada was still Muslim, and the formal unification of Spain did not happen until 1492, with the fall of Granada, when the Catholic monarchs signed the capitulation (surrender).[14] Even if differences between north and south, east and west were still very strong, the whole country was now united under the same Crown.

13 Ley 3º, Título XX. Partida 4ª.
14 This period has been traditionally known as the "Reconquest".

Several years after the conquest of Granada, in 1502, the subjects represented in the "Cortes" (General States of Spain), celebrated in Toledo, demanded that the Crown provide a Code of Law that would put order in the uncertainties, contradictions and gaps of the existing system. The petition gave birth to the "Leyes de Toro" promulgated in 1505 by Queen Juana, successor to her mother Isabel who had died a year before. The new code only abolished the "Siete Partidas" in case of contradiction, but it did not abolish it or other local codes for matters that had not been revised. In fact, regarding servants and slaves, the "Leyes de Toro" (1505), promulgated at the turn of the fifteenth century, maintained the validity of the medieval "Siete Partidas". Over fifty years later, King Philip II promulgated the "Nueva Recopilación de Leyes de España"[15] (New Compilation of Laws of Spain), printed in 1566. The new compilation included all the provisions, orders and decrees proclaimed by the king, who was the maximum legal authority. It was an important legislative corpus that covered a wide range of topics.

Slaves and Free Servants

The "Nueva Recopilación" did not include any new section devoted to slavery in general. And since slavery was a common phenomenon in the sixteenth century, it meant that legislation from the Middle Age was still in use. In fact, in most Andalusian cities of that period the number of slaves (whatever their origin) added up to 10 percent of the total population in urban areas,[16] in some periods even more. However, the percentage varies significantly from south to north and as we travel north their presence diminishes to 2–3 percent.[17]

15 From now on NRLE.

16 The percentage of women slaves and the reasons why they were more expensive than men is discussed in A. Martín Casares, *La esclavitud en la Granada del siglo XVI: género, raza y etnicidad,* pp. 236–243.

17 Alessandro Stella, *Histoires d'esclaves dans la péninsule ibérique*, Paris, 2001, pp. 76–77.

One can conclude that most slaves in urban areas were domestic workers as it has been recently verified that most of them were women.[18] Slave domestic workers included the following groups of people from the sixteenth century on: 1) Sub-Saharans from different ethnic groups who constituted the largest group of blacks,[19] 2) Berber and Arab North Africans, 3) Moriscos (Spanish Muslims converted by force to Christianity), 4) people from the Canary Islands, 5) Hindus or Tamils from India brought by Portuguese slave merchants and 6) Afro-Americans brought to Spain by their Spanish owners living in the Americas. The first three groups of slaves were the most numerous whereas the others only represented a small proportion.

The cities of Seville,[20] Cordoba[21] or Valencia purchased a significant number of black slaves from Portuguese and Spanish slave merchants. On the other hand coastal cities, such as Malaga or Almería, could more easily buy or capture white Arab slaves due to the proximity of north Africa.[22]

Most slaves brought to Spain as children or adolescents learned to speak Castilian very quickly but their ability to use this second language depended on the time their master took in teaching them. People whose instruction was abandoned spoke in the so-called "half language", black characters in literature generally changing 'l' for 'r' and 'r' for 'g' when speaking Castilian.

Unfortunately, most Spanish census of population do not indicate who were domestic workers and it is a very complex matter to give numbers for the whole country. I have analyzed the number of domestic servants – free and slave – in the city of Granada through the study of a census made in 1561 by the ecclesiastics.

18 Aurelia Martín Casares, "Free and freed blacks in Granada in the time of the Spanish Renaissance", in Kate Lowe and Tom Earle (eds), *Black Africans in Renaissance Europe*, Cambridge, Cambridge University Press, 2005.

19 They could be Muslims (since Islam had entered the area), Christians (since there were also Christian missions there) or animists (keeping their traditional religion).

20 A. Bernard, *Les esclaves à Séville au XVIIe siècle*, Doctoral Thesis, Université de Lyon II, 1998.

21 A. Ndamba Kabongo, *Les esclaves à Cordoue au début du XVIIe siècle (1600–1621)*, Doctoral Thesis, Université de Toulouse-Le Mirail, 1975.

22 In any case, Mediterranean trade also provided black slaves coming from the traditional trans-Saharan slave routes, Bernard Vincent, "Les noirs à Oran aux XVIe et XVIIe siècles", in B. Ares Queija and Alessandro Stella (eds), *Negros, mulatos, zambaigos: derroteros Africanos en los mundos ibéricos*, Sevilla, CSIC, 2000, pp. 59–66.

Figure 1. Domestic workers (free and slaves) and population in Granada, 1561

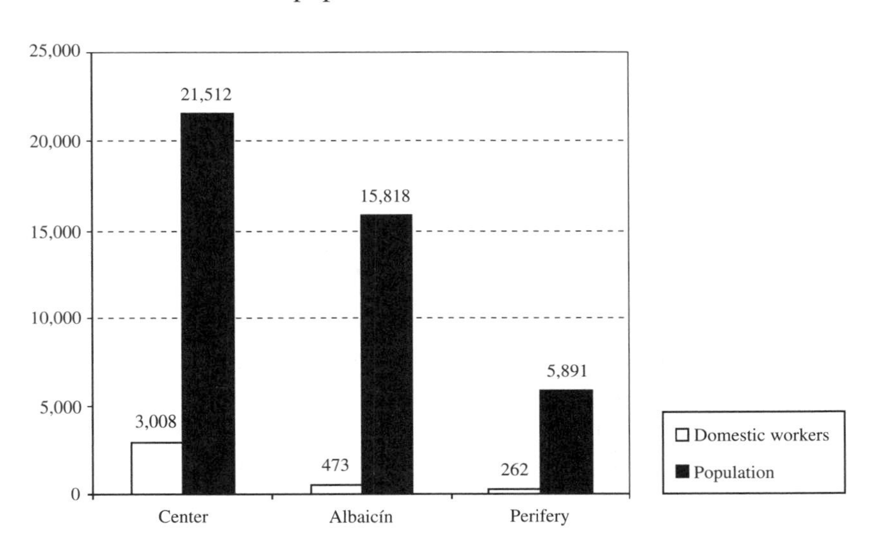

This census has the particularity of including all the people living in every house of the city, indicating the professions as well as other characteristics such as black, Morisco or slave. It is a precious source for studying the impact of domestic workers on the population of the city. In the city centre of Granada where the Christian population concentrated in 1561, the percentage of domestic workers – slaves and free people – oscillates between 10 percent and 23.40 percent depending on the district. A total of 3,008 people for 21,512 inhabitants (14 percent of the population). For every slave domestic worker there was an average of 2.6 free domestic workers.[23]

The first figure gives us an impression of the composition of free and slave domestic service in the city of Granada in relation to the total population. This graph shows the importance of domestic service and the second figure shows the numerical relationship between slaves and free domestic servants. I have not yet analysed the composition of the servant population by sex so I cannot give the results. For the slave population the number of women is higher during the whole sixteenth century and it rises

23 See the chapter on slave population in A. Martín Casares, *La esclavitud en la Granada del siglo XVI: género, raza y etnicidad,* pp. 91–138.

to 70 percent of the total number of slaves during the Morisco revolt since most men died at war.[24]

It's important to note that the census only takes into account people who could confess (referring to the Christian sacrament of confession) which happened around 9 years old, so younger servants are not included in the statistics.

The Royal Decree Concerning the Condition of Moriscos after their Revolt (1569-1571): Old Slaves and Young Servants

As I have mentioned, slavery was a widespread custom in Early Modern Spain which required the promulgation of several royal decrees, particularly concerning the condition of the prisoners taken during the Morisco revolt that took place in the Kingdom of Granada between 1569 and 1571.

Figure 2. Slave and free domestic workers in Granada, 1561

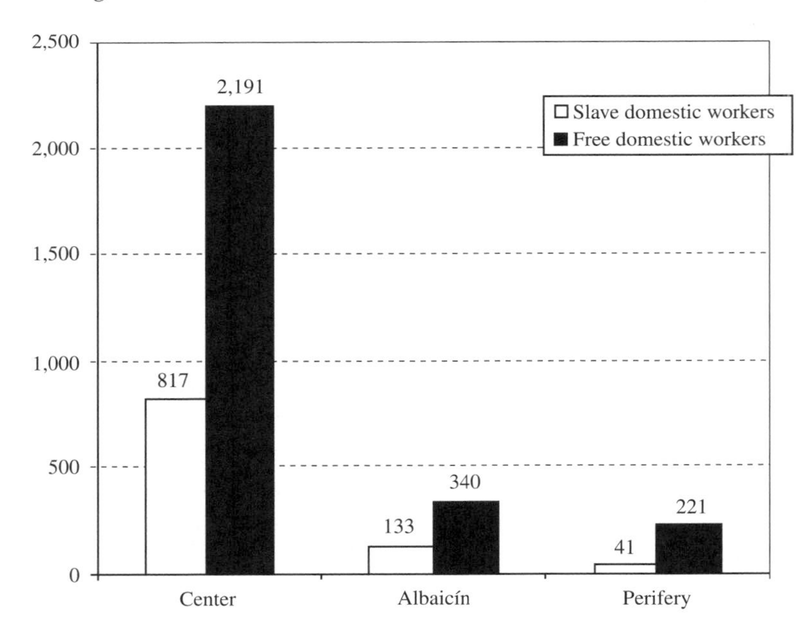

24 Aurelia Martín Casares, "Antropologia, genere e schiavitú (Granada, XVI sécolo)", *Genesis. Rivista della Società Italiana delle Storiche*, 1/2, 2002, pp. 157–172.

Indeed, the great legal question for Philip II was whether or not to enslave the Moriscos, since they were subjects of the Crown converted to Christianity through the sacrament of baptism and not all of them participated in the revolt. Philip II promulgated a decree regulating the situation on 20 July 1572.[25] The edict ordered that a register of all the Moriscos captured during the insurrection be made, indicating where they were born and captured, their age, physical features, height and face marks, profession, district where they resided. They were not allowed to change their place of residence unless approved by the priest of the district. Fugitives were punished by death.

As regards domestic service, the decree declares that Moriscos who were able to serve had to work in Christian' households. However, only one Morisco was allowed per household. The reason for isolating them was to prevent the formation of any kind of group solidarity. Legislation also stated that young children had to be raised by Christian masters who should teach them Christian customs. They could not speak Arabic, either at home or outside, under pain of very strict punishment. The Moriscos who took part in the war and were considered "captives of war" could be sold as slaves with the exception of boys under 10½ years and girls under 9½ years. Girls were sold a year earlier because they were supposed to be mature and responsible enough for work in the home earlier than boys. Younger children were considered free no matter what their sex but they had to be brought up *(criados)* by Christians and never see their parents again. The law states that they should serve in Christian households until the age of 20 and be set free thereafter.

Apart from legalizing the sale and purchase of converted Moriscos, the law regarding domestic service stated that children raised in the house could be formed according to the habits and demands of the family, no matter what their origin. Blood did not transmit heresy, raising *(criar)* children in the family circle made them vulnerable, docile and obedient and therefore suitable for servitude. Consequently, raising children for serving seems to have been a widespread tradition since medieval times that persisted into the Renaissance. Their exclusion from blood relationship put them in a defenceless position.

25 "Pragmática y declaración sobre los moriscos esclavos que fueron tomados en el reino de Granada. Y la orden que de ellos se ha de tener", Madrid, 20 julio 1572. The document has fourteen pages.

Nevertheless, documentation, such as contracts of sale and purchase, proves that many children, no matter their age, were sold as slaves as soon as the revolt began, and the royal edict mentioned above was largely ignored with the compliance of the authorities. However, judiciary records also report cases of Moriscos who litigated for their liberation, arguing that they were sold younger than legally stipulated by the king.

Servants in the Nueva Recopilación de Leyes del Reino (1566, Reprints: 1598, 1640, 1771)

Protecting Masters and Mistresses from Robbery and Aggression

Monarchs made several reprints (1598, 1640, 1771) of the Nueva Recopilación (NRLE), including new laws but maintaining the basic legal corpus. An innovation of the NRLE regarding domestic servants was the introduction of a whole section[26] with nine laws called: "De los lacayos y otros criados" (About lackeys and servants). It principally regulated the condition of people serving in wealthy households, since the law was intended to protect the privileges of noblemen. Thus it established punishments for people who bought goods from servants, since the law presumed they had stolen them from their masters' house.[27] The merchandise mentioned as susceptible of being sold by servants includes food, barley, straw, firewood, "other things used by servants" and jewellery. Slaves could not sell anything either. The Andalusian local ordinances specifically prohibited traders from buying cheese, oil, olives or jewels from slaves.[28] Hence, anyone buying goods from servants or slaves would be treated as a receiver of stolen goods.

26 Section number 20 (Título 20).

27 NRLE Ley 5. Libro 6º, Título 20. "Que los que compraren de criados algunas cosas de vianda o de servicio o alhajas de la casa sean habidos por encubridores de hurto."

28 "Los muy magníficos señores de Granada, estando juntos en el Cabildo, dixeron que por quanto son informados que los especieros y tenderos de esta ciudad que venden especias y cintas y otras cosas, compran de esclavos muchas cossas, así como queso, azeyte y aceitunas, y otras cosas que hurtan en la cassa y heredad de sus amos, y otras

The law also protected the nobility from verbal and physical aggression from their servants.[29] Insults and offences were considered a sign of infidelity and the severity of the penalty depended on the judges who would take into consideration the circumstances. If the aggression involved the use of arms and the servant who attacked was a nobleman ("hijodalgo") he would be sent to jail for 30 days and exiled for 2 years.

Luxury versus Productivity

Apart from protecting the master of the house, legislation also regulated the size of the staff of servants, since the king feared competition from aristocrats, and the number of servants was a sign of opulence and power. Law number 7 limits the number of servants any family could have, no matter its condition, to 18 people, counting gentlemen, lackeys, pages, butlers, accompanying servants and other servants high in the hierarchy.[30] Legislation affirmed that numerous servants were unnecessary and merely testified to sumptuousness and extravagance; so unprofitable servants should take a better job for the good of the Republic. It claimed that the number of servants did not increase or diminish the authority of the Prince and his Ministers and that the Royal house was the best example of austerity.

Neither noblemen nor noblewomen could have more than two lackeys or grooms.[31] However, Spanish Grandees could keep up to four lackeys. Both the master (or mistress) and the lackey were penalized, servants with

---

partes, y asimismo hurtan otras cosas como alhajas…" Ordinance dated 13-5-1528, in Recopilación de Ordenanzas de 1678. Archivo Municipal de Granada.

29 NRLE. Libro 6º, Título 20, Ley 3. "Que pone la pena en que caen los criados que injuriaren a sus señores."

30 Libro 6º, Título 20, Ley 7. "Que limita el número de criados que pueden haber en cada familia y declara a los que han de tener los consejeros y ministros."

31 The origin of this law was an edict promulgated by Philip II in Madrid, on 25 November, 1565. "Que ninguno pueda tener más de 2 lacayos o mozos de espuelas y la pena en que incurren el amo y los criados. Ni hombre ni mujer puede tener más de 2 lacayos, lacayuelos o mozos de espuela so pena de 20,000 maravedís y el lacayo será desterrado por 1 año del lugar donde sirviere. En las fiestas o justas en las que se acostumbra a sacar lacayos, por no ser aquello para continuo servicio sino para un acto y día sólo, se modere según donde se hagan las fiestas." NRLE. Libro 6º, Título 20, Ley 1.

exile for a year and lords (or ladies) with a certain payment. In order to avoid the law, masters made their servants pass for relatives, close or *protégés*, and aristocracy continued to have a large number of servants as confirmed by the repetition of the limitation of numbers of staff in the reprints of the NRLE.[32]

The large numbers serving in noble houses have given rise to the idea that servants were merely symbols of opulence.[33] The vitality of historiography regarding aristocracy and the luxury surrounding their manner of living may be the cause.[34] The staff of servants working in noble houses was numerous but it was also very hierarchical. There were two main types of domestic servant: the "oficios mayores de la casa" (superior house duties) and the "oficios menores de la casa" (inferior ones). The first were those limited by law and concerned lackeys, grooms, butlers,[35] pages, majors, etc. The second ones were not regulated by law and included a large number of people covering diversified jobs related to the primary necessities of the house: cooks, skivvies, maids, all purpose slaves, gardeners, etc. The social distance between a butler and a kitchen slave was insurmountable. But the main difference between slave and low-status free domestic servants was the fact of being or not being the property of the owner. In practice, their living conditions were frequently similar.

The "oficios mayores" implied professional specialisation, responsibility, better salaries, sumptuousness and sometimes personal relationship with the master, while the "oficios menores" were multipurpose and covered hard jobs. It's important to point out that the number of women ser-

32 NRLE. Libro 6º, Título 20, Ley 6. "Mi padre la hizo mandar el 25 nov de 1565, después en 1593 se mandó guardar por otra pragmática, no se ha observado como debía sino que se ha excedido el número de lacayos, buscando ocasiones y medios para defraudarla, y porque es muy conveniente al 'gobierno público' por cuya causa lo promulgo. De aquí en adelante se cumpla salvo en lo que toca a los Grandes que pueden tener 4 lacayos."

33 Aurelia Martín Casares and Bernard Vincent, "Esclavage et domesticité dans l'Espagne Moderne", in Alessandro Stella and Myriam Cottias (eds), *Dépendances serviles: une histoire comparée*, Paris, Editions de la Maison de l'Homme, 2004.

34 One of the first books regarding nobility in Spain was: A. Domínguez Ortiz, *Las clases privilegiadas en el Antiguo Régimen*, Madrid, Istmo, 1973.

35 A servant of the highest rank with an excellent salary consisting of 50,000 maravedís in Madrid at the time of Philip II. A. Guerrero Maylló, *Familia y vida cotidiana de una elite de poder. Los regidores madrileños en tiempos de Felipe II*, Madrid, Siglo XXI, 1993.

vants increases strikingly as we go down the scale. While men had the highest positions, the worst jobs were reserved for women. Any household needed, for its proper functioning, the performance of a large number of tasks labelled "oficios menores": taking care of garbage, sweeping, making beds, lighting fires and candles, carrying water, watering the floor, cooking, washing, sewing and ironing clothes, setting the table… an endless list of responsibilities. The fact that women throughout the ages have done these jobs has contributed greatly to the creation of a widespread image of domestic work as futile, inefficient and unproductive.[36] Furthermore, slaves and free women were also the key element among domestic workers in Early Modern Spain. This underestimation of domestic work is related to the strongly hierarchical nature and social division of labour, since women executed the least valued jobs. Its low visibility created the illusion that domestic service was an unproductive sector. Legislation restricting the number of servants never paid attention to slaves or women working in the kitchen since their function had nothing to do with sumptuousness but with hard productive work.

Working for Food, Housing and Clothing: Unpaid Workers

Domestic service was so widespread that even the lower classes employed servants.[37] But if aristocracy had numerous servants, lower-class people would have only one "all purpose servant".[38] Most low-grade servants, women and men, worked for food, housing and clothing. The legal for-

36 A. Martín Casares, "Las mujeres de los sectores populares en la Granada del siglo XVI", in VVAA, *Las mujeres y la ciudad de Granada en el siglo XVI*, Granada, Ayuntamiento, pp. 69–81.

37 M. T. Beltrán, "La accesibilidad de la mujer al mundo laboral: el servicio doméstico en Málaga a finales de la edad media", in VVAA, *Estudios Históricos y literarios sobre la mujer medieval*, Málaga, Diputación Provincial, 1990, p. 131.

38 Carmen Sarasúa, *Criados, nodrizas y amos. El servicio doméstico en la formación del mercado de trabajo madrileño 1758–1868*, Madrid, Siglo XXI, 1994, p. 108.

mula included in most service contracts was "they work for food, beverage, clothing,[39] shoes, housing and a bed to sleep in".[40]

Although some servants had working contracts, most did not. All-purpose service contracts did not demand any kind of specialization, and most servants were hired when children or adolescent. The hiring of child servants was related to two factors, firstly, the desire of a master to mould their characters, and secondly, the need of relatives to be rid of a mouth to feed. Adults engaged for domestic service were generally widows, unmarried women – and some men – and people freed from slavery. In the city of Granada, boys were hired mainly between 10 and 12 years old and girls at younger ages (around 8 years old). Boys also had higher salaries.[41] The youngest girl contracted in the documentation I have analyzed was three years old.[42] Poverty, death of parents and social exclusion were the reasons for entering domestic service. Since many of them were orphans, the curators signed the contracts.

However, even those whose salary was stipulated through a serving contract were in many cases not paid. Claims from domestic servants whose masters had died without paying them were frequent. Servants had three years in which to demand their salaries. But the NRLE stipulates that Prelates, Councillors and other Ministers' heirs should not be responsible for their relatives' debts concerning the salaries of servants unless stated in the testament or proved with documents signed by the deceased.[43] The testimony of the servants and witnesses was not taken into consideration.

Young apprentices in workshops also performed domestic work. In fact, their status was a hybrid condition between pupil and servant. Curators sometimes provided clothes for apprentices.[44] Apprentices were mainly boys and had a relatively better status than all-purpose servants.

39 A. Martín Casares: "Del vestido y la servidumbre en la Granada del siglo XVI", in Mª I. Moya and Garcia Wiedmar (eds), *Moda y sociedad: Estudios sobre educación, lenguaje e historia del vestido*, Granada, Universidad de Granada, 1998, pp. 355–365.

40 "Comer y beber y vestir y calzar y casa y cama donde duerma." Archivo de Protocolos del Colegio Notarial de Granada (from now on APG), Legajo 221, folio 297v, 1579.

41 I have studied 100 service contracts (1560–1590) preserved at the APG.

42 APG, Legajo 180, folio 448v, 1571.

43 NRLE. Libro 6º, Título 20, Ley 9.

44 "Le habeis de dar de comer e beber e casa e no otra cosa porque el vestido se lo tengo de dar yo."

Dismissal and Sexual Relationships

The NRLE regulated two other subjects: dismissal and sexual relationship with household people. Any servant who left his/her job voluntarily and without the compliance of his/her master was obliged to leave the region.[45] If the servant had been dismissed he/she could work in the same place at someone else's house.

Regarding sexuality, servants who had a relationship with any women of the house, no matter her condition or position, was penalized with a hundred lashes in public and two years' exile and the woman received the same penalty.[46] Although sexual exploitation by their masters of women domestic servants, slave or free, was the rule in Spain, victims of rape were represented as having an active role in order to consider them as guilty as men. The law specified that if the servant was a gentleman, or if the woman was a relative of the master, a young women brought up in the house ("doncella que cría en su casa") or a wet nurse, the penalty was more severe.[47] Wet nurses were common until the nineteenth century since most urban women did not breastfeed their children.[48]

The Novísima Recopilación de Leyes de España (1804)

During the seventeenth century there was a dramatic increase in the phenomenon of "esclavos cortados" – a phenomenon that Philip III tried to stop by prohibiting, in 1619, the presence of "esclavos cortados" in the country and invalidating their work permits. The king stated that enslaved persons whose owners put them to work outside their houses, even if they

45 NRLE. Libro 6º, Título 20, Ley 2. "Que los criados que se despidieren de sus señores no puedan asentar ni servir a otro señor en el mismo lugar."

46 NRLE. Libro 6º, Título 20, Ley 4. "Que pone la pena en que incurren los criados que se envolvieren y tuvieren acceso carnal con alguna mujer, criada o sirvienta de sus señores."

47 Mediators were also punished.

48 M. Vigil, *La vida de las mujeres en los siglos XVI y XVII*, Madrid, Siglo XXI, 1986, p. 126.

were obliged to give their master the wages they earned daily, lived in a freer condition which was prejudicial to the Republic. Up to a point, the "cortados" did have more autonomy, since they were not constantly under the supervision of their masters. In any event, men and women slaves working outside their masters' houses ("cortados") was a widespread phenomenon in seventeenth and eighteenth century Spain. In particular poor widows made a profit through this form of slavery. Such is the case of Doña María Bolea (1714), whose husband died in Oran, and her brother bought her a slave whom she put to work as a water-carrier, earning seven "reales" a day which allowed her to live.[49]

The political tendency in the eighteenth century was to soften the conditions of slavery in European Spain, although not at all in the American colonies. Regarding the Spanish peninsula, Charles IV promulgated in 1789 a Royal Decree recommending the amelioration of treatment towards slaves, but it was merely a recommendation and not a regulation. The British abolition movement had, no doubt, a considerable impact in Europe, which affected the Spanish rulers' position regarding slavery in the mother country. Nevertheless, one of the most celebrated journals of the capital of Spain ("Diario de Madrid") continued to published advertisements for the sale of slaves during the eighteenth century, most of them coming either from Africa or America.

Charles IV promulgated the "Novísima Recopilación de Leyes de España" (Very New Compilation of the Laws of Spain) in 1804. The "Novísima" retains all the laws gathered in the NRLE concerning domestic servants and it does not abolish slavery, since slaves sustained the Spanish colonies in the Americas. The only new regulation in this legislative compilation decrees the prohibition of renting lackeys and servants by the day.[50] A month was the minimum period allowed for employing servants either in the Court or outside.

Although slavery diminished drastically in European Spain after 1750, I have collected historical documents regarding slaves in the Spanish Court in Madrid during the nineteenth century. It is also true that they were better treated, and their humanity was more evident, while their assimilation to the animal world gradually disappeared, but this was not the

49 Archivo de la Chancillería de Granada, legajo 513, cabina 2566, pieza 25.
50 Libro 6º, Título XVI, Ley 4.

case in Cuba or Puerto Rico. If Great Britain abolished slavery in 1807, slavery in Cuba was not abolished until 1886.[51]

Gender and Domestic Work

Domestic workers used to live and sleep in their masters' houses, a circumstance that facilitated enormously the supervision of their productivity and implied their permanent availability. Their labour was basically uninterrupted and they had to be "ready to serve" their masters day and night. As I have pointed out, the division of domestic labour according to gender put the men to work in the stables taking care of horses, drivers or cooks, while women performed the less valued household tasks. While in most households there was only one servant, the staff of servants in a noble household was characterized by its great number and strict hierarchy.

Subsequently, with industrialization came the institutionalization of salaried relations of production. The creation of factories contributed to the separation of labour and personal spheres, and consequently the opposition work/family-domesticity strongly marked the roles assigned to women and men. Therefore, the domiciliary or extra domiciliary nature of work represents a central element in what is considered work.[52] Even today, domestic "obligations" are an argument that makes it more difficult for a women to enter and remain in the labour market. In our time, domestic work is still mainly done by women, apparently as a voluntarily "service", even though the reality is that it is a compulsory labour that women have to do because their socially created function is to take care of the family and the home. As Christine Delphy states: "Since domestic work, child-bearing and education are: 1) a women' responsibility and 2) unpaid

51 R. Scott, "Relaciones de clase e ideologías raciales: Acción rural colectiva en Lousiana y Cuba 1865–1912", *Historia social*, 22, 1995, pp. 127–149.

52 U. Martínez Veiga, *Mujer, trabajo y domicilio. Los orígenes de la discriminación*, Icaria-Institut Catalá d'Antropología, Barcelona, 1995, p. 25.

work, the conclusion is that women have a specific relationship with production, a relationship that is assimilable to servitude".[53]

The word "service" associated with "domestic" contributes to the construction of the ancestral collective imagery in Europe that conceptually relates the domestic sphere with the "action and effect of serving, helping and assisting". As the Dictionary of the Royal Academy of the Spanish Language[54] states, the infinitive "servir" (to serve) means: "to be subject to another person for any reason, even if it is voluntarily, doing what he wants or disposes", "to be an instrument, a machine or similar thing, for any particular purpose" and "to assist at the table bringing or distributing food and drinks".[55]

In short, "to serve" is related in the collective unconscious and the dominant ideology with subjection, gratification, helping, assisting, kitchen equipment, baseness, indecency, etc. In addition, the above-mentioned dictionary definitions present a manly image of the person to be served while the group of servants is presented as asexual and genderless. Therefore, the traditional role of women – free or slaves – in patriarchal societies throughout the history of Europe fits completely within the cited definitions. Women are, and have been customarily, the assistants, helpers and supporters serving all the members of the household, subjected to masculine power and left to inferior social positions, due precisely, among other reasons, to the so-called "domestic obligations" they have to perform graciously. At the same time, the social and symbolic order creates the impression that "women's domestic work" is done in an apparently "voluntary way".

53 C. Delphy, *Por un feminismo materialista. El enemigo principal y otros textos, Horas y horas*, Madrid, 1982, p. 13.

54 *Real Diccionario de la Lengua Española*, Madrid, 1992, pp. 1871 and 1872.

55 In order to understand the conceptual universe of "domestic service" in Spanish, I believe it is relevant to include here the meaning of the word "servicio" – service – as stated in the above-mentioned dictionary. "Present in benefit of an equal or a friend", "Portion of money offered voluntarily to the king for public property", "Set of dishes (silverware, chinaware), and other objects, to serve food, coffee, tea, etc." and "organization and staff intended to take care of the interests or satisfy the needs of the public or of a private or public entity". If we continue the search, we find that "servidumbre" – staff of servants – means: "all servants that serve the house at the same time", but it also means: "lavatory, toilet", and "servil" – servile – means "related to serfs and servants" but also "low, humble and of low esteem" and even "base, abject, grovelling, someone that acts in a servile way".

Consequently, the concept of "domestic service" takes us to a conceptual universe clearly influenced by the idea that people who perform domestic work are inferior, at different socio-cultural and economic levels, something presented as relating to their own will, their lack of talent, and even worse, to a blind adhesion to authority that emerges from their "natural" and "personal" condition.

I have tried to illustrate throughout this article that Early Modern Spanish legislation "served" the objectives of dominant social groups as well as maintaining the prevailing patriarchal order in society, and that most domestic servants were women of low status, coming from rural areas or in some way deprived. And I would like to point out that domestic work continues nowadays to be an "assigned role" for women (as opposed to an "acquired role", gained through personal talent) that they perform gratuitously, although it is economically essential for the good functioning of the Welfare State.

Domestic Service and the Law in Early Modern Japan

Mary Louise NAGATA

Laws and political policies form the framework for finding solutions for conflict. At the same time, laws and policies are often reactions to "problem" practices and are designed to prevent them. As such, laws and policies can reveal social norms such as the assumptions of how society and the social system ought to work. Laws and policies can also be the result of negotiation between people and the state through protest and other action.

This study addresses the legal and political environment of domestic service in Japan, 1600 to 1937, as it both reacted to and shaped the system of domestic service and labor in general. Sometimes laws and policies had the opposite effect from the intentions of the political and legal authorities and they changed in reaction to this disparity. At the same time, reactions to the constraints of laws and policies were sometimes violent protests and could effect changes in these laws. Thus, domestic service also shaped its legal and political environment in its interaction with other factors such as economic development and social structures.

For data the study uses a variety of sources. One source is labor contracts and miscellaneous documents from businesses in central Japan. A second source is the population registers and related research for two villages in north eastern Japan, two villages in central Japan and the city of Kyoto. A third source is secondary research on laws and policies in the regions that provide my original sources. For the twentieth century, secondary research has used sources such as women's magazines and "help wanted" advertisements. Local governments such as Kyoto City also conducted surveys of domestic service, both of women working as servants and of employers hoping to hire servants.

Japan was divided into roughly 260 domains under the Tokugawa regime. The number varies slightly over time because domains were sometimes disbanded by the central government and new domains were occasionally established. Each domain was under the administration of a domain lord who had his own economic policies for governing his domain. At the same time, most domains generally followed the policies of the central government, but could vary in how these policies were followed. Policies regarding labor migration and proto-industrial development were particularly important for shaping domestic service. Other important laws affected labor contracts, particularly pawn service contracts and debts in general.

In this study the interaction of domestic service and the law will be examined chronologically for convenience because each new development resulted from previous ones and effected new changes. The study is therefore divided into sections corresponding with centuries. The next section will address the seventeenth century and the events leading to the requirement of guarantors and labor contracts. The following section addresses the eighteenth century and the results of public and private competition for labor. Here we can easily see negotiations over law and practice. Then the study addresses the nineteenth century as one of structural changes under both the Tokugawa and Meiji regimes. Finally, the study addresses domestic service in the twentieth century followed by discussion and conclusions.

The Seventeenth Century: Labor Contracts and Guarantors

At the beginning of the seventeenth century, selling a person into service was still common and this was one of the standard ways of gaining a servant. Other methods included employing kin such as nieces, nephews or cousins and taking in the children of friends or other members of a larger network of people known and trusted by the employer. Thus, an informal network of contacts supplied domestic servants to those who needed them.

After a 1619 law prohibited the sale of people, the informal network became the main source of servants (Ishii 1979, 106–107). The sale of people devolved into two types of service agreements. One type was called "pawn service" in which a head of household borrowed money on the collateral of the labor of a member of his household. Sometimes the labor of the servant was considered the interest for the debt. Often, however, the servant received a wage for his service after the debt was repaid (Ishii 1979, 108–109).

The 1619 law actually prohibited the *permanent* sale of people so many families sent their children into service as a temporary sale and this developed into wage employment. In this agreement, the employer would pay the wage in advance for the agreed service period. The following contract written in 1753 gives an example of this arrangement. The written contract is a receipt for the advanced payment.

> Kiheiji of Kawachi province Tannan district Yamahigashi Shinden age 23 has been well known to us for years, so we stand as his guarantors and send him to work for you for a half term from this cock eleventh month until the coming dog seventh month fifteenth day so we certify. His wage is set at 85 monme of silver, which we have certainly received without mistake...[1]

When wages are paid in advance, one natural concern is keeping the servant working for the full contract period. Indeed, this was the problem negotiated during the seventeenth century. Since servants were recruited through informal relations at the beginning of the century, there was an assumption that these informal connections would provide their own enforcement. However, as the economy expanded and servants were recruited from a wider labor market, problems arose.

Usually the prospective servant would enter the household of the employer for a five-day trial period. If both parties were agreeable at the end of the period, then the contract would be finalized and the wage paid in advance. When the family of the servant had personal connections to the employer, then there was probably no problem. However, more and more employers had to use employment agents called *kuchiire* to recruit servants. In this case, the employer paid a commission to the agent to find a likely servant for him. The servant might have migrated from the rural countryside and a family representative might not be present for the final agreement and unknown to the employer. The employment agent sometimes would pocket the commission and disappear without producing the servant. Or the agent would receive the wage at the final agreement osten-

1 Guarantor Genjirō *et al.*, [to Sugiyama Zenzaemon], "Hōkōnin ukejō no koto", Labor contract, 1/11/1753, Sugiyama collection No. 87, Kyoto University Museum Archives, Kyoto. One *monme* equals 3.76 grams. Years were often identified by the Chinese calendar cycle of 12 years since the era could change at the whim of the political authorities.

sibly to send it to the family of the servant, but then pocket the money so that the servant's family received no compensation for his work. A third scam was for the agent to pocket the money he would later share with the servant. A few days later, the servant would abscond from the employer's household, sometimes stealing household valuables, and disappear. Actually, the employment agent would often send the servant to another household in a different area for the same process. The employer would lose money, labor and whatever the servant took with him. The agent would receive the commissions and share the wage and the value of the stolen goods with the servant (Nagata 2005, 111–112; Ishii 1979, 93–94).

These problems of contract enforcement were particularly acute during the latter half of the seventeenth century in the cities that were under the direct administration of the central government – Edo, Osaka and Kyoto. Rural villagers likely relied more upon the informal networks to recruit servants and enforcement was less of a problem during this early period. In an effort to control these problems the central government issued numerous laws. In 1665, servants were required to have a reliable guarantor to the contract agreement. The guarantor was required to at least be from the same province as the servant or have personal connections to the servant or his family. When the problems continued, the government enacted laws to punish the guarantors, in 1666–1668. One such law required the guarantors to have guarantors. The guarantor would be put in chains while the guarantor's guarantor found and returned the missing servant, replaced him, or reimbursed any losses incurred by the employer (Ishii 1979, 93–94).

One problem of enforcement was that many contracts were verbal. Without a written proof and the addresses of the servant and the guarantors, there was plenty of room for dispute and both servant and guarantor could easily disappear. Let me note that it was both legal and common to change one's personal name at this time. Moreover, surnames were not normally in use and technically disallowed for people who were not members of the warrior class (Nagata 1998). Of course, the religious and population investigation registers called *shūmon aratame chō* were already in common use at this time, so disappearing was not expected to be easy. However, finding an individual in the registers without knowing his present or previous address would have been extremely difficult. Moreover, urban registers did not record where people went when they moved away (Nagata 2002). One obvious action was for a contract to be drawn up that recorded all of the necessary information regarding the guarantors, their responsibilities and how to contact them (Nagata 2005, 112–113).

With the above background, the title of early modern labor contracts as "Guarantee of Service" is unsurprising. Labor contracts were usually written in three parts. The first part identified the worker with information as to name, age, family and residence as in the example given above. The first section also included any information regarding the terms of his service: from when to when for a period of so many months or years for a wage of so much as well as any details of payment, if specified. Finally, the first section always included the certification that the guarantors did indeed know the servant or his family and had known them for a long time.

The second part of the contract included promises that the servant would obey national laws as well as the laws of the employer's house and certified that the worker was indeed registered at some Buddhist temple and not a Christian or member of some other prohibited religion or sect. This last certification included specifics identifying the temple by sect, name and address. The following excerpt is an example of this part of the guarantee. Employers in Kyoto frequently had a further requirement. Kyoto municipal law prohibited any member of the warrior class without obvious business in the city from living there. One restriction was against renting or selling housing to such people. They were also restricted from finding employment (Akiyama 1980, 165–173).

> Her religious sect is traditionally Nishi Honganji. We have her temple registration and she is not a member of the prohibited Christian sect. If she should become one, tell us immediately. She will not turn her back on government prohibitions. Furthermore, she is neither a warrior, a masterless warrior nor the daughter thereof.[2]

The final section of the contract text was the guarantee that the guarantors would take care of any problems that should occur. Most contracts were specific on some details such as absconding or stealing. Others included guarantees that there would be no complaint if the servant suddenly became ill or died. In this section also, however, provisions were sometimes spelled out as to what care the employer would provide in case of illness.

2 Guarantor Roku'uemon, parent Kisanji, servant Shige, [to Kanaya Yasubei], "Hōkōnin ukejō no koto", Labor contract, 3/1776, Noguchi collection No. 289, Kyoto City Library for Historical Documents, Kyoto.

> He is to work diligently. If he should be of disservice or become ill, we will immediately find a replacement according to your direction or return his advanced wage. Of course, if he should run away with something or abscond we will find and return him and reimburse you for any lost items. As his guarantors we will take care of any difficulties that should arise so that he can work for you without delay and you will not suffer any problems.[3]

> Even after his contract period expires, as long as he continues working for you he is not to leave without notice. If this person should secretly conduct business on the side, cause you to lose money or profit, use an excessive amount of money, run away with anything or abscond, we the guarantors will certainly investigate your lost items and reimburse you so that you will not suffer from loss. No matter whatever other difficulties he may cause, we will go to the authorities and take care of it so that you will suffer no inconvenience.[4]

> If he should take anything or abscond we will immediately investigate and return any lost items so that you will suffer no loss. Whatever other difficulties Kinosuke should cause we will come the day following your notification, apologize and settle the matter so that you will not suffer the slightest trouble. If Kinosuke should become ill, then we will take him to a healing temple until he is well. Naturally, he will work diligently for you. We his guarantors will stand by this contract for however many years he works for you.[5]

Perhaps the most important part of any labor contract in early modern Japan was the signatures with witnessing marks. The contracts were written as letters addressed to the employer and usually signed by one or more guarantors, the head of the employee's home household and the employee. Each person signing the contract identified his or her relation to the employee and the contract agreement such as parent, brother, guarantor, village elder, village headman, servant, etc. Moreover, each signature is accompanied by a specific address such as "Ōmi Province, Takashima district, Kawanabe village" or "one block south of the corner of Yanagi-nobamba and Niōmon streets". These addresses were the protection for the employer that guaranteed he or any authorities could find the guarantors when problems occurred.

3 Guarantor Genjirō *et al.*, [to Sugiyama Zenzaemon]. "Hōkōnin ukejō no koto", Labor contract, 1/11/1753, Sugiyama collection No. 87, Kyoto University Museum Archives.

4 Guarantor Iketsuya Kahei, parent Hiranoya Ichibei, servant Shōhachi, [to Hiranoya Yasaburō], "Hōkōnin ukejō no koto", Labor contract, 10/1823, Endō collection No. 690, Kyoto City Library for Historical Documents.

5 Guarantor Kumamotoya Youemon, servant Kinosuke age 19, [to Toyota Matabei], "Ukejō no koto", Labor contract, 3/1860, Toyota collection, Kyoto City Library for Historical Documents.

The contracts also make it obvious that conflicts were not generally handled through the legal system. Indeed taking problems to the magistrate seems to have been a last resort. Instead, the guarantors including the servants' family were held responsible for settling any problems and only those conflicts that could not be solved in this fashion went to the courts (Nagata 2005, 113–125).

In summary, during the seventeenth century domestic service and other types of labor changed from informal dependent relations to formal wage contracts. As the economy expanded, informal connections through the kin group and other acquaintances proved insufficient for supplying the labor force. Therefore, employers had to recruit servants through formal employment agents and other routes. This meant that they often were taking total strangers into their households. This situation was ripe for many scams. The legal system instituted guarantors as the solution for the scams and labor contracts as written letters of guarantee were part of the solution.

The labor contract identified the servant, his term of service and his wage. Then it certified that he was registered with a Buddhist temple and therefore in the population registers. Moreover, the letter promised that he would obey the laws of the government and the rules of the employer's household. Finally, the guarantors promised to settle any problems, particularly reimbursing any losses and returning or replacing the servant if he absconded. However, this was only the beginning of the system as it developed over time. In the next section, I address the conflicts and changes of the eighteenth century.

The Eighteenth Century: Public and Private Competition for Labor

The incomes of local and central governments, domain lords and their retainers depended primarily upon the rice tax. During the seventeenth century the land under cultivation was expanding and this income was constantly increasing. By the early eighteenth century, however, this early expansion had slowed down. There were also other issues that are too complex to explain in this short paper and outside of the main topic. In any case, the various domain lords were most interested in maximizing their income from the rice tax and did not gain much, if any, income from proto-industrial production beyond what they could use themselves. At the same time, the national market for these industrial products was expanding, particularly for cotton and silk textiles, sake, and soy sauce brewing, and paper, not to mention mining and other products. As a result, domain lords tried to maximize their agricultural labor force while proto-industries also attracted a great amount of labor under the guise of domestic service and apprenticeship as well as casual labor.

Each domain had its own policies toward proto-industrial development and migration. Here I will give several examples of how laws and policies interacted with economic development and demography to affect labor migration for live-in employment. These examples also show how laws and policies could be the result of negotiation and conflict.

Settsu province in central Japan was located near Osaka, one of the three major cities of Tokugawa Japan and the economic center of the system. Osaka acted as the clearing-house for tax rice. The central government also licensed sake brewing for the national market in the villages of this province, especially Itami, Sannomiya and the five villages of Nada district (Yunoki 1987, 47–50).

The brewing industry attracted huge amounts of labor to Settsu. Of course, many were casual laborers working the winter season in the breweries, but there were also many spin-off professions such as coopers, malt producers and transport. This labor magnet naturally affected the policies of neighboring domains.

The policies of Tatsuno domain west of Settsu province were designed to allow for the migration of casual labor to the Settsu breweries. The domain required full and complete records of the out and return migrations of its people and set definite time limits. People could not leave until after the wheat harvest in the fall and were required to return before the rice-planting season in the spring. In 1754 the domain imposed a high tax upon villagers who were not back by the deadline, but this tax was widely protested. Twenty-three villagers protested on the riverbank of Tatsuno River that year that were arrested and chained. Eventually the domain recognized it could not enforce its restrictions without losing the labor the restrictions were designed to retain and the restrictions were eased in 1763. Instead, the domain required people leaving for labor migration to register and remain in the fields until the sixth day of the tenth month of each year. The people leaving for labor migration further increased during the Kansei era 1789–1801. The domain encouraged domestic industry such as soy sauce and sake brewing and encouraged the people of the domain to find their labor contracts locally during this era. Finally, the domain required villagers who would be away for the year to pay a fee to allow the village to hire replacement labor (Yagi 1981, 235–238).

Each domain had different circumstances and the legal negotiation could be quite different. Nihonmatsu domain in northeastern Japan provides another example of how domain laws and policies could interact with demographic and economic factors to produce results quite different from the intentions of the domain authorities.

The strain of rice under cultivation in Japan in the seventeenth and much of the eighteenth centuries was not suited to the climate of the northeast. As a result, there was either a poor harvest or no harvest more than once every two years. In the records, some decades show eight or more consecutive years of poor or no harvests. Since domain income relied upon the tax from the rice harvest that was paid half in cash and half in kind, years of poor or no harvest meant greatly reduced income for the domain. Unsurprisingly, the domain was in debt from the latter half of the seventeenth century (Nagata *et al.* 1998).

Proto-industry such as paper and silk and cash crops such as tobacco and indigo provided important income to the villagers in the domain in the early eighteenth century. In 1728, however, the domain lord prohibited or generally discouraged these developments as reducing his tax income since he was unable to directly tax these products. The domain authorities also prohibited migration out of the domain and there were no major industries in neighboring domains that might pull labor outside of the domain in spite of local laws, as was the case in Tatsuno. These harsh policies resulted in violent protests without greatly increasing the tax income. The protests culminated in a major peasant uprising in 1749. Tax rates were subsequently relaxed in years of poor harvests, but the prohibitions essentially continued until the Tenmei famine in the 1780s (Nagata *et al.* 1998).

Domestic service together with farm labor generally took the form of pawn service in this domain. The head of a household would borrow money on the collateral of the labor of a household member, often himself. Domain laws limited the length of the service contract to 3–5 years.

During the seventeenth century, inherited servants called *nago* or *fudai* were often sent into pawn service. By the mid eighteenth century, however, there were hardly any of these inherited servants remaining in these villages. Examination of the population registers of two villages in the domain, Niita and Shimomoriya, has shown that married family members, generally beginning with the head of household followed by his wife and then married son, were sent into pawn service (Nagata 2001; Nagata 2003). Of course, the greater the economic hardship, the more households borrowing money through pawn service. Since the household members entering into pawn service were usually married and entering service separately, this practice seems to have had a negative effect on fertility. In any case, fertility was greatly reduced during the eighteenth century and below replacement for its mortality regime (Nagata *et al.* 1998; Nagata 2003).

In the 1780s, particularly during the famine, domain surveys revealed that reduced population together with economic hardship had left many fields uncultivated and the population at risk. This was in spite of fertility incentives, out-migration prohibitions, and suppression of industrial development. Therefore the domain reversed its policies to encouraging proto-industry and cash crops and focused on developing a strain of rice that could prosper in the local climate. The changes took time, but at least the population decline slowed down and stabilized by the 1790s and the population began to grow from the 1840s as proto-industries such as the production of raw silk became established (Nagata *et al.* 1998). I will address how these changes affected domestic service in the nineteenth century in the following section.

The above cases reveal some of the ways in which law and policies could interact with social and economic conditions to constrain or encourage domestic service and labor migration. Moreover, while the laws were reactions against specific conditions or events and designed as preventive measures against undesirable conditions, they sometimes had unexpected results. Protests and uprisings also effected changes in the law. Thus laws and policies were the result of negotiation and change with further negotiation.

The Nineteenth Century: Structural Change and Domestic Service

The negotiations between people and political authorities through protests and other means during the eighteenth century resulted in a number of legal and political changes. Restrictions on labor migration eased for some domains and many domains moved to encourage rather than discourage proto-industry as a way of providing local income sources and maintaining the local population (Nagata 2005, 153–162). At the same time, this competition over labor also resulted in a change in the structure of employment so that more and more industries made use of casual labor where possible. Moreover, evidence shows that some employers also began to hire domestic service and farm labor on a casual labor basis. The advantage for the employers was immediate because they supplied fewer non-monetary services to casual labor employees who were hired by the day and only present when needed thus making them less expensive to use. Moreover, casual labor was easier to supply because political authorities did not see this as taking away the agricultural labor force and their tax base. If anything, the extra income earned by the casual labor increased the ability of peasants to pay their taxes. On the other hand, casual labor is invisible on the population registers because there is no long-term change in residence (Nagata 2001; Nagata 2003; Nagano 1986).

Although population registers are not the only source of information regarding domestic service, they are an important source. With the population registers of a community we can know how common domestic service was, who entered into service defined by the relations of the servants in their home households, and the timing of entering service in relation to other factors such as age or marital status. This information also allows us to see the role domestic service played in the social and economic system.

The population registers were compiled once every year and recorded all residents of a community in their households of residence, with their relation to the head of the household. This included, of course, servants. However, short contracts of less than a year and commuting arrangements in which the servant did not live-in meant that this short-term labor did not usually appear on the registers. The urban registers continued to record many servants including apprentices and other management workers in early modern businesses. The rural registers, however, reveal an apparent fall in labor migration, not just in the northeast where migration was discouraged, but also in central Japan where migration was common (Nagata 2003). This was a structural change. Other sources show that employment likely increased, but population register analysis shows that local destinations fell dramatically (Nagata 2001).

Nevertheless, these were merely new tendencies rather than sudden changes. As long as the registers were compiled, we can still see large numbers of domestic servants, or at least live-in employees described as servants. Moreover, the general pattern seems to have been a continuation of the earlier patterns of life-cycle like service in central Japan, especially Kyoto and the out-migration of non-inheriting kin from rural villages (Nagata 2003). However, a second major structural change made even this view of domestic service impossible. The system of yearly population registers ended in 1872 and changed to family registers with a census once every ten years. Unfortunately, there is no access to any census data that would show individual level social class or status. Therefore, the types of analyses and information that can be gained from the population registers, or census like data, are not possible after 1872. As a result, how common domestic service was in terms of what proportion of households employed servants, what portion of the population entered into domestic service, what classes or even the questions of feminization or whether domestic service continued to be a life-cycle profession or a life-long profession in the later nineteenth or early twentieth centuries are difficult questions to address with the available data.

Fortunately, there are other sources that provide other kinds of information. Domestic service in the late nineteenth and twentieth centuries has been addressed using a variety of sources such as magazines, books and textbooks published for women and providing advice for the wife on how to manage her servants and also advice for the young women who worked as servants. Also of interest is the study of advertisements of servant positions and women looking for employment as servants. Many regions in Japan also conducted surveys of women employed as domestic servants in the 1930s. I will address the twentieth century research in the following section.

The Meiji government set out on a course of modernization and westernization designed to enrich and strengthen the country, but primarily designed to gain the respect of western nations so they would revise their treaties with Japan that Japan saw as unequal and unfair. Part of this agenda included the establishment of mechanized factories and the encouragement of investment in modern industries. Of course, the proto-industrial development begun during the Tokugawa period was accelerated. These developments in turn accelerated trends that also began during the Tokugawa period such as the use of commuting labor rather than live-in labor in industry. There were also new developments since now women had more employment opportunities outside of domestic service such as in the newly mechanized and rationalized factories of the textile industry. Moreover, the tax system was converted to individual and household income tax rather than a tax on the rice production of villages. With the government no longer dependant upon the income from agriculture and eager to push non-agricultural industrial development, restrictions on labor migration were removed. The state also provided public education, so apprenticeship was no longer the only way to gain commercial or technical skills.

Government policy saw the economy as a dual structure. The major part of the economy continued to be "traditional" with trade, industry and employment continuing as it had previously. The spread of public education brought about some changes. Apprenticeship and service were no longer the main method for gaining basic skills in literacy and calculation. However, this merely delayed the beginning of apprenticeship or service rather than replacing it. Apprenticeship remained the main method for gaining more advanced technical skills, even after professional schools were established to provide training in the new technologies. Employers and artisans continued to see apprenticeship as the best way to develop expertise (Crawcour 1988, 403–406, 414–421; Gordon 1988).

Under these conditions, domestic service continued pretty much under the same conditions as before since apprentices and management employees in the traditional sector continued to live-in as servants and employers required other servants – usually maids – to assist in their maintenance. This situation can be seen in the advertisements in a women's magazine published in 1888 called *Jogaku Zasshi* or "Women's Studies Magazine". Employers were looking for kitchen help, babysitting, and sewing while the young women looking for employment preferred sewing and tried to avoid kitchen work. At the same time, both were amenable to work-study combinations in which a young woman would be allowed several hours a day to go to school and study in return for working for room and board or for a small wage. The advertisements also show a general assumption that maids were unmarried women in their late teens or early twenties (Yamaguchi 1967).

In short, the "negotiations" of the eighteenth century brought about the beginnings of change in the structure of industry, labor and employment practice. This can be seen in the moves toward commuting and casual labor in the early nineteenth century. Changes in the political and legal framework of society and political policies during the Meiji period only gave momentum to these changes already begun during the Tokugawa period. Domestic service at the end of the nineteenth century continued to look very much like it had in the early part of the century. However, the new trends begun from the late eighteenth century carried the seeds for new changes in the twentieth century, as we shall see in the next section.

The Twentieth Century: Domestic Service vs Other Employment

At the beginning of the twentieth century, domestic service continued to be a major source of employment for women as the "traditional sector" continued to be the mainstay of the economy until about 1920 (Crawcour 1988). One major legal and political change of the Meiji era was that local and national political authority fully encouraged modern industrial development instead of reluctantly giving in to it. One result was female factory employment in the textile industry that provided an alternative to domestic service or by-employment in traditional industries.

This change did not at first take much labor away from the services industry. Many women entered the labor market as domestic servants and subsequently went to work in factories before marriage. One young woman, Kagawa Haruko, published her diary of her experience as a maid and then as a factory worker in 1912. Domestic service as depicted by Kagawa was not very different from earlier periods. Maids were hired in their teens or early twenties and helped out with everything. Kagawa's employer was so pleased with her that the family offered to adopt her as their daughter, but she refused. This can also be taken as a sign of the times. New experiences as a factory worker or other employment were more attractive than remaining in her employer's household (Kagawa 1912/1996).

The economic and technical development that accompanied the First World War increased the importance of the modern sector in Japan's economy until it overtook the traditional sector in 1920: then began Japan's Industrial Revolution. Now women had many more opportunities for careers as office ladies or shop assistants in department stores as well as in the factories of the textile and other industries. Indeed, domestic service was certainly not the main or even the preferred choice of work for women. Umemura Matao estimates that only 7.7 percent of all employed women were domestic servants in 1906. This figure increased to 8.2 percent in 1918 and then dropped to 5.7 percent in 1920. From another viewpoint, however, Odaka Kōnosuke estimates there was one maid for every nineteen households in 1920 and one for every seventeen households in 1930. He also estimates that one out of every six employed women was a domestic servant (Hinna 1998).

These figures seem quite low compared to the impression of the early nineteenth century population registers. However, there was also some change in the structure of work and who was considered a domestic servant. Throughout much of the nineteenth century shop assistants were live-in servants and domestic servants also included young women working in inns, as kitchen help in restaurants or tea houses, and other similar service occupations as well as those helping with farm work. In the twentieth century estimates, however, Umemura and Odaka use a stricter definition of domestic servant as literally someone who helps with or does housework including cooking, sewing, and child-care, but only within a household. Part of this difference is a change in definition. However, this change also reflects a change in the structure of employment since the above service occupations would have been live-in occupations during much of the nineteenth century, but became separate commuting occupations by the early twentieth century. This also reflects a general change in larger businesses of separation between the family that owns and runs a business and the business itself and the concurrent separation of working and living space. Moreover, this evolution also effected a change in the working conditions of service positions no longer considered strictly domestic service in wages, hours of work and other factors that I will address below.

At the same time, there was a great demand for domestic service. Employing a maid became a symbol of relative affluence. According to Nishiyama Uzō in his study of Japanese architecture, middle-income housing advertised in a woman's magazine in 1906 and defined as around 165 meters square always included a room for maids (Hinna 1998). By 1918, however, households that wanted to employ maids began to find it difficult to find a maid to employ and the government began to study the problem. In a report on problems in female employment published in 1918, Morito Tatsuo identified four problems with domestic service: low wages, poor food and lodging, long hours, and overly servile labor relations (Hinna 1998). Women were apparently beginning to see domestic service as an unattractive job and this was beginning to affect the labor market.

By the 1930s the shortage in women willing to work as domestic servants as compared to the demand for servants led various local governments to conduct studies of domestic service. In Kyoto, for example, the city made a survey of women working as domestic servants or looking for work as such and households employing or hoping to employ domestic servants in 1933 and again in 1936. I summarize the results below.

From 1933 to 1936 the number of households looking to employ domestic servants showed little change. However, the number of women looking for employment as maids was greatly reduced at only 75 percent of the 1933 number while the number of women looking for other types of employment was greatly increased at 179 percent of the 1933 figure. Nevertheless, the total women looking for work was 130 percent of the 1933 figure while the women finding work was 165 percent of the 1933 figure. This shows how domestic service had become an unpopular career choice for the women of Kyoto who tended to look for and find other types of employment in great numbers. A closer look at the women who looked for work as domestic servants revealed that these women chose domestic service as a way to learn housework – something like serving apprenticeships as wives – rather than because they needed to work for economic reasons. Indeed, 32.7 of those surveyed indicated that they chose domestic service to learn housework, needlework or manners while another 17.7 percent chose domestic service for "self-improvement". Only 6.8 percent chose domestic service for economic reasons, 5.7 percent for family reasons and 2.4 percent because it was the local custom. The remainder had a wide variety of reasons each amounting to less than 1 percent of the respondents.

Most households employing maids only employed one or two maids and nearly all of the employer households were married couples. Around half of the employers had 1–3 children of primary school age or younger. While employers came from a wide variety of social backgrounds, 36.2 percent were employed in commerce and 16.7 percent were employed in industry. The latter group included activities as weaving, dyeing, spinning, tailoring and others related to the textile industry, as one might expect in Kyoto.

A little more than half of the women working as maids found work through informal contacts, either through family connections, friends or acquaintances. A third of the women used formal agencies such as the traditional employment agents (26.5 percent) or the city office (6.9 percent) for finding employment. A small number found their positions in magazine or newspaper advertisements. Similar to the contracts of the Tokugawa period, 58 percent of the women had guarantors to their contracts and the women who had guarantors were more often those who found work through formal agencies even though the formal agencies offered a separate guarantee of service. The reason given by the employers was that they did not know the background of the girls they employed well enough to trust them without a guarantor.

Of the women employed as maids, 92 percent had never been employed in any other type of work. Only 8.5 percent had worked before, mostly in factory work. On the other hand, a third of the maids remained in service for only six months or less and two thirds remained in service for eighteen months or less. These short service periods are also a carry over from at least the early nineteenth century system. About half of them changed employers once or twice, again for a variety of reasons: 11 percent left their position for employer convenience, 27 percent were dissatisfied with the employer or employer benefits and the remaining left for personal or family reasons. The most common reason for leaving a position was illness suggesting that conditions had not greatly improved since the 1918 study.

Working conditions were certainly difficult and hours were long. Most maids worked from the moment they woke up until they went to sleep. More than 70 percent worked for 17 hours per day from 5 or 6 a.m. until 10 or 11 p.m. and half of them had no free time. For those who had some free time, most had two hours per day. Similarly, 27 percent had no holidays off, but 58 percent had one or two free days per month. Wages were low compared to the number of hours they worked and were related to age and somewhat to how the maid found employment. Those who found employment through formal agencies tended to receive slightly higher wages and older girls tended to receive higher wages. However, most maids were aged 16–23 and this too was similar to the age patterns found during the Tokugawa period in the early nineteenth century (Urushiba *et al.* 1937).

In short, the surveys conducted by local authorities revealed that domestic service was a system that showed a great deal of continuity with the early modern system under the Tokugawa period in age patterns, contract length, reasons for employment, and other factors. Moreover, domestic service suffered from the trends begun in the eighteenth century. Women who were looking for work for economic reasons did not choose domestic service. There were plenty of other better paying positions available that had better working conditions and were better career choices. This was part of the reason why domestic service retained its traditional form as well as why it became unpopular. Under these conditions, it is no surprise that domestic service rapidly declined after the Second World War.

Changes in the career and job opportunities available to women as the economy changed and the unfavorable conditions of domestic service compared to other careers, however, are only one side of the story. The decline in the number of women looking for work as domestic servants also met with a response that perhaps hastened the decline as attitudes toward domestic service changed.

The change in attitude occurred not only on the part of women looking for work. Attitudes also changed with regard to employing domestic servants. In the women's magazines of the late nineteenth and early twentieth centuries there are many articles with titles that assume domestic service as a common part of family life. "Domestic service and preparing for marriage", "Using your servant", "What you need to know about being a servant", "The diary of a maid", are some article titles from magazines such as "Household journal" or "Women's study world".[6] After the First World

6 The original article titles and journals listed are "Yomeiri junbi to gejo" from *Katei Zasshi* (1899) and "Gejo no tsukai kata", "Gejo no kokoro e" and "Gejo nikki" from *Jogaku Sekai* (1902, 1906, 1910).

War, however, there is a definite change. *Shufu no tomo* or "The housewife's friend" was and continues to be one of the main journals published for married women on a monthly basis. In 1917 there are eight articles for maids with the title "What you need to know as a maid" with subtitles for laundry, cooking, or taking orders. From 1918, however, some articles begin to praise wives who do not employ servants. These titles include "Wives who do not employ servants should be honored", "Three benefits to doing away with servants", "Easygoing life without servants", and "The health and economy I gained by not hiring servants".[7] In other words, this and other journals began to encourage and teach married women to live without employing domestic servants (Yamaguchi 1967).

Already in the early nineteenth century there are records of villages where domestic servants were sometimes hired on a temporary or commuting basis such as three days per month for a year or for specific tasks (Nagano 1986). This form seems to have remained only minor form of service for nearly a century and was largely ignored in the journals and other literature. However, the general public began to pay more attention to these commuting service relationships from around 1920 and many women's journals began to advertise the advantages of employing housekeepers who did not live-in, but came once a week or were hired by the day as necessary. An association of housekeepers "Kaseifu kai, Hashutsu fu" was founded in Tokyo in 1918 for families to employ domestic servants in these commuting relations. The association provided women prepared to offer specialized services such as cooks, waitresses (personal maids), errand girls, seamstresses, laundresses, hairdressers, etc. (Yamaguchi 1967).

In summary, domestic service continued to be a common part of family life in Japan and a symbol of the middle and upper classes in the early twentieth century, but this changed after the First World War. When the modern and industrial sector of the economy overtook the traditional sector, the structure of work and employment changed. Family businesses largely separated the family and the business, as they had not done previously, and live-in apprenticeship stopped being the main way to gain technical training. This also meant there were more jobs and careers available for women as shop assistants and office workers as well as in facto-

7 The original article titles are "Jochū wo tsukawanu no wo shufu no meiyō to seyō" (10/1917), "Jochū wo haishite mitsu no rieki" (7/1918), "Jochū wo haishite ajiwatta kiraku na seikatsu" (7/1918), "Jochū haishi kara eta kenkō to keizai" (7/1918).

ries. These jobs also paid better wages with less hours than domestic service and consequently, fewer women chose to enter domestic service. Those women who entered service tended to see domestic service as a way to learn the tasks and duties of a housewife and the manners of affluent households. Moreover, they tended to find service positions through informal personal connections rather than through formal employment agencies. At the same time, the "apprentice wife" aspect of domestic service meant that domestic service retained its life-cycle aspect with most servants being young women ages 16–23 working for 6–18 months.

As the number of women entering domestic service fell while the demand remained rather high, society in the form of women's journals and other media began to encourage women to give up employing servants or employ part-time commuting housekeepers instead. At the same time, local governments established committees and associations to study and address the problems of domestic service such as low wages and long working hours. The propaganda encouraging women to stop hiring domestic servants may have resulted from these studies as a solution to the problem.

Discussion and Conclusions

This study has reviewed the relation between domestic service and the law from 1600 until 1937. This final section discusses the various ways law has affected domestic service over time.

Domestic service and the labor market in general in Japan underwent great changes during the early modern and modern periods often related to changes in laws and policies. The changes from selling people into service to service as wage labor with a labor contract and guarantors were related to legal problems and political policies sometimes directly and sometimes indirectly. Restrictions on labor migration and proto-industrial development also were lifted as a direct result of protests and other actions taken by rural villagers and these changes in law and policy brought further changes in domestic service and the structure of wage labor. The labor market competition between live-in labor such as domestic service and casual commuting labor such as that used in breweries, manufactories and later factories was another result of the eighteenth century protests and new policies for proto-industrial development under the Tokugawa system.

The fall of the Tokugawa regime and the modernization policies of the Meiji era accelerated these trends as well as bringing new changes to the labor environment. The introduction of public education meant that service and apprenticeship were no longer the main means for gaining technical training and basic education. The separation of the family from the business in family businesses was another important change, as more and more employed positions became commuting positions rather than live-in positions. In turn, this meant that women had more career choices and were less likely to turn to domestic service for economic reasons.

In spite of all these changes, domestic service in the twentieth century had many similarities with domestic service in the nineteenth century and even under the Tokugawa regime. Domestic service was still a life-cycle activity rather than a life-long profession. Girls still chose domestic service as a way to learn manners and gain experience in the tasks of a wife. Employers continued to require guarantors when they had no personal connections to a servant, but servants continued to find service positions through personal and informal connections more often than through formal employment agencies.

The persistence in the traditional form of the system was perhaps a major factor in the rapid decline in domestic service in the mid-twentieth century. There were many other job and career options for women that paid better and had better working hours and conditions than domestic service. The decline in the number of women looking for work as servants as compared to the demand for servants is therefore unsurprising. This disparity was a cause for concern during the interwar period. At the same time, social pressure against employing domestic servants also appeared. The Second World War largely brought a stop to the practice as employing domestic servants came to be considered an unnecessary luxury. This rapid change in attitude needs to be addressed further. Finally, even domestic service developed along the lines of commuting work with associations sending servants to work on a commuting basis or for specific tasks.

Domestic service in many countries followed a path of feminization and professionalization as service also changed from a life-cycle to a lifetime activity. This process, however, did not appear to take place in Japan. Service in Japan retained its life-cycle nature for live-in service. Moreover, although society perceived that servants were probably poor, uneducated girls from the countryside, these girls actually entered better paying jobs in factories and offices rather than domestic service. Servants were more often girls from more affluent families who used service as an apprenticeship for marriage. Domestic service in the strict sense of household work only may have undergone feminization during the eighteenth century or earlier, but live-in servants included apprentices even into the mid-twentieth century. Therefore, domestic service did not really undergo feminization until live-in apprentices and the traditional sector of the economy was surpassed by the modern sector after the First World War.

Domestic service, therefore, was greatly affected by the legal and political framework, not only directly, but also in how laws and policies affected the economy and the social system. There seems to be no simple and easy answer to the way domestic service developed and changed over time, or its decline in the mid to late twentieth century.

References

AKIYAMA, Kunizō, 1980, *Kinsei Kyōto chōsō hattatsu shi*, [History of the development of neighborhood groups in early modern Kyoto], Kyoto, Kyōto Hōsei Daigaku Shuppan Kyoku.

CRAWCOUR, E. Sydney, 1988, "Industrial and technological change, 1885–1920", in Peter DUUS (ed.), *The Cambridge History of Japan.* Vol. 6: The Twentieth Century, Cambridge University Press, pp. 385–450.

GORDON, Andrew, 1988, *The Evolution of Labor Relations in Japan: Heavy Industry, 1853–1955,* Cambridge, MA, Harvard University Press, 503 p.

HINNA, Kaoru, 1998, "Meiji makki kara Shōwa shoki ni okeru 'jochū' no henyō", [Change in 'maids' from the late Meiji to early Showa eras], *Shakai kagaku kenkyū, The Journal of Social Science*, Vol. 49, No. 6, pp. 31–87.

ISHII, Ryōsuke, 1979–1988, *Shinpen Edo jidai manpitsu*, [New collection of essays on the Edo period], Tokyo, Asahi Shinbunsha, 328 p.

KAGAWA, Haruko, 1996, *Jochū bōkō to jokō seikatsu*, [Domestic maid service and life as a female factory worker], in Tomoko YAMASAKI (ed.), Tokyo, Ōzorasha. Original edition, Tokyo, Fukunaga Shoten, 1912.

NAGANO, Hiroko, 1986, "Kinsei kōki joshi rōdō no henkan to tokushitsu", in Reiko HAYASHI (ed.), *Ronshū kinsei*, [Essays on early modern Japan], Tokyo, Yoshikawa Kōbunkan, pp. 103–138.

NAGATA, Mary Louise, 1998, "Name Changing Patterns and the Stem Family in Early Modern Japan: Shimomoriya", in Antoinette FAUVE-CHAMOUX and Emiko OCHIAI (eds), *House and the stem family in EurAsian perspective, Proceedings of the C18 Session, Twelfth International Economic History Congress*, August 1998, Kyoto, Nichibunchen, pp. 291–319.

–, 2001, "Labor Migration, Family and Community in Early Modern Japan", in Pamela SHARPE (ed.), *Women, Gender and Labor Migration*, London and New York, Routledge Press, pp. 60–84.

–, 2002, "Migration and Networks in Early Modern Kyoto, Japan", *International Review of Social History* (IRSH), 47, pp. 243–259.

–, 2003, "Leaving the Village for Labor Migration in Early Modern Japan", in Frans van POPPEL, Michel ORIS and James Q. LEE (eds), *The Road to Independence, Leaving Home in Western and Eastern Societies, 16th–20th Centuries*, Bern, Switzerland, Peter Lang, pp. 273–311.

–, 2005, *Labour Contracts and Labour Relations in Early Modern Central Japan*, London and New York, Curzon Routledge Press.

NAGATA, Mary Louise, KUROSU, Satomi and HAYAMI, Akira, 1998, "Niita and Shimomoriya or the Nihonmatsu Domain in the Northeastern Region of Tokugawa Japan", EurAsian Project on Population and Family History, *Working Paper Series* No. 20.

URUSHIBA, Kenryū *et al.*, 1937, *Kyōto shi ni okeru jochū ni kan suru chōsa*, [Investigation of maids in Kyoto city], Kyōto Shi Shakai Ka.

YAGI, Tetsuhiro, 1981, "Kinsei mura no seikatsu: nōson yojō rōdō wa dekasegi ni", [Early modern village life: surplus farm labor moves to labor migration], in *Tatsuno shi shi*, [Tatsuno city history] vol. 2, Tatsuno Shi Shi Hensan Senmon Iinkai ed., Tatsuno, Tatsuno City, pp. 235–238.

YAMAGUCHI, Michiko, 1967, "Kindai ni okeru 'jochū' zō no henkan: Meiji, Taishō ki no fujin zasshi wo chūshin ni", [Changes in the images of 'maids' in the modern period: examination of women's magazines during the Meiji and Taishō eras], Ōsaka Kyōei Joshi Tanki Daigaku Ronbun Shū Henshū Iinkai, [Ōsaka Kyōei Women's Junior College Essay Collection editorial committee], *Ōsaka Kyōei Joshi Tanki Daigaku Ronbun Shū*, pp. 63–77.

YUNOKI, Manabu, 1987, *Sake zukuri no rekishi*, [The history of sake brewing], Tokyo, Yūzankaku Shuppan, 363 p.

Political Reforms in the Domestic Service Sector – Aims and Impact

Karen JAEHRLING

Activities like cooking, cleaning, laundering, ironing, shopping, gardening etc. used to be considered as part of the reproductive sphere, the counterpart of the so called productive or market sphere. But this perspective is changing. It has become quite common to refer to these activities as the "domestic service sector", thereby pointing to the widely noticed trend of replacing unpaid work with market substitutes. This article deals with the political reforms that shape this process of "domestic outsourcing" (Bittmann, Matheson and Meagher 1999, 249). Concentrating on reforms in Germany, it analyses the varying means by which political interventions have tried to create additional employment and improve working conditions in this sector during the last ten years. As I will argue, even though the reforms have partly followed a sensible approach, the employment effects have been modest so far and tend to be highly overestimated. The findings of the research and evaluation projects at the Institut Arbeit und Technik (IAT) suggest that the high expectations raised by the political discussion do not take into account two central obstacles to the creation of regular employment in this sector: on the demand side, the low acceptance of prices that considerably exceed those on the informal market and, on the supply side, the difficulties in recruiting suitable employees, due to the fact that the knowledge and skills which are required in domestic services are not as low as is often assumed.

The Political Regulation of the Domestic Services Market – Some General Remarks

Before elaborating on the details of political reforms, I will begin with a short delineation of the general significance of political regulation in this area. Even though we refer to household activities as a service industry, this doesn't imply that there is a free game of Supply and Demand, free of state control and legislation. Basically, states assume two functions which influence the quantity and the quality of employment in this sector.

Firstly and most elementary, states *constitute* the market, that is they define the legal boundaries and the size of a market. In the case of the market for domestic services, they do this by acting as an employer on their own, through the provision of public services absorbing some of the services formerly provided by the family, thereby confining the scope of market activities (either *de jure* or *de facto*). And they do this by regulating supply and demand in the remaining areas, for example by restricting market access or by stimulating demand, thereby influencing the volume of traded services. Since the early 1990's this kind of political intervention has gained importance in many industries that used to be part of the public sector or were at least dominated by public companies – like the transport industry, the telecommunications industry or the health sector[1]. The provision of public services has since been partly replaced or supplemented by a policy regulating the services supplied by private contractors. Apart from regulations that *constitute* the market these policies also include regulations that *structure* the market: they frame the contractual relations in this market, which in turn has implications for the working conditions. It is useful to distinguish between three different basic models of contractual relationship.[2]

- Model 1: *a sales contract* between a domestic worker and the households demanding his or her service; in this case, the household act as a 'customer' and the domestic worker as a self-employed person. This bilateral relation (Model 1) can also be enlarged to a trilateral relation,

1 For the health sector see for example J. Le Grand and W. Bartlett, *Quasi-Markets and Social Policy*, Macmillan, Houndmills, 1993.

2 For a similar typology see Labruyère 1999, p. 4.

with an intermediary agency acting as a broker between the two sides without changing the nature of the contract (Model 1a).

- Model 2: *a contract of employment* between the domestic worker and the household demanding his or her services. In this case, the household acts as an employer and the domestic worker as a dependent employee. This bilateral relation (Model 2) can also be enlarged to a trilateral relation, with an intermediary agency acting as a broker between the two sides without changing the nature of the contract (Model 2a).
- Model 3: *a combination of both*, that is a contract of employment between a domestic worker and the service company employing him, and a sales contract between the company and the household demanding the service. In this case, the third party becomes the center of the contractual relationship.

Table 1. Models of contractual relations in domestic services

	Two parties	*Three parties*
Sales contract	Model 1	Model 1a
Employment contract	Model 2	Model 2a
Employment contract + sales contract		Model 3

Of course, these are only the basic legal alternatives and there are many hybrid forms to be found in real life. This is also due to the fact that an important share of the domestic services market is part of the informal economy, where written contracts have virtually no meaning. However, most of the employment relationships that can be found in the informal market resemble one of these variants. As to the link between contractual relation and working conditions, there are no direct and lineal implications. But the type of contract defines who is responsible for the compliance with laws determining the level of social security and with other laws related to working conditions, and this may have consequences as I will argue in the following.

Political Reforms in the Domestic Service Sector – Aims and Means

The following analysis addresses the question why, by what means and to what extent political reforms have affected the quantity and quality of employment in this sector. I will concentrate on reforms in Germany, since this has been the main focus of the research and evaluation projects at the Institut Arbeit und Technik (IAT).[3] But I will also point out the parallels with reforms in other European countries.

Throughout Europe, the *objectives* of recent political reforms in the domestic service sector have been quite similar. They are twofold and aim both at promoting regular employment and improving working conditions in this sector *and* at providing families and the elderly with affordable domestic help. There are several other aims linked to these main objectives, particularly combating informal work, and sometimes the reforms centre on specific target groups like the long-term unemployed.

Types of Financial Incentives

The most important means to achieve theses objectives have been financial incentives, either as direct payments or tax concessions, in order to reduce the costs of legal employment subject to social insurance. It is useful to rely on the three forms of contractual relationships outlined above in order to highlight important differences between the many varieties of financial subsidies. They are granted to different parties of the contractual relationship, thereby promoting one of the three forms of contractual relationships. For instance, one of the best-known subsidies that has been introduced in a European country in the 1990's is the *chèque emploi-service* (CES) in France which is granted to the demand-side, encouraging households to act as employers (Causse, Fournier and Labruyère 1998). The *chèque* facilitates the administrative tasks and entitles the employer to a tax credit amounting to 50 percent of his expenses up to a limit of

3 See C. Weinkopf 1997; S. Bittner, S. Strauf and C. Weinkopf 1999; S. Bittner and C. Weinkopf 2000; S. Bittner and C. Weinkopf 2002.

FF 45,000 per year (Le Feuvre 2000, 16). Another subsidy, the AGED *(Allocation de garde d'enfant à domicile)*, is a direct payment to families with children below the age of six, allowing them to engage a nanny. Hence, the employment relationships promoted by these subsidies come close to Model 2. By contrast, the law on "Home Service" *(hjemmeservice)* that was introduced in Denmark in 1994 encourages the creation of professional service companies. These companies are obliged to apply for a license, entitling them to a state subsidy equivalent to 50 percent of the expenditures for every "productive" working hour, i.e. every working hour sold to a customer. Hence, the contractual relationships promoted by this reform are similar to Model 3. But applying for a licence is also open to self-employed domestic workers, and an assessment of the employment effects of the reform revealed that the majority of domestic service firms covered by the scheme are very small, consisting mostly of one or two people, approaching the dominant form of contractual relations to Model 2 (Plougman and Buhl 1998).[4] The Dutch programme SVP *(Schoonmaakdiensten voor Particulieren)*, introduced in 1998, restricts access to financial subsidies from the state to companies employing long-term unemployed (Tijedens 2001, 20), thereby implementing Model 3.

Table 2. Models of contractual relations promoted by different financial subsidies

	Two parties	*Three parties*
Sales contract	Hjemmeservice (Denmark)	
Employment contract	Chèque emploi-service (France) Allocation de garde d'enfant à domicile (AGED) (France)	
Employment contract + sales contract		Schoonmaakdiensten voor Particulieren (SVP) (Netherlands)

4 See also "Assessing Domestic Service", *European Industrial Relations Review,* 313, 2000, pp. 26–27.

Political Reforms in Germany during the 1990's – The First Experiments

Political reforms in Germany have eventually resulted in the implementation of every model, one after another. In 1989, the federal government introduced a tax deduction scheme for households employing a domestic worker, thereby promoting contractual relationships similar to model 2. In the beginning, this scheme was restricted to families with at least two children under the age of 10 or a person in need of care, but it was extended to all households in 1997 (Weinkopf 2003a, 135). At the same time the government introduced a service voucher *(Haushaltsscheck)* following the French model, designated to reduce the administrative burden. Unlike in France, though, the scheme only covered employment relationships with wages higher than DM 630 (~ € 325). The reason for this is a particular regulation in Germany that exempts jobs with wages up until a certain level (termed *geringfügige Beschäftigung*) from social insurance contributions – and understandably the government wanted to restrict its subsidies to jobs subject to social insurance. Therefore only a minority of the households could benefit from this scheme, since the experiences to date both in France and Germany have shown, that the majority of the households cannot afford and often do not need more than 3–4 hours of paid domestic work per week (Bittner and Weinkopf 2002, 18). Not surprisingly then, the reform contributed only to a modest increase in regular employment, from ca. 34,000 in 1997 to 39,800 by the year 2000 (for details see Bittner and Weinkopf 2002, 19; Schupp 2002, 51).

These experiences, among other things, gave reason to other experiments at the regional and local level. Since the mid-1990s, many federal states and communities backed up companies and non-profit organizations acting as employers for domestic workers. At the end of the 1990s there were up to 100 of these professional service providers. By spreading the working hours of one employee over several households, they were able both to meet the demands of those households that only needed domestic help for a few hours per week *and* to offer their employees full time employment or at least an employment exceeding the *geringfügige Beschäftigung*. And as we know from a recent survey on working time preferences carried out in several European countries (Bielinski, Bosch and Wagner 2002) this is what a majority of employees, including women, prefer. Apart from that, there are reasons to believe that the chances of producing acceptable working conditions and of minimizing abuse will be greater if the available public financial support is channelled towards professional service providers rather than towards private households seeking to hire workers themselves. Companies are obliged to report and document many of their activities and to provide opportunities for workforce representation, while the regulations governing personal privacy act against the establishment of effective controls in private households. The isolation of domestic workers further aggravates the situation. Binding employment contracts, dismissal protection, regulation through collective agreements and health and safety issues at work can easily be ignored. It can be assumed that many people are even ignorant of the minimum regulations in this area as to register employees for statutory accident insurance. These theoretical considerations have been confirmed by our research. It consisted of a survey covering 84 professional service companies throughout Germany, and an in-depth-analysis of three service companies in North Rhine Westphalia, assessing the conditions for their success or failure in attracting customers and examining the working conditions in these companies. The results were that most of the employees, many of them with previous experiences as employees in private households, were appreciating

- that they were receiving their wages on a regular basis, even during their holidays and in case of illness;
- that they had the management backing them up in case of conflicts between the employee and the private household;
- and, above all, that they had social insurance (Bittner and Weinkopf 2002, 137ff.).

But these advantages come at a considerably higher price than those paid on the informal market. The price differential covers non-wage costs, such as social security contributions, and the granting of other benefits, such as paid holidays and sick pay, as well as overhead costs for the management and wages for "unproductive" working hours in case of insufficient incoming orders. Experiences to date show that even with sufficient incoming orders the percentage of "productive" working hours is unlikely to be higher than 70 percent of the working time, the remaining time being spent on commuting to and from work, sick leave, holiday, and qualification (Weinkopf 2003a, 138). According to the IAT-survey, even with the financial support from the state the average price charged to the customers was about € 12 in West Germany and € 9 in East Germany in 1998, and that was much more than what could be earned on the informal market, where prices could be as low as € 5 and even below, depending on the legal status of the employee (for details see Bittner, Strauf and Weinkopf 1999).

It therefore hardly comes as a surprise that the employment effects of these experiments were modest. At peak time, the number of regular jobs in service companies ranged between 1,000 and 2,000 nationwide. This is remarkable against the backdrop of the difficult conditions for creating such jobs. The willingness to pay higher prices than those prevalent on the informal market remains low and it therefore has to be considered as quite an achievement that the companies were able to generate at least some regular jobs. But it is a sobering experience if you compare the results with the expectations raised in the political discussion and also with the existing employment in the sector. Drawing on recent surveys the number of households employing a domestic help, either with or without paying social insurance, was estimated as high as 4.35 millions (for an overview see Bittner and Weinkopf 2002, 39; Schupp 2002, 58ff.).

But the problems *on the demand side* are not the only ones hampering the creation of additional employment. There is another bottleneck *at the supply side*, and this one is frequently ignored. Services to private households are often regarded as an area in which new employment opportunities for low-skill workers can be opened up. But the recruitment of suitable employees encounters several difficulties. First of all, domestic work remains a demanding work in terms of physical fitness. Many of the employees interviewed confessed that there is a big difference between doing domestic work for only a few hours per week and doing it full time, and this was something even the service companies were not able to change. Hence, not every low-skilled unemployed person can perform this kind of work. And secondly, the required skills are not as low as often assumed. Even if it is true that the level of technical skills required for such jobs tends to be low, a relatively high level of social skills is required. All approaches to promoting employment in this area require the services to be provided in individual households on a decentralized basis. Therefore, workers must be able to react flexibly to customer expectations and to work with minimum supervision. This also turned out to be one of the reasons for difficulties in the recruitment of suitable staff.

These experiences have to be taken into consideration when assessing proposals for present and future reforms. In the last part of my presentation, I will take a look on the very recent reforms implementing the recommendations of the Hartz Commission and analyse their compliance with these demands.

The Proposals of the Hartz Commission

The law implementing the recommendations of the Hartz Commission[5] came into effect in April 2003. The most important modification concerning employment in the domestic service sector is that so called "minijobs" in private households worth up to € 400 per month are taxed only an all-inclusive rate of 12 percent and are free from any other taxes or contributions to social insurance. Before that, the limit was € 325, and the all-inclusive rate for the employer was 22 percent. Combined to that, the households get a tax credit amounting to 10 percent of their expenses (up to a limit of € 510 per year). As already mentioned these jobs come with almost no social insurance. The employees are not provided with health and unemployment insurance, and their contributions to the pension scheme will not even add up to a pension that exceeds the public welfare benefit. That is to say, the core of the reform consists of a financial subsidy that encourages private households to act as employers, but this time including part-time jobs not covered by social insurance. It is now in the responsibility of the employees themselves to arrange for social protection in the case of illness, unemployment and age, hence the employment relationship is situated somewhere between model 1 and model 2. On the other hand, the scheme extends its financial subsidies to professional service companies, granting households a tax credit amounting to 20 percent of their expenses for services provided by these companies (up to a limit of € 600 per year). But this advantage is almost completely absorbed by the disadvantage of having to pay a sales tax of 16 percent in addition to

5 The so called "Hartz-Kommission", named after its chair Peter Hartz, was originally expected to develop proposals for the reform of the Federal Employment Agency, but finally came up with recommendations for the reform of the German employment policy. Its recommendations, presented shortly before the elections in September 2002, were widely discussed and had a very strong impact on a series of laws following the reelection of the government. The laws themselves were therefore also termed Hartz I, II, III and IV. The most important law for the domestic service sector is "Hartz II" ("Zweites Gesetz für moderne Dienstleistungen am Arbeitsmarkt", 23 December 2002).

the full social insurance contributions of both employers and employees. The price charged to the customer therefore is bound to be substantially higher in the case of the service company than it is in the case of the "minijob". Certainly, due to the tax credit and the reduced social insurance contributions, there is no big difference left between a "minijob" and informal work, so households may be encouraged to register their previously non-registered employees. But there are only few incentives for the employees themselves to transform their informal employment relationship into a formal relationship. This probably explains why one year after introducing the law there are only a few thousands more registered jobs in private households than before. In March 2004 there were around 47,000 jobs compared to around 24,000 in March 2003 (for details see the official statistics in Bundesknappschaft 2004, 11). Again, there is no evidence that this reform will contribute to a major increase in jobs in private households. And even if it will, the resulting jobs do not differ substantially from jobs in the informal labour market. The only winner seams to be the government, since this reform is much cheaper compared to former experiments, as it transfers the responsibility and costs for social protection to the individual employee.

Summary and Conclusion

Political reforms in the domestic service sector in Germany have shifted from model 2 to model 3 and finally (back) to model 1 of the typology outlined above, and this shift has implications for the working conditions promoted by state regulation. Whereas the first financial subsidies were restricted to jobs covered by social insurance, this is no longer true for the subsidies introduced recently following the proposals of the Hartz Commission. By passing the responsibility for social protection to the employee, they contribute to an individualization of the risks associated with working life – illness, unemployment, age. The majority of domestic workers being women, this reform reflects and reinforces the norm of the "male-breadwinner" family, where the job of the male spouse is the main source of income and social security for all family members (Ostner and

Lewis 1995, 184ff.). In our point of view, this shift points in the wrong direction; instead, our research confirms the assumption that a professionalization of the domestic service industry via service companies is best suited to address bottlenecks both on the demand side and on the supply side of the market, that is to raise the acceptance for decent prices and to overcome difficulties in recruiting employees. However, this would mean to adopt a long term perspective and to moderate expectations concerning employment effects in the short run.

References

BIELENSKI, Harald, BOSCH, Gerhard and WAGNER, Alexandra, 2002, *Wie die Europäer arbeiten wollen: Erwerbs- und Arbeitszeitwünsche in 16 Ländern*, Frankfurt a.M. [u.a.], Campus.

BITTMANN, Michael, MATHESON, George and MEAGHER, Gabrielle, 1999, "The Changing Boundary Between Home and Market: Australian Trends in Outsourcing Domestic Labour", *Work, Employment and Society,* 13, 2, pp. 249–273.

BITTNER, Susanne, STRAUF, Simone and WEINKOPF, Claudia, 1999, *Dienstleistungspools und Vermittlungsagenturen – Ergebnisse einer bundesweiten Befragung*, Graue Reihe Nr. 1999-05, Gelsenkirchen, Institut Arbeit und Technik.

BITTNER, Susanne and WEINKOPF, Claudia, 2000, "Dienstleistungspools am Scheideweg – Erfahrungen und Perspektiven der Förderung haushaltsbezogener Dienstleistungen", *WSI-Mitteilungen*, 53, 4, pp. 256–264.

BITTNER, Susanne and WEINKOPF, Claudia, 2002, *Dienstleistungspools NRW: Haushaltshilfe als professionelle Dienstleistung – Erfahrungen und Perspektiven*, Abschlussbericht der wissenschaftlichen Begleitung zu den Modellprojekten Dienstleistungspools NRW, Düsseldorf, Ministerium für Frauen, Jugend, Familie und Gesundheit des Landes Nordrhein-West.

BUNDESKNAPPSCHAFT, 2004, *Aktuelle Entwicklungen im Bereich der geringfügigen Beschäftigung*, Ausgabe 1/2004, Essen, Bundesknappschaft.

CAUSSE, Lise, FOURNIER, Christine and LABRUYÈRE, Chantal, 1998, *Les aides à domicile. Des emplois en plein remue-ménage*, Paris, Syros.

LABRUYÈRE, Chantal, 1999, "Professionnaliser les emplois familiaux. Un objectif affirmé, mais un processus encore à construire", *Céreq Bref* (Centre d'études et de recherches sur les qualifications), 125, pp. 1–4.

LE FEUVRE, Nicky, 2000, *Employment, Family and Community activities: A new balance for women and men (France),* Dublin, European Foundation for the Improvement of Living and Working Conditions.

LE GRAND, Julian and BARLETT, Will, 1993, *Quasi-Markets and Social Policy*, Houndsmill, Macmillan.

OSTNER, Ilona and LEWIS, Jane, 1995, "Gender and the Evolution of European Social Policies", in Stephan LEIBFRIED and Paul PIERSON (eds), *European Social Policy. Between Fragmentation and Integration*, Washington D.C., The Brookings Institution, pp. 159–193.

PLOUGMAN, Peter and BUHL, Sanne, 1998, *Self-Employment in Denmark Trends and Policy*, Paper presented at the Conference on Self-Employment, Burlington (Ontario), Canada 24–26 September 1998, www.ciln.mcmaster.ca/papers/seconf/denmark.pdf.

SCHUPP, Jürgen, 2002, "Quantitative Verbreitung von Erwerbstätigkeit in privaten Haushalten Deutschlands", in Claudia GATHER, Birgit GEISSLER and Maria S. RERRICH (eds), *Weltmarkt Privathaushalt. Bezahlte Haushaltsarbeit im globalen Wandel*, Münster, Westfälisches Dampfboot, pp. 50–70.

TIJDENS, Kea, 2001, *Employment, Family and Community activities: A new balance for women and men (the Netherlands)*, Dublin, European Foundation for the Improvement of Living and Working Conditions.

WEINKOPF, Claudia, 1997, "Beschäftigungsförderung im Bereich haushaltsbezogener Dienstleistungen", in Ute BEHNING (ed.), *Das Private ist ökonomisch. Widersprüche der Ökonomisierung privater Familien- und Haushaltsdienstleistungen*, Berlin, Edition Sigma, pp. 133–151.

WEINKOPF, Claudia, 2003a, "Förderung haushaltsbezogener Dienstleistungen. Sinnvoll, aber kurzfristige Beschäftigungswirkungen nicht überschätzen", *Vierteljahreshefte zur Wirtschaftsforschung*, 72, 1, pp. 133–147.

WEINKOPF, Claudia, 2003b, Minijobs und Gleitzone – Rettungsanker für zusätzliche Beschäftigung?, IAT-Report Nr. 2003-5, Gelsenkirchen, IAT.

ZIMMERMANN, Klaus, 2003, "Beschäftigungspotentiale im Niedriglohnsektor", *Vierteljahreshefte zur Wirtschaftsforschung*, 72, 1.

Promoting Domestic Workers' Human Dignity through Specific Regulation

Adelle BLACKETT

Dignity or Abolition*

Ambivalence characterizes the governance of private paid domestic work.[1]
Decent work is the aspiration of all workers.[2]

The study of domestic work "forces us to acknowledge… that, worldwide, millions of homes are workplaces, and millions of workplaces are homes".[3] But that domestic work has remained so essential to both productive and reproductive labour, yet so invisible and undervalued by the law across the ages remains one of its great paradoxes, richly explored in the papers at the Third European Union Network seminar.[4] The law at once jealously guards the public borders of the state through immigration laws, while reifying the private borders of the home despite the public

* I am grateful to McGill University for its support of this research through its Internal Research Development Fund, and to Loubna Farchakh and Ralph Mercedat for able research assistance.

1 Pierrette Hondagneu-Sotelo, *Doméstica: immigrant workers cleaning and caring in the shadows of affluence*, Berkeley, University of California Press, 2001, p. xi.

2 ILO Director-General, Decent Work Report of the Director General, International Labour Organization Conference, 87th Session, Geneva, 1999, available at http://www.ilo.org/public/english/standards/relm/ilc/ilc87/rep-i.htm.

3 See Shellee Colen and Roger Sanjek, "At Work in Homes II: Directions", in Roger Sanjek and Shellee Colen (eds), *At Work in Homes: Household Workers in World Perspective*, American Ethnological Society Monograph Series, No. 3. Washington, DC, American Anthropological Association, pp. 176–188 [as cited in Sara Dickey and Kathleen M. Adams, *Introduction: Negotiating Homes, Hegemonies, Identities and Politics* in Kathleen M. Adams and Sara Dickey (eds), *Home and Hegemony: Domestic Service and Identity Politics in South and Southeast Asia*, Ann Arbor, University of Michigan Press, 2000].

4 Servant Project, Barcelona workshop (December 2002).

activity that proliferates behind its doors. Restrictive regulation of the immigration dimensions of the trans-national "maid trade" stands in stark contrast to the abject neglect of the employment and labour law dimensions of domestics' workforce participation.

This chapter seeks to challenge this contemporary paradox. It is not, however, an attempt to review all of the ways in which this dichotomy leads to the profound marginalization of domestic workers in most industrialized societies, including throughout the European Union. Recent scholarship has effectively canvassed the extent to which these approaches provide a way for industrialized states to deliver a benefit to their citizens, largely on the backs of women and their families in subsidizing developing countries, often complicit in the exportation process.[5] Similarly, this EU Network Seminar has examined the under-regulation or under-enforcement of laws that apply to domestic workers' conditions of employment, illustrating the limited extent to which they capture the lived experiences attached to a series of occupations that have traditionally not even been considered real, skilled "work".[6] This paper will not retrace those steps.

This paper takes as its starting point that, short of significant reform, a ban on migrant domestic work, or "abolition", would be the only principled approach to ending the continued servitude of migrant domestic workers within the EU context, a position called for by some commentators.[7] Others come close to this proposal in their analyses, because of their

5 See in particular Bridget Anderson, *Doing the Dirty Work? The Global Politics of Domestic Labour,* London, Zed Books, 2000. See also Christine B. N. Chin, *In Service and Servitude: Foreign Female Domestic Workers and the Malaysian "Modernity" Project,* New York, Columbia University Press, 1998, p. 99, noting that "[w]hat had begun as a temporary solution soon became permanent for many South and Southeast Asian labor-sending countries as labor out-migration was incorporated in development policies"; Donna E. Young, "Working Across Borders: Global Restructuring and Women's Work", *Utah Law Review,* 2001, 1, p. 52, arguing that "Employers of domestic workers – who by virtue of their citizenship, class, and/or race are able to exploit global economic forces that drive women from their homes in search of remunerative jobs in other countries – plainly benefit from the law's unequal treatment of domestic workers".

6 See *Proceedings of the Servant Project,* Barcelona Seminar papers by Christer Lundh; Mary Louise Nagata; Suzy Pasleau and Isabelle Schopp.

7 See the discussion and diverging positions of principle expressed by Marie-Claude Belleau and Louise Langevin, "Le trafic des femmes au Canada: Une analyse critique

inability to extricate the identity of the domestic worker, whether migrant or not, as inherently in a position of servile subordination in the unregulated space of the domestic household.[8]

The historical approach of this EU Network Seminar has underscored the ambiguity inherent in attempts to distinguish between servitude and slavery when the two have coexisted,[9] as well as elucidate the meaning of "honour" in workplace relationships characterized by persisting overlaps between social "status",[10] "social class"[11] and race.[12] In the current context, the troubling overlap between domestic work and contemporary forms of slavery and forced labour[13] can make the appeal to abolition morally at-

---

du cadre juridique de l'embauche d'aides familiales immigrantes résidantes et de la pratique des promises par correspondance", Ottawa, Condition féminine Canada, 2001.

8 See e.g. Kristi L. Graunke, "'Just Like one of the Family': Domestic Violence Paradigms and Combating on-the-job Violence against Household Workers in the United States", *Michigan Journal of Gender and Law*, 2002, pp. 9, 131, 204, canvassing arguments for and against this position.

9 Note in particular the attention paid to this matter in Raffaella Sarti's paper, Servant Project, Barcelona workshop (December 2002).

10 In contrast, little attention is paid in contemporary legal academic scholarship to the worldwide status implications, even cultural expectation, of having paid domestic assistance in the home. In Western industrialized economies, it remains the case that the vast majority of working families cannot afford full time domestic assistance. These contrasting status dimensions warrant greater attention in analyses about the different interests at stake in domestic work analyses. For two notable exceptions see Christine B. N. Chin, as discussed infra part I and Bridget Anderson, "Just Another Job? The Commodification of Domestic Labor", in Barbara Ehrenreich and Arlie Russell Hochschild (eds), *Global Woman: Nannies, Maids and Sex Workers in the New Economy*, New York, Metropolitan Books, 2003, pp. 104, 113–114, arguing that employers "should also be aware that the very act of employing a domestic worker weaves them into a status relationship".

11 Similarly, the differences between the notions of honour, status, and social class in relation to domestic work warrant further exploration. The historical approach of the Barcelona Servant Project workshop should facilitate this kind of analysis.

12 See Donna E. Young, p. 3; Taunya Lovell Banks, "Toward a Global Critical Feminist Vision: Domestic Work and the Nanny Tax Debate", *Journal of Gender Race and Justice*, 1, 1999, p. 3, arguing for a global critical feminist analysis of domestic work.

13 See ILO, *Stopping Forced Labour*, Geneva, Global Report, 2001 pp. 29–30, available at http://www.ilo.org/dyn/declaris/declarationweb/globalreportslist?var_language=EN. See also A. Yasmine Rassam, "Contemporary Forms of Slavery and the Evolution of the Prohibition of Slavery and the Slave Trade Under Customary International Law", *Virginia Journal of International Law*, 39, 1999, pp. 303, 327–328; Joy M. Zarembka, "America's Dirty Work: Migrant Maids and Modern-Day Slavery", in Barbara Ehrenreich and Arlie Russel Hochschild (eds), *Global Woman: Nannies, Maids, and Sex*

tractive. Indeed, abolition would provide a stark way for the EU to attempt a clear break with the legacy of servitude so deeply intertwined with the workplace and cultural identity that is referred to as European. As a result, the tremendous ideological and ethical hurdles that accompany rejection of this claim are simply posited here for future reflection, but are by no means underestimated.

The abolitionist approach, however principled in the abstract, none the less requires one to look askance at the myriad of complex reasons why women decide to leave their homes to provide for their families abroad,[14] while also in some cases seeking to reclaim their own autonomy and identity in resistance to patriarchal expectations.[15] These reasons compel women to cross borders, whether they do so legally or not, and indeed whether they have full prior knowledge of the implications of their choices, or (as is usually the case) not.

An attempt simply to ban migrant domestic work would overlook the shifting boundary of legality, particularly when one recalls how many women perform this work beyond the shadow of the law: *les sans papiers…*[16] Legality and illegality are constructed in relation to the movement of persons and citizenship rights, in ways that perpetuate disadvantage for women and men who are defined as outsiders. These constructions leave work beyond the shadow of the law as the only realis-

---

Workers in the New Economy, New York, Metropolitan Books, 2003, p. 142; Kristi L. Graunke, pp. 150–171.

14 See Rhacel Salazar Parreñas, "The Care Crisis in the Philippines: Children and Transnational Families in the New Global Economy", in Barbara Ehrenreich and Arlie Russel Hochschild (eds), *Global Woman: Nannies, Maids, and Sex Workers in the New Economy,* New York, Metropolitan Books, 2003, p. 39, offering a thoughtful discussion of the hardship faced by families left behind.

15 For a succinct discussion of the reasons, pointing to a myriad of articles from around the world in the same collection that contribute to our understanding of this dynamic, see Janet Henshall Momsen, Conclusion: "Future trends and trajectories", in Janet Henshall Momsen (ed.), *Gender, Migration and Domestic Service*, London, Routledge, 1999. For a valuable discussion of the different migration theories, especially as they apply to women, see Joan Fitzpatrick and Katrina R. Kelly, "Gendered Aspects of Migration: Law and the Female Migrant", *Hastings International and Comparative Law Review,* 47, 1998, p. 22.

16 See in particular Bridget Anderson, "Overseas Domestic Workers in the European Union: Invisible Women", in Janet Henshall Momsen (ed.), *Gender, migration and domestic service,* London, Routledge, 1999, pp. 117–118, recalling that, in the EU, domestic workers account for an important part of the undocumented, and particularly vulnerable, pool of female labour.

tic option. Indeed, a ban on the status (migrant) rather than on the occupation (domestic worker) runs the risk of entrenching the workers' marginality, thereby accentuating the precarious character of their irregular situation.

And, of course, a ban on the occupation (domestic work in private homes, particularly of the live-in variety) would sidestep attempts to grapple with the root-causes affecting why women's traditional "labour of love" is so undervalued, de-skilled once it is taken as separate from "mothering"[17] and instead relegated to the realm of non-productive, un-skilled, "dirty" work for marginalized, racialized, "other" women.[18] Middle class women's "productive" labour market participation is made viable because "other" women are performing "their" invisible reproductive/"non-productive" work in the home. Gendered and racialized distributions of labour remain undisturbed.[19] Domestic work in transnational context therefore should force a problematization, not only of the persisting unequal domestic distribution, deskilling and undervaluing of women's work in industrialized countries in the EU, but also in the countries from which foreign domestic workers have come. Yet the status quo simply forces disenfranchised women to shoulder the brunt of the inequality, as their readily available labour in the home remains unacknowledged, indeed invisible, under the law. This is true even in states that have invested considerable energy into regulating domestic workers' conditions of employment, as they tend in practice to exclude from their scope those women who perform the labour on a clandestine basis.[20]

Arguably the most important factor that affects a decision on whether to promote a ban on migrant domestic work is that domestic workers tend

17 See generally Martha Fineman, *The Neutered Mother, The Sexual Family and Other Twentieth Century Tragedies*, 1995.

18 See in particular Dorothy E. Roberts, "Spiritual and Menial Housework", *Yale Journal of Law and Feminism*, 9, 1997, p. 51.

19 See Kristi L. Graunke, pp. 190–192, offering a difficult discussion of middle class women's inability/ failure to achieve a renegotiation of the domestic division of labour between men and women. Unfortunately, and as Kristi L. Graunke recognizes, these discussions may overemphasize the private capacity of women to strike individual bargains in the home when the broader society has not fundamentally challenged expectations of "mothering" and deeply racialized and gendered visions of domestic responsibilities. And, of course, many discussions on the topic assume a white, Western nuclear family containing a male breadwinner with whom domestic tasks may in theory be shared…

20 See S. Pasleau and I. Schopp's chapter in the present volume.

to call instead for decent working conditions, work that respects their human dignity.[21] Taking their concerns seriously would entail characterizing European identity in a manner that includes these "other" women, rather than attempting to close international borders on them in an attempt to seal out social inequities.[22] Indeed, for a Europe already characterized on immigration matters as "fortress Europe", to head down the abolitionist route without a clear mandate from the persons most affected by the decision would yield tremendous cynicism, if not outright alarm.

Short of a ban, domestic work in the EU requires robust legal regulatory interventions, of the nature that can only be promoted if domestic work is treated both and at once as work like any other, and as work like no other. In other words, its distinctiveness must be acknowledged in the specificity of the regulation, a specificity that valorizes its character as real work requiring recognized skills, with inherent social and economic value, and whose workers merit respect. Yet regulatory approaches (or the relative lack thereof) in relation to working conditions have reinforced the perception that "[p]aid domestic work is distinctive [...] in being regarded as something other than employment".[23] The explanations for this phenomenon abound, and involve a complex intertwining of the invisibility of work performed in the private, non-productive female sphere, diminished when the worker is a member of a subordinated, racialized, and often immigrant community who performs the labour of love for a menial pay, and

21 See e.g. *Building Respect! Migrant Domestic Workers in Europe share advice and experiences,* with contributions from workers and staff at WALING-WALING/UWA and KALAYAAN, UK, KASAPI, Greece, CCEM/ BABAYLAN, France, IN VIA/ POLSKA RADA SPOLECZNA, Germany, VOMADE/MPDL, Spain, CGIL, Italy, CFMW/ TNI, Netherlands, 1999, available online at http://www.solidar.org/ (At page 7, in a Charter of Rights for Migrant Domestic Workers in Europe: "We call for justice and equity for all migrant domestic workers; whether documented or undocumented; whether live-in or live-out; whether first or second generation; whether born in Africa, Asia, South America or Europe. Member states of the European Union must recognize the intrinsic dignity and crucial importance of domestic work and seek to educate their citizens accordingly.")

22 In this regard, it is worth noting that Raffaella Sarti's discussion of the French ordinance of 1762 is not only an important shift in its explicit move away from focusing obliquely on "slaves" to focusing directly on "negroes and mulattos"; it is also the first example in the Barcelona Network Seminar papers of explicit border controls (immigration regulations) in relation to domestic service.

23 P. Hondagneu-Sotelo, p. 9. This point has been underscored throughout the EU Barcelona Network Seminar.

a self-distancing from the occupation itself by the domestic worker hired to perform the myriad of household and child care tasks. Added to this is the informality of the employment process, often conducted through a range of niche-based networks and word-of-mouth referrals between high-end professional employers and the social networks of their domestic employees.

Consequently, this paper seeks to question what role law can be asked to play in attempts to change the profound under-valuation of paid domestic work, and the systematic exploitation of the women who perform the work. It takes first steps toward rethinking the role of law in the process not only of improving domestic workers' conditions, but also of fundamentally changing the social status of the work. It seeks to identify what regulatory approaches to the challenge of domestic work can most readily promote the human dignity of domestic workers. Basically, this paper asks what is required to recognize the contemporary international imperative of decent work. At its core is the assumption that if domestic work cannot be conducted in an atmosphere that affirms the inherent human dignity of the person who performs the work, then regulatory initiatives that are meant to preserve fundamental principles and rights at work should lead to their progressive but swift abolition.

Part I of this paper sets out the international regulatory context, in which the international imperative of human dignity at work has been prioritized. It canvasses the international mandate to ensure that domestic workers can effectively enjoy their fundamental principles and rights at work. It acknowledges the perceived paradox at the international level, in its general application of many norms to this category of workers by virtue of the fact that they have not been specifically excluded. None the less, given the dynamic interpretation of the Committee of Experts of the ILO, the landscape for specific regulation for domestic workers is generally clear. It argues that specific regulation is important at all levels, particularly at the national and regional levels, to ensure enfranchisement by this segment of the "non-productive" labour market, ill suited to the dominant regulatory modes that seek to capture fordist and increasingly post-fordist work relationships.

Part II of this paper underscores the critical need to regulate, on a specific basis, domestic workers' immigration status and terms and conditions of employment. Focusing briefly on examples that surround the issue of accommodation, it contends that one crucial element of change –

the legal requirement in some countries to live in the home of the employer – must be eliminated. But it also tries to imagine how the state could act, in a manner that draws constructively on immigration powers to monitor the conditions under which domestics work, and to ensure that fair employment conditions are known by workers and adhered to by employers.

Part III of this paper moves beyond the framework of state protective action, to the more affirmative, collective dimensions of the regulation of the work. It calls for a deeper thrust toward recognizing domestic workers' collective agency, through tailored attention to how to include domestic workers within the regulatory realm of collective labour relations. It argues that the freedom of association and right to bargain collectively are cardinal aspects of domestic workers' human dignity interest that need to be preserved. Again it tries to imagine a way through which a stronger state role in domestic service could facilitate domestic workers' exercise of their collective rights, in a manner that recognizes their specificity.

International Regulatory Approaches

Despite the growing knowledge of wide-scale abuse in domestic service, the topic has surprisingly not been the source of much sustained advocacy by mainstream international human rights groups.[24] Yet international human rights instruments, particularly those speaking directly to the workplace context and promulgated by the International Labour Organization (ILO), could hardly be clearer in their challenge to "eliminate discrimina-

24 See Dan Gatmaytan, "Death and the Maid: Work, Violence and the Filipina in the International Labor Market", *Harvard Women's Law Journal,* 20, 1997, p. 229. See also Karen Tranberg Hansen, "Ambiguous Hegemonies: Identity Politics and Domestic Service", in Kathleen M. Adams and Sara Dickey (eds), *Home and Hegemony: Domestic Service and Identity Politics in South and Southeast Asia,* Ann Arbor, University of Michigan Press, 2000, pp. 283, 290.

tion in respect of employment and obligation",[25] and in their application to "all workers".[26] A 1998 ILO working paper on this topic provides concrete examples to support the affirmation that

> [t]he ILO maintains that the specificity of domestic work is not adequate reason for uncritically excluding domestic workers from the scope of international labour protections. To the contrary, ILO supervisory bodies have repeatedly expressed their support for basic labour protections to be extended in a meaningful manner to domestic workers.[27]

Examples are cited in which domestic workers are specifically referenced in international labour standards. The argument is forwarded that, unless they have been excluded from the scope of a Convention, either in its terms or by a Member pursuant to use of a general flexibility clause, domestic workers are to enjoy the rights, freedoms and protections afforded to all workers, contained within ILO Conventions.[28] Particularly notable examples of this interpretative approach are the Freedom of Association and Protection of the Right to Organize Convention, 1948 (No. 87), and the Right to Organize and Collective Bargaining Convention, 1949 (No. 98), neither of which refers specifically to domestic workers, but both of which entitle them to the full gamut of freedoms of association and collective bargaining.[29]

There may be a perceived paradox in the international regulatory approach, which tends not to contemplate in any detail the specificity of domestic workers' conditions of employment, and the pleas in this paper for specific regulation at other governance levels. However, it is my contention that a specific international instrument, focused on domestic work, which addresses labour, social and immigration aspects could provide a helpful guide to regulators at the local, national and regional levels, but

25 ILO Declaration on Fundamental Principles and Rights at Work and its Follow-up, adopted June 18, 1998, 37 I.L.M. 1233, Available at http://www.ilo.org/public/english/standards/decl/declaration/text/index.htm [hereinafter ILO Declaration].

26 See the clarification by Juan Somavia, the Director General of the ILO of this principle in Decent Work, *op. cit.*

27 See Adelle Blackett, "Making domestic work visible: The case for specific regulation", p. 6 (Geneva: ILO Labour Law and Labour Relations Programme Working Paper 2, 1998), available at: http://www.ilo.org/public/english/dialogue/govlab/papers/1998/domestic/

28 *Ibid.*, pp. 6–11.

29 *Ibid.*, p. 7.

would largely only repeat the obligations to which member States have already overwhelmingly committed themselves. That, too, is the optimistic picture. The pessimistic picture is that any attempt at the international level to seek a consolidated, unified restatement as applied to this politically disenfranchised group would run the real risk of reducing the international protections to which domestic workers are entitled.

What may be needed, rather than more international norms, is a fervent commitment by leading states to privilege regulatory changes at the domestic and regional levels, particularly where there is the greatest willingness to undertake the kind of structural, societal rethinking necessary to change the profound disadvantage that characterizes this sector of the economy. In other words, greater attention is needed to determine what serious action can be taken within magnet states to shift the balance in favour of recognizing the inherent human dignity of domestic work.

Domestic work has received enhanced attention within the framework of the ILO's normative prioritizations, prioritizations which I argue compel a different approach to acting upon and thinking about globalization's impact on workers. In other words, if one of the societal requirements is regulation that is responsive to the new international division both of productive and reproductive labour, in a manner that recognizes and values the work fully, rather than permits a range of state and non-state actors to manipulate a reserve labour force, then a new framework for the conceptualization and regulation of domestic workers' labour must be interposed. This framework has recently and eloquently been articulated as a matter for international priority by an international community increasingly conscious of its "situation of growing economic interdependence",[30] through the recent ILO Declaration of Fundamental Principles and Rights at Work and its Follow-up. In its reaffirmation of dignity at work, the ILO Declaration stresses the centrality of enfranchisement and social justice for all workers.

In particular, the ILO Declaration, which calls in its preamble for special attention to the need to improve the conditions of migrant workers, places human dignity at the core of its understanding of workers' rights. This shift is not one of mere semantics. It is an attempt to prioritize the setting of international norms, rather than merely proliferating hundreds of standards that hold very limited prospects of being ratified, implemented

30 See ILO Declaration, *op. cit.*, preamble.

and enforced. It seeks in an interdisciplinary fashion to promote the broad-based yet deep respect by state actors of a core articulation of fundamental principles and rights.

Understandably within the EU, though perhaps less so as it embraces poorer nation States primarily from the East, the list in the ILO Declaration might seem rather primeval. The world looks to Europe for its often enlightened, comparatively sophisticated approaches to social policy. Yet focusing, as EU Network Seminar participants are doing, on the particular struggles of domestic workers over time in Europe provides an unavoidable reminder of the palpable and growing exclusions within the EU's highly developed regions. That domestic service should continue to abound now, in globalized, post-industrial capitalism, under the worst vestiges of paternalistic/ maternalistic forms of subordination that have coexisted in Europe through feudalism into early modern times,[31] slavery,[32] colonialism,[33] industrialization[34] and authoritarianism,[35] and within monarchic and monastic[36] spaces, gives tremendous pause. Domestic service is indeed a factor of European identity, one that exposes deep contradictions while underscoring the extent to which the most basic objectives outlined within the international framework, notably as concerns forced labour, the elimination of discrimination, and the freedom of association/right to bargain collectively, are mere dreams for many who live and work on European soil.

We also know that citizenship and legal immigration status (that ever moving target)[37] is an oft-relied-upon but ultimately misleading criterion

31 See in the *Proceedings of the Servant Project,* Barcelona Seminar Papers by Tomás Mantecón, Aurelia Martin Casares, Sheila McIsaac Cooper.

32 See *Ibidem*, Seminar Paper by Aurelia Martin Casares, Sheila McIsaac Cooper (addendum); Carolyn Steedman.

33 See *Ibidem* Seminar Paper by Carolyn Steedman. More explicit comparative attention to colonial relationships and legal structures within European society would invariably complicate the understanding of servanthood, slavery, and European identity, leading to deeper parallels to contemporary transnational dimensions of domestic work.

34 See in the *Proceedings of the Servant Project,* Seminar Papers by Suzy Pasleau and Isabelle Schopp; Claudia Alemani; Artemigia Ioli.

35 *Ibidem*, Seminar Paper by María del Carmen Muñoz.

36 *Ibidem*, Seminar paper by Ofelia Rey Castelao.

37 See in particular the work by Saskia Sassen on the porous, flexible divide between legality and illegality in immigration policy. See Saskia Sassen, *Losing Control? Sovereignty in an Age of Globalization*, New York, Columbia University Press, 1996. See also Kim Rubenstein and Daniel Adler, "International Citizenship: The Future of Na-

upon which to base the applicability of the fundamental principles and rights at work of domestic workers in Europe. Valuable recent studies have underscored the extent to which the State is central to this process of trans-national labour migration, despite economic rationalizations of the equilibrium price established for the migratory transactions that would suggest that "migrants are rational actors who have unobstructed access to information regarding the migratory process, the availability of jobs, and comparative wages in relation to the cost of living overseas".[38] Rather, and in a striking parallel to the links between the slave trade and servitude in European societies, many migrant domestic workers become "objects to be exported-imported, bought-sold, and controlled in the most demeaning ways"[39]; their commodification is a crucial aspect of the "maid trade".

For industrialized countries like EU member States, this approach provides two inter-related social benefits in an economic climate in which women's workplace participation is abundant. First, a permanent supply of migrant domestic workers relieves the state of some of the responsibility for social reproduction, as the full cost of raising some of the more privileged members of the future societal workplace is dislodged; similarly, care-taking for the aged and the disabled is subsidized by foreign domestic workers' labour. Foreign domestic workers schemes in some industrialized countries remain "privatized methods of dealing with the increasing crisis in the domestic sphere".[40] In some cases, the reliance on domestic workers becomes a cipher for class status, signalling a shift away from reliance on extended family members toward a particular vision of the modern, middle class nuclear family that assures that women's work is undertaken through the status symbol of a commodified foreign servant.[41]

---

tionality in a Globalized World", *Indiana Journal of Global Legal Studies*, 7, 2000, p. 519, identifying the consequences for "nationality" in a world where sovereignty is challenged by the process of globalization.

38 Christine B. N. Chin, p. 93; B. Anderson, *Doing the Dirty Work?*, Ch. 10 ('Your Passport Is Your Life' Domestic workers and the State).

39 C. B. N. Chin, p. 94.

40 Tanya Schecter, *Race, Class, Women and The State: The Case of Domestic Labour*, Montreal, Black Rose Books, 1998, p. 124; B. Anderson, "Overseas Domestic Workers", p. 117.

41 C. B. N. Chin, pp. 166–167 (discussing the case of Malaysia). Her analysis of consumption relationships reflects the contemporary shift in many Western industrialized societies to the reliance on paid housekeepers by many middle class families. See also B. Anderson, p. 120, arguing that "in the final analysis, domestic work is not definable

Second, the workplace ghettoization of migrant domestic workers ensures that privileged women from the majority culture can be freed to develop their public careers unencumbered by private "women's work". Industrialized countries can take credit for the gains in gender parity attained by these women, without having to measure them against the social and economic marginalization of foreign domestic workers.[42]

The continued yet varying racialization of female domestic workers is a crucial element enabling the state to continue to justify this marginalization.[43] Yet advocates of deeper government involvement in the recognition and socialization of the costs of reproductive labour have been unsuccessful at dislodging the core perception not only that this work is and remains most appropriately "women's work", but that its transferral to racialized women to liberate dominant culture women, allowing them to be "productive" societal members further and more problematically marginalizes this work, deepening its social and economic undervaluation.[44]

In the light of these dynamics within the EU framework, the compelling and longstanding claim of domestic workers for social justice calls out for particular attention. Indeed, within the preambular language of the Declaration, the ILO constituency proclaims that "the ILO should give special attention to the problems of persons with special social needs,

---

in terms of tasks, nor permanent availability, but in terms of a role which constructs and situates the worker within a certain set of social and economic relationships".

42 For a discussion of this State interest in the Canadian context, see T. Schecter, pp. 120–125. See also Mary Romero, "Bursting the Foundational Myths of Reproductive Labor Under Capitalism: A Call for Brave New Families or Brave New Villages", *American University Journal of Gender, Social Policy and the Law*, 2000, 8, p. 177.

43 See e.g. Judy Scales-Trent, "African Women in France: Immigration, Family, and Work", in Adrien Katherine Wing (ed.), *Global Critical Race Feminism: An International Reader,* New York, NYU Press, 2000, pp. 141, 149, discussing the difficulties faced by African women in securing cleaning jobs in the homes and businesses of dominant culture French society, and Rekha Narula, "Cinderella need not apply: A study of paid domestic work in Paris", in Janet Henshall Momsen (ed.), *Gender, migration and domestic service*, London, Routledge, 1999, pp. 148–160. See also B. Anderson, *Overseas Domestic Workers*, p. 117, remarking that "[w]hat is passing unnoticed is the racialisation of paid domestic work in Europe, and in particular, the important role played by non-citizens in sustaining the European family as a viable social, economic and reproductive unit"; Hope Lewis, "Universal Mother: Transnational Migration and the Human Rights of Black Women in the Americas", *Journal of Gender, Race and Justice,* 2001, p. 197.

44 See A. Blackett, *Making domestic work visible, op. cit.*, p. 4; T. Schecter, p. 125; C. B. N. Chin, pp. 102, 167.

particularly [...] migrant workers". And, in the ILO's recent global report entitled Stopping Forced Labour[45], an entire chapter is devoted to the priority to be given to the special condition of domestic workers. Domestic work is recognized to be central to the story of globalization.[46] Regulating domestic work specifically, creatively, and in light of international prioritizations that recognize the connection between the social and the economic in an increasingly integrated world, must similarly become central not only to how globalization is received, but also to how it is acted upon, shaped and reconfigured.[47]

Labour Protection: the Claim for Specificity

As alluded to above, domestic work, particularly when performed by foreign workers, is often considered to present insuperable barriers for regulation. Attempts are made to provide extensive controls upon entry, of the sort that restrict access and constrain the acquisition of rights of landing on the part of immigrant domestic workers. In other cases, domestic workers are largely considered illegal, particularly when there are no specific schemes permitting them to perform the labour that they undertake in European member states, despite the implicit reliance by the state on their work to foster deeper labour market access of its citizens. These women are controlled, indeed themselves paradoxically hyper-regulated, via their status as illegal migrants. Moreover, it is telling that although domestic workers are no longer excluded from the basic labour legislation of most countries, they remain fundamentally invisible.[48] This is so because "the

45 ILO, Stopping Forced Labour (Geneva: Global Report, 2001), Ch. 5, *Domestic Workers in Forced Labour Situation.*

46 See in particular Saskia Sassen, "Notes on the Incorporation of Third World Women in Wage Labor Through Immigration and Offshore Production", in Saskia Sassen, *Globalization and its Discontents*, New York, The New Press, 1998, p. 81. See also Helma Lutz, "*At your service Madam!* The globalization of domestic service", *Feminist Review,* 2002, p. 89.

47 Adelle Blackett, "Globalization and its Ambiguities", *Columbia Journal of Transnational Law,* 1998, p. 57.

48 A. Blackett, *Making domestic work visible*, p. 1.

specificity of their employment relationship is simply not addressed in most legislative enactments but that same specificity is relied upon – at the level of common practice – to justify denying them their status as 'real workers' entitled to the legislative protection that exists".[49]

Yet this relationship is not coincidental. The hyper-regulation through the immigration process ensures state control over the movement of persons across borders, the jealous preserve of industrialized states despite increasingly free movement of other factors of production, notably capital. The hyper-regulation also reinforces public perceptions of the racialized outsiders as undeserving "social pariahs",[50] who seek to exploit the generosity of industrialized states to take advantage of social benefits without offering a meaningful, skilled contribution to the society. The neglect of these women in employment legislation is therefore deemed to be justified, as they are considered fortunate simply to have been permitted to enter the country.

Regulation on the basis of domestic workers' human dignity would of course look markedly different. Specificity in labour regulation is proffered as a response to the invisibility that robs domestic workers of their social justice claims. It seeks to act on the recognition that "the private sphere of the employer is the public sphere of the employee".[51] Looking at the specificity of domestic worker must entail embracing the fact that domestic work is quite simply different from many other forms of work, but insisting upon the need to grapple with it, rather than sweeping it under the carpet of unregulated household affairs.

Indeed, it is not at all implausible to imagine that the immigration laws could themselves become the bases through which greater specific social protection of domestic work could be ensured. For example, states that heavily control the entry of domestic workers could easily proceed to register domestic workers *and their employers,* acting further and as of right to inspect the premises in which it is proposed that the domestic workers will live, informing the employers of their responsibilities and the

49 *Ibid.*, pp. 1–2.

50 See discussion of state surveillance and media characterizations of Filipina and Indonesian domestic workers' sexuality in C. B. N. Chin, p. 111. See also B. Anderson, *Overseas Domestic Workers*, p. 129, discussing the control over African women's bodies in Athens, including being required to undergo HIV/AIDS tests at their own expense.

51 See Lesley Gill, *Precarious Dependencies: Gender, Class and Domestic Service in Bolivia*, New York, Columbia University Press, 1994, p. 5.

employees' rights, and providing detailed information for the workers in question to ensure that they understand their rights, as well as how to vindicate them in the event of abuse. Contact information for civil society organizations and unions that act in defence of domestic workers could also quite easily be made available to domestic workers who enter through specific schemes or on particular work visas.[52]

In some cases, as part of the immigration process, model contracts are presented for signature between prospective employers and workers, which in the process carefully define minimum conditions for work that are applicable to domestic workers.[53] One benefit of this process of formalization is that it requires tasks to be itemized and to a limited extent defined. To some extent this may already occur, outside of the immigration process, particularly through some employment agencies; the profit-based motives can occasionally coincide with weeding out the most abusive employers at the mid to high-range levels.[54] Yet as Hondagneu-Sotelo notes, "[t]he agency operators say they do not list the numbers of hours of work required for the live-in jobs; the assumption is that the live-in is on call at all hours".[55] A process structured around the state could not only recognize the benefits that domestic work provides to European society; it could also assert state responsibility to ensure that laws apply in a meaningful fashion to domestic workers' conditions of employment.

Some forms of regulation in relation to domestic workers are simply quite difficult to justify. Particularly troubling are attempts to justify the legal imposition of "live-in" requirements applied exclusively to foreign domestic workers.[56] Not only is the general international rule that employ-

52 See e.g. Joy M. Zarembka, pp. 148–149, contrasting the kind of *encadrement* that was provided to au pairs under a J-1 visa, including the services of a counselor to assist in resolving any disputes, with the total absence of information under the domestic worker programme. Of course, serious difficulties have also been documented with au pair schemes.

53 In addition to some examples in South East Asia, see *Proceedings of the Servant Project,* Barcelona Seminar papers by Claudia Alemani and Artemigia Ioli; the latter two papers focus on domestic employment relations.

54 See the results of P. Hondagneu-Sotelo's study of California-based agencies, pp. 102–107.

55 P. Hondagneu-Sotelo, p. 104.

56 See for e.g. Citizenship and Immigration Canada, Chapter IP4, Processing Live-in Caregivers, and Chapter OP14, Processing Applicants for the Live-in Caregiver Program, available at http://www.cic.gc.ca/manuals-guides/english/

ers should not provide accommodation at the workplace.[57] The basis for focusing on foreign workers is usually grounded in the fact that citizens and permanent residents of the industrialized countries are most unlikely to accept to live-in. Hence, the regulation is in place precisely to satisfy a labour market demand for a form of labour that has been widely and repeatedly criticized in the available social science literature as providing tremendous ground for discrimination and other serious abuse.

In addition to maintaining that "live-in" requirements should be eliminated from domestic law, I would suggest that at a minimum, "live-in" work cries out for a deeper problematization of the appropriate spatial limits of workplace regulation. To remain a legally tolerated component of workplace relationships, a "live-in" option should carry with it the understanding that the employer must cede a certain degree of domestic "privacy" in recognition that the home has become both the workplace and dwelling of a particularly vulnerable category of worker. The employer's ability to enter into a contract entailing such otherwise unbridled subordination should be prepared to see that authority reasonably circumscribed. The employer should also only be able to obtain that labour market service at a financial premium,[58] the kind of premium that could only flow from the removal of live-in status as a requirement.

This approach goes beyond the admittedly close relationship between specific regulation and fiscality. Indeed, in some of the contexts in which specific regulatory initiatives are most developed, notably France, simplified tax schemes related incentives have been put in place to encourage employers and employees to declare their relationship. However, the levels and approaches sometimes lead to perverse consequences; the fiscal approaches themselves may encourage workplace actors to mask the full extent of the employment relationship, to benefit from being perceived as

57 See generally A. Blackett, *Making domestic work visible*, p. 15. As discussed in that paper, however, there are exceptions that could potentially be applied to domestic work, albeit with much greater recognition then that the worker is in fact at work throughout the live-in period. The exception implies a call for greater rather than lesser protective regulation.

58 The tendency, instead, is to allow for deductions from salary to pay for room and board. See, e.g., the French Convention Collective Nationale (CCN), Art. 5, discussed infra.

"casual" or "part-time" work.[59] Beyond its role of providing incentives for adherence to labour standards, the state needs to send a clear message that adherence to labour standards does not depend on the voluntary goodness of individual employers, but reflects a state recognition that domestic work is real work, warranting reasonable state scrutiny.

Yet it is the somewhat pessimistic contention of this paper that domestic work into the 21st century will not be able to foster a structural shift in characterization unless the underlying principles of paternalism/maternalism[60] are profoundly challenged, in a way that fundamentally shakes up the gendered and racialized characterization of domestic workers' identity. The protective strategies of legislative intervention cannot remove the profoundly rooted global social stratification; that is, there is always another category of particularly disenfranchised persons who can be enlisted beyond the shadow of the law to do the undocumented, unregulated work.

In the many narratives on domestic workers' lived experiences, the overwhelming realization is that paternalism, or "maternalism", continues to be the central determinant of whether domestics will receive fair treatment at work. This is true despite the "rights"-based focus of contemporary Western societies. In a rich account of the complex relational dimensions of domestic work, Hondagneu-Sotelo makes a strong case instead for "personalism"[61] or genuine respect for the human worth and dignity of

59 See B. Anderson, *Overseas Domestic Workers*, p. 121. For a detailed discussion of some of the regulatory approaches in France in the 1990s, see generally A. Blackett, *Making Domestic Work Visible*.

60 See in particular P. Hondagneu-Sotelo, who describes maternalism as embodying hierarchical, and somewhat manipulative practices to extract greater work and workplace "loyalty" from the domestic worker. Specifically, she identifies "a one-way relationship, defined primarily by the employer's gestures of charity, unsolicited advice, assistance, and gifts. The domestic employee is obligated to respond with extra hours of service, personal loyalty, and job commitment. Maternalism underlines the deep class inequalities between employers and employees. More problematically, because employer maternalism positions the employee as needy, deficient, and childlike, it does not allow the employee any dignity and respect" (P. Hondagneu-Sotelo, pp. 207–208).

61 According to P. Hondagneu-Sotelo, "[p]ersonalism, by contrast, is a two-way relationship, albeit still asymmetrical. It involves the employer's recognition of the employee as a particular person – the recogition and *consideración* necessary for dignity and respect to be realized. In the absence of fair wages, reasonable hours, and job autonomy, personalism alone is not enough to upgrade domestic work; but conversely, its absence virtually ensures that the job will be experienced as degrading" (P. Hondagneu-Sotelo, p. 208).

domestic workers. Hondagneu-Sotelo considers personalism to be separate from – but a necessary companion to – appropriate regulation of domestic workers' conditions of employment. It is my contention that this recognition of the human dignity of domestic workers must be mediated through workplace regulation that shifts the balance away from noblesse-oblige toward more egalitarian understandings of workplace interaction between individuals of equal human worth, whose self-actualization is intertwined. I am inclined to believe that, when domestic work relationships are infused with the "rule of law", and (as discussed in part III) when domestic workers are seen as agents in establishing, shaping and enforcing that law, through workplace democratic action (that is, collective bargaining) that "personalism" as a form of social citizenship is more likely to follow.

So the call for specificity in this paper is not grounded exclusively in "protective" state action. Domestic work complicates the public-private divide across the regulatory borders. In its attention to principles of participatory, inclusive democracy, this paper contemplates meaningful ways to facilitate the freedom of association and effective exercise of the right to bargain collectively for domestic workers. Inclusive democratic participation is affirmed to be central to enable domestic workers to claim full recognition of their human dignity.

Promoting Agency through Specificity: Dignity in Action

Collective relations are seen as the cornerstone vehicles through which workers can act to create the law that governs their workplace relationships. In other words, they are workplace actors, rather than the mere recipients of the largesse of a protective State. The premise of this form of workplace organization is that central to workers' identity is the acceptance that they are best placed to understand, discuss with employers, and establish, on a basis of equality of bargaining power achieved through worker union solidarity rather than individual subordination, the conditions under which the labour contract will be executed. They are also best placed to seek its day-to-day enforcement.

Yet collective labour relations in the twentieth century have moved away from craft-based models of organizing,[62] to rely overwhelmingly upon the industrial workplace characterized by fordist modes of production. Conveniently, the industrial models have contributed to the exclusion and further ghettoization of women's reproductive work, as well as the associated "non-productive" paid work in the home. And,

> despite overwhelming ratification of the ILO's leading Right to Organize and Collective Bargaining Convention (No. 98), 1949, effective collective bargaining remains elusive for the vast majority of workers. Globally, only a minority of workers benefit from the free and fair collective representation of their rights, needs and interests.[63]

Admittedly, there are not only barriers to the collective regulation of domestic workers' conditions of employment. There is at least one oft overlooked advantage. Unlike the classic paradigm of the movement of most factors of production, employers of domestic workers are not footloose multinational enterprises who move across oceans in search of cheap labour pools. Rather, domestic workers' employers are very much tied to place. In other words, the work does not, indeed will not, go away... This dynamic contains within it some points of strength for the organization of domestic workers in a collective form.[64]

Of course, the vulnerability of the domestic workers themselves is cited as a barrier, for they are the ones who cross borders, and they are preferably young, preferably single, preferably childless.[65] But the political science literature has established the extent to which that vulnerability

62 The examples of brotherhoods and their exclusionary practices, evoked in the discussion of Raffaella Sarti's paper, Barcelona Seminar, warrants greater attention. Similarly, the discussion of unionization initiatives in Norway contemplated in Sølvi Sogner's paper is particularly instructive.

63 See Adelle Blackett and Colleen Sheppard, *The Links Between Collective Bargaining and Equality*, ILO Declaration Working Paper No. 10 (Geneva: ILO, 2002); available at
http://www.ilo.org/dyn/declaris/declarationweb.download_blog?var_documentID=155
4. See also Adelle Blackett and Colleen Sheppard, "Collective Bargaining and Equality: Making Connections", *International Labour Review*, May 2004, p. 419 and p. 420.

64 P. Hondagneu-Sotelo, p. 242.

65 Maria Castro Garcia, "¿Qué se Compra y qué se Paga en el Servicio Doméstico?: El Caso de Bogotá", in Magdalena León (ed.), *La Realidad Colombiana: Debate sobre la mujer en América Latina y el Caribe*, Vol. I, Bogotá, ACEP, 1982, pp. 99ff.

is constructed, largely by the state.[66] Consequently, that form of organizing depends largely on the willingness of the state to act in a different way, to ensure that necessary migration schemes are not used to prevent workers from seeking to organize and to pull the cost of domestic labour farther downward.[67] This entails regulating upward the conditions of work, despite the resistance to workplace regulation in private homes. The state is needed to act as a counterbalance in recognizing that the private home in which domestic workers are employed has to some extent become a public place of work.

The challenge therefore is to changing, on a structural level, the position of domestic workers. It is my contention that a key part of advocating that change is, precisely, to be found in underscoring the unpalatable extent to which the contemporary status reflects a failure to break with vestiges of the past, status-based relationships that characterized the regulation of domestic labour, forced or "free". The underlying issue of the structural (and constructed) vulnerability of this category of workers will not go away merely through protective state interventions. One of the key ways in which "employees" in industrial and post-industrial society have been able to gain "respect" in the workplace has, precisely, been through a valorization of their ability to act as agents irrespective of whether they performed manual labour in a deskilled Taylorist industrial workplace, or in a traditionally female "caring" field. An insuperable part of this dynamic must entail providing the spaces within which the gendered and racialized characteristics of particular forms of work can be challenged.[68] Partly, this involves ensuring that domestic workers, whoever they are, are able to act collectively, in solidarity, and know that they are agents able to make the law that governs them. It is recognizing the philosophical basis of subordination in an employment relationship, wherever that relation-

66 In addition to C. B. N. Chin, see generally an early classic on the topic, Cynthia Enloe, *Bananas, Beaches and Bases: Making Feminist Sense of International Politics*, London, Pandora, 1989.

67 See T. Schecter, pp. 114–125, documenting the shift in Canada away from West Indian toward Filipina domestic workers once the former started to organize for their rights.

68 The implementation of equal pay for work of equal value has become an important vehicle through which to itemize and value the characteristics of work that has traditionally been labelled women's work. The EU experience in this matter, particularly in the relationship between legislative vehicles (Directives, national laws) and labour regulatory processes (collective agreements, collective negotiations, collective dispute resolution) can be instructive in relation to domestic work.

ship may take place, which grounds the claim for the right to bargain collectively. As a facilitator of the subordination, the state is also required to seek to mediate it. Indeed, collective bargaining and broader social dialogue systems provide the foundations that change the character of the relationship, by shifting the identity of the workers in the process of infusing equity into workplace relationships.[69]

The ILO's commitment to the "effective recognition of collective bargaining",[70] to be interpreted meaningfully, "cannot but include the realization that, to be effective, collective bargaining mechanisms must grapple with the need creatively to encompass all categories of workers, and more particularly those workers who have faced historical disadvantage of the kind that Convention No. 111 strives to eliminate".[71] Considering that the ILO has applied the collective bargaining principle "in an uncompromisingly broad manner, albeit one that recognizes a wide diversity of industrial relations systems",[72] the question becomes whether the notion is sufficiently flexible to permit collective relations to move effectively beyond the straight jacket of fordist modes of production. This question must be asked not only as concerns historical relationships like that of master and servant, but also to decidedly post-fordist technology-based economic organization.[73]

Yet the persistence, indeed vigorous resurgence, of domestic work, reminds us that it is not just a vestige of feudal and colonial times; indeed, it now responds to a new mode of production that stratifies and accentu-

69 See Alain Supiot, "Déréglementation des relations de travail et autoréglementation de l'entreprise", *Droit social,* 195, 3, Mars 1989, p. 204.

70 ILO Declaration, *op. cit.*

71 A. Blackett and C. Sheppard, p. 5.

72 Adelle Blackett, "Whither Social Clause? Human Rights, Trade Theory and Treaty Interpretation", *Columbia Human Rights Law Review*, 31, 1999, 1, p. 15.

73 Indeed, the ILO has championed the companion notion of "social dialogue", embracing participation by tripartite and tripartite-plus constituencies in a broad range of economic and social policy-making activities. At a pragmatic level, this is justified as ensuring the broadest possible participation by the broadest number of workers and representative stakeholders in labour market matters, with the overarching goal of promoting dignity at work. As Anne Trebilcock has aptly argued, tripartism is rooted in "the acceptance of societal pluralism". See Anne Trebilcock, "Tripartite Consultation and Cooperation in National-Level Economic and Social Policy-Making: An Overview", in Anne Trebilcock *et al.*, *Towards Social Dialogue: Tripartite Cooperation in National Economic and Social Policy-Making*, Geneva, International Labour Office, 1994, p. 1.

ates irregular but extended working hours, under-defined job boundaries, and relentless demands that make professional life for men and women increasingly less compatible with child care, elder care and other home care responsibilities. Collective relations in this sector are a way to interpose a form of social citizenship, of workplace democracy, into otherwise fundamentally paternalistic/maternalistic relationships.

In recognition of this need, domestic workers' associations have sprung up throughout many parts of the world. Although in a few cases they may be recognized as bona fide trade unions, in many cases they act outside of exclusionary collective bargaining laws.[74] They often also embrace a fairly broad vision of their mandate. They seek to provide needed legal information and action, as well as concerted initiatives to lobby politically to improve relevant laws. They also attempt to ensure that their constituencies have a range of moral support, social activities, training opportunities, information sessions as well as basic space for retreat and consolidation.[75] A few organizing efforts have also succeeded, including a recent initiative in one of the hardest countries to unionize workers, the United States, where homecare workers who assumed main responsibility for eldercare were successfully organized in an approach that coupled an emphasis on the one hand on better working conditions and respect for domestic workers, and on the other hand on better quality of care for the service recipients, or "clients". The organizing permitted elements of the employer's characteristics to be attributed both to a state entity established to facilitate unionization and to the "clients".[76]

It is no surprise, however, that I argue in favour of legislative reforms that are not confined to the dominant *industrial* relations tradition within

74 See A. Blackett, *Making domestic work visible*, pp. 6–11.

75 See generally Margaret Hosmer Martens and Swasti Mitter, *Women in Trade Unions: Organizing the unorganized,* Geneva, ILO, 1994, pp. 17–60, discussing different organizing initiatives with domestic workers, including migrant domestic workers, in selected parts of the world. See also eg. B. Anderson, *Overseas Domestic Workers*, p. 131 (noting the example of Dominican women in Barcelona, who tend to rent apartments in which a dozen or so workers can meet on their days off, share information, support one another and fulfill their child care needs).

76 See Linda Delp and Katie Quan, "Homecare Worker Organizing in California: An Analysis of a Successful Strategy", *Labor Studies Journal*, 27, Spring 2002, pp. 1–23 (available at http://www.iir.berkeley.edu/clrc/humanservices/delpquan.pdf). See also Labor Research Association, 13,000 Home Care Workers in Oregon Vote Overwhelmingly to Join SEIU; Union Election Was Largest in State's History (8 January 2002) available at http://www.laborresearch.org/print.php?id=87.

the places where organizing efforts are sought. The limits of traditional forms of workplace organization are great in relation to domestic work in private homes. Mere efforts to legislate nominal inclusion on the same terms as other workers are doomed to fail.[77] The barriers have been daunting in most systems, precisely because of the isolated conditions under which domestics work. The sense of group identity, particularly across citizenship, racial and ethnic divides, further complicates this process. The legislative extension of contracts to apply to domestic workers, ably evoked in the work on Italy,[78] and also present in France,[79] remains the classic example of using a pre-industrial collective organizing vehicle to respond to a contemporary regulatory challenge. As laudable as these initiatives may be, they none the less continue to pose direct difficulties. The first relates to the content of the norms themselves; the second relates to the decision-making process.

A good example of the first – normative – difficulty is found in the French *Convention collective nationale* (CCN), which recognizes that care-givers who may be called upon during the day or night should be remunerated at least for being "on-call" during some of those hours. The CCN attempts to delimit the scope of the "heures de présence responsable", and of regular work ("heure de travail effectif") defining them as those hours during which the employee may use her time for herself, while remaining vigilant and prepared to intervene, if necessary. It also

77 For an example of this in the Canadian context, see Judy Fudge, "Little Victories and Big Defeats: The Rise and Fall of Collective Bargaining Rights for Domestic Workers in Ontario", in Abigail B. Bakan and Daiva Stasiulis (eds), *Not One of the Family: Foreign Domestic Workers in Canada*, Toronto, University Toronto Press, 1997.

78 See *Il contratto collectivo nazionale di lavoro domestico, stipulato a Roma 8 marzo 2001 between the unions*, Fidaldo and Domina and the employers, Filcams-CGIL, Fisascat – CISL, Uiltucs – UIL, and Federcolf. See also Seminar Papers by Claudia Alemani, and Artemigia Ioli. For a comprehensive comparative account of immigration, labour and employment relations in Rome and Los Angeles see R. S. Parreñas, *Servants of Globalization: Women, Migration and Domestic Work*, Palo Alto, Stanford U. Press, 2001.

79 See Convention collective nationale des salariés du particulier employeur étendue par arrêté du 2 mars 2000 (CCN), *Journal Officiel de la République Française*, 11 mars 2000, available at http://www.legifrance.gouv.fr/WAspad/VisuSommaireCoco.jsp? lenum =3180.
See also A. Blackett, *Making domestic work visible*, pp. 12ff for a discussion of an earlier version of the French Convention collective nationale des employés de maison, du 3 juin 1980, étendue par arrêté du 26 mai 1982, *Journal Officiel,* 27 juin 1982, brochure no. 3180.

clarifies that performing work linked to childcare, notably preparing meals, doing the laundry, taking the child on a walk, cleaning up after them or their rooms, and any other family or other tasks, are considered to be "travail effectif", not on-call hours.[80] Despite the progress that recognition of "heures de présence responsable" reflects, the application of the concept runs the risk of leading some domestic workers to be required to work particularly lengthy periods of time that are in practice difficult to quantify and negotiate.[81]

The second difficulty is that participation by domestic workers in the process of establishing the workplace conditions that govern their relationships is likely to be quite limited. For example, even in the French context, where the right to organize and exercise collective action is regulated in the Labour Code,[82] the *Conventions collectives nationales* are perceived to be more regulatory than contractual in nature,[83] established and modified primarily by a tripartite "commission mixte" that is presided over by a representative of the Minister of Labour to negotiate conditions of employment on behalf of domestic workers.[84] Despite serious attempts to ensure that domestic workers' lived experiences are considered, vehicles by which to ensure that domestic workers can participate in the decision-making process remain inadequate.[85] Their agency, in other words, remains sorely tested. In less regulated contexts, mere statutory grants of collective bargaining rights can be meaningless without further regulatory attention. For undocumented workers, of course, the barriers to "industrial" collective action (other than massive public-solidarity campaigns to obtain legal immigrant status) may seem insuperable.

80 CCN, Art. 3. Note that night time sleeping hours for a domestic worker who lives on site in a separate room, even if required to be prepared to awaken and intervene, are remunerated at lower rates than the *heures de présence responsable*. See detailed discussion in Jean-Yves Kerbourc'h, p. 340.

81 See A. Blackett, *Making domestic work visible*, pp. 18–19. See also Anderson, 2000, pp. 167–168.

82 Arts. L. 131–2. See Jean-Yves Kerbourc'h, "Le régime du travail domestique au regard du droit du travail", *Droit social*, avril 1999, 4, p. 335.

83 See in particular Jean Pélissier, Alain Supiot and Antoine Jeammaud, *Droit du travail,* 21st ed., Paris, Dalloz, 2002, parag. 768–769 and Jean-Yves Kerbourc'h, pp. 335–337, 339–340.

84 J. Pélissier *et al.*, p. 864.

85 Jean-Yves Kerbourc'h notes, for example, that employees who are mandated by their union to participate in representative functions may receive time off of work, but are not paid for that time off, p. 338.

This latter difficulty brings the analysis full circle. The ability to exercise collective agency depends in large measure on a more broadly favourable regulatory climate, and in particular one that marshals immigration law not as a factor for repression, but rather as a channel through which fair labour conditions for an essential but exploited category of immigrant women workers can be maintained. In the EU context, in addition to pure pragmatism, a case can be made for a more coordinated, if not "directive" approach to this matter. These interventions can be grounded in the EU's inevitably broadened approach to the movement of persons within the community; the workforce demands imposed upon two-breadwinner, new economy households; and the deepening legal protections against gender discrimination as well as against racism and xenophobia.[86] The historical case that the EU Network is well-placed to present is that short of proactive regulatory engagements, the problematic vestiges of the relationship of servility are likely to continue, only compounding the proliferation of a profoundly inequitable, state-sanctioned working relationship under conditions that are contrary to the basic international aspiration of decent work.

Conclusion

What does it mean to assert, as does Anderson, that "in the final analysis, domestic work is not definable in terms of tasks, nor permanent availability, but rather in terms of a role which constructs and situates the worker within a certain set of social and economic relationships"?[87] Can a regula-

86 See Treaty of Amsterdam, Article 13 and EU Directive 78/00 of 27 November 2000. See also Mark Bell, Article 13 EC: "The European Commission's Anti-Discrimination Proposals", *Industrial Law Journal*, 2000, p. 79; Lisa Waddington, "Article 13 EC: Setting Priorities in the Proposal for a Horizontal Employment Directive", *Industrial Law Journal,* 176, 2000. However, one should not be naïve in assuming that domestic workers, without political clout, are readily able to militate in favour of social inclusion, without widespread societal support. For a discussion of the difficulties of political organizing on this topic in the Canadian context, see Schecter, *op. cit.*, pp. 107–138.

87 See B. Anderson, *Overseas Domestic Workers*, p. 120.

tory approach that looks at domestic work through meticulous attention to the particular, with the avowed aim of rendering the work highly visible offset the social status implications that the work invariably also encapsulates in contemporary consumption-based societies? Can specific regulation contribute to destabilizing, and over time dislodging deep-seated inequalities based on class, race, and citizenship status through which the gender relations of domestic work are mediated?

These questions only underscore the depth of the challenge. To a limited extent, they are answered through practice, but heightened historical awareness of the regulatory context and the ways that the contemporary discussion of options is cast would be invaluable. Indeed, more attention to changes in the nature of work from the eighteenth through the early twentieth centuries would likely yield further helpful points of comparison. Already, what the work of participants in the EU Network Seminar has revealed is that a necessary starting point must be to ensure that the vestiges of paternalistic interactions that signal unencumbered employer property rights are dislodged, to give way instead to a relationship that rests firmly on a foundation of domestic workers' rights and agency. The corollary for the state to permit employment relations in the home to continue must be that the state needs to exercise its authority to prevent the relationships from becoming exploitative. Otherwise, the only principled option, I maintain, is to ban (at least) migrant domestic work.

Effective regulation of domestic workers' conditions of employment and collective bargaining rights is one of the starkest examples of the need to "think beyond old categories, and beyond traditional territorial boundaries".[88] More than many other forms of work, it requires "the development of new, overlapping, or complementary approaches"[89] to ensure that domestic workers work in dignity.

88 A. Blackett and C. Sheppard, *op. cit.*, p. 17.

89 *Ibid.*

PART III

THE MAID, THE MASTER AND THE FAMILY

From Family Member to Employee: Aspects of Continuity and Discontinuity in English Domestic Service, 1600–2000

Sheila MCISAAC COOPER

Domestic servants have been a constant presence in English history since Anglo-Saxon times. Although their numbers have varied, only in the period after the Second World War did their population percentages decline radically, a trend that reversed itself in the later twentieth century as dual-career families sought domestic help. This paper addresses some major continuities and discontinuities in English domestic service, comparing service in the pre-industrial period to that in modern England. Although the important demographic and formative roles service played in early-modern society have disappeared, there exists in many relatively modest contemporary households demand for domestic workers to provide services that are often remarkably similar to those of the earlier period. However, although the service is often similar, the servant is considerably less so.

The Early Modern Period

British historians, amongst others, label the sixteenth through the eighteenth century as the early modern period. Falling as it does between the end of the Middle Ages and the era of industrialization, the early modern period also constitutes much of what we call the pre-industrial era. Throughout the period, what John Hajnal has identified as the northwest European marriage pattern was well established in England.[1] In north-

1 John Hajnal, "European marriage patterns in perspective", in D. V. Glass and D. E. C. Eversley (eds), *Population in History*, London, Edward Arnold, 1965, pp. 101–135.

western Europe first marriage came relatively late and at roughly the same age for both partners. Upon marriage couples set up independent households, which their children commonly left well before their own marriages. For the most part the young people moved into homes of others of the same or somewhat better social station, often into the homes of extended family, friends, or patrons. They became junior members of these families, generally as wage-earning servants or as apprentices. Peter Laslett called these young people, who came from across all social strata, life-cycle servants. That term has acquired wide currency in the historical literature.[2]

Early Modern Domestic Servants

The north-western European marriage pattern resulted in a long gap between puberty and marriage – ten to fifteen years. The widespread practice of sending adolescents and young adults of all social strata out of their natal homes as "life-cycle servants" helped to fill that gap. The percentages of young people involved are impossible to determine exactly as they vary from time to time, place to place, and definition to definition. Nonetheless, servants emerge very conspicuously in pre-industrial household listings and other census-type documents. These suggest that perhaps close to three-fifths of early modern English young people spent some time in service. Besides domestic servants and apprentices, life-cycle service included large numbers of servants in husbandry, i.e., agricultural servants.[3]

For most life-cycle servants, service was not and would not become a career although for apprentices, who were a subset of life-cycle servants, it was preparation for a career. On the other hand, the majority of appren-

John Hajnal, "Two kinds of pre-industrial household formation system", in Richard Wall, Jean Robin, Peter Laslett (eds), *Family Forms in Historic Europe*, Cambridge, Cambridge University Press, 1983, pp. 65–104.

2 Peter Laslett, "Family, kinship and collectivity as systems of support in pre-industrial Europe: a considerations of the 'nuclear-hardship' hypothesis", *Continuity and Change*, 1988, 3, 2, pp. 153–175.

3 See Ann Kussmaul, *Servants in Husbandry in Early Modern England*, Cambridge, Cambridge University Press, 1981, p. 3.

tices failed to stay the course. Non-apprentices too were often in service only briefly or were in and out of service between abbreviated stints as regular apprentices, periods at home, travel, or other activities. For servants as for their youthful fellows today this phase of the life cycle was a time for acquiring training and other education. Formal schooling in pre-industrial England was usually expensive and, with limited exception, gendered. Most of those who had extended formal instruction were young men destined for the Church, the law, sometimes medicine, or to maintain a social position. Pre-industrial society offered limited opportunity for those with extensive formal education. The economy demanded practical skills, skills more readily acquired in service (including apprenticeship). Thus service was largely a transient phase. A person's occupational status would have come from the fully adult role that he or she assumed afterwards – as housewife, shopkeeper, landlord, tenant, farmer, merchant, rentier, artisan, aristocrat, victualler, laborer, or some other job, including what Laslett has called "lifetime" servant.

The great majority of early modern domestic servants were life-cycle servants, but there were others, mostly lifetime servants. Laslett called them lifetime servants because they were older and their time in service had extended beyond young adulthood. Sometimes married or widowed, they frequently served as senior staff in multi-servant homes but they could be found serving in single-servant households. Lifetime servants often included butlers, stewards, housekeepers, and those in comparable authority. They were called lifetime servants because their period of service extended into or came later in the life cycle. Many spent most of their adult years as servants although many others did not remain servants for life. Some died in service while others retired or left, especially for shopkeeping, inn-keeping and other victualling trades, agriculture, or day labor. Nonetheless, they were not part or would not remain part of the society-wide, youthful exodus Hajnal had identified.

Two other types of domestic workers common in the pre-industrial period but virtually always non-resident were washerwomen or laundresses and charwomen or chars. Except for the occasional laundress in a very large household, these workers did not live with the families they served. Although usually non-resident, washerwomen often had regularly scheduled appointments with their employers. Charwomen, on the other hand, seldom had scheduled employment.

Charwomen were part of that great crowd of pre-industrial day laborers that the seventeenth-century demographer Gregory King felt depleted the wealth of England. Servants, on the other hand, shared the socio-economic rank of their masters and mistresses in King's analysis, which may reflect the social breadth of life-cycle service.[4] Lacking regular employment, a charwoman could be hired for the day or part of the day as needed. Occasional charring was done by women, frequently married ones, to help people whom they knew or to make a little extra money. Nevertheless, most charwomen were older, needy, and often widowed, and that would remain the case at least through the 1911 census. Those who had once been servants would have suffered serious erosion in status. Chars' lives were difficult, for employment was uncertain and, as irregulars, they got the heaviest, dirtiest of cleaning jobs. Working for different people, chars would have found the heavy, dirty jobs recurring working day after working day. While life-cycle service carried very little stigma until youthful service became increasingly *déclassé* in the later eighteenth and nineteenth centuries, charring was highly stigmatized very early and charwomen considered immoral and dishonest. Eliza Hayward in her preachy, eighteenth-century manuals for servants warned them not to consort with chars or to let a charwoman into the house.[5]

Not all servants in early modern England were English. Many came from other parts of the British Isles. These Scots, Welsh, and Irish, who often served fellow countrymen living in England, fell into the same life-cycle/lifetime categories as their English peers. So too did a group of servants from France and the Low Countries. Many were part of the Huguenot diaspora that resulted from the revocation of the Treaty of Nantes, and often served in Huguenot families or those of other French expatriates. French servants also found places amongst the staffs of larger households, where French ladies' maids were in demand. As trans-Atlantic trade swelled, Africans, especially boys, were also fashionable amongst the elites who so often included them in portraits. Although not insignificant, these two groups were relatively small.

4 For King's scheme, see Peter Laslett, *The World We Have Lost*, London, Methuen, 1971, pp. 36–37 (2nd edn).

5 Eliza Haywood, *A Present for a Servant-Maid*, Dublin, George Faulkner, 1793, pp. 29–30.

Ubiquity of Domestic Service

Labor needs of pre-industrial English households – even very small ones – were enormous. Sustaining an early-modern household of any size depended critically on human power – to haul water, to go to market, to gather wood, to build fires, to cook food, to launder, to spin yarn, to make cloth and clothing, to watch children, to tend the ill and infirm, to clean, etc.[6] For most households having servants was not an indulgence or a social indicator but indicative of the labor necessary to maintain the house and family. A large servant staff for those not engaged in farming, innkeeping or other labor-intensive business was a mark of social status or a symbol of what a later age would call conspicuous consumption.

A late-marriage regime, which limited the extended family, made life-cycle service an attractive option. It provided both labor to labor-short households, and family and training to servants often enough parentless. Relatively high mortality, late age at marriage, and limited life-expectancy led to a paucity of adult relatives. In addition to the nature of the work, mortality and disease took their toll so often that many households had only one effective adult. Life-cycle service let householders, in Naomi Tadmor's words, "sculpt a family".[7] At the same time service provided what Ann Kussmaul has termed an economically "elegant solution" because it moved labor from families where it had become superfluous to families that needed it. It would have been surprising if servants had not been ubiquitous in England in the pre-industrial era.

Because most households were small and far from wealthy, the majority of English families with servants had one or perhaps two of them. Large staffs of servants with a pronounced servant hierarchy like those described by J. J. Hecht were far less common.[8] Being a sole servant in the early-modern period did not mean isolation, however. Much of early-

6 Albert Gallatin, the early nineteenth-century American Secretary of the Treasury, estimated that eighty percent of all clothing was produced in the home. Quoted in Lucy Maynard Salmon, *Domestic Service*, London/New York, MacMillan, 1897, p. 215.

7 Naomi Tadmor, *Family and Friends in Eighteenth-Century England*, Cambridge, Cambridge University Press, 2001, ch. 1. Kussmaul, *Servants in Husbandry,* p. 26.

8 Joseph Jean Hecht, *The Domestic Servant Class in Eighteenth-Century England*, London, Routledge and Kegan Paul, 1956; see also Tim Meldrum, *Domestic Service and Gender, 1660–1750. Life and Work in the London Household*, Harlow, Longman/Pearson Education, 2000.

modern life was lived outdoors – delivering messages, hauling water, depositing night soil, marketing, gathering wood, doing laundry, chasing after children.

Housing and Family Life

Most early-modern families lived in confined quarters; a two-room cottage was common. If the roof had been high enough, the cottage might have had a loft or even become a house like the ubiquitous two-up, two-down. Even in larger homes daily living tended to be communal when parents, children, and servants – let alone apprentices – lived together. The environments of most servants would have resembled the environments they had left behind in their family homes, where privacy was minimal.

In the poorest of masters' cottages the entire family – servant included – would have shared very limited sleeping space. In other homes servants often shared rooms, sometimes beds, with family members or other servants of the same sex, if there were any. Larger houses had both more room and more residents. At Crosby Hall, Lancashire, in the eighteenth century the four or five female servants slept two to a room. The Hall also regularly accommodated some of the six or so male servants, largely in the "servants' chamber". Over time a number of retired former Crosby servants, many of them later also tenants, shared a servant's room or slept in the servants' chamber for a period. In addition to the master, mistress, their children, and the servants, others might spend a night or a series of nights. These included friends, family relatives, servants' relatives, itinerant artisans like the tailor, former servants, visitors caught by illness or storms, the priest, the doctor, and others including unexpected guests.[9] Privacy, unattainable in smaller quarters, was not easily found in some quite substantial homes.

Close living necessitated familiarity, but masters and servants were often quite familiar with each other before they shared a home. To be sure, social strata were real enough, and the elites did not send out as many

9 Nicholas Blundell, *The Great Diurnal of Nicholas Blundell of Little Crosby, Lancashire, 1702–1729*, 3 vols, The Record Society of Lancashire and Cheshire, n.d.

young people as they hired to serve. However, although servants aided by their families commonly sought to serve in households socially superior to those from which they came, much movement was lateral or nearly lateral. Many masters and servants were connected by intricate patterns of kinship including step and in-law relationships. Also prevalent, especially in smaller towns and the countryside, were client-patronage networks that matched landholders and tenants' children, clergy and parish young people, shopkeepers and customers' progeny, amongst others and thus helped foster social, commercial, and professional exchange.

Servants customarily participated in the general life of the household and often had quite a lot of fun. Diaries like that of Roger Lowe, Thomas Turner, or Nicholas Blundell record servants seeing and acting in plays, dancing, skating, celebrating holidays, meeting at the alehouse, trysting, playing instruments, cockfighting, and much else. Nonetheless, family life was often tumultuous, and servants like children were at times caught in abusive situations. Largely unlike children, servants had some legal protections and could relatively easily leave their service. Apprentices and parish apprentices, who were in effect indentured servants, encountered greater barriers. However, they all had rights under the law, and many used them. Court records show servants not only in struggles with masters or mistresses but caught between husband and wife or parent and child.[10] Even Crosby Hall, generally a happy home for servants, was often enough the scene of what its master called "a great falling out" with a servant. These events were usually "peeced" and of no lasting consequence but sometimes they led to departure or dismissal. Generational conflicts, whether between parent and child or master and servant were then as they are now a fact of life. Smaller homes, even that of the amiable diarist Parson Woodforde, had similar incidents. Sometimes the master or mistress initiated peace, sometimes the servant. Sometimes the episode dissipated, sometimes the sides parted in anger.[11]

10 For examples see William Lewis Sachse, *Records of the Norwich court of mayoralty, 1630–1631*, Norfolk, Norfolk Record Society, 1942, or Tim Meldrum's examples of London Consistory Court records in *Domestic Service and Gender*, p. 15.

11 *The Diary of Roger Lowe of Ashton in Makerfield, Lancashire 1663–74*, William L. Sachse (ed.), New Haven, Yale University Press, 1938; *The Diary of Thomas Turner of East Hoathly (1754–1765)*, Florence Maris Turner (ed.), London, Bodley Head, 1925; *The Diary of a Country Parson: the Reverent James Woodforde*, John Beresford (ed.), 5 vols, London, Oxford University Press, 1924–31.

The Major Tasks: Child-Minding and Cleaning

Servants in smaller families, where they generally served alone, necessarily had to be generalists, helping to perform whatever work was at hand. My analysis of all the extant returns from a 1689 national surtax on servants shows strong correlations between the presence of children and the presence of servants, between the presence of apprentices and the presence of servants, and between the presence of journeymen and the presence of servants. These correlations imply that the more dependents in a family, the more likely that the family would also include a servant, all other things being equal. Whatever else propelled the servant/master relationship, the need for more hands was especially critical.

Most tasks in early modern homes were gendered. Two of the most important tasks were child-minding and cleaning, which Caroline Davidson claims was "of central importance to housework after 1670".[12] The bulk of child-minding and cleaning was done by the wife/mother, if well, aided primarily by one or more female life-cycle servant, whom she supervised. Both the mistress and the servant performed a wealth of ancillary tasks including cooking, sewing, laundry, and marketing.

In the single-servant household the servant was much occupied with children, if there were any. Wealthier households with children often had a designated nursery maid, generally a life-cycle servant dedicated to child-minding but with other duties as well. Although descriptive reports, as opposed to prescriptive ones, of the daily life of an early modern nursery maid are fleeting, they turn up often enough to provide some idea of the scope of her duties. We see the constant presence, not only of the nursery maid but also of the generalist and of the affection, generally reciprocated, that she had for her young charge(s). Once out of service or serving in other families maids and the growing (or even grown) children would retain some of these ties.[13]

Cleaning of all kinds formed the central core of the general servant's job. The lack of piped hot water, which, as Davidson reminds us, remained missing from many English homes until the twentieth century, made cleaning very difficult. Meanwhile, domestic space per capita grew,

12 *A Woman's Work Is Never Done: A History of Housework in the British Isles, 1650–1950*, London, Chatto and Windus, 1982, p. 128.

13 See for examples, *The Great Diurnall of Nicholas Blundell.*

purchase of consumer goods increased, and hearths multiplied. Cleaning tasks expanded in turn, and the housewife worked harder, sought more help, reorganized or succumbed. If she could afford to, the housewife could affect reorganization by turning to local artisans and tradespeople. Spinning, producing cloth and clothing, mending, baking, brewing, mixing medicines, and much else could be transferred, at a price to be sure. Eschewing outsourcing, a family could take on a servant or an additional servant, or hire occasional labor like the washerwoman or the charwoman.

Increases in living area, consumer goods, and hearths were accompanied by other changes. Some were in living patterns that affected architecture and increasingly separated servants physically from the family. Others affected the workplace and increasingly saw it separated from the home. Both, along with fundamental economic changes that recognized the utility and social advantages of formal education, hastened the end of life-cycle service and the servant as family member. These changes underpinned the decline of apprenticeship and the increasing feminization of service as well.

It is difficult to view traditional service, especially life-cycle service, through a modern lens. The shadow of the late Victorian or Edwardian servant falls across the lens and tends to obscure her Stuart predecessor. One such shadow belongs to Hannah Cullwick, who left an extraordinary diary of what she was doing hour after hour, day after long day, inside the homes of various nineteenth-century mistresses. She became a servant after the demise of most life-cycle service (as we have come to define it after Hajnal and Laslett). As a servant, even in her teen years, Cullwick shared not a life-stage but one of class, which her religious faith helped to make more tolerable.[14] It is easy to think that pre-industrial servants needed no qualifications. That was not the case. Many were deemed unsuitable for service, most of them very poor and without exposure to simple material goods like forks or to basic cleaning routines appropriate for decidedly modest households. Courts frequently ordered young, unemployed miscreants to go into service, but the authorities were seldom able to enforce such sentences and usually did not try to. In the late seventeenth century and increasingly in the eighteenth, charity schools prepared poor children for service, inculcating some skills and some discipline – Cullwick was a product of one such remaining school. The link between

14 *The Diaries of Hannah Cullwick, Victorian maidservant*, Liz Stanley (ed.), New Brunswick, N.J., Rutgers University Press, 1984.

charity recipients and service came as middling and wealthier parents were investing in more formal education and devaluing service including apprenticeship for their children. Earlier, however, families had often educated their children before sending them into service. For example, the seventeenth century vicar Ralph Josselin's eldest surviving daughter, Jane, boarded with a schoolmistress for a period of terms before becoming servant to the dowager Lady Harlakenden.[15] In early eighteenth-century Norfolk, the mother of one girl and the uncle of another left money for the respective girl's education in the uncle's words to "better fit her for service". Neither girl needed to serve for the money. Indeed, the wealthy, childless uncle had left his niece real and personal property as well as money.[16] Rather, the training, stability, and social opportunity that service provided at that time were key to these decisions.

The Modern Period

Most western historians date the modern period from about the end of the eighteenth century, a time when domestic service had largely become *déclassé*. In the centuries that followed, domestic service underwent additional change. The trend to feminization of service continued, and at present English domestic workers are overwhelmingly female.

Starting in the sixteenth century, urbanization and the Crown's growing control of its more bellicose subjects began the feminization of service nationwide. Servants in husbandry and apprentices aside, between ten and twenty per cent of early-modern domestic servants were male. The figure was undoubtedly higher in the sixteenth century before cadres of liveried retainers – bodyguards and "tall men", threatening social symbols of the elite – became *passés*. The proportion of male domestic servants continued to drop as distance carriers and access to equipage displaced more and more footboys and footmen, once the indispensable messengers of landed

15 See Alan Macfarlane (ed.), *Diary of Ralph Josselin, 1616–1683*, London, Oxford University Press for the British Academy, 1976, pp. 364–538.

16 Will of Christopher Manning, 26 February 1693/94, Norfolk Record Office, ANW 197, vol. 71.

families and of thriving middlemen. At the same time the classic model of economically successful male maturation, apprentice/journeyman/master or servant/master, was giving way to the industrial model of schoolboy/manager or owner.

Demand for female domestic servants remained high, however, and their absolute numbers soared until the First World War. Thereafter demand slowed substantially, and after the Second World War domestic service began to seem outdated. Except amongst the wealthy, the institution was shriveling. Nonetheless, in the last three decades of the twentieth century demand for domestic servants has risen steadily, largely the result, as geographers Nicky Gregson and Michelle Lowe contend, of the rapid growth of dual-earner households.[17]

Modern Domestic Servants

Edward Higgs has argued that domestic service in Victorian England was a life-cycle occupation for young women, especially in areas where there was little opportunity for alternative employment and where country girls took places in provincial towns.[18] As we know, life-cycle service in early modern England was not a default career choice on the part of young women who needed to work but rather the destiny of large numbers of youths of all social classes when they left home. Yet as age of first marriage had dropped, mortality rates had declined, and education was becoming more widespread, life-cycle service was no longer a demographic imperative. The traditional marriage pattern in England was changing. Over time as middle-class families kept their children out of service and formal education became both more desirable and lengthier, jobs as servants were left to working-class youngsters. By the time increasing numbers of young men chose the growing industrial sector over service, life-cycle service as such had already been routed. Life-cycle service in the traditional sense survived in some rural areas notably in northern England

17 Nicky Gregson and Michelle Lowe, *Servicing the Middle Classes: Class, Gender, and Waged Domestic Labour in Contemporary Britain*, London/New York, Routledge, 1994, pp. 59–65.

18 Edward Higgs, *Domestic Servants and Households in Rochdale, 1851–1871*, New York, Garland Pub., 1986.

into the early twentieth century, but elsewhere it had largely disappeared. It succumbed to a falling age of first marriage, rising fertility, and falling mortality as well as to other, more purely economic and social factors.

Nonetheless, the pattern of having resident servants, many of them young and in single-servant households, continued throughout the nineteenth century and into the twentieth. So too did that of having staffs with senior servants and junior servants so familiar to us from novels and television series. As before, Scottish and Welsh women entered English service, and the Irish diaspora both before and after the Famine provided a large source of domestic workers. Doubtless many of these joined the ranks of non-resident laundresses and charwomen. Since the Second World War and with decolonization, relatively accessible air travel, the opening of eastern Europe, and structural economic change, migration from underdeveloped nations to western Europe has flourished. Many of these migrants became domestic workers in England, some brought in expressly for that purpose by both foreign and native employers.

Ubiquity of Domestic Servants

Demand for and supply of domestic workers fluctuated in twentieth-century England. The national census indicates that at any one point near the turn of the century about 15 percent of households, possibly fewer, must have employed domestic servants including "day girls". The ratio of domestic servants to family units dropped from almost 21.8 percent in 1891 to 17 percent in 1911. However, without the existence of multiple-servant households the ratio would have been substantially lower. Because documents differ both in form and content, we cannot readily compare like with like in our two periods. Yet, the percentages of early modern families with domestic servants at any one time in the early-modern period were considerably higher than these figures. Roughly 30 percent of such families had servants, excluding day labor, at a given period and most of these were female.[19] Similarly, although absolute servant numbers had never been so high as they were at the turn of the twentieth century,

19 P. Laslett, A. Kussmaul, and others based their estimates largely on early modern household lists from the Cambridge Group for the History of Population and Social Structure.

the percentage of the population that were servants was lower than that of pre-industrial England. Again, comparing like with like is difficult in part because we cannot control for age structure of the pre-industrial populations represented. Nonetheless, female domestic labor, once again including what the census called "day girls", fell from 4.7 percent to 3.8 percent of the population between 1891 and 1911. Estimates of the percentage of domestic servants not including day girls, i.e., women hired as domestics by the day or hour, at any one time in seventeenth and eighteenth-century urban populations range from 7.7 to 23.5 percent. Data from most sources seem to cluster in the lower half of that spectrum.[20] Estimates of life-cycle servants in early-modern England run in the neighborhood of 15 percent of the national population.

The absolute number of "female domestic indoor servants" increased from the 1881 census to that of 1901 and again to 1911. However, the increase did not keep pace with the growth in population generally or with the increase in the number of families in England. The male component of the domestic-servant population, a small fraction of the female, declined absolutely as well as relatively between 1901 and 1911. Thus the perceived servant shortage at the turn of the century, which led to "An Enquiry by the Women's Industrial Council", was real.[21]

Two world wars and the depression in between created very special conditions, the former by giving alternative employment opportunities to women and the latter by its staggering unemployment. Many erstwhile employers as well as servants went on the dole although for those households that could afford them gas stoves, vacuum cleaners, hot water heaters, and refrigerators significantly lessened the need for domestic help. There were, however, no appliances that minded children.

Our image and the reality of modern domestic service in England do not always gel. The most elite households continue to employ multiple servants. However, as two-earner families on the one hand and single parents on the other become more numerous, many very humble households are again employing domestic help as their early-modern predecessors did. Servant numbers are not entirely known, for many domestic

20 For a recent study of urban data see T. Meldrum, *Domestic Service and Gender*, pp. 13–15.

21 C. Violet Butler, *Domestic Service, an enquiry by the Women's Industrial Council*, London, G. Bell and Sons, 1916; for the American shortage, see L. M. Salmon, *Domestic Service*.

workers, especially cleaners, are paid in cash outside official purview, thus avoiding taxation. As many of these workers do not live with their employers, the ruse is readily maintained. Conversely, the number of households employing domestic workers is not known for the same reason. However, all reports indicate that the average modern household that employs domestic workers has just one, sometimes two.

Housing and Family Life

In some respects household relations between servants and their employers in England seem to fall broadly into three periods, and that is the case also with residence. From late medieval times to the end of the early-modern period, when life-cycle service was waning, servants commonly lived amidst the master's family. At this time community ties between servants' families and their masters often mitigated possibilities for abuse. Indentured parish apprentices did not usually have this cushion. Relatively few domestic servants unknown to the master were hired at hiring fairs; and employment agencies, which began to appear in London in the eighteenth century, were not an immediate success. For example, a model once started by the novelist Henry Fielding and his brother failed. For many years inns and taverns along the main highways into London served would-be employers but especially servants as information exchanges.

By the nineteenth century, the upper and middle classes had largely kept their children out of domestic service and humble homes increasingly had no servants. As a result, the importance to master and servant of ties of family and friendship and of patronage, which offered protection to the servant, had largely melted away, especially in urban areas. Domestic servants, while generally still resident, became physically and psychically more distanced from the families whom they served. Amongst other things social and class distinctions – including education, language, dress, and leisure activities; separation of workplace and home; more rigid allocation of space; and less prior familiarity – played a role in creating a widening gulf between householders and servants. Culturally the two had less and less in common. With the middling and upper classes no longer a source of servants, employers often had little acquaintance with or knowledge of prospective domestics, especially in cities. In London during the

1880s, for example, Marion Sambourne like her friends commonly used advertisements and agencies to find servants. Many of these, considered slatternly and ill prepared for households where polishing was important, were promptly dismissed although not easily replaced.[22] Increasingly working-class young women sought commercial or industrial work while would-be employers bemoaned a servant shortage.

The mid-century decline in demand for domestic workers provided a watershed. In the last half of the twentieth century, domestic work in England became increasingly comparable to other forms of employment. While necessarily still situated in family residences, domestic service has emerged as a better defined job with set hours and stated wages due at shorter intervals, often weekly rather than quarterly. As the middle classes who had given up servants embraced them once again, these changes became more marked, and others followed. Except for those in prestigious households, domestic workers increasingly tended not to live with their employers, so were not dependent on them for room and board, and they were in regular communication with others outside the employer's residence.

With lengthier compulsory schooling, domestic service has over time become primarily an adult occupation. Both age and training augment the worker's power. Vocational schools and polytechnics offer many courses, notably certification for nannies, that give domestic work some legitimacy as a specialty. Courses are not an innovation of the later twentieth century. Charity schools provided vocational training, and special programs in home economy or domestic science were instituted with some success a century ago. But widespread certification in a number of technical areas has helped to give those in the domestic sphere a more positive context.

Nonetheless, other factors still work against the employee. Both being the sole employee, as a domestic worker often is, and the isolation of the workplace in a family home increase the employer's power especially in matters like irregularity of payment, demand for overtime, and inappropriate tasks. Those domestic workers who have little qualification and limited alternatives are at greater risk. Their number includes school-leavers, non-English speakers, and undocumented workers. For them domestic service can be virtual enslavement especially if they are resident in

22 Shirley Nicholson, *A Victorian Household, based on the Diaries of Marion Sambourne,* London, Barrie and Jenkins, 1988, pp. 65–68.

the workplace. Recognizing the problem, charitable agencies have formed to help them.

The Major Tasks: Child-Minding and Cleaning

In the late twentieth century, the growing presence of wives and mothers in the paid workforce raised demand for domestic workers. Gregson and Lowe sampled advertisements for both male and female domestic help that employers placed between 1981 and 1991 in *The Lady*, a national magazine that has been the major source of "sits vac", and in two regional newspapers. The domestic-labor needs of late twentieth-century households that the advertisements reflect seem remarkably similar to labor needs of pre-industrial families. In all three modern publications the overwhelming majority of advertisers were seeking child-minders or cleaners.[23] The modern nanny and cleaner may have replaced the early-modern nursery maid, general servant, and charwoman, but their charges in many ways remain the same – children and dirt.

Modern child-minders run the gamut from live-in nannies to quasi-businesspersons minding children brought to the minder's premises. The person in charge of a minding business hardly qualifies as a domestic worker. However, for the other minders, whether a resident servant or an employee with her own residence, there often are problems of status inconsistency, for more than most they face the issue of whether they are employees or family members. Both they and the children's parents, especially mothers, may be confused about their roles, for the child-minder, regardless of professional credentials, is commonly emotionally involved with the children in her care as a family member would be. And where is the middle ground between family member and employee? She may attach herself to her young charges in a motherly or familial fashion only to learn that she is not considered a family member in any sense but a replaceable employee. Her affection for the family's children can lead her into role conflicts and often muddies her self-image as an employee.[24] In this respect she bears some resemblance to the nineteenth-century child

23 N. Gregson and M. Lowe, *Servicing the Middle Classes*, pp. 9–19, 242–8.
24 *Ibid.*, pp. 229–230.

minder. However, that nanny or nurse often had an accepted middling role as a family retainer. She was in a category of servants who were not members of the family. This group, including housekeepers and others, especially long-term servants, were part of a patronage system of employees to be cared for that was not legally but rather socially defined.[25] The early modern maidservant's role was clearer too. She was perceived as part of the family and played a role similar to an older sibling's or a young aunt's, a role both she and her master or mistress understood – subordinate but integral. The modern child-minder is in a much more ambiguous position.

The most striking change in the later twentieth century may have occurred with the rise, or re-invention, of the cleaner. The role of the non-resident, occasionally employed charwoman, despised over the centuries, has combined to an extent with that of the housemaid and emerged as the non-resident cleaner. From the char the cleaner takes flexibility of schedule. Like the char she is frequently older, even widowed. She often has the additional advantage of depending on cleaning for supplementary income or pocket money only, which gives her a form of independence that the worker minding the child in its parents' home usually does not have. Like the experienced housemaid, the cleaner has an aura of a practiced quasi-specialist and works without the close supervision that the char so often had to tolerate, largely because the cleaner's employer is generally employed herself and out of the house during working hours. Perceived by both herself and her employers as self-employed, the cleaner works to a schedule, often weekly.

Not all cleaners, however, fare so well. Those who come to England from developing countries are generally dependent on their jobs for support and are thus usually more vulnerable, which puts them at a disadvantage in their relationships with their employers. If they are in the country without documents, they are virtually powerless in the relationship.

25 For examples see Jonathan Gathorne-Hardy, *The Rise and Fall of the British Nanny*, London, Hodder and Stoughton, 1972.

From Family Member to Employee

The demand for help with child-minding and cleaning is one of the most striking continuities in English domestic service. We should not be surprised, however. These are tasks that machines can make easier but cannot totally displace. They are not only long-term but widespread. In 2002, Sembeyo Bobke, a poor Masai, received $38,000 from the British as damages for the loss of her son caused by abandoned munitions. She bought a vehicle and started a taxi business. Subsequently she hired a maid, Elizabeth Nosip, to "clean the house, fetch firewood and water, and to take [the] little girl to school".[26] Although we may deal with it in new ways, some domestic work will always be present.

The primary difference between such work in early modern times and in contemporary England lies with the conditions of workers and the conditions of work. What over time has been gained and what has been lost? The gains are relatively easy to see; the losses are a bit more elusive. The early modern servant was widely considered to be a family member as long as she remained in service. The modern domestic worker is legally an employee and generally thinks of herself that way although even modern domestic service is not as divorced from the family with all its emotional baggage as most employment is.

Being an employee in the modern British state has advantages. Servants have had some job and wage security since the medieval period; but modern laws regarding minimum wages, child workers, workplace safety, and sexual abuse as well as health, unemployment, and disability protection encompass much more. The Elizabethan poor laws were a marvel for their time, the flower of the Tudor welfare state, but they were not so far-reaching. And the seventeenth-century Act of Settlement made it difficult for the poor generally and those "out of service" in particular to move about the country to improve their lot. Earlier nineteenth-century legislation, notably the "new" poor law, was also harsh. Male household heads, who at one time could almost freely administer corporal punishment to any member of the household, have lost that right even in regard to their children.

26 "New wealth brings Masai mixed fortunes", *Guardian Weekly*, February 26–March 3, 2004, p. 21.

The utility of formal education and training that became apparent as the pre-industrial age closed lessened the proportion of youth entering domestic service. Their replacement by fully adult domestic workers largely with their own residences has helped to professionalize the working relationship. Early modern service entailed an enforceable contract written or not. However, lack of specie, fictive relationships between master and servant, difficulty of taking one's host to court, worry about recommendations, and other considerations made a servant a reluctant suitor. Today's employer of domestic workers understands she has the same obligations as other employers, whether she skirts them or not. When the hire is unreported, usually by mutual agreement to avoid taxation and other obligations, the worker has little protection.

The role of the government in making education compulsory as well as supporting training programs for domestic workers has helped to elevate domestic work into a more respectable occupation than it has often been in the past. While life-cycle service was understood to be temporary and perfectly socially acceptable, other forms of early domestic service often were not, especially if they involved day labor or when older workers were stuck in positions more appropriate for young people. Nineteenth- and early twentieth-century servants were possibly even less respected. Often house-bound and living in undesirable conditions, separated in smaller homes from normal intercourse with others, at times subject to excessively long hours and harsh discipline, Victorian servants were at considerable risk of many kinds of repression.

The modern period has seen domestic work sheltered under the umbrella of "the service industry", which encompasses a range of different jobs. With a safety net of sorts to depend on and more disposable income, both servant and employer can vacation in Majorca, even if in different hotels. Early modern life-cycle servants often had lifestyles similar to those of their employers, but their lifetime fellows and nineteenth-century servants seldom did. Too, loss of status was keenly felt by the impecunious, yet well-educated daughters and sisters of the financially straitened who were sent out as companions, governesses, and ladies' maids and often like Mary Wollstonecraft and the Brontës turned to their pens for a living.

The tide of change that swept across England in the early-modern period and especially in the eighteenth century necessarily affected domestic service. The life-cycle system that had been in place from at least the medieval period belonged to an economic, social, and demographic regime that mercantilism and capitalism would sweep away. Once that regime came under assault, life-cycle service necessarily retreated. It lasted longest where traditional agricultural society was still viable. Domestic service today and in the recent past has emerged from its nadir in the nineteenth and twentieth century when class identification pushed most domestics to virtual social oblivion. For that emergence we can be grateful although much remains to be done to maintain acceptable employment practices and to provide support for an underclass of immigrants among some others.

Having said that, we can look back with some affection to the early modern period. English society with limited use for formal education had found a viable way to train and educate the young while giving them shelter and responsibility away from home yet within a community. Life-cycle service offered a predominately safe transition between the parental household and independence, between childhood and adulthood. Life-cycle servants were fed, housed, clothed, trained, and paid in return for their labor. The arrangement benefited both the household head short of labor and the servant short of experience and sometimes of natal family. The facet of the north-western European marriage pattern that constituted service may have taken centuries of late antiquity to work out, but for further centuries it was a major strength of English life. However, in a changing economic climate, English parents who could afford to do so withdrew their children from service. Their sons went on to school and employment. Their daughters went home in many cases to some formal education and social training. Children from poorer families continued to go into service and out to labor, both marked by the absence of the broad social spectrum and often stigmatized by class.

In addition, for some middling and wealthy young women it was a particular loss. Service had taught their grandmothers to be instrumental – to market apples, to sell chairs, to handle money, to mix with people across social strata. Such activity had made many of them more competent and confident women although not angels in the house.

Irregular Migration and the Globalization of Domestic Work

Migrant Domestic Workers in Germany

Helma LUTZ and Susanne SCHWALGIN

This paper addresses a surprising social phenomenon: despite immense technological changes, domestic and care work in the post-modern household are increasingly taken over by maids, nannies, domestic workers and carers. In our age of information technology, the "new maids" are involved in domestic work in similar numbers as they did a hundred years ago. However, there are important differences between traditional maids and the maids of our days. One difference concerns the fact that currently domestic workers are often migrant women from Eastern Europe, East Asia and Latin America. A large number of them are illegalised in a twofold way. First, they do not hold a residence permit and second they are not registered as workers. Thus, they work in the twilight zone of the informal labour market.

This dual illegalisation results in a number of problems which makes their living and working conditions extremely unstable. Without a legal residence and work permit they are excluded from citizenship rights and are denied access to medical care, education (for themselves and their children), regular working hours, wage continuation in case of illness, paid vacation etc. Often they suffer from psychological stress and psychosomatic disorders resulting from the fear of being discovered and deported.

Under these circumstances, undocumented women seek employment as domestic worker. In contrast to other segments of the labour market private households seem to offer more protection against police controls of residence and work permits. In this respect the gendered character of domestic work is supposed to be an advantage. Domestic work is still unaddressed by public discourse and the household is still seen as a private sphere. Therefore, domestic work – as opposed to other segments of the informal labour market – is relatively safe from state control. Thus, at first glance domestic work seems to be a "space of protection" for illegalised migrant women. Simultaneously this "space of protection" may turn out to be a "dangerous space" because the denial of wage payment, injuries, sexual harassment and violence are not subjected to any control nor legal regulation.

However, precarious working conditions of domestic servants and the globalization of domestic work is not a new phenomenon at all. During the eighteenth and nineteenth century, European working class women adopted employment as domestic servant and child carer inside and outside Europe (Sharpe 2001; Henkes 1998; Harzig 1997), often accepting precarious working conditions. Although the now widely used term domestic worker or servant derives from a very different historical situation in the past and therefore, is an "old theme", in the context of globalization and the trans-nationalisation of life-courses new aspects come to the fore. One important result of the trans-nationalisation of domestic work is the emergence of multi-local and transnational households – including members on the move as well as those staying behind. How people manage these transnational households and what kind of lifestyle emerges from this is still un-addressed in social science research and requires further research, in particular in the case of Germany.

The research project "Gender, Ethnicity, Identity – the new maids in the age of globalization" aims at reducing this lack of research by exploring the relationship between processes of the globalization of domestic work on the one hand and the twofold illegalisation of migrant domestic workers on the other.[1] In the following part some aspects of this research project will be discussed.

We will start by roughly presenting the design of research. Second, we will describe the scope and shape of contemporary domestic work in Germany. In this context the question of (dis-)continuities between the new maids and the historical domestic servants is at centre stage. Third, we will present some preliminary results of our work in progress. One important insight is the fact that there are remarkable individual differences in the ways how migrant domestic workers deal with their living situation as illegalised migrants. These differences can only be examined

1 See www.uni-muenster.de/FGEI.

by focusing on resources which arise from their biographical experiences. Therefore, finally our paper examines "biographical resources" of undocumented migrant domestic workers in Germany, deriving from life history interviews. This raises the question in which respect domestic work constitutes a space of agency for illegalised migrants.

Research Design[2]

Migrant domestic workers should not be seen as mere victims or marionettes driven by the circumstances of globalization but rather as self-consciously acting subjects. They may be confronted with similar structural restrictions. However, they rely on different biographical and structural resources in order to manage their lives as transnational undocumented migrants. The complexity of factors which lead to individually different ways of dealing with illegalisation can only be explored by focusing on agency. Thus, the project's focus are the following questions:

- Which biographical and structural resources are mobilised in order to actively create and manage the migration process and a life as illegalised migrant?
- How do migrant domestic workers manage transnational households and lifestyles?
- How do they respond to biographical ruptures that may result from migration and illegalisation?
- How do they retrospectively remember and narrate these ruptures in order to integrate them in a meaningful way in their life stories?

2 The period of data collection was finished by the end of 2003. The data set consists primarily of 70 interviews with migrant domestic workers and their employers. The countries of origin of the migrant domestic workers are Poland, the Czech Republic, Hungary, Georgia, Ukraine and Lithuania for the Middle-Eastern European countries and Ecuador for Latin America besides Columbia, Uruguay, Peru, Chile and Brasilia. The overwhelming majority of the interviewees was female. Meanwhile more than half of the interviewees successfully legalised themselves by marriage, half of them live without a valid residence permit in Germany and only a small minority holds a temporary residence permit as students.

These questions are explored through life history interviews. Life history interviews evoke retrospective reflections and individual processes of making sense of one's life. In order to analyse social practices in a given situation participant observation was a second important method of our research.

Through participant observation, concrete social practices can be explored, as for example questions concerning the intercultural aspects of communication and relationship between employer and employees in the household. The employer-employee relationship is always embedded in hierarchically structured power relations. In this context interviews with employers are conducted, too.

Another focus of our project has been the exploration of networks (local and transnational networks respectively) that enable migrant domestic workers to organise migration, transnational household management as well as their life without papers. Thus, participant observation is not only conducted at the working place, but in other social spheres/spaces, too. For example church based communities seem to be an important social space for Polish and Filipina migrant domestic workers in order to find work, a place to stay as well as emotional support. German non-governmental organisations and self-organisation seem to play a similar role for domestic workers from Latin America in Berlin and Hamburg.

However, the possibilities of conducting participant observation were limited. These limitations are intrinsically linked to two important characteristics of the research field. First, private households are private spheres of the employers and consequently only accessible for participant observation in the limited time of an interview or visit. Second, the clandestine character of undocumented migration prevents undocumented migrants from claiming public spaces for themselves. Third, illegalised migrants seem to avoid public gatherings. Therefore, their social life relies mostly on informally organized networks in a private context. Furthermore, most migrant domestic workers have long working hours that leave little time for social or other activities. All these factors contribute to the fact that there are no sites of field research in the sense of locality where participant observation can easily be conducted.

The field research is differentiated by four categories:

- Regional differentiation – research locations are Berlin, Hamburg and Münster – a medium-sized town in the Northwest of Germany,

- differences with respect to the place of origin – although we do not focus on specific ethnic groups of migrant domestic workers we try to take into account ethnic or other particularities of their social networks,
- differences with respect to the tasks performed in the context of domestic work
- and differences with respect to parenthood, the parental status of the employer and the employee alike.

These methodical particularities will be further explored during the presentation of two case studies.

New Maids in the Age of Globalization and the Transnationalisation of Households

For a long time during the twentieth century it was expected that technological progress would eliminate the need for human assistance in households. However, today, at the threshold of the twenty-first century the numbers of domestic helpers working in European households are very similar to what they were a century ago. How could an activity that had certainly been deleted from the register of occupations by the end of the Second World War in Western European households have made such a vigorous comeback? The simplest answer that has been given by mainstream sociologists and economists is that professional working women today need help in coping with the double burden of family care and career. Hundred years earlier, the reasons had been different. Back then, domestic staff was part of the prestige of bourgeois families. Research on continuity and discontinuity in aspects of maid service in the twentieth century reveals many changes. As already mentioned, today's maids are increasingly recruited among migrant women from Asia, Africa, Latin America and Eastern Europe. They emigrate to the centres of the wealthy world to support and sustain their families back home. This trend does not only reflect the world-wide feminisation of migration (see Koser and Lutz 1998; Phizacklea 1998) and the international labour market's globalization but also the shift of exploitation and dependence from a national to an international context. In Western Europe the maids issue has evolved from one of class to one of ethnicity and nationality.

Unlike in the past, no reliable sources today quantify domestic service – yet another paradox in our world controlled by technology. According to the economic scientist Jürgen Schupp (2002, 65): "In Germany there are approximately 3 Million private households that employ a domestic worker on a regular basis; however less than 40,000 employees are registered for social insurance." In the context of an investigation for the International Monetary Fund his colleague Friedrich Schneider estimates that the new maids contributed approximately 5.5 Billion German Mark to the German Gross National Product (GNP) in the 1990s (Schneider and Enste 2000). Simone Odierna (2000) calculated 2.4 million sub-minimum types of jobs in private households without any social security. In their study of Bremen, Marianne Friese and Barbara Thiessen submit that one out of eight households uses hired help (Friese and Thiessen 1997). All these authors expect growth in this field of employment (see Gather *et al.* 2002).

Today, domestic work has emerged as an informal, feminised labour market for migrant women. These women are often recruited through family or friendship networks of employees and employers alike. Another form of recruitment is being performed by church based or commercial agencies as well as through newspaper advertisements. In Germany the internet is also being used to hire domestic workers from Eastern Europe, especially if care for the elderly is required.[3]

One example is a web-site that is established and run by a Sudeten German journalist. He promotes the website as a means to "improve the benefits of good neighbourhood for Germans and Czechs". On his homepage it is made clear that questions of labour and residence permits should be clarified by the employers themselves. However, all labour-seeking advertisements offer wages "according to negotiations" and not according to the legal standards that are required by the so called Riester-Modell. The Riester-Modell has been implemented as a legal possibility – similar to the former "guest-worker" model – to temporarily hire care workers for the elderly from Eastern European Countries (Poland, Hungary, the Czech Republic, Slovenia). The German Ministry of Work was in charge for the recruitment of these women. They were offered at maximum a three years

3 See www.tschechien.biz/index/html, 01-09-2003.

working permit as carers for those elderly people who can claim a specific need for care according to the German care insurance. The so-called Riester-Modell was implemented from the beginning of 2002 on until spring of 2003.[4] There had been plans to include the decree in the new law on the regulation of migration (Zuwanderungsgesetz) that was supposed to be put into force in 2003. As the implementation of the law on migration was delayed, the decree has been suspended. There are plans however, to re-establish it as part of the new migration law.[5]

The above mentioned German website which pretends to promote good East-West-neighbourhood-relationship, uses the internet as a means for labour-contact and -contracts; the costs for posting an advertisement are only 5 Euro. US-based websites in comparison, are much more advanced – commercial agencies use the internet for offering domestic workers from Asia on global scale per mouse-click.[6]

In any case local and transnational networks alike are essential to organize migration and a transnational lifestyle. These networks are especially important if children are left behind and if their care has to be organized with either family and kin members or with a paid care giver. Arlie Russell Hochschild has coined this phenomenon the "global-care-chain" (Hochschild 2000, 130–146). The emotional care that cannot be given to one's own children is addressed to the children of the employer, instead. Migration research refers to the exodus of the well-educated from the countries of origin as brain-drain. Worldwide female migration for the purpose of domestic work creates a similar pattern in the care work sphere. Here the care capital is reduced. Thus, similar to brain-drain, this migration pattern is called "care-drain" (Ehrenreich and Hochschild 2002). However, since the majority of the new maids are well educated, their migration combines both patterns: it has the effects of brain and care-

4 Detailed figures are available for the time period of February to December 2002. According to a report of the central agency of employment recruitment 1102 domestic workers were hired during this period. The overwhelming majority were female, only 79 were men. The domestic workers predominantely came from Poland (862 persons); the other countries of origin were Slovakia (103), Slovenia (4), Czech Republic (43) and Hungary (90): see Zentralstelle für Arbeitsvermittlung, 2003.

5 This information is based on a telephone conversation with an employee of the German Ministry of Economy and Work (Bundesministerium für Wirtschaft und Arbeit) in Bonn, 16 July 2004.

6 See e.g., http://www.filmo.com.

drain for the countries of origin, which turns into brain waste and care surplus in the destination countries.

We will be rather short about the question how transnational motherhood is organized.[7] In general it can be mentioned that two factors facilitate transnational mother-/parenthood. First, recent achievements in communication technology make at least oral communication easier. Frequent calls to children left behind and their care givers are in most cases possible and affordable. They may be a means to perform educational intervention despite immense geographical distances and enable mothers (in some cases fathers) to stay in touch with their children.

Second, transnational motherhood/parenthood cannot be analysed with the concepts of motherhood and family which exist in western industrial countries. As most of the women are not allowed to take their children with them, the physical closeness, seen as healthy and "normal" in the western upbringing of a child, is not given. Other bonds of belonging have to be developed between parents and children. Rhacel Parreñas calls the type of motherhood, which develops in the case of long mother-child parting "commodified motherhood" (Parreñas 2001). The tie between mothers and children is mostly expressed through material goods, financial aid and the payment for a good education. The psychological results, for example personal alienation, are often underestimated by the mothers. On the other hand, non-western constructions of motherhood do not measure a good mother according to her direct involvement in the upbringing of or her symbiosis with a child; this function can be handed over to a "social mother".

Therefore, research about household and family structures in the Caribbean, Latin America and Asia suggests that universalistic eurocentric notions of family and parenthood have to be dismissed. Mary Chamberlain (1997) describes traditional patterns of migration for young Caribbean women migrating to the United States, to Europe or to another Caribbean island in order to improve their living conditions, after they gave birth to one or two children. From generation to generation these children are left behind and educated by social mothers, grandmothers or other female kin. Chamberlain argues, that this concept of social motherhood facilitates migration of women. The social anthropologist Karen Fog Olwig (1993) explored similar patterns of child caring for the Islands of

7 For a more detailed examination of this phenomenon, see R. S. Parreñas (2002) and K. Shinozaki (2004).

Nevis in the Caribbean. Pierrette Hondagneu-Sotelo and Ernestine Avila (1997) describe processes of family "fragmentation" as a consequence of migration for Mexican and Latin American households. The number of households which rely on remittances earned by young women in the United States, Spain and Germany among other European countries is said to be constantly rising. How does daily life and work look like for these transnational migrants?

The tasks which are performed by migrant domestic workers cover a wide range of occupations. They range from cleaning private households to offices, washing, cooking and caring for children and the elderly to assisting at family celebrations and corporate events. In the Anglo-Saxon context these tasks are described as the three Cs – Cleaning, Cooking, Caring (Anderson 2000). In most cases, especially where care of children and the elderly is included, tasks cannot easily be separated from each other but they are performed in combination. However, the activities that are outsourced to migrant domestic workers are those which are considered unpleasant and distasteful.

The heterogeneity of tasks corresponds with the heterogeneity of employment situations. They range from a two-hour a week cleaning job to the 24-hour on call-service of the live-in maids or au pairs. The wages can be heterogeneous, too. According to our data material 8–10 Euro is the average wage per hour, although there are differences between the three cities Hamburg, Berlin and Münster. In Hamburg the wages per hour are higher than in Berlin and Münster. However in some cases wages per hour are less than 3 Euro or up to 10 Euro.

As mentioned before, a lot of migrant domestic workers are affected by double illegalisation as undocumented migrants and irregular workers alike. However, one preliminary result of our research project is that the residence status of migrant domestic workers may constantly change over the years: they may enter the country with a tourist visa, stay as overstayers if their visa are exceeded, and thus, becoming undocumented, renew their residence permit through enrolment as students and lose it once again, when their status as students expires. For most migrant women the step towards illegality is not easy at all, because they are well aware of the risk involved. Living in the twilight zone as undocumented migrant does not only mean to be deprived of labour rights, but of future perspectives, civil and social rights alike.

What are the reasons that lead women to migrate as undocumented domestic workers, despite the difficult living conditions of illegalised existence and the emotional costs they are paying for their migration?

Domestic Work as a Space of Opportunities for Undocumented Migrants?

We have to keep in mind, that female migrants first and foremost do not choose unstable working- and living conditions, but actively try to leave them behind. The most important regions of origin of migrant domestic workers are those that are – in contrast to the target countries of the global flow of migrants – regions in crisis. These unequal terms of trade have facilitated the emergence of a new export product: "care-work" which is offered mainly by women and to a much lesser extent by men.

Although the countries of origin to do not actively promote the export of care-work, they encourage this work indirectly because their economies considerably rely on remittances – as for example the Philippines where 5.6 Million women working out of the Philippines earn 8 billion dollars currency per year (Parreñas 2001).

Recent studies as well as our own results report that most domestic servants are well educated. For example women from Eastern-European countries have performed occupations that are devaluated after the system transformation. This devaluation process is twofold, it takes place in the country of origin as well as in the destination country. Destination countries are not interested in their professional expertise but rather in their "experiential expertise" – as for example in the fact that they have children of their own if they work as child carer, or in skills that are perceived as natural female. For East-European migrant domestic workers, who are the focus of our project, the following factors for migration can be distinguished:

- Young women, who have no opportunities to find a job in their countries of origin. By migrating they attempt to improve their working opportunities through foreign language skills or they aim at studying in Germany, or they only want to earn some money to finance a univer-

sity education back home. Moreover, these women are like other peers attracted by cosmopolitan dreams and try to realize them through migration.
- Divorced women who want to earn money for their living and the education of their children. Some of them may try to find a German marriage partner, because marriage would be the only possibility to bring their children to Germany.
- Women, who themselves or whose families encounter financial difficulties and thus attempt to work abroad as long as these problems have not been solved. Sometimes they try to realize other targets as the establishment of their own business. However, in many cases remittances develop their own dynamics as for example the family expects them to fulfil material desires that are developed by the constant flow of money.

In most cases migrant domestic workers do not attempt a life-long emigration, but a mobility flexible in time and space to overcome immediate financial problems. As Mirjana Morokvašic pointed out, Polish women "leave home in order to stay at home" (Morokvašic 1994). In the Polish case and that of other East-European migrant women this results in pendular migration instead of emigration.

A fourth group consists of young lesbian women and homosexual men form Eastern European countries who attempt to flee discrimination and taboos of homosexuality through migration.

This list mirrors a more or less socio-economic logic that is not only characteristic for East-European migrants, but for other groups, too. Yet, socio-economic reasons are only one of the reasons that foster migration. In contrast to Malgorzata Irek's study (Irek 1998) who in her research on Polish migrants in Berlin, argues that these women come along with illegality and behave according to a rational choice model – the maximisation of profit – the preliminary results of our data show enormous differences in the ways of *responding to illegality*. These differences are shaped by the following four *intersecting structural and biographical factors*:

- the *different modes of illegalisation*: an illegalised residence status and an illegalised employment situation;
- the *geographic proximity* between working places and places of origin;
- *individual differences* in the ways how migrant domestic workers deal with their living situation as illegalised migrants. These differences can

only be examined by focusing on *resources* which arise from their *biographical experiences*;
- *transnational relationships* to their places of origin and their families left behind, too.

In the following these intersecting factors will be exemplified by focusing on two case studies.

Ways to Deal with Illegality – Two Case Studies

Mrs A. came to Germany in the summer 1990. She was 30 years old, single, and had just finished her studies of economic science in Poland. Searching for an opportunity to bridge the unemployment gap, she worked as a cleaner in various households during the summer. She had entered Germany with a tourist visa and returned to Poland after three months. Another six months later she came back to Münster. A network of Polish friends supported her to find jobs as a domestic worker as well as accommodation. In order to legalise her residence status, Mrs A. successfully registered in an academic course in Economics at the University of Münster in the summer of 1992. During the following years she took on jobs in various households, looking for children, caring for old people and cleaning in both private houses and offices. Ten years later her residential status as a student ceased. At the moment of our interview she felt forced to choose between two alternatives – to stay in Münster illegally or to return to Poland. And she did no like any of them.

Mrs A. felt scared by imaging herself as a "sans papiers". For her being an honest person had been a central value. She already felt guilty of cheating or "playacting" as she called it, on her employers, having led some of them to believe for years that she was only working for them in order to support herself as a student, even though she hardly attended any classes. She pointed out the importance of being needed by her employers because she does "not like to feel as a robot". She developed friendly relations to one of the families employing her – she takes care of their child, who has learned Polish words from her, she cleans their household and helps out their parents as well. Moreover, her employers are her landlords;

she does not live as a live-in but rents her flat from them. She feels like a member of the family.

In the first place, it seems to be essential to her that she is respected and acknowledged by her employers; she derives satisfaction from the fact that she has a key function as a first port-of-call for the friends of her homosexual Polish network, as well as a communications role. In contrast to Mrs M. – the protagonist of the second case which we will present – Mrs A. does not have any plans for the future. During the interview she stated that not having a plan had been characteristic for all the years she had been living in Germany.

However, returning to Poland is definitely not an attractive alternative for her. For Mrs A. Münster has become the focus of her life ("I know my way around better in Germany"). Although she visits her place of origin in Poland several times each year she feels completely estranged from Poland. Even the fact that she could count on the economic and emotional support of her family does not dispel her doubts that she might be perceived a "migration loser" when returning to Poland. During her frequent visits to Poland she had felt uncomfortable with not being able to show the expected symbols of a successful migration as e.g. a car, a good job in Germany, money for establishing an own business in Poland or at least a German husband. For Mrs A. returning to Poland is therefore just as unattractive an option as staying in Germany illegally. Thus, she finds herself in a social trap, and at the moment of our interview it was not clear yet how she was going to get out of it.

Mrs M., the protagonist of our second case study, developed a rather different way of dealing with illegality. She had left Uruguay for Hamburg in 1994; at the time she had already been in her late 40's. In the beginning of the interview she stressed the fact, that her migration to Germany had not been motivated by economic reasons. She had just taken advantage of an opportunity, accompanying her daughter, who had fallen in love with a German man. After her arrival in Germany she could rely on a network of German friends whom she had got acquainted with through their common political activities in Uruguay. This personal network enabled her to find accommodation and places to work as a cleaner as well as access to important knowledge about how to get medical treatment as a *sans papiers*. Moreover, she got in touch with the German NGO "Nobody is illegal" and started to give public lectures about her life as an illegalised migrant.

In contrast to Mrs A., Mrs M. has developed plans during the course of her stay. First of all she experienced migration as an emancipating project since she separated from her husband after 27 years of marriage. After having lived and worked four years as undocumented migrant she decided to legalise her residential status by marrying a German. After legalisation she gained working permission and could take up jobs legally, but she decided to pursue the irregular work because her most important aim was to save as much money as possible. The purpose of saving, however, changed over time. While she first supported her son's university education in Uruguay and later started the renovation of her house in Montevideo, she is currently preparing for her return to Montevideo and saving money to establish her own business there.

During her years in Germany Mrs A. supported herself (and her family) by working as a cleaning woman. As she explained, she cleaned private households and offices due to the lack of German language skills that obstructed her to find a job in any other field: "I am cleaning because I cannot speak." On the one hand her argument describes a painful lack of other opportunities. On the other hand Mrs M. emphasized during our interviews that she prefers to clean in places where she is *not expected to speak*. In contrast to Mrs A. who needs to feel like "one of the family", she has no desire to cultivate close emotional relations with her employers; she even tries to avoid them.

The quite different ways of coping with illegality can only be explained by taking Mrs M.'s biography into account. In contrast to Mrs A. Mrs M. has already lived through several biographical ruptures before migrating to Germany. During the years of the military junta in Uruguay, she and her husband had been persecuted as political activists and had been forced to go underground in order to save their lives. Finally, she and her family had left the country and spent 12 years as political refugees in Argentine. In exile she had continued working in her old profession as a designer for the first years. After realising that this profession did not offer a future perspective due to ongoing computerization she had retrained as a specialist of gastronomy.

For Mrs M. her occupation as a domestic worker in Germany is not the centre of her life, but a means to follow other aims. Her political activism allows her to derive recognition beyond her occupation as domestic worker; she gives lectures and interviews and she has been the protagonist of a documentary on her life in Germany. Recently she started to write a book about her migration experiences. In addition, Mrs M.'s political engagement provides her with social relations to a circle of German political activists. This network is not only a resource for emotional support but a community of friends with whom she is well able to communicate (in Spanish) despite her limited language skills in German.

In both the cases sketched here, migration did not automatically result in experiences of crisis. However, the case of Mrs A. shows that a biographical crisis in the context of migration – which for her finally led to illegality – can occur even many years after the actual move has been made. In her case, the end of her residence status coincided with a severe crisis around the time of her 40th birthday, which led her to question the very meaning of life; both these developments threatened her stability and thus her biographical project. In the case of Mrs M. on the other hand, migration represents a "purposive means of continuing the biography" (Breckner 2002); even illegality is an aspect of this overall biographical process. Moreover, it is striking that Mrs A. who does not have any financial responsibilities for her family in Poland feels very much under pressure to present a successful migration project. She argued that she rejects remigration to Poland because she is not longer able to integrate in Polish social life. Mrs M. on the other hand, who shouldered considerable financial obligations towards her family in Uruguay, actively strives for remigration. Although she visited Uruguay only once during her years of absence, she does not expect any difficulties to re-integrate socially in Uruguay. Yet, both women have one thing in common – both of them actively keep up transnational relations with their families through daily phone calls. In the case of Mrs M., these communication practices can also be described as a transnational praxis of motherhood, since they enabled her to remain emotionally close to her son left behind.

Both case studies show that illegalised domestic workers develop individual ways of dealing with illegalisation and transnational relations. Even if they live in similar circumstances, the two cases demonstrate that these differences cannot be explained in terms of ethnic origin or geographical proximity to the place of origin. On the contrary different biographical resources as well as age differences and a different marital status should be taken into account to explain these differences. Moreover, different structural resources that are available for illegalised people in different German cities may influence these differences, too: Mrs M. could continue her political relations to German political activists in Hamburg without any problems, whereas Mrs A. could only rely on the Polish catholic church in case she would need support. Therefore, the exploration of the following four *intersecting structural and biographical factors* is at the core of our research project:

- the *different modes of illegalisation*: an illegalised residence status and an illegalised employment situation;
- the *geographic proximity* between their working places and their places of origin;
- *individual differences* in the ways how migrant domestic workers deal with their living situation as illegalised migrants. These differences can only be examined by focusing on resources which arise from their biographical experiences;
- *transnational relationships* to their places of origin and their families left behind, too.

Concluding we are coming back to our initial question: What are the substantial new aspects of the globalization of domestic work nowadays? In the beginning of this article it has been argued that the globalization of domestic work is not a new phenomenon since even during the eighteenth and nineteenth century young women from European countries adopted employment transgressing national borders. Comparing these historical migration flows of domestic workers with the globalization of domestic work nowadays the following particularities come to the fore.

First of all technological changes as well as global economic relations have increased and accelerated transnational mobility of human beings, ideas, capital e.g. in general. As one consequence, transnational migration, especially of females, has grown dramatically.

Second, the new maids show important differences comparing with their "European sisters of the eighteenth and nineteenth century". Whereas the latter migrated inside Europe or from the "European centres" to the "colonized peripheries" the new maids are moving from the East to the West and from the South to the North. The historical domestic workers adopted employment for a limited period of their lives. By working as domestic servants they bridged the years between adolescence and marriage. Besides saving some money for their dowries their employment as servants had been seen as an education as later house wives, too. Today, the average migrant domestic servant is not only older than her historical sister, but she is well educated, too. Moreover, an increasing number of today's maids are mothers who left their children behind. Third, the shape of domestic work and the composition of employers in Western countries (European countries and US) have changed since the end of the Second World War. Historically, hiring one or more domestic workers was not only a bare necessity to manage the burdens of the household without technological facilities. Employing domestic servants was a question of prestige and therefore of performing class differences, too. In comparison today's employers cover a wide range of household types, e.g. from single households, single parents, double-income-no-kids-couples to parents with one or more children. Most of them belong to the middle class. For them hiring a domestic workers is not a matter of prestige but of managing their careers and their households and children as flexible as it is demanded by the new global economy's labour markets. Thus, the transnational mobility of migrant domestic workers facilitates their upward social (educational) mobility. However, these two types of mobility show important differences. The mobility of most employers is at least somehow regulated in the framework of Western national welfare states. In comparison the overwhelming majority of migrant domestic workers are illegalised, as was shown, in a twofold way. Whether they will be able to organize themselves as a political force on a national and/or transnational level – as their historical sisters did some 150 years ago – is an open question. However, it is most important to study the phenomenon as both "old" and "new" at the same time and thereby underline continuities and discontinuities. Social inequalities and exploitation processes have certainly changed over time; but the organization of the private sphere including the organisation of emotions shows lots of well known former elements from a century ago.

References

ANDERSON, Bridget, 2000, *Doing the dirty work? The global politics of domestic labour*, London, Zed Books.

BADE, Klaus/Rat für Migration e.V., 2001 (ed.), *Integration und Illegalität in Deutschland*, Osnabrück, IMIS.

BASH, Linda, GLICK-SCHILLER, Nina and SZANTON BLANC, Christina, 1994, *Nations Unbound. Transnational Projects, Postcolonial Predicaments and Deterritorialized Nation States*, Langhorne, PA.

BRECKNER, Roswitha, 2002, "Migration – ein biographisches Risiko. Zum Zusammenhang von Migration und Biographie", in J. ALLMENDINGER (ed.), *Entstaatlichung und soziale Sicherheit*, Opladen, Leske und Budrich, pp. 236–253.

CASTELLS, Manuel, 2002, *Das Informationszeitalter II. Die Macht der Identität*, Opladen, Campus.

CHAMBERLAIN, Mary, 1997, *Narratives of Exile and Return*, London/Basingstoke, Macmillan.

EHRENREICH, Barbara and HOCHSCHILD, Arlie Russel (eds), 2002, *Global women. Nannies, maids and sex workers in the new economy*, New York, Metropolitan Books.

FRIESE, Marianne and THIESSEN, Barbara, 1997, *Modellprojekt Mobiler Haushaltsservice – ein innovatives Konzept für die Ausbildung und Beschäftigung von Hauswirtschafterinnen*, Universität Bremen.

GATHER, Claudia, GEISSLER, Birgit and RERRICH, Maria S. (eds), 2002, *Weltmarkt Hausarbeit. Bezahlte Hausarbeit im globalen Wandel*, Münster, Westfälisches Dampfboot.

HARZIG, Christiane (ed.), 1997, *Peasant Maids – City Women: from the European Countryside to Urban America*, Ithaca, Cornell University Press.

HENKES, B., 1998, *Heimat in Holland. Deutsche Dienstmädchen 1920–1950*, Straelen, Straelener Manuskripte.

HOCHSCHILD, Arlie Russel, 2000, "Global care chains and emotional surplus value", in Will HUTTON and Anthony GIDDENS (eds), *On the edge. Living with global capitalism*, London, Jonathan Cape, pp. 130–146.

HONDAGNEU-SOTELO, Pierrette and AVILA, Ernestine, 1997, "'I'm here, but I'm there'. The Meaning of Latina Transnational Motherhood", *Gender and Society*, 11, 5, pp. 548–571.

IREK, Malgorzata, 1998, *Der Schmugglerzug. Warschau-Berlin-Warschau*, Berlin, Das Arabische Buch.

KOSER, Khalid and LUTZ, Helma (eds), 1998, *The new migration in Europe: social constructions and social realities*, Basingstoke *et al.*, Macmillan.

LUTZ, Helma, 2000, *Geschlecht, Ethnizität, Profession. Die neue Dienstmädchenfrage im Zeitalter der Globalisierung*, Münster.

–, 2002a, "Transnationalität im Haushalt", in Claudia GATHER, Birgit GEISSLER and Maria S. RERRICH (eds), *Weltmarkt Privathaushalt. Bezahlte Haushaltsarbeit im globalen Wandel*, Münster, Westfälisches Dampfboot, pp. 86–102.

–, 2002b, "In fremden Diensten. Die neue Dienstmädchenfrage im Zeitalter der Globalisierung", in Karin GOTTSCHALL and Birgit PFAU-EFFINGER (eds), *Zukunft der Arbeit und Geschlecht*, Opladen, pp. 161–182.

–, 2002c, "*At your service, madam!* The globalization of domestic service", *Feminist review*, 70, pp. 89–104.

MOROKVAŠIC, Mirjana, 1994, "Pendeln statt Auswandern. Das Beispiel der Polen", in Mirjana MOROKVAŠIC and Hedwig RUDOLPH (eds), *Wanderungsraum Europa. Menschen und Grenzen in Bewegung*, Berlin, Ed. Sigma.

ODIERNA, Simone, 2000, *Die heimliche Rückkehr der Dienstmädchen*, Opladen, Leske & Budrich.

OLWIG, Karen Fog, 1993, *Global culture, island identity: continuity and change in the Afro-Carribean community of Nevis*, Chur *et al.* Harwood.

PARREÑAS, Rhacel Salazar, 2001, *Servants of Globalization. Women, Migration and Domestic Work,* Stanford, Stanford University Press.

–, 2002, *The care crisis in the Philippines: children and transnational families in the new global economy*, in Barbara EHRENREICH and Arlie Russel HOCHSCHILD (eds), *Global women. Nannies, maids and sex workers in the new economy,* New York, Metropolitan books, pp. 39–54.

PHIZACKLEA, A., 2001, *Geschlechterparameter in der Migration*, in Jochen BLASCHKE (ed.), *Ost-West-Migration, Perspektiven der Migrationspolitik in Europa*, Berlin/Hamburg, Edition Parabolis, 2001, pp. 137–157.

SHARPE, Pamela (ed.), 2001, *Women, Gender and Labour Migration. Historical and Global Perspectives*, London/NewYork, Routledge.

SHINOZAKI, Kyoko, 2004, *Making sense of contradictions: Examining negotiation strategies of "contradictory class mobility" in Filipina/ Filipino migrant domestic workers in Germany*, in Thomas GEISEN (ed.), *Arbeitsmigration. WanderarbeiterInnen auf dem Weltmarkt für Arbeitskraft*, Frankfurt, IKO.

SCHNEIDER, Friedrich and ENSTE, Dominik, 2000, *Schattenwirtschaft und Schwarzarbeit. Umfang, Ursachen, Wirkungen und wirtschaftspolitische Empfehlungen*, München.

SCHUPP, Jürgen, 2002, "Quantitative Verbreitung von Erwerbstätigkeit in privaten Haushalten Deutschlands", in Claudia GATHER, Birgit GEISSLER and Maria S. RERRICH (eds), *Weltmarkt Hausarbeit. Bezahlte Hausarbeit im globalen Wandel,* Münster, Westfälisches Dampfboot, pp. 50–70.

THIESSEN, Barbara, 2002, "Bezahlte Hausarbeit. Biografische Befunde zur Gestaltung von Arbeitsbeziehungen im Privaten", in Claudia GATHER, Birgit GEISSLER and Maria S. RERRICH (eds), *Weltmarkt Hausarbeit. Bezahlte Hausarbeit im globalen Wandel*, Münster, Westfälisches Dampfboot, pp. 140–153.

ZENTRALSTELLE FÜR ARBEITSVERMITTLUNG, 2003, "Erfahrungsbericht zu der Vermittlung von Haushaltshilfen zur Beschäftigung in Haushalten mit Pflegebedürftigen nach § 4 Abs. 9a Anwerbestoppausnahmeverordnung (ASAV)", Bonn, 2003, July 28th (unpublished report).

www.uni-muenster.de/FGEI/: Forschungsprojekt Gender, Ethnizität, und Identität. Die neue Dienstmädchenfrage im Zeitalter der Globalisierung (Stand Dez. 2002).

www.tschechien.biz/index/html (Stand 09.01.2003).

Calling the Tune: Domestic Workers' Earnings and Intra-Household Gender Relations in Turkey

Gül ÖZYEGIN

"We [women] worked but never saw the face of money." This is how most of the rural migrant Turkish women I studied, who are employed as domestic workers in the middle-class homes of Ankara, expressed the absence of wages in their past lives as peasant women, when I asked them if they earned wages back in the village. Indeed, these women were characterizing an important part of their lives as a transition from unpaid family workers to urban, "individualized" wage earners. The basic patriarchal organization of the Turkish peasant family and its economic and social life allow women no direct control over money when women do not receive individual wages. Although female labor is central to the production process, this production system is characterized by the absence of autonomous female economic activity and independent female earnings (Sirman 1988; Berik 1987; Kandiyoti 1990). Furthermore, when women are employed as wage laborers their wages are negotiated by and paid to the head of the household, and, as a result, women have no control over cash flow. Now, as wage earners, these women have become major contributors to their household economy. Does finally "seeing the face of money" affect these women's lives in terms of greater control over resources and allow them participation in decision-making processes from which they were previously excluded? How and in what areas of life are women able to translate economic agency into decision-making authority? How do women feel about earning wages? What role, if any, does earning wages play in the alteration of their subjectivities? Does earning wages put them in circumstances to challenge patriarchal authority?

In this paper, I investigate these questions comparatively as they pertain to the two groups of rural migrant women, who share similar migratory histories and socio economic profiles. However, their different social locations in the urban space create differences in the dynamics involved in women's ability to control their income and to translate income into decision-making influence.

As many have demonstrated, women's earnings neither inevitably translate into their exercise of independent control over their money, nor automatically increase their decision-making authority in households (Safilios-Rothschild 1990; Standing 1985; Blumberg 1991; Blumstein and Schwartz 1991). There are many reasons for this. Women's subordinate position in the labor market rarely allows them to achieve wage and status parity with men, rendering the relative size of women's monetary contribution to the household economy smaller than men's. Inferior earnings provide women with low bargaining power inside the family, lending them no special leverage in household politics of redistributive practices. Gender and family ideologies naturalize and legitimize gendered relationships to money and authority.

In this paper, I build on these ideas of women's control over earned income and their spending practices in my examination of Turkish domestic workers' experiences with their earnings. I probe two sets of interrelated dichotomies in the literature, subsistence/surplus spending and maternal altruism/self-interest, that inform main parameters of the discussion in assessing women's empowerment in relation to income earning. My aim is to posit an analysis of Turkish domestic workers' experiences that encompasses the interaction of these dichotomies.

Research Context

Turkey is a large increasingly modern and industrial nation with a population exceeding 65 million, which has undergone social transformation so rapidly that it has been described as a society "on the brink of a social mutation" (Tekeli 1990, 3). One aspect of change is an ongoing urbanization that is drawing the rural population into the big cities in a process one social scientist calls "depeasantization" (Kiray 1991). The impact of these social and economic transformations on women and gender relations is not uniform in Turkey. Migration of peasant women often results in their "housewifisation" (Senyapili 1981b, 214). Most women, especially married women in rural migrant communities, are not allowed to work outside the home because of patriarchal opposition to women's employment, and, thus, they show the lowest urban female participation in wage labor (Ayata and Ayata 1996). Economic hardship in many migrant households does not erode deep-seated male objections to women's employment. Only 16.5 percent of the urban female population in metropolitan areas were employed in 1994. Recent studies conducted on women's informal occupations in urban settings suggest that the labor of migrant women is becoming increasingly informalized (Cinar 1991; White 1991). Women are confined to particular branches of the informal sector, concentrated in those activities that occur within the home and are compatible with their roles within the domestic sphere. Informal wage-earning activities reinforce women's dependent status as wives and mothers rather than as income earners.

A recent national survey of the division of labor by gender in Turkish families reveals that housework and childcare are territories of work occupied solely by women. Women have sole responsibilty for household tasks and childcare. The only area of work that men share with women is grocery shopping. There is no significant difference between urban and rural families' pattern of gendered division of labor (KSSGM 1998, 50–57). The most recent findings on some aspects of decision making indicate that routine household spending decisions are mostly made by women (Ozbay 1990) representing a shift from the male-dominant decision-making profile found in the national survey of Turkish family structure in 1968 (Timur 1972). And more importantly, controlling for such factors as social class and women's social status as employed wives or housewives, decisions pertaining to women's physical mobility, women's employment, birth control, and sex belonged to men indicating the pervasiveness of male domination in Turkish society.

This Study

This paper draws upon a larger study of two groups of rural migrant women now living in Ankara, the capital of Turkey. These rural migrant women work in private homes as domestic workers, where the terms and conditions of their labor are neither officially determined nor regulated. I distinguish the two groups of women by the proximity of their homes to their work places. The first group of women I studied are the wives of doorkeepers of middle and upper-middle-class apartment buildings and I refer to this group (N=103) as *wives of doorkeepers* in this paper. Unlike the majority of rural migrants, doorkeeper (*kapici* in Turkish – literally means "doorkeeper") families live and work in middle and upper-class areas where husbands are employed as doorkeepers[1] and wives as domestic workers. Doorkeeper families live in the basements of the buildings in which their services are required. Wives of doorkeepers constitute a prime pool from which middle-class tenants recruit waged domestic labor. Because of this, wives of doorkeepers rarely navigate the domestic labor market, but hold a virtual monopoly over domestic service.

The second group (N=57) of domestic workers consists of those who live in squatter settlements in the margins of the city and commute daily to upper-middle-class neighborhoods for work. I refer to them as *women of squatter settlement* in this paper. The two groups experience urban space in quite different ways. While *women of squatter settlement* negotiate the diverse contexts and dynamic pace of urban life, and the domestic labor market, wives of doorkeepers remain firmly attached to their apartment houses. Wives of doorkeepers can undertake paid domestic work without leaving the home or the oversight of their husbands. Squatter women, however, are accustomed to long daily commutes across subcultural and geographic boundaries Indeed, the latter embodies the constraints placed on female spatial mobility in Turkey.

The comparison between wives of doorkeepers and squatter settlement women offers a vantage point for delineating the conditions under which women are able to retain control over their earnings. Both groups of women have undergone a radical transition from unpaid family laborers

1 The doorkeepers' main duties include operating central-heating systems, performing maintenance duties, taking out the residents' trash, buying and distributing fresh bread twice a day, grocery shopping for the residents, providing building security, collecting monthly maintenance fees from tenants, and disposing of refuse from coal-burning furnaces. Duties may also include walking tenants' dogs, tending gardens, or taking tenants' children to school. The closest North American term for this job is "janitor" or "super", or the "concierge" in France, though none of these fully describe the Turkish doorkeepers' work and occupational identity. For a study of janitors in the United States during the 1950s, see Ray Gold (1952).

(as peasant women) to individual wage earners as domestic workers. The institution of doorkeeping perpetuates the familiar patriarchal structures, albeit in modified forms by enabling men to maintain their traditional control over women's labor and earnings. The imprecise boundaries between the locus of work and of home allows for the peripheral involvement of household members other than the official jobholder, the doorkeeper husband. In contrast to squatter settlement women, doorkeeper wives retain the "unpaid family laborer" status from their rural past, despite working as wage earners. The doorkeeper's job structurally reinstates some of the terms of the peasant conjugal contract that defines men as absolute holders and managers of the earnings of those under their authority and protection. Cash wages owed to the doorkeeper wives are occasionally paid to husbands (just as they were in the village). Thus, in these cases, cash does not even find its way into women's hands, let alone enter into their pockets.

With a few exceptions, the women in this study come to Ankara with no previous urban experience. During the time of my survey in 1990, the majority of these migrant women had lived in Ankara for a fairly long time, roughly eleven years on average. They range in age from 18.5 to 66.0 years with a mean age of 33.2. The women in the squatter settlement group are, on average, 6.4 years older than the wives of doorkeepers. The mean age of marriage is 17.6 years for the doorkeeper group and 16.7 for the squatter settlement group. Length of employment in domestic service ranged from one month to 37.0 years with a mean of 7.7 years. Nearly half of the women are illiterate, and only 3 percent have as much as a middle school education. The two groups are similar in terms of number of years in primary school and literary rate. The two groups have similar household characteristics. Eighty-nine percent of the doorkeeper households and 81 percent of the squatter settlement households were nuclear. Though, the doorkeeper households were smaller, with an average of 4.3 members compared with 5.3 members in squatter settlement household. Doorkeeper families have an average of 2.6 children living at home, while squatter families average 3.1.

Method

Three sources of field data: a survey, participant observation, and in-depth interviews provide the empirical foundation of my analysis. The fact that the majority of domestic workers in Turkey are wives of doorkeepers offered a unique opportunity for drawing a representative sample. The apartment buildings that house this group of domestic workers and employers provided me with a frame for random sampling. I selected 103 domestic workers in the doorkeeper group by using a mixed sampling strategy (systematic and random). In addition, I interviewed a total of 57 domestic workers from four different squatter settlement neighborhoods. Due to the lack of an adequate sampling frame, though, a representative sampling procedure for this group was not possible. Instead, this group was chosen by a snowball method. The survey included forty questions probing issues related to domestic financial arrangements, ranging from sources of income in the household, income-pooling strategies, allocation of income into different spending categories to patterns of money control. In addition to these questions, the survey instrument contained questions pertaining to spending decisions in four areas: the purchase of food, the purchase of household durables, the purchase of electrical appliances, and the purchase of clothes for religious holidays. It also included one question on how saved money was spent and two questions pertaining to the raising of their children. In addition, three questions were designed to explore decisions about both self and social life, including questions about birth control and sex ("when to have sexual intercourse"). Finally, the questionnaire included a question about who has the "last word" in important family matters and its normative counterpart: who should have the word? The survey probed for open-ended responses to many questions, including "how they define/see the impact of earning wages on their marriages".

I and my two research assistants administered the survey through face-to-face interviews. For another source of field data, I took part in many informal gatherings of women for drinking tea and chatting. I was also invited to circumcision and wedding ceremonies and to women's periodic "acceptance-day" *(kabul gunu)* gatherings. I spent a considerable amount of time in their homes, casually socializing, watching television and eating meals with them, their husbands and children, and their neighbors. I became a constant presence in their communities. This status allowed for considerable informality: participating in daily routines without setting-up particular meeting times and without radically interrupting the rhythm of work or leisure. For example, I assisted women as they folded laundry, prepared food, and bargained with the street peddlers. On a few occasions I accompanied them on visits to a doctor's office or to stores when they went into debt to purchase a set of steel cookware or fancy sheets. Qualitative data offers me interpretative lens for understanding the grounded complexities of the lives of these women. Although the doorkeeper sample is based on a representative sample, the snowball sample of squatter women limits the generalization of my findings.

Theoretical Underpinnings

In the last three decades feminist scholars have made great progress in denaturalizing a household model which had been the hallmark of a diverse range of theories from the New Home Economics to Marxists economic and development theories. These theories identify the household as a sharing and pooling unit without considering the relations of power that structure it. The concept of the moral economy of the household, common to these views, assumes that the internal economy of the household is governed by principles of reciprocity, consensus, solidarity and altruism (Wolf 1992; Folbre 1988; Berk 1985; Harris 1988 for criticism of the New Home Economics and Marxist models). According to this model, adaptive household strategies are "objectively" beneficial for all members of the domestic group. This model not only ignores differences of gender and age in family experiences, but also underestimates conflict and adversarial negotiations concerning money or distributional practices within the household (Dwyer and Bruce 1988; Hartmann 1981; Thorne and Yalom 1982; Harris 1988; Hondagneu-Sotelo 1994).

Indeed, a growing body of empirical research has shown that income and other financial resources are not always pooled and reallocated according to the family's collective well being and resources such as food, education and health care are distributed unequally by gender and age in households (Dwyer and Bruce 1988; Hartmann 1981; Whitehead 1988; Maher 1988; Hoodfar 1988; Fapohunda 1988; Mencher 1988; Charles and Kerr 1987). There are also important differences in the ways men and women spend household earnings under their control. Women devote more of their incomes than men to subsistence and nutrition, while men withhold their earnings for individual spending (Whitehead 1988; Maher 1988; Bolak 1995; Delphy 1979; Pahl 1980; Wilson 1987; Dwyer and Bruce 1988; Kiray 1985; Celle de Bowman 2000). White (1981) describes women's close attachment to the collective or family aspects of consumption as reflecting "maternal altruism", a powerful ideology that effectively creates barriers to women disposing of their income freely in the market.

Blumberg's (1991) cross-cultural studies show that wives' incomes affect their power only to the extent that they retain control over that income. Patriarchal organization of gender relations assign women as wives and daughters no authority in allocation and distribution of their earnings, which are often regulated and controlled by the male head of household. Thus, limiting the role of earned income in making differences in their own lives. Blumberg further argues that women's empowerment is especially limited in low-income households where women, even when they have full control over money, cannot translate their income into increased power for themselves because subsistence incomes allow for little discretionary spending (Safilios-Rothschild 1990; Standing 1985; Blumberg 1991; Blumstein and Schwartz 1991).

In this chapter, I attempt to empirically probe these two dichotomies; one that delineates sharply spending for subsistence and surplus and the one that casts women as maternal altruists and men as self-interested and individuated actors. Subsistence and surplus level spending are neither empirically tangible given nor universally applicable categories. Meanings of "subsistence" and "surplus" are not only culturally defined but also shift depending on the income level and social class. Similarly, the dichotomy that casts women as maternal altruists and men as self-interested and individuated actors needs to be empirically specified within the normative context of gender order in a given society. I argue that this dichotomous framework bypasses the importance of women's consumption decisions in defining female identity. My analysis will suggest that the boundaries between the maternal altruism and self-interest in Turkish migrant women's lives are permeable.

In what follows I first examine allocation of women's income in the household and distinguish the main money control patterns, discussing women's experience in money control in relation to the levels of women's contribution to the household economy. I then examine strategies women employ to create conditions in which they can autonomously dispose of portions of their income. Here, scrutinizing the distinction between subsistence and surplus spending, I address the crucial question of what women do with money at their disposal and suggest, as alternative to maternal altruism and subsistence/surplus explanations, a different way of looking at the worth of women's and men's personal spending money. Finally, I examine women's perception of decision making according to women's different contributor status and money control systems.

Findings and Analysis

"The Money That Comes In Daily, Goes Out Daily": Allocation of Women's Income

A pattern of gender-specific purchasing, where husband's and wife's incomes are channeled into different spending categories, characterizes most of the households' spending practices in this study. Nearly 40 percent of the women in the doorkeeper sample reported that their earnings go toward specific expenditures, primarily for food but also including clothing, household durable goods, children's education, and their daughters' trousseau. In the squatter settlement group, a much higher percentage of women (78 percent) reported that their income paid for subsistence and nutrition, primarily for kitchen expenses.

Meanings attached to husbands' and wives' financial contributions and the devolution of their incomes to specific expenditures are related to differences in the ways in which husbands' and wives' earnings enter the household, reflecting differences in the frequency of payment for women and men. In these households, women receive their wages daily, whereas men receive their cash wages monthly. Thus, there is a built-in tendency to spend women's wages on food and other daily expenditures and men's wages on fixed expenditures that require monthly payments, such as installments for consumer goods and other monthly bills (rent, utilities, phone, etc.) Many women noted that "The money that comes in daily, goes out daily". But this expression is more readily translated into practice for women in the squatter settlement group who, on the way home from work, spend a great proportion of their daily wages on food shopping.

Yet this clear-cut channeling of women's earnings into gender-specific spending areas does not always mean that women control spending in these areas. Even when women's earnings are earmarked for particular kinds of expenditures, they are consolidated in a "common pot", which is often controlled by the husband. With the exception of a small number of cases (N=8) in the squatter settlement group where only "abstract" pooling is present, *as far as the members of the nuclear family are concerned,* all households in this study pool their income and other financial resources.[2] Nonetheless, the control of money, rather than the presence of pooling, is a crucial factor that allows us to assess the relations between power and income for women.

Women's Level of Contribution and Control of Money

In order to compare the control women have over the disposal and distribution of their incomes at different contribution levels, I subdivided the sample into three groups according to the relative size of women's contribution to household income. Women whose contribution is equal to or higher than 60 percent of the total household income are classified as "major" contributors; those who contribute 40 to 60 percent are classified as "equal"; and those who made up less than 40 percent of the total income are categorized as "minor."

In the doorkeeper group, the proportions of major, equal and minor contributors are 44.1 percent, 38.2 percent and 17.6 percent, respectively,

2 Perhaps, as argued by Fapohunda (1988), having knowledge of a spouse's income, knowing where that income is spent and the existence of joint financial planning are good measures of existence of pooling. According to this criterion, households in my study are pooling-households. First, the majority of women had full knowledge of their husbands' income (at least the stable part of it). In cases where they did not, this was more an effect of the unpredictability of the informal petty cash earning activities than an instrument of intra-household power or separation of budgets. Second, they had full knowledge of how their husbands spent their money. Third, as explained in this paragraph, they had an understanding that each spouse's income would go to particular items of spending and investment – regardless of who controlled the money and who had decision-making power.

which means that the overwhelming majority of women are the main source of household income (Table 1). In the squatter group, 13.7 percent of women are major contributors, 49.0 percent are equal contributors and 37.3 percent are minor contributors.

Do different proportions of male and female contributions produce differences in control and redistribution within the household? Control signifies a capacity to enforce direction and disposal of money against competing claims. Control over money is a difficult concept to measure, because the important distinction between "execution of money" (management and/or budgeting) and "control" often gets blurred. Pahl (1983) analytically distinguishes between "control" that concerns major intra-household decisions of a "policy-making" kind and "management" that puts policy decisions into action. The concept of control as I use it here covers both the senses of "policy-making" and "management".

Table 1. Women's level of contribution to the household income

	Doorkeeper		Squatter	
	%	N	%	N
Major contributor	44.1	45	13.7	7
Equal contributor	38.2	39	49.0	25
Minor contributor	17.6	18	37.3	19
Total	100.0	102	100.0	51

Table 2. Control of money

	Doorkeeper		Squatter	
	%	N	%	N
Male control	61.8	63	37.3	19
Female control	17.6	18	37.3	19
Shared control	20.6	21	9.8	5
Separate	n.a.		15.7	8
Total	100.0	102	100.0	51

Two items from the survey instrument produced a four-part categorization. The following have been used in assigning each woman to a specific control category: 1) who physically holds the household money – the wife, husband or neither (neither holds but there is a designated place where money is kept), and 2) who manages the household money. The four categories developed from these two variables are "Male control", "Female control", "Shared control", and "Separate control" (Table 2).

Under *Male control* system, household money is held and administered by the husband. It basically takes two forms. In the first the husband holds and manages the money, and the wife rarely deals with money after handing over her wages. Alternatively, the husband controls the money but delegates the daily management of a portion of it to the wife in the form of *partial housekeeping allowance.* In the majority of doorkeeper households, money is under male control (62 percent). In the squatter settlement group, male and female control are equally distributed (37 percent). It is only among minor contributors that I found the second variant of the male-control system, the partial housekeeping allowance system.

If the husband's and wife's earnings are combined and she manages the money, either held by her or kept in a place where she has exclusive access, it is defined *Female control* system. This system is more prevalent in the squatter settlement households. *Shared control* system presents a pattern of joint conjugal financial control and management where the money is either held by the woman or is kept in a designated place to which both the husband and the wife have access. *Shared control* is the second prevalent mode among the doorkeeper households (21 percent), while its proportion is the smallest in the squatter group (10 percent).

In *Separate control* system each spouse holds and manages his or her own money. Physical pooling does not take place. A gender-specific division of responsibilities for expenditures constitutes one of the bases for the separately controlled system. While women's and men's incomes are allocated to gender-specific expenditures across the sample as I explained earlier, within the separate control system women and men assume control of gender-specific spending. Each spouse keeps his/her own earnings separately; they control and manage them separately – what Pahl (1983) calls the "independent management system". I found this system only in the squatter households (16 percent).

One would expect women who are major contributors to the total household income to maintain control of financial resources. That is, major contributors would be the least represented under the male-controlled money system. This expectation is confirmed in the case of the squatter group in which 57 percent of households where women are major contributors are female-controlled. As the women's contribution increases, the proportion of squatter settlement households with money under male control decreases and those under female control increases (Table 3).

Table 3. Level of contribution by type of control over money

	Doorkeeper Group				*Squatter Group*			
	Major	Equal	Minor	Total	Major	Equal	Minor	Total
Male	64.4	53.9	72.2	61.8	14.3	32.00	52.6	37.3
Female	20.0	15.4	16.7	17.7	57.1	36.00	31.6	37.3
Shared	15.6	30.8	11.1	20.6	0.00	16.00	5.3	9.8
Separate	n.a.	n.a.	n.a.	n.a	28.6	16.00	10.5	15.7
Total	45	39	18	102	7	25	19	51

However, in the case of the doorkeeper group, no *linear* relationship is apparent between who controls the money and the level of women's contribution. Instead, the relationship appears to be hyperbolic. While nearly three quarters of the minor contributors are under male control, a much smaller proportion of major or equal contributors are under male control. Yet, the proportion of *equal* contributors under male control is smaller (54 percent) than that of the *major* contributors (64 percent) under the same type of control.

The overall proportion of doorkeeper households under female control is not very large either. While 82 percent of doorkeeper wives are either major or equal contributors, only 15 percent of these households are under female control. Indeed, incidence of female control is relatively uniform despite differences in contribution levels.

In the doorkeeper group, then, the type of control and the size of contribution are relatively independent factors while the two are closely correlated in the squatter group. This striking difference results from the doorkeeper husband's job, which allows him to exert substantial control over household money. His home-bound and shopping-centered work informs the internal structure of the household economy, constraining women's control over their earnings. Wives interpret their limited relationship with money in terms of a traditional conjugal contract that defines men as leaders of the household. In the modern form of this traditional idea, they believe that the husband's job places him in an objectively privileged position to decide what is needed in the household and how it can be obtained.

Comparable "Worth" of Women's and Men's Personal Spending

The degree to which women can claim any part of their earnings for themselves or for discretionary purposes varies. Three groups emerged: "non-claimers", "known-claimers", and "clandestine claimers". Thirty percent of the doorkeeper wives and 57 percent of the squatter women set aside some portion of their income as money under their exclusive control. The frequency and the amount set aside vary considerably in both groups. Some regularly reserve a portion of their daily wages while others withhold money as they need it. About a quarter of women in the doorkeeper group and a third in the squatter settlement group are "clandestine claimers" who set aside money without the knowledge of their husbands.

In both the doorkeeper and squatter groups, a strong relationship exists between male control of household money and women setting aside money for discretionary use. There is, however, a difference in the relation between control type and clandestine withholding in the two groups. In the doorkeeper group, eight of the nine clandestine claimers are in the "money under male control" group. In the squatter group, clandestine claimers are evenly distributed across types of control.

Men also claim personal spending money, with nearly 20 percent of doorkeeper husbands and 52 percent of squatter settlement men withholding some portion of their income. A larger percentage of doorkeeper husbands do not hold back money for two reasons. First, the majority of these husbands have exclusive access to the household money. When asked whether their husbands set aside money for their personal use, these wives said "all money is his money". When money is under his control, the doorkeeper, as well as the squatter settlement husband, can spend it for personal use without designating it as "his set-aside money". The same explanation may apply to women whose set-aside money becomes more visible when men control all household money. Second, since the doorkeeper works inside the apartment and its vicinity, he has less work-related expenses requiring personal spending money. In contrast, among the squatter group, where men work away from home, a much higher proportion keep personal spending money regardless of the type of control in the household. Both groups' percentages of set aside-money still fall below those of women's. Interestingly, the direct relationship between setting aside spending money and men's control observed among women is more strongly mirrored among husbands. More men in the households where money is under female control appear to keep personal spending money than in households where men control money themselves.

Men's personal money is spent on cigarettes, work-related expenses (transportation) and routine socializing activities such as trips to coffee houses, the modal "recreational" activity among lower class Turkish men. Men's personal spending patterns cause no conflict unless they are markedly irresponsible (husbands with gambling and drinking problems.) Indeed, women believe a man should not go around without any cash in his pocket – for, as I will discuss below, day-to-day male-gendered routines require more visible personal cash.

Women's "personal" spending money is usually channeled into collective and non-personal expenditures. A great proportion of women spend their discretionary funds on children's education and clothing (61 percent in the doorkeeper and 34 percent in the squatter group). Such expenses might include sending children to *kurs* (private courses outside the school system) or to extra-curricular courses (for instance a mother from the doorkeeper group sends her artistically gifted 11 year old daughter to an art class) and providing children their daily allowance for school.

Many women also invest discretionary money in golden bangles and gold coins which serve as security and savings. Although women use golden bangles and chains as ornaments to display wealth and self-worth, these goods also serve as savings for the well-being and security of the family. Such jewelry is converted into money when an urgent need arises. However, the moment of conversion occurs most typically when a big sum of cash is needed for property investments (house and land) or when the family marries off a son. Savings in the form of collecting gold bracelets and coins also frequently functions as an informal banking and loan mechanism in the women's community, where women borrow and pay back gold instead of cash. Women open credit accounts in neighborhood stores to buy items to beautify their homes such as drapes, tablecloths, towels, blankets, expensive steel pot sets, fancy tea pots and sets of coffee cups to be displayed in glass cabinets. Women also spend discretionary money on sheets, comforters and similar items as well as on material to make embroidered household items for a daughter's trousseau.

As described thus far, these patterns of discretionary spending and what women's income pays for are fully consistent with other cross cultural findings: women devote their income to subsistence and nutrition and they tend to closely identify their discretionary spending interests with home and children (Whitehead 1988; Maher 1988; Delphy 1979; Pahl 1980; Wilson 1987; Dwyer and Bruce 1988; Kiray 1985). Should we, then, conclude that Turkish migrant women's altruistic behavior benefits their families and children at the expense of their own autonomy and empowerment?

I suggest that we should not automatically assume that "maternal altruism" necessarily entails negative consequences for women. We should, instead, empirically demonstrate the actual meanings and consequences of "maternal altruism". Accepting the proposition that women do not benefit from their earnings *because* of their maternal altruism risks ignoring cultural meanings of such spending and the ways it defines identity. Even though women in this study channel their earnings into home and children-centered spending categories, like their counterparts in similar contexts, they often cherish independent access to and control of money, even for apparently "subsistence" level spending because their consumption decisions enhance their status as mothers and housewives. Spending categories that are closely associated with these women's aspirations for modernity and urbanity, for example, stews – which can be made with or without meat – are an important part of the Turkish diet. Some women interviewed felt they had provided something out of the ordinary for their children when they were able to add meat to such dishes. Clearly, in these women's lives, adding meat is a "surplus" level act. These women rarely worry about their ability to feed hungry children. Instead, they wonder if they can bring them bananas (the most expensive fruit in Turkey), buy their family *kabob* from the corner *kabob* shop, or serve their guests pastry from the bakery rather than homemade cookies.

The conceptual framework that proposes that women do not gain power from discretionary spending unless, like men, they spend on themselves is workable only in circumstances where men and women participate in the *same sphere of activities* (especially leisure consumption). We need to qualify such assumptions to express cultural contexts where women's social identity depends upon their role in the family and where there is a generalized gender segregation, such that equal gender spheres cannot be presupposed.

What happens when the activities that women and men engage in and the possible terrains of sociability are gender-segregated? By borrowing the notion of "comparable worth" from the wage-equity movement (Steinberg and Haignere 1991), we can assume a comparable worth of women's and men's personal expenditures even when women do not spend their "personal money" on items and leisure activities that are deemed to be personal. Although men and women operate within partially divergent gender domains with distinct conceptions of value and prestige, they may perceive themselves as gaining "comparable" degrees of status and self-esteem from different forms of spending.

Thus, maternal altruism may be a highly feasible form of investment in a cultural sphere with good returns of fulfillment and social recognition. As rational and self-interested actors, these women devote their "personal" money to home and children-centered spending categories to enhance their status as wives and reputations as good mothers. Seemingly private, altruistic spending can be experienced as enhancing the status and self-image of the spender. To deny the benefits derived from "altruism" spending disregards women's agency and empowerment and belies their own perceptions of their lives and decisions.

What I am suggesting is that the "worth" of a wife's entertaining her friends by baking chocolate cake (plain cake has a rural, unprestigious identity), serving instant coffee (a prestige item in the Turkish context) rather than cheaper traditional coffee, along with cubed sugar over the less expensive loose sugar because it signifies urban, modern refinement or sending her daughter to an art class are comparable in status value to her husband's treating his friends with coffee in the coffee-house or smoking high-priced imported Malboros rather than Turkish cigarettes.

Moreover, intra-gender competition is not an exclusively male phenomenon as is often assumed in the literature. Women compete among themselves for recognition and identity within their gender sphere – and, in financial terms, such competition can be just as costly as men's if not more so. Women are judged, gain worth, judge themselves, and find fulfillment according to culturally established standards of womanhood.

Women's Influence in Household Decision Making

How do women perceive decision making within the household? On the whole, doorkeeper wives seem to have a more limited influence in household spending decisions in all categories than the wives in the squatter settlement group, a discrepancy reflecting their different positions in the money control systems discussed earlier. Yet their decision-making profiles are almost identical in the areas of decisions concerning self, sex, and overall decision making.

As I described earlier, the survey instrument contained questions pertaining to decisions in four areas of spending as well as one question on how saved money was spent. There were two questions pertaining to the raising of their children. Three questions were designed to explore decisions about both self and social life, including questions about birth control and sex (when to have sexual intercourse). Finally, the *questionnaire* included a question about who has the "last word" in important family matters and its normative counterpart: who should have the word? For each decision, the respondent was asked to state which of the following choices best described the household arrangement: 1) "I have all"; 2) "I have more than him"; 3) "Equal"; 4) "He has more than me"; and 5) "He has all". Table 4 presents resulting total scores for the doorkeeper and squatter groups based on a *summary ratio index*.[3] Women in both doorkeeper and squatter households claim to have a pronounced influence on

3 In order to quantify the claimed relative weight of women's versus men's decisions in such matters I developed a *summary ratio index*. Decisions were defined as husband dominant when respondents answered 4 or 5, female dominant when respondents answered 1 and 2, and equal when respondents answered 3. The ratio index involved the sum of all female dominant decisions plus 1/2 of equal decisions divided by male dominant decisions. The formula can be represented as follows:

$$\text{Decision Influence Ratio} = \frac{1 + 2 + (\text{half of } 3)}{4 + 5 + (\text{half of } 3)}$$

The result is a ratio whose size shows the relative *aggregate* reported influence of the wife over that of the husband *within any specified group* in the sample. A score of 1.00 indicates "equal influence"; scores less than 1.00 indicates less influence than men, and scores over 1.00 indicate higher influence than men. Obviously, this ratio does not lend itself to a literal, naturalistic interpretation. Instead, it should be taken as a conceptually defensible measure of women's claimed influence in decision making. The justification for inclusion of the reported mid-point (i.e. "equal influence") in such a ratio is in the substantial social meaning of these women reporting an "equal influence" with their men. Since the women in my sample belong to a culture that is thoroughly patriarchal, it would be highly misleading to underestimate the weight of the "mid-point". Reporting to have an "equal say" in certain items may signal a claim to have very un-patriarchal powers in the family, and this measure is designed to capture that possibility.

purchasing and savings decisions.[4] While the fact that most figures are below 1.00, therefore indicating less influence than men, the results for certain items in this survey are striking, for they suggest a level of women's influence that is markedly different from conclusions reached in other studies on decision-making profiles of Turkish families. It is also important to emphasize that the wife's increased participation in decision making is really an index of shared decision making rather than evidence of autonomous decision making.

Women generally claim to have more influence on purchases that directly benefit them, including household technology that would reduce their work load, than they do on purchases related to electronic gadgets, a male domain. Women have less say in deciding how much to spend on food than men, even though a greater proportion of women's earnings go toward food-related expenses. This finding is not unexpected in the context of the income control patterns of these households, but it does deviate from the more general cross-cultural pattern found in similar contexts where women have predominant or exclusive influence. The score on this item for the doorkeeper group is smaller than that of the squatter group, indicating the significant role of the doorkeeper husbands as agents of food-related purchases.

Besides purchasing decisions, women in the doorkeeper group also have markedly less influence than men in decisions concerning expenses associated with children's education and how to bring them up (0.67 and 0.86 respectively). A substantial difference in this area of influence between women in the doorkeeper and in the squatter households is also evident. Squatter settlement women claim to have more influence than their husbands in making decisions concerning children (1.08 and 1.15), reflecting again the sharing of childcare responsibilities by the doorkeeper husbands and the virtual absence of such involvement in the squatter group. In both groups, husbands have considerable influence over whom their wives may associate with. Although the score which reflects women's influence on choice of associates is very high for both groups, the size of the score for this item should not be considered comparable in

4 Furthermore, Elliott and Moskoff (1983) found that the responses in their sample to similar family decision items clustered on the mid-point, decreasing the real variation which they believe that there was. My formula, by dispersing the mid-point toward the extremes, also takes care of this problem – albeit with a considerable fiat of mathematical aesthetics.

size to the scores of any other decision-making items. In the doorkeeper group, for example, 50 percent of the women report having the say on this matter, 19 percent report having equal say with the husbands, and 31 percent report that the husband decides with whom she may associate. Corresponding percentages for the squatter group are 57.4 and 39, respectively. The fact that husbands are involved at all (as "equal" or "more" influential) in such directly personal decisions at such high proportions is indicative of the extent of patriarchal control of women's social interactions in these families.

Birth control is the only area of decision making in which husbands do not have any predominant or exclusive influence. Questions pertaining to birth control were asked only of those respondents who reported practicing birth control in response to a previous question; therefore, these scores, apply to a subset of a sample and should be interpreted with caution. If and when a "decision" on the birth control is present, women are the predominant decision makers in this domain (1.97 for the doorkeeper group and 6.20 for the squatter settlement group). In the doorkeeper group, 31 of the 46 women who use birth control (mean age 30.3) reported that it was a joint decision whereas 15 women (mean age 31.1) stated that it was exclusively their decision. In contrast, 13 women (mean age 35.1) out of 18 (those who use birth control) in the squatter settlement group reported that using birth control was their own decision, and 5 women (mean age 33.4) said that this decision was made jointly with the husband. Women seem to have less influence on the decision of when and how frequently to have sex. The ratios are almost identical for both groups (0.20 for the doorkeeper group and 0.16 for the squatter group).

The ratios on "overall decision making" indicate that the last word belongs to the husband (0.13 in both groups and constitutes the lowest ratio). This response is consistent with my analysis of men's influence on "woman's association". This unspecific item contrasts well with a question that frames the same issue with a normative orientation, "Who do you think should have the final say about important decisions affecting the family?". While only 22 percent of the wives of doorkeepers and 12 percent of the women in the squatter group report having equal or more influence on important matters that affect the family, 65 percent and 55 percent of the women uphold the normative view that women ought to have equal or more influence.

Table 4. Women's influence in decision making.
Doorkeeper and squatter. Totals

	Doorkeeper	N*	%**	*Squatter*	N*	%**
Consumption & saving decisions						
Food	*0.64*	81	79.41	*0.82*	30	58.82
Household electronics	*0.45*	102	100.00	*0.65*	43	84.31
Household durables	*0.74*	102	100.00	*0.87*	44	86.27
Clothing	*1.36*	99	97.06	*1.59*	44	86.27
Children's education	*0.67*	76	74.51	*1.08*	26	50.98
Savings & investment	*0.45*	95	93.14	*0.61*	45	88.24
Marital & self-related decisions						
How to raise children	*0.86*	96	94.12	*1.15*	44	86.27
Birth control	*1.97*	46	45.10	*6.20*	18	35.29
Woman's association	*1.46*	102	100.00	*1.45*	49	96.08
When to have sex	*0.20*	97	95.10	*0.16*	39	76.47
Who has the "Last Word" and Who should have it						
Who has the last word on important family matters	*0.13*	102	100.00	*0.13*	49	96.08
Who should have the last word	*0.55*	102	100.00	*0.44*	49	96.08

* N is the number of applicable responses to the item.
** PCT is the proportion of applicable responses to the item in the total number of cases.

Do Women's Higher Earnings Translate into Greater Power?

How do women's earnings and control of money affect decision making for the doorkeeper and the squatter groups? As Table 5 shows, in the doorkeeper households, a positive relationship occurs between the level of women's contribution to the household income and their influence in decision making in the spending areas, indicating that major and equal contributors have more influence than minor contributors. Across the board, major and equal contributors have more influence than their minor counterparts, except in the case of household electronics. The most notable observation, however, is the existence of a small marked difference between "major" and "equal" contributors – being a major contributor does not immediately entail having more influence than an "equal" contributor.

As shown in Table 6, in the squatter settlement households, major contributors tend to participate in purchasing decisions to a greater extent than minor contributors. With the exception of decisions concerning food and savings, equal contributors have more say than minors. The difference is especially marked in the area of self, sex, children's education, and clothing purchases. Child raising is the only area in which there is a reverse relationship between the level of contribution and decision making.

In the doorkeeper group, control of money is closely related to decision-making power, and generally speaking, women who belong to households where money is under their control have a greater influence in all decision-making areas than women who are in households where money is under male control. This difference is especially pronounced in decisions concerning food and children. Parallel observations can be also made in the case of the squatter settlement group, where a strong association exists between women's greater control of money and their greater influence in decision making in all areas

Table 5. Women's influence in decision making by the proportion of female monetary contribution to household in doorkeeper group

	MAJOR	N*	%**	EQUAL	N*	%**	MINOR	N*	%**
Consumption & saving decisions									
Food	*0.63*	31	68.89	*0.83*	33	84.62	*0.36*	17	94.44
Household electronics	*0.38*	45	100.00	*0.56*	39	100.00	*0.38*	18	100.00
Household durables	*0.70*	45	100.00	*1.00*	39	100.00	*0.44*	18	100.00
Clothing	*1.67*	44	97.78	*1.39*	37	94.87	*0.80*	18	100.00
Children's education	*0.68*	32	71.11	*0.75*	28	71.79	*0.52*	16	88.89
Savings & investment	*0.51*	40	88.89	*0.61*	37	94.87	*0.13*	18	100.00
Marital & self-related decisions									
How to raise children	*1.15*	44	97.78	*0.75*	35	89.74	*0.55*	17	94.44
Birth control	*1.94*	25	55.56	*2.09*	17	43.59	*1.67*	4	22.22
Woman's association	*2.00*	45	100.00	*1.36*	39	100.00	*0.80*	18	100.00
When to have sex	*0.28*	41	91.11	*0.16*	39	100.00	*0.13*	17	94.44
Who has the "Last Word" and Who should have it									
Who has the last word on important family matters	*0.15*	45	100.00	*0.15*	39	100.00	*0.06*	18	100.00
Who should have it	*0.53*	45	100.00	*0.63*	39	100.00	*0.44*	18	100.00

* N is the number of applicable responses to the item.

** PCT is the proportion of applicable responses to the item in the total number of cases.

Point of Saturation

The preceding observations suggest that women's agency as decision makers is based on their control and disposal of their earnings. Comparing higher contributors with minor contributors, we clearly see the influence of earning power on decision making. However, this relationship does not seem linear: "major" contributors (i.e. those who contribute over 60 percent of total household income) have less, not more, influence than equal contributors (i.e. those who contribute between 40 to 60 percent of total household income). Like those discussed earlier, this finding is consistent with the non-linearity *(curvilinear)* of the relationship between contribution level and male or female control of money. Just as the size of women's contributions does not ensure them control over money, contribution size does not automatically translate into a proportionately increased influence in household and self-related decisions. The "major" contributors who are under either female or shared control are clearly more influential in most decision areas than the corresponding groups among the "equal" contributors.

The intriguing fact is that the women who make a "major" contribution but whose money is controlled by men are worse off than the corresponding group of women who make only an "equal" contribution.

How then do we explain this predominance of male control arrangements under conditions where women are the major contributors? It is possible to conclude that wives' earnings generate increased decision-making influence as long as those earnings are subordinate or equal to husbands' earnings.[5] When women's earnings surpass those of their husbands, men appear to exercise increased control in decision making. The threat entailed by women's economic power is countered by an increased exercise of patriarchal prerogative.

5 This finding is consistent with Safilios-Rothchild's (1990) observations in the cases of Greece, Honduras, Kenya.

Table 6. Women's influence in decision making by the proportion of female monetary contribution to household in squatter group

	MAJOR	N*	%**	EQUAL	N*	%**	MINOR	N*	%**
Consumption & saving decisions									
Food	*3.00*	4	57.14	*0.65*	14	56.00	*0.71*	12	63.16
Household electronics	*0.71*	6	85.71	*0.78*	24	96.00	*0.44*	13	68.42
Household durables	*1.40*	6	85.71	*1.00*	24	96.00	*0.56*	14	73.68
Clothing	*1.40*	6	85.71	*3.00*	22	88.00	*0.78*	16	84.21
Children's education	*2.00*	6	85.71	*1.44*	11	44.00	*0.50*	9	47.37
Savings & investment	*1.00*	6	85.71	*0.50*	21	84.00	*0.64*	18	94.74
Marital & self-related decisions									
How to raise children	*2.00*	6	85.71	*0.90*	20	80.00	*1.25*	18	94.74
Birth control	*5.00*	3	42.86	*8.00*	9	36.00	*5.00*	6	31.58
Woman's association	*0.71*	6	85.71	*2.43*	24	96.00	*1.00*	19	100.00
When to have sex	*0.00*	5	71.43	*0.31*	19	76.00	*0.07*	15	78.95
Who has the "Last Word" and Who should have it									
Who has the last word on important family matters	*0.50*	6	85.71	*0.07*	24	96.00	*0.12*	19	100.00
Who should have it	*0.40*	7	100.00	*0.39*	23	92.00	*0.52*	19	100.00

* N is the number of applicable responses to the item.
** PCT is the proportion of applicable responses to the item in the total number of cases.

Conversely, women under such conditions do not seem to seek to increase their influence commensurately with their earnings, perhaps because continued gains involve different kinds of costs for women and result in increasing marital conflicts. Women, therefore, may be more likely to avoid using their superior earning power as leverage for intra-household bargaining once they clearly become the dominant income providers. There seems to be a threshold, a saturation point, beyond which women cannot – or imagine they cannot – proceed.

The data clearly underscore the extent to which men reassert male control of female income once that income clearly surpasses their own. Interviews with domestic workers further illuminate women's attempts to change the dynamics of their marriages with money and male response to such an attempt.

Table 7. Women's influence in decision making by "control of money" in doorkeeper group

	Men	N*	%**	Women	N*	%**	Shared	N*	%**
Consumption & saving decisions									
Food	*0.42*	47	74.60	*2.09*	17	94.44	*0.55*	17	80.95
Household electronics	*0.34*	63	100.00	*0.64*	18	100.00	*0.68*	21	100.00
Household durables	*0.70*	63	100.00	*0.57*	18	100.00	*1.10*	21	100.00
Clothing	*1.26*	60	95.24	*1.77*	18	100.00	*1.33*	21	100.00
Children's education	*0.58*	49	77.78	*0.86*	13	72.22	*0.87*	14	66.67
Savings & investment	*0.39*	59	93.65	*0.68*	16	88.89	*0.48*	20	95.24
Marital & self-related decisions									
How to raise children	*0.64*	60	95.24	*1.62*	17	94.44	*1.24*	19	90.48
Birth control	*1.84*	27	42.86	*3.00*	6	33.33	*1.89*	13	61.90
Woman's association	*1.47*	63	100.00	*2.00*	18	100.00	*1.10*	21	100.00
When to have sex	*0.14*	58	92.06	*0.38*	18	100.00	*0.27*	21	100.00
Who has the "Last Word" and Who should have it									
Who has the last word on important family matters	*0.09*	63	100.00	*0.29*	18	100.00	*0.17*	21	100.00
Who should have it	*0.47*	63	100.00	*0.71*	18	100.00	*0.68*	21	100.00

* N is the number of applicable responses to the item.

** PCT is the proportion of applicable responses to the item in the total number of cases.

Zehra Kibar (a pseudonym), wife of a doorkeeper, described a Sunday afternoon when she and her husband took their two children, an 8 year old girl and a 10 year old boy, to the amusement park *(Genclik Parki)*. At the beginning of this outing, the boy misbehaved – did something that made his sister cry. The father decided to punish the boy on the spot: first he lightly smacked him and then declared that the boy would not get the ice-cream he was promised and was eagerly anticipating. Zehra intervened, turning to her husband and saying "the boy is going to get his ice-cream. I'll pay for it. In fact, my money is paying for this whole outing". A marital argument ensued and continued at home; the husband accused her of using her money to undermine his authority. "Who do you think you are?" he asked. The boy did not get his ice-cream: Zehra could not act in direct defiance of her husband's wishes. Her defiance of his will was limited to the mere assertion of a disposal right. Going further than that by actually buying the ice-cream would be costly.

Table 8. Women's influence in decision making by "control of money" in the squatter group

	Men	N*	%**	Women	N*	%**	Shared	N*	%**	Separate	N*	%**
Consumption & saving decisions												
Food	*0.24*	13	68.42	*3.40*	11	57.89	*0.00*	1	20.00	*1.00*	5	62.50
Household electronics	*0.20*	15	78.95	*1.25*	18	94.74	*0.67*	5	100.00	*1.00*	5	62.50
Household durables	*0.36*	15	78.95	*1.25*	18	94.74	*0.67*	5	100.00	*3.00*	6	75.00
Clothing	*0.14*	8	42.11	*3.00*	12	63.16	*1.00*	2	40.00	*1.67*	4	50.00
Children's education	*0.30*	15	78.95	*1.71*	19	100.00	*0.11*	5	100.00	*0.20*	6	75.00
Savings & investment	*0.58*	15	78.95	*3.00*	18	94.74	*1.00*	5	100.00	*11.00*	6	75.00
Marital & self-related decisions												
How to raise children	*0.58*	15	78.95	*1.77*	18	94.74	*1.67*	4	80.00	*1.33*	7	87.50
Birth control	*4.00*	5	26.32	*7.00*	8	42.11	Women only	1	20.00	*7.00*	4	50.00
Woman's association	*0.89*	18	94.74	*1.92*	19	100.00	Women only	5	100.00	*0.75*	7	87.50
When to have sex	*0.13*	13	68.42	*0.19*	16	84.21	*0.25*	5	100.00	*0.11*	5	62.50
Who has the "Last Word" and Who should have												
Who has the last word on important family matters	*0.06*	18	94.74	*0.23*	19	100.00	*0.00*	5	100.00	*0.17*	7	87.50
Who should have it	*0.50*	18	94.74	*0.33*	18	94.74	*0.67*	5	100.00	*0.45*	8	100.00

* N is the number of applicable responses to the item.

** PCT is the proportion of applicable responses to the item in the total number of cases.

Table 9. Women's influence in decision making and female level of contribution controlled by control of money in the doorkeeper group

	Major Contributors						Equal Contributors					
	Male Control	N*	Female Control	N*	Shared Control	N*	Male Control	N*	Female Control	N*	Shared Control	N*
Consumption & saving decisions												
Food	0.42	17	1.29	8	0.71	6	0.89	18	2.00	6	0.38	9
Household electronics	0.26	29	0.64	9	0.75	7	0.56	21	0.33	6	0.71	12
Household durables	0.61	29	0.64	9	1.33	7	1.33	21	0.33	6	1.00	12
Clothing	1.55	28	3.50	9	1.00	7	1.38	19	1.40	6	1.40	12
Children's education	0.40	21	1.33	7	3.00	4	0.89	17	0.50	3	0.60	8
Savings & investment	0.33	26	1.33	7	0.75	7	0.82	20	0.71	6	0.29	11
Marital & self-related decisions												
How to raise children	0.71	29	5.00	9	2.00	6	0.73	19	0.67	5	0.83	11
Birth control	1.83	17	1.67	4	3.00	4	2.20	8	n.a.	2	1.33	7
Woman's association	2.22	29	5.00	9	0.56	7	1.21	21	1.40	6	1.67	12
When to have sex	0.19	25	0.64	9	0.27	7	0.08	21	0.20	6	0.33	12
The "last word" and who should												
Who has the last word on important family matters	0.07	29	0.50	9	0.17	7	0.11	21	0.20	6	0.20	12
Who should have it	0.49	29	0.50	9	0.75	7	0.45	21	1.40	6	0.71	12
Socio demographic characteristics (Means)												
Age	33.3		29.0		26.9		32.4		28.0		26.8	
Age at marriage	17.7		17.0		17.1		17.9		17.5		17.4	
Years worked in domestic service	7.0		4.1		4.5		7.9		6.8		5.2	
Duration in the city	*15.6*		*12.0*		*9.7*		*14.6*		*10.5*		*9.4*	

* N is the number of applicable responses to the item.

** PCT is the proportion of applicable responses to the item in the total number of cases.

Table 10. Measures of the patriarchal authority and women's responses to patriarchy in the doorkeeper group

	N*	*Who has the Last Word?* PCT** who say "Men do"	*Who should have the Last Word?* PCT** who say "Men should"
Total of doorkeeper group	102	*78.4*	*35.3*
Level of monetary contribution			
Major contributor	45	*75.6*	*35.6*
Equal contributor	39	*76.9*	*33.3*
Minor contributor	18	*88.9*	*38.9*
Control of money			
Under male control	63	*85.7*	*42.9*
Under female control	18	*61.1*	*27.8*
Under shared control	21	*71.4*	*19.0*

* N is the number of applicable responses to the item.
** PCT is the proportion of applicable responses to the item in the total number of cases.

This cost might even mean facing physical male violence. It may explain why women like Zehra do not attempt to exercise such disposal rights more actively. Wife-beating is quite common in rural migrant families and studies demonstrate a close connection between domestic violence and money issues (Erman 1998).

But Zehra's experience is also representative of the possibilities earning and claiming money open to women's subjectivities, it testifies to the salience of self-worth through economic agency and explains why women in this study are markedly critical of their husband's patriarchal authority. Only about a third of the women think that "Husbands should have the ultimate say". Women feel that familial authority should be based on the resources one contributes to the household rather than gender. They cannot, however, directly demand more power or authority.

When asked, "Who has the ultimate say in important family matters?" women, departing from previous responses pertaining to specific consumption decisions, indicate that the husband has the final word. Over three fourths of the women, regardless of their level of contribution to household income, said that the ultimate word is their husbands'. It is possible that women achieve "equal participation" in a range of specific household decisions while traditional male domination is maintained at structural levels. The overall decision-making score is not therefore a summary of other item-specific scores, but is instead a measure of "idealized authority" reflecting the husband's traditional institutionalized role. These husbands' traditional authority does not derive from their roles as providers (i.e. the resources they are capable of bringing in), but rather it emanates from their position in the traditional patriarchal family.

Conclusion

This present study reaffirms that the relationship between women's earnings and claiming decision-making power are far from direct and simple. Women's monetary contribution to their households is not directly correlated with independent control over money or with decision-making authority in the household. The contrast between the doorkeeper wives and the squatter settlement women starkly demonstrates the irrelevance of the size of women's contribution to the household budget. Due to male control of money in doorkeeper households, the wives of doorkeepers are much higher contributors to household income than the squatter settlement women, yet they claim less influence in decision making than the latter. This study identified a point of saturation: women's earnings enhance decision-making influence up to a point, as long as those earnings are subordinate or equal to the husbands' earnings. When women pass this point and begin to earn more than their husbands, husbands perceive this as a loss of their patriarchal power and compensate by exerting control over decision making. Decision-making profiles of the two groups of women are almost identical in the areas concerning the self, sex, and overall decision making and show similarities with other studies demonstrating powerfully that non-economic decisions are resistant to challenge by women's income. Neither the size of earnings nor the control of it translates into women's autonomy. Yet, women's earnings and controlling money has generated a situation in which men's unquestioned authority as husbands has become less taken-for-granted and where women have started questioning naturalness of arbitrary male authority.

At a theoretical level, Turkish rural migrant women's experiences reveal the limitations of dichotomous frameworks: they obscure rather than illuminate the many ways that women embrace wage earning as the key to successful motherhood and good reputation as housewives while they simultaneously articulate the significance of financial independence/ autonomy within marriage for their sense of self worth and the way they express self-confidence. Women's definition of the self through the roles of wife and mother does not mean that they ignore the value of their labor in monetary terms or that the ideology of family unity or identity of interests destroys their sense of individuality. As this study showed, women have their own self-interests, often divergent from men and act on them with their earnings. They actively manage and attempt to increase their standing in the family and the community with their spending decisions. Their earnings offer a capacity to participate in an increasingly pervasive urban consumer culture and to invest into their children's education and upward mobility. This fusion of maternal altruism and self-interest in the definition of migrant women's identity underscores the need for conceptual frameworks that accommodate contradictions in women's lives.

References

AYATA, Sencer and AYATA, Ayse, 1996, "Konut, Komsuluk ve Kent Kulturu" (Housing, Neighborliness, and the Urban Culture), *Housing Research Series 10*, Ankara, T.C. Prime Ministry, Housing Development Administration.

BERIK, Gunseli, 1987, *Women Carpet Weavers in Turkey: Patterns of Employment, Earnings and Status*, Geneva, International Labor Office.

BERK, Sarah Fenstermaker, 1985, *The Gender Factory*, New York, Plenum Press.

BLOOD, Robert and WOLFE, Donald M., 1960, *Husbands and Wives*, New York, Free Press.

BLUMBERG, Rae Lesser, 1991, "Income Under Female Versus Male Control: Hypotheses from a Theory of Gender Stratification and Data from the Third World", in Rae Lesser BLUMBERG (ed.), *Gender, Family, and Economy: The Triple Overlap*, Newbury Park, Sage.

BLUMSTEIN, Philip and SCHWARTZ, Pepper, 1983, *American Couples: Money, Work, and Sex*, New York, William Morrow.

–, 1991, "Money and Ideology: Their Impact on Power and the Division of Household Labor", in Rae Lesser BLUMBERG (ed.), *Gender, Family, and Economy: The Triple Overlap*, Newbury Park, Sage.

BOLAK, Hale Cihan, 1995, "Towards a Conceptualization of Marital Power Dynamics: Women Breadwinners and Working-class Households in Turkey", in Sirin TEKELI (ed.), *Women in Modern Turkish Society*, London and Atlantic Heights, NJ, Zed.

CELLE DE BOWMAN, Olga, 2000, "Peruvian Female Industrialists and the Globalization Project", *Gender and Society*, 14, 4, pp. 540–559.

CHARLES, Nicola and KERR, Marion, 1987, "Just the Way It Is: Gender and Age Differences in Family Food Consumption", in Julia BRANNEN and Gail WILSON (eds), *Give and Take in Families: Studies in Resource Distribution*, London, Allen and Unwin.

CIFCI, Oya, 1990, "Women in the Public Sector", in Ferhunda OZBAY (ed.), *Women, Family and Social Change in Turkey*, Bangkok, Unesco.

CINAR, Mine, 1991, *Labor Opportunities for Adult Females and Home-Working Women in Istanbul, Turkey*, The G.E. von Grunebaum Center for Near Eastern Studies, Working Paper No. 2. Los Angeles, University of California.

CINAR, Mine, EVCIMEN Gunar and KAYTAZ, Mehmet, 1988, "The Present day status of small-scale industries sanatkar in Bursa, Turkey", *International Journal of Middle East Studies*, 20, 3, pp. 287–301.

DAVIS, Kingsley, 1988, "Wives and Work: A Theory of the Sex-Role Revolution and Its Consequence", in Sanford M. DORNBUSCH and Myra H. STROBE (eds), *Feminism, Children and the New Families*, New York, The Guilford Press.

DELPHY, Christine, 1979, "Sharing the same table: consumption and the family", in Christopher Charles HARRIS (ed.), *The Sociology of the Family: New Directions in Britain*, Keele, University of Keele.

DPT, 1992, "Turk Aile Yapisi Arastirmasi", *DPT Yayinlari*, No. 2313.

DUBEN, Alan, 1982, "The significance of family and kinship in urban Turkey", in Çigdem KAGITÇIBAŞI (ed.), *Sex Roles, Family and Community in Turkey*, Bloomington, Indiana, Indiana University Press.

–, 1985, "Turkish families and households in historical perspective", *Journal of Family History*, 10, 1, pp. 75–97.

DUBEN, Alan and BEHAR, Cem, 1991, *Istanbul Households: Marriage, Family and Fertility 1880–1940*, Cambridge, Cambridge University Press.

DWYER, Daisy and BRUCE, Judith, 1988, *A Home Divided: Women and Income in the Third World*, Stanford, Stanford University Press.

ELLIOTT, Joyce and MOSKOFF, William, 1983, "Decision-Making Power in Romanian Families", *Journal of Comparative Family Studies*, 14, 1, pp. 38–51.

ERKUT, Sumru, 1982, "Dualism in values toward education of Turkish women", in Çigdem KAGITÇIBAŞI (ed.), *Sex Roles, Family and Community in Turkey*, Bloomington, Indiana, Indiana University Press.

ERMAN, Tahire, 1998, "The impact of migration on Turkish rural women: four emergent patterns", *Gender and Society*, 12, pp. 146–168.

ESPINAL, Rosario and GRASMUCK, Sherri, 1993, "Gender, Households and Informal Entrepreneurship in the Dominican Republic", Unpublished paper. Presented at the

XVIII Annual Convention of the Caribbean Studies Association, Kingston and Ocho Rios, Jamaica, 24–29 May.

FAPOHUNDA, Eleanor, 1988, "The Nonpooling Household: A Challenge to Theory", in Daisy DWYER and Judith BRUCE (eds), *A Home Divided: Women and Income in the Third World*, Stanford, Stanford University Press.

FOLBRE, Nancy, 1988, "The Black Four of Hearts: Toward a New Paradigm of Household Economics", in Daisy DWYER and Judith BRUCE (eds), *A Home Divided: Women and Income in the Third World*, Stanford, Stanford University Press.

GOLD, Ray, 1952, "Janitors vs. Tenants: a Status-income Dilemma", *The American Journal of Sociology*, 57, pp. 487–93.

GRASMUCK, Sherri, 1991, "Bringing the Family Back", in *Towards an Expanded Understanding of Women's Subordination in Latin America,* Paper presented at the meetings of the Latin American Studies Association, XVI International Congress, Washington D.C.

HARRIS, Olivia, 1988, "Households as Natural Units", in Kate YOUNG, Carol WOLKOWITZ and Roslyn MCCULLAGH (eds), *Of Marriage and the Market: Women's Subordination Internationally and Its Lessons*, London, Routledge and Kegan Paul.

HARTMANN, Heidi, 1981, "The Family as the Locus of Gender, Class, and Political Struggle: The Example of Housework", *Signs*, 6, 3, pp. 366–94.

HOCHSCHILD, Arlie R., 1987, *The Second Shift*, New York, Viking.

HOODFAR, Homa, 1988, "Household Budgeting and Financial Management in a Lower-Income Cairo Neighborhood", in Daisy DWYER and Judith BRUCE (eds), *A Home Divided: Women and Income in the Third World,* Stanford, Stanford University Press.

HONDAGNEU-SOTELO, Pierrette, 1994, *Gendered Transitions: Mexican Experiences of Immigration*, Los Angeles, University of California Press.

KADININ STATUSU VE SIRUNLARI GENEL MUDURLUGU (KSSGM), 1998, *Turkiye'de Kadinin Durumu*, Ankara, Takav.

KANDIYOTI, Deniz, 1990, "Rural Transformation in Turkey and Its Implications for Women's Status", in Ferhunde OZBAY (ed.), *Women, Family, and Social Change in Turkey*, Bangkok, Unesco.

KIRAY, Mübbecel, 1985, "Metropolitan City and the Changing Family", in *Family in Turkish Society*, Ankara, The Turkish Social Science Association.

KIRAY, Mübbecel, 1991, "Introduction: A Perspective", in Mübbecel KIRAY (ed.), *Structural Change in Turkish Society*, Bloomington, Indiana, Indiana University Press.

KUYAŞ, Nilüfer, 1982, "Female Labor Power Relations in the Urban Turkish Family", in Çigdem KAGITÇIBAŞI (ed.), *Sex Roles, Family, and Community in Turkey*, Bloomington, Indiana, Indiana University Turkish Studies.

MAHER, Vanessa, 1988, "Work, consumption and authority within the household: A Moroccan Case", in Kate YOUNG, Carol WOLKOWITZ and Roslyn MCCULLAGH (eds), *Of Marriage and the Market: Women's Subordination in International Perspective,* London, CSE Press.

MENCHER, Joan, 1988, "Women's Work and Poverty: Women's Contribution to Household Maintenance in South India", in Daisy DWYER and Judith BRUCE (eds), *A Home Divided: Women and Income in the Third World,* Stanford, Stanford University Press.

OLSON, E., 1982, "Duo Focal Family Structure and an Alternative Model of Husband-Wife Relationship", in Çigdem KÂGITÇIBAŞI (ed.), *Sex Roles, Family and Community in Turkey*, Bloomington, Indiana, Indiana University Press.

OZBAY, Ferhunde, 1989, "Family and household structure in Turkey: Past, present and future", Paper presented at the conference on Changing Family in the Middle East, Amman, Jordan, 16–18 December.

–, 1990, "Changes in women's occupation inside and outside the home", in Şirin TEKELI (ed.), *From Women's Perspective: Women in Turkey in the Eighties*, Istanbul, Iletisim Yayinlari.

PAHL, Jan, 1980, "Patterns of Money Management within Marriage", *Journal of Social Policy*, 3, 9, pp. 313–35.

–, 1983, "The Allocation of Money and the Structuring of Inequality within Marriage", *The Sociological Review*, 31, May, pp. 237–262.

PAPANEK Hanna *et al.,* 1988, "Women Are Good with Money: Earning and Managing in an Indonesian City", in Daisy DWYER and Judith BRUCE (eds), *A Home Divided: Women and Income in the Third World,* Stanford, Stanford University Press.

SAFILIOS-ROTHSCHILD, Constantina, 1970, "Study of Family Power Structure: 1960–69", *Journal of Marriage and the Family*, 32, November, pp. 539–552.

–, 1976, "A macro and micro-examination of family power and love: an exchange model", *Journal of Marriage and the Family,* 38, pp. 355–62.

–, 1984, "The Role of the Family in Development", in Sue Ellem M. CHARLTON (ed.), *Women in Third World Development,* Boulder, Westview Press.

–, 1990, "Socio-economic Determinants of the Outcomes of Women's Income-Generation in Developing Countries", in Sharon STICHTER and Jane L. PARPART (eds), *Women, Employment and the Family in the International Division of Labor,* Philadelphia, Temple University Press.

SENYAPILI, Tansi, 1981a, *Ankara Kentinde Gecekondu Gelisimi*, Ankara, Kent Koop Yayinlari.

–, 1981b, "A New Component in Metropolitan Areas: Gecekondu Women", in Nermin Abadan UNAT (ed.), *Women in Turkish Society*, Leiden, E.J. Brill.

–, 1982, "Economic Change and the Gecekondu Family", in Çigdem KAGITÇIBAŞI (ed.), *Sex Roles, Family, and Community in Turkey*, Bloomington, Indiana University Press.

SIRMAN, Nuket, 1988, "Peasants and Family Farms: The Position of Households in Cotton Production in a Village of Western Turkey", Unpublished Ph.D Thesis, University of London.

STANDING, Hilary, 1985, "Resources, wages, and power: the impact of women's employment on the urban Bengali household", in Haleh AFSHAR (ed.), *Women, Work, and Ideology in the Third World,* London, Tavistock.

STEINBERG, Ronnie and HAIGNERE, Lois, 1991, "Separate but Equivalent: Equal Pay for Comparable Worth", in Mary Margaret FONOW and Judith A. COOK (eds), *Beyond Methodology*, Bloomington, Indiana University Press.

TEKELI Sirin, 1990, "The Meaning and Limits of Feminist Ideology in Turkey", in Ferhunde OZBAY (ed.), *Women, Family and Social Change in Turkey*, Bangkok, Unesco.

THORNE, Barrie and YALOM, Marilyn (eds), 1982, *Rethinking the Family: Some Feminist Questions*, New York, Longman.

TIMUR, Serim, 1972, *Turkiye'de Aile Yapisi*, Ankara, Hacettepe University.
–, 1981, "Determinants of Family Structure in Turkey", in Nermin Abadan UNAT (ed.), *Women in Turkish Society*, Leiden, E.J. Brill.
WHITE, Jenny, 1991, "Women and Work in Istanbul: Linking the Urban Poor to the World Market", *Middle East Report*, November–December, 18–22.
–, 1994, *Money Makes Us Relatives*, Austin, University of Texas Press.
WHITEHEAD, Ann, 1988, "'I'm hungry, mum': the politics of domestic budgeting", in Kate YOUNG, Carol WOLKOWITZ and Roslyn MCCULLAGH (eds), *Of Marriage and the Market: Women's Subordination in International Perspective*, London, CSE Press.
WILSON, Gail, 1987, "Money: Patterns of Responsibility and Irresponsibility in Marriage", in Julia BRANNEN and Gail WILSON (eds), *Give and Take in Families: Studies in Resource Distribution*, London, Allen and Unwin.
WOLF, Lauren Diane, 1992, *Factory Daughters*, Los Angeles, University of California Press.

Women Breadwinners in the Margins: Filipina Domestic Workers in Rome, Italy

Margaret MAGAT

Whether working as domestics, nannies, nurses or prostitutes from Amsterdam to Qatar, the ubiquitous presence of Filipina women around the world is testimony to the globalized economy. Human labor is the number one export of the Philippines and Filipina domestic workers make up the majority of the service sector (Go 1998; Imson 1999a). This work is based on my dissertation which focuses on Filipina domestics in Rome, Italy and examines the disjuncture of their everyday life brought on by mass mediation and migration (Appadurai 1996). I attempt to trace the complexities linking labor migration to the creation of a Filipino diaspora, seeking to identify the processes in which the women maintain their ethnicity and ideas of selfhood.

What role do Filipina women play in the growing feminization of international migration in the southern European context and why has their ethnicity become synonymous in many countries with the term "maid"? (Chell-Robinson 2000; Lazaridis 2000; Constable 1997). In this work, I will address the day-to-day experiences of Filipina domestics as they negotiate their lives and their work with their Italian employers, while attempting to carve a space for themselves.

With a population of about 72 million, the Philippines has an estimated 4.5 million documented overseas contract workers (and millions more undocumented) who work in more than 140 countries worldwide. In the last two decades, Europe has witnessed a "New Migration" which has transformed traditional countries of emigration such as Italy and Spain into countries of immigration (Koser and Lutz 1998; Cole 1997; Anthias and Lazaridis 2000).

Although there are now women of various ethnicities working as domestics in Italy, such as Somalians and Latin American women, Filipina women make up the majority of domestic workers in the country (Caritas 2000; King 2000), as well as elsewhere in the world (Alabastro 1995; Cohen and Vertovec 1999; Parreñas 1998, 2001). In places such as Saudi

Arabia, Greece, Singapore, and Hong Kong, the wide scale phenomenon of mostly educated Filipinas working as maids has led to their ethnicity becoming synonymous with their occupation (Chell-Robinson 2000; Lazaridis 2000; Constable 1997). In Italy, my informants have told me that the Italian word *Filippine* is the vernacular term for "maid", while, in Hong Kong, the term *banmui* translates to "Philippine girl" and it also means "servant" or "maid" (Constable 1997).

One scholar attempts to explain the preponderance of Filipino domestics and service workers. Mina Ramirez (1987) argues that, with the Spanish arrival in 1521, Filipino labor has been devalued. Because Filipinos traded their gold and food for useless trinkets, inequitable trading exchanges became the norm and this set the stage for Filipinos to undervalue themselves in jobs as domestics and laborers, despite their college degrees. The devaluing of labor continued during the American colonization, and was cemented by the Marcos administration when foreign companies were lured to invest by labor costs 35 to 50 percent lower in Manila than Singapore or Hong Kong. In effect, Filipinos were treated as second-place citizens in their own country, preparing them to be second-class citizens abroad.

Filipina women first flocked to Italy to work as domestic workers in the early 1970s (Andall 1998 and 1999; Chell-Robinson 2000), although some long-term migrants claim that Filipinas arrived as early as the late 1960s (Magat 2000–2001). However, it is after 1974 that the large influx of Filipinas to Italy began in earnest. That year, then-President Marcos launched the Overseas Employment Program as an attempt to solve staggering unemployment and to inject much-needed foreign currency into the Philippine economy (Cariño 1998; Imson 1999b; Parreñas 1998). The export of "manpower" had been publicized as a temporary solution to stimulate the economy, but now, the Philippines heavily relies on the remittances sent by workers. Remittances from the millions of "overseas contract workers" (OCWs) who are obligated to send 50–70 percent of their salaries (Stahl and Arnold 1999) brought in about $7 billion in 1998 (Vanzi 1998).

The demand for domestic workers in Italy has been fueled in part by lack of childcare and elderly care centers and the large numbers of Italian women working outside the home. Factors such as ease of entry into Italy and its geographic location, a thriving underground economy requiring flexible and cheap labor, and insufficient regulation along with a long-standing culture of migration in the Philippines have lured an estimated 200,000 Filipinos, both documented and undocumented, to work in Italy, making this the largest concentration of Filipinos in Europe. This is a conservative estimate from the Philippine ambassador to Italy, and it contrasts sharply with the 65,000 official estimate from the *Caritas 2000* study. More than 60 percent of Filipinos here are Filipina women, both single and married, working as domestic workers. Among themselves, Filipinos joke that Rome is the "Hong Kong" of Europe since it is fairly easy to enter and obtain service jobs.

Fieldwork was conducted between November 2000 and June 2001, with qualitative interviews of Filipinas at bus stops and piazzas, supplemented by participant observation of their cultural activities. Priests, nuns, Italian and Philippine officials as well as several active feminist non-government workers were among those interviewed. Filipinas are the preferred domestics of choice in Italy – indeed, they like to joke that they are the Mercedes-Benz of domestics –, and hiring a Filipina is a status symbol for many Italian families due to the majority of the women being educated and English-speaking. Nevertheless, due to the low-status of domestic work in Italy and elsewhere, Filipinas suffer experiences similar to other migrants. In particular, class and ethnicity conflicts with Italian employers, as well as discriminatory experiences and cultural misunderstandings with others.

Although some employers go out of their way to ensure that their live-in employee is satisfied, my fieldwork suggests that many Italian women employers engage in what Pierre Bourdieu (1977; 1994) termed "modes of domination". Several Filipina women told of how their employers would buy them small gifts or give them some spending money on occasion. Consequently, they are unwilling to complain whenever necessary because they do not want to appear ungrateful. "Generous" gestures such as the giving of second-hand clothes and pocket money (Lazaridis 2000) may be seen as "gentle, hidden exploitation [...] the form taken by man's exploitation of man whenever overt, brutal exploitation is impossible" (Bourdieu 1994, 186).

Debra, a woman in her 40s, has been in Rome for the last eighteen years. She and her husband, a part-time domestic worker and security guard, live in their own apartment with their son. Their apartment is free, courtesy of the building that her husband patrols. This is an unusual situation in Italy, as most two-bedroom apartments are shared by several families, up to eight Filipinos living together. Debra remains very grateful for her life in Italy, and despite the heavy load of her job which takes a toll on her health, she refuses to say anything bad about her employer. One time, her niece began to complain that Debra was being worked too hard, but Debra immediately hushed her, pointing out that her employer gives her second-hand clothes and small gifts from time to time. In return, Debra goes beyond the call of duty, even continuing to work despite being just released from the hospital after an operation. Her husband and niece expressed their concern, but despite her weakened condition, Debra would not listen.

Other examples include the lack of a room or space of their own to entertain friends on their days off. Many of the women interviewed mentioned that they only have a pull-out sofa bed. Consequently, their employers in fact, end up indirectly controlling the women's free time, where she can spend it, and how. The "hidden exploitation", to use Bourdieu's term, is also made worse by the Filipino cultural trait of *utang ng loob.* This trait, roughly translated to mean "debt from the heart", refers to the belief of many Filipinos that once someone does something for them, they are obligated many times over to return the favor and be loyal to that person no matter what. This debt of gratitude can vary in strength, but often it can be so strong that many feel it can never be repaid, and for the rest of one's life, one is obligated, even if the person is a manipulative employer. This can also be seen in the following case.

Selica,[1] 26, has been working as a domestic worker in Italy since she was 14 years old. A *petite* woman, she is not a college graduate like many other Filipinas, but she is an intelligent person who dreams of doing something else. An operation for emergency appendicitis two years ago has made her reflect about her work and what is lacking in her life. Now, she says, her work as a domestic worker is literally "killing" her.

> When I want to go out, I want to go out, but in my job, I cannot do what I want to do… I feel like a robot. When I wake up in the morning, I feel just like a machine. I have to wake up, I have to prepare breakfast, I have to dress the children and in the same routine. I feel so suffocated [her voice rises]! And I, for the whole day, I have to stay in that house, and what do you think? I feel depressed. I feel more than just like in jail. Everyday is the same thing.

1 Some names were changed to protect the individual's privacy.

Like most Filipino migrants, Selica sends regular remittances to family. Each month, Selica earns $500, and accommodation and food is included in her contract as a live-in domestic worker. But most of the time, what she sends home is never enough. Often, there are relatives who fall sick, or younger siblings who need funds for schooling. Recently, she has had to finance her sister's debut or coming-of-age party, a ritual that is popular in Philippine society. Selica spent about five months salary, equivalent to more than 4 million lire.

Selica would like to look for an additional job, but as a live-in, she cannot leave the house except on Thursday afternoons and on Sundays. She has complained to her employer about her workload, and she has shared her desire for future schooling as well. The employer promised that in the future, Selica could use Tuesday evenings to take classes. Selica is so grateful that she now does extra work on her time off to repay her employer, even though it was just a verbal promise. Selica's Filipino cultural trait of *utang ng loob* or debt of gratitude enables her employer to perpetuate the "gentle exploitation" identified by Bourdieu. Now, she cannot say no when her *signora* asks her to stay for a while to iron or find clothes on Sundays. In addition, Selica says the *signora* often takes advantage of Selica's genuine affection for the children by appealing to her to dress and take care of the children on her time off although the *signora* herself could have done it easily.

An analysis of the dynamics of the servant-employer relationship through gender alone would not be sufficient to illuminate the various conflicts brought on by differences in class and ethnicity. Migration scholars like Jacqueline Andall (1998; 2000) have pointed out in their work that not only gender, but class and ethnicity are needed to call attention to the inequalities and asymmetrical relationship between Italian female employers and employees. Andall points to the Italian State and the Catholic Church for rendering female migrants "doubly invisible" by not addressing their needs as women and mothers. Italy continues to have unequal divisions of labor in the home, while organizations like the ACLI-COLF formed in the 1950s for domestic workers continue to emphasize the needs of Italian employers over those of their migrant employees. At all times, female domestics are urged to cultivate a "harmonious" relationship with their employers and avoid conflicts with them (Andall 1998, 126).

Annie Phizacklea (1998) also includes class and ethnicity in her analysis of female labor migration. Like Andall, Phizacklea points out that the labor of domestic workers from Philippines and Mexico "allow women in more affluent countries to escape the drudgery of housework in conditions which sometimes approximate to a contemporary form of state-facilitated slavery" (Phizacklea 1998, 33). Evelyn Nakano-Glenn (1992) identifies this as a "racial division of reproductive labor." This racial division allows women with more class privileges to evade housework by giving it to other women, and it also enables white males to continue disregarding their share of reproductive labor. In addition, the consideration of class, ethnicity as well as gender can uncover the employer's small acts of domination which lead to oppressive work and living situations for Filipinas and other domestic workers. A closer investigation of the dynamics of the Italian employer-Filipina employee relationship can reveal the ways power relations can exist among women as well as men (Anthias 2000; Foucault 1980).

The Filipina women I interviewed were very aware that Italy is a better place to live in for a domestic worker than, for example, Saudi Arabia. Some women say that their employers consider them like family, with some Italians attending the weddings and family celebrations of their maid, paying for the dresses and whatever else is needed. One Italian employer willingly became the babysitter while the Filipina mother worked around the house. Part of the problem lies, however, in the fact that a great number of Filipina migrants have college degrees and they experience "deskilling" in becoming domestics (Chell-Robinson 2000; Constable 1997). There are many narratives about Italian employers who are surprised when they discover that their Filipina maid is well-read or can add and subtract better than they can. Recounting her own experience, one Filipina woman said,

> My employer was so surprised to see I can compute taxes in my head. He doesn't know I was a CPA in the Philippines for fifteen years.

Strict linguistic and training requirements block Filipino access to the Italian formal economy, although there are some signs that as the community matures and families are increasingly reunited, other jobs may open up, namely in home health, where Filipinos can exercise their nursing skills as *assistenti* or caretakers, earning twice the amount of a live-in domestic (Chell-Robinson 2000; Magat 2000–2001). A recently approved law now allows Filipina nurses to be hired in Italy. There were also two instances where I have observed Filipinos helping in pharmacies, but these examples are still few and far between.

Italy's tight labor market, strict language requirements, and the fact that Italian degrees are preferred, make it very difficult for the women to find work suited to their education and skills, and so they work for years as domestics. For those who are not college graduates like Selica, the possibility of being something else is almost too painful to contemplate. She told me that sometimes, she wishes that she could just stop dreaming. "Non voglio piu sognare. Stano qui, stano lavoro, basta! Mi no", she said, switching to English. "I want to grow as a person."

Appadurai suggests that "the central problem of today's global interactions is the tension between cultural homogenization and cultural heterogenization" (1996, 32). This is exemplified in Italy where assimilation to Italian culture is expected and where cultural differences are generally not tolerated (Triandafyllidou 2000, 202). Despite their place in the migrant hierarchy, racism and intolerance are increasing, with many of the Filipina women being spat at or harassed. The cost of assimilating to Italian culture is quite high, with some women indicating to me that they have forgotten how to prepare their own food ways. Since they are always cooking for their Italian employees, they do not have the chance to cook for themselves and they forget their own cuisine through the years.

Gianfausto Rosoli (1993, 297) and others have noted that ethnicity has not been an issue in Italy except in recent years and that more arrivals from Asia and Africa will increase the already fractured sense of national identity. How do Italians receive the presence of the Filipina women (and other foreigners)? Their reactions can be seen in what I call "space wars". The "space wars" help demonstrate how Italian society considers migrant workers and exemplify Appadurai's theory of the clash between cultural homogenization and cultural heterogenization. It is space, or lack of it, which fuel public outcry over Filipinos and other migrants, seen not only in Italy but in places like Hong Kong and Singapore where, sometimes, fashionable streets lined with pricey boutiques become mini-Filipino villages where food is hawked, relationships made, and one's selfhood and ethnicity are reinforced (see for example, Tam 1999).

In Rome, the public spaces are the areas where changes due to migration become apparent. Due to lack of Italian reception areas, leisure facilities and housing, the piazzas and Termini station and other public transportation centers (besides the churches) are the places where Filipino migrants and other migrants meet and gather. Many of the public spaces are spatially divided according to ethnic and gender demarcation (Chell-Robinson 2000, 116). Although the division may not be always strict, in places like the Termini station where there is about one acre of space, the distinctions are nevertheless clear. Chell-Robinson calls these transformed spaces "social maps" (p. 116). Since numerous Filipino men are unemployed and are seen as loitering, many in the Filipino community fear that their presence in public places are giving Filipinos a bad reputation for gambling, drinking and womanizing (see for example, Cuchapin 2000). It is due to what Chell-Robinson calls this "unemployed mass of men" in piazzas and Termini station that the migrant phenomenon is seen as largely male.

> The use of public space is increasing the complex set of assumptions and attitudes used in reference to migrant women, due to this image of the migrant phenomenon as male, non-white, unproductive and uncontrolled. These are images unlikely to lead to the adjustment of migrant and national groups (Chell-Robinson 2000, 117).

If there is space available, it is carved out by force, and is soon taken away. Rhacel Parreñas (1998) describes the bustling sub-community set up under a bridge in Rome beside the rat-infested section of the Tiber River. Here in what was once a shanty for Albanian refugees, Filipinos patronize make-shift restaurants, food shops with homegrown Filipino vegetables and imported goods, hair salons and tailoring businesses put up in wooden stands. One can get a haircut, shop as well as sit-down and eat on wooden benches brought in to accommodate diners. However, my fieldwork confirms that the Filipinos are now barred from Mancini. This sub-community no longer exists, and once again, the Filipinos are forced to go to Termini station and other public spaces. Since apartments are usually quite expensive, another alternative for Filipinos to have space is to rent a two-to-three bedroom apartment and have as many as ten or more people share in the rent.

As domestic workers, Filipinas are usually relegated to the margins of society, but Stuart Hall argues that margins can be spaces of power besides being spaces of weakness (1999). Filipinas know they are marginal in Italian society, but they also recognize the Italians' preference for Filipina domestic workers and that ultimately, they have the power to quit. Scholars have noted that there is informal hierarchy of immigrants in Italy, influenced by what Italians perceive to be the culture and race of the immigrant (Chell 1997; Iosifides 1997; Booth and Cole 1999, 198–199). At the top are Filipinos, who are seen as clean, hardworking and Catholic to boot. Some women do not hesitate to use this stereotype to their advantage. Whenever her frustrations with her employer get to be too much, Selica threatens to quit and look for another job. Also in her favor is the fact that the children adore her, as she is the one who is raising them. To prevent her leaving and causing the children to be unhappy, her employers inevitably beg Selica to remain and their treatment of her improves for a short while before they forget and she again is unhappy.

This tactic of directly or indirectly using the children's affection as leverage to obtain better work conditions and a higher salary is not uncommon, said Father Bati, who is the chaplain and head of the Filipino church center, Santa Pudenziana in Rome. "If Filipinas want to increase their salary, they say they are going to leave for another job, with a higher salary", said Father Bati. "Then the Italian child will cry, asking how much will it take to make them stay, and the child will beg the parent to increase the salary." This power that the domestic can wield over her employer has its drawbacks in Italy, however. Not everyone can do this. Many women have no papers at all, or if they do, they are afraid to quit as this would put their legal status to be in Italy in jeopardy.

Father Nonong, a Filipino priest who also works with the Filipino community in Rome, said: "Women have to be aware of their power. If they are not aware of their power, there is no power at all."

James Clifford points to the "diasporic predicaments" that women migrants are faced with everyday. Although they may earn income in often exploitative situations, "new areas of relative independence and control can emerge" (Clifford 1997, 259). Women should be seen as active agents, not passive victims (Orsini-Jones and Gattullo 2000). In her work with migrant women in Spain, Angeles Escrivá (2000, 219) reports that despite the loss of status as a domestic worker, women migrants gain social mobility, welfare and educational exposure. Floya Anthias notes that Filipina women renegotiate gender roles, gaining more power in their families with their new economic resources and social responsibilities (2000, 36). However, agency is often limited to structural and institutional contexts. One Filipina woman who worked as a domestic and earned supplementary income acting as a maid in Italian soap operas and films could not find other roles on screen, as well as off (Magat 2000–2001).

Cultural practices and consumption have fueled the culture of migration in the Philippines. Filipino migrants send regular *balikbayan* (literally "coming home") boxes filled with imported electronic goods, clothing, steaks and even washing machines and whole Christmas trees (Okamura 1998). Like the contracting labor agencies and remittance banks, the material culture of transnational migration has been "institutionalized".

According to Clifford, transnational practices, which describe *balikbayan* boxes, exemplify accommodation as well as cultural resistance to the host country (Clifford 1997, 251). Cultural expressions in the Filipino diaspora like *balikbayan* boxes have developed out of necessity in dealing with the long distance from loved ones and diasporic conditions. They maintain the culture of migration by symbolizing immigrant success (Rafael 2000, 260).

The consumption patterns of Filipino migrants may also be seen as markers of ethnicity. Many Filipino domestics in Rome save up for designer furs and sunglasses, even Mercedes-Benz cars, jeopardizing their goals of building their dream house in the Philippines. Their penchant for designer styles can be seen in the following popular joke: an Italian woman told her maid to put the "pollo" or chicken, in the freezer. Instead of putting the chicken in the freezer, the newly arrived Filipina puts the Ralph Lauren Polo designer shirt in the freezer. This joke reflects the importance of designer labels. It is not unusual to meet Filipinas with haute couture clothes and $350 designer glasses, bought with the average $500–600 a month salary.

Krystyna Romaniszyn (2000) notes that consumption is provoked by the rule of "spread-of-infection", where people are seen as buying more if they observe their friends buying. There is a social dimension to consumption, a point also made by Appadurai. Consumption is an active affair, not a private one and is socially and culturally controlled. One is pressured to consume by others, to keep up with appearances. Romaniszyn expands this point, saying "consumption expresses culture, and generates it [...] the consumption styles adopted become that part of a migrant's way of life which is perceived by the host society, and by which migrants express their ethnic culture" (Romaniszyn 2000, 139). Filipino domestics in Italy bring their consumption habits to a new level, using it to mark themselves apart from other migrants. Once they return to the Philippines for good or for a visit, postponed consumption occurs with the presentation of gifts, the endless party-giving and the showcasing of the new wealth and prestige.

The social norm that is generated by consumption propels further migration as other Filipinos aspire not only to earn money to help their families but to keep up with the new levels of consumption. The pressure to earn and the way to earn it, via migration, becomes a new social value or a required behavior which further feeds the local culture of migration. According to Romaniszyn, labor migration may be interpreted as a rite of passage, which allows individuals to cross the line into adulthood and acquire social prestige (Romaniszyn 2000 quoting Gmelch 1987, 266).

An NGO activist in Rome stated frankly that the materialism of Filipino migrants was "sickening". But Appadurai claims that consumption is a form of agency. "Where there is consumption there is pleasure, and where there is pleasure there is agency" (1996, 7). It also seems that Filipinos may want to have top material goods to transcend their status. Are their consumption patterns forcing many into an endless cycle of debt and attempts to pay it off through hard work as domestics? Paola Sanna, an Italian businesswoman who works with Filipinos in Rome, believes that Filipinos are much more materialistic than Italians because they want to assert themselves.

> "We [Italians] don't spend much money to have an identity," said Sanna. "A lot of Filipinos here, they want to identify themselves that they are not domestics. I think this is exaggerated, they spend a lot of money in things that in reality are not so important. If you dress from head-to-toe in Valentino, Louis Vuitton, what's the difference? You are always yourself."

Nelly Tang, a Filipina NGO activist, agrees with Sanna. According to Tang, to boost self-esteem, migrants wear expensive jewelry and clothes. Then to compensate for long-lost years, Filipino parents working in Italy buy designer clothing for their children who remain behind in the Philippines. For those children who are reunited with their parents after years of separation, the spoiling continues with more material goods once they are in Italy. Tang has seen parents buy cell phones or *telefonini* for their children as young as eight years old, and she claims this is bad because children do not understand the value of money. She argues the young generation soon presume that it is easy to get money, and they do not appreciate what work went into obtaining it.

"Ang consumerism ay malakas sa ating Pinoy, kesa mga Italians" (consumerism is very strong in Filipinos, more so than Italians), notes Tang.

> When they were in the Philippines, they didn't realize this would be their kind of work. They were professionals, then when they arrive in Italy, their job is to be a domestic. So to assuage their ego [...] they wear jewellery and other material things. That's what they are using to feel and look good.

Tang and others also believe that Filipino consumerism is another sign of colonial mentality.

Due to three hundred years of Spanish colonization, more than 80 percent of the Philippine population is Catholic, and the fact that Rome is the capital of the Catholic faith attracts many migrants. The main church is the designated basilica for Filipinos called Santa Pudenziana, near Termini Station. Since 1995, church officials have run Centro Filipino, located in Santa Pudenziana, an office catering to the social, legal, and other needs of migrants. It is in the spaces around the church and inside the hall that Filipino cultural performances take place. Food is hawked in a side hall of the church, while teenagers play volleyball inside an inner court. On their days off, as mentioned, Filipinos can flock to piazzas, bus stations or the Termini station. But many choose to go to their local church center; out of more than nine hundred Catholic churches in Rome, Filipinos have formed small communities around fifty or so churches. This means that they go to that particular church to meet friends, organize cultural activities, and eat home-made Filipino foods. In San Silvestro, for example, the space above the church is filled every Thursday afternoon and Sunday with vendors hawking Filipino foods like *lumpia* or egg roll, noodles called *pancit*, or other native snacks and drinks. But church is not the place for those who want more secular activities, such as gambling. The piazzas and transportation hubs continue to draw gamblers as well as food vendors who compete with self-styled businesses, such as those renting videos and books from the Philippines.

However, the role of the Catholic Church in the lives of the Filipina women cannot be underestimated. Some women consider themselves as the "new apostles of Christ" (Parreñas 1998). Priests like Father Nonong and Father Bati see Filipinos in Italy as "evangelizers" for Jesus. This is because Filipinas have access to the private sphere of Italian families and they wield influence over the child, and consequently over their employers. Several women have said that when they take the children to church, sometimes the parents follow. Even if the employers do not attend the church, they trust the Filipinos to go out with their children. In this case, religion helps to alleviate tension between the women and their employers.

Various cultural groups are created within the confines of a particular church center. The most notable of these groups is the *Karilagan* singing group, which is based in Santa Pudenziana. The majority of its members are domestic workers who must adhere to the rigorous and strict schedule of the group's rehearsals and performances during their days off. I contend that such groups represent the family left behind in the Philippines. For many Filipinos, whether in *Karilagan* or another group, such church groups act as their guide to their social and cultural lives, dictating their scarce hours of freedom. Indeed, there are even church groups who dictate the love life of its members, with many women telling me that their group resents their dating and prefers their members to be "old maids" since boyfriends take them away from the group's activities.

The dominant stereotype of Filipinos as just domestics is an image that the *Karilagan* singing group would like to subvert. The group sings in four different languages, showing off their cosmopolitan knowledge, never mind the fact that most members are domestics. They perform in cultural events all over Italy, and typical reactions from Italians range from one of surprise to shock that their domestic worker has impressive linguistic capability. During one December 2000 concert, I observed the ease in the way they performed their repertoire. Bing Crosby songs including *A White Christmas* were sung with affecting nostalgia, although many of the singers had never seen snow or even been to America (see Appadurai 1996). *Good 'ol Bing* was followed by several Latin hymns, one or two Italian songs, with the finale composed of a joyous performance of several Tagalog Christmas folksongs. In less than an hour, the singers in effect had demonstrated their histories, their embodied Spanish-Catholic-American colonialisms, along with their experiences of the here and now.

I commented to Esther, a singer, about Karilagan's ability to sing songs in different languages.

> Yes, in a concert, we sing how many songs, from Tagalog, to English, to Italian and Latin songs. Imagine, how could we have sung it if we weren't affected by it [colonialism]? We sang Tagalog songs because it's ours, we sang English songs

> because we have to sing it and we know English and we were colonized by Americans as well. And then we sang Italian songs, because we are here in Italy and we know how to sing in Italian and to cater to Italians in the audience. And then we sang Latin songs because it's the original language of the Catholic religion, which the Spaniards brought.

What will happen as the community matures and grows? Filipina migrants, as well as other female migrants, should be recognized for their role as the main breadwinners of their family. Their needs must be addressed. Besides social networks and Church organizations, the female migrant cannot rely on the Italian government for social services. Cultural facilities must be established and more places where they can turn to for help.

At present, the Filipino migrant situation in Rome is very much in a state of flux, although the community is showing signs of maturing. Replacement migration is occurring, with mothers being replaced by daughters as they retire from domestic work. The new migration flow means that younger women are flocking to Italy, and they delay having their own families. How will this affect Philippine society in the future? Another issue is the presence of more and more teenagers, either second generation Filipino Italians, or Filipino teenagers who have just arrived. I was told by church and Philippine embassy officials that hundreds of Filipino teenagers became undocumented migrants after arriving in Rome for the World Youth Day held in August 2000. Many of these teenagers are said to be the children of working Filipina domestics, and they never left. Due to recent reunification laws, more women are being reunited with their husbands and children. But the men have a difficult time finding jobs, and one of the problems is the prevalence of Filipino men attaching themselves to several women at the same time to support them and help them acquire work by gaining the trust of their girlfriend's employer. Another problem is the tension between the mother and the now-rebellious child, who grew up away from the mother for years. The rebellion shows in many forms: drug-taking, truancy. It is not unusual to see groups of young Filipinos gathered in piazzas during the week. Some children have forsaken school altogether to take up domestic work with their parents. Therefore, the high value traditional Filipinos place on education disappears once they are in Italy. The long-term effects could be that Filipinos in the future will no longer be the most desirable domestics.

This brings up the haunting possibility that for generations to come, the Filipino community in Rome will be a community almost exclusively made up of members specializing as domestic workers. Pursuant to this is the belief expressed by several of my field consultants that most Filipinos in Italy no longer aspire to take up other professions. Only time can tell whether the second and third generation of Filipinos in Rome will be forever a class of domestic workers. It is my hope that they will not.

References

ALABASTRO, Ruben P., 1995, "Philippine exodus leads to death row", *The Washington Times,* Friday, 22 September 1995, p. A15.

ANDALL, Jacqueline, 1998, "Catholic and State Constructions of Domestic Workers: The Case of Cape Verdean Women in Rome in the 1970s", in Khalid KOSER and Helma LUTZ (eds), *The New Migration in Europe. Social Constructions and Social Realities,* London, Macmillan Press, pp. 124–142.

–, 1999, "Cape Verdean women on the move: 'immigration shopping' in Italy and Europe", *Modern Italy,* 4, 2, pp. 241–257.

–, 2000, "Organizing Domestic Workers in Italy: The Challenge of Gender, Class and Ethnicity", in Floya ANTHIAS and Gabriella LAZARIDIS (eds), *Gender and Migration in Southern Europe. Women on the Move,* New York, Berg, pp. 145–171.

ANTHIAS, Floya and LAZARIDIS Gabriella (eds), 2000, *Gender and Migration in Southern Europe. Women on the Move*, New York, Berg.

ANTHIAS, Floya, 2000, "Metaphors of Home: Gendering New Migrations to Southern Europe", in Floya ANTHIAS and Gabriella LAZARIDIS (eds), *Gender and Migration in Southern Europe. Women on the Move*, New York, Berg, pp. 15–47.

APPADURAI, Arjun, 1996, *Modernity at Large*, Minneapolis, University of Minnesota Press.

BOOTH, Sally S. and Jeffrey E. COLE, 1999, "An unsettling integration: immigrant lives and work in Palermo", *Modern Italy*, 4.2, pp. 191–205.

BOURDIEU, Pierre, 1977, *Outline of a Theory of Practice*, Trans. Richard Nice, Cambridge, Cambridge University Press (or. ed. Genève/Paris, Droz, 1972).

–, 1994, "Structures, Habitus, Power: Basis for a Theory of Symbolic Power", in Nicholas B. DIRKS, Geoff ELEY and Sherry B. ORTNER (eds), *Culture/Power/History: A Reader in Contemporary Social Theory*, Princeton, Princeton University Press, pp. 155–199.

CARIÑO, Benjamin V. (ed.), 1998, *Filipino Workers on the Move: Trends, Dilemmas and Policy Options*, Manila, Philippine Migration Research Network.

CARITAS DI ROMA, 2000, *Immigrazione. Dossier Statistico 2000*, Roma, Anteren.

CHELL, Victoria, 1997, "Gender-Selective Migration: Somalian and Filipina Women in Rome", in Russell KING and Richard BLACK (eds), *Southern Europe and the New Immigrations*, Sussex, Academic Press, pp. 75–92.

CHELL-ROBINSON, Victoria, 2000, "Female Migrants in Italy: Coping in a Country of New Immigration", in Floya ANTHIAS and Gabriella LAZARIDIS (eds), *Gender and Migration in Southern Europe. Women on the Move*, New York, Berg, pp. 103–123.

CLIFFORD, James, 1997, *Routes*, Cambridge, Harvard University Press.

COHEN, Robin and VERTOVEC, Steven (eds), 1999, *Migration, Diaspora and Transnationalism*, Cheltenham, UK and Northhampton, Mass., Edward Elgar Publishing.

COLE, Jeffrey, 1997, *The New Racism in Europe: A Sicilian Ethnography*, Cambridge, Cambridge University Press.

CONSTABLE, Nicole, 1997, *Maid to Order in Hong Kong. Stories of Filipina Workers*, Ithaca & Lon., Cornell University Press.

CUCHAPIN, Pagasa, 2000, *I Nuovi "Eroi": Etnografia dell'immigrazione Filippina in Italia*. Ph.D. dissertation, Università degli Studi di Roma, La Sapienza, May.

ESCRIVÁ, Angeles, 2000, "The Position and Status of Migrant Women in Spain", in ANTHIAS, Floya and Gabriella LAZARIDIS (eds), *Gender and Migration in Southern Europe. Women on the Move*, New York, Berg, pp. 199–225.

FOUCAULT, Michel, 1980, *Power/Knowledge: Selected Interviews and Other Writings, 1972–1977*, Colin GORDON (ed. and trans.), New York, Pantheon.

GMELCH, George, 1987, "Return Migration to Rural Ireland", in Hans Christian BUECHLER and Judith-Maria BUECHLER (eds), *Migrants in Europe: The Role of Family, Labor and Politics*, New York, Greenwood Press, pp. 265–281.

GO, Stella P., 1998, "Towards the 21st Century: Whither Philippine Labor Migration?", in CARIÑO, Benjamin V. (ed.), *Filipino Workers on the Move: Trends, Dilemmas and Policy Options*, Manila, Philippine Migration Research Network, pp. 9–44.

HALL, Stuart, 1999, "Cultural Identity and Diaspora", in Robin COHEN and Steven VERTOVEC (eds), *Migration, Diaspora and Transnationalism*, Cheltenham, UK and Northhampton, Mass., Edward Elgar Publishing, pp. 299–314.

IMSON, Manuel, 1992, "Overseas Employment: An Indispensable Program", *Overseas Employment Info Series* 5.2, December, pp. 13–27.

–, 1999a, Personal communication via telephone, 25 February, Philippine Embassy, Washington D.C.

–, 1999b, Personal interview, 19 March, Labor Attaché, Philippine Embassy, Washington D.C.

IOSIFIDES, Theodoros, 1997, "Immigrants in the Athens Labour Market: a Comparative Study of Albanians, Egyptians and Filipinos", in Russell KING and Richard BLACK (eds), *Southern Europe and the New Immigrations*, Sussex, Academic Press, pp. 26–50.

KING, Russell, 2000, "Southern Europe in the Changing Global Map of Migration", in Russell KING, Gabrielle LAZARIDIS and Charalambos TSARDANIDIS (eds), *Eldorado or Fortress? Migration in Southern Europe*, New York, St. Martin's Press, pp. 3–26.

KOSER, Khalid and LUTZ Helma (eds), 1998, *The New Migration in Europe. Social Constructions and Social Realities,* London, Macmillan Press.

LAZARIDIS, Gabriella, 2000, "Filipino and Albanian Women Migrant Workers in Greece: Multiple Layers of Oppression", in Floya ANTHIAS and Gabriella LAZARIDIS (eds), *Gender and Migration in Southern Europe. Women on the Move*, New York, Berg, pp. 49–79.

MAGAT, Margaret, 2000–2001, Fieldwork based on interviews with Filipina domestics in Rome and participant-observer research, November 2000–June 2001.

NAKANO-GLENN, Evelyn, 1992, "From Servitude to Service Work: The Historical Continuities of Women's Paid and Unpaid Reproductive Labor", *Signs*, 18,1, pp. 1–44.

OKAMURA, Jonathan, 1998, *Imagining the Filipino American diaspora: Transnational Relations, Identities, and Communities*, New York, Garland Pub.

ORSINI-JONES, Marina and GATTULLO, Francesca, 2000, "Migrant Women in Italy: National Trends and Local Perspectives", in Floya ANTHIAS and Gabriella LAZARIDIS (eds), *Gender and Migration in Southern Europe. Women on the Move*, New York, Berg, pp. 125–144.

PARREÑAS, Rhacel Salazar, 1998, *The Global Servants: Immigrant Filipina Domestic Workers in Rome and Los Angeles*, Sociology dissertation, University of California, Berkeley.

–, 2001, *Servants of Globalization: Women, Migration and Domestic Work*, Stanford, Stanford University Press.

PHIZACKLEA, Annie, 1998, "Migration and Globalization: A Feminist Perspective", in Khalid KOSER and Helma LUTZ (eds), *The New Migration in Europe. Social Constructions and Social Realities*, London, Macmillan Press, pp. 21–38.

RAFAEL, Vicente, 2000, "'Your Grief is Our Gossip': Overseas Filipinos and Other Spectral Presence", in Vicente RAFAEL, *White Love and Other Events in Filipino History*, Durham and London, Duke University Press.

RAMIREZ, Mina, 1987, *The Socio-Cultural Presuppositions of Filipino Outmigration*, Scalabrini Migration Center.

ROMANISZYN, Krystyna, 2000, "Clandestine Labour Migration from Poland to Greece, Spain and Italy: Anthropological Perspectives", in Russell KING, Gabrielle LAZARIDIS and Charalambos TSARDANIDIS (eds), *Eldorado or Fortress? Migration in Southern Europe*, New York, St. Martin's Press, pp. 125–144.

ROSOLI, Gianfausto, 1993, "Italy: Emergent Immigration Policy", in Daniel KUBAT (ed.), *The Politics of migration policies: settlement and integration: the first world into the 1990s*, 2nd ed., New York, Center for Migration Studies, pp. 281–306.

STAHL, Charles W. and ARNOLD, Fred, 1999, "Overseas Workers' Remittances in Asian Development", in Robin COHEN and Steven VERTOVEC (eds), *Migration, Diaspora and Transnationalism*, Cheltenham, UK and Northhampton, Mass., Edward Elgar Publishing, pp. 170–196.

TAM, Vicky C. W., 1999, "Foreign Domestic Helpers in Hong Kong and their role in childcare provision", in Janet HENSHALL MOMSEN (ed.), *Gender, Migration and Domestic Service*, London and New York, Routledge, pp. 263–276.

TRIANDAFYLLIDOU, Anna, 2000, "'Racists? Us? Are you Joking?' The Discourse of Social Exclusion of Immigrants in Greece and Italy", in Russell KING, Gabrielle LAZARIDIS and Charalambos TSARDANIDIS (eds), *Eldorado or Fortress? Migration in Southern Europe*, New York, St. Martin's Press, pp. 186–206.

VANZI, Sol, 1998, "$7 Overseas Filipino Workers' Earnings (OFW) Buoy Economy in '98" Retrieved 15 January 1998 from the website: *Philippine Headline News Online*, www.newflash.org/199812/hlframe.html.

Gender Inequalities in the New Global Economy

Rhacel SALAZAR PARREÑAS

With or without men, women cross borders. In globalization, more of them are doing so in response to the high demand for low-wage domestic work. Women from Mexico and Central America move into the households of working families in the United States; Indonesian women to richer nations in Asia; Sri Lankan women to Greece and the Middle East; Polish women to Western Europe; Caribbean women to the United States and Canada, and Filipina women to more than 160 countries the world over.[1] In this paper, I will look at the flow of migrant domestic workers in globalization in order to illustrate inequalities of gender and citizenship that, first, plague women, second, reinforce relations of inequality between women, and third, deny the human rights of migrant women. I examine these inequalities of gender and citizenship by looking specifically at women's work in the family.

Despite the increase in women's labor market participation in both poor and rich nations, the work of nurturing the family remains women's work. Yet the burden of housework is not a convenient platform for alliance but instead is a source of inequality between women. As Mary Romero succinctly puts it, housework is not a bond of sisterhood but instead a bond of oppression. This is because, to unleash the burden of housework, women, as Evelyn Nakano Glenn has pointed out, rely on the commodification of this work and purchase the low-wage services of poorer women. In globalization, it is migrant women workers from the global south who are increasingly freeing women in the global north of this burden. This bears significant consequences to relations between them as the advancement of one group of women is at the cost of the disadvantage of

1 See Noeleen Heyzer, Geertje Lycklama á Nijeholt and Nedra Weekaroon (eds), *The Trade in Domestic Workers: Causes, Mechanisms, and Consequences of International Labor Migration*, London, Zed Books, 1994; Abigail Bakan and Daiva Stasiulis (eds), *Not One of the Family: Foreign Domestic Workers in Canada,* Toronto, University of Toronto Press, 1997; Rhacel Salazar Parreñas, *Servants of Globalization: Women, Migration and Domestic Work,* Stanford, CA, Stanford University Press, 2001; and Pierrette Hondagneu-Sotelo, *Doméstica*, Berkeley, University of California Press, 2001.

another group of women. This is a central challenge to our efforts for building transnational feminist alliances in globalization.

The flow of migrant domestic workers from poor to rich nations generates troubling care inequities that speak of race and class hierarchies between women and nations. In the case of migrant-based economies with patriarchal households such as the Philippines, the movement of domestic workers and women threatens the quality of care available in the country. We can argue that the migrant flow of domestic workers indicates a contemporary colonial trade relationship with the global south sending neither raw materials nor manufactured goods but instead their supply of care workers to the global north. In the Philippines, for instance, care is now the country's largest export, surpassing the amount of foreign currency generated by electronics manufacturing. Most migrant workers from the Philippines, approximately two-thirds of them, are women and the labor that they provide to the citizenry of other nations is mostly care work.[2] While approximately two-thirds of Filipina migrant women are employed as domestic workers, the majority of professional emigrants who either leave as contract workers or permanent migrants are nurses.[3] Remittances – mostly from migrant care workers – constitute the economy's largest source of foreign currency, totalling almost $7 billion in 1999.[4] Care as the largest export from the global south to the global north raises the question of who is left to provide for the care needs of those left behind in the poor countries of the south.

The growing reality of transnational motherhood calls attention to this question. As a result of the systematic extraction of care from the Philippines, a great number of children are growing up without the physical presence of their migrant parents. It is estimated that a quarter of the Filipino youth population – nine million children – are growing up in transnational households.[5] Assuming that women with children can provide better quality care than other women, employers often prefer their migrant nannies to be mothers themselves. What this means is that migrant mothers

2 Rhacel Salazar Parreñas, *Servants of Globalization.*

3 R. S. Parreñas, "The Care Crisis in the Philippines", 2003.

4 Bureau of Employment and Labor Statistics, "Remittances from Overseas Filipino Workers by Country of Origin Philippines: 1997–Fourth Quarter 1999", *Pinoy Migrants, Shared Government Information System for Migration* http://emisd.web.dfa.gov.ph/~pinoymigrants/.

5 Personal interview with Father Paolo Prigol of the Scalabrini Migration Center, 27 August 2001.

who work as nannies often face the painful prospect of caring for other people's children while being unable to tend to their own. Rosemarie Samaniego, a mother in Rome, describes this predicament.

> When the girl that I take care of calls her mother "Mama," my heart jumps all the time because my children also call me "Mama". I feel the gap caused by our physical separation especially in the morning, when I pack (her) lunch, because that's what I used to do for my children... I used to do that very same thing for them. I begin thinking that at this hour I should be taking care of my very own children and not someone else's, someone who is not related to me in any way, shape, or form... The work that I do here is done for my family, but the problem is they are not close to me but are far away in the Philippines. Sometimes, you feel the separation and you start to cry. Some days, I just start crying while I am sweeping the floor because I am thinking about my children in the Philippines. Sometimes, when I receive a letter from my children telling me that they are sick, I look up out the window and ask the Lord to look after them and make sure they get better even without me around to care after them. [Starts crying.] If I had wings, I would fly home to my children. Just for a moment, to see my children and take care of their needs, help them, then fly back over here to continue my work.[6]

For a large number of women, the experience of migration involves the pain of family separation. This emotional burden is one that directly results from the exportation of care and its consequent effect of transnational motherhood.

It is not just mothers but also children who lose out from this separation. Between 2000 and 2002, I spent 18 months in the Philippines where I conducted 69 in-depth interviews with children of migrant workers.[7] Among these children, I found a great number have come to expect a lesser amount of care from their migrant mothers. This includes Ellen Seneriches,[8] a 21-year-old medical student in the Philippines and daughter of a domestic worker in New York. She states,

6 This excerpt is drawn from R. S. Parreñas, *Servants of Globalization*, p. 119.

7 I gathered these interviewees through a non-random snowball sampling in schools, community organizations, and public spaces in my field research site. I supplemented these interviews with 31 interviews with their guardians; a survey questionnaire with 228 elementary and high school students with migrant parents; and interviews and focus-group discussions with guidance counselors, priests, and representatives of nongovernmental and governmental organizations in the area.

8 Ellen Seneriches and the names of the other children I quote in this chapter are all pseudonyms.

> There are times when you want to talk to her, but she is not there. That is really hard, very difficult… There are times when I want to call her, speak to her, cry to her, and I cannot. It is difficult. The only thing that I can do is write to her. And I cannot cry through the e-mails and sometimes I just want to cry on her shoulders.

Children such as Ellen, only 10 years old when her mother left for New York, often repress their longing to reunite with their mothers. Understanding the limited financial options available to families in the Philippines, they sacrifice by putting their emotional needs aside. This is often done with the knowledge that their mothers divert their care to other children in the global economy of care work. As Ellen describes,

> Very jealous. I am very, very jealous. There was even a time when she told the children who she was caring for that they are very lucky that she was taking care of them, while her children back in the Philippines don't even have a mom to take care of them. It's pathetic, but it's true. We were left alone by ourselves and we had to be responsible at a very young age without a mother. Can you imagine?

While their mothers give their care and attention to other children, children such as Ellen receive a lesser amount of care from their mothers, a sacrifice made more painful by their jealousy over these other children.

As shown by the story of Ellen, geographical distance in transnational family life engenders emotional tensions among children. By asserting this claim, I do not mean to imply that migrant mothers do not attempt to ease these tensions. In fact, they do. For instance, in the case of Ellen, although her mother has not returned once to the Philippines in twelve years – a situation explained by her undocumented status in the United States, Ellen knows that her mother struggles to maintain close ties with her children. As she describes,

> I realize that my mother loves us very much. Even if she is far away, she would send us her love. She would make us feel like she really loved us. She would do this by always being there. She would just assure us that whenever we have problems to just call her and tell her. And so I know that it has been more difficult for her than other mothers. She has had to do extra work because she is so far away from us.

The efforts of Ellen's mother to "be there" indicate that migrant mothers do not necessarily abandon their traditional duty of nurturing the family.

Instead, like Latina domestic workers in Los Angeles, they reconstitute mothering and provide acts of emotional care from a distance.[9]

Yet, despite these efforts of migrant mothers, children in transnational families still do suffer as they lose out in family intimacy. They can only wait for the opportunity to spend quality time with migrant parents. Yet, waiting tends to be a painful process. As Theresa Bascara, an 18-year-old college student whose mother has worked in Hong Kong since 1984, describes:

> When my mother is home, I just sit next to her. I stare at her face, to see the changes in her face, to see how she aged during the years that she was away from us. But when she is about to go back to Hong Kong, it's like my heart is going to burst. I would just cry and cry. I really can't explain the feeling. Sometimes, when my mother is home, preparing to leave for Hong Kong, I would just start crying, because I already start missing her. I ask myself, how many more years will it be until we see each other again?

In general, children in transnational families do lose out. They are denied the intimacy of the daily routine of family life. As Theresa continues,

> Telephone calls. That's not enough. You can't hug her, kiss her, feel her, everything. You can't feel her presence. It's just words that you have. What I want is to have my mother close to me, to see her grow older, and when she is sick, you are the one taking care of her and when you are sick, she is the one taking care of you.

Sacrificing the routine pleasures of receiving and giving emotional care is what a great number of children in the Philippines are doing to help keep their families intact. This sacrifice works to the benefit of those at the receiving end of the global transfer of care work – the employer, their family, and the local economies that utilize the freed employer's labor.

In globalization, the growing exportation of care and the consequent emergence of the transnational family result from women passing down their family responsibilities to other women. This implies that a care inequality defines the relationship of women in the global economy. Equally significant, it also indicates that public accountability for care remains slim. As we can assume that structural adjustment policies have sapped sending countries of the care provisions afforded by the state, I make

9 See Pierrette Hondagneu-Sotelo and Ernestine Avila, "'I'm Here, But I'm There': The Meanings of Latina Transnational Motherhood", *Gender and Society*, 11, 5, 1997, pp. 548–71.

these points by looking at the case of various receiving nations that employ migrant domestic workers.

In the industrialized countries of Asia, the Americas and Europe, the number of gainfully employed women has climbed dramatically in the last forty years. For instance, in France, an additional 2 million women entered the labor force between 1979 and 1993, a 21 percent jump in the number of employed women.[10] In Italy, there has been an increase in the number of married women in the labor force.[11] In the US, three out of four mothers with school-age children are in the paid labor force, the majority working fulltime.[12] Similarly in Italy and Spain, women tend to keep their full-time jobs even when they have young children at home.[13] Yet, women still face a "stalled revolution".[14] They face a double day indicating that the division of labor in most families does not mirror the increase in their share of labor market participation

I would like to point out that the double day is not only indicative of continued gendered inequalities between men and women in the family, but it also demonstrates the inadequacy of state welfare support for the family. This is the case in the United States, as well as various nations in Western Europe. Notably, the United States has the least welfare provisions among rich nations in the global economy as families are without access to universal health care, paid maternity and parental leave, government-provided childcare, or family care giving allowances.[15] The absence of a sense of communal responsibility for care in the United States is reflected for instance in the care of the elderly. Studies have shown that

10 See Pauline Conroy and Aoife Brennan, *Migrant workers and their experiences*, Dublin, Interact2, 2002.

11 V. A. Goddard, *Gender, Family, and Work in Naples,* Oxford and Washington, D.C., Berg, 1996.

12 Scott Coltrane and Justin Galt, "The History of Men's Caring", in Madonna Harrington Meyer (ed.), *Care Work: Gender, Labor and the Welfare State*, New York and London, Routledge, 2000, p. 29.

13 *La Documentation Française, Les migrations internationales*, Cahier Français, 307, Paris, 2002.

14 Arlie Russel Hochschild (with Anne Machung), *The Second Shift,* New York, Avon Books, 1988.

15 Francesca Cancian and Stacey Oliker, *Caring and Gender*, Thousand Oaks, CA, Pine Forge Press, 2000, p. 116.

family members, usually women, provide approximately 80 to 90 percent of their care without any formal assistance from the government.[16]

Although providing more benefits than the United States, the welfare regimes in various European countries also follow a conservative model of the family. The comprehensive publicly funded preschool system in France stabilizes the family life of dual wage earning couples, but feminists have argued that the "strongly entrenched division of labour within the household" still hurts women.[17] This is for instance shown by the burden of elderly care falling mainly on women in the family in countries such as France, as it is not supported with residential care provisions. Other countries such as Greece, Italy and Spain have relatively low welfare provisions.[18] In contrast, the socially democratic Scandinavian nations provide the most gender sensitive public benefits for families. Sweden for instance promotes gender equality by providing gender-neutral parental leave and universal entitlements in the form of allowances, subsidies, and direct services for the elderly and single parent households.[19]

Social patterns of welfare provisions seem to influence the direction of the migratory flows of foreign domestic workers. Notably, nations with very low welfare provisions, i.e. nations that keep the care of the family a private responsibility, particularly the United States and southern European nations such as Spain, Greece, and Italy have a greater presence of foreign domestic workers. In contrast, countries with social democratic regimes such as those in Scandinavia, where the benefit system abides by universalism and provides large-scale institutional support for mothers and families, are less likely to rely on foreign domestic workers.

Thus, it seems that the lesser public accountability there is for the family the greater the need for the labor of foreign domestic workers. This suggests that a movement against the neo-liberal state regime would lead to greater recognition of the high worth of the care of the family and the lesser burden of the double day for women in the labor force. Without doubt, women in industrialized countries have come to take advantage of

16 Jennifer Mellor, "Filling in the Gaps in Long Term Care Insurance", in Madonna Harrington Meyer (ed.), *Care Work: Gender, Labor and the Welfare State*, New York and London, Routledge, 2000, p. 206.

17 Eleonore Koffman, Annie Phizacklea, Parvati Raghuram and Rosemary Sales, *Gender and International Migration in Europe: Employment, Welfare and Politics,* New York and London, Routledge, 2000, p. 143.

18 *Ibid.*

19 F. Cancian and S. Oliker, 2000, p. 118.

their greater economic resources than women from developing countries: they do this by unloading the caregiving responsibilities of their families to these other women. As my discussion shows, those who receive less gender-sensitive welfare provisions from the state do so much more than others. And those who are able to negotiate with their male counterparts in the family for a fairer gendered division of labor are equally less likely to do so. This indicates that greater state and male accountability for care would likely lead not so much to a lesser need for domestic workers but greater recognition of the worth of domestic labor.

In addition to state welfare policies, state immigration policies also lock the unequal bond of housework between women. The state protects its pool of low-wage domestic workers and consequently secures the lack of male and state accountability for care work in the family by limiting the human rights of migrant domestics. Despite their economic contributions, migrant domestic workers suffer from their limited incorporation as partial citizens of various receiving nations.[20] By this I mean they face restrictive measures that stunt their political, civil, and social incorporation into host societies. From an economic standpoint, this is not surprising. Receiving nations curb the integration of migrants so as to guarantee their economies a secure source of cheap labor. By containing the costs of reproduction in sending countries, wages of migrant workers can be kept to a minimum; i.e., migrants do not have the burden of having to afford the greater costs of reproducing their families in host societies. Moreover, by restricting the incorporation of migrants, receiving nations can secure their economies a supply of low-wage workers who could easily be repatriated if the economy is low.

As such, migrants are usually relegated to the status of temporary settlers whose stay is limited to the duration of their labor contracts. Often, they cannot sponsor the migration of their families, including their own children. This is the case in Middle Eastern and Asian receiving nations, which are much more stringent than other countries. Accounting for the nuances engendered by differences in government policies, the restriction of family migration comes in different degrees and levels of exclusion. Temporary residents in Italy have been eligible for family reunification since 1990. Likewise in France and Germany, dependents of migrants were granted the right to work in the 1980s. However, family reunifica-

20 See Chapter 2 of *Servants of Globalization: Women, Migration, and Domestic Work*, 2001.

tion remains a challenge to many immigrants in Europe. In France, for instance, they are discouraged by the increase in years of residence to qualify for family reunion as well as the decrease in the age for eligibility as a dependent from 21 to 18 years old.[21] Labor conditions in domestic work also hamper the ability of migrants to reunify their family.

Eligibility for full citizenship is available in a few receiving nations including Spain, Canada, and the United States. In Spain and Canada, migrant Filipinas are eligible for full citizenship after two years of legal settlement. Despite the seemingly more liberal and inclusive policies in these nations, political and social inequalities still mar the full incorporation of migrant workers. In the United States, for instance, obtaining a green card through employer sponsorship – while more difficult to secure these days – has been described by Shellee Colen based on her study of West Indian domestics in New York as a "form of state-sanctioned indenture-like exploitation" because the petition requires the worker to stay in the sponsored position until the green card is obtained (usually two or more years). This process of legalization, as my research on migrant Filipina domestic workers also shows, can take up to a decade before women qualify to petition for the migration of their children, when their children are too old to qualify for dependent status and immediate family reunification. In other words, the law often makes it too late for children to reunify with their migrant domestic mother in the United States.

Without doubt, the imposition of partial citizenship on migrant domestic workers benefits employers. The guest worker status, legal dependency to the "native" employer, ineligibility for family reunification, and the labor market segmentation of foreign women to domestic work guarantee host societies a source of secure and affordable pool of care workers at the same time that they maximize the labor provided by these workers and constrain their ability to care for their own family, particularly their own children. This works to the benefit of the employing family, since migrant care workers can give the best possible care when they are free of caregiving responsibilities in their own families. Yet, the experience of partial citizenship for migrant domestic workers points to a central irony in globalization. Migrant domestic workers care for rich families in the global north as they are imposed with social, economic, and legal restrictions that deny them the right to nurture their own families. The elimination of these

21 E. Koffman *et al.*, 2000, p. 68.

restrictive measures would at the very least grant foreign domestic workers the basic human right of a family.

In globalization, women inhabit a paradoxical position regarding family care work. While women from the global north view the care work for the family as a burden to be passed on to poorer women, often from the global south, this latter group of women see it as a human right denied to them by restrictive migration policies in various host societies. However, the division of care labor between women does not completely work to the advantage of the employing women in the global north. Though freed of the care work for the family, they are still plagued by the structural gender inequities that relieve men and the state of responsibility for care.

Imposing sub par labor conditions on migrant domestic workers only maintains and avoids the root causes of these inequalities. As I agree with Hondagneu-Sotelo's argument in her book *Doméstica*, I do not mean to suggest that society should ban the employment of migrant domestic workers.[22] Instead, employing families should develop a greater sense of accountability for migrant domestic workers and their families. They can do this by advocating for the elimination of policies that restrict family migration and more generally limit the citizenship rights of migrant workers. Not doing so would maintain the gender inequalities that plague employed women and promote the maintenance of the international division of care work, the relegation of care work to women, the lack of public accountability for this work, and finally the devaluation of this labor. Addressing the human rights concerns of migrant domestic workers could only benefit the larger population of women in our global society.

22 Pierrette Hondagneu-Sotelo, 2001, *Doméstica*, Berkeley, CA, University of California Press.

The Dynamics of the Mistress-Servant Relationship

Pothiti HANTZAROULA

This essay is an attempt to investigate the process by which a serving subjectivity was produced in women. The making of the self in the service of others is about a specific subordinate subject position produced in the relationship between mistress and maid. The lineaments of the formation of subordinate subjectivities are explored through the narratives of women who worked as servants in Athens between 1920 and 1945.[1] Their memories are not used as vehicles that convey the experience of oppression but as "guides to social identity".[2] Their meaning is drawn from the effects of the experience of service on the subject and from the ways they illuminate the process of the formation of class identities. As identity is formed through the relationship with one's own past, memories are selected for their contribution to constructing relationships and personal identity. Thus, memory will be treated here as a source of subjectivity, that is, as an important source of conception of ones' own self. Events that have changed the course of the existence of an individual are transformed through memory into "event-signs", and constitute the knowledge of one's own existence. It is the selection of these events that manifests a truth when memory re-inscribes the past in the present.

Domestic servants have been excluded from the narratives of class as their experience was assigned to the private sphere and constructed as immune from the market and class conflict. Dealing with domestic service involves the exploration of experiences of oppression that had not been recognized as such and with subjects denied admission to the history of class relations. Historical scholarship on domestic service has too evaded the question of class. Whereas the relationship between employers and domestics is seen as crucial for the formation of the identity of white middle-

1 My sample includes twenty interviews that I collected between 1996 and 1997 with women who worked as domestic servants in Athens.

2 James Fentress and Chris Wickam, *Social Memory*, Oxford, Blackwell, 1992, p. 88.

class women, the contribution of this relationship to the formation of subordinate identities has not been adequately explored.[3] Another stream of scholarship approached domestic service as a cultural bridge between the labouring poor and the middle class and viewed servants as cultural amphibians who adopted middle-class values and transmitted elite behaviour and values to the masses. Moreover, scholars divested servants of any individuality treating even their autobiographical accounts as "typical" illustrations of an occupational group or as products of middle-class class and gender fantasies.[4] Contesting this assumption, scholars argued that the mistress-servant relationship resembled more a battlefield where different cultures, and different systems of meanings, were contested. Been rather trapped in a vicious circle described as reproduction/resistance,[5] they argued against the diffusion of middle-class values and based their argument on servants' resistance to middle-class definitions of femininity.[6]

A major shift towards exploring the intersection of gender, race and class in the mistress-maid relationship came from the sociological work on minority domestic servants in the United States. The central preoccupation of these works is a confrontation with the exploitative relationship between paid domestic workers and white female employers. Judith Rollins employed the term maternalism to denote the benevolent and patronizing attitudes of employers in order to perpetuate their authority and their unequal relationship to servants.[7] Bonnie Thornton Dill discusses the notion of "maternalism" but argues that racial differences were an obstacle to the exercise of maternalism on the part of employers and that do-

3 Phyllis Palmer, *Domesticity and Dirt: Housewives and Domestic Servants in the United States, 1920–1945*, Philadelphia, Temple University Press, 1989.

4 "This makes Hannah Cullwick's diary, with its detailed record of childhood memories, conditions of work and work performed, wages, hours, recreations, relationships among fellow servants, and many other details, a unique and precious document. However, it must be remembered that she was writing it for Munby's eyes alone, a further way in which he could dominate and even create her life." Leonore Davidoff, "Class and Gender in Victorian England: The Case of Hannah Cullwick and A. J. Munby", in *Worlds Between: Historical Perspectives on Gender and Class*, London, Polity Press, 1995, p. 117.

5 Pamela Fox, *Class Fictions: Shame and Resistance in the British Working-Class Novel, 1890–1945*, Durham, Duke University Press, 1994.

6 Ann McClintock, *Imperial Leather: Race, Gender and Sexuality in the Colonial Contest*, London, Routledge, 1995, pp. 133–180.

7 Judith Rollins, *Between Women: Domestics and Their Employers*, Philadelphia, Temple University Press, 1985.

mestic workers appeared in many cases rather to "mother" their employers.[8] Women tried to gain autonomy and control over their tasks and to resist employers' objectification and depersonalising attitudes towards them by choosing employers who display human and personal recognition and treat an employee with dignity.

Mary Romero's book on Chicana minority women is one of the few works that inserts the concept of class in the study of domestic service. She adopts a Marxist-structural approach and argues that the domestic-employer relationship should not be seen as a continuation of pre-industrial, feudalistic master-servant tradition[9] but analysed within the context of capitalism. Critical of previous work that analysed domestic service in a social psychological framework, Romero argues that the relationship should be better "conceptualised as an employee-employer relationship and as an instance of class struggle".[10] Thus, the relationship should be treated like other employee-employer relationships under capitalism, in which the control over the work process is an arena of contest between workers and employers. In the case of Chicana domestic servants, their attempts are focused on restructuring the occupation to resemble a businesslike arrangement.

Rhacel Parreñas, in her work on migrant Filipina domestic workers in Los Angeles and Rome, coins James Scott's term the "hidden transcript" which denotes the discourse that domestic servants employ outside of the view of employers. Their individual acts of immediate struggles are rooted in the collective consciousness of a shared struggle among domestic workers. This hidden transcript enables them to feel more empowered and demand better working conditions and salaries.[11]

Building from the previous studies, I will argue that every interpersonal relationship cannot be exhausted in a face-to-face interaction but rests on a whole network of beliefs, values, and practices that extends beyond the confines of this interaction and informs it. Rather than separating the organisation of labour from the felt experience of service, the structure of service employment from social relationships, this essay uses

8 Bonnie Thornton Dill, *Across the Boundaries of Race and Class*, New York, Garland Publishing, 1994.

9 See J. Rollins, *Between Women*.

10 Mary Romero, *Maid in the USA*, New York, Routledge, 1992, pp. 130–131.

11 Rhacel Salazar Parreñas, *Servants of Globalization: Women, Migration, and Domestic Work*, California, Stanford University Press, 2001, pp. 194–195.

servants' testimonies in order to illuminate the process by which servants produced a subordinate subjectivity through their relationship to mistresses. The testimonies presented here illustrate that class "happens in human relationships".[12] These women's subjectivity was not an outcome of the internalisation of inferiority because the notion of internalisation implies that the subject was absent from the process of its making. On the contrary, domestic servants were active in its constitution as they were formed by the circumstances they were describing.[13] Liz Stanley has pointed the "doing" aspect of class which indicates a possession, and a knowledge of being working class that subordinate groups use to achieve empowerment, in order to resist, effect, influence, control the relationship of labour.[14] It is this possession and articulation of a particular understanding of the self that constitutes the texture of subjectivity.

One of the most important characteristics that distinguish domestic service from other types of employment is its total character in the sense that the totality of time, the body as well as the labour power of the individual who enters into this particular labour relationship are at the disposal of the employer in an absolute manner. All the activities of the individual subjected in domestic service, duties and chores but also sleep, food, and movement as well as communication beyond the confines of the employers' household are controlled and organised by the employers. The barriers that define a clear separation between leisure, work and sleep are dissolved. This total character of domestic service, defined by the possession of servant's time, movement, labour power and contact with the outside world by a single authority, that of the employer, resembles what Erving Goffman defines as a total institution.

Erving Goffman in his book *Asylums* defines total institutions as "a place of residence and work where a large number of like-situated individuals, cut off from the wider society for an appreciable period of time, together lead an enclosed, formally administered round of life".[15]

12 Edward Palmer Thompson, *The Making of the English Working Class*, London, Penguin, 1980 (1st ed. 1963), p. 8.

13 Carolyn Steedman, "The Price of Experience: Women and the Making of the English Working Class", *Radical History Review*, 59, 1994, p. 115.

14 Liz Stanley, *The Auto/Biographical I: The Theory and Practice of Feminist Autobiography*, Manchester/New York, Manchester University Press, 1992, p. 169.

15 Erving Goffman, *Asylums: Essays on the Social Situation of Mental Patients and Other Inmates*, New York, Anchor, 1961, p. xiii.

As Goffman argued, one of the basic functions of total institutions is to create a new person by treating the body as memory. Aiming at the violent elimination of all the traits that composed the identity of an individual and at their substitution with new ones, they place an enormous effort on apparently insignificant details such as dress, bearing, physical and verbal manners. This process of "disculturation" is achieved through technologies that target both body and soul. As Pierre Bourdieu has pointed out, in these technologies a whole cosmology is instilled, an ethic, a metaphysic, a political philosophy.[16]

This essay will consider the total character of domestic service articulated in the technologies that were employed by employers in order to produce a docile body in their service. These technologies will be approached from the point of view of those who were subjected to them through their effects on subjectivity. These technologies consist of the "welcome", corporal mechanisms of subordination, such as dress, gestures, and postures, divisions of space, testing of honesty, restrictions on food, restrictions on contact, defacement, and physical violence.

Technologies of Entering

The technology of "welcome" aimed at establishing the rules of communication between employer and employee. At the same time, the first encounter with employers was a liminal experience, which allowed the grasping of the transformations of identity and the rupture that the meeting with a different culture produced in the self.

> When I first entered the house, it was the first time I went of course, they opened the door, we entered, and her water pipes had broken. The tubs broke and there was water everywhere, inside the house, a flood, and I didn't know any of these things in the village. I was standing there looking like an idiot. And she started shouting at me. "Quickly, move on, sop up the water, why do you stand like an idiot, don't you see?" This happened the moment I entered, I would never forget that. How could I know, "take the mop, take the bucket", I didn't know any of

16 Pierre Bourdieu, *Outline of a Theory of Practice*, Cambridge, Cambridge University Press, 1977, p. 194.

> these things. And I was sick because I always feel dizzy in the car and I vomited, and she started shouting at me. I finally picked up the bucket to sop up the water. This stayed with me, because I didn't burst into tears, but it was very bad for me. [Stavroula]

Memory reconstructs the first encounter with employers as a traumatic displacement that arises out of the self occupying an alien social space (note here the frequent use of the phrase "I didn't know"). Siegfried Kracauer has talked about situations of self-effacement, or homelessness, like exile, and the states of mind in which the self is a stranger who does no longer belong to a place. In these situations the mind becomes a *palimpsest*, in the sense that the self the person was continues to exist beneath the person he is about to become, his identity is bound to be in a state of flux.[17] Stavroula came to Athens from a village of north-western Greece at the age of seven. Her employers picked her up with their car and brought her to Athens. On finding herself in an alien place, in a social space to which she did not belong, her identity was in a state of flux, of becoming. She was not only cut off abruptly from a familiar social space, but also from the material culture connected with this space. Her look was vacant because what she saw was not pregnant with memories. The objects around her are unrecognisable. Her mode of existence is that of the stranger to her self, while the expression of emotions was curtailed as tears presuppose reciprocity.

The self in a state of flux is not empty from memories as the knowledge of the past determines understanding the experience of the present situation.[18] The lack of knowledge of a particular social space, and in consequence of the language that conceptualises these images, impeded the communication between the newly arrived servant and the employer. Here the process of stepping out of one's culture is not an act of freedom as Kracauer put it. There is no possibility to make the "other" culture her own. Instead a whole range of technologies extending from the body to the mind were used by the employers to establish boundaries and keep the servant "in her place". These technologies, performed immediately at the moment of entering the house, accentuated the sense of displacement and alieness, and served as an initiation into the new culture. It was through

17 Siegfried Kracauer, *History: The Last Things before the Last*, New York, Oxford University Press, 1969, p. 83.

18 David Connerton, *How Societies Remember*, Cambridge, Cambridge University Press, 1989, p. 2.

this encounter that Stavroula came to consciousness of herself not as a family member but as a worker.

The control of communication rests with the employers and a specific tone of voice is employed to restrict contact. Shouting was a common strategy of intimidation on the part of the employers, and it set the rules of communication. The immediate allocation of tasks to the newly arrived servant is the initiation ritual for the new identity, that of the worker for the family. Moreover, these strategies serve as an "obedience test".

Let us move to another interviewee who entered domestic service at the age of ten. During the Second World War she was sent into service by the Patriotic Institution for the Protection of Children. The "welcome" entailed a series of humiliations, degradations and abasements.

> When they brought me to her [employer], they started to tell me "sweep there, wash there", and I was small and I bent, how could I know to kneel, how could I know the chores. Finally, when they put me to wash the dishes, from which they had eaten, they did not give me any food because there wasn't any left, and I neither spoke, nor could I speak, because I saw them I don't know how… Sometimes they gave me some juice from the food, to eat, to put on bread… I remember, and this has remained with me until now, and I tell this to my daughters and I'm still crying. I was licking their dishes, they ate and I was licking their dishes. They didn't take me to feed me, they took me as a skivvy. And I was a child that didn't know. To leave from a family in which we ate off plates of tin in order not to break them because we were a lot of children and to find yourself in a house in which they ate off plates of china, these seemed to me very alien things. In my fantasy. [Eleftheria]

The articulation of the first encounter with employers indicates that entering service was a rite of passage, a move to a new social space and identity. The structuring of the narrative in oppositional terms is employed to illustrate difference, to set self-identity in opposition to the employer's identity. The withdrawal from the familiar world and the social background in which it was embedded was a cultural shock, as girls could not even recognise the objects and the spaces of the new world. The correspondence between social space and the symbolic properties attached to this space produce certain dispositions which constitute the class *habitus*. The asymmetrical relationship to material things in the employer's house and the employee's exclusion from and thus illegitimate relationship to property constituted the hierarchy and positioned those who lacked both the legitimate possession of things but also the symbolic properties and dispositions attached to these things as subordinate. The house was the space where class distinction was made concrete, and where one's own identity was recognized as different and inferior to that of the employers.

Corporal Mechanisms of Subordination

The body has become an object of inquiry as a site of knowledge and of conditioning mainly through normative discourses. Scholars have not been so much concerned with the practices through which social knowledge is conveyed, and with the ways in which the body enacts social subordination. Neither have they investigated the effects of control on real bodies and its emotional dynamics. As David Connerton argued: "In all cultures much of the choreography of authority is expressed through the body."[19] He also considered that it is possible to discern social inequalities through the ways people use their bodies in relation to the bodies of others. This section will explore the incorporating practices through which bodies were constituted as inferior. Since social hierarchies are not just expressed through the body but are constituted and established in the body, we shall explore the training of bodies in the service of others. Dress, gestures, postures, and facial expression were means for constructing hierarchical relationships, and they will be examined here from the standpoint of the wearer.

The apron constituted the symbol that displayed the employers' status. The circumstances in which employees put on an apron varied according to the social status of their employers. In upper-class households, in which everyday life, and especially eating, had a ritual character, servants wore aprons inside the house; aprons were of different colours and made of different kinds of material according to the tasks servants performed. Upper-class households usually had two to three servants: a cook, a chambermaid and a person who attended at the table, and sometimes also a chauffeur. Dress varied according to the tasks each one performed and according to the formality of situations. When the chores and the cooking were performed lighter colours and cheaper materials were used for the

19 *Ibid.*, p. 74.

uniform. During serving the person who attended at the employer's table wore a black dress and white apron. For formal dinners with guests, the staff had black dress, white apron, cuffs and bonnet.

> In the morning we put on an apron with straps while we did the chores. As soon as we finished you had to shower, this was obligatory in order not to smell when you serve them, and we put on the black dress, white apron and white cuffs. [Aggelina]

In lower-class households, employers put greater importance on the use of aprons outside the house. Dinners did not have the formality of upper-class households, while everyday life was devoid of a ceremonial character. These differences also indicate the different functions of the apron. Wearing an apron signalled the possession of an individual in the service of others. For lower middle-class women, social recognition was not a given, but had to be proved. For that reason, in lower-class households with only one servant, the apron was part of the employer's strive to participate in dominant values and it was used only outside the house in order to display the privileged position of women. Going shopping or accompanying the mistress or the couple on Sunday, a servant wearing an apron signified the respectability of her employers. The servant's body mirrored the well-being of the household, its neatness, order and cleanliness. It was in this sense a body, and by extension a person, without any identity apart from that of servant, a projection of middle-class respectability.

> This lady, because I was a good child, I was of good stuff [*kalis pastas*], put me taffeta ribbons, I had very long hair. The only bad thing with this woman is that she put me an apron. She took me with her; we went to the cinema. Or they wanted to go to a confectionery with the children and she took me with her. But she wanted me to wear an apron always. [...] She sent me for bread, for vegetables, she said to me you will buy this and that. I went out always wearing an apron. It was out of the question that I should go out without wearing an apron. And every time I went out, I had to wear a new apron, a clean one.
>
> – Why did she do that?
>
> I don't know. I too wonder about that. Now my daughter says that she wanted to show that she had a servant. I don't think that she was so petty as to want to show that she had a servant. I don't know. It was a kind of principle, I don't know, it was a repressed desire [*to apothimeno*]. Let me take a handkerchief. [Eleftheria]

Yet the apron was not solely the symbol or expression of social superiority, but its infliction constituted social hierarchies. Through the apron, employers constructed a different person. Stripping their employees' body of all those characteristics that constitute a person's identity, such as clothes, was a means to achieve defacement. This technology of defacement was part of the process of disculturation, that is, of creating a new individual, of reconstructing an individual in the service of others. Personal possessions are important elements out of which an individual builds a self, as we have seen in Eleftheria's account, which stresses ribbons and long hair as items of self-identity and reward. Through the infliction of the apron, the control of the individuals over their own body and self was curtailed and substituted with the domination of employers over the bodies of employees. This domination extended, as we have seen above, to the control of excretion. Showers were obligatory before serving at table in order to eliminate smell.

The apron was a stigma symbol for those who wore it, not only because it was a manifestation of the social status of the bearer and of the confinement that domestic service entailed, but also because it solidified the image of a person in the service of others and displayed the symbolic possession of the body beyond the employer's house. The emotions that the infliction of the apron produced were devastating for self-esteem and hurt these children who were in an ambivalent position in a family. In some cases the apron was also an arena of conflict between couples. Eleftheria's mistress, who had married the errand boy [*psychogios*] of her father, argued with her husband about Eleftheria wearing the apron outside the house.

> Her husband said, "please, tell Eleftheria to take off the apron". And they had an argument on this issue. The husband wanted me to take off the apron but she didn't want. As I told you I obeyed. I obeyed her more than Kostas, her husband.

Coming from a lower-class background the husband not only was aware of the stigma that a uniform attaches to a person but he intervened to prevent Eleftheria's exposure to a stigmatic identity.[20] It is possible that

20 For the embarrassment that the use of uniform provoked and the resistance to it in other working environments, see Effi Avdela, "Amfisvitoumena noimata: prostasia kai antistatisi stis Ektheseis ton Epitheoriton Ergasias, 1914–1936" [Contested meanings: protection and resistance in the Reports of the Inspectors of Labour, 1914–1936], *Ta Istorika/Historica*, vol. 25, nos. 28–29, December 1998, pp. 200–202; Antonis Liakos, *Ergasia kai Politiki stin Ellada tou Mesopolemou: To Diethnes Grafeio Ergasias kai i anadisi ton koinonikon thesmon* [Labout and politics in Inter-War Greece: The International Labour Office and the emergence of social institutions], Athens, Idrima Erevnas kai Paideias tis Emporikis Trapezas tis Ellados, 1993, p. 389.

Eleftheria's master as a servant in the merchant enterprise of his wife's father had been wearing an apron. In this implied identification between the mistress' husband and Eleftheria, the power and control lay with the mistress. The imposition of the apron was a point of conflict between employer and employee. Those who climbed to the top of a servant's career and became cooks resisted wearing an apron outside the house.

> – Did you wear an apron when you went out?
>
> No way I would go out with the children wearing an apron. [Anastasia]
>
> She didn't force me to wear an apron. Other [employers] did. There was no way I could wear an apron outside. I wore it in the house, but as soon I got out of the house, I put the apron aside. I put it away. [Eirini]

Postures, gestures, and speech also played an important role in the construction and reproduction of difference. Standing erect while talking to employers, standing while the employers were dressed, never addressing to employers unless they were encouraged by them to do so, bowing and curtseying when visitors were in the household were some of the essential rules of behaviour in the household. Eleftheria was astonished with the changes her sister's body had undergone since she had been employed as a servant in an upper-class household. She remembers the stiffness of her body when Aggelina was talking to them and the changes in her vocabulary. Dressing up was also a ritual procedure for middle-class women.

> When she was getting dressed, I had to stand like a soldier before her, and to give her this and that. Like a soldier. All those hours I had to stand like a soldier. She put on the make up, she took off the make up, and in order to go out she had to put this and that. Three times a week she played cards. [Artemis]

> I was kind to them. I bent for them. Those days shoes had buttons, so you had to button their shoes. [Eva]

These narratives help us to understand the incorporation of bodily practices and the transformations that bodies underwent in service. Women who went into service as children stress persistently in their accounts the way they had to adapt their bodies to the demands of domestic work. These changes are inscribed in their memories but also imprinted on their bodies as their continuing obsession with cleanliness and order show.

Rituals of deference such as curtseying, bending and standing erect before employers and guests constituted a memory of the body, and were reproduced after service, and moreover transferred to future generations. Let us see how these ritual gestures of respect and obedience, which were taught in a work environment, were used by people outside this environment, in situations in which they felt inferior. Eleftheria refers to her relationship with her husband and his kin.

> He imposed many things on me. And I accepted it either because I had been taught to obey or because I felt inferior toward Nikos because of poverty and because I married without a dowry. [...] My mother threw me in with Nikos' kin and I didn't know how to guard myself. Do you understand? Because it was a family different from mine. But one thing saved me. [...] I had learned from this [the employer's] family to behave, to talk, and to be silent when it was appropriate. She told me, "you will not talk if they don't ask you. Whatever you see, you will say I didn't see anything". She gave me good things. And these proved useful in my subsequent life. And in the family of Nikos I didn't speak; I only listened to them.

The above testimony illuminates the process through which social inequality takes the form of social principle. Self-censorship constitutes one of the mechanisms of obedience through which a person learns her place in the employer's house, which here is reproduced when faced with the fear of exposure in the eyes of those who possessed cultural and economic capital. The employer's house was a place of reform in which an individual went through a form of conversion consisting of the elimination of presence, desires, and opinions, in short of the suppression of individuality. Invisibility as well as respect towards social superiors was the aim and achievement of this training. The appropriation of the codes of bodily practices before socially superior individuals was considered valuable and it arose out of "a feeling of a gap between the socially legitimate body and the body which one has and is".[21] The unease and awkwardness experienced due to the inability to incorporate a socially legitimate body, and the fissure between a body one wishes to have and the body one sees through the condemning eyes of others leads the person to conform and to perpetuate the practices of bodily inferiority. "Unable to incarnate an acknowledged model", Eleftheria resorts to adapting to a dominated position, one learned in service, out of the fear of exposure. The recognition of authority is produced though the sense of failure and cultural unworthiness.[22]

21 D. Connerton, *How Societies Remember*, p. 91.

22 Pierre Bourdieu, *Distinction: A Social Critique of the Judgement of Taste* (trans. Richard Nice), Cambridge, MA, Harvard University Press, 1984, p. 386.

Corporal and psychological abuse exercised by employers was a mechanism of control enforced particularly on children, and it threatened the bodily and psychic integrity of those who were subjected to it. Violence was widespread in service, as is documented in police reports and in the interviewees' testimonies. It was a mechanism that aimed at the total elimination of the individuality and autonomy of the other.

This abuse of children by employers was what made service unbearable. Children who were in a vulnerable psychic state as they had experienced loss of parents and the violence of war found themselves in conditions that not only did not provide any support but aggravated psychological disturbances.

> I will tell you what she did. She had diabetes and she didn't eat sugar. Well, I made the coffee, and dipped some bread in it to eat. We had to fast and she didn't give us milk. [...] I make the coffee, and she tastes it and because it was sweet, she slapped me with her rings. She delivered many women and when they did not have money to pay, they gave her jewellery. She wore them. Her hands were full of jewellery. She tried the coffee and because it was sweet... "I told you to drink it without sugar", but how can I drink it bitter. I can't drink it like that; I was a little girl, 12–13 years old. Even 14 or 15. Is the coffee drinkable like that? She slaps me and I started bleeding. That's how she used to beat me: with the back of her hand straight in the mouth. She beat me and I left and I went to Makriyanni, where the American Relief was. And the building is still there, opposite to the Columns of Zeus Olimpios. [...] There it was the Club of the Working Girl where young women went to eat because it was cheap. I don't know where they worked. Those who were in a house. So, I left twice. She [the employer] came and found me there, she said, "our children are on the streets". I told her "you go, I don't have any children". Then Lykourezou came, there were other ladies as well. She told her, "Madam, don't exercise such pressure on children, you break their nerves, and don't you understand that they are just children? You make great demands on children". [...] And I told Lykourezou, "do you see my mouth? She beats me". She said, "let's go". And they [ladies] said, "stay here until she calms down". But I couldn't calm down. I was hitting the table with my fists; I turned the table upside down. "She is criminal", I shouted, "she beats me, she will kill me, I don't go anywhere". They cajoled me, they said in fifteen days time we'll take you. In fifteen days they came. She had changed her attitude. She behaved like a different person. Let me put my glasses on. With all these tears that they don't know how to burst and damage later the body, all this suffering, when the child is needy, when she suffers... [Evdoksia]

> When they sent her the invitation from the Near East, then she dressed me up and she gave me a doll and I had a doll then. Then I held a doll in order to go there. [Evdoksia]

The above testimony is an illustration of the deep antagonism and conflict embedded in the mistress-servant relationship. Evdoksia refuted her positioning as a member of the family ("I do not have any children"), a denial and a form of defiance directed both against her foster mother as well as against the institution that positioned her as a foster child. The hand full of rings that slapped her was not the hand of her mother that symbolized shared property and inheritance rights. It was the hand of an employer who possessed both property and the power to exclude her from the consumption of goods.

For girls who were placed as servants by Near East Relief it was required that their employers disclose information about their economic status. They were also required to deposit an amount of money in the orphan's name for an agreed-upon number of years. Additionally, Near East Relief officials were supposed to scrutinise the family and social life of the employers and to watch closely, through home visits, the welfare of children. In the case of Evdoksia, none of the above rules was seriously applied.

Hair cutting was a form of punishment that aimed at humiliating children and young women in service. It was one of the corporal practices in total institutions that marked the passage to a different form of life stripping the person of a visible characteristic as well as a sense of individuality. When performed in domestic service, it reveals also the antagonism felt by mistresses who wanted to have total possession of children. Contact with the outside world threatened their control over girls and set at risk the institution of fostering, which was established to secure life-long service. Feelings of jealousy were part of their fear of the undermining of their authority and their sexuality, but also expressed the allocation of responsibility for the management of sexuality to female employers. The elimination of the maid's sexuality was a means to keep sexuality to the confines of the conjugal couple. Damage to the body, and especially to the face, inflicted by mistresses are illustrations of the struggle for the control of sexuality and of the manifold relationships of force that take shape and come into play in families.

> I had this life of beating. She sent me to her cousin to give her a note. And she wasn't there. And she asked who brought it? Eleni? No. Who, Konstantina? No. The beautiful one who wears her hair in plaits. Me, the poor one, the pretty one with the plaits. She put me standing. My mistress, why do you cut my hair? And she beat me. And she left my hair in the shape of the fez; she cut it all around the

> head and left me a crest. And I was an eighteen-year old girl. She wanted me not to walk like this but like that. And I had to wear a bodice in order not to show my breast. But it showed. She made me bodices of canvas. She beat me. [Panajiota]
>
> I put the clock ten minutes earlier in order to be on time at school. And she realized that. One morning as I was combing my hair, she came, I always had a forelock when I was small, and she took the scissors and cut my hair to the roots. How could I go to school like that? I told you, there are a few things that I will never be able to forget. She didn't want me to look at myself in the mirror. [...] She abused me all the time. And when we went out, she dressed me and she used to say hypocritically, Stavroula, my beloved child. [Stavroula]

Corporal violence was exercised against children and also against young women. Not only the interviewees' testimonies but also the police reports were rife of incidents of mistreatment of children by their employers. The director of the Police Headquarters draws from these reports several cases of children who were found severely beaten and expelled by employers hanging around in the streets of Athens. He adds that there were numerous incidents of children resorting to police stations because they had been beaten by employers against whom there was no persecution.

> A pensioner, an ex civil servant of the State in a town of Old Greece, received, before departing, a poor orphan girl, at most ten years old, in order to serve him with the promise of providing her with a dowry as is usually the case with these problematic protectors in order to avoid paying these poor creatures who serve them. It is unimaginable what this poor girl went through and the number of beatings she was subjected to by the wife of this mister. The most tragic is that as punishment they put her down a well and locked the cover.[23]
>
> The accused A... wife of G. S., doctor, age 33, having in her service for nine years Soultana, unknown surname, age around 13, abused her frequently, and specifically on 18 February 1932 threw hot water on her and caused burns to her face. The night of 19 February 1932 she threw her out of the house with the words 'go wherever you want'.[24]

23 Pavlos Nirvanas, "Ta doulakia" [The little slaves], *Estia*, Friday, 9 July 1926.

24 Aristotelis Koutsoumaris, "I zoi kai I ekmetallefsi ton mikron ipiretrion" [The life and exploitation of little female servants: measures that have to be taken], *Ellinis*, no. 5, 1934, p. 197.

The Division of Space: Forms of Symbolic Violence

The places servants slept in and ate illustrate the imprint of social inequality in domestic space. For the majority of the interviewees a room was a luxury that very few enjoyed. Only two out of twenty interviewees had a room of their own. These rooms were tiny and dark and were usually located in the basement or next to the kitchen.[25] They did not have heating even in the 1960s when flats in multi-storey blocks had central heating. Neither did they have wardrobes. Aspasia put her socks in a drawer in the kitchen and was scolded by her employer who asked her to put them under her mattress. In upper-class houses, a room was shared between the domestic staff. Sleeping on the floor, in a corridor, in a *patari*, in the laundry room, in the kitchen and even under the kitchen table did not reflect the lack of space in the middle-class house but a violation of all areas of the self. Moreover, the space accorded to a body, as well as the space claimed for her body in physical space, were fundamental for experiencing one's sense of social value and also for constructing social difference.

The two-table pattern, as Elvin Hatch had called the separate eating arrangements for workers and family in households, was a symbolic marker of social distance.[26] Employers ate only with people they considered their social equals in their dining room, while servants ate in the kitchen. Ioanna, who nursed an elderly person, considered herself different from the maid of all work.

> They distinguished us in many issues, in many… Flora went out on Sunday with her cousins. In the afternoon. Because she had to stay in the morning in order to cook and wash the dishes after they had their meal. And afterwards we [with her employers] went out. We went to the theatre, to the movies.

25 "The existence of the so-called rooms for domestic servants, especially those in blocks of flats, in which they are forced to sleep, is alone enough to attach a stigma in our civilization", Aristotelis Koutsoumaris, "Social provision for the protection of the child in our country", *To Paidi*, no. 41, January–February 1937, p. 21. "The loft proved extremely hot in the summer and freezing cold in the winter; we assigned the attic to the servant, and he, too, abandoned it after a while", Penelope Delta, *Anamniseis, 1899* [Memoirs, 1899], ed. by Pavlos Zannas and Alexandros Zannas, Athens, Ermis, 1990, pp. 383–384.

26 Elvin Hatch, *Respectable Lives: Social Standing in Rural New Zealand*, Berkeley, University of California Press, 1992, pp. 140–143.

> – Did you eat with them?
>
> No, no. I ate with Flora. We had a nice table in the kitchen. I didn't want to offend Flora. No, it wouldn't be appropriate. I did offer my services too in this house. Together. She was a very good woman.

This perception of the self as different emanates from her position in the household and the underlying hierarchical relationships. Ioanna was not paid but she did a service job. The restriction on contact both with her parents and with the other domestic staff imposed by her employers was a form of control that aimed at safeguarding her long-term service. At the same time, sharing a number of middle-class attitudes such as accompanying employers in the theatre and better clothing put her in an in-between space. The separate eating arrangements, apart from her serving duties, indicate that she was not a social equal of her employers. This ambivalence in identity is illustrated by the explanation about her segregation from employers at meal time. On the one hand, it was done on the ground of not offending Flora, the maid of all work. On the other hand, it was appropriate to her status arrangement as she too was a servant.

As Hatch argues:

> Systems of social standing, or prestige structures, and the concept of person are rooted in the same body of cultural ideas. The moral notions by which the individual identifies what is significant about others and so orders them into hierarchies of standing also form the conceptual scheme by which the individual defines, measures and shapes his or her own self-identity.[27]

Separate eating arrangements for agricultural labourers and land owners marked social difference in rural society. The sense of the self that emerged through this form of social standing was rooted in work and in the position of a particular occupation in the system of hierarchy in a particular community.

> – When you went to this house in 1934 did you see your mother?
>
> Yes, she came to the house, because she was a noble person, a very nice soul she had, very good person my mother, she was ashamed to sit at the table with us because her hands were a mess. [Galini laughs]
>
> – Was she working?

27 *Ibid.*, p. 180.

> Yes, agricultural labour, how could we live otherwise? And she was ashamed to eat, yes.
>
> – Did you eat with them?
>
> Yes, but when my mother came I ate separately. They had me as their own child.

Her mother's refraining from eating with Galini's employers was an expression of respect to social superiors and of conforming to the moral codes of rural society. The internalisation of the social structures that legitimise distinction and their transfer to the next generation are expressed in Galini's understanding of this specific situation. Galini's mother was not in a labour relationship with the employers of her daughter. Her mother's refraining from eating with those employers is, rather, a manifestation of knowing her place in the world, of having a sense of her own place expressed through excluding herself from what she was already excluded from by the system of hierarchy. Here, it is the body that bespeaks social inferiority bearing the traces of manual work, and becomes the most indisputable materialization of class. As Bourdieu pointed out, "The seemingly natural features of the body [...] reveal the deepest dispositions of the habitus".[28] Exclusion derives from her mother's knowledge that she does not possess a legitimate body that would allow her to eat with her daughter's employers. The marks of labour on her body revealed that she did work that was ranked low in the hierarchy of occupations. This low status of labour transferred its devaluing marks through the body to the self. That the value of the self is rooted in work is also manifested in Galini's effort to disentangle her mother's character, her inner self, from the labour she performs and from the marks of labour on her hands. Galini knows from her mother's shame that a (female) body that bears the scars of manual work can transfer its class marks to the self. If delicate and clean hands are signs of respectability, because they illustrate the freedom from manual work, then hard, dirty and worn hands tell of a lack of respectability. That Galini insists so much on her mother's kindness suggests that there is constantly an imagined or true audience (myself) that might question her mother's worth in relation to the form of labour she performed. Shame produces defensiveness against an external construction of superiority. Galini's laughter was an expression of the embarrassment she felt about her mother's body.

28 P. Bourdieu, *Distinction*, p. 190. See also, Pierre Bourdieu, *In Other Words: Essays towards a Reflexive Sociology*, Cambridge, Polity Press, 1990, p. 110.

The meaningful practices and perceptions generated by the class habitus, defined as "the subjective but not individual system of internalised structures, schemes of perception, conception, and action common to all members of the same group or class and constituting the precondition for all objectification and apperception"[29] can be illustrated in Galini's willing self-exclusion from things from which she was already excluded, that is, access to her employers' goods:

> After two days he waited for his children to come from America and they cooked and slaughtered the chicken. They were wealthy people, yes, and they said, o gosh, the food is not enough; we have to make something more. And I interrupted and said, I don't mind if I don't eat. This stayed with them until they died. Because I said, "I don't mind not to eat", as if my portion would be enough for the rest. [Laugh]

Testing of Honesty and Restrictions on Food

Testing of honesty was the most widespread practice by which employers harmed the self-esteem of the women who were subjected to it. Money and jewellery were put under carpets and beds, wallets under pillows, and even food such as currants and chocolates were hidden under beds or displayed as tests to prove the honesty of domestic staff. The interviews with employers confirm this strategy: employers talked with pride about laying traps that aimed at discovering the honesty of their servants. Yet, all the interviewees knew that these were tests and felt humiliated about the employers' automatic doubting of their honesty. The accusation of theft was also a strategy by which employers got rid of domestic staff when they no longer needed them and sometimes it was a form of revenge when servants and foster children abandoned their posts. Questioning of honesty was a structural element in the relationship of the middle-class with the lower classes.

> They were bitter when they learned that I was engaged. They thought that I would leave. I will tell you something that was a thorn in my flesh. When I left she said, I am ashamed to say this because I didn't do it, that she had lost a tablecloth. And

29 P. Bourdieu, *Outline of a Theory of Practice*, p. 86.

> then my cousin said, go and talk to them. I went crying and begged them, and I told them that I had no idea about this thing. But since I left this thing remained, that I stole the tablecloth. [Galini]

The meaning of theft was also class-defined. For servants as well as for the working class in general stealing food was a strategy of survival and a solidarity mechanism for the family.[30] During the Occupation Aggelina together with the cook had a skeleton key of the cellar where employers stored food and they gave food to their parents and relatives:

> There was hunger. But the rich did not starve, it was us who starved. [Aggelina]

In many cases food was distributed secretly from employers' stores, but this required access and control of food and so was something that was only possible for servants in the privileged position of the cook. Often theft was a compensation for the lack of salary. In one newspaper report the removal of the master's clothes by two maids was their retaliation for the withholding of their salaries.

While depriving domestic staff of food was not considered an offence even when it set at risk the employees' survival, taking food was an offence that led to punishment.

> They had in a box figs and raisins, now I was a child, I was hungry and I opened it and took some and they considered me as a thief, that I stole it. Well, I stole it as it were. Yes, I took it, but I didn't do it with the aim to steal. I was hungry, that's why I stole, do you understand? And I remember she punished me. This was the first and last time I did it. She forced me to stand and she screamed: "thief", "thief". [Eleftheria]

During the Occupation the employers' exploitation of their employees reached unprecedented levels. As we have already seen with Eleftheria, situations of crisis such as the war, orphanhood and refugeedom became for the middle-classes opportunities for extreme exploitation and for the

30 This kind of theft has been defined by Stephen Humphries as social crime. This term was used by Humphries to encompass the minor crimes against property committed by working-class children and condoned by the working-class community as legitimate, despite their illegality. What oral testimonies suggested to Humphries was that social crime was "a rational discriminating activity in the context of class inequality and the day-to-day demands of the family economy", Stephen Humphries, *Hooligans or Rebels? An Oral History of Working-Class Childhood and Youth 1889–1939*, Oxford, Blackwell, 1981, p. 151.

most exploitative contracts. Both the war in Asia Minor and the Second World War created an enormous number of destitute children who hired their labour just for food and boarding. These children were a cheap labour force and there are indications that a large number of families employed more servants than they would have done if they had had to pay a salary. Besides, children and young women who were orphans or poor were employed without remuneration by families that otherwise would not have been able to afford servants. Aggeliki was an orphan child from Smyrna. After the invasion in Fokaies its inhabitants became captives of war. Her father and brothers were killed and the baby was thrown in a lake. During their forced march her sister was taken by soldiers and raped. Aggeliki found her in Athens several years after the war. Her sister, who worked as a servant in Athens, introduced her to a compatriot whose employers wanted a girl to serve at the table. Aggeliki found a post in this family whose head was an MP and who kept four servants, all refugees. Two of them were minors; there were three women and one boy.

> It was in Skoufa street, number 8. It was the house of an MP. He had his wife and three daughters. He had two refugee girls and a boy for the office. The young daughter disliked me. She chased me and beat me on the head. This happened every day. But there was something worse. They bought for us half kilo of bread to eat for lunch and dinner. In the morning we had nothing. Just tea. The lady locked up their food. You didn't see either bread, or cheese, or olives.

In her second post, Galini abandoned her employers because they starved her, while Aspasia, who entered service without payment, that is only for food, changed posts six times during the Second World War because the food provided was less than that her family received with her ration. Access to food depended also on the position of the servant in the household. Many employers locked away sugar, coffee and even bread. The inventiveness of employers concerning the control of food knew no limits. Evdoksia, who in 1922, after the war, in Minor Asia was given by the Near East Relief for adoption to a midwife, remembers:

> She locked away the bread, for me not to eat it. [...] When she cooked meat, do you know what she did? She removed the meat and gave me the bone. She didn't even give you proper food. She cheated me. She sent me into the other room and put water in my milk. [Evdoksia]

Penelope Delta, a writer, lived together with her mother-in-law in Athens, who had undertaken total control over the housekeeping. She locked away the sugar and coffee and gave them by the spoonful to servants in order to prepare the coffee.[31] Keeping the keys of drawers and wardrobes and locking the food were widespread practices of employers, while the counting of items was a typical advice to mistresses in conduct literature.[32] Another employer would put water in the coffeepot with the remains of coffee after she made herself coffee and give it to her servant. In many cases, not only the food but also the bread provided was different for servants. A segregated market with lower quality goods was used by employers for feeding servants.

> They bought white bread and ate it. We had black. You could find whatever you wanted in this bread. I cut a slice; there was a piece of rope inside. I told this to the mistress and she said, "What's the matter? It is fine". I cut another piece, and I found a worm. The bread was like cotton. The knife stuck when you cut it. "You will eat this bread", she said. She cut a little piece and she pretended that she ate it. And she didn't buy it every day. She bought 7 kilos. [Panajiota]

The position of cook was considered the top of a servant's career not only because of a higher salary but also due to the privileged access to food. In a dialogue between two Folegandrian women, one who entered service in 1930 and the other in 1952, we can get an idea about the power of being a cook.

> Margarita. Did you eat different food from the employers?
>
> They never gave me food. I had the food. [Anna]

Food appears here as a possession; its control and distribution attached a certain power to cooks. Artemis worked after the war until the middle of the 1990s as a day worker for families of ship owners and industrialists.

> All this wealth, they ate the best, we had soup. The cook said, this is what the mistress ordered me to cook.
>
> – Did the cook eat the same food as you?
>
> She of course didn't eat the same.

Distinctions in the consumption of food were not only due to an attitude of thrift on the part of employers, but also set boundaries and maintained

31 Penelope Delta, *Anamniseis, 1899*, p. 424.

32 Aikaterini Varouksaki, *Oikiaki Oikonomia* [Housekeeping], Athens, 1923, p. 174.

social distance. Barriers in space and in consumption were mechanisms to keep these two worlds within a household apart and to prevent them merging. Other goods that belonged to mistresses, such as cream, should not be touched. On the other hand, the barriers of time were completely dissolved. The employees' full time was placed at the convenience of employers and their leisure time either did not exist or was not respected.

> They called me while I was eating, and I went chewing. Girl, go out and empty your mouth and come in. And I went and I took the bread out of my mouth and I presented myself. When we ate, she had to come while we were eating and we had to stand up. She spent all day in the kitchen, and you had to stand from morning till night. [Panajiota]

> – Did you eat well?
>
> I told you she put me in the kitchen and she gave me a plate with food and I paid through the nose for that. She put the baby on the carpet to shit. And then she called me while I was eating to clean. I was sixteen years old and I had taught the child the way I knew. And I had an old box but when she saw it she made such a fuss about it. [Vania]

Defacement

One of the forms of psychological violence exerted against domestic staff was defacement. The mechanisms of this forced removal of identity varied according to the needs of employers. The institution of fostering constituted an informal form of adoption that aimed not so much at securing cheap labour but at establishing a contract of life-service based on bonds of fictive kinship. Fostering, as a strategy by employers was oriented towards the future, and constituted an investment that aimed at securing care in old age as well as care of future generations. Based on loyalty and on ties of affection, it blurred the boundaries between employment and kinship. On the part of poor people it was a strategy to attach their daughters to people of a higher social class with the prospect of endowment or a lump sum after the death of the employer. Children who entered this contract and relationship experienced the worst form of exploitation and psychological and corporal abuse.

This pattern of domestic service deviated from the institution of service that was firmly and intrinsically embedded in the local economy as in Folegandros and the other Cycladic islands. In these islands both the profession and migration were organised by the community and its networks of solidarity in Athens functioned as a safety valve for children and young women against mistreatment.

There are nuances in the ways this type of relationship was experienced by the interviewees, but it is a common denominator that it is perceived by the interviewees as a labour relationship and as a form of exploitation. As we shall see in the following testimonies, foster mothers are called "alien hands". "Alien hands" is a typical phrase used in Greek to convey the position of a child or an adult in a family that is not the parental family. It speaks about the way the child or the adult relates to this family rather than about status. The strength and the emotional weight that this phrase carries are drawn from a verse of a popular song: "The alien hands are knives" [*Ta ksena heria einai maheria*]. In this phrase the subject's relationship to the family is not one of affectionate bonds but is felt as hostile. Moreover, this relationship is perceived both in bodily as well as in psychic terms, the one informing and attaching meaning to the other: the hands that are meant to caress or embrace are transformed into knives that wound (invisible wounds that cause psychic pain), their warmth being substituted by the freezing feeling of metal. This phrase is telling about how this particular relationship was understood: that is, not as a familial relationship but as an alienating experience. Rather than being expressed in terms of love, it felt like slavery.

> She took me to do the chores. She wore me out. I was a small child but she had great demands. It didn't matter for them that we were children. We were worn out in the "alien hands". It was not like now, the servant is better off than the mistress is. You are afraid of talking to her. In those days it was different. They had you for a penny. In the beginning she took me for twenty drachmas. I was her skivvy. A skivvy. [Evdoksia]

Fostering was a labour relationship but under the worst working conditions. When children could not respond to their duties, employers did not hesitate to break the contract and send them back to their parents, or even to leave them in the streets, as in the case of Evdoksia, who was an orphan child from Asia Minor without relatives. Even employers who had adopted children from kin sent them back to their parents and exchanged them with another child when they were not satisfied with the services they offered.

> This aunt of mine could not have children. She [her mother] gave me to her. But I pissed and she was very tidy. I stayed for one-two years and she said to my mother "Marina, I cannot keep the child". And she took the other, Rita. And she made her life unliveable. She beat her because she did not do the chores the way she wanted. Rita was beaten a lot in order to learn to do the chores properly. After she ironed the clothes she put her to iron them again. [Evaggelia]

Fostering not only formed part of the rehabilitation policy of public and private organizations concerning refugee children from Asia Minor or poor children during the Second World War. It constituted also one of the welfare policies used by rural communities to deal with orphan children. There the priest or the teacher decided the destiny of such children, and service was proposed as the solution to orphanhood.

Let us return to the question of removal of identity. Employers aimed at establishing a long-standing relationship of dependency grounded on total domination over foster children. Already, in the negotiations between parents and employers, the object of exchange was not the labour power of the daughter but the whole self. In order for domination to be achieved, employers exercised various forms of psychological as well as corporal violence. When fostering took the form of migration, employers' control of correspondence and visits by parents and relatives aimed not only at breaking off the bond between parents and daughters but also at concealing the appalling living conditions and mistreatment of these children.

The restriction on information that was directed to parents or kin was exercised systematically and the technologies employed combined control both of the written word and of personal contact.

> My father came. It was Tuesday when he came to the shop. The masters told him that she is out with the lady. And he comes on Wednesday, this time in the afternoon. With the knock of the door, I go out. "I don't know", he said, "are you my child?" "Daddy", and then he hugged me and kissed me. "Welcome, welcome, *koumbare*." She took the *koumbaros* and sat in the dining room, as if he was her lover. And the *koumbaros* left and she didn't let the girl enter the dining room. So that I could not be present. Now, what they said, what they did, only God knows. The *koumbaros* left, goodbye, goodbye, I didn't see him or hear him. [Panajiota]

> My cousin came to see me in the hospital. And the master told him, there is no such name here. And I was in the operating room. [Panajiota]

The conditions of living were brutal: beatings, deprivation of food, sleeping on the ground and hard labour. Blocking of Panajiota's right to see her father was done on the purpose to concealing these conditions. At the same time, it implied that Panajiota constituted for both parties simply an item of economic exchange without rights and substance. All her earnings after twenty years in service were taken from her and given to her brother. The case of Stavroula is similar. She had not seen her parents for three years.

> But my aunt came occasionally to see me, to ask me whether I was satisfied, but I couldn't tell her that it wasn't good, because she [the employer] was there all the time, she was next to me constantly. [...] They [the employers] read all my letters. And at some point I wrote a letter to my father, it was after two and a half years I was there. I had a friend, a very good friend, and I told her that I had a bad time there and I wanted to leave. I wrote a letter and I gave it to her to send it. Now I don't know what happened, she was caught, and she didn't send the letter. And I got in trouble, of course. She controlled all my letters. She controlled everything I wrote. [...] When we went in the summer to Menidi, she didn't let me go to the village. I waited two and a half years to see them. And my mother wanted to come and see me. And she came to Menidi and I didn't let her go, I started crying, I said that I wanted to leave. [Stavroula]

These limitations of contact were also imposed on those whose parents lived in Athens.

> – Did you see your mother?
>
> No, she didn't let her see me. She said your mother will never come to see you again. I was crying as a child for my mother. Because I knew who my mother was. [Artemis]

> No, they did not let me go to my parents. They were afraid that I would be attracted and I would leave them. They wanted me always there with them. And outside the house, when we went for shopping, they called me Miss Fotiadis. [Ioanna]

The removal of the family name was the ultimate act of removal of identity. In this action the desire for life-long possession of an individual in the service of employers was inscribed, which did not differ from slavery. We have seen the case of Ioanna, whose employers not only did not let her visit her parents but also had given her their family name. Panajiota too had the family name of her employers and even her kin called her by this name. Stavroula's employers imposed on her to send letters to her parents signed with their name.

> They didn't have children and they wanted me to be their child and everything to be given to me after their death. And they wanted me as a complete child, to write their name in the letters I sent. And of course I didn't want, my name was Margariti. But they forced me and I ended up signing with both names. [Stavroula]

This act of defiance, of refusal to submit to total possession springs from the cognition of a labour relationship that violated all the boundaries of the self. Middle-class women pressed for this relationship to remain under their total control, disguised as a familial relationship. Women tried to escape, but the imprint of it stayed with them.

Restrictions on Contact

The restriction on contact with the outside world imposed by employers can be traced in the arrangement of leaves for domestic staff. All the interviewees were allowed half a day off once a week late in the afternoon, after they had cooked, served the employers and washed the dishes. In households with more than one servant, employees were more disadvantaged as they had a day off once a fortnight. In reality this was not a day off but an afternoon. For the urban population, whose houses were located in settlements which were distant from the employer's house, visiting their parents required walking long distances because either there was no frequent transportation or they wanted to save money from the ticket fare. Goffman defines total institutions as the establishments whose encompassing and total character is symbolised by the barriers against social intercourse with the outside.[33]

> Where could you go? She said, you will be back at eight in the evening. She didn't allow me to be out later. You couldn't leave early, because they had lunch on Sunday and you had to clean the kitchen. It was already three, four o'clock, and one hour walking to go and one to come back, where could you go?

Distress and loneliness in service is very often documented in the interviews. It was a result of institutionalisation and minimum contact with familiar persons.

33 E. Goffman, *Asylums*, p. 14.

In the second house, although I wanted to go this house, my problem was that I wanted to go out to walk. I cried alone so many times, especially on Sunday when I saw people pass by with kids. I said, these people are having a walk. I was desperate, I said if only I was with my brother running in the fields. [Margarita]

I had such a nice life in the village. I took off my shoes and I ran in the snow. I can't forget that. These thinks have stayed with me. [...] I felt suffocated in Athens. [...] Every night I cried. Every night. I had an image of Virgin Mary above my bed and they wanted to take it away. [...] Every night I prayed to Virgin Mary to escape from this life. [Stavroula]

I was crying, I wanted to be in my house with my mother. They said you will get used to it. But it took a long time to get used to it. I was very sad, and cried a lot, but I became accustomed slowly. [Eva]

A day's work meant a whole day in the service of others. Time was defined by employers' needs.

There was no time left to do your own thing. [Anastasia]

They paid you. The people paid to have you. [Margarita]

Are you kidding? Of course. Any time they wanted you, the bell would ring, and you would go up and be occupied with something. [Anastasia]

The Association of Domestic Personnel (servants) was represented at the first conference of women in 1946.[34] The Servants' Union had 250 members.

Our life is miserable from all aspects. We wake up very early and we work until midnight. And if the needs of our masters demand that we do not sleep, we are obliged to work for twenty-four hours. The conditions under which we work are hard and exasperating.

Our payment is restricted to a plate of food and a few drachmas that are not even enough for a pair of socks. If we dare to complain they will say: "We feed you, we accommodate you, and you do not have expenses." But listen to what we eat. Nothing in the morning because sugar is too expensive and there is no need for the servant to drink something hot. For lunch they will eat meat and hors d'œuvres and fruit, but for us it will be beans or chickpeas or any cheap food depending on the season. They accommodate us. Where do we sleep? In the light wells, in lofts, in

34 Talk by the representative of the Association of Domestic Personnel, First Panhellenic Conference of Women, May 1946 (President Avra Theodoropoulou, Secretary Roza Imvrioti), Archive of Roza Imvrioti.

> *pataria* or in damp and dark basements, in which they wouldn't even put their animals if they didn't have servants. But we don't only live under hard conditions of non-paid work, we live also under constant humiliation and disregard.
>
> In many houses they beat us and all the time they constantly threaten us with expulsion. And when they speak to us their look shows that they are speaking to people of the lowest status. And this would not be so strange if we met this attitude only from the class of our employers, which aims at disparaging us and in various ways makes us believe that we are inferior beings in order to handle us more easily in their own interest and for their comfort. But this evil is general in our sector. In the same way that our employers despise us, equally the state despises us and does not pass any protective legislation for us. In the same way they all despise us. There are houses in which they treat us as human beings, but these are exceptional. We ask women to raise their voices for us and to help us to work under the same conditions.

This description of the conditions of service labour and the understanding of the experience of service as well as the structure of feeling that arises from the subjection to this particular labour relationship by the representative of the Association bear profound similarities to the interviewees' testimonies. The class-based perceptions of domestic servants explored so far are illuminating about the process through which women came to achieve through their relationship to their mistresses a consciousness about the conditions that shaped them as subordinate. As E. P. Thompson argued:

> Class is a social and cultural formation (often finding institutional expression) which cannot be defined abstractly or in isolation, but only in terms of relationship with other classes; and, ultimately, the definition can only be made in the medium of *time* – that is, action and reaction, change and conflict. When we speak of *a* class we are thinking of a very loosely defined body of people who share the same categories of interests, social experiences, traditions and value-system, who have a *disposition* to *behave* as a class, to define themselves in their actions and in their consciousness in relation to other groups of people in class ways. But class itself is not a thing, it is a happening.[35]

35 Edward Palmer Thompson, "Peculiarities of the English", in *The Poverty of Theory and Other Essays*, London, Merlin Press, 1978, p. 295.

Conclusion

I have tried to show how class consciousness was formed in a realm where class-based feelings are supposed to be absent. The interviewees experienced their relationship to mistresses as a class-based relationship. That this understanding did not lead to the only form of class politics that is recognised as such by analysts does not mean that it is not political. Class is not an objective category of historical analysis but a form of identity that is constructed in specific historical and social circumstances. Historians pointed out that the history of class formation was written out of class struggle, privileging a particular kind of politics and excluding other forms of consciousness. As Carolyn Steedman argued, this formulation of class and the epic story of class formation in which it was crystallized did not only exclude women's experiences of class but it was also untypical of the experiences of many men too.[36] The memories presented here provide accounts not only of how social conditioning was inscribed on one's body, language, and appearance in this particular relationship of labour but also of how these women came to understand themselves as products of this relationship.

36 Carolyn Steedman, "A Weekend with Elektra", *Literature and History*, vol. 6, no. 1, Spring 1997, p. 18.

Part IV

Servant Adaptability to the Labour Market, Past and Present

Mistresses of Themselves? Female Domestic Servants and By-Employments in Sixteenth-Century Scottish Towns

Elizabeth EWAN

In August 1507, James Wardlaw built a new house on his Edinburgh property. As part of the process, he promised his neighbour, Alexander Mauchane, that he would make a common passage through his building to the backlands beyond, and that the corbel stone supporting the roof of the passage should be "as high as any servant maid of Alexander Mauchane may bear a measurable tub with water on her head without any stop or impediment caused by the said corbel".[1] The domestic servants who carried out essential household tasks for their employer were an important part of the everyday traffic using the passage. As this agreement suggests, female domestic servants were ubiquitous in sixteenth-century Edinburgh, as they were throughout Scotland and the rest of contemporary Europe.

Much literature on early modern female domestic servants has emphasized the negative aspects of their position. Young, away from their parents and birth community, their time entirely at the disposal of their employers who were entrusted by the authorities with the responsibility for monitoring and disciplining their behaviour, domestic servants lived hard lives which were endurable only because time in service was a temporary phase of the life cycle, to be ended for women only upon marriage.[2] As will be discussed below, however, other studies have modified this picture, pointing out that servants did have a certain degree of independence in some aspects of their lives, including, for example, the choice of marriage partners. There are also some examples of what appears to be inde-

1 Walter Macleod and Marguerite Wood (eds), *Protocol Book of John Foular 1503–13,* Edinburgh, Scottish Record Society, 1940–1941, no. 336 (my translation).

2 Madona Hettinger, "Defining the Servant: Legal and Extra-Legal Terms of Employment in Fifteenth-Century England", in Allen Frantzen and Douglas Moffat (eds), *The Work of Work: Servitude, Slavery, and Labor in Medieval England*, Glasgow, Cruithne Press, 1994, pp. 206–228; Kim Phillips, *Medieval Maidens: Young women and gender in England 1270–1540*, Manchester, Manchester University Press, 2003, pp. 120–135.

pendent action on the part of groups of female servants. For example, in London in 1573 a pamphlet apparently written by, or at least in the name of, a group of maidservants, pointed out that their labour was indispensable to their employers, and that if the employers made their life intolerable, they could always withdraw their services. In Edinburgh a century and a quarter later, female servants submitted a petition to the town council seeking permission to establish a relief fund for those fellow servants who fell into poverty.[3]

This article focuses on female domestic servants and argues that there was scope for independent action on their part, not just in the choice of marriage partner, but in earning money for the dowry for that marriage through by-employments not under the control of their employer. One of these activities, money lending, was practised by both male and female servants, but two others, laundering and brewing, grew out of the skills which girls learned from their mothers and mistresses and which they would use themselves in caring for their own families later in life if they did indeed marry.

It is only recently that the female domestic servant has begun to be examined by historians of early modern Scotland. A study of the master and servant relationship in an introduction to Scots law for historians in 1958 focussed almost entirely on male servants and mainly on apprentices and journeymen.[4] The only general survey of women in the early modern period pays very little attention to domestic service, while a study of women and work in eighteenth-century Edinburgh omits service from among the female employments discussed.[5] However, the situation of female servants in the seventeenth and eighteenth centuries is beginning to be revealed, with studies of such topics as female migration patterns, household rela-

3 Ann Rosalind Jones, "Maidservants of London. Sisterhoods of Kinship and Labour", in Susan Frye and Karen Robertson (eds), *Maids and Mistresses, Cousins and Queens. Women's Alliances in Early Modern England*, New York, Oxford University Press, 1999, pp. 28–29; Rab A. Houston, *Social Change in the Age of the Enlightenment*, Oxford, Clarendon Press, 1994, pp. 89–90.

4 Thomas B. Smith, "Master and Servant", in *Introduction to Scottish Legal History*, Edinburgh, Stair Society, 1958, pp. 130–144; *Id.*, "Master and Servant. Further Historical Outlines", *Juridical Review*, new series, 3, 1958, pp. 215–229.

5 Robert Allen Houston, "Women in the economy and society of Scotland 1500–1800", in Robert Allen Houston and Ian D. Whyte (eds), *Scottish Society 1500–1800*, Cambridge, Cambridge University Press, 1989, pp. 118–147; Elizabeth Sanderson, *Women and Work in Eighteenth-Century Edinburgh*, Houndmills, Macmillan, 1996.

tions, testaments, wet-nursing, and illegitimacy.[6] Some aspects of the lives of later sixteenth-century servants have been discussed in a recent Master's thesis, and in two studies of the social discipline of the Reformation church.[7] However, the female domestic servant is still largely invisible for the first half of the sixteenth century.

One difficulty is a lack of sources. The documents which have been used so effectively for studies of servants in England,[8] for example, do not exist for Scotland for the sixteenth century. There are no comprehensive poll tax lists or census data on urban town dwellers, although more evidence becomes available in the seventeenth century. The earliest survey of inhabitants to include female servants is a 1636 list of the inhabitants of Old Aberdeen.[9] Servants make up 19 percent of the people listed; female servants outnumber male servants by about 3:2. The next such lists do not appear until the poll tax of 1694. An analysis of this source for Edinburgh

6 Ian D. Whyte and Kathleen A. Whyte, "The Geographical Mobility of Women in Early Modern Scotland", in Leah Leneman (ed.), *Perspectives in Scottish Social History*, Aberdeen, Aberdeen University Press, 1988, pp. 83–106; R. A. Houston, *Social Change*, pp. 87–101; Winifred Coutts, "Women, Children and Domestic Servants in Dumfries in the 17th Century", *Transactions of the Dumfriesshire and Galloway Natural History and Antiquarian Society*, 61, 1986, pp. 73–83; Gordon Desbrisay, "Wet Nurses and Unwed Mothers in Seventeenth-Century Aberdeen", in Elizabeth Ewan and Maureen Meikle (eds), *Women in Scotland c.1100–c.1750*, East Linton, Tuckwell Press, 1999, pp. 210–220; Gordon Desbrisay, "Twisted by Definition: Women under Godly Discipline in Seventeenth-century Scottish Towns", in Yvonne G. Brown and Rona Ferguson (eds), *Twisted Sisters. Women, Crime and Deviance in Scotland since 1400*, East Linton, Tuckwell Press, 2002, pp. 137–155; Rosalind Mitchison and Leah Leneman, *Sexuality and Social Control: Scotland 1660–1780*, Oxford, Basil Blackwell, 1989.

7 Janay Nugent, "Servants' Lives: Youth in Lowland Scotland, 1560–1650", unpublished MA thesis, University of Guelph, 1997; Michael Graham, *The Uses of Reform*, Leiden, E.J. Brill, 1996; Margo Todd, *The Culture of Protestantism*, New Haven, Yale University Press, 2002.

8 P. Jeremy P. Goldberg, *Women, Work, and Lifecycle in a Medieval Economy. Women in York and Yorkshire c.1300–c.1520*, Oxford, Clarendon Press, 1992, especially ch. 4; Marjorie McIntosh, "Servants and the Household Unit in an Elizabethan English Community", *Journal of Family History*, 9, 1, 1984, pp. 3–23; Vivien B. Elliott, "Single Women in the London Marriage Market: Age, Status and Mobility, 1598–1616", in R. B. Outhwaite (ed.), *Marriage and Society*, London, Europe, 1981; Ilana K. Ben-Amos, "Women apprentices in the trades and crafts of early modern Bristol", *Continuity and Change*, 6, 1991, pp. 227–252.

9 Robert Tyson, "Household size and structure in a Scottish burgh: Old Aberdeen in 1636", *Local Population Studies*, 1998, pp. 46–54.

has shown that in that town female domestic servants were the largest occupational group, and that there were 100 female servants for every 33 male servants.[10] Edinburgh may have been somewhat exceptional because of the large number of wealthy aristocratic and merchant households, but studies elsewhere suggest that it was common for towns to have a large female servant population, both in the seventeenth century and earlier. One in ten Scottish girls was in service in one of the four main towns of Scotland in the 1690s.[11]

For the sixteenth century, however, only one listing of citizens, made in Edinburgh in 1558, includes servants and because this was drawn up for military service, only male servants are included.[12] We are thus forced to rely on qualitative rather than quantitative evidence in looking at how common it was to employ servants in the sixteenth century. The makers of local legislation seem to have assumed that most households would have included servants. In 1556 all merchants and craftsmen and other indwellers of Edinburgh were ordered to send their servants with torches to accompany the provost on certain festival days.[13] Moreover, national legislation ordering all idle and masterless people to pass to service was presumably based on the belief that there were sufficient positions of service for them (or at least most of them) to pass to. As early as 1425 sheriffs had been given the power to arrest idle men and force them to find masters or to work in crafts within forty days.[14] This applied mainly to rural workers but in the sixteenth century towns began to pass their own legislation. In Edinburgh in 1512 the town council ordered that any youthful poor who could work were to take up service or leave the town. In

10 Helen Dingwall, *Late 17th Century Edinburgh. A Demographic Study,* Aldershot, Scholar Press, 1994, pp. 22, 28–29, 132–134.

11 Merry Wiesner, *Women and Gender in Early Modern Europe*, Cambridge, Cambridge University Press, 1993, p. 92; Olwen Hufton, *The Prospect Before Her*, New York, Knopf, 1996, pp. 80–1; Rab A. Houston and William W. J. Knox, "Introduction: Scots and their Histories", in Rab A. Houston and William W. J. Knox (eds), *The New Penguin History of Scotland*, London, Penguin Press, 2001, p. xxxiv.

12 Michael Lynch, *Edinburgh and the Reformation*, Edinburgh, John Donald, 1981, pp. 9–10.

13 James D. Marwick (ed.), *Extracts from the Records of the Burgh of Edinburgh,* Edinburgh, Scottish Burgh Records Society, 1869–92, ii, pp. 7–8, 38, 73, 260.

14 Thomas Thomson and Cosmo Innes (eds), *The Acts of the Parliaments of Scotland 1124–1707*, Edinburgh, Record Commission, 1814–75, ii, p. 11, c. 20.

1536 all beggars who did not enter service were to be imprisoned and then banished.[15]

What evidence there is for the sixteenth century suggests that in many ways the experience of Scottish servants resembled that of servants elsewhere in northwest Europe. In 1988 Peter Laslett outlined several characteristics of service, suggesting common traits found in most north-western European countries.[16] Most young people from rural families undertook a period of service or apprenticeship from their early or mid-teens to their early or mid-twenties. Service was a stage of the life cycle, during which young people made the transition from childhood to adulthood. It was expected that servants would be young (some Scottish records refer to them interchangeably as "servants" and "children"),[17] although some people remained servants for their lifetime, and some widows returned to service later in life. In 1567 the Scottish Parliament ordered that any vagrant's child aged 5–14 could be put to work for any who liked until age 24 if male, 18 if female.[18] For women service tended to be domestic service, although some girls were apprenticed formally, and probably many more received informal apprenticeship.[19] Service provided training for adult life. Girls learned the domestic skills they would need as mistresses of their own households when they married, including brewing and laundering, and often additional craft and retailing skills which enabled them to assist their husbands in their work. They also learned skills which would sustain them if they did not marry. Wages earned in service allowed them to save towards setting up a household. Life-cycle service thus provided the underpinning for the north-western marriage pattern of relatively late female marriage age, companionate marriage and the establishment of new nuclear families.

15 J. D. Marwick (ed.), *Records of Edinburgh*, i, p. 137, ii, p. 73.

16 R. A. Houston and W. W. J. Knox, "Introduction", pp. xxxiv–v; Peter Laslett, "The Institution of Service", *Local Population Studies*, 1988, pp. 55–60. Recently it has been suggested that service may not have been quite as common for girls from urban families, Merry E. Wiesner, "Having Her Own Smoke: Employment and Independence for Single women in Germany, 1400–1750", in Judith M. Bennett and Amy M. Froide (eds), *Single women in the European Past 1250–1800*, Philadelphia, University of Pennsylvania Press, 1999, p. 200.

17 Edinburgh City Archives [ECA], SL1/1/4, fo. 10v; J. D. Marwick (ed.), *Records of Edinburgh*, ii, pp. 307, 308.

18 T. B. Smith, "Master and Servant", pp. 221–222.

19 I. K. Ben-Amos, "Women apprentices", pp. 228, 239–243; K. Phillips, *Medieval Maidens*, pp. 133–134.

The mechanisms by which servants were hired are not easily discernible in the surviving records, although occasional glimpses are caught of the existence of hiring fairs. For example, it appears to have been common for people from Selkirk to go to Edinburgh to hire maids at Martinmas. In late October 1519 the town authorities of Selkirk forbade the inhabitants to go to Edinburgh for any cause apart from this, because of fears of spreading of the plague. This statute suggests that maids were important enough to the economy that the only exception to the plague regulations was made for them, although it might also imply that the women came from outside Edinburgh so that there was less danger of them bringing back the infection with them.[20] Other servants found employment through kinship links – in Dumfries in the early seventeenth century, servants included the sister of one woman and the stepdaughter of another.[21]

Contracts generally seem to have been for six months or one year, with changes in service generally taking place at two fixed terms of the year, Martinmas (11 November) and Whitsun (15 May). Such terms remained common at least in the rural areas in Scotland until the twentieth century. Urban terms probably reflected rural terms as so much of the labour came from the countryside. Rents, rural and urban, were commonly paid at Martinmas and Whitsun. Individual contracts could, however, vary – in Edinburgh in 1561 Alison Ramsay was ordered to pay Janet Somervell 8s for service from Martinmas to the following Easter. In Perth in May 1547 Isobel Adeson contracted for a twelve-week term of service.[22] Contracts were sealed by the payment of "arles" or "earnest money" to the servant. For example in 1513 Will Fergus of Aberdeen admitted to the court that he had feed himself to Cuthbert Monroe for one year by taking a plak (a coin) of arles. In 1536 in Selkirk Helen Hesloip hired Helen Lorimer as a servant and gave her a penny arles "as custom is".[23]

One indication of a relative level of independence on the part of servants is the frequency with which they seem to have broken their contracts and moved to another master or mistress. The frequency of ordinances,

20 John Imrie *et al.* (eds), *The Burgh Court Book of Selkirk 1503–45,* Edinburgh, Scottish Record Society, 1960–69, p. 54.

21 W. Coutts, "Women, Children", p. 78.

22 Marguerite Wood (ed.), *Court Book of the Regality of Broughton and the Burgh of the Canongate 1569–1573*, Edinburgh, Oliver & Boyd, 1937, p. 300; Perth Council Archives, Perth Burgh Court Records, B59/12/3, fos. 2r-v.

23 Aberdeen City Archives [ACA], Aberdeen Council Registers, vol. 9, p. 225; J. Imrie (ed.), *Court Book of Selkirk*, p. 175.

such as that of Dundee in 1567, prohibiting such behaviour and forbidding prospective employers enticing away another's servant, suggests that, as elsewhere in Europe,[24] the practice was widespread. In Dundee in 1521 Janet Husband, servant to Jonkyn Henrison, took service with Wille Mair's wife before her first term was up. Her new employer was forced to pay Jonkyn the fee he had promised Janet. In 1523 Janet Retre was found by the court to be one man's feed servant and was ordered to leave another man's service immediately and return to her former employer.[25] The movement of servants was probably made easier by the fact that most contracts were oral, unlike apprenticeship agreements which would often be written down. Thus in Stirling in 1529 in a dispute between Simon Brown and Janet Crookston he had no proof that she was his servant, and had to entrust his case to her oath whether she was or not. In Selkirk in 1515 a woman took malt from William Ker. Ker tried to recover payment for the malt from Allan Forsyth, believing that he was her employer, but Allan denied that she was his servant. In 1519 another Selkirk man and his family and friends had to swear that a horse-stealer was not their servant and indeed had never been their servant. Among those swearing to this were Adam's servants.[26]

It has been argued that the institution of life-cycle service, especially urban service, gave young people a large measure of independence and freedom, in particular in choice of marriage partners, although just how complete this independence from parental control was has been the subject of some debate.[27] Young people moving to the towns would be able to make new contacts and would have a much greater control over marriage choice. Although they were under the control and moral and religious discipline of their employers for the term of their contract, servants, unlike apprentices, were free to change employers frequently, and many did so. During their years in service they met prospective marriage partners.

24 Alex Warden (ed.), *Burgh Laws of Dundee*, London, Longmans, Green, 1872, p. 33; M. E. Wiesner, "Having Her Own Smoke", pp. 201–202.

25 Dundee City Archives [DCA], Book of the Kirk, fos. 29r, 148r.

26 Stirling Council Archives [SCA], Stirling Court Book, B66/15/1, fo. 194v (1529); J. Imrie (ed.), *Court Book of Selkirk*, pp. 33, 50, 56–57.

27 P. Jeremy P. Goldberg, "Marriage, migration, servanthood and life-cycle in Yorkshire towns of the later Middle Ages: Some York cause paper evidence", *Continuity and Change*, 1, 2, 1986, p. 155; P. Jeremy P. Goldberg, "Female Labour, Service and Marriage in the Late Medieval Urban North", *Northern History*, 22, 1986, pp. 25–26; V. B. Elliot, "Single Women", p. 86; M. E. Weisner, *Women and Gender*, pp. 57–58.

Largely free of parental control, especially if they were among the large number of young people who migrated to the towns from the countryside, they had much more freedom of choice in marriage partners than they would probably have had if they had remained in the parental home or community.

Scottish evidence suggests that this held true for Scottish servants as well. Court cases from the later sixteenth century show that servants were very mobile and that they were relatively free to contract marriage with whom they liked. The records of the St Andrews kirk session (local parish court), beginning in 1559, support this.[28] These court cases took place just as the Protestant Reformation (1559–60) was beginning to be established in Scotland, and while the rulings of the court were influenced by the new ideas of the Reformers, the actions of the litigants seem to reflect behaviour which had a longer history. Many of the litigants in marriage cases were servants, as were many of the witnesses. Among the servants it appears to have been common for a man and a woman to contract marriage with one another, either privately or in front of friends – rarely is there any reference to parents. Studies elsewhere suggest that many servants migrating to cities had lost one or both parents. This may also have been the case in Scotland – one servant who brought a marriage claim against her former lover was supported by her two brothers as she had no parents to help her.[29] The ease and independence with which servants could enter into marriage is shown by the description of the marriage of Patrick Gourlay and Margaret Wilson in 1568. A witness said that he was present in Christen Braed's house one day when Patrick went down to the stream where her servant Margaret was washing clothes, and said to her "Since we should end this matter let us go to it". Immediately they came into the house and John Brown asked Patrick Gourlay "ar ye content to have this woman to your wyf?" and he said "Ye". And in like manner he asked Margaret if she was content to have Patrick to her husband and she said "Ye". And then John Brown said "I shall lay your hands together, lay your hips where you will!".[30]

28 David Hay Fleming (ed.), *Register of the Minister, Elders and Deacons of the Christian Congregation of St. Andrews*, Edinburgh, Scottish History Society, 1889–90.

29 V. B. Elliott, "Single Women", p. 90; D. H. Fleming (ed.), *Register of the Ministers*, i, pp. 212–220.

30 D. H. Fleming (ed.), *Register of the Ministers*, i, p. 301.

There was one other aspect of domestic service in Scotland, however, which seems to have been little discussed in studies of servants in other countries at this period, and that is whether servants, like so many other people in late medieval and early modern towns, were able to engage in more than one occupation at a time. Did servants spend their entire working time on their employer's tasks or were they able to supplement their income in other ways? Studies of women's work in several European medieval and early modern towns have suggested that many married women found it necessary to supplement the income provided by their husband's business in order to make ends meet, and that many people, men and women, engaged in more than one occupation, despite legislation against such practices.[31] Could this be true for servants as well? They might not have to support a household, but one of the main goals of a period in service was to save resources towards setting one up in the future. Did they have other ways of making money besides service? If they did, these would also be good training for later life, especially for women, who would be less likely to have one main trade.

Non-wage earnings have been examined in some studies of domestic servants but mainly in the form of room and board and perks and vails, not by-employments. It was common for servants to receive the cast-off clothing of their employers, and it has been argued that many counted on these so that they could be sold for extra income. Such clothes could also be saved by female servants as part of their trousseau. But these forms of supplemental income were dependent on the whim of the employer, and helped to underline the dependency of the servant.[32] There were also, of

31 Merry Wiesner Wood, "Paltry peddlers or essential merchants? Women in the distributive trades in early modern Nuremberg", *Sixteenth-Century Journal*, 12, 1981; M. Kowaleski, "Women's Work in a Market Town: Exeter in the Late Fourteenth Century", in Barbara A. Hanawalt (ed.), *Women and Work in Preindustrial Europe*, Bloomington, Indiana University Press, pp. 145–164. For Scotland, see H. Dingwall, *Late 17th Century Edinburgh*, pp. 79, 202; Margaret H. B. Sanderson, *A Kindly Place? Living in Sixteenth-Century Scotland*, East Linton, Tuckwell Press, 2002, p. 67.

32 Tim Meldrum, *Domestic Service and Gender 1660–1750*, Harlow, Pearson, 2000, pp. 195–205; O. Hufton, *Prospect Before Her*, p. 172; Margot Finn, *The Character of Credit. Personal Debt in English Culture 1740–1914*, Cambridge, Cambridge University Press, 2003, pp. 30, 82–84.

course, illegal means – theft by servants was a common problem.[33] But were there other legal ways to save money for a dowry?

The picture is sketchy, but it does appear that Scottish female servants could undertake other work as well. Evidence exists of them engaging in three types of activities outside the service work done for the household and craft of their employers.

These were money-lending, laundering and brewing. Money lending by servants has been noted in passing in other studies, but other separate employments have not. Most studies suggest that the employer owned all the time and labour of the servants. Merry Wiesner suggests that female servants in Europe rarely received any official time off, although London maidservants of the later sixteenth century appear to have had Sunday afternoons free.[34] Jeremy Goldberg in his study of York can find very little evidence in the records of how servants might spend any spare time although some English servants spent it in betting or playing cards, as Coventry legislation in 1452 forbade them from doing this on festival days.[35] Evidence that Scottish servants did engage in some other profitable activities – besides betting – as well as their duties to their employers, however, appears in legislation in Edinburgh in the first half of the sixteenth century.

Money Lending

The role of women in money lending has been noticed in several works on credit, and the involvement of servants has also been noted in some studies, notably in Havering in Essex.[36] Cissie Fairchilds has commented on

33 Garthine Walker, *Crime, Gender and Social Order in Early Modern England*, Cambridge, Cambridge University Press, 2003, pp. 172, 179; G. Desbrisay, "Twisted by Definition", p. 149.

34 M. Wiesner, *Women and Gender*, p. 93; A. R. Jones, "Maidservants of London", pp. 27–28.

35 J. Goldberg, *Women, Work and Life-Cycle*, p. 184.

36 Marjorie McIntosh, *A Community Transformed. The Manor and Liberty of Havering, 1500–1620*, Cambridge, Cambridge University Press, 1986, p. 63. See also Deborah

the role of French servants in money lending, although she sees it as a characteristic of the growth of a more "capitalistic" outlook among servants in the eighteenth century.[37] In fact, money lending was practised by servants much earlier than this. On a small scale, it was a common activity among women throughout Europe, in Scandinavia, Germany, England and elsewhere.[38] Wiesner suggests that German servants might invest their savings in small loans. In German cities they also had the opportunity of putting their money in a more risky investment, the city lottery. In Havering, McIntosh suggests that many servants became part of the local credit network, loaning and borrowing anything from a few pence to several pounds. As Fairchilds points out, servants would gain experience in managing money and credit in their task of purchasing household supplies for their employers.[39]

In Scotland there is evidence of women money lending. Two Edinburgh women appeared in court over their practice in the 1570s. Marion Robertson lent £3 to Margaret Aitkin who had pledged one gown, one pot and a candlestick for payment. At the time of her court appearance, Marion had received 18d a week in interest for five weeks from Margaret.[40] Edinburgh widows were involved in money lending in the later sixteenth century and seventeenth centuries.[41] Such ventures were sometimes risky and the creditor might be forced to go to law to try to recover her money. As a result, the activity sometimes becomes visible to the historian.

Was money lending also practised by women servants in the sixteenth century? There is evidence that it was, although it only enters the records because of concerns about the plague in the late fifteenth and early sixteenth century. One of the commonest items to be pledged for loans was

Simonton, *A History of European Women's Work 1700 to the Present*, London, Routledge, 1998, p. 105.

37 Cissie Fairchilds, *Domestic Enemies: Servants and Masters in Old Regime France*, Baltimore, The Johns Hopkins University Press, 1984, pp. 60, 77–79.

38 William Chester Jordan, *Women and Credit in Pre-Industrial and Developing Countries*, Philadelphia, University of Pennsylvania Press, 1993, pp. 19–20, 32–33.

39 Merry Wiesner, *Working Women in Renaissance Germany*, New Brunswick, Rutgers University Press, 1986, pp. 91–92; M. McIntosh, "Servants and the Household", pp. 12, 18; C. Fairchilds, *Domestic Enemies*, pp. 78–79.

40 "Extracts from the Buik of the General Kirk of Edinburgh", in *Miscellany of the Maitland Club*, vol. 1, pp. 106–7. For another woman money-lender see *ibid.*, p. 112.

41 Keith Brown, "Noble Indebtedness in Scotland between the Reformation and the Revolution", *Historical Research*, 62, 1989, p. 271.

clothing.[42] The town authorities believed that plague could be spread by infected clothing and at times of outbreaks they attempted to control the movement of all cloth. In 1500 the Edinburgh council decreed that no servant was to take any clothing without the knowledge of the master or mistress, under pain of burning on the cheek or banishing from the town. It could be argued that "taking cloth" does not necessarily mean taking it in pledge but in 1502 a similar statute was combined with a prohibition on "wedwives", women who took pledges of any kind. In 1505 the prohibition on wedwives was repeated, although this time the prohibition was limited to cloth of any type, wool, linen, silk or other; added to this was the stipulation that no manner of servant woman, maidens or others take in pledge or lay in pledge any cloth.[43] Servant women were obviously involved in small-scale credit, and may even have taken advantage of the earlier prohibition on wedwives to take a larger share of the market for themselves, forcing the council to take official notice of them for the first time. Perhaps they also got around the earlier restrictions on cloth by accepting other articles as pledges; hence the second statute might be a response to a complaint by the wedwives that unless they were allowed to do likewise, they would lose all their livelihood to the servant women. A renewed outbreak of plague in the 1530s led to new restrictions on cloth pledges, but this time the council tried to close all loopholes by directing the restriction at "all manner of person, man or woman".[44]

Wedwives may not have been greatly respected. There was at least one wedwife in Haddington, but she and her daughter were sentenced to be banished from the town in late 1538.[45] Interestingly, in the seventeenth century, there seems to have been a relationship between wedwives and servants. In the late seventeenth century, when an employment agency was established by the town council of Edinburgh for domestic servants, it was to replace wedwives and wedmen who had earlier feed servants.[46] It appears that pawnbrokers had acted as employment agents for servants, perhaps having good knowledge of who was in the market to hire them.

Servants' conditions of employment meant that they were well set-up to engage in small-time money lending. Payment was usually in the form

42 R. A. Houston, *Social Change,* p. 43.

43 J. D. Marwick (ed.), *Records of Edinburgh*, i, pp. 78, 96, 106–107.

44 *Ibid.*, ii, pp. 44–45.

45 National Archives of Scotland [NAS], Peebles Burgh Court Records, B30/9/2, fo. 94r.

46 R. A. Houston, *Social Change*, p. 153.

of a yearly fee which would be paid at the end of the period of service, providing them with extra money which could be lent out. It was also common for part of a servant's wages to be paid in cloth, clothing and/or shoes. Janet Husband was hired by Will Mair's wife in Dundee in 1521 for 5s, an apron and a pair of shoes.[47] Female servants especially were often paid in cloth, being expected to make their own clothes. A Dumfries servant in the early seventeenth century was paid 5 merks of fee, and 4 ells of cloth, while another was paid 4 merks to purchase linen and harden to make her clothes.[48] This meant that they had goods to pledge in order to borrow as well as lend.

Unfortunately, only a few records specifically show named servants lending money, although some single women of unclear status who appear in this role could be servants.[49] Marion Wigholme servant of Thomas Reidpath in Canongate had lent silver a number of times and also given ale on credit, to a total value of £3 9s Scots to Patrick Syffeir and Gelie Mure his spouse; she went to court to recover it in 1593.[50] One servant involved in money lending was Isobel Guthrie, the servant of Walter Cousland in Stirling. In 1528 she lent money to Agnes Crag in return for a pledge for a term of three weeks. The agreement is registered in the town court with Isobel's employer standing surety for Isobel.[51] This is the only instance in these court records – does this mean that such an action by a servant was unusual in Stirling? Or were there some unusual circumstances behind this particular transaction? It is not clear. Evidence of money lending by servants does appear occasionally in other court records. Marion Dennem, servant to William Lamb in Canongate, sought to recover "lent silver" as well as payment for bread which she had furnished several times to Agnes Mak, wife of Robert Lawson.[52] Patrick Black of Dundee owed 50s to Isobel Morris, servant of George Rollok, in 1556 – it seems likely that this was a loan as no fee or purchase is mentioned.[53] This was a large sum representing more than a year's wages. In Canongate in 1592 Thomas Daill owed £10 to Bessie Aikman servant to Grissell

47 DCA, Dundee Book of the Church, fo. 29r.
48 W. Coutts, "Women, Children", p. 77.
49 Erskine Beveridge (ed.), *The Burgh Records of Dunfermline*, Edinburgh, W. Brown, 1917, p. 6.
50 ECA, SL150/1/6, pp. 86–87.
51 SCA, Stirling Council Minutes, B66/15/1, fo. 143v.
52 M. Wood (ed.), *Court Book of Broughton and Canongate*, pp. 5, 18.
53 DCA, Dundee Burgh Court, iv, fo. 27v.

McFain – this was a large enough sum that a written obligation of repayment had been drafted and was subsequently shown to the court.[54] Occasionally the debts surface in wills – the wills of a Dumfries merchant and a local farmer include debts for borrowed money (distinguished from fees) to their female servant of £40 and £15 (plus interest) respectively.[55] Most servants, however, were probably involved in very small-scale money lending and informal transactions which would be unlikely to come to court. One instance which did come before the court occurred in Canongate in 1569. Marion Louf, the servant of Janet Turnbull, had lent 13s 8d to Steven Busby in 1568. He had repaid the loan, giving it to Janet on her servant's behalf, but Janet had withheld it, and Marion had to sue her mistress in order to get the money as well as 18s in unpaid wages. Janet may have had reason for withholding the money as shortly afterwards Marion was ordered to pay her mistress 20s for damage she had suffered due to Marion's negligence in the last harvest.[56]

Marion's withheld wages (even if, in this case, justified by the circumstances) remind us that in a sense most servants were involved in involuntary money lending to their employers, through the withholding of wages, although this was partially compensated by the employer providing food and lodging.[57] Servants' wages in the sixteenth century seem to have ranged from £1 6s 8d Scots to £3 for men and 14s to £2 for women.[58] The fee for service was agreed at the beginning of the contract, but not paid until the end. Probably, as for example in Renaissance Venice, employers advanced money to their servants if they needed it before the end of the contract, and deducted it from the final payment.[59] Employers might also make loans to servants. In 1545 John Gray servant of Thomas Kinpont borrowed 32s from his master – this was a large enough amount that it was registered in the court book of Stirling to ensure repayment.[60] On the other hand, some servants made loans to their employers. Janet Somerville

54 ECA, SL150/1/7, pp. 2–3.

55 W. Coutts, "Women, Children", p. 78.

56 M. Wood (ed.), *Court Book of Broughton and Canongate*, pp. 46, 54.

57 Dennis Romano, *Household and Statecraft. Domestic Service in Renaissance Venice 1400–1600*, Baltimore, Johns Hopkins University Press, 1996, p. 147; T. Meldrum, *Domestic Service*, p. 197.

58 M. H. B. Sanderson, *A Kindly Place,* p. 38. A pound Scots was worth about 1/12 of a pound sterling by the end of the sixteenth century.

59 D. Romano, *Housecraft and Statecraft*, pp. 130–131.

60 SCA, B66/15/2, fo. 16r.

lent her mistress Alison Ramsay 4s in 1560. She had to go to court in 1561 to recover not only the loan, but also her unpaid wages for her six month's service, and her promised gift of 3s.[61] Studies of servants in Renaissance Venice and eighteenth-century France have revealed evidence of similar loans by servants to their employers.[62]

Indeed, given the problems that some servants had with their employers over money, money lending may have been the most sensible way to look after any assets they had gathered. Several had to go to court to recover money and other goods which they had left in safe-keeping, or so they thought, with their employer. Sharing rooms with other servants, it probably seemed safer to leave money and valuables with one's employer, than trying to keep them safe oneself.[63] However, this strategy could bring its own problems. Margaret Wightman of Selkirk complained to the court in 1517 that her employer's wife not only owed her 7s for her year's fee but also was holding onto 7s, a kerchief and 2 collars that she had given her in safekeeping. The court found in her favour.[64] Isobel Adeson of Perth, who had served Effie Boswell for twelve weeks in 1547, had to sue her employer for the return of a black kirtle, a pair of hose, five kerchiefs, two black collars, two linen collars, a buckram apron, and several other items of clothing.[65] Isobel may have accumulated this sizeable wardrobe as an alternative to fees, as she had agreed to serve Effie for a pair of new hose and a pair of shoes. Catherine Diksoun of Edinburgh had left clothes in a locked chest with her mistress, but had to sue her both for her property and her fee when she left her service in 1594.[66]

A study of sixteenth-century Scotland suggests that there, as in other contemporary societies, it was very common for servant's wages to be in arrears.[67] Most town courts records include cases of servants suing their

61 "Extracts from the Records of the Burgh of the Canongate", in *Miscellany of the Maitland Club*, vol. 2, Edinburgh, Maitland Club, 1840, p. 300.

62 D. Romano, *Housecraft and Statecraft*, p. 147; C. Fairchilds, *Domestic Enemies*, p. 79.

63 D. Romano, *Housecraft and Statecraft*, p. 147.

64 J. Imrie (ed.), *Court Book of Selkirk,* pp. 42–43.

65 NAS, B59/12/3, fo. 2r–v.

66 ECA, SL150/1/7, p. 139.

67 M. H. B. Sanderson, *A Kindly Place*, p. 39. For England, see A. R. Jones, "Maidservants of London", pp. 22–23.

employers for unpaid wages.[68] Legislation was passed in 1579 stating that servants' fees had to be pursued within three years[69] – the need for such a statute of limitations suggests that unpaid fees were very common indeed. In 1570 Elizabeth Wallace and her husband pursued her former mistress Elizabeth Ker for her wages for five half-year terms, a total of £5, for Wallace's service to Ker in a tavern. Sometimes disputes over unpaid wages could turn ugly. On 14 August 1570 Alison Snype, who owed her servant Katherine MacNab 6s of her fee, struck Katherine on the head "to the effusion of her blood in great quantity" – a court ordered Snype not only to pay the unpaid fee but also fined her for assault and ordered her to make amends to her servant.[70]

Wills from the seventeenth century show that most people making wills had lent out money during their lives – the wills are biased towards the elite, but it seems likely that the practise of making small loans was common at all levels of society. There were servants among those making wills in early seventeenth-century Dumfries.[71] A study of the Panmure estates in Forfarshire in the seventeenth century concluded that unmarried servants along with widows and elderly people must have been major sources of credit within the community. The authors suggest that such lenders may have been more business-like because they had more limited earning power. This, along with their low social status, helped put the lending relationship on a less personal basis and made it more attractive to those who had to borrow.[72] It seems likely that urban servants might play a similar role, although probably some money lending went on between servants as well. A recent study of sixteenth-century testaments shows some servants dying with debts owed to them. Katherine Watson who

68 For example, NAS, Burntisland Council Records, B9/11/1, fos. 51v–52r; ACA, Aberdeen Council Register, vol. 9, p. 356; DCA, Dundee Burgh Court vol. 4, fo. 140r; NAS, Haddington Burgh Court, B30/10/1, fo. 150r.

69 J. Irvine Smith, "The Transition to the Modern Law 1532–1660", in *Introduction to Scottish Legal History*, p. 35.

70 M. Wood (ed.), *Court Book of Broughton and Canongate*, pp. 280, 262.

71 W. Coutts, "Women, Children". See also H. Dingwall, *Late 17th Century Edinburgh*, pp. 113–4, 273.

72 Ian D. Whyte and Kathleen A. Whyte, "Debt and Credit, Poverty and Prosperity in a Seventeenth-Century Scottish Rural Community", in Rosalind Mitchison and Peter Roebuck (eds), *Economy and Society in Scotland and Ireland 1500–1939*, Edinburgh, John Donald, 1988, pp. 75–76; W. C. Jordan, *Women and Credit*, p. 35.

died in 1585 had lent out money which was still unpaid at the time of her death.[73]

Much money lending in towns was small-scale and servants could thus provide a crucial service for the poor households of the town. Studies of women borrowers in European towns in the late medieval/early modern period have suggested that they usually borrowed from the lower levels of society, although not the lowest.[74] Servants would fit this category well.

Money lending was an activity which could be carried out without devoting a lot of extra time to it, unless of course it went wrong and a debtor had to be taken to court. What about laundering, the second of these extra activities?

Laundering

Like money lending, laundering (of clothes, not money) was an activity that many women, married and unmarried, engaged in, not only for their own families but also for payment. Unlike money lending it was an almost exclusively female employment. It was a very common task for domestic servants, and it usually took place away at the nearest stream or loch, some considerable distance from the house and the supervision of employers. Hence the marriage proposal mentioned above, between Patrick Gourlay and Margaret Wilson in 1568, when Patrick went to the stream to approach Margaret away from her master and mistress.

Some servants took advantage of these conditions to earn themselves extra money by doing the washing of people outside their employer's household. As well as the family laundry, they might wash, as the Edinburgh town council put it, "this woman's collar and that woman's kerchief". They collected the extra laundry by the town gate as they went out beyond the walls to the washing places. Once again, it is thanks to the threat of plague that this activity becomes visible. In May 1530, the Edinburgh council, determined to keep out all infected cloth from any possible source, forbade servants to wash any clothes other than that belonging to

73 M. H. B. Sanderson, *A Kindly Place*, pp. 62–63.
74 W. C. Jordan, *Women and Credit*, p. 43.

their employers. The ordinance does not seem to have been entirely successful as it had to be repeated again in December of that year.[75] Edinburgh may have been a particularly good source of such extra work. After it became the administrative, financial and political capital of Scotland from the later fifteenth century, many nobles and churchmen kept houses there to be near the king's court, the parliament and the law courts, but as they were not there all year they might not keep a full complement of servants, and would require extra labour for such tasks as laundering.[76] Small households, as well, often needed to hire extra help to do the laundry, and may have given work to these servants. Since servants could wash extra clothes at the same time as they were doing their employer's laundry, the time spent on this does not seem to have been overly begrudged by their employers (if indeed they were aware of it).

Brewing

The third and final activity is one that was associated very strongly with women in the medieval and early modern period, and that is brewing. We probably know more about this female economic activity than most, thanks to the work of recent scholars.[77] Brewing was one of the tasks associated with housewifery; wives were expected to know how to brew, and most households had their own brewing equipment, often passed down through the generations. Because ale spoiled fairly quickly, it seems to have been the practice in many households to brew a surplus and sell the

75 J. D. Marwick (ed.), *Records of Edinburgh*, ii, pp. 44–45.

76 Rosalinda Marshall, *Virgins and Viragos, A History of Women in Scotland from 1080 to 1980*, London, Collins, 1983, pp. 151–152. On laundering generally see O. Hufton, *Prospect Before Her*, pp. 83–84.

77 Judith Bennett, *Ale, Brew and Brewsters in England: Women's Work in a Changing World 1300–1600*, Oxford, Oxford University Press, 1996; Nicholas Mayhew, "The status of women and the brewing of ale in medieval Aberdeen", *Review of Scottish Culture*, 10, 1996–97, pp. 16–21; Elizabeth Ewan, "'For Whatever Ales Ye': Women as Consumers and Producers in Late Medieval Scottish Towns", in E. Ewan and M. Meikle (eds), *Women in Scotland*, pp. 125–36.

extra to supplement the household income, then to purchase small amounts of ale until the next brewing.[78]

Women in all the Scottish burghs were heavily involved in brewing. Because ale was one of the staples of the town diet, its production and sale were heavily regulated, and as a result brewing is more visible than many other urban activities. The names of many brewers are known because they appear in the courts charged with infractions of brewing regulations.[79] The names show that brewing was an activity carried out by women at all social levels, from the wives of prosperous burgesses to poor widows.

Servants' involvement in brewing appears both in legislation and in lists of brewers. As employees, they were active in all of the processes of producing ale, from making malt, to brewing, to selling the final product. They helped the mistress with brewing ale for the household and in selling it, sometimes in the house, sometimes in the street or at the market. Female servants were often employed in taverns and alehouses to serve customers ale and wine; the alehouse keepers and taverners themselves were often women.[80] Selling drink gave them valuable retail experience that they could use later in life. Some servants handled quite large amounts of money in the course of their duties. Alison Robertson who had been hired by Mr Robert Purves to sell wine in his tavern in May 1569 also handled larger sales – in November 1569 Purves took her to court to recover £22 6s 8d she had received for wine bought by Robert Stanis.[81] In 1593 Margaret Trumbill owed £6 10s to her former mistress for ale and beer which she had sold while in her service; her mistress also recovered from her the price of some tin vessels which had been stolen forth of the cellar and tavern through her negligence. Janet Stevenson, servant of Marion Pennycuik in Leith, owed £90 to her mistress for wine accounts in 1589.[82] Selling drink also gave women experience of dealing with difficult customers. One woman in Dunfermline shut the door on a customer who had become

78 Judith Bennett, "The Village Alewife", in B. Hanawalt (ed.), *Women and Work in Preindustrial Europe*, pp. 20–36; E. Ewan, "For Whatever Ales Ye", p. 128.

79 For example, ACA, Aberdeen Council Registers, vol. 8, pp. 391, 509–10, 561; J. D. Marwick (ed.), *Records of Edinburgh*, ii, pp. 24–26, 45–46; E. Beveridge (ed.), *Burgh Records of Dunfermline*, pp. 29, 41.

80 R. Marshall, *Virgins and Viragos*, pp. 153–154.

81 M. Wood (ed.), *Court Book of Broughton and Canongate*, pp. 112–113.

82 ECA, SL150/1/7, p. 53; SL150/1/6, p. 411.

rowdy. He later sued her for not giving him the drink for which he had paid.[83]

It appears that some household heads entrusted both brewing and selling to their female servants. In Edinburgh in the late 1520s and 1530s, as part of a policy of gaining more control over the brewing industry, the town council required brewsters to provide sureties that they would observe the town statutes in brewing and selling ale. A number of men stood as sureties for their wives, but others became sureties for their servants.[84] Still others became surety for women described as their brewsters; for example, Robert Glen stood surety for his brewster in 1530.[85] This suggests that brewing may have been a full-time occupation for some women. Possibly the sureties were alehouse-keepers, who hired full-time brewsters. Unfortunately not enough biographical evidence survives for these men to determine this.

Why would employers need to provide surety for their servants in this specific activity, when in law they were already responsible for them?[86] The answer lies in the fact that some servants carried on their own brewing business, apart from their work for their employer. In 1530 the Edinburgh council discussed female servants who "brewed on their own adventure", that is, on their own initiative and at their own risk. The phrase "on his own adventure" was more usually applied to merchants engaging in overseas trading ventures. Its use in association with servants suggests that the council did not disapprove of this activity. It appears that, in return for use of her employer's brewing equipment, the servant gave a portion of each brewing to her mistress. The rest of the ale was hers to sell. The council required such servants to give sureties that they would obey the town statutes,[87] which explains why we find employers standing surety for their servants. Nor were these servants women who were hired only part-time for brewing. The legislation calls them "feed servitrices" which means full-time female servants hired for a term of at least six months.

The practice of hiring out equipment went further than this. Some women, when they left service, set up as brewsters on their own. They were helped to do this by the fact that they could hire the necessary

83 E. Beveridge (ed.), *Burgh Records of Dunfermline*, p. 132.

84 ECA, Dean of Gild Court Records 1529–1557, fos. 60r–62v, 69v–73r, 75r–78r.

85 J. D. Marwick (ed.), *Records of Edinburgh*, ii, p. 25.

86 T. B. Smith, "Master and Servant. Further Historical Outlines", pp. 215–220.

87 J. D. Marwick (ed.), *Records of Edinburgh*, ii, pp. 24–25.

equipment, perhaps even from their former employers, with whom they could continue the brewing relationship established during their time in service. The council indeed became concerned that too many women were doing this.[88] Their concerns were both economic and moral. Such women were providing competition to other brewsters, especially burgess wives; periodically towns attempted to limit brewing to burgess wives and widows, although such attempts were largely unsuccessful.[89] Even worse, though, was the fact that these former servants were living independently. Brewing provided them with enough of a livelihood to live on their own, unmarried and outside a household. "Masterless" women, as well as masterless men, were increasingly regarded with suspicion and dislike by the authorities in the sixteenth century, not just in Scotland, but throughout Europe. There were many attempts to force unmarried women to live within households by ordering them to take up domestic service.[90] In December 1597 the kirk session of Stirling ordered Janet Nicholl, the daughter of a maltman who had been living by herself, to enter into service by Whitsun. At the same time, they decreed that no other unmarried woman be allowed to dwell alone in a house.[91] The Edinburgh council ordered that no servant was to pass from service without a licence except to get married or, interestingly enough, to enter a brothel. It appears that even the morally-questionable artificial household of the brothel was preferable to women living on their own. The council also ordered that all brewsters were to own their equipment and not hire it, making it more difficult for them to raise the necessary capital to begin their brewing enterprise.[92]

The town's attempts to regulate independent women brewers were not very successful, for in 1553 the council, having found most of the town's brewsters guilty of contravening the statutes, was forced to warn those who hired out cauldrons to the brewsters that the penalty for a second violation was "the dinging [striking] out of the cauldron bottom" and that

88 *Ibid.*, ii, p. 27.

89 E. Ewan, "For Whatever Ales Ye", p. 130.

90 M. Wiesner, *Women and Gender*, p. 99; M. McIntosh, *Controlling Misbehavior in England, 1370–1600*, Cambridge, Cambridge University Press, 1998, pp. 110–111. For Scotland, see E. Ewan, "Crime or Culture? Women and Daily Life in Late Medieval Scotland", in Y. G. Brown and R. Ferguson (eds), *Twisted Sisters*, pp. 126–128; G. Desbrisay, "Twisted by Definition", pp. 138–9.

91 "Extracts from the Register of the Kirk Session of the Burgh of Stirling", in *Miscellany of the Maitland Club*, vol. 1, pp. 128–129.

92 J. D. Marwick (ed.), *Records of Edinburgh*, ii, p. 40.

this would be carried out no matter whose cauldron it was.[93] This was probably no more successful than the earlier legislation. Helen Dingwall, in her study of late seventeenth-century Edinburgh, has argued that domestic servants often sold ale as a sideline.[94]

Employers do not seem to have objected to their servants engaging in these activities; there are no complaints about servants' by-employments in the surviving sixteenth-century town records which I have examined to date. The town council of Edinburgh, comprised of employers of servants, was concerned about the spread of plague through these activities, not the work itself. All these activities could be carried on while the servant was doing work for the employer and so they were minimally disruptive. Could it be that employers may even have welcomed them as they provided an excuse for employers to pay their servants less? This would explain how servants hired for room and board only could save towards their future, without relying exclusively on their employer's generosity in providing gifts, although probably most such servants were young children whose burden of support was thereby transferred from their parents, or from the authorities in the case of orphans, to their employers.[95] It is also possible that allowing servants to make extra money helped keep them working for their employers – the London maidservants' pamphlet of 1573 warned that if employers made their life intolerable, they could always withdraw their services.[96]

All these activities, like many of women's economic undertakings, grew out of domestic duties. Those who engaged in them outside service were predominantly women. The activities were part-time, low-status, and required minimal investment. They were thus well-suited to servants' resources of time and money. A period in service, then, not only provided women with some degree of marital choice and with training in the skills needed to maintain their own households, but in its introduction to the world of by-employments, it prepared many women for a possible future role in the "economy of makeshift".

As with so many of women's activities, such work was virtually invisible in contemporary records; concerns about servants laundering for households other than the employer's, brewing for their own profit, and

93 *Ibid.*, ii, pp. 177–178.

94 H. Dingwall, *Late 17th Century Edinburgh*, pp. 150, 202.

95 D. Romano, *Household and Statecraft*, pp. 131, 140.

96 A. R. Jones, "Maidservants of London", pp. 28–9.

money lending mainly make an appearance in sixteenth-century town records because of plague regulations. Were the female domestic servants of Scotland unusual in being able to supplement their income in this way or did servants elsewhere have similar opportunities? Perhaps future studies of servants elsewhere will reveal whether it is the Scottish servant or the Scottish evidence that is unique.

The Three Colours of Domestic Service in Belgium at the Start of the Twenty-First Century

Suzy PASLEAU and Isabelle SCHOPP

Since 1975, (in)direct job creation has been one of the guidelines of the labour-market policy in Belgium. Like the other member states, Belgium is now following the collective and individual recommendations set out by the European Community. Despite a number of initiatives, Belgium is considered as a "bad pupil" by the European authorities (employment rate in 2003 at 59.6 percent as against 63.2 percent in France, 65 percent in Germany, 72.9 percent in Sweden, 75.1 percent in Denmark and 64.3 percent for the whole of the European Community). The target to be reached for 2010 is 70 percent in general and 60 percent for women. Belgium, in fact, suffers from a lower employment rate than its neighbours (under-employment of young people on account of the obligation for them to stay in school until the age of 18; of older people because of attractive early retirement regulations; but also of women over 40 and under-skilled workers) and from insufficient activity in the service sector. It would appear, however, that the latter is the sector that, at present, is the greatest employment provider.[1]

In order to increase job-demand in the service sector in general and especially in personal services, Belgian politicians must take into account recent economic, social, demographic and cultural developments that have occurred at family level and within society.[2] The rising number of work-

1 Cf. Extraordinary European Council in Lisbon on the subject "Employment, economic reforms and social cohesion – for a Europe of innovation and knowledge". Among other things, it is established that the European employment strategy must be reactivated, strengthening the guide-lines and fixing further concrete targets. Among the four areas pin-pointed figures growth of service-sector employment. See also Belgian national action plan on employment, 2001.

2 "For socio-cultural reasons, families are less available for care of the aged at precisely the time when the aging of the population and the growing demand for autonomy by old persons increase the need for care" (M. Saintrain and C. Streel, *Définir les services de proximité: une démarche prospective*, in Bureau Fédéral du Plan, *Le développement des services de proximité. Balises pour un débat*, Brussels, 1996, p. 32).

ing women, the spread of the two-income household model, the increase in the number of one-parent families, the aging of the population and the growing demand for a better quality of life give rise to new needs in day-to-day management (housework, child-minding, caring for the old or sick, goods-delivering, etc.). These needs cannot or can no longer be met in the same way as before (family, neighbours, friends) and thanks to certain traditional services organised by the public sector (but more and more strictly rationed) and now require outside assistance from the public at large. For private domestic service, there are three possibilities on offer: taking on a salaried domestic servant, employing an undeclared worker or using the "middle way" through the personal services system (*Agences locales pour l'Emploi* or local employment agencies [A.L.E] and the voucher system).[3]

As opposed to "domestic workers" defined as such because they are under contract and receive wages declared to the income tax authorities (with social security contributions/national insurance paid by the employer), there are all those who work informally (with no contract or social security) and therefore cost their employers less.[4]

Whether Belgian or of foreign nationality, many servants – if not the majority – belong to the black economy, a veritable socio-economic plague denounced by the European Parliament in November 2000.[5] For fear of losing other sources of income or of being expelled as illegal, they prefer to remain hidden, in the anonymity and indifference of the big towns; this is particularly the case for migrant domestic workers, sometimes victims of "domestic slavery", another problem discussed by the Council of Europe Parliamentary Assembly in June 2001.[6] Between these two clearly distinguished categories, other domestic workers carry on their

3 "The connection between personal services and domestic services rests on the matching of personal services with activities potentially carried out by households for themselves in the private sphere or for which they may have the technical-economic possibility of playing the role of employer" (*Ibidem*, p. 28).

4 Suzy Pasleau and Isabelle Schopp, *The role of domestic service in EU*, paper presented during the Seminar "Informal/Undeclared Work. Research on its changing nature and policy strategies in an enlarged Europe" organized by the DG Research and DG Employment and Social Affairs, Brussels, 21 May 2003.

5 Parlement Européen, "Résolution sur la normalisation du travail domestique dans l'économie informelle", 30 November 2000, *The Official Journal*, 13 August 2001.

6 Assemblée Parlementaire du Conseil de l'Europe, *Recommandation n° 1523 sur l'esclavage domestique*, 26 June 2001; *Idem*, *Directive n° 575 sur l'esclavage domestique*, 26 June 2001.

activity within the framework of the personal services system following a trajectory that is sometimes called "grey" or semi-official.

In the present chapter, we present the three colours of domestic service in Belgium (white, grey and black) through a definition, a quantification when possible, and a description of the measures adopted in their favour. In order to combat undeclared employment in domestic service, there are more and more political initiatives designed to make white domestic service financially more attractive to employers, develop grey domestic work on a wider scale and move the latter towards the formal economy. Particular attention will therefore be paid to personal services, i.e., individually oriented or family services, these being divided into five categories: housework (maintenance, cleaning, laundry and gardening), child minding (baby-sitting, caring for sick children, psycho-motricity sessions, help with school-work), care for the aged (home care, technical and administrative assistance, meal delivery), certain services related to mobility (accompaniment of persons with physical disabilities, shopping and decorating jobs (repairs, painting, tiling).

"White" Domestic Workers

The O.N.S.S. *(Office National de Sécurité Sociale)* gives the following definition: "domestic workers are persons who provide mainly manual labour in the house (laundry, ironing, cleaning, etc.) for the household needs of the employer (an individual person) or his/her family".[7]

Excluded from this category are:

- employees who – on a company's behalf – perform the same tasks in private households;
- employees who perform these tasks for a community whose members do not, strictly speaking, constitute a household (ex. a convent);
- employees who maintain the common areas of an apartment block.

7 Office National de Sécurité Sociale (O.N.S.S.), *Instructions générales aux employeurs*, February 2002, p. 27.

The O.N.S.S. distinguishes between these "domestic workers" and "other home employees", who include: "those who provide intellectual services for the household (for example, private chauffeur, handyman, gardener)".[8]

All home helps, however, are included in this definition. In order to make white domestic services more attractive – essentially to employers – several measures have been taken:

- Certain categories of domestic employees are exempted from social security enrolment. "Not declared (effectively) to the O.N.S.S. are the following: domestic employees who never work 4 or more hours per day for the employer; those who work daily 4 hours or more, but for whom the total number of hours worked at 4 or more hours per day is under 24 hours per week, for one or several employers." Hidden behind these exemptions are many ways of getting round the legislation, and so, numerous cases of non-declared domestic employees. The occupation of a live-in domestic servant is, however, always subject to O.N.S.S. declaration.
- Exemption from employer contributions for engaging a person on full unemployment benefit (for at least the last 6 months), or on social security benefit, as a household employee. "Individuals who engage a household employee are exempted, during the entire length of the contract, from employer contributions to the O.N.S.S. (with the exception of annual holiday contributions)." This exemption is limited to the recruitment of a single household employee per individual employer (Royal Decree n° 483 of 22 Dec. 1986 modified by Act of 01/11/1987, Act of 13/02/1998 and Act of 12/08/2000).

  In June 1999, the number of beneficiaries stood at 613 and for the first quarter of the year 2000, at 153. This second measure has very limited impact. This results in part from the complete exemption from employer's national insurance contributions that applies to domestic employees (or cleaning personnel) working for a limited number of hours (cf. previous measure). Moreover, one must take into account the competition of black labour and of the unemployed who work with the A.L.E.

8 *Ibidem*; "les aides familiales, aides-ménagères, gardiennes d'enfants effectuent des 'travaux directement reliés aux besoins immédiats de la personne gardée'" (Raffaëlle De Groot and Elisabeth Ouellet, *Plus que parfaites. Les aides familiales à Montréal, 1850–2000*, Montréal, Les éditions du remue-ménage, 2001, p. 60, note 3).

- Fiscal advantage for "the individual engaging a household employee (= domestic workers + other household personnel) who can thus deduct from the totality of net income (income from property, liquid assets, professional and other income) a sum corresponding to 50 percent of wages and national insurance payments" under certain conditions (Royal Decree of 10/01/1992).

  In 1999, the number of household employees stood at 154 (cf. *Rapport d'évaluation 1999 de la politique fédérale de l'emploi* drawn up by the Ministry of Employment and Labour). This third measure has also had a limited impact, for the same reasons as those given for the previous measure. Furthermore, the person engaged must have been on unemployment or social security benefit for a total of 6 months. It is therefore necessary to be in long-lasting precarious circumstances in order to have some hope of getting paid work?
- Simplification of formalities (since January 2003) with the institution of DIMONA (or Déclaration immédiate de l'emploi).

For the counting of "domestic workers", there are traditionally two types of possible statistical sources: (1) administrative sources (constituted by the different Social Security organisms which, for their own use, draw up statistics) and (2) the various general and specific censuses carried out by the I.N.S. (National Institute of Statistics). These two types of source are used in complement. The Social Security data are of a purely administrative nature as far as they result from the employer's obligation to make a quarterly declaration of all employees. The statistical data obtained are profoundly influenced by the procedure and regulations at the origin of this obligation.

- In the private sector are concerned salaried employees, working – that is bound by a labour contract – in Belgium and subject to Social Security. Not therefore included are paid workers who avoid this system (cf. existence of a specific social insurance system; non-compulsory affiliation to a social insurance system). Thus, not all domestic staff (although subject to Health/Invalidity, pension, annual holiday and Unemployment insurance) are subject to compulsory Social Security enrolment (cf. exception above). In consequence, estimations of this socio-occupational category rest on the number of "household staff" insurance policies ("industrial injury" insurance imposed by the 10 April 1971 Act) registered by the Ministry of Social Care *(Ministère de la Prévoyance Sociale)*. [The fact of subscribing to such insurance does not mean that the domestic worker is declared to the O.N.S.S. since a "household" staff" insurance is always anonymous! In the case of a more serious accident, medical expenses (hospitalisation, invalidity, etc.) can mount up quickly. If the victim is not enrolled in Social Security, the Industrial Injury Fund can attack the employer for the refund of expenses incurred by the O.N.S.S. And yet this insurance is not very expensive (€ 40-65 a year).]

Table 1. Domestic workers registered by Belgium Office National de Sécurité Sociale (ONSS)

Years	*Men*	*Women*	*Total*
1993	944	84960	85904
1994	930	84818	85748
1995	930	86580	87510
1996	1068	89398	90466
1998			93616
1999	1113	93826	94939

Source: O.N.S.S.

– *L'enquête par sondage sur les forces de travail (EFT)* (Work-force poll) [= socio-economic poll organised by the I.N.S., carried out on (48,000) households and coordinated at European level by the European Community Office of Statistics EUROSTAT. Since 1999, it has been continuous, which allows, among other things, measurement of seasonal phenomena. The main aim is to class the population of working age (15 and over) in three distinct exhaustive groups (in work, unemployed and non-working) and to provide descriptive and explanatory data on each of these categories]. This poll is addressed to all individuals independently of their occupational status. It also aims to study casual labour (it would appear, however, from the answers given, that nobody works "on the side"; there isn't any such thing as "black work"). It allows for a spontaneous declaration of the situation (thus, does a job-seeker working in an A.L.E. consider herself as a worker in work or as unemployed?). Beside these qualities and others, the results of an EFT (poll) are always marred by random variations; the answers may also be erroneous.

The *ten-year census* provides much precious information on the socio-occupational structure of the population in Belgium. In addition to the under-declaration by those questioned in the census, its main drawback is the lack of a precise definition of the socio-occupational group "domestic servants" or a list of the occupations considered (cf. use of the expression "and assimilated"). The data from the latest census (2001) not being available yet, we have to rely on those of 1991. Of the nine categories placed in the sub-group of "domestic service staff, horeca *(hotel/restaurant/catering)...*" (N° 91), let us consider two or three on the basis of occupations and type of employer mentioned in the *Code des Professions*[9]: Valets and chambermaids, servants and assimilated; child minders and home helps; domestic cleaners. [The category "cleaners, handymen, cleaning ladies and assimilated" refers to personnel employed for the upkeep of buildings.]

Table 2. Domestic workers according to the 1991 Belgium census

Categories	*Men*	*Women*	*Total*
Valets and chambermaids, servants and assimilated	274	3079	3353
Child minders and home helps			
Domestic cleaners	1483	61,855	63,338
Total	1757	64,834	66,691

Source: I.N.S., *Population censuses,* 1991. For categories, see Annex below.

According to the different sources, numbers for domestic workers differ. The analysis of official statistics (provided essentially by the I.N.S., O.N.S.S., INAMI *(Institut National d'Assurance Maladie et Invalidité)*, etc.) on "domestic workers" circulating within the formal economy are at fault through manifest under-estimation.[10]

9 Issued in 1993, the *Code des Professions pour le recensement de la population et des logements au 31 décembre 1991*, Brussels, pp. 115–117, gives detail of each category and identifies the employers' sector of activity. Thus, the category "valets and chambermaids, servants and assimilated" groups 12 occupations of which 2 belong explicitly to the "private" sector (servant and domestic). See Annex below, p. 453.

10 Already in 1964, J.-L. Yernaux, "Les taux féminins d'activité. Leur évolution en Belgique, 1866–1962", *Revue Belge de sécurité sociale*, August 1964, p. 1104, mentions the fact that for domestics there are no official statistics. We must therefore be satisfied with estimations.

"Black" Domestic Workers

As to black labour ("moonlighting" or work "on the side"), there is no clear juridical definition. In fact, this general terminology is used to designate very different situations:

- Clandestine employment of foreign workers in violation of the law regulating foreigner's rights;
- Employment of workers not declared to compulsory social insurance;
- Undeclared employment enjoyed by a worker who is on unemployment benefit or who has other private social insurance;
- Work carried out by working men/women during their free time, in violation of a collective agreement;
- Work carried out under a false denomination (by wrongly-called self-employed persons);
- Employment of workers who have not been declared to the fiscal authorities either by the employer or the employee.

By definition a shady phenomenon, black labour cannot really be apprehended in quantitative terms since it eludes official statistics.

Black labour affects various sectors: building and horeca sectors, the garment industry, horticulture, taxi companies, cleaning firms, the personal services sector (housework, child minding, etc.). If it is convenient for employers, it is also convenient for employees, but not always. No regulation protects the latter: no guaranteed minimum wage, no notice in case of "dismissal", no paid holidays, etc. While the unemployed person who is caught risks a suspension of his/her rights for a limited period, the clandestine foreign worker risks expulsion.

In October 1999, Laurette Onkelinx, Minister of Employment and Labour, presented a directive on the battle against illegal working. She distinguished between the two facets of "black" labour. The micro-economy presents the visible facet. This concerns the non-working mother who minds the neighbour's children, the unemployed person who does odd jobs. For the Minister, these proximity services represent a gold-mine for employment.[11] But families cannot or will not pay the true cost of these services. The "underground" facet of black labour exists within businesses

11 *Le Soir*, Thursday 28 October 1999, p. 1.

(false self-employed, laundering...). The Minister's plan of action turns on a triple axis: action – prevention – repression. The action plan advocates intervention by local authorities through vouchers[12] and the ALE's. This means, then, a "laundering" of certain forms of black labour, made less attractive by appropriate fiscal measures (= reduction of social payments). Household demand is made "solvable" in order to satisfy the needs. As to prevention, the government has set on foot a vast campaign to inform businesses and individuals of the dangers of black labour (prosecution, imprisonment, fines). It also allows professional federations to take civil action against fraudulent companies and grants law-abiding businesses a social label. As to repression, it will particularly target black labour networks often linked to organised crime. The battle against the exploitation of illegal workers will also be stressed.

On 10 October 2000, a Report on the normalisation of domestic labour in the informal economy [*Rapport sur la normalisation du travail domestique dans l'économie informelle*] (by Miet Smet, PPE-Belgium representative) was examined and voted by the Commission of women's rights and equality of opportunity of the European Parliament. It mentions the legislation of several member states (United Kingdom, Italy, Portugal), and advocates the elaboration of a European definition of domestic labour (which must be recognized as a full occupation and figure in employment guide-lines). It also wishes to see produced and updated statistics on the phenomenon of undeclared domestic labour. It further establishes the fact that workers as well as employers must be informed of their rights and obligations with regard to the work-contract. It proposes a series of measures to combat the growing proportion of undeclared domestic workers (simplification of administrative formalities concerning declaration of engagement to be carried out by private employers, a fiscal deductibility for domestic services in order to reduce the cost-disparity between "black" and declared employees). Because of the large number of migrant women employed in this sector, the Commission recommends the setting up of specialized reception centres responsible for providing the necessary help in drawing up a file for the procedure leading to a temporary residence permit.

Most foreign domestics are employed at home and work for international diplomats and functionaries or for single individuals. Some of these

12 *Ibidem.*

migrants can be truly considered as domestic slaves. The Committee against Modern Slavery (CCEM) has laid down five criteria which demonstrate the difference between an international domestic and a slave:

- Identity papers (generally the passport) are confiscated by the employer. The worker is thus deprived of all legal existence and finds him/herself in a state of total dependence;
- the domestic slave is sequestrated and fear of the police is inculcated;
- he/she works 15 to 17 hours a day, seven days a week and receives little or no wage;
- his/her living conditions are contrary to human dignity (no private room, little food, beating and sexual exactions);
- family ties are broken and isolation is complete (the domestic does not have a mastery of the language of the country he/she is living in).

In May 2001, the Council of Europe paid special attention to domestic slavery. Like the European Parliament, it noted that domestic services are increasingly ensured by migrant women and that many of them find themselves in a state of slavery. It recommends setting up a vast campaign of prevention in the domestic migrants' original countries (whatever the risks run by the workers), the creation of an indemnity fund for the victims and legal measures in country of destination (protection of victims and repression of slavery). The Council of Europe also favoured the introduction of a domestic charter elaborated by the RESPECT network.[13] This charter would give the possibility of restoring dignity to domestic workers by recognising domestic work as authentic labour and instituting rules to be respected as to work contract, wages, hours…

Even if there is no doubt that the main activity of migrant women is domestic labour, its irregular nature makes it difficult to quantify. In Belgium there are no official figures that could give a precise idea of the number of foreign servants. In an attempt to better grasp the phenomenon,[14] a campaign has been inaugurated by *Solidarité mondiale* (World Solidarity), an association originating from the Christian Workers' Movement (M.O.C.), with petitions saying "Give a face to international

13 This European network created in 1998 groups individuals and migrant workers' organisations, and fights for the respect of migrant domestics (illegal or not).

14 See S. Pasleau and I. Schopp, "'Late and early' legislation for domestic workers in Belgium in the twentieth century", *Proceedings for the Servant Project*, vol. III (seminar in Barcelona, December 2002).

domestic staff". The M.O.C. puts at 8,000 the number of Philippine servants working in Belgian families. In Antwerp, the Indian diamond merchants employ servants from their own country. In Brussels, Polish cleaning ladies are in great demand. In this case, it is a question of external staff who make frequent visits to Poland. The *Solidarité mondiale* campaign concerns the totality of international domestic staff suffering from exploitation, not only cases of slavery.

"Grey" Domestic Workers

Since the end of the 1980s,[15] initiatives have therefore been taken in Belgium to compensate for the weakness or incapacity of private sector enterprises in responding satisfactorily to the personal service needs of households (home help, child minding, care of the aged, etc.). Since neither the public nor the private sector seems adequate as a direct producer or supplier, public authorities must themselves encourage or favour this type of work. They must, however, act in logical steps: the sector's poor development being mainly due to socio-cultural reluctance, they should, firstly, adopt a local awareness-heightening policy; since the absence of a market results from a lack of supply, they must then organise the production of such services themselves, that is develop a technical, administrative, legal and financial, etc. backing for structuring the supply; since the development of personal services is hampered by the lack of "solvency" in the demand, they must, finally, ensure a low, or at least a lowered, cost of the service (subsidies to either demand or supply). By developing day-to-day personal services, the public authorities stimulate demand among the final interior economic agents: households.[16]

15 Cf. 1995 Belgian government declaration and Belgian pluri-annual employment plan, October 1995, following the 1993 European Commission White Paper and the December 1994 Essen Summit.

16 "In national accounting, households are both producers and consumers of services when the workers are directly subordinate to them and they therefore assume responsibility for payments and are subject to legal employer obligations (insurance, national insurance contributions, etc.)." These elements correspond to the definition of domestic services (M. Saintrain and C. Streel., p. 15).

Personal/Proximity Services

Since no accepted definition yet exists of the general concept of "proximity services", let us quote a chance example. They "designate services to individuals or collectivities relating to the framework and activities of daily life". They group various activities: home deliveries, preparation and/or delivery of "meals on wheels", local transport in rural areas, development of multi-service centres in desertified or outlying zones, cleaning and home help, laundry, ironing, sewing jobs, upkeep and minor house repairs, garden upkeep, assistance to disabled persons, aid to old people, tele-care, care of the sick, administrative and social assistance, school-work support, psychological aid, local security, house-minding and looking after domestic animals, reinsertion policy on an economic basis, renovation of public housing, patrimony conservation, recycling of waste, tourism, certain cultural activities, etc. This long list shows that "proximity services" designate not only activities taking place within the private sphere but also, and increasingly, outside it. In particular, the use of "black" labour goes to prove that households are not prepared, without some financial incentive, to pay high enough prices to make some of these activities viable in the formal economy. This is of course the case for everything connected with housework and domestic service!

Proximity services belong to the new sources of employment (defined in 1995 by the European Community), covering, however, a wider area (example, new information and communication technologies, identified as new sources of employment in the leisure field, are never quoted among proximity services). They constitute a "transversal" activity sector insofar as service providers may belong to either the public or the private sector (and, within the latter, be paying or not). Moreover, they generate an added social value by responding to new needs. Integrating these new services into the regular economic circuit requires them to be revaluated as real work, indispensable to society. They must be quality services but also accessible to the greatest number. Accessibility is then guaranteed by a social pricing system presupposing that proximity services ensure improvement in the quality of life for all.

Although the (re)insertion of the long-term unemployed does not represent an absolute priority for proximity services, it is a secondary goal to be pursued, a fortiori in a context where employment policy aims to raise the employment rate and create long-term jobs. Proximity services, in fact, offer the means of integrating risk groups into the labour market, both by the creation of new posts and by the very nature of the services offered. In the context of an economy marked by ever-increasing technology, which encourages the elimination of under-productive work, proximity services provide the low-skilled with the opportunity to become active. They demand a new type of skill, not necessarily linked to a diploma, but rather social, relational and communication capacities. It is also necessary to ensure continuation of these jobs. The needs to be satisfied are numerous and among them, some are no doubt met through the informal, black circuit.

At present, proximity services show a diversity of both demand and offer, which does not always make their development any easier. This development, however, does not follow the same course as the production of traditional goods/services: it is more an interactive process between different local actors (users, informal circuits, workers). Several Member States have encouraged personal services, mainly through subsidies, fiscal or para-fiscal deductions, etc.: *service vouchers* linked to a dependence-insurance which allows individuals to be aided by home services in Germany; the *service-voucher* for home services, the *employment-service voucher* for personal care, available from recognized organisations, and the *work-voucher* (experimentally, at local level) proposed to aged or less able persons for helping services (accompaniment or delivery of home meals) in France; the *service-voucher* for child minding in Finland and in Great Britain; the *"home-service voucher"* for housework services in Denmark; the *"banenplan"* in the Netherlands, etc.

From the historical point of view, the desire of the Belgian public authorities to develop home help (housework) and child-minding services gave rise to subsidies designed to develop these services. These subsidies helped the providers of these services to become professionalised. In the context of the socio-economic crisis in the eighties (massive unemployment, big budget deficits), a new direction was taken in public authority policy: priority was given to measures in favour of job creation and reduction of unemployment figures. The providers of housework and child-minding services were thus confronted with a reduction in structural subsidies. Today, the development of proximity services as a whole faces a state of permanent uncertainty as to means of financing. Moreover, the cost of these services is often higher than what the user is willing or able to pay. After a brief experiment with "service-vouchers" and parallel with A.L.E. development, the federal government, together with the Regions, finalised in 2001 and 2003 a proposal for the introduction of new vouchers.

The Local Employment Agency System (A.L.E.)

A.L.E creation in "communes" (local authority areas) or groups of communes (since 1987 and particularly since 1994) aims to satisfy, on one hand, the demand for a certain number of activities not to be found in the regular work circuits and which do not compete with the latter, and, on the other, the demand for employment by long-term unemployed persons, those on minimum benefit and some of those on social benefit, who have difficulty in finding their place in the labour market. These persons are allowed to receive, on top of their benefit, a net hourly wage of 3.72 euros for working in clearly defined activities. Time worked concurrently with the drawing of benefit is limited to a maximum of 45 hours per month. The user (individuals, local authorities, education establishments and non-profit associations [ASBL]) buy from the A.L.E. vouchers of a value ranging from € 4.96 to € 7.44 for one hour worked. This sum is exonerated from para-fiscal payments and is deductible up to a maximum of € 1983.15 a year. For individuals, the work that can be carried out concerns: help with housework (laundry, ironing, dish-washing, cleaning, cooking, etc.), help with gardening jobs, help with child-minding, accompanying children or sick persons, help with carrying out administrative formalities. Long-term unemployed persons (after two years on benefit or six months if the recipient is over 45) are automatically enrolled in an A.L.E. (young persons new to the labour market, persons on minimum benefit and older unemployed persons may also enrol). Since 1 January 2000, the A.L.E. is the employer of workers enrolled in an A.L.E. and the latter are given a permanent written labour-contract.

Some statistical data: at 30 June 2000, 99 percent of the 589 Belgian communes have an A.L.E.; 81 percent of those working for an A.L.E. are women. In 1999, one person works on average 29 hours per month, which makes a total of 12,632,441 hours, equivalent to 7,315 full-time jobs! Work-offers are made by 74 percent of individuals (46 percent of these activities concern help with housework, 4 percent help with gardening, 1 percent child-minding or help with sick persons, 49 percent in mixed activities).

Table 3. Persons working in the A.L.E. system

At 30 June	*Men*	*Women*	*Total*
1995	2655	8153	10.808
1996	4097	15.339	19.436
1997	5264	20.835	26.099
1998	6852	28.240	35.092
1999	7500	31.000	38.500
2000	7578	32.471	40.049
2001	6213	31.467	37.680

Source: O.N.E.M.

The political vision behind the A.L.E. system is two-fold. On one hand, to save from exclusion a certain number of long-term low-skilled unemployed, who are the hardest to re-employ. On the other, to anticipate latent requirements for proximity services, needs which are at present unsatisfied because of their too high cost, or which are provided for in the informal circuit. The system has largely responded to these expectations: it allows some extra income to quite a large number of unemployed (see table) and also brings new activities into the regular or formal circuit. Moreover, it proves advantageous on account of its wide flexibility: job-seekers who are difficult to re-employ can again be motivated to accept work because it can be done in a sufficiently flexible way and within a globally limited length of time.

The initiatives taken do not, however, meet with unanimity in public opinion. Publicity campaigns organised by the A.L.E.s, which have popularised the figures of *"Gaston au gazon et Sabine à la cuisine"* ("Sean in the lawn and Karen in the kitchen") have crystallised the controversy and resulted in sometimes virulent argument, in particular within parliamentary debate. The promotion of proximity services marks a direction, both topical and disputed, in economic and social policy. The A.L.E. voucher lowers the cost of work but is often negatively perceived because it causes confusion between proximity service employment and casual labour, "odd jobs" with no permanence or proper statutes.

On account of the relatively "generous" conditions awarded to the unemployed who work for an A.L.E., this system also reinforces, in large measure, the risk of a financial employment-trap, so that transfer from an A.L.E. to a regular circuit is not easy. The financial incentive for transfer from the (semi-official) A.L.E. worker status to the regular labour-market is too modest, even inexistent [the change from an A.L.E. activity, even a limited one, to a part-time job in the regular circuit is of no financial advantage! One-parent or one-income families also nearly always see a loss of income when accepting a part-time job in the regular circuit]. Moreover, the financial traps are intensified by the fact that an unemployed person working in the A.L.E. system can remain there permanently. Finally, a recent government initiative designed to encourage employers to take on A.L.E. workers in the regular circuit through an activation allocation of € 495.79 per month does not increase the incentive for the A.L.E. worker himself to make the change.

In the opinion of some, the A.L.E. system creates "new servants". The A.L.E. employee is considered as a worker but some important rights considered as established are brought into question. Thus, according to the 7 April 1999 Act, no wage is due during non-working periods of the A.L.E. contract (art. 17 and 19): the worker has no right to a wage in case of sickness or accident or, similarly, if he is absent when responding to a job-offer or for family reasons; the 4 January 1974 Act concerning public holidays is not applicable to A.L.E. workers (art. 25); the 4 August 1996 Act concerning welfare of workers (appropriate clothing) is not applicable (art. 27), etc.

The New Voucher System

So far, the efforts made by public authorities in order to ensure solvency in the demand for personal proximity services have hardly been convincing (cf. experiment with service-vouchers (1999) limited for a few months to interior decoration and terminated on account of soaring budget costs).

In early May 2001, the Federal government – following the lead of numerous foreign countries – approved a draft bill on the development of a service voucher system which would constitute an alternative for services generally rendered by the black economy. The purpose is clear: the service-voucher system aims to promote the use of proximity-services helpful to households. These are new services, highly labour intensive, in which there is a call for low or medium-skilled workers. Unlike the A.L.E. system, they provide paid work created by businesses which have to be approved by the Regions.

For the consumer, the service vouchers are comparable to A.L.E. vouchers. He buys service-vouchers from an issuing body (€ 6.20 an hour) and with these, he can pay someone for three types of personal proximity services: home housework, home child-minding and minding of aged, sick or disabled persons. The worker (occupied at least part-time on the basis of a normal work contract) hands in the voucher to his enterprise, which is approved by the public authorities for offering proximity services, as proof of his activities. This enterprise can be either an A.S.B.L. or a private enterprise. It sends the voucher to the issuing body which pays the enterprise with a cheque covering the real cost of the service given (+/- € 23.55 an hour). The difference between the amount paid by the consumer and that paid by the enterprise is made up by the public authorities.

This project raises, however, some more questions: how far does this system guarantee equal access for all citizens, or, in other words, is the value of a voucher adjusted according to income? How far does this system offer an optimal alignment with existing A.L.E.s? [There is the impression that as long as there is no clear vision of the future of the present A.L.E. system, the proposal will compete with the latter for recruitment. The obligation for the approved enterprises to draw up "normal" part-time work contracts is a positive measure, but it could have perverse effects on account of the shortage now existing on the labour market. A traditional work-contract offers less flexibility than the present A.L.E. regime which proposes made-to-measure work for risk-groups.] Only the future will give the answer.

In Conclusion

The emergence of proximity services in general can be interpreted as connected with a macro-economic dynamic leading a new generation of activities from the private to the public sphere, whether this movement is part of a long-term historical evolution or whether it is produced by a socio-political drive on an European scale. During the nineties, a certain disaffection or a diminished availability for household tasks became more marked within families themselves, who then had to call on other agents. Confronted with the scale of black labour in domestic services (and so, income loss for the state), Belgian public authorities have encouraged, through (in)direct aid, the A.L.E. system and the voucher system. The former aims primarily to satisfy the demand for a certain number of activities not covered by the regular labour circuit and which do not compete with it. It also supplies the demand for work by the long-term unemployed, those on minimum benefit and some of those on social benefit, who have difficulty in finding their place on the labour market. The second system directly creates employment: service-vouchers propose jobs to low or medium-skilled persons for supporting certain proximity services (cleaning and child-minding). Nevertheless, from the limited response to one or other of these systems, we cannot foresee a large-scale transfer of domestic workers from the black to the grey and then to the white economy.

References

CHADEAU, Ann and FOUQUET, Annie, 1981, *Le travail domestique, essai de quantification*, Paris, Archives et Documents, INSEE.

DUSSUET, Annie, 2001, "'On n'est pas des domestiques!'. La difficile professionnalisation des services à domicile", *Sextant*, 15–16, pp. 279–295.

La documentation française, 1998, *Emplois de proximité*, Paris.

FOUQUET, Annie, 2001, "Le travail domestique, du travail invisible au gisement d'emplois" in J. LAUFER, C. MARY and M. MARUANI (eds), *Masculin-Féminin: questions pour les sciences de l'homme,* Paris.

MATEMAN, S. and RENOOY, P. H., 2001, *Undeclared Labour in Europe. Towards an integrated approach of combating undeclared labour*, Amsterdam [Regioplan Publication nr. 424].

MOZERE, Liane, 1999, *Travail au noir, informalité: liberté ou sujétion?,* Paris, L'Harmattan.

Van HAEGENDOREN, M. and VERREYDT, G., 1993, "Informele economie in het dagelijkse leven van vrouwen", in *Onderzoekgroep sociale wetenschappen*, 8.

Annex

91 Personal Services, Horeca, ...

913 Valets and chambermaids, servants and assimilated
- 91300 Chambermaid
- 91301 Valet
- 91302 Room attendant
- 91308 Hotel servant
- 91309 Floor page (Hotel)
- 91315 Laundry maid (Hotel)
- 91320 Servant (Private)
- 91321 Domestic (Private)
- 91322 Housemaid
- 91380 Couchette attendant
- 91390 Footman
- 91391 Floor attendant

917 Child-minders and home helpers
- 91700 Governess
- 91710 Nursemaid
- 91711 Nurse (Private)
- 91731 Wet Nurse (Private)
- 91740 Child-minder
- 91750 Home helper
- 91751 Family helper
- 91752 Caring helper (for the aged)

918 Domestic cleaners
- 91850 Charlady
- 91850 Cleaning lady (domestic)

Gender, Care and Globalization as seen from Norway

Lise WIDDING ISAKSEN

An unequal division of labour at home, recruitment difficulties in the welfare state and a shortage of public services pave the way for increased commercialisation and legal and illegal immigration by women. Will the labour of poor women be the salvation of the women-friendly welfare state of the future?

At present, the welfare state is still the main supplier of those care services that are necessary for the functioning of everyday life. But the welfare state's recruitment difficulties, the growing number of women in paid employment and the commercial market's interest in producing welfare services may lead to more and more people finding new ways of solving their care problems. In the 1960s and 1970s we built up the Norwegian welfare state through the utilisation of the reserve pool of labour represented by women. This care reservoir is now exhausted, resulting in a care shortage among the population to which the commercial market, the welfare state and the institution of the family relate in different ways.

In Norway as in other western societies, we are experiencing a change in the demographic composition of the population. Improved living conditions and increased life expectancy have led to a situation where increasing numbers of children have the pleasure of growing up with both grandparents and great grandparents. The number of those over eighty is increasing and those over 85 constitute the fastest growing group. On the other hand, fertility of Norwegian women has increased and birth patterns have changed. Because today's young women take more years of education than previously, they postpone giving birth for the first time. Women in this group are the mothers of small children until they are well into their forties. In addition, we have groups of women who are now in their fifties and who gave birth when they were in their early twenties. Many of these women are grandmothers in full-time work. It is normal for the grandmothers of today's young children to be in full-time jobs. What is new is that grandmother also has a mother and/or father who is still alive and who may need help on a daily basis. In family networks, women in the 45–60 age range can be said to be sandwiched because they are in demand as care workers, both as grandmothers and as daughters. The concept of double work in this generation does not merely refer to the combination of salaried work and care work but also to the fact that they may have double care responsibilities. They may be needed both as relief in looking after their working children's children and at the same time be required to offer a "helping hand" to their increasingly frail parents.

In 1980, 45 percent of women between the ages of 40 and 54 were in full-time employment. In 1997 56 percent of the same age group were in full-time jobs, 28 percent worked between 20 and 36 hours a week and 16 percent spent between 1 and 19 hours a week in paid employment (Statistics Norway 1997).

In the 1970s, when the Norwegian Storting was debating the implementation of the new home help service, Jo Benkow described middle-aged women as "freed hands" (Isaksen 1984). He was communicating a common perception that women between the ages of 40 and 60 were an available care reservoir which could be utilised as a kind of free benefit in solving society's care problems. It was assumed that this group had grown-up children and, to a much lesser extent than today, parents who were still alive. Even though present-day reality is quite different, public debate about issues of social policy indicates that the realities of the employment situation nonetheless do not seem to have sunk in. The care reservoir is no longer available and this has a number of social implications.

Firstly, it means that the help previously provided by daughters in the family network has now been reformulated as a demand for public care. Secondly, it means that since public care is not capable of satisfying the increased demand, present-day families are overburdened by care duties. In other words, we are dealing with an increasing gap between supply and demand, both of formal and informal care services. Central social institutions like the family, the commercial market and the welfare state have adjusted to this situation in different ways, depending on the type of care in question.

Absent Fathers and Sons

We have not succeeded in solving the problems of gender equality in the division of labour within families. It is still women who bear the main responsibility for housework and care work at the same time as they pursue full-time careers. "Absent fathers" still constitute a major problem in the everyday lives of families with small children. When it comes to the family's care for elderly fathers and mothers in need of help, the picture is one of "absent sons". The division of labour is even more unequal here than in the case of child care. While today's young fathers talk publicly about changing nappies and giving their children baths, we have still not arrived at a situation where masculine men in their forties and fifties can talk about their experiences of changing their incontinent mothers or fathers' nappies or of helping them to take a bath.

The welfare state is characterised by a shortage of qualified labour and by the increasingly industrial organization of home-based care services. Even though more elderly people than before are receiving help, each individual elderly person receives less help. This means that the pressure on the family's care capacity is increasing.

The failure in recruitment to the care professions is particularly acute in the sector with the lowest prestige and the hardest jobs – the care for the elderly sector. There is a big shortage of nurses at precisely the time when fewer people are applying for training for such professions. According to a survey from Oslo University College, moreover, only just over half of those currently taking registered general nursing courses actually want to work with seriously ill patients after the end of their training (*Sykepleien* 19/2000). Applications for training as enrolled nurses and similar are also low. This may result in a situation where, if it became possible to shorten waiting lists for nursing homes for instance, the lack of qualified staff and financial resources might force those responsible to seek alternative solutions.

One such alternative solution may be to export elderly patients to the Mediterranean countries. Eleven municipalities in Vest-Agder are working on building apartments for the elderly in Spain. 22 municipalities want to purchase nursing home places in Bærum's planned nursing home in Altea, and Betanien nursing home in Bergen was planning to open a nursing home in the same area in the autumn of 2001. Altea's deputy mayor and head of building and development, Jacinto Mulet, wants to make the municipality a centre for Norwegian senior citizens. The municipality is short on industry and the Spanish welcome such a development because it creates jobs and income for local inhabitants (*Dagbladet*'s online edition, 1 October 2000).

Another solution is to import qualified staff from other countries. The Norwegian employment service Aetat is currently endeavouring to recruit doctors and nurses, from the Czech Republic, Hungary and Poland in particular. But active efforts are also being made in countries such as Germany, France, Italy, Austria and Finland. The employment service has also organised a separate project called "Aetat health service recruitment" and it has already recruited 1,300 health workers. An agreement has already been signed with Poland for the recruitment of nurses and active endeavours are now being made to sign agreements with the Czech Republic, Hungary and the Philippines. Norwegian diplomats are also being co-opted in the employment service's drive to recruit nurses and doctors for Norwegian hospitals. At present, the target is 500 new health workers annually. The recruitment of health personnel from other countries has been going on since 1997. Until recently it was possible to recruit health personnel from the other Nordic countries because there was a certain amount of unemployment there. Now they need their trained health personnel themselves. Pursuant to the European Economic Area (EEA) Agreement, Norway is not allowed to recruit labour actively in other EEA countries before it has been ascertained that such labour is not available in Norway. The gap between supply and demand is increasing in the EEA area too and there is no manpower reserve of health workers which can be exported. Competition for health workers is therefore increasing in the EEA area, making recruitment from countries like the Philippines more attractive (Aetat insert in *Dagbladet*, 27 March 2001, 12).

Despite the shortage of trained nurses, those who go abroad to train as nurses run the risk of the rigid set of regulations governing authorisation as Norwegian registered general nurses on their return.

Commercial Care Services

The shortage of both public services for caring for the elderly and adequate child care services at a time when families are being sandwiched in the time squeeze between work and family life, has led to the growth of services in a private commercial market. For middle class families who have not succeeded in achieving a more gender equal division of labour at home, the gender-based conflicts can be resolved by outsourcing them from the family. To avoid small daily disputes on how to divide responsibilities, firms such as City Maid help solve the problem. These problems can also be solved by employing cleaners working undeclared.

In a newspaper article about the growing new underclass, the anthropologist Marianne Lien writes about the development of informal women's networks in Oslo that help to procure cleaners from the Baltic countries, Poland and other poor countries for undeclared work. One of the cleaners she knows of is an Estonian woman who is sole provider for two teenagers. By doing housework for undeclared earnings, she manages to pay for her children's education. Her sister looks after her children while she is in Norway on a tourist visa. When she returns home, it is her sister's turn to travel to Norway to work ("Magasinet", *Dagbladet*, 21 April 2001).

According to the au pair agencies, an increasing number of families solve the problems of child care by employing a foreign au pair. It has become generally more acceptable to use the services of professional agencies such as "Alantis AuPairbyrå" and "Inter Aupair" to manage the combination of full-time employment, lack of gender equality in the home and family life. Now that care practice is no longer a requirement for training as a pre-school teacher or similar, au pairs nowadays tend to be young girls from Eastern Europe. The most frequent nationalities are Russian, Latvian, Polish, Lithuanian and Slovakian ("Magasinet", *Dagbladet*, 20 January 2001). According to the agencies, they are queuing up to come to Norway. And virtually no one wants an au pair from an African country. The normal wage for an au pair is between NOK 2,500 and 4,000 per month.

Not only private families come up with private solutions to narrow the gap between the supply and demand for care services. More and more employers are offering their employees services as fringe benefits. Two years ago Postbanken launched its quality-of-life package. It offers flexible schemes for parents of small children and help with cleaning, ironing, folding clothes, changing beds, window cleaning etc. In Telenor, female managers (not male) are offered help at home so that the time thus freed can be experienced as an improvement in their quality of life in general and their enjoyment of work in particular (*Dagbladet*, 30 March 2001).

Since there is also a shortage of flexible public care services for the elderly, firms like "Human Omsorgsassistanse (Humane care assistance)" in Stavanger have sprung up. In return for a fee of NOK 200 per hour they sell "surrogate child services", i.e. they sell services to people who do not have the time to accompany their elderly mother or father to the doctor's or hairdresser's. According to the firm's owner, the market for such services is growing.

"Falken Husvenn (Falken house friend)" is another firm. It markets itself as "a good friend of the family". In a full-page advertisement for this firm (BT, 24 November 2001) there is a photo of an old lady who wants "someone's company to enjoy, someone to laugh with and someone to help with the preparations for get-togethers of old friends". She says that her children visit "quite often", but she misses having someone to talk to. Falken Husvenn provides services "in which everything is done to promote personal contact and assistance". The services are based on *security, care, professional health services and practical help*. The house friends are intended to be "like a friend of the family".

The most recent addition to such market-based services is "Hjelp (Help) 24" which is a service offered by the insurance company Gjensidige NOR. They offer help with housework, gardening, cleaning, preparing meals and changing car tyres. From 1 January 2001, Akademikererne's home contents insurance (available through membership of the Norwegian Association of Researchers) was extended to include membership in "Hjelp 24". The insurance company If Skadeforsikring has recently launched the service "Handverkeren (Craftsman)" whereby company craftsmen help customers to wallpaper the bathroom and build a new patio if they should need it (*Dagbladet*, 3 April 2001).

The Status of Care Workers

Among young women of today there are few who envisage their lives including long periods at home. Most of them see themselves combining children and family life with stable careers. Care work at home has always carried low status, but now the status of public paid care work is also falling. The recruitment difficulties in the health sector are an acute expression of this.

In a recently published book called *Modermordet (Matricide)* (Bakken 2001) it is claimed that one of the reasons that so few people want to become nurses is that it is not perceived to be particularly attractive to be identified with the "caring mother figure". The emergence of this cultural shift at a time when the need for carers is increasing may have dramatic consequences. "The natural link between women and nursing has been broken", says the author. To be caring and other-oriented is fast becoming associated with having failed in one's self-realization project. These characteristics appear to be linked to a loser identity. But the signals in this area are contradictory and multifarious.

Bente Slaatten, head of the Norwegian Nurses Association, claims that nurses do actually *want* to be nurses but that poor wages, disgraceful working conditions and extra shifts are tiring people out. Surveys carried out by the Nurses Association show that the vast majority wants to work in the field in which they have been trained and that it would be possible to get 10,000 nurses to return to work with patients if wages and working conditions were improved.

Given the gender-based division of labour in the family and the price of pre-school services, many women nurses find that they are left with a pittance once nursery school fees and transport costs have been paid. Higher wages and bigger increments for evening and night work may, however, bring more nurses back to the nursing sector, claim nurses interviewed in the newspaper *Bergens Tidende* (4 April 2001).

Since normal collective bargaining has not succeeded in satisfying demands for better wages and working conditions, new methods are being tried out. Laila Dåvøy, former Minister of Labour, leader of the Norwegian Nurses Association and now employed by the temporary staffing agency Olsten in Bergen, now wants to employ health personnel under private sector auspices and to enter into agreements with institutions and hospitals or municipalities. She believes that this will mean public savings in terms of resources because it takes time and effort to hire temporary staff. ECON reports, however, show that it costs employers NOK 230,000 *more* per man-year to hire nurses from agencies compared with a normal nursing man-year. Whether or not this figure is correct is perhaps not so important in the context. For individual nurses the most important factor may be that by allowing themselves to be employed and hired out by Olsten Norsk Personal they can increase their earnings by NOK 75,000 per year (*Bergens Tidende*, 4 April 2001).

Recruitment difficulties and changed perceptions of the value of care work are both expressions of a process of change taking place in both the public and private care cultures. And they are changing because of other, more far-reaching social changes such as increased individualization, greater market orientation and globalization of the economy.

Individualisation

One of the most fundamental characteristics of care work is its orientation towards others. To help others who are incapable of managing on their own and to do so in a manner which does not insult the person being helped is an important ethical principle. Today, the majority of women state that they are in paid employment because they want to realise themselves and lead a meaningful life. This meaningful self-realisation is linked to the ideals of stimulating challenges and lifelong learning. The foundation of the care profession can in many ways be said to go hand in glove with "a meaningful life" if one finds contributing to helping people who need assistance rewarding and interesting. But, if care becomes primarily a question of what a meaningful life is to *me*, then we are looking at an inverse care motive (Bakken 2001). If it is true that today's young people find it unattractive to be identified with "the caring mother figure", this may contribute to reinforcing a cultural crisis which will have its strongest impact on the welfare state but which will also have consequences for the gender-based division of labour within family networks. The employment of women outside the home has come to stay. Former care cultures in families and in the welfare state were and still are based on one sex making itself available to meet the needs of others. This will to sacrifice is now in the process of disappearing. This cultural capital is basically in the process of being exhausted (Bakken 2001).

The fact that the care professions are both symbolically and literarily now experienced as "dirty jobs" is another expression of cultural change (Isaksen 1996). Today, the majority of university students are women and they are studying subjects such as law, social sciences, the arts and medicine. They do not regard themselves as care providers either at home or outside the home. For the welfare state on the other hand, which has now entered a period in which services are being rationalised and costs cut, efforts are being directed at emphasizing the family's moral responsibility or "utilising the family's own care resources" as it is referred to in the parlance of the care and nursing bureaucracy. In practice this means that they are looking for greater effort from women. But why are men not included in this picture?

A survey of unemployed young men in several European countries shows that a majority preferred continued poverty and unemployment to a job in the care sector (*The Economist*, 28 September–4 October 1996). As regards men who *have* chosen care jobs such as nursing, not many stay for long by the hospital bed. They frequently end up in specialized departments such as intensive care and surgery, i.e. in departments which carry high status because they use advanced technological equipment and which are in harmony with masculine ideals (Vigdal 1995). Men working in female professions are often regarded as "weak" and unsuited to "real work". SINTEF researchers who evaluated the project "Bevisste utdanningsvalg (Conscious educational choices)", a project aimed at getting boys to make untraditional choices, concluded that cultural opposition was the greatest hinder to endeavours to get more boys to make untraditional choices (Buland and Havn 2001).

Male nurses sometimes face ridicule from other men who regard care work as "washing bums and carrying bedpans". They also find intimate care problematic because of its associations with homosexuality and because patients prefer female nurses to perform physically intimate work.

Now however, male nurses have taken up the challenge and organised themselves in the Norwegian Association of Male Nurses which was founded on 24 November 2000. The founders claim that while the majority of male nurses are their families' main providers, the majority of female nurses work part-time. The organisation's main aim is to achieve higher (providers') wages. They claim that female nurses are an employer's dream because they "bow and scrape and prefer not to mention money", says press spokesman and founder of the association Geir Kåsa to *Bergens Tidende*, 3 March 2001.

Globalization

The individualization and globalization of our culture creates several scenarios for the future of care solutions. If attempts to solve the division of labour between women and men in the home do not succeed and women are no longer able or willing to work double, this could lead to an increase in the market for both legal and illegal services. For middle class men (and increasingly also women) whose ideals are based on conceptions of making a career in a culture dominated by global "business class" masculinity, it may be difficult to combine this with being a stable father, son and husband. A good income may make it possible to buy oneself out of domestic gender-equality conflicts by hiring domestics, au pairs, professional "house friends" and cleaners, with the consequences this might have for one's own emotional and social feeling of belonging, for the children and the rest of the family. In the 1950s the "problem of seamen's families" was a central issue among researchers into the family. Then, it had to do with young boys' lack of stable role models and the adjustment difficulties that followed in its wake. The sociologist Erik Grønseth and several of his colleagues started a project dealing with how it might be possible to achieve spouse-divided working hours in order that both mothers and fathers could spend more time overall with their children and families. Fifty years later, we are facing a different reality, but we have still not managed to solve these problems.

It is also possible that several differentiated public and private care cultures may emerge. The welfare state will possibly take the form of an hourglass in which fewer people stay in the middle section, more people become upwardly socially mobile and more people experience downward social mobility. The latter may become the servants of the upwardly mobile. If we can use the metaphor of a "bath" to describe this, it could be said that the contrasts are between those occupying the upper levels, who take "luxury baths" in well-being centres with access to aroma therapy baths, colour therapy, massage baths etc., thus contributing to relaxation and well-being after a strenuous working day and those at the bottom on the other hand – the elderly who are bathed by community nurses and care workers, are bathed for reasons of hygiene every other week, and then in combination with what are called "evacuation days", i.e. days on which the care patrol arrives in the morning and administers an enema then returns later in the forenoon to "empty the user" after lifting him/her on to a chair whose seat is in the form of a toilet bowl. Then the elderly person is wheeled or carried to the shower and washed in a rather industrial manner. They are washed by people wearing knee length plastic stockings and throwaway gloves. What little bodily contact they experience is the feeling of heat from a hand protected by plastic.

Care work may come to be perceived as immigrants' work. Some might legitimize this by claiming that "immigrants come from cultures in which they really respect the elderly. That is why they are more suited to it than we are". This is most probably a case of the values of motherliness, warmth and care becoming associated with images of subjugation and the will to sacrifice. These values stand in opposition to individual self-realisation as young (post) modern individualists seem to understand it.

The import of care-providing women from poorer countries can be explained in numerous ways. As regards the import of nurses from Poland, the employment service Aetat says that "countries like Poland have expressed a desire to export health personnel because this could clear a path for the export of labour from other sectors in which Poland has major unemployment problems. Moreover, many of the nurses and doctors will return home having gained new experience" (*Dagbladet,* 10 March 2001).

The export of care workers has already become a growth industry for poor countries. In the 1990s, 55 percent of Philippine emigrants were women. Alongside the electronics industry, the money sent home by these women is the country's largest source of foreign currency (Hochschild 2001). The group of islands is also building up its own educational institutions which are being tailored to meet the demand for care workers in western countries.

But what kind of cultural capital are we importing? Is it "just" manpower? One aspect is the moral issue related to our helping to empty poor countries of health personnel they need themselves. Another less-debated aspect is linked to the question of how the lack of solutions to gender-equality projects in private homes and our hesitation to pay (well enough) for public services, may help to create "absent mother" problems in the care cultures from which we import this labour. To put it bluntly one could say that the West's "absent father" problems are being solved by creating "absent mother" problems in poor countries. Even though it is poverty that is the driving force behind this phenomenon, it should not under any circumstances be the only way in which women can provide for their families. However, this does not free western countries from a certain moral responsibility. This could be said to be today's global dimension to the old slogan that "the private sphere is also political". Norwegian families choosing to keep peace at home by employing someone else to do work that may cause conflicts, may well be contributing to robbing children in the Third World of their mothers' presence in everyday life. In the terminology of globalization this is an example of "stretched social relations", i.e. how the sum of the decisions made in social relations at the micro-level in one country can lead to both institutional and individual consequences in countries on the other side of the world.

If we look back at the history of various types of labour import, we could in somewhat oversimplified terms say that the slave trade was about the import of muscle power/manual labour; the import of IT expertise from, for instance, India could be said to be part of a kind of brain drain of the Third World and the import of care labour is a form of "mother theft". This may mean that care is regarded as a commodity or a kind of competence that can be imported and exported on a par with other goods and services. But the import of care workers is distinct from the import of other types of labour in that those who come are brought here to take care of small children and people who are ill or dying. This requires more than technical or professional competence alone. Both public and private care work is rooted in the deepest emotional structures of our culture and is about how we relate to human dignity, shame, pain and suffering.

So far, we know little about what conceptions are associated with the import of care workers. It is not necessarily only rooted in the conception that it does not matter who performs the work as long as it is done in a medically and technically adequate manner. It may also be based on the view that some cultures' care workers are better suited than others. The fact that families who employ foreign domestics seem to prefer women to men and to accept women from European cultures but not from African ones, may indicate that the work is not only seen as being gender-specific but also culture-specific. In Denmark for instance, the appointment of African male nurses in the community health service gave rise to a heated debate on whether it was right to expect 85-year-old women to be washed and personally attended to by African men (Sjørup 2001).

Research Challenges

It is no accident that this article is primarily based on information gleaned from daily newspapers. It reflects the fact that there is a lack of systematic empirical research on how the commercial market forces are actively positioning themselves in relation to the problems of the welfare state and the family. The relationship between the state and the market is undergoing change and we know little about what groups are being targeted by commercial service providers, who is being appointed to the jobs being created and what rights they are being offered.

On the level of principle, the challenge is not merely to the idea that care for society's dependants is a collective responsibility that should be organised by the public sector and be based on those performing and those receiving services having important rights. The idea of the welfare state as a women-friendly state is also being challenged.

If it is the case that the welfare state's recruitment difficulties are being solved by the import of qualified labour from countries where wages are substantially lower than here, then this may result in a raising of status for those who come. In the long term however, it may contribute to health and care work becoming cemented as low paid women's work, and thereby less attractive for young job seekers and potential students. There is already a widespread view among the younger generation that care is about subjugation and the will to sacrifice, and as Halvorsen (2001) demonstrates, several commercial institutions are contributing to reinforcing this image.

If we perceive society as more than the sum of its individuals and regard it more as the sum of its relationships, it will be easier to raise the question of what the social consequences might be for those family networks which for several complicated reasons “export” their mother’s, wife’s and daughter’s presence and caring capacity to another country. How do families in the Baltic countries and Eastern Europe experience this? And how might it contribute to cementing a lack of gender equality in Norwegian families? And: what moral and political dilemmas will we face in the future if we continue to solve our “absent father” problems by creating “absent mother” problems in impoverished parts of the world?

The emergence of a new domestic help institution based on women coming to this country on tourist visas and who have none of the rights of employees, is an expression of several complicated phenomena. The tacit acceptance of their presence, however, expresses cultural discomfort because they demonstrate that problems on the home front remain unsolved despite (at least) 30 years of campaigning for gender equality. In a historical perspective there is nothing new about more than two adults being required to manage all the obligations entailed in the bonds of family networks. It is the political and moral problems involved in solving care problems through importing cheap labour at one end of the scale and through exporting those in need of care at the other that must be put on the public agenda. If the situation in the future is one in which Estonian women on tourist visas clean our houses, au pairs from Lithuania look after our children, our sick grandmothers are sent to Spain while home helps in Norway come from Murmansk and surgeons are assisted by nurses from the Czech Republic – how will this affect the power and gender aspects of the interaction between the state, the market and the family? And what social, political and cultural changes will it entail? This represents a major challenge for research into women and gender issues in the years ahead.

References

BAKKEN, Runar, 2001, *Modermordet (Matricide)*, Oslo, Universitetsforlaget.

BULAND, Trond and HAVN, Vidar, 2001, “Bevisste utdanningsvalg (Gendered educational choices)”. Working paper, SINTEF Teknologiledelse, Norwegian University of Science and Technology, Trondheim.

HALVORSEN, Grethe, 2001, *"Den stramme kvinnen (Firm-bodied women)". A textual analysis of weekly magazines' construction of the female body during the period 1988–98*, Degree thesis, Dept. of Sociology, University of Bergen, 2001.

HOCHSCHILD, Arlie R., 2001, "Globale omsorgskjeder (Global care chains)", *Kvinneforskning* (Journal for Women's Research), Oslo, Norway, 2.

ISAKSEN, Lise Widding, 1984, *"Omsorg i grenseland (Public and Private Care Work)". Home help recipients' experiences of public and private dependency*, Master Thesis, Dept. of Sociology, University of Tromsø.

–, 1996, *"Den tabubelagte kroppen (The Body Tabooed)", Body, gender and taboos in modern care work*, Ph.D., Dept. of Sociology, University of Bergen.

Statistics Norway, *Labour market statistics*, 1997.

SJØRUP, Karen, 2001, "Nye dimensjoner i omsorgen (New dimensions in care)", *Sygeplejen*, 9, pp. 42–45.

PARREÑAS, Rhacel Salazar, 2001, *Servants of Globalization: Women, Migration and Domestic Work,* Stanford, Stanford University Press.

VIGDAL, Roar, 1995, *Om menn i sykepleien (On men in nursing)*, Master thesis in sociology, Dept. of Sociology, University of Bergen.

Irish Domestic Servants and English National Identity

Bronwen WALTER

The Irish are by far the largest and longest-established migrant labour group in Britain.[1] They have settled in British cities in large numbers throughout the nineteenth and twentieth centuries, filling gaps in the "unskilled" labour force. Apart from the massive outpouring following the catastrophe of the 1840s Famine their numbers have responded closely to demand for labour in Britain.

The areas of work in which Irish people have been continuously in strong demand have been domestic labour for women and construction work for men. However men's work "on the buildings" has been much more visible and is synonymous with the pervasive image of "Paddy".[2] Irish women have had a lower profile, despite outnumbering men in most decades and being even more strongly clustered in a single occupational group.[3] In Britain there has been no equivalent image of "Bridget", although this was a well known collective name for servants in the USA.[4]

I want to argue that Irish women servants have played a key, but unrecognised, role in constructions of English national identities through their widespread presence as paid workers in English homes. But because

1 Useful overviews include: Graham Davis, *The Irish in Britain 1815–1914*, Dublin, Gill and Macmillan, 1991; Colin Holmes, *John Bull's Island: Immigration & British Society, 1871–1971*, London, Macmillan, 1988; John Archer Jackson, *The Irish in Britain*, London, Routledge and Kegan Paul, 1963; Enda Delaney, *Demography, State and Society: Irish migration to Britain 1921–1971*, Liverpool, Liverpool University Press, 2000.

2 Liz Curtis, *Nothing but the same old story*, London, Information on Ireland, 1985, p. 56. For a broader class view, still focusing on men, see Roy Foster, *Paddy and Mr Punch: connections in Irish and English history*, London, Allen Lane, 1993.

3 Bronwen Walter, *Outsiders inside; whiteness, place and Irish women*, London, Routledge, 2001, pp. 87–94.

4 Hasia Diner, *Erin's daughters in America: Irish immigrant women in the nineteenth century*, Baltimore, The Johns Hopkins University Press, 1983, p. xiii; Kevin Kenny, *The American Irish: a History*, Harlow, Pearson, 2000, p. 152.

the Irish are classified as "white" the significance of this role has been overlooked in theorisations which link national identity formation to the home. We need to problematise constructions of whiteness in different time periods in order to examine the place of Irish female servants in these constructions.

The home has played a major role in constructions of British national identity. It carries powerful messages about who "really" belongs in the nation in terms of class, gender and "race".[5] As workers who contribute in vital ways to the functioning of "respectable" English homes, domestic servants are closely linked with these constructions. But their invisibility as workers is linked to their invisibility in academic discourse.[6]

For the purposes of this paper two important periods will be examined. The first is the second half of the nineteenth century, when the "cult of domesticity" was at its height in England according to Anne McClintock.[7] The second period is the 1950s, a decade when Wendy Webster argues that notions of Englishness came to be constructed around the home, a private and apparently classless definition, in contrast to the 1930s representation of two nations defined regionally, North/South standing for rich/poor, employed/unemployed.[8] In both periods class, gender and colonial relationships were undergoing rapid change and representations of the home were used to secure versions of national identity.

The 1870s–90s

This was a period of crisis both abroad and at home.[9] In the colonies there was imperial rivalry from Germany and the US, whilst at home there was growing unrest in Ireland over demands for Home Rule and fears about

5 Wendy Webster, *Imagining Home: Gender, 'Race' and National Identity 1945–64*, London, UCL, 1998.

6 Leonore Davidoff, *Worlds Between: Historical Perspectives on Gender and Class*, Cambridge, Polity, 1995, p. 1.

7 Anne McClintock, *Imperial Leather: race, gender and sexuality in the colonial contest*, London, Routledge, 1995, p. 46.

8 W. Webster, *Imagining Home*, p. 72.

9 Jose Harris, *Private lives, public spirit: Britain 1870–1914*, London, Penguin, 1993, p. 5.

dark, uncontrollable inner cities where the population was seen as "a race apart".[10] McClintock and others argue that the cult of domesticity was a central element in countering these threats to the dominant group and asserting the authority of white, middle-class English males.[11] Boundaries of gender, class and "race" were thus established through the othering of both women and the working classes. This took place through a process of disavowal of the social and economic value of female manual and domestic work in order to credit wealth-generation and independence to the "master of the house".[12]

The cult of domesticity thus defined not only femininity but crucially also masculinity.[13] Middle-class men needed to mark their separation from men in the two other major strata of society, that is the aristocracy and the working classes.[14] The former were characterised by their lack of money, since they had continued to depend on the declining asset of land, rather than seize the opportunities of commodity capitalism. The latter were identified by their lack of property. Control of both money and property had therefore to be clearly assigned symbolically to middle-class men and the cult of domesticity allowed boundaries to be drawn which accentuated this.

The key aspect of women's domestic service was that it was paid labour in a space, the home, which was represented as the antithesis of the market place. Exclusive male rights to the generation of money could only be asserted by the suppression of knowledge of women's contribution to the economy. The domestic sphere must therefore be portrayed as "natural" and outside the cash nexus. Thus the notion of paid women's work in the household was highly threatening and had to be hidden from sight.[15] This led to the invisibility of the work performed both by middle-class and working-class women so that "the domestic labour of women suffered one of the most successful vanishing acts of modern history".[16]

Middle-class women performed the "labour of leisure", whereby the appearance of idleness was cultivated by all, but only achievable in reality

10 Frederick Engels, *The Condition of the Working Class in England 1845*, trans. W. Chaloner, Oxford, Blackwell, 1971.

11 A. McClintock, *Imperial Leather*, p. 48.

12 *Ibid.*, p. 169.

13 *Ibid.*, p. 5.

14 *Ibid.*, p. 153.

15 *Ibid.*, pp. 163–165.

16 *Ibid.*, p. 137.

by the richest. Idleness was not therefore the absence of work but the conspicuous consumption of leisure in order to highlight men's ability to create wealth through work.[17] However the main burden of the work involved in maintaining this outward appearance was thrust onto paid domestic servants. In addition to carrying out household maintenance, servants performed work to underpin the symbolic aspects of middle-class women's leisure, including the provision of elaborate costumes which prohibited any strenuous movement, and the cleaning and polishing of large numbers of emblems of household prestige.

What McClintock does not pursue is the national origins of the servant classes in England on whom this structure was built. I suggest that the racialisation of the servant underclass incorporated an understanding of their Irishness, in a similar way to arguments about the discourse of "slums". As Jennifer Davis[18] argues, this was dependent on pre-existing racialised representations of the Irish. *Punch* cartoons of the 1860s to 80s demonstrate greatest use of simianised images of the Irish.[19] Although men were the focus of public attention, these notions would have applied equally to Irish-born domestic servants significantly reinforcing their "otherness".

However the importance of Irish women's contribution to the servant workforce has been overlooked. Although it has been widely acknowledged that domestic service was the principal source of paid work for Irish women, no connections appear to have been drawn between representations of the Irish and the symbolic roles of servants as representing the "other" to white middle-class men. This is part of a wider failure to acknowledge Britain's long history as a country of immigration,[20] which can also be seen in the work of historians of domestic service. For example, in Leonore Davidoff's path breaking work *Mastered for Life*, first published in 1974,[21] about the significance of domestic service in nineteenth century

17 *Ibid.*, pp. 160–162.

18 Jennifer Davis, "Race and the residuum: the Irish origins of the English underclass", paper to King's College Social History Seminar, Cambridge, UK, 1996.

19 L. Perry Curtis, *Apes and Angels: The Irishman in Victorian Caricature*, Washington, Smithsonian Press, 1997, pp. 29–45.

20 Parokos Panayi, "The historiography of immigrants and ethnic minorities: Britain compared with the USA", *Ethnic and Racial Studies*, 19, 1996, pp. 823–840.

21 "Mastered for Life: servant and wife in Victorian and Edwardian England", *Journal of Social History*, 7, 1974, pp. 406–459.

Britain, the contribution of Irish women is left in a strange limbo. In a footnote Davidoff, adds:

> Note that during this period Britain had neither an indigenous nor imported ethnically or religiously disadvantaged population *(with the possible exception of the Irish).* Such groups often make up the majority of domestic servants and thus blur the effects of the master-servant relationship. Contrast [this] with the American experience.[22] (my emphasis)

Again in a later overview she elaborates on the "particular obsession" in England in the mid-nineteenth century with denoting distinctions between sections of the population, especially when confronting a growing waged and urban working class.[23] However, she identifies this obsession as "paradoxically partly due to lack of external differentiation", earlier describing "the remarkable homogeneity of the English nation *with the constant exception of Irish Catholics*" (my emphasis). In this theorisation, class differentiation alone is seen as a sufficient explanation, leaving the Irish as an anomaly, which, on the one hand, disturbs the homogeneity of the English nation but, on the other, is not sufficiently different to be classified as an external group.

The failure to note the ethnic origins of the servant workforce is part of a much wider erasure of the work of domestic servants in nineteenth-century Britain, which remains extraordinarily intact. The lack of information, or even debate, about domestic servants' social and economic place in nineteenth- and twentieth-century Britain or their personal experiences, is sharply at odds with their numbers. Overall figures from Censuses show that this was the second largest category of employment after agricultural work. Numbers rose from 750,000 in 1851 to 1.3 million in 1891 and never fell below one million until the late 1930s.[24] Yet in her 1974 article Davidoff described nineteenth-century residential service as an "exceptionally elusive" area of study.[25] Even when women's history was embraced in the 1970s, little attention was paid to this topic. More than twenty years later, in her overview of research on the topic in 1995, Davi-

22 L. Davidoff, *Worlds Between*, p. 35.

23 *Ibid*., p. 5.

24 Mark Ebery and Brian Preston, "Domestic Service in late Victorian and Edwardian England, 1871–1914", *Reading Geographical Papers*, Reading, Department of Geography, 1976, p. 20; Jane Lewis, *Women in England 1870–1950*, Sussex, Wheatsheaf, 1984, p. 156.

25 L. Davidoff, *Worlds Between*, p. 19.

doff continues to describe it as "swept under the carpet".[26] This is despite its intriguingly anomalous position, outside both the private world of the family and the public world of the paid workforce, which she argues should provide particular interest to historians.

Part of the explanation for academic neglect is that residential domestic servants in England were also remarkably hidden during their own lifetimes, and have therefore left few traces. Contemporary representations are very meagre, again contrasting with the outpouring of commentary in the United States of America. Hasia Diner stresses this historical visibility in her discussion of her data sources on Irish immigrant women, about 80 percent of whom were employed as domestic servants.

> The major problem… I encountered in putting together this study of immigrant Irish women was the mountains of material from government, charity and church sources, particularly at the local level, seemed almost insurmountable.[27]

In Britain, by contrast, Davidoff points out "Considering the numbers involved, both autobiography and fiction were strangely silent".[28] In addition, popular images of working women in the nineteenth century also ignored servants, focussing instead on "mill girls, or possibly the milliner or seamstress".[29] Again these absences are congruent with the physical and symbolic invisibility of servants within British households. In the first place, they were literally hidden from the view of the outside world within the homes of their employers. In fact Davidoff argues that unlike servants in continental Europe, those in England were unusually segregated:

> The intense privacy of the English middle-class household in individual dwellings often surrounded by gardens in isolated settings or suburbs separated from working-class districts, made English domestic service exceptionally confining.[30]

This underlines the difference between Irish men's working lives in the open air, as construction workers, visible to passers by and Irish women servants' confinement behind closed doors.

The absence of servants from public discourse was not therefore an indication of their lack of importance, but rather a measure of the inadmis-

26 *Ibid.*, p. 1.
27 H. Diner, *Erin's daughters in America*, p. 155.
28 L. Davidoff, *Worlds Between*, pp. 3–4.
29 *Ibid.*, p. 21.
30 *Ibid.*, p. 21.

sibility of their power.[31] Not only did they represent the necessity for, and middle-class men's dependence on, women's paid work, but their relationship with middle- and upper-class children placed them in an extraordinarily important position. Servants raised children and played a key role in the early experiences of middle-class men, while mothers were excluded from close contact by the necessity to appear untouched by manual labour.[32] Children also represented disorder and dirt, which meant that they too had to be segregated into particular parts of the house and fed at separate times. Boys spent more time with nurses and domestic servants than with their own mothers, before being sent off to boarding school, ironically being closely influenced by the very class from whom their fathers protected themselves. It can be speculated that the Catholic beliefs of Irish servants were transmitted much more directly in this way as well as stories from Irish oral traditions, but confirmation awaits evidence from personal or perhaps literary sources.

Irish women in paid domestic work have been rendered invisible in Britain as part of the wider process of denying the importance of this form of labour. However a fascinating extension of this idea is the possibility that their national/ethnic origins have also contributed to the construction of invisibility of the servant class as a whole through the double association of their externally and internally racialised identities.

In order to examine this connection more fully, detailed work needs to be undertaken to assess the nature and extent of Irish women's participation in the residential domestic labour force. This work has not been possible until recently because the published Census tables have not linked occupation with birthplace. Again the effect of this statistical representation has been to emphasise the homogeneity of the population rather than to allow the diasporic importance of migrant labour to be taken into account. All that can be gleaned from existing sources is that over the course of the nineteenth century Irish women became a much more important and sought-after source of domestic labour.

However it is now becoming possible to make Irish servants at this important late nineteenth-century period visible. In a project based at the Essex Data Archive run by Kevin Schürer and Matthew Woollard, a 5 percent sample of the 1881 Census has been made available in a form

31 A. McClintock, *Imperial Leather*, p. 164.

32 *Ibid.*, p. 236.

which allows cross tabulations by occupation and birthplace.[33] We can therefore begin to quantify Irish women's contribution to the domestic labour force for the first time and assess their relative importance in different types of household and in different geographic locations. I have recently set up a small project to analyse the findings, focussing in the first instance on domestic servants in London, where the middle classes were most heavily concentrated in 1881.[34]

Preliminary examination of the 1881 5 percent sample suggests that Irish women were still a relatively small proportion of the domestic service labour force in 1881 and that numerical values alone would not support the strength of the hypothesis outlined above. They made up 3.4 percent of the total in London, more than the Scottish and Welsh totals combined (2.8 percent) and the foreign-born (1.2 percent), but the great majority of domestic servants in London in 1881 were still English-born women (81.6 percent). Despite the small proportions, however, Irish women had become much more widespread amongst English households than in the 1850s. Lynn Lees described a situation where very large numbers arrived in Britain from conditions of extreme poverty in Ireland and were seen as a particularly undesirable birthplace group for such work.

> Irish servants abounded in London. Allegedly saucy and incompetent, they seem to have taken up the less desirable posts in the metropolis. And many more Irish women wanted such jobs than could find them… One said in 1853 that positions were almost impossible to find. Girls usually had to accept work either in a pub or with an East End Jewish family, where they were paid only one or two shillings a week plus board. In any case, the priest claimed that they usually quit or were fired, their final recourse being prostitution or begging.[35]

The 1881 data shows that Irish servants were located in middle-class English households in London at all levels of the domestic service hierarchy, and indeed were over-represented in some "upper ranks", such as cooks (12.9 percent of Irish-born servants, compared with 10.2 percent of English-born). At the same time fewer lived in with their employers (29.0 percent, compared with 50.1 percent of English-born servants) which may indicate a lower level of acceptability, although it could simply reflect

33 Kevin Schürer and Matthew Woollard, *The 5 percent sample of the 1881 Census of Great Britain*, Colchester, University of Essex, 2000.

34 British Academy Small Grant SG-37492.

35 Lynn Lees, *Exiles of Erin: Irish migrants in Victorian London*, Manchester, Manchester University Press, 1979, p. 95.

their greater average age. Irish-born women in 1881 were most numerous in the 45–49 age group, whereas English-born women had largest numbers aged 15–19. More detailed analysis of the data is in progress and will involve comparing the types of domestic service performed by Irish servants and those from other birthplaces and analysing both the social status of the employing householders and composition of the households in which they were located. This will throw light on their economic, social and cultural roles within English households.

It may be that numerical expansion of Irish servants took place on a larger scale in immediately succeeding decades. Certainly by the 1930s Irish servants were viewed as indispensable to the English economy.[36] In a memo from the British Minister of Labour in 1932, when repatriation to ease unemployment levels during the Depression was being considered:

> If it were decided to repatriate all persons in this country born in the Irish Free State there might be some temporary dislocation in the case of employers, particularly in Liverpool and Glasgow [...] but there is no doubt that under present conditions the total number of workers born in the Irish Free State *with the possible exception of those engaged in domestic service*, could be replaced rapidly and without much difficulty by workers born in Britain.[37] (my emphasis)

The precise timing of this shift, therefore, remains to be determined. What is clear is that Irish women were both available and in demand to fill growing gaps in the paid domestic labour market. In Ireland, girls benefited from the higher levels of education in the second half of the nineteenth century so that most were literate before emigration.[38] Moreover girls from higher status backgrounds began to take up this form of work. Those who would have been forbidden by their fathers to take up domestic work in rural Ireland because of the decline in status involved were under no such ban in London. Domestic service became increasingly unpopular in Dublin towards the end of the nineteenth century.[39] In 1881 it

36 Louise Ryan, "Aliens, Migrants and Maids: Public Discourses on Irish Immigration to Britain in 1937", *Immigrants and Minorities,* 20, 2001, pp. 25–42.

37 Sean Glynn, "Irish immigration to Britain, 1911–1951: patterns and policy", *Irish Economic and Social History,* 8, 1981, p. 63.

38 Donald Fitzpatrick, "'A share of the honeycomb': Education, emigration and Irish women", *Continuity and Change*, 1, 1986, pp. 217–234.

39 Mona Hearn, "Life for domestic servants in Dublin, 1880–1920", in Maria Luddy and Cliona Murphy (eds), *Women surviving: studies on Irish women in the nineteenth and twentieth centuries*, Dublin, Poolbeg, 1990, pp. 148-179.

accounted for 48 percent of all female employment, but by 1911 this had declined to 29 percent. Irish servants preferred emigration, often simply to do the same work in America or Britain, or even endure unemployment at home, which increased by 5 percent between 1901 and 1911.

In Britain Irish women's urgent need for work made them more willing to accept the subservience necessary to please English employers.[40] Working-class English women seized opportunities to move into "white-blouse" work, mainly teaching, retailing, office work and nursing. Jobs in these areas increased by 161 percent between 1881 and 1911, while manufacturing and domestic service expanded at the much lower rate of 24 percent.[41] But for middle-class homes, employing servants was increasingly an essential mark of gentility.

Irish women were strongly encouraged to enter domestic service in preference to other types of work by the Catholic church. They presented it as fulfilling the ideal of Catholic womanhood, preparing young women for marriage and child raising by learning domestic skills and saving money. Domestic service also had attractions for women. The provision of board and lodging was an important bonus for new arrivals. Moreover, in 1900 a housemaid could earn £18–20 a year, plus board and lodging, which was close to the annual income of the best paid group of women workers, those in cotton textile mills. In addition, the private workplace protected Irish women from discrimination widely experienced in factories, though not necessarily from exploitation. Thus domestic service persisted as the major area of Irish female employment contrary to the general trend among the peer group of British women, whose employment in personal service in England and Wales fell from 42 percent to 23 percent between 1901 and 1951.[42]

40 Melanie Tebbutt, "The evolution of ethnic stereotypes: an examination of stereotyping, with particular reference to the Irish (and to a lesser extent the Scots)", in *Manchester during the late nineteenth and early twentieth centuries*, unpublished M.Phil. thesis, University of Manchester, 1983.

41 J. Lewis, *Women in England 1870–1950*, Sussex, Wheatsheaf, p. 156.

42 J. Lewis, *Women in England*, p. 156.

The 1950s

The second period chosen is the 1950s, again a time of major change both "at home" in England and in Britain's relationships with its colonies. "At home" the post-war period was associated with a more inclusive construction of Englishness. The economic depression of the early 1930s had produced sharp regional and class divisions, especially between North and South. It was believed that the prosperity of the immediate post-war period would lead to a new "classless" society.[43] Overseas, Britain was rapidly losing its grip on its colonies and simultaneously attracting their labour to Britain itself.[44]

The new inclusiveness of Englishness was symbolised by the home, a place apparently outside the class hierarchies of public spaces, including the workplace. The massive building expansion literally produced estates of similar-looking housing throughout the country and rising wages reduced differences in spending power and lifestyle between different parts of the population. The home was the location where the welfare state was consumed most fully, through health services, education as well as housing itself. Alistair Bonnet argues that the spread of the welfare state after the First World War was the major factor in the extension of whiteness to the indigenous population as a whole.[45] Entitlement to welfare services became interlinked with the racialised notion of "our people".

The new focus on the home as the prime location and symbol of Englishness placed white "English" women at the centre. Their central function was to be homemakers, and above all "good mothers". The boundary was now being constructed not within the home but between the home and the "outside world", literally those who visibly represented such a world in their bodies. Gender and "race" were thus the main components and the key "others" were "black" migrant men.

Migrant women, both "white" and "black", were omitted from this construction but in fact played a vital role in supporting the existence of

43 W. Webster, *Imagining home*, pp. 69–71.

44 Stephen Castles, *Here for Good: Western Europe's New Ethnic Minorities*, London, Pluto Press, 1984, pp. 41–46.

45 Alistair Bonnet, *White identities: historical and international perspectives*, Harlow, Prentice Hall, 2000.

"English" homes, by enabling indigenous women to perform their primary work as wives and mothers. Whereas the "good mother" devoted her life to children and husband, only taking on part-time paid work, migrant women filled the full-time jobs for which female labour was required, in domestic service and various branches of the expanding welfare state. However only "white" migrant women were permitted to work inside the homes of indigenous English women as nannies and cleaners. "Black" women were not seen as suitable for this work; instead they were distanced from the personal lives of "white" English people and given public domestic work, for example hospital and office cleaning.[46] Irish women were thus placed at the heart of 'English' households, crucial maintainers of the "good homes" in which "English" children were being raised whilst their own were the "latch-key children" seen as a threat to social stability by academics such as John Bowlby.[47]

The apparent shifting of the Irish across the black/white binary did not therefore mean that they had ceased to be "other", but that their invisibility had increased. The 1950s was a decade when "No Black, No Irish, No Dogs" signs were widespread in advertisements for accommodation in English cities, indicating that the Irish were not seen to be entitled to rent English houses or settle in English neighbourhoods.[48] Throughout the 1950s there were fierce debates about including the Irish in legislation to control immigration. They were finally given a special status of freedom of movement on grounds of expediency, because of the difficulties in controlling the border in Northern Ireland and because of the value of a flexible labour force.[49]

The oral histories of two women, Mary and Margaret, who migrated in the 1930s and 1950s respectively, to Bolton, a cotton textile industrial town in Lancashire, illustrate the ambivalent position of Irish servants.[50] On the one hand they were desperately needed by English women em-

46 W. Webster, *Imagining home*, pp. 158–159.

47 John Bowlby, *Child care and the growth of love*, Harmondsworth, Penguin, First published 1953.

48 Mary Lennon, Marie McAdam and Joanne O'Brien, *Across the water: Irish women's lives in Britain*, London, Virago, 1988, pp. 141–143.

49 Mary Hickman, "Reconstructing deconstructing 'race': British political discourses about the Irish in Britain", *Ethnic and Racial Studies*, 21, 1998, pp. 288–307.

50 I completed ten oral histories with Irish-born women in Bolton in 1993–94 funded by an Economic and Social Research Council Research Grant for the project "Hidden Irishwomen; gender and migration to Britain 1951–1991", R000234790.

ployers to fill domestic labour shortages, but on the other they could still be ostracised as racially inferior, a continuing residue of nineteenth-century attitudes.

Mary had arrived in Lancashire from the rural west of Ireland as a young, single woman in her early twenties, and moved to Bolton to look for work during the Second World War.[51] She found a job in a large house with five servants, but the employer then visited her home to withdraw the offer because one of the other servants refused to share a room with her.

> *Mary:* The others [servants] were all English, and because they had to share – well, that's what she told me. She came to see me where I was staying out at Moses Gate, on the Saturday, because I should have started on the Monday, and she said, I'm very sorry, through no fault of your own, she said, we have four – no, five – no, five, I would be the fifth, because the other one had left, she said, and she said, unfortunately you would have to share a room with this English girl and she doesn't want to share a room with an Irish girl. But that was the only nastiness I ever – well, it wasn't nasty even, when I came over. And then I went for another job at Moses Gate, but they were Jews so my cousin's wife wouldn't let me take it, wouldn't let me take it because they were Jews. So anyhow, I went to an Irish dance and I met this Irish girl, and she said, well, I can give you an address, she said, she's got home because of the war, she's frightened and she's gone home and she hasn't come back.

Mary's experience shows the ease with which domestic work could usually be found, as she quickly replaced another Irish girl who had returned to Ireland. Her story also revealed other layers of racism, in her own Irish family, this time against Jewish employers.

During the War Mary met and married an Irishman, also from the west of Ireland, who worked as a coal miner in Bolton. They had five children, one of whom died. However her husband died of a coal-related disease when the children were still at school and Mary took on several paid jobs to support the family. She refused to apply for welfare benefits, fearing that she would be judged an unfit mother because she had heard a friend's experience of anti-Irish stereotypes of alcoholism.

> *Mary:* In them days I done three jobs, cleaning jobs, and they came up from the town hall and I was told to pack in my jobs and they paid me. I said, no way, because when I was travelling to Hickston I met this – she's of Irish descent, and she told me a tale about the town, you know. She said she was helped, because her husband died young, and she said this day she was taking in washing, this day she

51 B. Walter, *Outsiders inside*, pp. 218–223.

> was washing, and I suppose there were no washers in them days, and she had a pint jug on the table and she said, this man that came from the town hall nearly knocked her over. He thought the water was beer, and had that been beer her help would have stopped. So I think that stopped with me, you know?
> *B:* So you wouldn't take it?
> *Mary:* No, I wouldn't take it, no.
> *B:* So did you work all the time when you had children?
> *Mary:* Oh, I worked all the time.

She explained that the children helped with the domestic chores at home and that a neighbour also assisted. But the main responsibility for managing her own household, whilst working in several other women's at the same time, fell to her.

> *Mary:* Well, they'd tidy up and that kind of thing if I was out, you know, but when I went to work in the morning like, I always cleaned, so I didn't go out until they were gone to school, and then I finished at twelve till one, then I was home to get an evening meal ready for them, and then I used to go on a snackbar after my husband – well, I didn't go to work until after my husband died.
> *B:* So you did two jobs?
> *Mary:* I did three some days, I went to three houses. Then weekends I worked on the dog track two nights a week, I worked on a football ground Saturday afternoons, I went onto the dog track at night. Everywhere there was money to be earned.
> *B:* So your children brought themselves up as far as...?
> *Mary:* Well, they did really, they did, but I had a good neighbour though that – I was only ten minutes' walk away from them at night, where I worked in the snackbar from where I lived on Manchester Road.

The "Irish" home in England could not therefore be run by a home-based mother, as was the ideal image of an "English" home. In order that the "English" home could be clean, and the mother freed to devote her energies to her children's upbringing, working-class, including migrant, women provided invisible services. Their "whiteness" helped to produce this invisibility and obscure the dependence of constructions of Englishness on the labour of Irish women.

Margaret came to Bolton from Dublin to marry an Englishman she had met when he was on holiday there.[52] She had worked in domestic service before she emigrated. After her own children were born she looked for cleaning and childcare work which would enable her to combine her own

52 B. Walter, *Outsiders inside*, pp. 238–240.

domestic responsibilities with paid work. Again she was in demand as a worker in English homes and had no difficulty finding employment.

> *Margaret:* I think when my two children were young, you see, I needed a job, to help out, and I thought, the only thing – I love housework, and I worked out that I could take the children with me when there were holidays. I told my employers that from the word go. And the lady that I helped out at first, she had a mentally handicapped son, and I'd gone up to visit a friend of mine one evening. He husband used to play for Bolton Wanderers. And when I got there she said, oh, Lillian next door is in the most awful state, she said, she doesn't know where to turn. You know she's got twin girls and she's got a handicapped son David, and she's just found out she's expecting again, and she just does not know where to turn, and she's thinking of having the child terminated. Well, that was a big shock to me because I didn't like that, you know. I said, oh, my goodness, I said, I hope she doesn't do that because I doubt she'd be able to live with it herself afterwards. But she said, she'd have to do something, she said, she's going to have to either get somebody to help her in the house, because her husband was a big businessman anyway. And I said, well, I think we can help one another really. I knew the job, and Lillian needs help. So it was only supposed to be until the baby was born, so I ended up with her three years.
> *B:* So it was childcare plus housework?
> *Margaret:* Yes.
> *B:* General helping in the home?
> *Margaret:* Yes, and it suited both of us.
> *B:* And your children could play with her children?
> *Margaret:* That's right. And then when I left there, I found out another lady, she used to foster children, and I went to work for them. But it didn't work out because they both were at college, and they used to say to me, when you're finished, just put the baby in the cot for her sleep, because we'll be home shortly after you leave. And I thought, no.
> *B:* No, I agree.
> *Margaret:* No, no, I'm not doing this, so I used to take the baby home with me, if they weren't home. I'd wait, sometimes quarter of an hour, half an hour. And I used to bring the baby home. Leave a note, taking baby home with me, please collect. And they were using me really, and I thought, no, I'm not having this. So I said no, I'd be too frightened. And they said, we'll be home. But, I said, you're not home shortly afterwards, it's proved that you're not home. Because I mean they'd come for her an hour later. And I said, you forget that I'm the last one in the house with the baby, and if anything happened it's me that would get it, you know.
> *B:* You'll feel bad anyway, even if it's not your responsibility, won't you?
> *Margaret:* Oh yes. I wouldn't do it. So then a couple of months later I – the lady next door actually said to me, I said, I've answered a job out of the paper, help needed, new house in –, well, it's off Chorley New Road, – Drive, it was called, and it was a phone number so I phoned up, and this man said, could you come and see us? He was a solicitor. And I said, well, I'll come this evening. He said, I can't pick you up but I'll bring you home. And I said to the lady next door, I said, I've

just answered a job, and she said, oh, I'm nearly sure my daughter works for that solicitor, in the office. And it seems when he put the phone down he said to Alice, where's – Avenue? Don't you live near there? And she said, why? And he said, I've just had a lady on the phone and she's answered the advert. He said, she's Irish. So Alice said, what number? He said, sixteen. She said, it's my next-door neighbour. So of course he asked her then, you see, was I all right, and Alice said, oh, I think you'll please one another really. So I went out and got the job, and stayed there for quite some years really, seen all their children grown up and doing well for themselves.
B: So what were you doing there?
Margaret: Housework, and then they had another baby and it was then mostly to mind the baby, while they were out at college – well, he was working and she was out doing the university bit.
B: It worked well? You were happy?
Margaret: Oh yes. It was like another family really. Yes. Just two mornings a week, from nine o'clock till one, which suited me fine.

Margaret's paid domestic work enabled two English women to gain further qualifications and thus to enter the labour market at a higher level. She was valued for the home-making and child-rearing skills she had brought from Ireland and her willingness to undertake these tasks for relatively low pay. In the 1950s English women were expected to have their children cared for in their own homes, rather than send them to nurseries for collective care. After the Second World War, nurseries were closed down as part of the re-establishment of the individual home as the appropriate place for English children to be raised.[53] But Margaret herself was unable to conform to these English ideals. Lack of public day care provision meant that her own children were taken to her workplace.[54] The "care chain", which has now been globalised, for example, by the recruitment of Filipina and East European migrant workers in Ireland who leave children in their own countries,[55] was in this case performed by one woman taking on a double load of childcare.

The life histories of women like Mary and Margaret have remained hidden within the private confines of English and Irish family narratives.[56]

53 Penny Summerfield, *Women workers in the second World War: Production and Patriarchy in Conflict*, London, Routledge, 1984, pp. 186–191.

54 W. Webster, *Imagining home*, p. 143.

55 Pauline Conroy, "Migrant women – Ireland in the international division of care", *Women's Studies International Forum*, forthcoming.

56 M. Lennon, M. McAdam and J. O'Brien, *Across the water: Irish women's lives in Britain*, London, Virago, 1988, p. 9; Louise Ryan, "'I'm going to England': women's narratives of leaving Ireland in the 1930s", *Oral History*, Spring 2000, pp. 42–43.

They are also invisible in the production of official statistics. Once again the Irish origins of the domestic service class have been overlooked and again they cannot be identified in present-day Censuses. Although we know that Irish-born women were heavily concentrated in the Personal Service category in 1991, for example, which at 1.5 million workers remained the largest single category for women and the second overall to metal manufacturing and engineering, no breakdown is given which would allow domestic service to be examined on its own.[57] Thus although there are marked overall similarities in the employment patterns of Irish and African-Caribbean women at each Census from 1961 to 1991, for example, there are important differences at a more detailed scale which cannot be measured precisely. These would illuminate the ambivalent ways in which the apparent "whiteness" of most Irish women works both to mask their racialised difference and to provide them with a means of "passing" within English society.

Conclusions

Homes have been important sites for constructions of national identity which has depended on particular constructions of gendered, classed and raced Englishness. I have argued that the presence of Irish domestic servants has contributed to these constructions in shifting and complex ways. Whilst their gender provided an additional "other" to the masculinity of later nineteenth-century Englishness, in both periods their class contributed to constructions of middle-class English femininity by removing the need for middle-class women visibly to perform "women's" manual labour. In the 1870s and 80s this facilitated representations of "ladies of leisure" removed from the creation of wealth and the "dirt" of "housework". In the 1950s "good mothers" needed to give priority to their children's wellbeing, but to ensure that their houses conformed to high standards of cleanliness which required additional manual labour from paid domestic workers.

57 Mary Hickman and Bronwen Walter, *Discrimination and the Irish Community in Britain*, London, Commission for Racial Equality, 1997, p. 248.

The racialised Irish origins of this group of servants made a specific contribution to such national constructions. In the later nineteenth century the Irish were openly racialised which gave an added dimension to the "internal racialisation" of the working classes in Britain.[58] By the mid-twentieth century Irish women had become recognised as archetypical servants and were therefore allowed inside a boundary that was being drawn between those belonging inside and outside the home/homeland. But this was a measure of expediency at the domestic level just as it was at the national scale. The Irish were in the process of being defined as "white" through the hardening of the official black/white binary in the 1960s but despite apparent homogeneity, the category contained a diverse range of identities who were not necessarily protected from ongoing racialisation.

58 Robert Miles, *Racism after "race relations"*, London, Routledge, 1993, pp. 88–97.

Was Bridget's Experience Unique?

A Comparative View of American Domestic Service over Time and Space

Margaret LYNCH-BRENNAN

Domestic service was the chief occupation of employed women in the United States of America in the nineteenth century. From the 1840s to the 1930s, streams of young, unmarried girls from rural Ireland crossed the Atlantic to work in this occupation in middle-class homes in the United States. By comparison with other European countries, Irish emigration was notable for the high number of females in the stream; by the end of the nineteenth century, more Irish daughters than sons left Ireland for the United States. As David Fitzpatrick points out, "Ireland's abnormally heavy female emigration ensured that American domestic service would become very much an Irish domain...". And so it was, for in Boston in 1850, almost 72 percent of domestic servants were natives of Ireland, while overall, 60.5 percent of the women employed in America in 1900 who were Irish natives were domestic servants. The Irish Bridget or Biddy, the generic nickname given to all Irish domestics, was so closely associated with domestic service that Blaine McKinley claims that "After 1850 domestic servants and the Irish became virtually synonymous". Bridget was very familiar to readers of popular American literature where, from the mid-nineteenth century on, in cartoons as well as text, her faults and foibles, in particular her ignorance of American housekeeping methods, were decried and derided. Employers complained of "Bridget's ignorance and awkwardness" and declared "these Irish servants are the plague of our lives"[1]. (See Figure 28, p. 585 and Figure 29, p. 586.)

1 F. Dudden, *Serving Women. Household Service in Nineteenth-Century America*, Middletown, Wesleyan University Press, 1983, p. 1; A. Grossmann, "Women in domestic work: yesterday and today", *Monthly Labor Review*, August 1980, pp. 17, 18; H. Diner, *Erin's Daughters in America. Irish Immigrant Women in the Nineteenth*

Following the Great Famine of 1845–1852, circumstances peculiar to Ireland, including changes in land inheritance patterns and family life among the Irish peasantry, as well as the lack of employment opportunities in Ireland, accelerated emigration. In the post-Famine period, Irish parents of limited means could not provide for the future of all their children in Ireland. Instead, land (i.e., the family farm) was left to only one son, and the dowry or fortune required for the arranged marriage called a "match" was provided to only one daughter. The remaining children of traditionally large or "long" Irish families had to find their futures outside Ireland, and so, many emigrated to the United States.[2]

Girls from rural Ireland became familiar with the United States through the "American Letters" written home by expatriate relatives and friends; these letters are said to have made emigration seem both attractive and possible to the Irish. They willingly decamped for the United States, where they hoped to find employment, "adventure", and husbands. In a chain migration in which family members continued over time to bring relatives from Ireland to the United States, they flocked to cities, particu-

---

Century, Baltimore, The Johns Hopkins University Press, 1983, pp. 30–31; D. Fitzpatrick, "'A Share of the honeycomb' education, emigration and Irish women", in M. Daly and D. Dickson (eds), *The Origins of Popular Literacy in Ireland. Language Change and Education Development 1700–1920*, Dublin, Department of Modern History, Trinity College Dublin and Department of Modern Irish History, University College Dublin, 1990, p. 173; D. Fitzpatrick, *Irish Emigration 1801–1921. Studies in Irish Economic and Social History*, Ireland, Dundalgan Press, 1984, first quote from p. 32; B. McKinley, "'The Stranger in the Gates' Employer Reactions Toward Domestic Servants in America, 1825–1875", Ph.D. diss., Michigan State University, 1969, p. 152, second quote from p. 282; D. Katzman, *Seven Days a Week. Women and Domestic Service in Industrializing America*, New York, Oxford University Press, 1978, p. 67; "Your Humble Servant", *Harper's New Monthly Magazine*, June 1864, third quote from p. 53, fourth quote from p. 54.

2 P. Jackson, "Women in 19th century Irish Emigration", *International Migration Review*, 18, 4, 1984, pp. 1009, 1010, 1012, 1014, 1017, 1018; D. Fitzpatrick, "The Modernisation of the Irish Female", in P. O'Flanagan, P. Ferguson and K. Whelan (eds), *Rural Ireland 1600–1900. Modernisation and Change*, Cork, Cork University Press, 1987, pp. 163, 164, 168, 169, 174–175; D. Fitzpatrick, "A Share of the honeycomb", pp. 167, 175; T. Guinnane, *The Vanishing Irish. Households, Migration, and the Rural Economy in Ireland, 1850–1914*, Princeton, Princeton University Press, 1997, pp. 158–160.

larly in the American Northeast, where the demand for servants exceeded the supply.[3]

In America, the Irish were *different* in that they were *not* Anglo-Saxons. Their generally peasant class origin and culture, as well as their ethnicity and Roman Catholic religion, marked them as the *other* in the United States where, in the mid-nineteenth century, being American was considered synonymous with being Protestant. Religion was bound up with the Irish experience in America because anti-Catholicism was so widespread. In fact, John Higham identifies anti-Catholic nativism, and Anglo-Saxon nativism (or the belief in the superiority of Anglo-Saxons), as two of the three themes running through the history of American nativism, and contends that "Anti-Catholic nativism... completely overshadowed every other nativist tradition". As Irish girls entered service in the United States, the private home in urban, middle-class America became the most familiar frontier of contact between Irish immigrants and middle-class Americans. There the Irish immigrant domestic and her American mistress faced each other across a gulf of class, cultural, ethnic and religious differences that adversely affected employer-domestic relations.[4]

In the nineteenth century, with industrialization, urbanization, with the rise of the middle class and the spread of gentility in America, standards of cleanliness rose. With a new-found affluence attributable to the economic benefits of industrialization, middle-class American women had the

3 A. Schrier, *Ireland and the American Emigration*, Minneapolis, University of Minnesota Press, 1958, pp. 40–41, 111; D. Fitzpatrick, *Irish Emigration 1801–1920,* pp. 24–25; Mrs. J. Sadlier, *Bessy Conway or the Irish Girl in America,* New York, D. & J. Sadlier, 1861, reprint, New York, D. & J. Sadlier, 1863, p. 7; J. Nolan, *Ourselves Alone. Women's Emigration from Ireland 1885–1920,* Lexington, University of Kentucky Press, 1989, quote from p. 73; D. Fitzpatrick, "Irish Emigration in the Later Nineteenth Century", *Irish Historical Studies*, XXII, no. 86, 1980, p. 129; D. Fitzpatrick, "Emigration, 1801–70", in W. E. Vaughan (ed.), *A New History of Ireland*, vol. v, Ireland under the Union, I, 1801–70, Oxford, Clarendon Press, 1989, pp. 602, 603; D. Katzman, *Seven Days a Week*, p. 177.

4 C. Fanning, *The Exiles of Erin. Nineteenth-century Irish-American Fiction*, 2nd ed., Chester Springs, Pa., Dufour Editions, 1997, p. 1; E. Levine, *The Irish and Irish Politicians. A Study of Cultural and Social Alienation*, Notre Dame, Indiana, University of Notre Dame Press, 1966, p. 63; J. Higham, *Strangers in the Land. Patterns of American Nativism, 1860–1925*, New Brunswick, N.J., Rutgers University Press, 1984, quote from p. 6, see also pp. 5–8, 9, 11, 26, 79–87, 95, 131, 149–150, 157, 262–263; B. McKinley, "The Stranger in the Gates", pp. ii, 283; H. Diner, *Erin's Daughters*, p. 94.

means to free themselves from housework by hiring servants. Consequently, there was a popular demand for live-in domestic servants in private homes in urban America. Servants brought status to the employing families, marking positively their class station. The employment of servants was so important to a family's status that to keep up appearances even people of limited means hired servants.[5]

In hiring live-in domestics, including maids-of-all-work, chambermaids, child nurses (nannies), waitresses and cooks, the mistress (the term used for female employers) of the middle-class home was provided with the opportunity of supervising, rather than executing, domestic work in her home. By employing servants, mistresses also obtained time for leisure pursuits such as reading, writing letters, taking morning naps, and making formal social calls. They also procured time to do good works through activity in "the voluntary organizations known as the 'benevolent empire'", working on "temperance, moral reform, Sabbatarianism, domestic and foreign missions, and aid to the poor".[6]

Middle-class American mistresses did not want green, untrained Irish girls for their servants. So some employers phrased their advertisements for domestics in such a manner as to directly or obliquely indicate that no Catholics or no Irish need apply, Irish and Catholic being deemed equivalent terms. In 1868, one such ad stated that a woman was wanted "to take the care of a boy two years old, in a small family in Brookline". It stipulated that "Positively no Irish need apply". Mistresses wanted white, native-born American girls for servants, but native-born Americans eschewed the occupation because of its low status – servants were stigmatized by their employment. Instead, it was Irish girls who met the middle-class demand for servants; they constituted the largest portion of

5 F. Dudden, *Serving Women*, pp. 115, 126–27, 137–145, 148; S. Hoy, *Chasing Dirt. The American Pursuit of Cleanliness*, New York, Oxford University Press, 1995, pp. xiv, 5, 7; S. Strasser, *Never Done. A History of American Housework*, New York, Pantheon Books, 1982, pp. 163–164; D. Katzman, *Seven Days a Week*, pp. 46, 59, 269; J. Rollins, *Between Women. Domestics and Their Employer,* Philadelphia, Temple University Press, 1985, pp. 52–53; *The Boston Pilot*, 6 March 1852, p. 6.

6 For the purposes of this paper, the terms *domestic, domestic servant, servant, employee,* and *worker* will be deemed synonymous, as will *service* and *domestic service*. A. Neal, "The Crisis", *Godey's Lady's Book and Magazine*, May 1857, pp. 519, 520; J. Kasson, *Rudeness and Civility. Manners in Nineteenth-century Urban America*, New York, Hill and Wang, 1990, pp. 173–74, 210; F. Dudden, *Serving Women*, pp. 155–192, quotes from p. 241.

the immigrants in domestic service in the second half of the nineteenth century.[7]

In some ways live-in domestic service met the needs of Irish immigrant girls. The salary live-in servants earned was considered good in comparison with wages earned by other working women. With room and board provided, Irish domestics could save their wages to remit money home to their families in Ireland. The "American money" they sent greatly improved the material life of the Irish at home. The room provided to Irish domestics, however, was often less than desirable, and usually provided a marked contrast with the living space of the employing family. Many times servant quarters were cheerless, poorly furnished rooms in attics that often lacked heat and running water; such attics were hot in the summer and cold in the winter. Not all servants had their own rooms, either, as some were expected to share a room with other servants or with the children for whom they cared. Board or food was not always such a great benefit for live-in servants, either. Sometimes the food provided to servants contrasted unfavorably with that of the family for whom the servant worked; it might have been of lesser quality or quantity. Lack of adequate nutrition to perform the physically challenging work of domestic service was a problem for some servants.[8]

For live-in servants the work week was generally seven days long, and the work day was between 10 and 12 hours long, making both the work week and work day longer than those of most other working women. In addition, domestics were on-call to employers at all times. Usually, their time off was limited to one afternoon and one evening per week, often Thursday and Sunday. Domestic work was exhausting. Irish immigrant

7 *Boston Evening Transcript*, 3 August 1868, quotes; L. Salmon, *Domestic Service*, New York, The Macmillan Company, 1897, pp. 65, 163; D. Katzman, *Seven Days a Week*, pp. 14, 44, 162–163, 241–42; D. Sutherland, *Americans and Their Servants. Domestic Service in the United States from 1800–1920*, Baton Rouge, Louisiana State University Press, 1981, pp. 4, 5, 38–39; S. Strasser, *Never Done*, p. 164.

8 R. Dorr, *What Eight Million Women Want*, Boston, Small, Maynard & Company, 1910, pp. 252–53; L. Salmon, *Domestic Service*, pp. 93, 98–99; A. Schrier, *Ireland and the American Emigration*, pp. 110, 108, 109, 112; B. McKinley, "The Stranger in the Gates", pp. 215–216, 251, 253, 255; H. Spofford, *The Servant Girl Question*, Boston, Houghton, Mifflin, 1881, reprint, New York, Arno Press, 1977, p. 39; H. Campbell, *Prisoners of Poverty. Women Wage-Workers, Their Trades and Their Lives*, Boston, Roberts Brothers, 1887, reprint, 1889, p. 230; H. F. Cleary, interview by author by telephone, 31 July 1996, tape recording; F. Dudden, *Serving Women*, p. 196; D. Katzman, *Seven Days a Week*, p. 110.

domestic Hannah Collins attested to this in 1898 when she wrote to her friend and fellow Irish domestic Nora McCarthy, "I hope someday will come when I wont have to work so hard... I do hate to get up every morning I am so tired". As David Katzman points out, service work "involved the hiring of a person rather than just the obtaining of her labor", that is, servants were hired for their time, rather than just for specific tasks – the employer expectation was that the servant should work constantly. As one author put it, in the view of some employers, "the Irish Bridgets... are the machines" whose purpose is "to do a certain quantity of work of a particular kind..."[9].

In addition to being heavy, physical work, domestic service provided no benefits such as vacation time or sick leave. On-the-job injuries could impede a girl's ability to support herself, for not all employers would keep on a servant who could not work. Irish domestic Kate Monohan apparently suffered such an on-the-job injury. In 1897 she wrote to Nora McCarthy asking to be excused for taking so long in replying to Nora's last letter. Kate said "my dear friend It was owing to a Sore hand which I had for a week or two past that I have not answered your letter Sooner I burned my fore fingers & could not handle my pen for Some time but they are all better now with the exception of one which is quite Sore yet".[10]

Servants were forbidden to have "followers" (boyfriends) and they were rarely allowed to entertain friends and relations in the houses in which they worked. So, for the newly arrived Irish immigrant girl who worked as the single servant, the "maid-of-all-work", in a household, domestic service provided a lonely *entrée* into American life. Irish domestic

9 D. Katzman, *Seven Days a Week*, second quote from p. 107, pp. 110, 111, 112–3; F. Dudden, *Serving Women*, pp. 178–9; G. Laughlin, *Domestic Service. A Report Prepared Under the Direction of the Industrial Commission*, Washington, D.C., General Printing Office, 1901, p. 759; B. McKinley, "The Stranger in the Gates", p. 32; H. Collins, *Elmira, New York, to Nora McCarthy, 24 May 1899*, transcript in the author's hand, original in the hand of Dr. Patricia Trainor O'Malley, Bradford, Massachusetts, (hereinafter referred to as O'Malley Collection) first quote (to preserve the authenticity of their written language, throughout this paper I will reproduce the language of Irish domestics as they wrote it, without either correcting it or writing [*sic*] after misspellings); A. Neal, "The Servant Question", *Godey's Lady's Book and Magazine*, October 1857, pp. 327, 328; R. Tomes, *The Bazar Book of Decorum. The Care of the Person, Manners, Etiquette, and Ceremonials*, New York, Harper & Brothers, 1871, third and fourth quotes from p. 230.

10 K. Monohan to Nora McCarthy, 13 February 1897, transcript in the author's hand, O'Malley Collection.

Mary Malone attested to the loneliness of servant life when she wrote home in 1877 that she was "verry lonseom and down harted". For the house in which she worked was her work place, not her home, as Hannah Collins acknowledged when she wrote "I aint got any home here". While working in a multiple-servant household probably provided some relief from the isolation of this occupation, most households employed only a single servant.[11]

Culture in rural Ireland permitted women to be verbally assertive, as the Irish proverb "a woman's tongue is a thing that doesn't rust" indicates. Their assertiveness contrasted with the submissiveness expected of urban, middle-class American women in the cult of domesticity. Popular American literature of the period was rife with stories of the assertive Bridget, who manifested agency when she played her trump card and quit, sometimes for what seemed (to the employer) ridiculous reasons such as marrying a fellow Irishman. While the annoyed and exasperated mistress left behind was faced with finding and training a replacement servant, the demand for servants ensured that there was always another job available for the Irish Bridget. Word-of-mouth, via friends and relatives, or use of the employment agencies for servants that were called intelligence agencies, constituted the means Bridget used to secure a new job.[12]

11 R. Dorr, *What Eight Million Women Want*, pp. 266–67; R. Tomes, *The Bazar Book of Decorum*, p. 231; C. Dickens, "Servants in America", *All the Year Round*, 3 October 1874, p. 585; M. Malone, Fearport (Fairport, New York?), to her brother in Ireland, 24 January 1877, transcript in the author's hand, original in the hand of Professor A. Schrier, Cincinnati, Ohio (hereinafter referred to as Schrier Collection); H. Collins to Nora McCarthy, envelope dated 22 July 1899, O'Malley Collection.

12 P. Sayers, *An Old Woman's Reflections. The Life of a Blasket Island Storyteller*, trans. from the Irish by Seamus Ennis, Oxford, Oxford University Press, 1962, quote from p. 81. Assertive Irish women are evident in the work of Irish author William Carleton. See for example W. Carleton, "Shane Fadh's Wedding", in vol. 1, *Traits and Stories of the Irish Peasantry*, 1853, reprint, Freeport, N.Y., Books for Libraries Press, 1971, p. 120, and "Phelim O'Toole's Courtship", in vol. 2, *Traits and Stories of the Irish Peasantry*, pp. 206, 329; K. Sutherland, "Cooks", *Godey's Lady's Book and Magazine*, May 1852, pp. 393, 394; "Our Domestic Service", *Scribner's Monthly Illustrated Magazine*, November 1875, p. 273; "Bridget", *Harper's Bazar*, 11 November 1871, p. 706; A. Neal, "Fetch and Carry", *Godey's Lady's Book and Magazine*, February 1857, p. 113; C. Dickens, "Servants in America", pp. 585, 586; R. Bowker, "In Re Bridget-The Defence", *Old & New*, 4, 1871, p. 497; "Your Humble Servant", *Harper's New Monthly Magazine*, June 1864, p. 55; "Katie is Leaving – Again", *The New York Times Magazine*, 31 August 1941, p. 10; "Morals and Manners of the Kitchen", *The Nation*, 2 January 1873, p. 7.

Irish girls did not lose their self-esteem in service, despite its low status. The Irish servant girl, said to have absorbed from American culture a "hatred of superiority of all kinds", seemingly disregarded the distinction in class between mistress and maid. As one employer declared, "servant-girls understand themselves to be politically and theoretically our equals...". Irish domestics did not consider themselves to be members of a servant class. They did not anticipate spending their entire lives in service, but rather thought of service merely as a job through which they would pass on the way to their real goal of marriage and having a family of their own.[13]

The Irish ethnic community not only provided a network through which new jobs could be obtained, but also provided homeless domestics with housing between live-in jobs. In 1898, Hannah Collins wrote to Nora McCarthy "its so nice for you to have your sisters home to go to Sundays and when you are tired or out of work". Irish domestics also spent their limited time off with each other and the Irish community: they visited with one another, went to the Irish dances, and met at church, not only to worship, but to get the latest news on the Irish community. So important was Catholicism to Irish domestics that in 1852, "Bridget", the Irish domestic correspondent to *The Boston Pilot*, declared, "If it wasn't for the [Catholic] Church we couldn't get along at all". Many Protestant employers, however, were strongly prejudiced against Catholicism, and sometimes tried to force their Irish servants into participating in Protestant family prayers and undertook other means to convert them to Protestantism. The devotion to Catholicism of the Irish Bridgets, which required them to go to mass every Sunday and holy day of obligation, caused employer's dismay as it adversely affected household arrangements and mealtimes.[14]

13 "Morals and Manners of the Kitchen", *The Nation,* 2 January 1873, first quote from p. 7; H. Spofford, *The Servant Girl Question,* second quote from p. 89; V. DeForest, "Biddy's Blunders", *Godey's Lady's Book and Magazine*, April 1855, p. 329; J. Nolan, *Ourselves Alone*, pp. 68, 79; A Thankful Husband, "How My Wife Keeps Her Maids", *Harper's Bazar*, 4 December 1909, p. 1231.

14 H. Collins to Nora McCarthy, 21 September 1898, O'Malley Collection; O. O'Callaghan, Philadelphia, to his mother, Kilmacthomas, County Waterford, Ireland, 26 March 188?, transcript in the hand of the author, original in the hand of Professor Kerby Miller, Columbia, Missouri (hereinafter referred to as Miller Collection); "The Servant Question", *The Nation*, 26 October 1865, p. 528; C. Dickens, "Servants in America", p. 585; A. Greaney, "Young at Heart: Oldest Irish Woman Dies in Boston", *The Irish Voice* (New York), 29 July–11 August, 1998, p. 36; M. C. Horan, interview by Paul E. Sigrist, Jr., 24 April 1991, Interview EI-39, transcript, Oral History Collec-

Modern scholars of Irish immigration agree that domestic service provided an acculturating experience for Irish domestics and facilitated the rise of the Irish into the American middle class. Hasia Diner, for example, claims that domestic service offered Irish women "a first-hand peek at how Americans lived" and she points out that observers said that it was Irish women who "brought the family 'up', civilized them [the Irish family] by introducing the manners and accouterments of the middle class". Irish nanny Helen Flatley Cleary, who came to the United States in 1928, concurred, saying that in domestic service, she "learned a lot of the ropes". Indicative of the female role in the rise of the Irish is that few daughters of Irish domestics followed their mothers into service. Instead, teaching school became the occupation of choice for second-generation Irish females. Irish women, who tended to marry Irish men, pushed their families upward into the middle class while they retained their religion and certain Irish cultural attitudes. In doing so, Irish women pioneered a new way to be American – they showed that one could be concurrently *both* Irish and American.[15]

tion, Ellis Island Immigration Museum, New York, New York (hereinafter referred to as the Ellis Island Collection), p. 54; M. C. Harney, interview by Paul E. Sigrist, Jr., 11 October 1991, Interview EI-107, Ellis Island Collection, pp. 35, 36; H. Spofford, *The Servant Girl Question*, p. 59; Bridget, "Troubles in Families", *The Boston Pilot*, 21 February 1852, p. 7; D. Sutherland, *Americans and Their Servants*, p. 40; F. Hartley, *The Ladies' Book of Etiquette, and Manual of Politeness*, Boston: J. S. Locke, 1860, reprint, Davenport, Iowa, Amazon Drygoods, 1993, p. 239; J. Sadlier, *Bessy Conway*, pp. 205–207, iii; "Bridget", *Harper's Bazar*, 11 November 1871, p. 706; Veritas, "Trouble in Families. Servants as they are Nowadays, No. V", *Boston Daily Evening Transcript*, 9 February 1852, p. 4

15 I use acculturate to mean "adapt to or adopt a different culture", as defined in *The Oxford American Dictionary and Language Guide*, New York, Oxford University Press, 1999, p. 8; H. Diner, *Erin's Daughters*, pp. 51, 94–98, first two quotes from p. 140; H. F. Cleary, interview by author, tape recording, 31 July 1996, for third quote; J. Nolan, *Ourselves Alone*, pp. 81–82; E. A. Ross, *The Old World in the New: The Significance of Past and Present Immigration to the American People,* New York, The Century Company, 1914, pp. 35–36, H. J. Desmond, "A Century of Irish Immigration", *The American Catholic Quarterly Review,* 25, 1900, pp. 522–523; A. M. Greeley, "The Success and Assimilation of Irish Protestants and Irish Catholics in the United States", *Sociology and Social Research,* 72, 1988, pp. 231–232.

Other Domestic Servants over Time and Space

As I conducted research on Irish domestics for my doctoral dissertation, I wondered how the Irish experience compared with that of women from other ethnic and racial groups who, over time, have also worked in service in various locations in the United States. To find out whether the Irish experience was unique, I decided to research the experiences of other women in service. My starting point was to learn who the contemporaries of Irish domestics were. The 1870 federal census was the first to try to accurately record all female employment, and it indicated that domestic servants were concentrated in two areas of the United States: urban areas where immigrants, the Irish in particular, dominated the occupation, and the South where African-American women were dominant. According to this census, there were 145,956 Irish-born servants, 42,866 natives of Germany working as servants, and 11,287 natives of Sweden, Norway, and Denmark working too as such. Irish servants prevailed in the north-eastern states of Connecticut, Maine, Massachusetts, New Hampshire, New Jersey, New York, Pennsylvania, and Rhode Island, as well as the states of California, Illinois and Ohio. In contrast, German servants were dominant in Indiana, Iowa, Nebraska and Wisconsin, while Scandinavians were preponderant in Kansas and Minnesota. By 1900, 60.5 percent of Irish-born women worked in domestic service in the United States, 42.6 percent of German immigrant women were domestic servants, and 67.6 percent of wage-earning Swedish immigrant women worked in service.[16]

16 R. Cowan, *More Work for Mother. The Ironies of Household Technology from the Open Hearth to the Microwave*, New York, Basic Books, 1983, pp. 120, 121–22; S. Strasser, *Never Done*, pp. 163, 164; D. Katzman, *Seven Days a Week*, pp. 49, 65, 67; F. Walker, "Our Domestic Service", *Scribner's Monthly Illustrated Magazine for the People*, 11, 1, November 1875, p. 277; J. Lintelman, "'Our Serving Sisters' Swedish-American Domestic Servants and Their Ethnic Community", *Social Science History,* 15, 3, Fall 1991, p. 382.

Scholarship

Scholarly investigation into the experiences of domestics other than the Irish varies by group. Scholarship on German immigrant domestic servants in the United States in the nineteenth and twentieth centuries, for example, is sparse, at best. Only one scholarly work on German immigrant women in domestic service in the United States appears to exist – Silke Wehner-Franco's German-language *Deutsche Dienstmädchen in Amerika* 1850–1914 *(German Servant Girls in America 1850–1914).* Laurence Glasco, however, does make some mention of German immigrants in domestic service in his study of ethnic groups in Buffalo, New York in 1855. And Carol K. Coburn conducted some research on German-American girls in domestic service in Block, Kansas, in the period 1913–1937. Joy Lintelman, on the other hand, has produced some rather detailed work on Swedish immigrant domestic servants in the late nineteenth and early twentieth centuries.[17]

In the early part of the twentieth century, the number of African Americans in service in the urban North grew as Southern Blacks migrated North. Concomitant with the increased presence of African-Americans in domestic service in the North, the number of Irish immigrants working in domestic service in the cities of the Northeast declined. Susan Strasser succinctly sums up what then transpired: "Bridget, the stereotyped, full-time, live-in servant of the nineteenth century, left the scene, replaced by Beulah, the part-time black maid of the twentieth." By 1920, African-American women comprised the major servant group in the urban North, and by 1944, they comprised more than 60 percent of do-

17 There is an English-language review of Silke Wehner-Franco's book: D. Schneider, *American Historical Review*, 102, 1, February 1997, pp. 199–200. L. Glasco, "The Life Cycles and Household Structure of American Ethnic Groups. Irish, Germans, and Native-born Whites in Buffalo, New York, 1855", *Journal of Urban History* 1, 3, May 1975, pp. 339–364; C. Coburn, "Learning to Serve. Education and Change in the Lives of Rural Domestics in the Twentieth Century", *Journal of Social History* 25, 1, 1991, pp. 109–122; J. Lintelman, "'America is the woman's promised land' Swedish Immigrant Women and American domestic service", *Journal of American Ethnic History*, 8, 2, Spring 1989, pp. 9–23; J. Linterman, "Our Serving Sisters", pp. 381–395.

mestic workers. For this reason, much scholarly study of domestic service focuses on African-Americans.[18]

Research dealing with women from other ethnic and racial backgrounds working in domestic service in twentieth-and twenty first-century America has also been undertaken. Most of the scholarly literature consists of case studies of domestic servants from particular groups, in certain geographic locations in the United States in specific timeframes. Evelyn Nakano Glenn's work, for example, concerns Japanese women in northern California and shows that, agricultural work aside, domestic service was the usual occupation of both Japanese immigrant women and their American-born daughters until the Second World War. Vicki Ruiz points out that domestic service was the major occupation of Mexican women in the United States from 1900–1950, and her case study concerns undocumented (i.e., illegal) Mexican national women working in domestic service in El Paso, Texas in the 1980s. Also in the 1980s, Mary Romero studied American-born female Chicana (of Mexican descent) domestics working in the Denver, Colorado area, and in the mid-1980s, Shellee Colen studied West Indian immigrant domestic workers in New York City. From 1986–1988, Pierrette Hondagneu-Sotelo investigated undocumented Mexican immigrant women working in domestic service in the

18 S. Strasser, *Never Done*, p. 176, quote from p. 178; D. Katzman, *Seven Days a Week*, p. 273; E. Clark-Lewis, "'This Work Had a End' African-American Domestic Workers in Washington, D.C., 1910–1940", in C. Groneman and M. B. Norton (eds), *"To Toil the Livelong Day". America's Women at Work, 1780–1980*, Ithaca, Cornell University Press, 1987, pp. 196–211; E. Clark-Lewis, *Living In, Living Out. African American Domestics in Washington, D.C., 1910–1940*, Washington, D.C., Smithsonian Institution Press, 1994; B. T. Dill, "'The Means to Put My Children Through': Child-Rearing Goals and Strategies Among Black Female Domestic Servants", in L. Rodgers-Rose, *The Black Woman,* Beverly Hills, Sage, 1980, pp. 107–123; B. T. Dill, "'Making Your Job Good Yourself.' Domestic Service and the Construction of Personal Dignity", in A. Brookman and S. Morgen (eds), *Women and the Politics of Empowerment*, Philadelphia, Temple University Press, 1988, pp. 33–52; T. Harris, *From Mammies to Militants. Domestics in Black American Literature*, Philadelphia, Temple University Press, 1982; E. B. Kaplan, "'I Don't Do No Windows' Competition Between the Domestic Worker and the Housewife", in V. Miner and H. E. Longino (eds), *Competition: A Feminist Taboo?,* New York, The Feminist Press, 1987, pp. 92–105; P. Palmer, *Domesticity and Dirt. Housewives and Domestic Servants in the United States, 1920–1945*, Philadelphia, Temple University Press, 1989; J. Rollins, *Between Women*; S. Tucker, "The Black Domestic in the South. Her Legacy as Mother and Mother Surrogate", in C. M. Dillman (ed.), *Southern Women*, New York, Hemisphere Publishing, 1988.

San Francisco Bay area of California. In the mid-1990s, she undertook a case study of Latina (Mexican and Central American women) domestic workers in Los Angeles, California. In the late 1980s, Leslie Salzinger studied two Latina cooperatives for domestic servants in the San Francisco Bay area of California. Others who have produced scholarly work on domestic service in the United States in 1990s–2000s include Doreen J. Mattingly, who conducted a study of Mexican immigrant domestic workers in San Diego, California in 1993–4; Jennifer Bickham Mendez, who conducted a case study of a commercial cleaning service in California in 1994; Michael J. Pisani and David W. Yoskowitz, who completed a case study of Mexican immigrant domestics in Laredo, Texas in 2000, and Rhacel Salazar Parreñas, who studied Filipina domestics in Los Angeles, California.[19]

19 E. N. Glenn, "The Dialectics of Wage Work: Japanese-American Women and Domestic Service, 1905–1940", in E. Dubois and V. Ruiz (eds), *Unequal Sisters: A Multicultural Reader in U.S. Women's History,* New York, Routledge, 1990, pp. 345–372; E. N. Glenn, "From Servitude to Service Work: Historical Continuities in the Racial Division of Paid Reproductive Labor", *Signs,* 18, 1, 1992, pp. 1–43; E. N. Glenn, *Issei, Nisei, War Bride: Three Generations of Japanese American Women in Domestic Service*, Philadelphia, Temple University Press, 1986; V. Ruiz, "By the Day or the Week: Mexicana Domestic Workers in El Paso", in V. Ruiz and S. Tiano (eds), *Women on the U.S.–Mexico Border: Responses to Change*, Boston, Allen & Unwin, 1987, pp. 61–76; M. Romero, *Maid in the U.S.A.*, New York, Routledge, 1992, p. 6; S. Colen, "'Just a Little Respect': West Indian Domestic Workers in New York City", in E. Chaney and M. G. Castro (eds), *Muchachas No More: Household Workers in Latin America and the Caribbean*, Philadelphia, Temple University Press, 1989, pp. 171–194; P. Hondagneu-Sotelo, "Regulating the Unregulated? Domestic Workers' Social Networks", *Social Problems*, 41, 1, 1994, pp. 50–64; P. Hondagneu-Sotelo, *Doméstica: Immigrant Workers Cleaning and Caring in the Shadows of Affluence*, Berkeley, University of California Press, 2001, pp. 8, 16, 17; L. Salzinger, "A Maid by Any Other Name: The Transformation of 'Dirty Work' by Central American Immigrants", in M. Burawoy *et al.*, *Ethnography Unbound: Power and Resistance in the Modern Metropolis*, Berkeley, University of California Press, 1991, pp. 139–160; D. Mattingly, "Job Search, Social Networks, and Local Labor-Market Dynamics: The Case of Paid Household Work in San Diego, California", *Urban Geography*, 20, 1, 1999, pp. 46–74; D. Mattingly, "Making Maids: United States immigration policy and immigrant domestic workers", in J. H. Momsen (ed.), *Gender, Migration and Domestic Service*, New York, Routlege, 1999, pp. 62–79, J. B. Mendez, "Of Mops and Maids: Contradictions and Continuities in Bureaucratized Domestic Work", *Social Problems,* 45, 1, February 1998, pp. 114–135; M. J. Pisani and D. Yoskowitz, "The Maid Trade: Cross-Border Work in South Texas", *Social Science Quarterly,* 83, 2, June 2002, pp. 568–579; R. S. Parreñas, *Ser-*

Commonalties and Distinctions in Servants' Experiences

As an occupation, domestic service has been an integral part of the rural-to-urban migration for many women. Most Irish and Swedish immigrant domestics, for example, migrated from rural areas of their home countries to work in service in urban America. Many African-Americans domestics migrated from the rural South to urban America to work in service. And German-American girls migrated from rural to urban parts of Kansas to work as domestics. In contrast, the Latina domestics from the Amigos cooperative that Salzinger studied in 1988 were from urban areas. Likewise, Hondagneu-Sotelo claims that the Latina immigrant domestics in Los Angeles that she studied in the 1990s hailed from cities in their home countries. Domestics' reasons for migrating to work in service in America, too, have been consistent over time and space. They migrated for economic reasons – to improve their lives – and they entered domestic service because it was the best occupational venue available to them. And a review of the literature indicates that certain employers' reasons for hiring domestics – to provide the employer with more leisure time, and to fill the employer's status and emotional needs also – have remained much the same over time and space, regardless of the ethnic or racial group to which the domestic belonged.[20]

To varying degrees, most domestics considered in the scholarly literature have faced class and ethnic, as well as cultural and/or linguistic dif-

---

vants of Globalization: Women, Migration and Domestic Work, Stanford, Stanford University Press, 2001.

20 D. Katzman, *Seven Days a Week*, pp. 69, 202–204, 208–209, 273; J. Lintelman, "'America is the woman's promised land", pp. 10, 14; E. Clark-Lewis, "'This Work Had a End': African-American Domestic Workers in Washington, D.C., 1910–1940", p. 196; C. Coburn, "Learning to Serve", pp. 110, 111, 114; L. Salzinger, "A Maid by Any Other Name", p. 143; P. Hondagneu-Sotelo, *Doméstica,* p. 48; S. Colen, "'Just a Little Respect", p. 172; D. Mattingly, "Making Maids", p. 68; J. H. Momsen, *Gender, Migration and Domestic Service*, p. 11, and M. J. Pisani and D. Yoskowitz, "The Maid Trade", pp. 570, 572; on reasons for becoming domestics, R. S. Parreñas, *Servants of Globalization,* p. 184; J. Rollins, *Between Women*, p. 102, and E. B. Kaplan, "'I Don't Do No Windows'", p. 95, all on employer reasons for hiring domestics; P. Palmer, *Domesticity and Dirt*, pp. 4, 13–14, 138–139, 144, on hiring servants of color to confirm status; J. Rollins, *Between Women*, pp. 105, 107, 121, 131, 147, 156, 157, 180, on hiring African-Americans to meet emotional needs and to validate the employer's social class; M. Romero, *Maid in the U.S.A.*, pp. 112–113, 131.

ferences with their employers. Scholars argue that, in general, historically, domestic service has been an occupation deemed especially proper for women of color. And, so, according to the literature, race and color have intersected negatively with domestic service. This was the case for Irish immigrants, who were initially viewed by white, native-born Americans more as a separate race than as an ethnic group. African-American, Japanese, Latina (including Central American and Mexican) immigrants, American-born Chicanas (of Mexican descent), and West Indian women have all suffered from the intersection of race and color with domestic service. The experience of African-American women in domestic work, in particular, has entwined with racism.[21]

The literature also demonstrates that Irish immigrant domestics were not the only women to confront discrimination in recruitment and advertising for domestic work. Mexican domestics, too, faced such discrimination. As recently as the 1980s, an ad in an El Paso, Texas, newspaper read "Wanted: European housekeeper".[22]

Over time and space, regardless of the worker's ethnic or racial background, certain aspects of live-in domestic service have remained fairly consistent. For example, despite technological improvements, housework remains hard, physical work. Also, a supposed advantage of live-in service is that it provides the domestic with room and board. Yet with regard to board or food, Palmer discloses that employers often provided servants of color with food that was inadequate in amount, leaving them hungry. Similarly, Colen mentions that inadequate food was provided to West Indian immigrant domestics in New York City in the 1980s. And Hondagneu-Sotelo declares that the food provided to some Latina domestics in Los Angeles in the 1990s was sometimes of very poor quality or was so insufficient that they felt compelled to buy their own food. Also, Palmer notes that the room employers provided for the live-in domestics she stud-

21 D. Clark, *The Irish in Philadelphia: Ten Generations of Urban Experience*, Philadelphia, Temple University Press, 1973, p. 129; D. Clark, *The Irish Relations: Trials of an Immigrant Tradition*, E. Brunswick, N.J., Associated University Presses, 1982, p. 163; "Morals and Manners of the Kitchen", *The Nation*, 2 January 1873, p. 7; E. N. Glenn, *Issei, Nisei, War Bride: Three Generations of Japanese American Women in Domestic Service*, Philadelphia, Temple University Press, 1986, p. xi; P. Hondagneu-Sotelo, *Doméstica*, pp. 13–14, 18–19; 55–56; S. Colen, "Just a Little Respect", pp. 172, 189; M. Romero, *Maid in the U.S.A.*, pp. 71–72, 93–95. 98; P. Palmer, *Domesticity and Dirt*, pp. 13–14, 138–39, 144; J. Rollins, *Between Women*, pp. 8, 9, 180.

22 V. Ruiz, "By the Day or the Week: Mexicana Domestic Workers in El Paso", p. 71.

ied often was as unappealing as that provided to Irish servants, consisting, as it sometimes did, of a room over the employer's garage. West Indian domestics and live-in Latinas in Los Angeles, too, found it objectionable that sometimes they were expected to share a bedroom with the children for whom they cared.[23]

In general, employers have used physical space to separate themselves from servants. Employers of Irish domestics, for example, presided over houses in which, by design, servant spaces were separated from family spaces. Some employers of German-American domestics separated them from the family by making them eat in the kitchen, and others made their German-American domestics use the back, rather than the main, entrance to the house. Employers also physically separated themselves from their African-American domestics by relegating them to the kitchen when the domestics were not busy with chores in other rooms. It rankled live-in West Indian domestics, too, that they were not permitted to eat meals with the family for whom they worked, but rather were expected to eat in the kitchen. Whether or not they would or should eat with their employers was an issue for Latina domestics in Los Angeles, too. Not all servants desire inclusion at the family dinner table, though. Parreñas, for example, tells of a Filipina domestic in Los Angeles who refused her employer's offer to eat her meals with the employer's family, saying she would be more comfortable eating alone because "This is where I sleep, but it is not the same as being in your own home". Her comment points to an aspect of live-in domestic service that has been true over time and space: the house in which a domestic lives is her workplace, not her home. Hondagneu-Sotelo makes an ironic observation with regard to employers attempting to confine domestics to particular areas of the home. She tells us that some exhausted employers in contemporary Los Angeles, unwilling to expend the emotional energy personal interaction with their live-in Latina domestics would require, confine *themselves* to bedrooms to avoid dealing with their lonely employees.[24]

23 B. Ehrenreich, *Nickel and Dimed: On (Not) Getting By in America*, New York, Henry Holt, 2001, pp. 88–90; P. Palmer, *Domesticity and Dirt*, p. 83; P. Hondagneu-Sotelo, *Doméstica*, pp. 31, 33–35, 125, 217; S. Colen, "'Just a Little Respect'", p. 181.

24 B. McKinley, "The Stranger in the Gates", pp. 236–277; A. J. Downing, *The Architecture of Country Houses*, D. Appleton & Company, 1850, reprint, New York, Dover Publications, 1969, pp. 278, 309, 326, 350, 360; C. Coburn, "Learning to Serve", p. 114; J. Rollins, *Between Women*, p. 52; T. Harris, *From Mammies to Militants*, p. 15; E. B. Kaplan, "I Don't Do No Windows", p. 97; S. Colen, "Just a Little Re-

Most live-in domestics have shared the experience of working long hours and being on-call to their employers. In addition, most live-in servants have had very limited time off. Swedish immigrant domestics and the domestics of color that Palmer studied, for example, got the same limited time off, usually Thursdays and Sundays, that Irish maids had gotten. And in the 1990s, some Latina domestics in Los Angeles got only Sundays off. In addition, Latina domestics in Los Angeles, like the Irish maids of old, have found that their employers do not want them entertaining friends inside the employer's home. So, live-in domestic work is isolating and lonely work today, as it was in the past, and domestics' complaints of being treated as if they are invisible echo over time and space. It is no wonder, then, that Hondagneu-Sotelo found that Latina domestics in Los Angeles sought some personal relationship with their employer to validate their humanity, while time-pressed employers wanted a more distant, business-like relationship to minimize the amount of emotional energy they expended on their domestics.[25]

German immigrant domestics and their more modern sisters in service have experienced employer attempts to cheat them of their wages. In addition, the African-American and West Indian experiences in domestic service, as well as the Latina experience in service in Los Angeles, mirror the Irish experience in that they rarely included paid holidays, vacation or sick leave. Chicana domestics in Denver, too, failed to receive the benefits of paid vacations and social security because most of them worked off-the-books. Many Japanese domestics worked off-the-books, too. Despite the fact that by the 1970s certain protections covered domestic workers, Bonnie Dill Thornton claims that many employers failed to extend social security coverage, minimum wages, and unemployment insurance to African-American domestics and she points out that enforcement of such requirements is difficult. As Colen mentions with regard to West Indian

---

spect", p. 181; R. S. Parreñas, *Servants of Globalization*, quote from p. 166; P. Hondagneu-Sotelo, *Doméstica*, pp. 173–74, 182, 204.

25 J. Lintelman, "America is the woman's promised land", p. 17; P. Palmer, *Domesticity and Dirt*, p. 77; P. Hondagneu-Sotelo, *Doméstica*, pp. 11, 32–33, 63, 66, 142, 145, 177, 196, 197, 201, 206, 227; R. S. Parreñas, *Servants of Globalization*, p. 169; T. Harris, *From Mammies to Militants*, p. 12; D. Mattingly, "Job Search", p. 52; J. B. Mendez, "Of Mops and Maids", pp. 130–31; C. L. MacDonald, "Manufacturing Motherhood: The Shadow Work of Nannies and Au Pairs", *Qualitative Sociology*, 21, 1, 1998, p. 35; E. McLaughlin and N. Kraus, *The Nanny Diaries*, New York, St. Martin's Press, 2002, p. 274.

domestics in New York, and Hondagneu-Sotelo specifies with regard to Latina domestics in Los Angeles, the problem today is not the lack of governmental regulation of domestic service. Instead, the problem is either ignorance of the required regulations or failure to comply with them, both of which are exacerbated by the fact that the rules governing domestic service are generally not enforced.[26]

Employer fear that domestics will steal from them is apparently widespread. For, like employers of Irish servants, the literature indicates that employers of Swedish immigrant domestics, Japanese domestics, African-American domestics, West Indian domestics, Latina and Mexican national domestics all feared their employees would steal from them. Employer's ridicule of domestics has not been limited to the Irish, either. Like the Irish maids who were the butt of "Biddy" and "Bridget" jokes, Mexican national domestics in El Paso were the subject of derisive "stupid maid" stories. In addition, across the board, it appears that domestics have faced possible sexual harassment or exploitation at the hands of their employers' husbands, for Irish immigrant, Swedish immigrant, German-American, African-American, Mexican national and Latina domestics all encountered this problem.[27] Over time and space, immigrant women have also accrued a similar benefit from their work as domestics – the ability to save money to use to support their families. Like the Irish, Swedish servants sent money home, as did Japanese immigrant, and West Indian immigrant

26 A German House Servant, "Seeing America From the Kitchen", *Living Age*, 28 February, 1925, p. 465; M. Romero, *Maid in the U.S.A.*, pp. 128, 129, 148; V. Ruiz, "By the Day or the Week" p. 70; L. Martin and K. Segrave, *The Servant Problem: Domestic Workers in North America*, Jefferson, N.C., McFarland and Company, 1985, pp. 60, 74, 128, 144, 150, 151; E. B. Kaplan, "I Don't Do No Windows", p. 94; S. Colen, "Just a Little Respect", pp. 173, 186; P. Hondagneu-Sotelo, *Doméstica*, pp. 12, 21, 107–108; E. N. Glenn, *Issei, Nisei, War Bride*, p. 175; T. B. Dill, "Making Your Job Good Yourself", p. 35.

27 B. K. Bradbury, "The Servants of the Ogden Codman Family: The Relationships of Class, Ethnicity and Gender in Nineteenth Century Domestic Service", MA Thesis, Tufts University, 1993, p. 80; J. Lintelman, "Our Serving Sisters", pp. 384, 385, 386; E. N. Glenn, "The Dialectics of Wage Work", p. 362; T. Harris, *From Mammies to Militants*, pp. 4, 5, 18-19; S. Colen, "Just a Little Respect", p. 185; P. Hondagneu-Sotelo, *Doméstica*, pp. 47, 66, 163; V. Ruiz, "By the Day or the Week", pp. 69, 70; F. Dudden, *Serving Women*, pp. 214-217; C. Coburn, "Learning to Serve", p. 114; E. B. Kaplan, "I Don't Do No Windows", pp. 101-102; D. Bolden, "Forty-two Years a Maid, Starting at Nine in Atlanta", in Nancy Seifer (ed.), *Nobody Speaks for Me! Self-Portraits of American Working Class Women*, New York, Simon Schuster, 1976, p. 146; J. Rollins, *Between Women*, pp. 150-151.

domestics in New York City. Latina and Filipina domestics in Los Angeles, and Mexican immigrant domestics in San Diego sent home remittances, too. African-American domestics who migrated from the South to Washington, D.C. to work in service also sent money home.[28]

Scholars agree that throughout the nineteenth and twentieth centuries domestic service was a low-status occupation that stigmatized its workers. One hallmark of the demeaning nature of the work that has incensed domestics over time and space is being required to scrub on their hands and knees. Interestingly enough, however, regardless of their employers' perception or treatment of them, most domestics, like the Irish, do not seem to have accepted the idea that they were lower-status beings because they worked as domestics. Lintelman argues that Swedish immigrant girls working in cities in the urban Northeast and Midwest believed they had improved status as servants in America compared to their past positions as domestics in Sweden. She argues further that another reason Swedish women did not feel demeaned in service is that the Swedish community viewed domestic service more positively than did native-born Americans. And it is clear, too, that German-American girls thought that their status rose, rather than declined, in domestic service. And, according to Dill, although the Black domestics she studied "were keenly aware of the low social status of their occupation, ... they rarely presented themselves as defeated by it. Instead, they portrayed themselves as having been actively engaged in a struggle to assert their individual worth". Even though some of the West Indian domestics Colen studied had held higher-status jobs in their home countries before coming to America, they did not feel that working as domestics made them lesser beings than their employers. They, like the Irish, saw domestic service not as a lifetime career, but rather as a "stepping-stone" to other employment and a better life. Some of the Latinas Salzinger studied, too, ostensibly moved down the class ladder from higher-status work in their home country to domestic work in the United States, but they, too, refused to see themselves as having fallen downward occupationally. Instead, they were proud of the good work they did and the good pay they earned. Some of the Latinas of Hondagneu-

28 J. Lintelman, "America is the woman's promised land", p. 15; E. N. Glenn, "The Dialectics of Wage Work", p. 354; S. Colen, "Just a Little Respect", p. 186; P. Hondagneu-Sotelo, *Doméstica*, p. 65; R. S. Parreñas, *Servants of Globalization*, pp. 160, 249; D. Mattingly, "Making Maids", p. 68; E. Clark-Lewis, "This Work Had a End", p. 209.

Sotelo's case study in Los Angeles formerly had held higher-status jobs in their home country. They disliked being domestics but, she avers, they also "do take pride in their work, and... are extremely proud of what their earnings enable them to accomplish for their families". Most of the Filipina domestics Parreñas studied were educated, and some came from families that employed maids in the Philippines. Working as domestics would seem to have caused them to slip down the occupational ladder, and they were sensitive about this. They comforted themselves, however, that while their occupational status declined, they gained financially in that, as domestics in Los Angeles, they earned more than professionals in the Philippines. Indicating how important it was for them to hold on to their view of themselves as having some status, Filipina domestics called themselves "the educated domestics" to distinguish themselves from other domestics such as Latina and African-American domestics.[29]

Their own ethnic and/or racial community constituted an important support for domestics. During their limited leisure, Swedish servants, like Irish immigrant domestics, kept in close contact with their ethnic community. Also, between jobs, Swedish domestics, like Irish domestics, found housing with friends in their ethnic community. The Japanese community, too, provided support for Japanese domestics and the African-American community did so for African-American domestics. In addition, the West

29 D. Katzman, *Seven Days a Week*, pp. 44, 242–244; A German House Servant, "Seeing America From the Kitchen", p. 464; E. N. Glenn, "The Dialectics of Wage Work", pp. 345, 358; T. B. Dill, "Making Your Job Good Yourself", p. 34, first quote from p. 36, p. 51; J. Rollins, *Between Women,* pp. 58–59, 107–108; J. B. Mendez, "Of Mops and Maids", p. 122; B. Ehrenreich, *Nickel and Dimed*, p. 83; J. Lintelman, "America is the woman's promised land", pp. 11, 14, 16, 18; J. Lintelman, "Our Serving Sisters", pp. 382–383, 392–393; a 1906 article indicates that the conditions of domestic service in America were far better than conditions in Germany, so one might logically infer that German immigrant servants in America felt that their status improved in this country, see W. W. Whitelock, "The Servant Question in Germany", *Harper's Bazar*, May 1906, 40, 5, p. 467, but a German immigrant domestic argued in 1925 that "A cook's vocation in the United States is presumably not much pleasanter than in Germany, in spite of the higher pay and the more comfortable room..." see A German House-Servant, "Seeing America from the Kitchen", p. 463; C. Coburn, "Learning to Serve", p. 114; T. B. Dill, "Making Your Job Good Yourself", p. 34, first quote from p. 36, p. 51; J. H. Colen, "Just a Little Respect", pp. 173, 187, second quote from p. 189; L. Salzinger, "A Maid by Any Other Name", pp. 139, 145–146; P. Hondagneu-Sotelo, *Doméstica*, pp. 150–51, third quote from p. 12; R. S. Parreñas, *Servants of Globalization*, pp. 19, 150, fourth quote from p. 174.

Indian community, too, supported and encouraged the domestics from its ranks.[30]

All of the domestic servants cited in the literature, not just the Irish, showed agency. Since employment contracts clearly spelling out expectations are still uncommon, mismatches between the employer's and the domestic's expectations of what will be entailed in the job can and do lead to tense employer-employee relations. So, when German immigrant, African-American, Japanese, Latina and West Indian domestics were very unhappy in their work situation, like the Irish, they voted with their feet and quit. Immigrant Mexicana cleaners in San Diego, too, found that quitting was their "bargaining chip" in dealing with employers.[31]

Through their agency, African-American domestics are acknowledged as having effected a positive improvement in the occupation. Unlike young, single, Irish, German, and Swedish immigrant domestics, African Americans tended to be married women for whom service was often a lifelong occupation. Since African-American women had their own families, they preferred to return home at the conclusion of a day's service work, rather than to live in with their employers. As a result, African-American domestics are credited with engineering the transformation of domestic service from mainly live-in to mainly live-out or day work. Bonnie Thornton Dill maintains that in doing so, they gained increased individual freedom, lessened their isolation from their families and the African-American community, and reduced their hours of employment. African-Americans, however, were not alone in bringing about the switch to day work. Married Japanese-American domestics from 1905–1940 also preferred day work because it afforded them the flexibility of earning money while simultaneously fulfilling their family responsibilities in their own homes. Chicana domestics in Denver in the late twentieth century, as well as undocumented Mexican immigrants in San Francisco in the late 1980s, too, preferred day work to live-in service. Latina domestics in Los Angeles in the mid-1990s, too, preferred day work as cleaners to live-in

30 J. Lintelman, "'America is the woman's promised land", pp. 7, 13–14; J. Lintelman, "Our Serving Sisters", pp. 389, 393; E. N. Glenn, *Issei, Nisei, War Bride*, p. 179; T. B. Dill, "Making Your Job Good Yourself", pp. 47, 48, 50; J. H. Colen "Just a Little Respect", p. 188.

31 A German House Servant, "Seeing America From the Kitchen", p. 464; T. B. Dill, "Making Your Job Good Yourself", pp. 39, 41; E. N. Glenn, "The Dialectics of Wage Work", p. 363; P. Hondagneu-Sotelo, *Doméstica*, pp. 61, 138, 155; J. H. Colen, "Just a Little Respect", p. 187; D. Mattingly, "Job Search", quote from p. 64.

work because it permitted them to have a family life. Their preference highlights the fact that domestics who live out tend to be married, while those who live in tend to be single.[32]

Japanese domestics in the period 1905–1940 also demonstrated agency in insisting on working on a task, rather than a time, basis. Further, they purposefully selected employers who would be absent from the home when the work was performed. In doing so they derived greater occupational autonomy because absent employers have little opportunity to interfere with a domestic's execution of the work. For similar reasons, late twentieth-century Chicana domestics, too, preferred to work for employers who were absent from the home while they worked. And, in the mid-1990s, many Latinas in Los Angeles, too, worked alone in private homes for absent employers.[33]

Chicana domestics working at the end of the twentieth century also showed agency in their struggle with employers "to restructure the work as a small business by transforming it from wage labor to an occupation involving labor services". In this transformation, while working for multiple employers on a set schedule, individual Chicanas "define the work on the basis of a contract – by the house or the apartment – rather than as hourly work". According to Romero, in defining themselves as "expert cleaners or housekeepers" Chicana household workers sought to distinguish themselves from servants, per se. In her 1994 work, Hondagneu-Sotelo refers to Romero's 1992 work to point out that this flat-rate, job-work form of domestic service represents yet another transformation (the first was the switch from live-in to day work) in the nature of the occupation.[34]

32 J. Lintelman, "Our Serving Sisters", p. 390; C. Harzig, "The Role of German Women in the German-American Working-Class Movement in Late Nineteenth-Century New York", *Journal of American Ethnic History*, 8, 2, Spring 1989, p. 101; C. Coburn, "Learning to Serve", pp. 111, 112; D. Katzman, *Seven Days a Week*, pp. 44, 80–82, 89–92, 198–199, 273; T. B. Dill, "Making Your Job Good Yourself", pp. 34, 35; Palmer, *Domesticity and Dirt*, pp. 68–69; E. N. Glenn, "The Dialectics of Wage Work", pp. 355, 357–358; M. Romero, *Maid in the U.S.A.*, pp. 143, 145–148; P. Hondagneu-Sotelo, "Regulating the Unregulated?", p. 54; P. Hondagneu-Sotelo, *Doméstica*, pp. 38, 49–50.

33 E. N. Glenn, "The Dialectics of Wage Work", pp. 362–363; M. Romero, *Maid in the U.S.A.*, pp. 153; P. Hondagneu-Sotelo, *Doméstica*, pp. 78, 121.

34 M. Romero, *Maid in the U.S.A.,* first quote from p. 147, second and third quotes from p. 155; P. Hondagneu-Sotelo, "Regulating the Unregulated?", p. 51.

When the Irish dominated the occupation in the Northeast, in comparison with factory pay, the wages domestic service offered were good. Over the first half of the twentieth century, however, salaries for domestic servants increasingly lost ground against those paid to factory workers, making domestic service both low-status and low-paid work. More recently, however, domestic work has again been cited as offering attractive pay. For example, Romero avows that for Chicana women in the 1980s, "In comparison with other jobs they had held, domestic service usually paid more...". In her 1990s case study of Mexicana cleaners in San Diego, Mattingly makes a similar point, noting that the hourly wages of the domestic workers she studied exceeded the minimum wage. According to Hondagneu-Sotelo, in the mid-1990s, Latina domestics in Los Angeles found live-out work to pay better than live-in work, and found that the wages earned in live-out house cleaning compared favorably with factory work pay. And, as previously noted, Filipina domestics earned more as domestics in Los Angeles than they would as professionals in the Philippines.[35]

Their English-speaking ability would certainly seem to have provided Irish domestics with a decided advantage over non-English speaking or limited-English speaking German, Scandinavian, Japanese, Central American, Mexican and Latina immigrants. Former Irish domestic Mary Feely Harren, who came to the U.S. in 1927, apparently believed that her English language facility was an asset because she mentioned that the girls who did housework "that come from Sweden and Norway and Germany... didn't speak a word of English when they come here. But they learned. Some of them took care of the kids for a couple of months until they learned enough that they could get by on".[36]

Mattingly's case study in San Diego in the 1990s led her to conclude that English-speaking was an asset, for she found that English-speaking cleaners earned more than those without English-language facility, partly because they were better able to seek out new jobs and to negotiate wages with employers. For Latina domestics in Los Angeles in the 1990s, Hon-

35 D. Chaplin, "Domestic Service and Industrialization", in R. F. Tomasson (ed.), *Comparative Studies in Sociology: an Annual Compilation of Research*, vol. 1, Greenwich, CT., JAI Press, Inc., 1978, p. 110; L. Martin and K. Segrave, *The Servant Problem*, pp. 68–69; M. Romero, *Maid in the U.S.A.*, quotes from pp. 12–13; D. Mattingly, "Job Search", p. 55; P. Hondagneu-Sotelo, *Doméstica*, pp. 44, 51; R. S. Parreñas, *Servants of Globalization*, pp. 19, 150.

36 M. Harren, interview by author, 4 August 1996, tape recording.

dagneu-Sotelo, too, links the acquisition of better-paying domestic jobs with English-language facility. Also, Parreñas declares that Filipina domestics in Los Angeles see their English-language ability as an asset to them in their work. Interestingly enough, however, both Glenn and Hondagneu-Sotelo (in her 1980s work) claim that the language barrier was sometimes advantageous to domestics. Glenn declares that since Japanese women could not understand their employers, they were oblivious to "insulting or denigrating comments". Similarly, Hondagneu-Sotelo tells us that in the late 1980s, a novice Mexican immigrant domestic in San Francisco was advised by a more experienced domestic "to simply smile" at, rather than to speak to, her employer to stave off conversational attempts by the employer that might have wasted the domestic's time and money.[37]

Unlike some other countries, the United States has never had a governmental program to recruit foreign domestics to live and work here. Irish women in the period 1840–1930 came to this country first, and then found their way into employment in domestic service. These Irish women were *legal* immigrants. In this respect, their position is greatly distinguished from that of some more recent domestics. Mattingly notes that undocumented immigrants are much more likely to work as domestics than are legal immigrants, for service is one of the few employment options available to them. Hondagneu-Sotelo points out that the undocumented earn less as domestics than do those who are in the United States legally. Recent undocumented immigrants employed as domestics include West Indian, Mexican and Central American immigrant women. Ironically, also among them in the 1980s were well-educated but undocumented Irish immigrant women. Regardless of their education, class, race, or ethnic background, undocumented domestics earn less money than do documented domestics, and are more vulnerable to employer exploitation than are legal immigrant domestics.[38]

37 D. Mattingly, "Job Search", p. 63; P. Hondagneu-Sotelo, *Doméstica*, pp. 36, 45, 51; R. S. Parreñas, *Servants of Globalization*, pp. 178–79; E. N. Glenn, "The Dialectics of Wage Work", quote from p. 361; P. Hondagneu-Sotelo, "Regulating the Unregulated?", final quote from p. 57.

38 D. Mattingly, "Making Maids", p. 66; P. Hondagneu-Sotelo, *Doméstica*, pp. 20, 21; P. Hondagneu-Sotelo, "Regulating the Unregulated?", p. 59; R. S. Parreñas, *Servants of Globalization*, pp. 167, 168; J. H. Colen, "Just a Little Respect", pp. 173, 174, 175; P. Hondagneu-Sotelo, "Regulating the Unregulated?", p. 59; A. Rossiter, "Bringing the Margins into the Centre: A Review of Aspects of Irish Women's Emigration from a British Perspective", in Ailbhe Smyth (ed.), *Irish Women's Studies Reader*, Dublin,

Domestic service functioned as an acculturating occupation for Irish, German and Scandinavian immigrants, and for German-Americans. In the twentieth century, however, according to the literature, domestic service did not serve to acculturate many women of color, including Japanese and African-American women. Latinas appear to constitute an exception to this rule, for Hondagneu-Sotelo's study of Latina domestics in Los Angeles in the 1990s indicates that, in some respects, domestic service functioned as an acculturating occupation for them.[39] She notes, for example, that newly arrived Latinas tended to begin work as live-in domestics, especially as live-in combination nanny/housecleaners. Over time, however, as they developed their English-language skills and learned about other types of domestic employment, they moved on to the greater autonomy and independence offered by life as a live-out domestic, and usually ended up working solely as house cleaners. According to Mattingly's study of immigrant Mexican women, however, the Immigration Reform and Control Act (IRCA) has had a negative effect on mobility out of domestic service. For she argues that before this law passed, women could move out of domestic service into other employment. She contends, however, that "After IRCA, the opportunities for undocumented immigrant women to move out of domestic service became so limited that it now seems that household work is once again becoming an occupational ghetto".[40]

Every woman's experience in domestic service is dependent on a number of factors, including her personality, her employer's personality, the personalities of other members of the employing family, and the amount of work required of the domestic. Good employers exist along with the bad. Swedes believed that employers thought more highly of their domestics than they did of Irish servants. They contended that employers praised

---

Attic Press, 1993, p. 192; "Counting the Uncountable", *The Irish Voice*, 4 January–10 January 1995, p. 17; E. McLaughlin and N. Kraus, *The Nanny Diaries*, p. 36; J. Rollins, *Between Women*, p. 151; "Enslaved in land of the free", *The Albany Times Union,* 20 August 2000, p. B–7.

39 C. Hartzig, "The Role of German Women in the German-American Working-Class Movement in Late Nineteenth-Century New York", *Journal of American Ethnic History*, 8, 1989, pp. 87–108; J. Lintelman, "Our Serving Sisters", p. 390; C. Coburn, "Learning to Serve", pp. 111, 112, 115, 116; D. Chaplin, "Domestic Service and Industrialization", p. 108; E. N. Glenn, "The Dialectics of Wage Work", p. 345; T. B. Dill, "Making Your Job Good Yourself", p. 34; J. Rollins, *Between Women*, p. 55; P. Hondagneu-Sotelo, *Doméstica*, pp. 48–49.

40 P. Hondagneu-Sotelo, *Doméstica*, p. 49; D. Mattingly, "Making Maids", p. 72, quote.

their Swedish domestics; thus proud Swedes were led to proclaim that their domestics were "more reliable and hardworking than Irish women" and were thus "more sought-after for domestic positions". A 1906 report indicates, however, that Swedes may have over-estimated the esteem in which their domestics were held by employers. While praising them for being "hard workers, industrious, honest, efficient", the author of this report goes on to say that Swedish domestics are "not as rapid as the quick-motioned Irish girl".[41]

Religion was important not only to Irish domestics but to Swedish immigrant, German-American, African-American and West Indian domestics as well. As Irish servants were actively involved with the Roman Catholic Church, so too Swedish servants were great supporters of their church. Protestant Swedish churches in America counted domestics "as their best members". German-American servants in Kansas were good supporters of the Missouri Synod of the Lutheran Church, particularly its Ladies' Aid Society, which they turned into a money-generating organization. And African-American servants' desire to participate in their churches was one reason they favored day work, which made religious practice much more possible than live-in service. Dill also indicates that for African-Americans, the church "provided a place in which domestic workers could achieve status based upon their participation, making their occupational performance relatively unimportant". Recent scholarship, however, makes little or no mention of the relationship between religion and modern-day domestics. Overall, the information available indicates that the Irish experience in domestic service is distinguished from that of other women in that, only for Roman Catholic Irish domestics, was religion a strong point of contention between mistress and servant. Whether and how much religious discrimination was a problem for other Catholic domestics is simply unknown at this time.[42]

41 J. Lintelman, "America is the woman's promised land", p. 15; J. Lintelman, "Our Serving Sisters", quotes from p. 390; M. G. Smith, "Immigration as a Source of Supply for Domestic Workers", *Bulletin of the Inter-Municipal Research Committee* II, no. 8, May 1906, final two quotes from p. 8.

42 J. Lintelman, "Our Serving Sisters", quote from p. 391; C. Coburn, "Learning to Serve", p. 117; E. Clark-Lewis, "This Work Had a End", pp. 209–211; E. Clark-Lewis, *Living in, Living out*, pp. 136, 169–170; T. B. Dill, "Making Your Job Good Yourself", quote from p. 50; P. Hondagneu-Sotelo, *Doméstica*, pp. 225–26; S. Colen, "Just a Little Respect", p. 188. It is estimated that about 33 percent of German immigrants were Roman Catholics, the remainder were Protestant (Lutheran or other), see K. N. Con-

Conclusion

This comparative review of domestic service evidences many similarities and some differences in the experience of domestics over time and space in America. The Irish experience in domestic service, however, appears to be distinguished from that of all other domestic servants, in at least one respect – only Irish women appear to have dealt with intense religious discrimination in this occupation. Irish immigrant domestic servants strongly resisted the efforts of their white, middle-class, Protestant, female employers to interfere with their religious practice and dissuade them from their Catholicism. Consequently, after dealing with Irish immigrant domestics, employers no longer felt so free to interfere with a servant's religious beliefs. After the Irish experience, religion ceased to be a point of contention between employers and domestics in the United States. The Irish, then, can be credited with making domestic service in the United States more modern in that, as a result of their experience with American employers, religion became irrelevant to the occupation. So, in at least this one respect, the Irish Bridget's experience in domestic service was unique.[43]

---

zen, "Patterns of German-American History", in R. M. Miller (ed.), *Germans in America: Retrospect and Prospect*, Philadelphia, The German Society of Pennsylvania, 1984, p. 22. Nothing in the literature I reviewed indicated that German Catholic servants faced the same sort of conflict with their mistresses over religion that Irish Catholic domestics faced.

43 D. Katzman, *Seven Days a Week*, p. 164.

Were Servants Paid according to their Productivity?

Carmen SARASÚA

Wages, or, more generally, remuneration, are a fundamental element in the study of any working group. Wages express in different ways the economic and social value of work; they are a good indicator of the legal position of workers, since only free workers can contract their work; they help us to see the place of an occupation in the labour market, that is, in relation to other occupations. And they are the best indicator of the workers' standard of living, since, in a market society, wages are the main or only source of income for workers, and thus they determine their purchasing power.[1]

Wages have also been a central element of economic analysis. Standard or neoclassical economics defines wages as the price for labour, the main object of economics being to understand how prices are determined by supply and demand. So economics provide economic historians with a solid framework to interpret workers' wages. Yet in the last decades a number of scholars, mainly from economic history but also from labour economics, have pointed to the shortcomings and limitations of this theoretical framework to account for such crucial facts as wage differentials among workers, particularly race, age and gender gaps.

In this paper the main features of what we know about the remuneration of domestic workers in the eighteenth and nineteenth centuries are outlined, and an attempt is made to see if the theoretical framework provided by economic theory can help us to interpret them. I suggest that our historical evidence on how remuneration of domestic servants was fixed and paid illustrates the limitations of mainstream economic analysis to account for wages in the service sector in general, and for wages of domestic service and gender wage differentials in particular. I conclude that

1 I would like to thank Antoinette Fauve-Chamoux and Raffaella Sarti for providing me with the opportunity of discussing the history of domestic service within an international research network, and Peter Scholliers and Leonard Schwarz for generously commenting on a first version of this paper.

the notion of wages as cultural constructs, rather than market prices, is more useful to understand domestic workers' wages.[2]

Origins of Neoclassical Economic Theory: Domestic Service as Unproductive Work

Before the marginalist theory of the late nineteenth century, two important notions contributed to shape prevalent ideas about wages, and particularly about servants' wages. The first was the notion of wages as *subsistence* or *living wages*. Until the end of the eighteenth century, European economic thought linked wages to the cost of living, that is, to the price evolution of the basic food items, mostly grain. Wages were the means by which workers paid for their own subsistence. If the prices of food and rent rose, wages had to follow, or governments had to face an increase in poverty and in the already large number of beggars. Since most domestic servants were living-in servants, that is, servants living in their masters' houses, being fed and clothed by them, the idea of wages as subsistence wages led employers to regard the monetary part of their servants' wages as unimportant: servants did not need them.

A second notion contributing to a certain de-legitimation of servants' wages arrives with Adam Smith. In what is considered to be the origin of western economic thought, *The Wealth of Nations* (first published in 1776), Adam Smith defined domestic service (and service occupations in general) as non productive, and as such, as an occupation creating no wealth to pay for the wages received. As Smith was vindicating the productive character of manufacturing and trade, in contradiction to the French physiocrats, who claimed that agriculture was the sole source of

2 By servants I refer here to domestic servants, working mostly at home on domestic chores. Wages are broadly defined so as to include money but also food and lodging as well as other perquisites. See Peter Scholliers and Leonard Schwarz, "The wage in Europe since the sixteenth century", in Peter Scholliers and Leonard Schwarz (eds), *Experiencing Wages. Social and Cultural Aspects of Wage Forms in Europe since 1500*, New York, Berghahn Books, 2003, pp. 3–19.

new wealth, he used "menial servants" as example of non productive occupations:

> It seems [...] altogether improper to consider artificers, manufacturers and merchants, in the same light as menial servants. The labour of menial servants does not continue the existence of the fund which maintains and employs them. Their maintenance and employment is altogether at the expense of their masters, and the work which they perform is not of a nature to repay that expense. That work consists in services which perish generally in the very instant of their performance, and does not fix or realize itself in any vendible commodity which can replace the value of their wages and maintenance. The labour, on the contrary, of artificers, manufacturers and merchants, naturally does fix and realize itself in some such vendible commodity. It is upon this account that, in the chapter in which I treat of productive and unproductive labour, I have classed artificers, manufacturers and merchants among the productive labourers, and menial servants among the barren or unproductive (p. 639).[3]

In the chapter on productive and unproductive labour in the *Wealth of Nations*, he had, in fact, explained that servants' labour was unproductive because it created no value (value being understood as a vendible commodity):

> The labour of a manufacturer adds, generally, to the value of the materials which he works upon, that of his own maintenance, and of his master's profit. The labour of a menial servant, on the contrary, adds to the value of nothing. Though the manufacturer has his wages advanced to him by his master, he, in reality, costs him no expense, the value of those wages being generally restored, together with a profit, in the improved value of the subject upon which his labour is bestowed. But the maintenance of a menial servant never is restored. A man grows rich by employing a multitude of manufacturers: he grows poor, by maintaining a multitude of menial servants (p. 314).[4]

Smith accepts that service occupations (not only domestic servants, but lawyers, physicians, public officers, create no value through their work) may be necessary and useful, and of course deserve to be paid: "The labour of the latter [servant], however, has its value and deserves its reward as well." However, service workers, and domestic servants in particular, had less social and economic legitimacy to earn wages. By opposing the

3 References to Adam Smith, *An Inquiry into the nature and causes of the wealth of nations…* (first published in London, W. Straban and T. Cadell, 1776, 2 vol.), are taken from the Edwin Cannan's edition, New York, The Modern Library, 1937 (based on the 5th edition, 1789).

4 *Ibid.* This paragraph was already in the first edition, 1776, Book II, chap. 3.

behaviour of the manufacturer to that of the employer of servants, Smith is criticizing the dominant lifestyle of the upper classes of his time, and trying to incentive a new model of industrious bourgeois. The maintenance of "a multitude of menial servants" is the best example of irrational behaviour he can think of.

The idea of services, and particularly domestic services, as unproductive labour was maintained by economists after Smith. In his 1820 *Principles of Political Economy,* Malthus limited himself to a slight correction to Smith's principle:

> He defined productive labour as that labour that produced material wealth. He objected, however, to the term *unproductive labour* because he believed it connoted that such labour was unimportant. He preferred 'to substitute the term *personal services* for unproductive labour'.[5]

In the second half of the nineteenth century, Marx reinforced this classical undervaluation of service work, particularly of domestic service: as domestic servants failed to create surplus labour, they were "living not from capital but from revenue", and as such defined as *non-productive, relatively idle* workers.[6] This definition of domestic workers as unproductive, closer to paupers or rentiers than to factory workers, had important implications for political practice and for social consideration in general: since only workers producing surplus value were exploited, political activism and trade unionism made sense only among the truly exploited class. The same process that constructed factory workers (particularly male factory workers) as the real working class, constructed domestic workers (and female workers in general) as alien to it. For nineteenth-century revolutionaries as well as for twentieth-century trade unionists – one of whose main activities was pushing for higher wages – domestic workers were too

5 E. K. Hunt, *History of Economic Thought. A Critical Perspective*, Belmont, Wadsworth Pub., 1979, p. 71.

6 "The creation of surplus labour on the one side corresponds to the creation of minus labour, relative idleness (or *not-productive* labour at best), on the other. This goes without saying as regards capital itself; but also holds then also for the classes with which it shares; hence of the paupers, flunkeys, lickspittles, etc. living from the surplus product, in short, the whole train of retainers; the part of the servant class which lives not from capital but from revenue", Karl Marx, *Grundrisse. Introduction to the Critique of Political Economy*, quoted in Edward Higgs, "Domestic servants and the households in Victorian England", *Social History*, 8, 2, 1983, pp. 201–210.

close to the bourgeoisie and too distant (physically as well as mentally) from the "real" working class.

A main contribution to economic theory, and in fact what is considered to be the foundation of neoclassical economic thought, took place in late nineteenth century with the marginalist theory, which assumes that wages equal the marginal product of labour. Wages, thus, express workers' productivity. Increases in productivity are achieved through capital investment, that is, mechanization. Marginalist theory of wages mirrored the age of industrial labour and mass production, but failed to account for productive sectors difficult to mechanize, like parts of the service sector, which has nevertheless became the main productive sector of western economies in the twentieth century.

Wages as Cultural Constructs

Since the 1960s, many labour economists have disagreed with this theoretical framework to explain labour markets, particularly wage levels and wage differentials, and have pointed to the relevant role played by *institutions* in shaping long term economic behaviour. For their part, social and economic historians working on wages and other forms of remuneration argued that customs, traditions, and conventions played a fundamental role in fixing wages. The definition of wages as customary rather than market wages accounts better for, among other questions, the too suspiciously stable evolution of wage levels in pre-industrial times.[7]

Working since the 1980s to understand the gender wage gap, feminist historians have also made an important contribution to this critique of economic analysis by pointing to the fact that the very large gap between female and male wages in pre-industrial and industrial times cannot be explained solely by differences in productivity. They have gone beyond defining skills and qualifications as cultural rather than purely technical features. Gendered notions of "fair" and "appropriate" wage influenced what employers paid their workers. The institution of the "family wage", the notion of a salary for male workers sufficient to maintain their fami-

7 P. Scholliers and L. Schwarz, "The wage in Europe since the sixteenth century", in P. Scholliers and L. Schwarz (eds), *Experiencing Wages*, pp. 3–24.

lies, expanded during the second half of the nineteenth century and was supported both by mostly male trade unions and employers.[8] Employers bought industrial peace by agreeing to employ male instead of female workers, who were much cheaper and in many trades less militant due to their lower union affiliation. By defending their right to earn wages higher than those of women in order to preserve their role of heads of households, male workers were above all defending their right to have a paid occupation in preference to women. And they gained a social recognition that they, as much as middle class men, had a right to have housewives to take care of them, their homes and their children. Women workers were the only losers of this historic deal, as they increasingly lost their industrial jobs and were forced to employ themselves in undervalued and little paid occupations, such as home manufacturing, domestic service, or prostitution. In this process, market forces played only secondary roles. Wages were socially and culturally constructed as "woman's wages" or as "man's wages", as much as in the U.S. wages were constructed along race and ethnic lines. This approach seems more useful to understanding how servants' wages were fixed. Individual skill or capacity, that is the productivity of individual workers, helps to provide us with an approach to workers' pay, but it may be rather simplistic in view of the complexity of the process of wage fixation. Let us now turn to the historical evidence on domestic servants' wages.

What Do We Know about Servants' Wages?

Wages and remuneration in general is not a well known aspect of domestic service history. Authors refer to the silence of the sources, the private and non-written character of the contracts, the wide variety of domestic occupations, and the importance of the non-monetary components of do-

8 Alice Kessler-Harris, *A Woman's Wage. Historical Meanings & Social Consequences*, Lexington, The University Press of Kentucky, 1990. See, however, J. Burnette, "An investigation of the female-male wage gap during the industrial revolution in Britain", *Economic History Review*, 1997, pp. 257–281, for a classical vision of gender wage differences as the result of differences in productivity.

mestics' remuneration, among other questions, to account for this gap. My own research confirms this difficulty: studying domestic service advertisements from eighteenth and nineteenth century Madrid newspapers, I found only a few ads where salaries and other benefits were explicitly mentioned.[9]

Despite all the uncertainties about them, wages play a central role in the way crucial features of domestic service have been explained: the fact that service was the main occupation in most European towns until the second half of the nineteenth century, the decision of rural youngsters to migrate to the city, the preference of wealthiest employers for male domestics, the increasing feminisation of service in the nineteenth century, etc. This makes remuneration a crucial aspect of the history of domestic service. And although we are not yet in conditions to write a history of domestic workers' remuneration, it is possible to reconstruct its main characteristics:

a. Large differences in servants' wages, reflecting complex servant hierarchies, personal characteristics of the servants, and employers' decisions;
b. Importance of in-kind remuneration;
c. Nominal wages lower than in other occupations, but higher real wages, particularly in periods of price inflation, due to boarding as a part of remuneration;
d. Irregularity of money payments;
e. Highly valued qualitative aspects of domestic service;
f. Lower ability to bargain collectively for wages and working conditions.

Differences in Servants' Wages

Studies of domestic service point to large differences in domestics' wages, social status and working conditions. These differences were particularly apparent in the eighteenth and nineteenth century among servants of the

9 Carmen Sarasúa, *Criados, nodrizas y amos. El servicio doméstico en la formación del mercado de trabajo madrileño, 1758–1868*, Madrid, Siglo XXI, 1994. Remuneration and wages in pp. 216–226.

nobility and wealthy bourgeoisie, who employed large numbers of them and developed a complex hierarchy, to a large extent identified by differences in remuneration.

It is difficult to clearly identify the factors accounting for these differences in remuneration: skill and experience played an important role (as human capital theory would predict), but the personal characteristics of the servant (race, legal status, age, gender, and class) were fundamental as well. Large differences in the remuneration of domestic servants can also be attributed to employers' individual decisions. In her study of domestics in nineteenth century Florence, Casalini finds "truly surprising wage differences", that reveal "the wealth and generosity of employers". In the 1870s and 1880s, whilst the waitress to princess Olga Tubersckoj made 90 lire per month (plus housing and food), the male servant of a priest was making 100 lire a year. There were those happy simply to receive food and housing, whilst others received 20, 25 or 30 lire a month.[10] This total discretionality contradicts the very idea of a labour market, in which workers with similar skills obtain similar remunerations. The personal decisions of employers seem to reflect their appreciation for particular servants, as well as their desire to show their wealth.[11]

Among the systematic sources of differences in the remuneration of domestics, gender was probably the most classic. The wages of male servants were much higher than the wages of female servants, to the point that, as T. Veblen argued in his *Theory of the Leisured Class* (1899), male servants reflected better the wealth and status of their employers, and thus choosing to employ male servants was an obvious way of expressing the employer's higher status. Whilst in the eighteenth century domestic service was performed by both women and men (it was still the largest male occupation in most European cities), from the later years of the century it became a predominantly female occupation, given the increasing alternative occupations for men in transportation, manufacturing and the building trades.

Was domestic service badly paid because it was a feminised occupation or did it become feminised because it was badly paid? My research

10 Maria Casalini, *Servitù, nobili e borghesi nella Firenze dell'Ottocento*, Firenze, Olschki, 1997, p. 189.

11 As for the gender wage gap, Casalini argues that in the highest ranks of the occupation, male servants' wages were higher but often excluded food, because they were not forced to spend all of their daily workday at home.

suggests that feminisation led to a devaluation of domestic service, further reinforced by the fact that the middle-classes (including "poor" middle class families, such as those of shopkeepers, civil servants, teachers, etc., which to a large extent could not afford men's wages) were now the main employers of domestics.[12]

There is abundant evidence of domestic service being one of the very few occupations regarded as morally and socially adequate for women, as opposed to factory jobs. But we also know that, whenever an occupation has been recommended as suitable for women, women's social obligation to accept much lower wages than men was determinant. For instance, opponents to minimum wage for women in the U.S. in the 1920s argued that women should instead be more willing to become domestic servants, where they could live with lower wages and even save part of them.[13]

Importance of In-Kind Remuneration

Unlike most other wage workers, a majority of domestic servants were (and a certain percentage still are) live-in workers, that is, workers living in their employers' house, as part of the household (in fact, the group of servants received the name of "family" in the eighteenth century). Being a living-in servant meant that at least part of their remuneration was in kind: it consisted of food and lodging, plus working clothes and shoes and other perquisites. These non-monetary components of their remuneration constituted around three quarters of the total wage, according to most accounts.[14]

12 For a discussion of servants' employers in 19th century England, Leonard Schwarz, "The declining number of servants in England, 1650–1900", paper presented at the Conference on Models of Domestic Service, Munich, 2003, *Servant Project Proceedings,* Liège, 2005.

13 "But women, objecting to their endless hours, close supervision, and live-in conditions, frequently refused them", A. Kessler-Harris, *A Woman's Wage*, p. 45.

14 For mid-19th century Paris, "the monetary wage represented less than half of the total value of the servant's wage", Theresa McBride, "The Modernization of Woman's Work", *Journal of Modern History*, 49, June 1977, pp. 231–245. Quote in p. 240.

Fritz Hodne, Ola Grytten and Jorund Alme have shown the evolution of the monetary and non-monetary components of domestic servants' wages in Norway.[15] Living conditions were so bad for workers, particularly for children and women, that living in a comfortable house and eating every day was enough recompense for most of them:

> To understand how children could be pressed into such servitude, one has to recall the general economic conditions of the time. In the 1890s thousands of Londoners were homeless, sleeping in the parks, on the Embankment or in the recesses of London bridge. However badly a servant might be accommodated, it was no doubt better than the prevailing housing conditions for the poor in the London of the 1890s...[16]

This means that a qualitative feature of the servant wage (the fact that it was paid mostly in kind) compensated the quantitative aspect of wages being lower than in other occupations. The domestic servant was not only able to eat better herself or himself, but also to help unemployed or poor relatives, an image common in literary sources.

Boarding as the main or only component of domestics' remuneration helps also to better explain the social composition of domestic servants' employers. Edward Higgs has argued that the idea of domestics as a form of conspicuous consumption (that is, well paid domestics working for the middle and upper classes) fails to account for the "large numbers of girls recruited from the workhouse, who were paid little, if anything".[17] Workhouse inmates that "could be employed at board cost", as well as poor female relatives, worked in massive number for working class families. Sixteen percent of heads of his mid-nineteenth century sample of households accommodating living-in servants "were artisans, clerks or semi-skilled and unskilled workers" (p. 207). Not only girls or workhouse inmates; poor widows and many other women found their living this way: "Single *señor*, not being able to maintain a maid servant, offers an independent room, with coal, lighting, species, vegetables and water to a wid-

15 Fritz Hodne, Ola Grytten and Jorund Alme, "Norwegian real wages: trends in prices and wages, 1850–1950", in Peter Scholliers and Vera Zamagni (eds), *Labour's Reward, Real wages and economic change in 19th and 20th century Europe*, Aldershot, E. Elgar, 1995, pp. 61–75. Data is based on the first Norwegian cost of living index, calculated in 1913 by the statistical office of the city of Oslo.

16 Frank Victor Dawes, *Not in front of the servants. A True Portrait of English Upstairs, Downstairs Life*, New York, Taplinger, 1973, p. 24.

17 E. Higgs, "Domestic servants in Victorian England", p. 201.

ower or married woman, to assist him" (*Diario de Avisos de Madrid*, February 7, 1759).

Although not paid in cash, boarding was as fixed a component of the servant's wage as the money part: the worker knew exactly what to expect, in terms of quantity and quality, about food, clothes and housing, and when it should be paid. Components of boarding were mentioned in the contracts or advertisements more often than money wages: chocolate was mentioned as part of the boarding in many advertisements in the second half of the eighteenth century in Spain.[18]

Nominal Wages Lower than in other Occupations, but Real Wages Higher, Particularly in Periods of Price Inflation, due to Inclusion of Boarding

Boarding as part of the remuneration made the sector very attractive to workers in times of price inflation: during the second half of the eighteenth and the early decades of the nineteenth centuries, with rising commodity prices in Europe eating up most of the purchasing power of nominal wages, servants did much better than workers who were paid mostly or totally money wages, and so living-in domestic service was one of the most looked-after occupations.

For McBride, "the most common motivation for the migration of domestics to Paris was the attraction of substantially higher wage levels".[19] In the second half of the nineteenth century, a male servant might earn 2.5 to 3 times as much there, and a female servant twice as much. Higher wages existed in large cities for every occupation, but they were eaten up by the much higher cost of living.

> Because they were boarded, however, Parisian servants did not suffer much from the Parisian cost of living; their decision to come to Paris made more economic sense than that of other lower-class elements (p. 239).

18 "40 reales y chocolate", were offered as a monthly wage to a maidservant in the *Diario de Avisos de Madrid*, on July 18, 1758. "46 reales y dos libras de chocolate", also to a maid servant, on September 20, 1760, Sarasúa, *Criados, nodrizas y amos*, p. 217.

19 T. McBride, "The Modernization of Woman's Work", p. 237.

In Norway, and probably in other parts as well, the long-term tendency of the monetary part of servants' wages to increase was interrupted only during the First World War, when price inflation arrived to the highest levels.[20] In fact, boarding gained weight as part of servants' remuneration every time that a social or economic crisis took place. Early nineteenth-century Spanish cities, devastated by the Napoleonic troops, witnessed dramatic changes in their labour markets. Civil servants and soldiers became unemployed due to the government's inability to pay their wages, and employees in the trades were laid off, because of the general crisis. As advertisements published in the Journals during 1812 prove, the main strategy used by these new unemployed and homeless from the middle classes was to offer themselves as domestics, simply for food and housing. In times of crisis, then, boarding became a privilege for most workers, who were ready to work simply for it.

Yet the value attached by servants to boarding as part of their remuneration changed during the nineteenth century. Domestic workers (male domestic workers in particular), were now in an urban and industrial environment, with new job opportunities in industry and trade, jobs with a fixed working schedule and more independence. Furthermore, working class culture heavily rejected the concept of personal service. Increasingly, being housed and fed at the master's house appeared less attractive. William Tayler, a footman writing in 1837, described the life of a servant "as something like that of a bird shut up in a cage. The bird is well housed and well fed but is deprived of liberty".[21] In Spain, conservative voices lamented at the end of the nineteenth century the fragility of religious beliefs and traditional life among working-class women. The worst manifestation of this "sinister change" was their "sick preference for the dangerous life of the cigar-maker, instead of occupying themselves in domestic service".[22]

This changed perception suggests that the in-kind component of domestic servants' remuneration was less valued, and this probably forced the composition of the remuneration to change.

20 F. Hodne, O. Grytten and J. Alme, "Norwegian real wages: trends in prices and wages, 1850–1950", p. 69.

21 John Burnett (ed.), *Useful toil. Autobiographies of Working People from the 1820s to the 1920s*, London, Penguin Books, 1984. The quote is about William Tayler, footman, p. 185.

22 Geraldine Scanlon, *La polémica feminista en la España contemporánea (1868–1974)*, Madrid, Siglo XXI de España Editores, 1976, p. 86.

Fig. 13
A Servant Cook in a Wealthy Household. Engraving, 1862.
Museo Municipal, Madrid.
Frequent are the references to “sisa”, this servant practice to “fiddle the basket handle” when shopping, apparently benefiting from a semi institutionalized privilege. In France the kitchen maid used the same way to keep some coins after shopping
(“faire danser l’anse du panier”).

Highly Valued Qualitative Aspects of Domestic Service

Living in the employer's house also meant a closer, more personal relation with the family, which often opened the door to important benefits, such as gifts and inheritance. Privileged domestics were "protected" in many ways by the family. Wet nurses are a good example: they developed a very special relationship with the family's children and were regarded as "second mothers" for them. The interest of domestics in developing these relationships of patronage can be shown in the case of late nineteenth-century Florence, where more than one third of domestics had members of the highest ranks of society attending as witnesses to their weddings.[23]

In some periods and for certain types of servants, domestic service was an attractive occupation for these qualitative aspects. This was so for two main reasons. Firstly, because in large cities, and in periods when regional differences were still intense, rural young women were ready to trade high wages for friendly environments. In late nineteenth century *Morriña*, a novel by the famous Spanish writer Emilia Pardo Bazán, the young maid-of-all-work from Galicia working in Madrid complains bitterly of a previous stay with a non-Gallego family: she would not understand the language spoken (Spanish), and would lament she never heard about her homeland. "For half the pay and double workload I want to serve someone from my country."[24]

Secondly, domestic service was also attractive because closeness to the employers meant a real possibility of upward social mobility, which for many historians of domestic service was a reality for domestic servants. Upward social mobility was partly achieved through savings (which tells about the importance of money wages for many domestics), but also through acculturation, the contact with middle class values, rituals, behaviour, and language. A young man or woman who entered service

23 M. Casalini, *Servitù,* p. 194.

24 See 3rd ed., Barcelona, Impr. De Henrich y ca., 1895.

entered also life in a different social environment. Many of them were able to acquire the skills needed for a new occupation, including literacy.[25]

Irregularity of Money Payments

A second implication of servant wages being mostly in kind is that masters saw the money payment as not really needed by servants, and thus not required to be paid on a regular basis. This is evident from the many instances we know of masters paying their servants only once a year, or at their deaths, as many employers' wills show by mandating delayed wages to be paid to their servants;[26] or by masters simply not paying their servants at all. Because servants received their money wages when their subsistence was already paid for, and very often only once a year, those who really received their money had a much higher capacity to save and to spend than other workers. They were able to lend money to their families or even to their masters.

In his study of the eighteenth century French trades, Sonenscher found "an essential difference in the natural law tradition between the status of wages journeymen and the status of domestic servants".[27] This essential difference in legal status conditioned to a large extent the forms of remuneration for their work:

25 Theresa McBride, "Social mobility for the lower classes: domestic servants in France", *Journal of Social History,* 1974, pp. 63–78; J. Jean Hecht, *The domestic servant class in eighteenth-century England,* London, Routledge and Paul, 1956, particularly ch. VII, "The rewards of service: social advancement"; Raffaella Sarti, "Il servizio domestico: un canale di mobilità sociale? Il caso di Bologna (fine '700-inizio '900)", in *Società Italiana di Demografia Storica. Disuguaglianze: stratificazione e mobilità sociale nelle popolazioni italiane (dal secolo XIV agli inizi del secolo XX),* Bologna, Clueb, 1997, vol. I, pp. 145–167.

26 In the Netherlands, "Payment once a year (or sometimes twice a year) was the norm for living-in staff, such as servants, farmhands and maids. Since this payment was on top of room and board, the actual amount of money involved did not have to be that much, especially not once advances of, say, one guilder pocket money per week had been deducted", Jan Lucassen, "Wage payments and currency circulation in the Netherlands from 1200–2000', in *Jaarboek voor Munt- en Penningkunde*, vol. 86, 1999 (published in 2001), pp. 1–70. Quote from p. 6.

27 Michael Sonenscher, *Work and Wages. Natural law, politics and the eighteenth-century French trades*, Cambridge University Press, 1989, p. 70.

> The usual phrases [...] concerning the payment of wages in eighteenth-century France... were 'le prix de son travail', 'le prix d'une journée de travail', 'le prix de la façon', and, less currently, 'le salaire', or, finally, the word 'gages'. This last term was indicative of the difference between those employed for limited periods, who were usually journeymen or labourers, and those employed for longer periods. It was used almost exclusively in connection with payments to domestic servants. There were good reasons for this limited usage. The terms 'le prix d'une journée' or 'le prix de son travail' denoted the contractual and limited nature of the engagement. Labour was hired for a certain price for a certain duration. [...] The status of domestic servants was somewhat different, since they had engaged themselves to their masters or mistresses (and were therefore *'à leurs gages'*), for extended periods [...] In addition, they worked in their employers' households (rather than a *boutique* or *atelier*) and used their possessions. The nature of the engagement was therefore more extensive. The wages of servants were the price of their engagement: the wages paid to journeymen were the price of their labour.

More important than the irregular character of money payments is to what extent servants received directly the money payments they were entitled to:

> Servants did not always receive wages directly. The merchant Pierre Lacoste paid a chambermaid's wages directly to her peasant father. Similarly, Monsieur Flahaut sent foodstuffs or coals to the parents of servant girls, or paid rents on fathers' farms for girls who served the Flahaut family from 1811 to 1877.[28]

Simonton concludes: "Instead of saving, some girls had no funds at their disposal." Not paying wages directly to servants but to their fathers was relatively common concerning female servants of rural origin, young and unmarried. But for adult, married female servants, the point is that they often had no actual capacity to spend their wages, since all family earnings were administered by husbands or fathers.[29] This widespread practice contradicts the notion that labour markets are formed by individuals who own their labour and are able to freely contract in the market, earn their wages and use them for their own needs.

28 Deborah Simonton, *A History of European Women's Work. 1700 to the Present*, London/New York, Routledge, 1998, p. 105. She is quoting examples from Scott and Tilly and Margaret Darrow.

29 As the paper by Gül Özyegin on Turkish domestic workers shows, in the present volume.

Lower Ability to Bargain Collectively for Wages and Working Conditions

Domestic service was performed in private homes, not in factories or workshops. This space and symbolic privatisation of the work place of domestic workers had important implications for their wages. Firstly, because workers were isolated, they had little opportunities to communicate with co-workers, and so discussion of labour problems was extremely difficult. Secondly because, as a result of this identification with the private realm, domestic service was seen as a private relation between the employer and the employee, rather than as a work relation. Unions' pressure to improve workers' conditions and state intervention to guarantee workers' rights, were almost totally absent from domestic service. Protective legislation, including working day limitation, child labour prohibition, regulation of night work, and minimum wage, were never applied to domestic servants, as labour inspection never arrived to the sector. The tradition of economic and social policy described in the first pages, which regarded service work, and particularly personal and domestic services, as non-productive, had no doubt much to do with this absence.

Can Domestic Servants' Productivity Be Defined and Measured?

Productivity is a basic indicator of economic performance. But this economic concept was developed to account for industrial factory production, and its capacity to account for production in other sectors, particularly in the service sector, is very limited.

There are two basic ways of purchasing work: by the time (by hour, day, month or year), and by the task. When purchasing labour by time, the main problem of employers is to monitor the intensity of work (which explains the endless variety of devices to control whether the worker is actually at work). When paying labour by the task (the piece rate system), the main problem is not the time (since the worker is the one interested on working as rapid as possible), but the quality of the work done. Most domestic workers were paid by time, usually by the year if they were living-in servants. In the case of servants living and working at the employers' home, the problem of monitoring the intensity and quality of the work done was to a large extent solved. Middle-class employers lived physically close to their servants, so they knew at any moment where the domestics were and what they were doing. In larger households, masters employed a housekeeper whose job was precisely to monitor the work of the rest of the domestics. Working hours were long, beginning at 5 or 6 and ending at 11 or 12, and days off one (sometimes half a day) a week. Most importantly, living-in servants were always "on call": they could be called at any moment, at night, or in their day off, and in fact they were. As for the work intensity, many examples in the literature show domestic servants not working when masters are gone. This is why a traditional way to control servants' work in their masters' absence was to fix up tasks to be done.

The relation between domestic service and productivity poses at least three problems: first, the service sector has a lower potential than industry or agriculture to incorporate technological innovations (such as mechanization) or organizational innovations (such as mass production) and thus to intensify production. Second, because most services involve an important element of interpersonal relationship, intensification and speeding up of the working process in services oppose itself to the quality of what is delivered in a more intense way than in other sectors. And thirdly, in the service sector, workers can be hired to do no work other than displaying their employers' wealth. I will examine these three problems now.

Lower Potential for Services to Mechanize

The service sector has a lower potential to incorporate technological innovations, and particularly to mechanize. Technical innovations that have an impact on labour productivity are the responsibility of employers, who have to pay for them. In the industrial sector, technological investments took place only if owners had prospects of increasing benefits, either by lowering labour costs or by intensifying production. Mass production has been a powerful incentive to mechanization in industry, but is not possible in the service sector, much less in personal services. Development of mass production has historically been favoured by three conditions:

a. The first condition is production spatially concentrated in a work space, be it a factory or a commercial centre. The fact that domestic service takes place at the individual homes of the employers prevents the technological innovations associated with spatial concentration of production to be incorporated.
b. The second condition favouring mass production and mechanization is the labour process being divided into small operations to be constantly repeated. Division of labour was, according to Adam Smith, the most basic technique to intensify productivity, and was the basis for the Fordist revolution in industry, based upon chain production. Yet this division of labour can rarely be applied to services, particularly personal services. Unlike public services, personal services are by definition, individual: only one person is required to feed a child, to take care for an elderly person, to cook lunch for a family. The worker is required to do the entire service, not just a small part of it, so it makes no sense to cut the working process into small pieces. Chain production and mechanization are in fact the very opposite to personal services.
c. The third condition is the product being standard. Mass production in both industry and agriculture has required a certain degree of standardization of the unit of output, a process that arrives at the extreme in industrial chain production. Personal services cannot be standardized. This is also the reason why piece rates have never been a system of remuneration in domestic service, because piece rate wages require the quantity of work to be measured.

In sum, domestic service fulfils none of the conditions that favoured the adoption of technical innovations and were fundamental to increase productivity. As a result of this lower potential of services to incorporate new technologies (technologies which developed precisely to speed up mainly the industrial and agricultural production process), the amount of time required by some of the tasks performed by domestic workers is not very different today from the time required a century ago (with the exception of laundering).

A second consequence of this lower potential of services to increase labour productivity is the lack of competition among service workers. Competition among workers, fuelled by mass migration since the late nineteenth century, was the driving force behind technological innovation in industry and agriculture, particularly international competition. It was because of the higher productivity of American agricultural workers that European farmers were forced to mechanize. But except for some highly qualified occupations (precisely the ones that are more technological, like health services), markets for services were not international until very recently. The reason is that the personal characteristics of the worker, be these real or perceived (such as for instance regional stereotypes of cleanness) are very important in domestic service. Domestic services include physical proximity between the employer and the employee; access on the part of the employee to the employer's most private spaces and valuable possessions (for instance, the employee is responsible for the employer's children). This explains why the worker's language, country or region of origin, gender, age, race and physical appearance, become determinant in personal services. This is why personal networks have always been a main source for hiring domestic workers. In the absence of personal recommendation, letters of reference from peers, and stereotypes, work very powerfully. What this means in economic terms is that domestic workers are not easily replaceable: employers will not necessarily replace a domestic worker by another solely because the latter is cheaper. In other words, there is no competition through prices, and thus a basic element to increase productivity is absent in domestic service. The internationalization of markets for services that is taking place nowadays (including international migrations) is different from international markets for agricultural and industrial goods developed since the eighteenth century: flows of foreign services do not mean increasing *competition* and price reduction (and thus an incentive to technological modernization). Foreign domestic workers arrive because of an insufficient local supply of domestic workers. There is no competition and thus no need to reduce prices. This process takes place in other services as well: Spanish nurses are being hired in large numbers in England not in competition with English nurses (and thus not because they are paid less), but due to an insufficient supply of English nurses.

Quantity vs. Quality in Service Production

In the industrial sector, the concept of productivity is related to the intensification of the worker's effort and the speeding up of the production process. We can ask ourselves if this makes sense in domestic service. Did masters look for cooks who could cook very fast or rather were they looking for sophisticated cooks, able to cook French dishes, and probably taking lots of time to prepare a meal? Did masters look for servants able to clean very fast, or was extreme rapidity interpreted as a job badly done? Was a wet nurse more valued (and her salary was higher) if she was able to feed five children in the same time that other wet nurse fed only one? The concept of productivity associated to speeding up of the working process makes no sense in cleaning or cooking, much less in caring. *In personal services, quality seems often opposed to quantity.*

Employers disliked fast cleaning and even mechanical innovations allowing for lighter work because these conflicted with the idea that a good quality service is only possible through much time and effort. At the end of the nineteenth century a letter published in the English newspaper *The Sphere* expressed the discomfort of employers at increasing rapidity:

> Home is rapidly becoming the place that one seeks only when it is impossible to go elsewhere. The servant who takes an interest in her work seems no longer to exist, and in return for high wages, we get but superficial service. Where is the maid to be found who takes pride in the brilliance of the glass used upon the table or remembers of her own initiative to darn the damask? Every sort of contrivance now lessens labour (carpet sweepers, knife machines, bathrooms, lifts) in spite of this the life of a housewife is one long wrestle and failure to establish order.[30]

The problem of the quality of services becomes further complicated in the case of domestic service, which has a large component of personal service. In domestic service, the standard of a good job, the only possible definition of a job well done, is to please the master: a job well done is a job the master likes. A different master may have a completely different idea of how the floors should be cleaned or the laundry done. This introduces an element of intense singularity, and also makes it impossible not only to observe anything close to "mass production" or standardization of

30 Frank Victor Dawes, *Not in front of servants. A True Portrait of Upstairs, Downstairs Life,* p. 28.

the service, but also serves to question the very idea of domestic workers' productivity. Expanding the concept of productivity so as to include *qualitative productivity* (raising quality), as opposed to physical productivity (physical output or quantity per hour of work) seems a possible solution to account for domestic servants' remuneration.[31]

The Paradox of Leisure Workers

Servants have also historically been hired to do no work: rather, they were hired to display the master's wealthy lifestyle. The function of exhibiting the master's wealth by doing no work besides accompanying the master or being available to him or her, was described by Thorstein Veblen in *The Theory of the Leisured Class*. What mattered here was not what the servant did (the tasks performed), but their simple existence and public display as servants. The paradox described by Veblen consists in that these servants' function was not work, but leisure, exactly like middle-class housewives in the nineteenth and much of the twentieth century were educated and trained to do no work (that is, no paid work). How can economic analysis account for these highly rewarded workers whose duty was wearing expensive clothes and to be near their masters, never doing any manual work?

Were Servants Paid according to their Productivity?

My initial question was aimed at discussing which theoretical framework was best appropriate to understand and interpret domestic workers' remuneration. As we have seen, standard wage theory was developed mainly to account for industrial labour, and many forms of labour do not fit this model. In particular, the notion of productivity, basic in the neoclassical

31 Reinhold Reith, "Wage forms, wage systems and wage conflicts in German crafts during the eighteenth and earlier nineteenth centuries", in P. Scholliers and L. Schwarz (eds), *Experiencing wages*, pp. 113–138.

economic analysis, fails to account for how workers, particularly in the service occupations, are hired and their labour rewarded. The notion of qualitative productivity could be an alternative concept for these occupations. As standard wage theory is based on the notion of labour's productivity, it fails to account for how wages have historically been established in domestic service.

By studying domestic workers' remuneration, both historical and contemporary, it is possible to see that wages are much more than payment for a commodity in the market, and also to observe the importance of personal relations in fixing "labour's reward". The importance of the personal characteristics of the worker, culturally defined, characteristics such as race, gender, age or class, are then translated into the perception of the worker's qualification and worth. And, as a result, they became fundamental in determining the worker's remuneration. By looking at domestic service, we can see that even the more basic notions of economic theory, such as markets, fail to account for the complexities of labour relations. In sum, domestic servants' remuneration shows us that probably all wages should be analysed as cultural artefacts rather than within a supply and demand framework.

Servants were not paid according to their productivity, because productivity has little to do with domestic service. Speeding up the work process is not what servants' employers were looking for. On the contrary, rapidity and mechanization are usually seen as opposed to a quality service. Employers were reluctant to purchase electric domestic appliances and tended to prefer domestic workers doing domestic chores "old style", either by hand or with traditional non-electric appliances. Domestic service includes personal services as well, and in this case (wet nursing, care of children, elderly and sick persons, attention to members of the family in general), permanent personal availability is the quality demanded.

To a large extent, servants were paid simply following the employers' desires and decisions, taken personally and in view of personal cases. Personal satisfaction with personal services played a major role in the determination of both the forms and the amounts of remuneration. This is not to deny that there was a market for domestic servants, and that average wages for different domestic occupations existed. Domestic service is not an exceptional case in the workings of historical and current labour markets. Rather, domestic service shows to what extent values, traditions, and socially constructed roles shape supply and demand, and "labour's reward", in history as well as in our days.

Domestic Service in Precolonial India

Bondage, Caste and Market

Shireen MOOSVI

The history of domestic servants in pre-colonial India has not received much attention so far, apparently because this class is supposed to have played little role in production, being confined by its very definition to the service sector. The absence of previous studies in the field is one reason why I seek to cover in the compass of a single paper the entire history of domestic service in India from the proto-historic times to the end of the eighteenth century. In an initial effort like the following, description necessarily occupies much space; but I hope the study brings out some of the complex interplay between domestic service, slavery, caste and market that has had a written history in India of over 2,500 years. I should add that the second and third parts (covering the period from the thirteenth to the eighteenth century) are based mostly on my own research while I have largely relied on secondary sources for the information assembled in the first section of the chapter.

From Proto-Historic Times to the Thirteenth Century

It is practically certain that as Gordon V. Childe's "Urban Revolution"[1] took place, states arose and the wealthy became increasingly differentiated from the needy, the richer began to command the services of the poor and of the captives of war and rapine. In the Indus Civilization (2500–

1 Gordon V. Childe, *New Light on the most ancient East; the Oriental Prelude to European Prehistory*, London, K. Paul, 1934.

2000 BC), the great excavations at the city of Mohenjo Daro (Sind), each larger house had a single entrance leading to a courtyard around which were placed its various rooms. Many servants, whether slave or free, must have lived and worked within the rooms of each such house.[2] It can perhaps be legitimately assumed that the woman kneading flour or grinding grain depicted in a clay figurine from Harappa could be such a servant (Fig. 14).[3]

In the subsequent period of de-urbanization and the spread of the Aryans (the latter phase usually dated 1500–1000 BC), our earliest preserved text, the *Rigveda*, suggests a society where much servitude existed. In one *Rigvedic* hymn, the gifts of fifty *vadhus* or (slave-)women, and in another, that of a hundred *dasas* or male slaves, is gratefully acknowledged (or solicited!) by the priestly composers. Clearly, these slaves were meant for domestic and pastoral work since horses, cattle, camels, asses, etc., are also sought in gifts.[4]

It is, however, with the second urbanization, beginning about the sixth century BC, that we begin to get a more elaborate picture of domestic labour. We owe to Dev Raj Chanana an elaborate analysis of the information in early Buddhist literature, comprising mainly the *Tipitaka* and the *Jatakas*, parts of which go back to the fifth century BC. In "middle-class households", it was usual to have at least one *geha-dasi*, "domestic woman slave". Such a slave was one named Kali, said to be "clever at preparing the rice, making the beds and lighting the lamps" and "rising early to milk the cows". The fact that the scope of the woman slave's duties *(dasi-bhoga)* was contrasted to the daughter-in-law's work *(sunisabhoga)*, suggests that there were so few free-born maidservants in ordinary households that they could be ignored. The *dasi-bhoga* according to the later commentator Buddhaghosha included "work in the fields, removal of filth, fetching of water".

2 Irfan Habib, *The Indus Civilization*, New Delhi, Tulika, 2002, pp. 38, 42, 58.

3 See Gregory L. Possehl, *The Indus Civilization: A Contemporary Perspective*, New Delhi, 2003, pp. 182–183.

4 *Rigveda*, VIII: 19.36; and VIII, Valakhilya, 8.9. See English translation by Ralph T. H. Griffith, *The Hymns of the Rigveda*, ed. J. L. Shastri, Delhi, 1973, pp. 409 and 469.

Fig. 14
Woman (servant?) hand-milling flour or kneading dough.
Terracotta from Harappa, 2500–2000 B.C.

In larger households the various domestic chores could be performed separately by different categories of servants, who could be both free-born and slave. We are told of the cook who "is very tired [...] he cuts wood, washes the utensils... gets up early to cook the *yagu* (a kind of soup) [...] serves it to all and thus suffers a lot of hardship"; or of women slaves assigned to the hard duty of continuously bringing water from the well since early in the morning; or of other women slaves who had to husk rice all day long and who, sweating profusely, fell down exhausted. Men served as doorkeepers *(dvarika)* and as gardeners (*uyyana-pala*, etc.); these too could be slaves. Personal attendants *(pada-mulika)* of the master, who also ran errands for him, enjoyed a high position among the servants. To serve mistresses there were women attendants *(pesana-darika)*, who were usually slaves *(dasis)*. The *dhatis*, or wetnurses, could be both free-born and slaves. To look after the sexual needs of the master there were women servants known as *nataka-itthis*. Their status was quite servile because they could be gifted away as well as inherited.[5]

The emphasis on the suffering of the slaves and servants in Buddhist literature as found in the statements analysed by Chanana and elsewhere[6] might mainly stem from the well-known Buddhist doctrine that all life is sorrow *(dukha)*. But there is also an element of compassion here. The Buddha himself prohibited the sale of a human being *(sattavanijja)* by any lay follower.[7] The Buddhist Mauryan emperor Asoka (269–32 BC) in his celebrated edicts inscribed over the length and breadth of South Asia enjoined, as the first element in his law of Piety *(dhamma)*, "seemly behaviour to slaves and servants *(dasa-bhataka)*" in Rock Edicts IX and XI. The requirement is restated in Rock Edict XIII and Pillar Edict VII; in the latter Edict the same kind of conduct is also prescribed in relation to "the poor and the destitute".[8] The pairing of slaves *(dasa)* with servants *(bhataka)* needs to be noted, as suggesting that they were thought to be at the lowest level of society and/or performed the same kind of work.

5 This and the preceding paragraph are based on Dev Raj Chanana, *Slavery in Ancient India*, New Delhi, 1960, pp. 45–52.

6 See, for example, the Buddha's remarks in the *Samannaphala Sutta* quoted by Beni Madhab Barua, *Inscriptions of Asoka*, Calcutta, 1943, Part II, p. 308.

7 *Ibid.*, p. 308.

8 For an excessively literal translation of the edicts see *ibid.*, pp. 187, 189, 191, 213–14. For a more readable (though old) version, see V. A. Smith, *Asoka*, Oxford, 1909, pp. 167, 169, 172, 194.

In the evidence considered here, which brings us to the Mauryan times (the late fourth and the third century BC), domestic service and servitude are not set within the framework of the caste system, which had already emerged in a recognisable form by the fourth century BC. Megasthenes, the Seleucid envoy to the Mauryan court, c. 300 BC, held that the Indians were divisible into seven castes, specified by occupation, and separated from each other by endogamy. In extracts from Megasthenes' *Indika*, preserved mainly in the works of Diodorus, Strabo and Arrian, slaves and servants are included in none of the seven castes.[9] Indeed, Megasthenes says that there were no slaves in India, a statement which Strabo countered with a report from Onesicritus.[10] It is likely, on the other hand, that slaves and servants were not included among the recognised castes, because they were not recognised as members of society at all. Indeed, the *Milindapanho* (first century AD) explaining why the word "villagers" in certain contexts need not include all villagers, mentions among those excluded "the female and male slaves, servants and workers" *(dasi-dasa bhataka kammaraka)*.[11]

In the classic text on ancient Indian law, the *Manusmriti* (first century BC), those who perform personal service are not only held in scorn but are also excluded from the three "twice-born" Aryan *varnas* or castes, and put among the Sudras, the lowliest of the castes. "Service is called *savritti* (dog's mode of life)", and so a Brahman "should avoid it", the Manu says (IV.6). The Sudra, on the other hand, must "serve meekly" the three twice-born castes (I.91; VIII.410); and he has to be "the servant of his betters" (X.335). The traditional association of domestic service with slavery is here continued: "But a Sudra, whether bought or unbought, he (the Brahman) may compel to do servile work... A Sudra though emancipated by his master is not released from servitude" (VIII.413–14). And his property can be seized just like that of a slave (VIII.417).[12]

9 Translations of the extracts may be consulted in R. C. Majumdar, *The Classical Accounts of India,* Calcutta, 1960, pp. 224–226, 263–268.

10 *Ibid*., p. 271.

11 *Milindapanho*, ed. V. Trenckner, London, 1962, p. 147; transl. Rhys Davids, Oxford, 1890, pp. 208–209 (translation slightly modified here). Note that the *Milindapanho* repeats the words *dasa* and *bhataka* used in the Asokan edicts.

12 The references within brackets are to chapters and verses of *Manusmriti*. These will enable one to trace the passages also in G. Buhler, *The Laws of Manu*, Oxford, 1886, the translation that I have used.

Even when not actually slaves, those who undertook domestic service had little protection. The well-known erotic manual, the *Kamasutra* (second century AD) tells us that women who worked for hire in villages were vulnerable to the employer's sexual advances,

> when rendering forced labour *(vistikarma)*, when entering the (store-)house, when bringing material in or taking it out, when repairing/cleaning the house, when working in the fields *(ksetrakarma)*, when taking cotton, wool, flax, hemp and tree bark and bringing [in return] the yarn...

Apparently these women servants were not slaves, and had homes of their own, but were still treated by their masters as just *charshanis*, women of easy virtue.[13]

During the Gupta period (300–500 AD), a distinction begins to be made in the legal texts of what was unclean and clean in domestic labour. Narada describes as unclean such work as sweeping the gateway, the privy and the road, removing the leavings of food, ordure, etc., and rubbing the master's limbs or shampooing the secret parts of his body. Both Narada and Brihaspati lay down that only slaves, presumably of the Sudra caste, could be employed to do such work.[14] The notorious theory of "pollution" in the Indian caste system can be here seen to be at work. Much of the domestic work was actually done by women, many of whom were slaves.

The *Amarakosa*, a dictionary assignable to the sixth–eighth centuries AD, cites the word *dasisabham* ("multitude of female slaves"), as a typical expression for multitude.[15] Bana (seventh century) tells us of how the dying king Prabhakaravardhana (d. 600) called out to twenty women attendants, one after another by name, each to carry out some chore to relieve his pain, ranging from massaging and shampooing to story-telling.[16] Queens, princesses and presumably noblewomen had women personal attendants, aiding them in everything: the Ajanta cave painting (Cave XVIII, sixth century) of "the Queen's Toilet" shows the queen surrounded

13 *Kamasutra*, 5.5.5 and 6. I am indebted for the translation to Professor S. R. Sarma (formerly Professor of Sanskrit, Aligarh Muslim University).

14 Cited by Ram Sharan Sharma, *Sudras in Ancient India*, Delhi, 1958, pp. 227–228.

15 *Ibid.*, p. 229.

16 E. B. Cowell and F. W. Thomas (trs.), *The Harsa-carita of Bana*, Indian reprint, Delhi, 1961, pp. 144–145.

by attending women (Fig. 15).[17] But there were other things also for them to do: Bana speaks of older women servants dyeing cloth by the tie-and-die method.[18] An Ajanta painting (Cave I) shows three maids processing cotton from seed-separation to yarn-spinning apparently in a royal household (Fig. 19).[19]

There is no doubt that if the vast Sanskrit literature of the first millennium is more extensively explored we would learn much more about the mode of organisation of the lesser households and the place of both free and slave servants in it. Where a set of rather late (1230–31 AD) Sanskrit documents from the Chaulukya kingdom of Gujarat lift the veil, there is little doubt that the life of a maid-slave in an ordinary household was a most piteous one. In the four "slavery-deeds" *(dasi-patra)* four girls, two of 16 years, the others of 10 and 12, are respectively concerned. In two cases (Documents I and II) they were captured in plundering raids by Rajaputra chiefs *(rana, ranaka)*, and then sold; in the remaining two cases (Documents III–IV), abandoned by their families, they offered themselves *gratis* as slaves, to obtain sustenance (but no stipulated wages, or fixed payments in kind). Of these two latter one was of a high-caste *(Rajaputri)*. The masters in two cases are merchants, in the third a usurer. The kinds of work to be taken from the girl-slaves is similar in all the four cases:

> cutting [vegetables], grinding [corn], smearing the floor [with cow-dung], sweeping, bringing fire-wood, carrying water, etc.; throwing away human excreta, milking the cow, buffalo and goat, churning the curd and carrying butter-milk to the field; and field-work, such as bringing the fodder, weeding and cutting grass, etc. (quotation taken from Document II).

The girl could ask for nothing; she had to obey the master and all members of the family; she could be beaten and tortured. If this led to her death or suicide, no sin would attach to the master, while she herself would be reborn as a she-ass, etc. She could not maintain any connection with her

17 The painting has been widely reproduced. I take my reproduction from Kanaiyalal H. Vakil, *At Ajanta*, Bombay, 1929, Fig. V (p. 39).

18 See E. B. Cowell and F. W. Thomas, p. 125, transl. to be modified in the light of remarks by V. S. Agrawala, "References to Textiles in Bana's *Harshacharita*", *Journal of Indian Textile History,* Ahmedabad, Vol. IV, p. 66.

19 D. Schllingloff, "Cotton Manufacture in India", *Journal of the Economic and Social History of the Orient,* XVII, 1, 1974, pp. 89–90, with Fig. 3 on p. 88. See also Ishrat Alam, "Textile Tools as Depicted in Ajanta and Mughal Paintings", *Technology in Ancient and Medieval India*, ed. A. Ray and S. K. Bagchi, Delhi, pp. 130–131.

family, including her husband. There is not a word about protecting the slave from any sexual advances. Slavery is to be her lot for her whole lifetime.[20]

These documents shed light on slavery's two other relationships: with the caste system and the market. The fact seems to be clear that domestic slavery meant an utter loss of caste, an absolute break with the woman slave's family and an assignment to her of menial duties irrespective of her original caste. The fact that a Rajaputri, a woman of the superior Kshatriya caste, could become a slave of a merchant, that is, a Vaishya, lower in caste-ranking, shows that in practice no heed was paid to the legal rule that a slave belonging to a higher caste could not be owned by a person of a lower caste. Life in many matters was above caste!

As to the market, in the first case (Document I) the 16-year old girl was sold by her captor "at the crossing of the four roads" – that is publicly – for 504 *drammas* of a special sort. In the second case (Document II) a girl of the same age was sold by her captor to his creditor, for 60 *drammas*, adjusted against the debt owed. The other two girls just gave themselves up to slavery in desperation (Documents III and IV). Clearly, public and private sales both occurred, and a kind of slave market existed from which servile domestic servants could be drawn.

From the Thirteenth Century to Mughal India

From the thirteenth century on, our quantum of information about social matters increases substantially, though not as much as one would like it to. This is because with the establishment of the Delhi Sultanate (1206–1526), we have an increasingly large body of historical material in Persian, where traditions of writing histories, memoirs, reports, etc., were fairly strong and much attention was paid to dates and chronology.

Since, in the Islamic world, slavery (and slave-recruitment through raids) was as established a feature as in Ancient India, there was not much

20 The documents are translated and analysed by Pushpa Prasad, "Female Slavery in Thirteenth-Century Gujarat: Documents in the *Lekhapaddhati*", *Indian History Review*, New Delhi, XV, 1–2, pp. 269–275.

difference, *prima facie*, between the two cultures with regard to the preponderance of slaves in domestic service. The eleventh-century poet of Lahore, Mas'ud Sa'd Salman claimed in a verse how he, his slave *(ghulam)* and slave-girl *(kaniz)* could live on a mere pittance.[21] Clearly, this was the concept of the smallest household: the poet was out in the world with a male attendant and a concubine or maid-servant (for the word *kaniz* could mean either).[22] In the late thirteenth century, an impecunious student (the young mystic Nizamuddin) and his widowed mother, at Badaun, a town in western Uttar Pradesh, had yet a maid-slave *(kanizak)*.[23] In mid-fourteenth century we read of a merchant whose food was cooked and served to him by a *kanizak* or maid-slave.[24]

Not all servants were, of course, slaves; and favoured slaves used also to be freed. A man of modest means, the military captain and poet Hasan Sijzi of Delhi had a slave-servant Malih. On 1 February 1308 Hasan Sijzi took him to his preceptor Nizamu'ddin and there declared him free. In 1318 Malih was still with Hasan Sijzi as his "manumitted servant" *(`atiq-i khidmatgar)*, yet defying his master's request to free a small child he had bought whose parents were begging him to restore her to them. Malih himself had a family of his own, with four daughters, one of whom he married away in November 1317. Apparently, Malih had now a separate hut or household of his own.[25] The slave-servants were not naturally always happy with their lot, and Muslim mystics *(sufis)* were often asked to pray for the recovery by the masters of their escaped slaves, to supplement thereby the efforts of the police officials *(kotwal)*.[26] On the other hand, it is only fair to say that the saint Nizamu'ddin (d. 1324) praised the action of a fellow-divine of Badaun, who had seen an old maid-slave *(kanizak-i*

21 Quoted in *Farhang-i Sururi* [of 1619], ed. Dabir Sayaqi, Teheran, 1341 Solar/1963, III, p. 1214.

22 There seems no difference in sense between the words *kaniz* or *kanizak*, despite the latter being the diminutive form. In Hasan Sijzi's record of conversations with the mystic Nizamuddin (early 14th century), *Fawa'idu'l Fawad*, ed. Muhammad Latif Malik, Lahore, 1386/1966, pp. 339–340, 426, *kanizak* means a maid-slave, not a concubine; but elsewhere *kanizak* is used for both, as in Barani, quoted in footnote 31 below.

23 Hamid Qalandar, *Khairu'l Majalis*, ed. K. A. Nizami, Aligarh, 1959, p. 191.

24 *Ibid.*, p. 93.

25 On Malih, see *Fawa'idu'l Fawad*, pp. 5–6, 168, 263, 296, 308, 339. Unless Malih's daughter at her marriage was only eight years, Malih must have married before he was freed. One does not know how slaves' marriages in actual life were arranged.

26 *Fawa'idu'l Fawad*, pp. 425–426; *Khairu'l Majalis*, p. 184.

zal), lately enslaved, cry as she sat grinding grain (Fig. 20),[27] thinking of her son, and thereupon had himself taken her to the edge of the rebel tract *(mawas)* and let her go back to her people.[28]

In the more aristocratic households where there was much concern for the seclusion of the women, eunuchs were employed to carry out such tasks as guarding the harem. Marco Polo notes, in connection with his return voyage of 1292–95, how Bengal supplied such slaves to meet the demand of "all the Barons who keep them".[29] The trade, indeed, continued down to the seventeenth century.

The reason why domestic servants tended mostly to be slaves was obviously due to the plenitude of slaves obtained through capture in the various raids and expeditions conducted all the time all over India as the Sultanate expanded and consolidated its authority. Ibn Battuta found in 1334–35 at Delhi that "female captives there are very cheap because they are dirty and do not know civilized ways. Even the educated ones are cheap, so that no one there needs to buy [untrained] captives".[30]

The plenitude was reflected in prices at the slave markets. When 'Ala'uddin Khalji (1296–1316) fixed prices of all articles, including grain, cloth, slaves and cattle, the prices of slaves at Delhi were as follows in terms of silver *tankas*:[31]

Maid-slave	5	to	12
Female slave for concubinage	20	to	40
Untrained boy	7	or	8
Experienced male slave-servant	10	to	15
Handsome boy-slave	20	to	30

The low rates for human chattel can be appreciated when one notes that the most inferior horse *(tattu)* was priced at 10 to 25 *tankas* and a milch

27 From Mahmud Shadiabadi, *Miftahu'l Fuzala* (1468–69), British Library MS Or. 3299, f.119a.

28 *Fawa'idu'l Fawad*, pp. 278–9, 339–40. This act of compassion could be held to be theologically reprehensible since the woman, presumably converted to Islam upon enslavement, was obviously going to return to the Hindu fold, and the divine ('Alau'ddin Usuli) had thus colluded in apostasy.

29 Henry Yule (tr.) and Henri Cordier (ed.), *The Book of Ser Marco Polo*, 3rd revised ed. with Supplement, Indian reprint, Delhi, 1994, II, p. 115.

30 *The Travels of Ibn Battuta, A.D. 1325–1354*, transl. H. A. R. Gibb, Indian reprint, New Delhi, 1993, III, p. 741.

31 Ziya Barani, *Tarikh-i Firoz-shahi*, ed. Syed Ahmad Khan *et al.*, Bibliotheca Indica, Calcutta, 1862, p. 314.

buffalo at 10 to 12 *tankas*.[32] A captive girl-child was actually purchased for 5 *tankas* at Devagiri (Maharashtra) in 1318[33] Similarly low prices (slave girl for maid-service only, 8 tankas; girl fit for service as well as for concubinage, 15 *tankas*) at Delhi were reported in the reign of Muhammad Tughluq (1324–51).[34]

There is, therefore, no doubt that the glutted marts not only reduced slave-prices but also depressed wages of free-born servants as well. The historian Barani wrote that given the prices fixed in Ala'uddin Khalji's time, a person then offered himself to work as a servant *(chakar)* at 8 *tankas* only whereas at the time of his writing (1350s) such a person would not accept anything less than 50 *tankas* (presumably per annum).[35]

One need not, therefore, be surprised that immense multitudes of slave-servants accumulated in aristocratic households, the largest naturally in the royal establishments. 'Afif, writing, c. 1400, tells us that Sultan 'Ala'uddin had 50,000 slaves, and Firoz Tughluq (1351–88) as many as 180,000, of whom 40,000 were royal attendants at the court, and 12,000 employed as artisans in royal departments *(karkhanas)*. Concubines could also be quite numerous: Firuz Tughluq's principal minister Khan Jahan Maqbul had 2,000 of them.[36] There is an admonition made in mid-fourteenth century by Shaikh Nasiruddin that when one is poor one thinks of God; but when rich, only of slave-girls *(kanizaks)*.[37]

32 *Ibid.*, pp. 331–14. Cf. Irfan Habib in *Cambridge Economic History of India*, I, ed. Tapan Raychaudhuri and Irfan Habib, Cambridge, 1982, p. 91.

33 *Fawa'idu'l Fawad*, p. 339.

34 Extracts on India from al-'Umari's *Masalik al-Absar*, as *A Fourteenth-Century Arab Account of India under Sultan Muhammad bin Tughluq*, transl. Iqtidar Husain Siddiqi and Qazi Mohammad Ahmad, Aligarh, n.d., p. 51.

35 *Tarikh-i Firoz-shahi*, first version, MS: Bodleian Library, Elliot 353, f.144b. This piece of information would not be relevant to our purpose if *chakar* meant not an ordinary domestic servant, but a soldier (in which sense *chakar* is definitely used in *Khairu'l Majalis*, p. 146). In the latter case the rate given (8 *tankas* then, 50 later) could represent the monthly wages for a horseman.

36 Shams Siraj 'Afif, *Tarikh Firoz-shahi*, ed. Wilayat Husain, Bib. Ind., Calcutta, 1891, pp. 267–273, 288–289, 399–400.

37 *Khairu'l Majalis*, p. 122.

Mughal India

In our description of domestic service in pre-colonial India our provisional scheme of periodization has so far been based simply on the scale of information available. Mughal India (roughly sixteenth to eighteenth century) constitutes from this point of view a distinct third period, since during these three centuries the amount of our knowledge expands dramatically. For the first time, with Abu'l Fazl's *A'in-i Akbari* (1595),[38] the magnificent official survey of the Mughal Empire and administration, we have a treasure-house of all kinds of data, including wage, price and other statistics. Primary documents and memoirs, along with very detailed formal histories and biographies, enable us not only to have a massive amount of source material to draw from, but also, for the first time perhaps, to consider questions that we cannot even raise for earlier periods.

The very first important thing we are able to do is to obtain some idea of the extent of the service sector (which, of course, would include both domestic and non-domestic services) in the Mughal Empire. I was enabled to conclude from the statistical data in the *A'in-i Akbari*, supplemented from other sources, that around 1595 over 22 percent of the revenues reserved for Imperial use were spent on personal services, while the nobility spent over 20 percent of its income on the same item. This was a fairly high proportion of expenditure when we consider that the major part of the budgets of both the Emperor and the nobility had necessarily to be used to maintain their troops and revenue-collection machinery. Even among ordinary cavalrymen, personal services appear to have accounted for 14 percent of their salary income, out of which they had also to maintain their horses.[39] The conclusion drawn from these figures as well as those of the expenditure on "direct consumption" in the households of these classes and on the horses and other animals maintained by them, is that the "distribution of surplus took place [in the Mughal Empire] according to a pattern in which a major part of it took the shape of food-crops

38 Abu'l Fazl, *A'in-i Akbari*, ed. H. Blochmann, Bib. Ind., Calcutta, 1867–77, 2 vols.

39 Shireen Moosvi, *The Economy of the Mughal Empire, c. 1595 – A Statistical Study*, Delhi, Oxford University Press, 1987, pp. 224–295, esp. table on p. 294.

and fodder and maintained a [large] population unconnected with material production".[40]

Given this situation, it is not surprising that domestic servants constituted a large part of the population. Abu'l Fazl puts them as the fourth group in a four-fold division of those on whom the functioning of the imperial structure rested: such servants, he says by way of illustration were the *khawas* (personal attendants), *qurchi* (house-guards), *sharbatdars* (drink-servers), and *abdars* (water-men), *toshakis* (keepers of the wardrobe), etc.[41] He then goes on to describe in some detail, for each department of the imperial household, the functions, wages and numbers of the servants employed.

The personal establishment of the Emperor included the large harem (often called the *Darun*, the interior). Women servants were assigned various duties for which they received monthly salaries. Some of them worked even as sentries or guards of the palace and some as supervisors *(darogha)* over other maid-servants. Even when the imperial camp was on the move, separate enclosures were provided in the encampment for the female servants and slaves *(khasan)* of the Emperor, besides those of the wives and other relations. The female guards *(urdu-begis)* and other "pious" women-servants *(zanan-i parsa)* were also alotted separate cells. These women-servants appear to belong to a lower category than the concubines.[42] The monthly salaries of the female-servants and concubines *(parastaran-i huzur)* varied greatly, from Rs. 51 to 20 and Rs. 40 to 2. These cash stipends were supplemented by other privileges such as food from the imperial kitchen and gifts on various occasions. These *khasan* and *parastaran-i parsa* in the imperial harem numbered over 4,500. Besides them eunuchs also served inside the harem; they were required to guard the exterior of the harem while Rajput soldiers were deployed at a respectable distance for the guard-duty outside the palace.[43] The numbers

40 *Ibid.*, p. 295.

41 Abu'l Fazl, *A'in-i Akbari*, I, pp. 4–5.

42 There seems to be a distinction between the *khasan* and *parastaran/zanan-i parsa*: the former could be those from whom concubines were drawn while the latter were employed only as servants. Thus the higher salaries of Rs. 51–20 were perhaps for the former category while the lower grade of Rs. 40–2 was paid to the latter (*A'in-i Akbari*, I, pp. 40–41).

43 *A'in-i Akbari*, I, pp. 40–41.

and salaries of these men are, however, not given. (See Fig. 21 for a Mughal painting of the inside of the Imperial harem with its personnel.)[44]

There remains a question mark over the free or slave status of many of the women attendants. Many wet-nurses of the young princes such as the famous Maham Anaga (d. 1562), the wet-nurse of Akbar, were free-born women of status. But it seems to have been a different case altogether with the bulk of the harem staff who are generally designated *parastaran*, literally meaning "devoted ones" but usually personal attendants, and, in given contexts, women servants generally, sometimes including concubines.[45] The term *khawas* (variant: *khasan*), can apply, as may be seen from the use of the term by the Emperor Jahangir (1605–27), to the concubines, of whom a sister and two brothers of his were born.[46] It would seem that, by and large, *parastaran* was the broader term and included all attendants; but in no case has the term been used for a free-born woman, so that it is likely that they were all female slaves in origin. It is not clear if Akbar's order of emancipation of the imperial slaves in 1582, to be touched on below, included women in its scope or covered only men-slaves of his who were made free. The context suggests that in practice the latter was probably the case. However, it is likely that formally the women attendants were no longer held to be unfree, and the word *kaniz* is scrupulously avoided by Abu'l Fazl for use with reference to any of the imperial women servants. A term *saheli* (in Hindi meaning the female companion of a woman) came to designate the women servants of royal and aristocratic households. A biographical notice of Jahangir's queen Nur Jahan tells us of what she did when, after her marriage (1611), she took charge of the Imperial harem:

> She got all the *sahelis* of the Palace who were between 12 to 40 years of age married to *ahadis* (gentlemen troopers) and *chelas* (manumitted men slaves). As for women from the age of 40 to 60 or 70 years who were within the Palace, she made

44 Fig. 21 is from the *Akbarnama*, National Museum MS, painted c. 1600: the scene depicted is the birth of Murad, painted by Bhura with faces by Basawan: reproduction in W. G. Archer, *Indian Miniatures*, Greenwich, US, 1990, Plate 20.

45 The word *parastar* is defined by Jamaluddin Husain Inju, *Farhang-i Jahangiri* (1608–09), Samar-i Hind Press, Lucknow, 1876, p. 312 (s.v. *parastar*): "(man-)slave, slave, slave-girl, servant, obedient person."

46 Jahangir, *Toozuk-i Jehangeeree*, ed. Syeed Ahmad, Ally-gurh, 1864, pp. 14–15. In his brother Murad's case he calls her mother "one of the *khawas's* and *khidmatgars* (servants)", making it obvious that she was a servant who was made a concubine.

> them free to choose whether they would leave the Palace and find a husband for themselves or stay within the Palace.[47]

The implication is obvious that the younger *sahelis* became, in effect, free married servants, while the older ones could leave the Palace if they could find a home. However, originally, they must have been all slave-girls.

Coming to the "External" *(Birun)* part of the Imperial Palace-establishment, its personnel comprised numerous men servants of all kinds. Slave labour does not seem to have been used here at all. In 1582 Akbar had freed all his slaves, though keeping them in his service if they so wished, to continue as his *chelas* ("disciples").[48] In the Encampment department alone there were a thousand tent-pitchers, and carpet-setters *(farrash)*, five hundred spade-wielders *(beldar)*, a hundred water-carriers *(saqqa)*, fifty carpenters *(durodgar)*, tent repairers *(khaimadoz)* and torch-bearers *(mash'alchis)*, thirty leather-workers *(charamdoz)* and one hundred and fifty sweepers *(khakrob)*.

The monthly salaries of the Encampment staff ranged from Rs. 3.25 to 6.[49] In most of the "external" imperial departments servants were paid monthly salaries or daily wages, and were divided into ordinary servants and their heads *(mirs)*. The monthly salaries within the same departments varied greatly: for example while the highest salary in the department of "Illuminations" was Rs. 60, the lowest was only Rs. 2 a month.[50] On the other hand, in the painting department the distance between the maximum and minimum pay of the servants was not so large: the highest was Rs. 30 and the lowest Rs. 15.[51] But this was probably due to the fact that we are here dealing with skilled painters whose salaries were generally high.

The salaries were paid on the basis of nature and quality of work: generally, religion, race and caste do not appear to have played much role here. When in a number of departments Irani and Central Asian servants are mentioned, the account does not indicate at all that either these were better paid or placed higher in the hierarchy.

47 Shaikh Farid Bhakkari, *Zakhiratu'l Khawanin* (completed 1650), ed. Syed Moinul Haq, II, Karachi, 1970, p. 49.

48 Abu'l Fazl, *Akbarnama*, Vol. III, ed. Ahmad Ali, Calcutta, 1873–87, pp. 379–80, Br. Mus. MS Add. 27, 247, ff. 327b–328a.

49 *A'in*, I, p. 42.

50 *A'in*, I, p. 45.

51 *Ibid.*, p. 118.

An interesting case is here provided by the palace guards (*khidmatyas*, lit. servants) who belonged to the outcastes *(Chandals)* in the Indian caste order. Akbar is credited with paying much attention to them: he appointed them as palace guards and gave their headman the title of "Khidmat Rai" and a rank of some honour. This encouraged others also, says Abu'l Fazl, to employ them as house-guards.[52]

The lowest (in status) of all servants were the sweepers *(khak-rub, ja-rub-kash, kannas)*, who belonged to the so-called "menial" castes. Characteristically, Akbar renamed them *halal-khor*, i.e. people who worked hard to earn their pay (as against *haram-khor*, the idle).[53] Their remuneration, despite this improved nomenclature, was still on the lowest rate, two *dams* per day (i.e. Rs. 1.50 a month) or even less. Table 1 below sets out the range of wages paid to servants of various kinds in the Imperial Palace, as given in the *A'in-i Akbari*.

The designations and functions of the servants in the establishments of the aristocracy were almost exactly the same as in the imperial household, though in each individual household the numbers were much fewer. As a matter of fact the establishment of a Mughal noble appeared to be just a minor replica of the imperial household: the harem on the pattern of the imperial harem consisted of wives, usually three or four, living in separate apartments in the same palace and having "10 or 20 or 100" slave-girls each in accordance with her status. They all received cooked meals from a single kitchen. Besides female slaves, two or more eunuchs were engaged for each wife to look after her affairs and serve as guards. These eunuchs, though originally purchased slaves, generally brought from Bengal, exercised much power and influence in the harem or the *andarun* or *darun*, the inner apartments.[54] Some high ranking nobles maintained two separate kitchens, one for the *andarun* and the other for the *bairun* or *Diwankhana*

52 *Akbarnama*, Vol. III, p. 604.

53 *A'in*, I, p. 144. The very common explanation that *halal-khor* means one for whom to eat everything is lawful, is not at all tenable, though this is as old as Thevenot (Jean de Thevenot, "Relation de Hindostan, 1666–67", in S. N. Sen (ed.), *The Indian Travels of Thevenot and Careri*, New Delhi, 1949, p. 89), and is authenticated by Henry Yule and A. C. Burnell, *Hobson-Jobson*, ed. William Crooke, London, 1886, pp. 409–410, s.v. *halalcore*. The attribution of the term to Akbar seems credit worthy since there is no example of its use before his time.

54 Franciso Pelsaert, 'Remonstrantie', c. 1626, tr. Moreland and Geyl, *Jahangir's India*, Cambridge, 1925, pp. 64–68.

(the outer apartments used by men).[55] In the kitchen of grandees Iranian, Central Asian, Kashmiri and even European, and Brahman (the highest Hindu caste) cooks were employed.[56] The task of preparing the menu, laying out the dinning carpet and supervising the serving of food fell to a servant called *sufrachi* (one who laid the "table"). This was considered so important and respectable that Akbar's trusted minister, Abul Fazl's son acted for his father as a *sufrachi*.[57]

Other important servants in the kitchen were the *bakawal* who obtained the materials for the kitchen, and the *chashnigir* (taster), who first tasted the food before it was served, though the *bakawal* also performed the latter duty.[58] Each aristocratic household maintained a separate department for providing water *(abdarkhana)* and a *suchi khana* (cellar).[59] *Farrash's* were employed to spread carpets and (during marches) for pitching tents; *mash`alchis* (torch-bearers) for carrying lamps and candles; and *mahauts* for looking after elephants, grooms *(sa'is)* for horses, *sarban* for camels, and *bailwan* for bullock-carts.[60] Palanquin-bearers *(kahars)* formed an essential part of the retinue since the grandees usually rode on a palanquin requiring six men.[61] (See Fig. 16.)[62]

Other servants were also maintained, for display: one servant for marching on the side of the palanquin holding a spitoon, two more to fan the master and to drive away the flies, four footmen to march in front to clear the way and a number of decorated horsemen to follow in the rear;[63] and a *kafshbardar* to keep or carry shoes.[64]

55 Shaikh Farid Bhakkari, *Zakhirat-ul Khawanin*, Syed Moinul Haq, Karachi, 1970, II, p. 97.

56 *Ibid.*, p. 170.

57 *Ibid.*, I, 1970, pp. 72–73.

58 According to Babur the *chashnigir* was the Indian word for the Turkish *bakawal* (*Baburnama*, tr. A. S. Beveridge, London, 1921, II, p. 541).

59 Anonymous, *Bayaz-i Khushbui*, MS. India Office (London), I.O. 828.

60 F. Pelsaert, pp. 67–68.

61 Francois Bernier, *Travels in the Mughal Empire 1656–68*, tr. A. Constable, revised V. A. Smith, London, 1916, pp. 282–283.

62 For Fig. 16 Palanquin-men and porters in "Prince Salim greets his mother", Akbarnama National Museum MS., see Archer, *Indian Miniatures*, Plate 21.

63 F. Pelsaert, pp. 60–63.

64 *Zakhiratul Khawanin*, II, p. 143.

Fig. 15
The Queen's Toilet. Ajanta painting, Cave XVIII, 6th century A.D.

Fig. 16
Palanquin-men and Porters in "Prince Salim greets his mother" in *Akbarnama*, National Museum MS, c. 1600. The palanquin was carried at any one time by two persons, as we see in this painting, Four others (not shown in the painting) were needed to relieve them after short periods to maintain speed of movement.

Fig. 17
"Cooks" from illustration of *Baburnama* (Persian translation of 'Abdu'r Rahim Khan Khanan), British Museum MS, painting from Akbar's atelier, c. 1600. Note how the cooks covered their mouths.

Fig. 18
"Torch-men" *(mash'alchis)* from *Padshahnama*, Windsor Castle MS, painting from Shahjahan's atelier, c. 1650. Note they are carrying both covered candles *(shama')* and torches *(chiragh)*.

Table 1. Wages of Servants in the Imperial Establishment (External), in rupies

Department	Monthly Salaries in Rs.	
	Highest	Lowest
A. Staff in		
Illumination *(Chiragh Afrozi)*	60	2
Atelier *(Tasveerkhana)*	30	15
Armoury *(qurkhana)*	10	2.5
Kitchen *(Matbakh)*	10	2.5
Musical Band *(Shikoh-Saltanat)*	8.5	1.8
Encampment	6	3.25
B. Animal Stables		
Groom	4.25	2.6
Farrash	3.25	
Water carrier	1.25	
Sweeper	1.25	
C. Cattle Transport		
Attendant		3–3.75
Head carter		3.5
Carter		3.0
Head Carpenter		3.5
Ordinary Carpenter		3
D. Others		
Khidmatiya (palace guard)	4.5–2.5	
Meurah (runner/messanger)	4.5–2.5	
Kahar (Palanquin bearer)	9.6–4.8	
(best coming from Bengal and the Deccan)	4–3	
Chela (manumitted slave) (in addition presumably to food)	30–0.75 monthly	
Gatekeepers: Head	5–3	
Ordinary	3–2.5	
Elephant Stable (Rs/month)		
Mahot (sits on the neck)	5.5	1.5
Bhoi (sits on the back)	2.75	1.25
Meth (fodder collector)	3	2.6

Note: Daily payment rates have been converted into monthly rates through multiplication by 30.

For maintaining gardens and orchards, the grandees employed a considerable number of gardeners. A manual on household management, written during the reign of Shahjahan (1628–58) even prescribes how many gardeners were to be maintained in the great gardens of Agra.[65]

The treatment meted out to the servants and slaves engaged in the aristocratic households often depended on the temper of the master. Some like Abul Fazl did not even like to scold them directly;[66] on the other hand, one was such a hard task master that he made even the torch-bearers *(mash'alchis)* and musicians *(kalawant)* work as building workers so that they should not remain idle in the day time.[67] Another, a physician and administrator, who possessed three hundred slave-women *(kanizak)*, kept each one of them occupied from early morning till late evening on the basis of the maxim that if women are kept idle, they fall prey to mischievous plots. Moreover, he allowed them very little for their sustinance.[68] There was, however, some disapproval of physical ill-treatment. The historian Badauni speaks approvingly of the refusal of a mystic at Kalpi (Uttar Pradesh) even to speak to a visiting local governor who had beaten and abused his servants.[69]

Outside the ranks of the aristocracy there was also a considerable employment of domestic servants by "middle-class" groups. Pelsaert writing c. 1626 at Agra noted that "Peons or servants are exceedingly numerous in this country, for everyone – be he mounted soldier, merchant, or king's official – keeps as many as his position and circumstances permit".[70]

Bernier, the French traveller, 1656–68, agreed that servants in the army were "indeed numerous";[71] and Fryer (1672–81) remarked more specifically that "however badly off a [cavalry] soldier is, he must have three or four servants".[72] Bernier, who was himself employed by a Mughal noble Danishmand Khan as a "two-horse cavalier", was unable to do with less than three servants though he had no family and maintained no kitchen, since his servants procured on payment for him food from the royal

65 *Biyaz-i Khushbu'i* ff. 109b–111a. See also Irfan Habib, "Economic and Social Aspects of Mughal Gardens" in *Mughal Gardens*, ed. J. L. Wescoat and J. Wolschke-Bulmahn, Washington, 1996, pp. 132–34.

66 *Zakhirat-ul Khawa*nin, II, pp. 376–377.

67 *Ibid.*, pp. 341–342.

68 *Ibid.*, II, p. 97.

69 Badauni, *Muntakhabu't Tawarikh*, Bib. Ind., Calcutta, 1864–69, III, pp. 6–7.

70 F. Pelsaert, p. 61.

71 F. Bernier, p. 380.

72 *A New Account of East India and Persia, being Nine Years' Travels, 1672–81*, Vol. I, London, 1909, p. 341.

kitchen in the Fort, where there was much excess food to be sold for profit by the kitchen staff.[73]

Unlike the aristocratic households where servants were appointed for specific duties,[74] the servants working for lower officials and ordinary people had to perform varied functions. Thus Muhammad A'zam, *chobdar* of Annand Ram Mukhlis, the *vakil* or agent of the Governor of Lahore at the Mughal Court, was also the suprintendant of his master's two-horse stable; and Lachchhi Ram, a *khidmatgar* of Mukhlis cooked meat cutlets *(kabab)* for him while another *khidmatgar* also worked as a cook.[75] Mukhlis also makes a reference to his maid-slaves *(kanizan)*.[76]

Servants were as easily dismissed as hired. Two Kashmiri Brahman cooks were summarily dismissed by Mukhlis simply because they had crossed over the river before him and left him hungry on a journey.[77]

Beatings could occur, though Mukhlis himself, after he had hit a *beldar* (labourer), felt perturbed over whether it had been the right thing to do.[78]

Except for the rather vague reference to *kanizan*, (slave-girls) who were probably left at the house at Delhi, when Mukhlis left home, none of his male servants were slaves.[79] No European travellers or European Companies appear to have used slaves as servants in their factories. Yet some other evidence suggests that men-slaves were commonly owned by small men as well. In his verses the satirical poet Ja'far Zatalli (1710) suggests that a small household could consist of the master, his wife, a man-slave and a slave-girl. In deprecation of his own poor circumstances, he says:

73 F. Bernier, p. 251.

74 F. Pelsaert, p. 62, "... in the houses of the great lords each servant keeps himself strictly to his own duties...".

75 Anand Ram Mukhlis, *Safarnama-i Mukhlis,* ed. S. Azhar Ali, Rampur, 1946, pp. 91, 96.

76 *Ibid.*, pp. 54 and 57.

77 *Ibid.*, p. 12.

78 *Ibid.*, pp. 105–106.

79 *Ibid.*, p. 50.

> I do not have a servant or person or slave *(ghulam)* [to attend to me]
> Nor a slave-woman or a loving wife.[80]

Seventeenth-century marriage contracts from the Port of Surat seek to prevent the husband from possessing or subsequently acquiring a *kanizak* or *dah*, whom he might treat as a mistress. In one case the husband was, indeed, prosperous for the dower *(mahr)* was fixed at Rs. 3,000, and one might expect that he could easily afford a *dah*. But, in another, there is nothing to suggest such prosperous circumstances.[81] Such a condition is made a part of a contract given in an accountancy manual of Aurangzeb's reign, so that the fear of wives that their husbands might in time acquire slave girls was quite a widespread one.[82]

We have so far looked at the domestic servants from the point of view of their employers or masters. We can now turn to them as a class and, first, see what kind of skills were required of them. Divided as it was into various professions contemporaries yet had a word for the class as a whole, namely *shagird-pesha* (lit. "of the profession of pupils"!).[83]

Cooks *(bawarchi)* obviously represented one distinct category within this class. "Those who do the cooking, tuck in their sleeves and skirts, and cover their mouth and nose", says Abu'l Fazl[84] (see Fig. 17).[85] There were *bakawals* who supervised the cooking and tasted the cooked food. The *rikabdars* (keepers of table-crockery) put the bread, yogurt, chutnies, etc., in the dishes. The actual service at the meals was performed by the *sufrachi*.[86] This is the "tsaftergir or head servant" who, Pelsaert says, "sits in the middle and serves each guest according to his rank, the senior first".[87]

80 Na'im Ahmad (ed.), *Kulliyat-i Ja'far Zatalli*, Aligarh, 1979, p. 132. See also p. 108 for a satirical marriage contract where it is assumed that a husband would at least have a *dah* and a *ghulam*.

81 Volume of Documents 1583–1648: Bibliothèque Nationale de France, Paris, Blochet Supl., Pers 482, ff.201b–217a–b.

82 Nand Ram, *Siyaqnama*, pub. Naval Kishor, Lucknow, 1879, pp. 88–89.

83 For use of this word in this sense, see Tek Chand Bahar, *Bahar-i 'Ajam,* (c. 1740), s.v., and Mirza Qatil, *Haft Tamasha*, pub. Nawal Kishor, Lucknow, 1875, p. 135. It seems to have come into use in India in the seventeenth century on the analogy of *chela* ("disciple"), the designation given to manumitted slave-servants by Akbar.

84 *A'in-i Akbari*, I, p. 54.

85 "Cooks" from illustration of MS of the Persian translation of the *Baburnama* British Museum, Or. 3174, f.253a (Hamid Suleiman, Miniatures of the *Babur-nama*, Tashkent, 1970, Plate 34).

86 *A'in-i Akbari*, I, p. 5.

87 F. Pelsaert, p. 68.

It was his task to see how each dish was received by the master and his guests.[88]

Within the house, the *farrash* (from *farsh*, floor) "attends to his [master's] tent on the way [i.e. on a journey], spreads carpets, both on the march and in the house, and looks after the *diwan-khana*, or sitting room", where the master of the house received guests and, on occasion, took his meals.[89]

Lights within the house were provided by the *mash'alchi*, the torchman. Babur had spoken slightingly of the absence of the candle *(shama')* and torch *(mash'al)*, and the use in India, instead, of a peculiar contraption: the lamp-man *(deoti)* held in his left hand a burning wick carried on a tripod, and in his right a gourd containing oil to keep the lamp burning. When there was work to be done at night "these dirty lamp-men *(chirkin deoti)* bring these lamps *(chiragh)*, go close up and there stand".[90] An improvement was made in Mughal India by the replacement of the *deoti* by the *mash'al*, the carrier henceforth being known as *mash'al-chi*, who "looks to his torch, and lights lamps and candles in the evening".[91] (See candles and torches carried by the *mash'alchis* in Fig. 18.)[92]

The *chobdar* ("stick-man"), holding a mace, acted as usher, announced visitors, accompanied the master when going out, as a kind of herald, and carried letters and messages[93] (see Fig. 22).[94]

The term *khidmatgar* had a wide range, though literally meaning "servant"; but it was especially employed in the context of domestic service to

88 *Zakhiratu'l Khawanin*, I, pp. 72–73; II, pp. 282–283.

89 F. Pelsaert, pp. 61–62.

90 Babur, *Baburnama*, Turki text, ed. Eiji Mano, Kyoto, 1995, p. 467; A. Beverdige's transl., London, 1921, II, pp. 518–19. *Deoti* in more recent usage applies to the lamp only.

91 F. Pelsaert, p. 62.

92 See M. C. Beach and E. Koch, *King of the World: The Padshahnama* (MS in Royal Library, Windsor Castle), London, 1997, Plate 23. The volume was painted, c. 1650.

93 See quotations in Henry Yule and A. C. Burnell, *Hobson-Jobson*, ed. W. Crooke, London, 1886, p. 204. Also Mukhlis, *Safarnama*, pp. 96–99.

94 Fig. 18 is part of an illustration in the British Museum MS of the *Baburnama*, from which Fig. 16 is also derived (Hamid Suleiman, *Miniatures of the Baburnama*, Plate 34).

the personal attendant of the master, though here too looseness in the use often occurred.[95]

The water-man *(saqqa)* supplied water within the house, poured it down to help clean floors and privies inside and threw it about to settle the dust outside. He did so by carrying the water in a large buffalo-skin leather bag (Fig. 23).[96]

The sweepers (*khakrob, jarubkash*, etc.), renamed by Akbar *halalkhor* (see above), were responsible for practically the entire sanitary work. "The Halalcour are the scavengers of the Towns; they make clean the public and private Houses, and are payed for it Monthly."[97] Their services were, perhaps, the most essential of all.

How these servants looked at themselves and their own status remains largely a closed book to us, and so Mirza Qatil's observations recorded at Lucknow in 1811 turn out to be of great value, despite their rather late date. Qatil says that among the Hindus since caste determined status, it remained unaltered even if a Khatri took service as the lowly carrier of a water-pot under his wife's uncle as master. On the other hand, a low caste-man such as a Kahar, whose caste-profession was to transport baggage or carry palanquins, could never rise in the social scale whatever the profession he actually pursued. Among the Muslims it was, however, otherwise: here occupations actually undertaken determined status.[98]

Qatil describes in some detail how Muslim domestics of various categories saw their own ranking within the class of servants. Footmen *(piyadgan)* who escorted their masters and watched over their property *(ashya)* regarded themselves as superior to the *shagirdpesha*, or the general run of domestic servants, though they could not wear the kind of clothes or eat the food that the latter were able to do. Among the *shagirdpesha*, the *khidmatgars* (personal attendants) regarded themselves as above the rest, followed closely by *chobdars*, and, somewhat below both, the *farrash's*. However, Qatil felt that since *chobdars*, whether Hindu or Muslim, belonged entirely to the low-status caste of Kallals, their status

95 See the use of this word in Mukhlis, *Safarnama*, pp. 54, 57, 85. Nandu, a Kashmiri Brahman (Pundit), described on p. 57 as a *khidmatgar*, is stated on p. 105 to have been employed for cooking.

96 From *King of the World: Padshahnama*, Plate 23.

97 Jean de Thevenot's "Relation de Hindostan, 1666–67", in S. N. Sen (ed.), *The Indian Travels of Thevenot and Careri*, New Delhi, 1949, p. 89. The text has been modified by the editor's corrections on p. 314.

98 *Haft Tamasha*, pp. 27–28.

was, perhaps, not really as high as that of the *khidmatgars* as well as the *farrash's*, whose ranks impecunious and illiterate persons of the genteel class *(shurafa-zadas)* could join from time to time. However, whatever the degree of gentility of the *khidmatgars*, they were always treated as inferior by the masters. The barber *(dalak)*, whether as domestic servant or as independent professional, was held to be of low status in society, despite being called such high-sounding names as Hakim (physician), and was by the master treated at par with the *khidmatgars*.

In Qatil's view, the cooks *(bawarchi)* could not aspire to the status of a *khidmatgar*, though undoubtedly some persons of higher rank had been taking the profession of cooks. He noticed that prosperous cooks of obscure origin were now giving themselves airs and calling themselves Sayyids (descendants of the Prophet), and so of theoretically great respectability. They sought to marry off their daughters to men claiming genteel status. The *rikabdars*, *kabab*-makers and bread-makers were all of the same status as cooks and inter-married freely among themselves.

The lowest status among Muslim domestics, Qatil adds, was assigned to the water-carrier *(saqqa)*, the washer of cooking utensils, the *kahar* (porter) of the kitchen and the palanquin-bearer.[99] Such professions were regarded as *paji*, "vile or contemptible".[100]

From the social aspects, we may now turn to the economic. In considering the influence of the market on the supply of domestic services, the cases of unfree and free (or hired) domestics must be considered separately. In the first instance we deal essentially with slave-prices, in the other with wages and salaries.

With slave-prices our initial difficulty is that open slave trade came under ban under Akbar (1556–1605) during his early years (1562–63) and henceforth, except for regions affected by severe famines,[101] open sale of slaves in the market (and so their "market" prices) are simply not recorded in official or private documents. It could for an earlier time (c. 1510) be recorded that a noble of the Lodi empire "used to get his slave-girls *(dah)* and men-slaves *(ghulam)* from the market and then put them under a

99 *Ibid.*, pp. 134–137.

100 *Ibid.*, p. 28, where the lowly *(razil)* professions are listed as of "*khidmatgar* (personal attendant), water-man, elephant-driver, *farrash*, druggist *(`attar)*, sweatmeat seller, bread-maker".

101 Cf. Irfan Habib, "Akbar and Social Inequities", *Proceedings of the Indian History Congress*, 53rd session (Warangal), Delhi, 1993, pp. 300–301.

teacher to learn their prayers, etc.".[102] In 1591 Badauni, a critic of Akbar, still recognized that the practice of selling children into slavery had "abated somewhat" by the 1590s when he wrote his text on ethics.[103] Akbar's successor Jahangir (1605–27) extended the ban to the trade in eunuchs from Bengal.[104]

The acquisition of slaves and slave-girls by purchase continued, though by private means. When Akbar's counsellor Hakim Abu'l Fath in 1582 wished to get a concubine for his brother he purchased two "beautiful" *dahs*, one from Tamar Khan Badakhshi, the other from Khwaja Murad, at the capital city (Fatehpur Sikri), but not from a market.[105]

While it may be assumed that part of the slave population grew by internal reproduction, it also grew partly by the same means as earlier: Raids on recalcitrant peasants and rebels brought in captives, who were made into slaves. A model document in an accountancy manual of Aurangzeb's reign (1659–1707) shows how sale would follow captivity. A woman, Seoti, captured in a raid by a commander 'Abdullah Khan, was sold by him to a retainer of his, 'Inayatullah, against an unspecified deduction made in his salary. The woman was now being sold by him as a *dah* for a consideration of Rs. 40 to one Nur Muhammad.[106] Prices of slaves are not quoted in the Mughal Empire as in the fourteenth century (see previous section of the present chapter). They never appear on official reports of daily prices in different markets that have survived. Nevertheless, even if the sales remained private and prices therefore not directly determined by competition, these must have been affected ultimately by the state of supply. Rs. 40 (some ten months' wage at the time, see below) was by no means a low price, and may suggest that a contraction in the supply of domestic slaves was taking place, relative to demand. When manumission took place, it could also be against payment. In 1623 at Surat slave-woman *(kanizak)*, Sandal, was freed by her mistress on a payment of 30 *mahmudis* (= Rs. 12).[107] The amount probably came out of the slave-woman's earnings outside the home, or arrears of some "pocket-

102 Rizqullah Mushtaqi, *Waqi'at-i Mushtaqi*, ed. Iqtidar Husain Siddiqi, Rampur, 2002, p. 71. Mushtaqi wrote his book in 1572.

103 Abdu'l Qadir Badauni, *Nijatu'r Rashid*, ed. S. Moinul Haq, Lahore, 1972, pp. 239–240.

104 *Tuzuk-i Jahangiri*, ed. Syeed Ahmad, Aligarh, 1864, pp. 71–72.

105 *Ruq'at-i Hakim Abu'l Fath Gilani*, ed. M. Bashir Husain, Lahore, p. 22.

106 Nand Ram, *Siyaqnama*, pub. Nawal Kishor, Lucknow, 1879, p. 88.

107 MS Blochet, Supl. Pers. 482, f.194a–b.

money" allowed here. Such payment should not, therefore, be compared with prices at which women slaves were sold for domestic work or concubinage.

Coming to wages, the major source for us remains the *A'in-i Akbari*. Because of the difficulty in comparing wages of skilled servants, it is best to take the wages of the lowest paid domestic servants. From the table of wages compiled from the *A'in-i Akbari*, and true presumably for Lahore (then the imperial capital) in 1595, it is obvious that the lowest wages were those of the water-carrier and sweeper in the Animal Stables, amounting to Rs. 1, and 25 *dams* or Rs. 1.62 per month. Since the *A'in-i Akbari* also provides us with prices for various goods including cereals as well as cloth, it was possible for me to work out the purchasing power of the lowest wages in the *A'in-i Akbari* and compare them with those prevailing around 1871–72 in northern India, for which reliable figures of wages and prices could be obtained. The broad result was that the lowest paid domestic servant could buy more of cereals, butter, and salt and a little less sugar, but much less cloth. Overall the real wages fell by half over the entire period.[108] This is in general line with the other evidence for de-urbanization and de-industrialization over the nineteenth century. While this must have created a general contraction of demand for unskilled labour including domestic services, there is the further factor of the long-term inflation that might also have caused wages to lag behind prices. Despite the romance in Anglo-Indian novels attaching to the world of the "ayah" (children's nurse), the "bearer" (butler), the "khansama" (cook) and "peon" (orderly, office attendant), who looked after the sahibs, the lot of domestic servants in general was far worse after over a hundred years of British rule than it was under Akbar, when too it was by no means a thing to write home about.

108 Shireen Moosvi, *The Economy of the Mughal Empire, c. 1595*, pp. 331–336. It should be mentioned here that the considerable evidence about wages we have from other sources shows that the wages quoted in the *A'in-i Akbari* were by no means higher than normal. In 1626 F. Pelsaert reports, for example, that the ordinary servants received Rs. 3 or 4 per month at Agra, the then imperial capital (*Jahangir's India*, pp. 62–63). In 1714, the monthly wage of a *khidmatgar* (personal servant) at Delhi, now the capital, was Rs. 7 per month (C. R. Wilson, *Early Annals of the English in Bengal*, II(2), Calcutta, 1911, pp. 355–256). These are considerably higher than the *A'in's* wage-rates for the lowest-level servants, though doubtless, the sluggish "Price Revolution" in India might have been partly responsible for this difference.

Part V

Some Portraits
Domestic Workers – Past and Present

Fig. 19
Women servants separating cotton from seeds by "Indian cotton-gin" (right), separating fibres by pestle-and-board (left), and hand-spinning yarn (centre). Ajanta painting, Cave I, 6th century A.D.

Fig. 20
Woman (servant?) turning hand mill to grind flour. Miftahu'l Fuzala MS illustration (1469).
(Courtesy: British Library). Compare with Fig. 14: same work done with pestle-and-board, which must have been extremely onerous.

Fig. 21
The Inside of Part of Imperial harem: *The Birth of Prince Murad. Akbarnama* MS illustration (c. 1600). (Courtesy: National Museum.) Note the various kinds of women harem staff: those within the Queen's apartments and those in the general area of the harem. The men within the harem (there are none in the Queen's apartments) are presumably eunuchs. Standing outside the door are men-guards or *chobdars*.

Fig. 22
Chobdars (Stick-men) from illustration of *Baburnama* (Persian translation of 'Abdu'r Rahim Khan khanan) British Museum MS, painting in Akbar's atelier, c. 1600. See also Fig. 21.

Fig. 23
Water-man *(saqqa)* in *Padshahnama*, Windsor Castle MS, painting from Shahjahan's atelier, c. 1650. Note the leather-bag containing water.

Fig. 24
La Garde attentive. Jean-Baptiste Siméon Chardin, c. 1747, n.d., National Gallery of Art, Washington.
A care-giver is preparing a boiled egg in the kitchen, before serving it.

Fig. 25
The Studious Servant. Théodule Ribot, c. 1850, Art Gallery and Museum, Glasgow.

Fig. 26
Woman at the Fountain. François Bonvin, 1861,
Musée du Louvre (RMN), Paris.

Fig. 27
The Scourer. François Bonvin, 1873, Musée St Denis, Reims.

THE PATENT GRIDIRON.

BIDDY.—" If ye plase, Ma'am, your new fanglings have dropped me mate in the fior! What'll I do?"

MISTRESS —" Well, Biddy, Professor Cook tells us that only the carbonaceous portion undergoes combustion, so I suppose you can quickly rescue the fibrinous residue!"

BIDDY.—" Faith, Ma'am, an' if it's this rat trap of a toasting fork ye mane, I wish it gone busted like the mate, shure I niver lost my stake thro' my fryin' pan that way."

Fig. 28

The patent gridiron. Canadian Illustrated News, 12 May 1877, Archives Publiques du Canada (APC, C–65833).

SCIENCE AT A DISCOUNT.

COOK.—"Please 'm, I've come down to give you notice once more, for the likes o' this I never did see, nor will I stand. 'Ere's Miss Amelier a poking her glass thing-a-bob inter my mince pies to try their tempers, and well I knows as it tries mine, a lettin' down the 'eats and coolin' the hoven. Has for Perfesser Cook, I'm tired o' 'earin' of 'im, and I don't b'lieve there's no sich person as 'ud talk sich nonsense."

Fig. 29
Science at a discount. Canadian Illustrated News, 4 January 1873, Archives Publiques du Canada (APC, C–58960).

Fig. 30
How to Dispense with Servants in the Dining Room.
William Heath Robinson, 1921, The British Museum, London.
A satiric answer to the "servant problem", the lack of servant felt by the early 20th middle class: imaginative machineries active for serving meal, automatically and together, to the family and the pet. Published in the Christmas number of the *Sketch*, 1921 (untitled "Heath Robinson Patents for Doing Away with Servants".

Fig. 31
Portrait of Shirani, a Care Giver Born in Sri Lanka, 1952, with her employer, 1999. Plus que Parfaites, Montréal, 2001, p. 120.

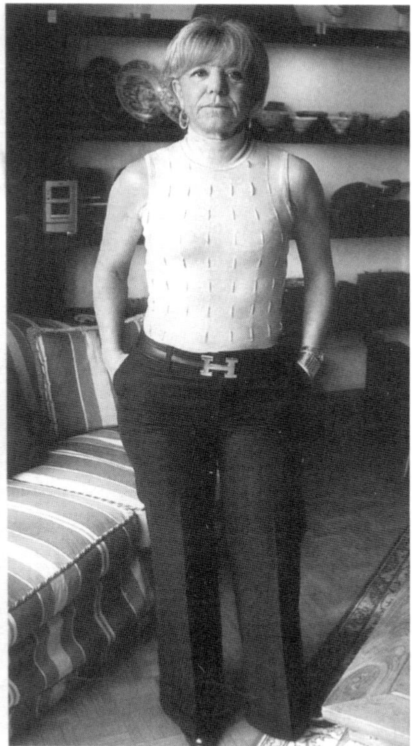

Fig. 32
An Ukrainian woman employed as domestic worker in Milan, Italy and her Italian employer. *Gente*, 27 March 2003, p. 40.
Before migrating to Italy, the Ukrainian woman, who has a specialization in zootechnique, taught at University, published scientific essays in genetics and managed a farm with 1200 cows. She decided to migrate after having lived for three years with no wage. As an irregular migrant, she applied for regularization in Italy, but she was sent back to Ukraine. Her story was told in a popular Italian magazine (Roberta Pasero, "Era l'angelo della nostra casa ma l'hanno espulsa come una ladra", *Gente*, 27 March 2003, pp. 40–41).